Lawrin Armstrong

USURY AND PUBLIC DEBT IN EARLY RENAISSANCE FLORENCE: LORENZO RIDOLFI ON THE *MONTE COMUNE*

Money, politics and law were intimately linked in the merchant republics of medieval and Renaissance Italy. Nowhere was this more evident than in the realm of public finance. Beginning in the twelfth century, governments borrowed money from citizens to meet expenses that exceeded ordinary revenues; by 1350, most had converted their outstanding debts into permanent funds serviced by consumption taxes and levies on subject territories. Loans were usually compulsory, but ruling classes preferred them to taxes: not only did loans pay a return in the form of interest, but they could also be sold to recoup part of the lender's capital.

Despite the blessing of elites, deficit financing was highly controversial. In Florence, the creation of the funded debt was associated with social upheaval and remained a factor in political struggles for over a century. Debts in Florence and elsewhere also raised legal and moral questions that became the focus of growing controversy in the later Middle Ages. Lawyers and theologians rarely questioned the reliance of governments on debt, but many considered the payment of interest to government creditors a violation of the ban on usury, which law and theology defined as any charge for a loan.

The defence of public debt offered by the Florentine lay canonist Lorenzo Ridolfi (1362-1443) in his *Treatise on Usury* was the most influential contribution to the debate and quickly became the standard canonical authority on the problem. *Usury and Public Debt in Early Renaissance Florence* presents an edition of the relevant portions of Ridolfi's treatise based on the autograph manuscript in the Biblioteca Nazionale di Firenze and a running commentary on the text. The introduction examines Ridolfi's text in the light of earlier writers on the debt problem and situates it in the broader sociopolitical and cultural context of early *Quattrocento* Florence. This study will be of interest to legal historians, to historians of medieval political economy and economic thought, and to students of early Renaissance Florence.

Frontispiece. Masaccio, *The Tribute Money*
Detail, Brancacci Chapel, S. Maria del Carmine, Florence.
(Reproduced with the permission of Scala/Art Resource, New York.)

STUDIES AND TEXTS 144

Usury and Public Debt in Early Renaissance Florence:

Lorenzo Ridolfi on the *Monte Comune*

by

Lawrin Armstrong

Pontifical Institute of Mediaeval Studies

Acknowledgements

This book has been published with the help of a grant from
the Canadian Federation for the Humanities and Social Sciences
using funds provided by the Social Sciences and
Humanities Research Council of Canada.

National Library of Canada Cataloguing in Publication Data

Armstrong, Lawrin D. (Lawrin David)
Usury and public debt in early Renaissance Florence :
Lorenzo Ridolfi on the Monte Comune / Lawrin Armstrong.

(Studies and Texts ; 144)
Includes bibliographical references and index.
ISBN 0-88844-144-4

1. Debts, Public – Italy – Florence – History – To 1500.
2. Finance, Public – Italy – Florence – History – To 1500.
3. Usury laws (Canon law). I. Title. II. Series: Studies
and texts (Pontifical Institute of Mediaeval Studies) ; 144.

KJA2066.5.A74 2003 336.3'4'09455109024 C2003-901407-X

Pontifical Institute of Mediaeval Studies
59 Queen's Park Crescent East
Toronto, Ontario, Canada M5S 2C4

Manufactured in Canada

www.pims.ca

For Johanna

Advocati dicuntur in legibus militare, sicut milites armis, et magis sunt necessarii reipublicae, quam milites.

Bartolus of Sassoferrato on *Code* 2.7.14

Der öffentliche Kredit wird zum Credo des Kapitals. Und mit dem Entstehen der Staatsverschuldung tritt an die Stelle der Sünde gegen den heiligen Geist, für die keine Verzeihung ist, der Treubruch an der Staatsschuld.

Karl Marx, *Das Kapital*, vol. 1, ch. 24.6

Si può trovare un criterio unitario per caratterizzare ugualmente tutte le diverse e disparate attività intellettuali? . . . L'errore metodico più diffuso mi pare quello di aver cercato questo criterio di distinzione nell'intrinseco delle attività intellettuali e non invece nell'insieme del sistema di rapporti in cui esse (e quindi i gruppi che le impersonano) vengono a trovarsi nel complesso generale dei rapporti sociali.

Antonio Gramsci, *Quaderni del Carcere*, 12.1

Contents

Illustrations viii
Preface and Acknowledgements ix
Abbreviations xiii

Introduction 1
1. Ridolfi and the Ruling Class 7
2. The Public Debt 28
3. Usury and the Public Debt Controversy 53
   A. The Usury Prohibition 56 □ B. The Public Debt □ Controversy 65
4. Ridolfi on the Public Debt 85
   A. The Criterion of Intention 85 □ B. Compulsory Loans 87 □ C. The Public Debt Market 93 □ D. Government Annuities 98
5. Law, Politics and Public Debt 100
6. The Edition 112
   A. Description of F_1 112 □ B. Contents of F_1 112 □ C. The Status of F_1 113 □ D. The Manuscript Tradition 120 □ E. Orthography and Format 121 □ F. Unedited Questions 123 □ G. The Venice Edition of 1584 126

LORENZO RIDOLFI, *TRACTATUS DE USURIS* 129

Prima Particula 131
Secunda Particula 155
Tertia Particula 210

Commentary
   Part 1 261 □ Part 2 295 □ Part 3 349

Glossary 381
Appendix: Notes on Ridolfi's Authorities 307
Bibliography 407
   A. Manuscripts Cited 407 □ B. Printed Primary Sources 408 □ C. Secondary Sources 414
Index of Citations 433
General Index 447

Illustrations

Masaccio, *The Tribute Money*. Detail, Brancacci Chapel, S. Maria del Carmine, Florence — *frontispiece*

BNF, Fondo principale II, III, 366 (Lorenzo Ridolfi, *Tractatus de usuris*), fol. 83r–detail — 118

BNF, Fondo principale II, III, 370 (Lorenzo Ridolfi, *Consiliorum liber tertius*), fol. 233r–detail — 119

Preface and Acknowledgements

Money, politics and law were intimately linked in the merchant republics of medieval and Renaissance Italy. Nowhere was this more evident than in the realm of public finance. From the twelfth century onward, the governments of Florence, Venice, Genoa, Lucca, Pisa and Siena borrowed money from citizens to cover costs, especially the costs of defence or territorial expansion, that could not be met out of ordinary revenues. By 1350, most cities had converted their outstanding debts into permanent funds serviced by taxes on subject territories and tariffs on food, services and imports called gabelles. Although loans usually took the form of compulsory levies, the merchant-oligarchs who dominated the city-states considered them preferable to taxes on private property, which they were largely successful in resisting throughout the later Middle Ages. As they observed, money they paid in taxes was lost forever, whereas loans secured by consumption taxes and rural imposts not only paid a steady return in the form of interest but in cities such as Florence and Venice could be sold on government-certified markets to recover at least part of their capital.

Despite its benefits to economic elites, who, as in any regime of regressive taxation, profited from a system that siphoned wealth upward, deficit financing was highly controversial. In Florence, whose public debt is at the centre of this study, the creation of the *monte comune*, the communal "debt mountain," between 1343 and 1345 was associated with challenges to the traditional balance of domestic political power and remained a factor in class and factional struggles for well over a century. The establishment of public debts in Florence and elsewhere also raised legal and moral questions that became the focus of growing controversy during the fourteenth and early fifteenth centuries. Theologians and lawyers rarely questioned the reliance of governments on debt, but many considered the payment of interest to government creditors and to those who bought credits on the market a violation of the ban on usury, which theology and law defined as any increment on the principal of a loan.

Debate over the usurious dimensions of public debt erupted in Florence within a few years of the *monte comune*'s creation and occupied several generations of lawyers and theologians. The defence of the debt offered by the lay canonist and politician Lorenzo Ridolfi (1362-1443) in his *Tractatus de usuris* (*Treatise on Usury*) was the most influential contribution to the debate. Ridolfi wrote between 1402 and 1404, at a time of military and political crisis, when the fiscal policies of the Florentine political elite were under attack, but over the longer term his treatise was enshrined as the standard canonical authority for defenders of public debts and speculative markets in government debt not only in Florence but elsewhere in Italy.

The text presented below is not a complete edition of the *Tractatus de usuris*, but is confined to the sections (about a third of the treatise) that reflect the dispute over the *monte comune*, a choice dictated by the constraints of academic publishing and by the attention historians have devoted to the public debt and to the debt controversy over the past forty years. The edition includes Part 1 of the treatise, the beginning of Part 2 and Part 3, Question 5, the *Questio montis* (Question of the Debt) itself. Part 1 outlines the underlying assumptions of the usury prohibition and introduces the canonical distinction between lenders' primary and secondary intentions. The opening sections of Part 2 elaborate on creditors' moral intentions with reference to the decretal *Consuluit* (X 5.19.10), and Questions 11-18 deal with annuities based on productive property, to which theorists often assimilated government loans. The *Questio montis*, subdivided by Ridolfi into eight *dubia* or sub-questions, is virtually a treatise in itself. I have excluded the remaining questions of Parts 2 and 3 because they have no direct bearing on the *monte* debate. I have also omitted an appendix to the *Questio montis* in which Ridolfi reports and glosses the opinions of earlier writers on the debt problem. Julius Kirshner has already edited part of this section from the manuscript on which the present edition is based, and I have recently published a critical edition of the *Questio de monte* of Francesco da Empoli, of which Ridolfi provides a synopsis. Where pertinent to Ridolfi's own argument this material is summarized in the introduction or commentary and noted in the *apparatus fontium*.

The introduction reflects the modern scholarship on usury and public debt and draws upon the rich historiography of early Renaissance Florence to develop a sociopolitical reading of Ridolfi's defence of the *monte*. My analytical perspective is Marxist, and for this I offer no apologies: with Eric Hobsbawm I can say that "historical understanding is what I am after, not agreement, approval or sympathy." However unfashionable it has become, historical materialism has lost none of its power to elucidate the reciprocal relationship between class and economic factors on the one hand and ideological phenomena such as law and theology on the other, and is therefore ideally suited to an inquiry of the kind undertaken here.

The remaining components of the book explain technical aspects of the treatise that might present barriers to the reader. Like lawyers in all eras, Ridolfi employed technical and mystifying jargon. Moreover, like all medieval lawyers, he used scholastic modes of reasoning and supported his analysis by abbreviated references to legal, theological and biblical authorities. As a guide through this semantic, methodological and intertextual jungle,

I have provided a commentary that summarizes Ridolfi's sources and analyzes his reasoning, a glossary of specialized terms and an appendix describing Ridolfi's principal medieval authorities.

*
* *

It is a pleasure to acknowledge the many professional and personal debts I incurred preparing this book. It originated as a doctoral thesis at the Centre for Medieval Studies, University of Toronto, where I profited from the scholarship and supervision of John H. Munro of the Department of Economics and Centre for Medieval Studies. I first encountered the usury problem in Professor Munro's economic history seminar and the book owes its completion in great measure to his unfailing interest and encouragement. The members of my advisory committee, A. George Rigg, Joseph Goering and Giulio Silano of the Centre for Medieval Studies and Joseph Shatzmiller now of Duke University, generously gave me the benefit of their expertise in Latin, text editing and canon law.

No one can study the public debt controversy without reference to the work of Julius Kirshner of the University of Chicago, and my debt in this regard is clear in the footnotes. But I am also grateful to Professor Kirshner both for his warm encouragement of this project and for his generosity in providing access to his unpublished research on the controversy. Kenneth Pennington of the Catholic University of America kindly allowed me to consult his unpublished bio-bibliography of medieval canonists and supplied references to several rare canonical sources. I am especially indebted to Luca Boschetto, who first introduced me to the Archivio di Stato di Firenze and provided me with many important references. The anonymous referees for the Canadian Federation for the Humanities and Social Sciences, John Najemy of Cornell University, Mark Leier, Tina Loo, Paige Raibmon and Paul Dutton, friends and colleagues in the Department of History of Simon Fraser University, suggested many revisions that improved the final version of the manuscript. I also wish to thank Ron B. Thomson of the Pontifical Institute of Mediaeval Studies for his patient production of this book. The many flaws that remain are entirely my own responsibility.

I am grateful to several bodies for financial support. Thesis research was supported by fellowships from the Social Sciences and Humanities Research Council of Canada, the Ontario Ministry of Colleges and Universities, the School of Graduate Studies, University of Toronto, Massey College and Trinity College, University of Toronto, and the Centre for Reformation and Renaissance Studies, University of Victoria College. The Social Sciences and Humanities Research Council Small Research Grant and the President's Research Grant programmes of Simon Fraser University underwrote supplementary research on the public debt controversy. A fellowship at the Villa I Tatti Harvard University Center for Italian Renaissance Studies and the hospitality of the Waldensian community of the Istituto Gould in 1999-2000 allowed me to reexamine several manuscripts in Florentine libraries. I am also grateful for a Lila Wallace-Reader's Digest publication subsidy from the Villa I Tatti, which covered the cost of illustrations.

This project would have been impossible without access to many libraries and archives and the patient assistance of their curators. In particular, I wish to thank the Biblioteca Nazionale Centrale di Firenze for permission to consult the manuscript on which the edition is based and several other manuscripts and early printed editions in its collection. I am particularly grateful to Jean Bettaney of the BNF for her patient help and good humour, and to her family for their hospitality. I should also like to thank the Archivio di Stato, the Biblioteca Medicea-Laurenziana, the Biblioteca Riccardiana and the Biblioteca Berenson, Florence, the Biblioteca Angelica, Rome, the Biblioteca Apostolica Vaticana, the Biblioteca Capitolare Feliniana, Lucca, the Bibliothèque nationale de France, Paris, the Österreichische Nationalbibliothek, Vienna, the Bayerische Staatsbibliothek, Munich, the Staats- und Stadtbibliothek, Augsburg, the law division of the Library of Congress, Washington, DC, the Pontifical Institute of Mediaeval Studies Library, Toronto, the Fisher Rare Book Library, University of Toronto, the Bruce Peel Special Collections Library of the University of Alberta, Edmonton, and the Special Collections Division of the Main Library of the University of British Columbia, Vancouver. I am especially grateful for the efforts of the inter-library loan department of the Bennett Library, Simon Fraser University.

My biggest debt is to my wife, Johanna Will-Armstrong, to whom I dedicate the book.

Bielefeld
31 December 2002

Abbreviations

AFP	*Archivum Fratrum Praedicatorum*
AFH	*Archivum Franciscanum Historicum*
ASF	Archivio di Stato di Firenze
ASI	*Archivio storico italiano*
BNF	Biblioteca Nazionale Centrale di Firenze
CCSL	*Corpus Christianorum: Series Latina*
CL	Classical Latin
comm.	commentary
CSEL	*Corpus Scriptorum Ecclesiasticorum Latinorum*
DDC	*Dictionnaire de droit canonique*
F_1	BNF, Fondo principale II, III, 366
It.	Italian
ML	Medieval Latin
PL	*Patrologia Latina*
RQ	*Renaissance Quarterly*
TUI	*Tractatus universi iuris* (Venice, 1584)

Legal Abbreviations

Auth.	*Authenticum*, constitution of Justinian
C.	Codex Iustiniani
C.	*causa* (in citations of *Decretum Gratiani*)
c.	*canon* (in citations of *Decretum Gratiani*)
c.	*capitulum*, *canon* (in the text)
Clem.	*constitutio clementina*, constitution of Clement V
coll.	*collatio* (in citations of the *Authenticum*)
D.	*distinctio*, division in the first part of *Decretum Gratiani*
Decretum Grat.	*Decretum Gratiani*
dictum Grat.	*dictum Gratiani*, comment of Gratian before or after a fragment
Dig.	*Digesta Iustiniani*
Extrav. comm.	*Extravagantes communes*
ff.	*Digesta Iustiniani* (in the text)
gl. ord.	*glossa ordinaria*
Inst.	*Institutiones Iustiniani*
l.	*lex*, law in Justinian's *Corpus* (in the text)
n.	*numerus*

Nov.	*Novella Iustiniani*
q.	*quaestio*, division within a *causa* of *Decretum Gratiani*
rubr.	*rubrica*
VI	*Liber sextus decretalium Bonifacii VIII*
v.	*sub verbo*, gloss to a law or decretal
X	*Decretales Gregorii IX* (*Liber extra*)

Legal citations in the introduction, *apparatus fontium* and commentary proceed from larger to smaller units of text. For example, Dig. 12.1.2.2 means *Digest*, book 12, title 1 *de rebus creditis*, *lex* 2, paragraph 2, and X 5.19.10 means *Decretales Gregorii IX*, book 5, title 19 *de usuris*, *capitulum* 10 *Consuluit*. Roman law citations comply with the format of the *Corpus iuris civilis*, ed. Theodor Mommsen, Paul Krueger, Rudolf Schoell and Wilhelm Kroll, 3 vols. (Berlin: Weidmann, 1872-95; repr. 1954). The *apparatus fontium* indicates where the organization of the medieval vulgate text of the *Corpus iuris civilis* used by Ridolfi differed from that of the modern critical edition by supplying the medieval citation in brackets from Franca Sinatti D'Amico and Hugo Nicolini, *Indices corporis iuris civilis iuxta vetustiores editiones cum criticis collatas*, Ius Romanorum Medii Aevi subsidia, no. 1, 3 vols. in 5 (Milan: Giuffrè, 1964). Canon law citations refer to the *Corpus iuris canonici*, ed. Aemilius Friedberg, 2 vols. (Leipzig: B. Tauchnitz, 1879; repr. Graz: Akademische Druck- u. Verlagsanstalt, 1959).

BIBLICAL ABBREVIATIONS

Abbreviated titles of books of the Bible are from the Stuttgart Vulgate: *Biblia sacra iuxta vulgatam versionem*, ed. Roger Gryson et al., 4th rev. ed. (Stuttgart: Deutsche Bibelgesellschaft, 1994), xliii.

Act	Acts of the Apostles	*Iob*	Job
1 *Cor*	1 Corinthians	*Lc*	Luke
2 *Cor*	2 Corinthians	*Mc*	Mark
Dt	Deuteronomy	*Mt*	Matthew
Ex	Exodus	*Os*	Hosea
Ez	Ezechiel	*Prv*	Proverbs
Gal	Galatians	*Ps*	Psalms
Hbr	Hebrews	*Rm*	Romans
Ier	Jeremiah	1 *Tim*	1 Timothy
Io	John		

Introduction

The Florentine lay canonist Lorenzo di Antonio Ridolfi finished writing his *Tractatus de usuris* in February 1404.[1] In the prologue, he defines the scope of the treatise as "the whole topic of usury" (23-24), declaring that

> my intention is to set forth everything connected with the abyss of usury so that, having assembled this material in the form of a *summa*, I might have recourse to it when the need arises (14-18).

He then outlines the structure of the treatise: after introductory sections on the nature of the usury prohibition in general, there follow almost 160 questions analyzing usurious contracts and restitution. Among these, the problems surrounding the *monte comune*, the consolidated debt of the Florentine republic, and the *prestanze* (obligatory loans) on which it was based receive the most elaborate treatment. The *Questio montis,* itself subdivided into eight subsidiary questions and supplemented by annotated abstracts of earlier writers on the debt problem, is the largest single component of the treatise. All told, the *monte* and related topics occupy a third of the text.

Despite Ridolfi's highly formal treatment of it, the *monte* was anything but an abstraction for contemporary Florentines. The debt had been controversial ever since its inception in the mid-1340s. Although disputants often framed their arguments in the language of law and moral theology, debate had always reflected class and factional struggles within the commune.[2] Controversy entered a new phase during the prolonged conflict with Milan between 1390 and 1404. As commerce dried up under the impact of blockade and repeated *prestanze* made heavy demands on private wealth, the

[1] Ridolfi states in the *explicit* that he completed the treatise on 14 February 1403 (3773-74 [references are to line numbers in the edition]). Since the Florentine year began on 25 March, the date corresponds to 14 February 1404 modern style. Dates in the introduction and commentary are in the modern style. Unless otherwise indicated, translations are my own.

[2] See below, pp. 28-52, 65-84 *passim*. On the origins of the controversy, see also Julius Kirshner, "Storm over the *Monte Comune*: Genesis of the Moral Controversy over the Public Debt of Florence," *AFP* 53 (1983): 219-76; and Lawrin Armstrong, "The Politics of Usury in *Trecento* Florence: The *Questio de monte* of Francesco da Empoli," *Mediaeval Studies* 61 (1999): 1-44.

nonelite merchants and lesser guildsmen of the political class became increasingly disenchanted with the policies of the patrician oligarchs who controlled the government. The leadership's decision in the fall of 1402 to prolong the war and demand additional war credits, even after the collapse of the Milanese campaign had eliminated the immediate threat to Florence, only magnified tensions that had been building since 1390.

It was in this context that Ridolfi wrote his treatise.[3] No one was better placed to serve as an apologist for the *monte*. Of patrician descent, Ridolfi enjoyed a high profile in Florence as a leading lawyer and a lecturer in the university. More significantly, he was a key figure in the regime and active in formulating its policies. Experienced in the interpretation of legal norms and versed in the mechanics of public finance, Ridolfi felt, in his own words, "compelled by these troubled times to explain for the spiritual good of my fellow citizens what is consistent with law and conscience in the matter of the public debt" (7-9). Not surprisingly, he concluded that the moral welfare of his fellow citizens was identical with the interests of the regime of which he was a leader. But as his emphasis on conscience indicates, the defence of the *monte* demanded more than illustrations of its utility to the republic's dominant group. The government's dependence on *prestanze* and the trade in debt credits that it fuelled could be construed as a violation of the ban on usury, which law and theology defined as any charge for a loan. As a defender of the debt, Ridolfi was obliged to confront the accusation that by compelling citizens to become its creditors the government was in effect creating a population of usurers.

Because Ridolfi's vindication of the *monte* was part of a wider medieval debate about usury, it has attracted the attention of historians studying the origins of modern theories of credit. In his pioneering study of the usury doctrine, John Noonan concluded that Ridolfi's analysis of the public debt marked a liberal turn in the interpretation of the usury prohibition.[4] Noon-

[3] Internal evidence allows us to date the composition of the treatise to 1402-1404. In a gloss on his summary of the *Questio de monte* of Francesco da Empoli appended to the *Questio montis*, Ridolfi observes that buyers of *monte* credits run the risk that share prices may fall, "as the year 1402, when the duke of Milan occupied Bologna, bears witness" ("testis sit annus 1402 quo dux Mediolani ciuitatem Bononie occupauit" [F_1 fol. 91r; *TUI* 7, fol. 44vb]). The duke of Milan, Giangaleazzo Visconti (d. 1402), captured Bologna on 26 June 1402, with the result that the price of shares, which was already depressed, fell even further (Gene A. Brucker, *The Civic World of Early Renaissance Florence* [Princeton: Princeton University Press, 1977], 181, n. 376). The *terminus ad quem* of February 1404 derives from the *explicit*; see above, p. 1 n. 1.

[4] *The Scholastic Analysis of Usury* (Cambridge, MA: Harvard University Press, 1957), 125. For a discussion, see below, p. 93.

an and others correctly emphasize that Ridolfi's treatise quickly became the standard authority for fifteenth-century apologists for state debts in Florence and elsewhere, but in my view the text's doctrinal originality has been exaggerated.[5] As a review of Ridolfi's sources shows, his analysis represented a consolidation and refinement of earlier legal and theological apologies rather than a radical departure from them. Ridolfi's objective was not, as Noonan suggests, to subvert the traditional usury ban, but rather to show that the operations of the debt were entirely consistent with it.

Noonan's interpretation may be attributed in part to his method. Since the publication of Hans Baron's influential study of civic humanism in 1955, Renaissance intellectual history has benefited from the work of social historians who have charted the class, patronage and political networks within which intellectuals moved.[6] With few exceptions, however, historians of law and economic theory have remained immune to this change, continuing to view their subjects from the perspective of theoretical developments largely undetermined by material factors.[7] The weakness of this

[5] On the dependence of later writers on Ridolfi, see Noonan, *Scholastic Analysis of Usury*, 126-32, 166; Amleto Spicciani, *Capitale e interesse tra mercatura e povertà nei teologi e canonisti dei secoli XIII-XV* (Rome: Jouvence, 1990), 101-2, 179-83, 187-88; Julius Kirshner, "From Usury to Public Finance: The Ecclesiastical Controversy over the Public Debts of Florence, Genoa and Venice, 1300-1500" (PhD thesis, Columbia University, 1970), 131-33, 139-40, 200-213; idem, "Reading Bernardino's Sermon on the Public Debt," in *Atti del simposio internazionale cateriniano-bernardiniano, Siena, 17-20 aprile 1980*, ed. Domenico Maffei and Paolo Nardi (Siena: Accademia senese degli Intronati, 1982), 550-51, 558-59, 563; and the *apparatus fontium* of Bernardino of Siena, "*Sermo* XLI," in *Opera Omnia*, vol. 4: *Quadragesimale de evangelio aeterno, sermones XXVII-LIII* (Quaracchi-Florence: Typographia Collegii S. Bonaventurae, 1956), 307-46.

[6] Hans Baron, *The Crisis of the Early Italian Renaissance: Civic Humanism and Republican Liberty in an Age of Classicism and Tyranny*, 2 vols. (Princeton: Princeton University Press, 1955); revised edition in one volume (Princeton: Princeton University Press, 1966); reference is to the revised edition. On the social networks of the civic humanists the basic study is Lauro Martines, *The Social World of the Florentine Humanists, 1390-1460* (London: Routledge and Kegan Paul, 1963). For recent discussions reflecting the impact of social history on the interpretation of humanism, see James Hankins, "The 'Baron Thesis' after Forty Years and Some Recent Studies of Leonardo Bruni," *Journal of the History of Ideas* 56 (1995): 309-38; and the essays collected in idem, ed., *Renaissance Civic Humanism: Reappraisals and Reflections* (Cambridge: Cambridge University Press, 2000), esp. 75-223.

[7] Among the exceptions are Lauro Martines, *Lawyers and Statecraft in Renaissance Florence* (Princeton: Princeton University Press, 1968); Julius Kirshner on law and the history of economic theory; and Thomas Kuehn on private law. The notion of law as an autonomous discipline divides legal historians from historians who use

approach is that it obscures how the usury debate was implicated in real economic, social and political relations. As Jacques Le Goff argues, the usury prohibition was more than an expression of abstract moral or legal principle: it was also an ideological weapon in the struggle to define the nature of medieval societies themselves.[8] For the merchant elites of the Italian city-states, whose financial activities were heavily dependent on credit, the stakes were nothing less than the legitimacy of the most sophisticated commercial economy in Europe.

Much of what follows will be concerned with the arguments Ridolfi inherited from earlier writers on usury and his own assessment of the *monte*'s moral and legal status. I depart, however, from the traditional approach to scholastic law and economics by emphasizing how the debt controversy—and Ridolfi's contribution to it—reflected class and political interests. Therefore, before turning to the controversy itself I situate Ridolfi in the sociopolitical context of early Renaissance Florence and review the politically divisive history of the *monte* from its foundation in 1343-45 to

---

legal sources to study past societies. The problem is discussed by Julius Kirshner in "Some Problems in the Interpretation of Legal Texts re. the Italian City-States," *Archiv für Begriffsgeschichte* 19 (1975): 16-27; and idem, "*Ars imitatur naturam*: A *Consilium* of Baldus on Naturalization in Florence," *Viator* 5 (1974): 289-331, esp. 323-24. See also the remarks of Thomas Kuehn, *Law, Family, and Women: Toward a Legal Anthropology of Renaissance Italy* (Chicago and London: University of Chicago Press, 1991), 7-11. On Ridolfi's text, see Lawrin Armstrong, "The *Tractatus de materia montis* of Lorenzo Ridolfi," in *Proceedings of the Twelfth International Economic History Congress, Madrid, 1998, Session D: Recent Doctoral Research in Economic History*, ed. Clara-Eugenia Núñez (Madrid: Universidad Nacional de Educación a Distancia and Fundación Fomento de la Historia Económica, 1998), 15-23. Odd Langholm reflects the traditional approach to the history of economic theory in a recent series of important studies. See, for example, *Price and Value in the Aristotelian Tradition: A study in scholastic economic sources* (Bergen, Oslo and Tromsø: Universitetsforlaget, 1979), 24, where Langholm explains his decision to base his account of medieval concepts of value exclusively on the exegetical tradition of Aristotle *Ethics* 5.5, remarking that "the casuistic economic literature of the Middle Ages contains much wisdom, but to the student of general theory it raises serious problems of interpretation, since the discussion tends to get involved in a mass of circumstantial detail. The description of the exchange situation in *EN* V, 5 is devoid of such detail. All we are presented with are the exchangers as bare types: the builder, the shoemaker, and their products. This very much increases the generalizing potential of comments on the text."

[8] See "The Usurer and Purgatory," in *The Dawn of Modern Banking* (New Haven and London: Yale University Press, 1979), 25-52; and idem, *Your Money or Your Life: Economy and Religion in the Middle Ages*, trans. Patricia Ranum (New York: Zone Books, 1988), esp. 47-64.

the early fifteenth century with particular attention to the class interests served by the fiscal system.[9] The fifth section of the introduction, "Law, Politics and Public Debt," integrates the legal and theological debate into the larger sociopolitical picture. Making use of Antonio Gramsci's concept of "hegemony," I argue that Ridolfi's apology for the *monte* should not be interpreted as an abstract theoretical exercise but rather as part of a broader elite strategy to generate consent to its political programme at a moment of instability and crisis.

[9] In this, I am particularly indebted to the work of Lauro Martines, Anthony Molho and John Najemy, who have argued for a greater emphasis on class consciousness and conflict in the study of medieval and Renaissance Florence. See in particular Lauro Martines, *Power and Imagination: City-States in Renaissance Italy* (Baltimore: Johns Hopkins University Press, 1979), 45-46, 191-217; Anthony Molho, "Cosimo de' Medici: *Pater patriae* or *Padrino*?" *Stanford Italian Review* 1 (1979): 9-18; and the essays of Najemy cited below p. 8 n. 3.

1
Ridolfi and the Ruling Class

In the estimate of the memorialist Vespasiano da Bisticci (1421-98), Lorenzo Ridolfi "was inferior to no citizen of an age when Florence was rich in distinguished men."[1] Writing some forty years after Ridolfi's death, Vespasiano represented him as a model Florentine. Of patrician descent and honourable profession, Ridolfi enjoyed a reputation for learning and integrity matched by a distinguished record in public office. Modern scholarship confirms Vespasiano's judgement. Until 1434, Ridolfi numbered among the dozen most influential men in the republic and was one of three lawyers who played a leading role in government.[2] The scholarship also provides

[1] "Non fu meser Lorenzo in ogni cosa inferiore a ignuno cittadino che abbia avuto la città di Firenze ne' sua tempi, quando la città fioriva d'uomini singulari" (*Le vite*, ed. Aulo Greco, 2 vols. [Florence: Istituto Nazionale di Studi sul Rinascimento, 1970-76], 2: 136; trans. William George and Emily Waters, *Renaissance Princes, Popes, and Prelates: The Vespasiano Memoirs: Lives of Illustrious Men of the XVth Century* [New York: Harper and Row, 1963], 319). There is a biographical notice of Ridolfi in Thomas Diplovatatius, *Liber de claris iurisconsultis, pars posterior*, ed. Fritz Schultz, Hermann Kantorowicz and Giuseppe Rabotti, *Studia Gratiana* 10 (1968): 342-43. For modern sketches, see Johann Friedrich von Schulte, *Die Geschichte der Quellen und Literatur des canonischen Rechts*, 3 vols. (Stuttgart: F. Enke, 1875-80; repr. Graz: Akademische Druck- u. Verlagsanstalt, 1956), 2: 393-94; Guido Carocci, *La Famiglia dei Ridolfi di Piazza: Notizie storiche e genealogiche* (Florence: Giuseppe Civelli, 1889), 36-38; and Federico Martino, "Umanisti, giuristi, uomini di stato a Firenze fra Trecento e Quattrocento: Lorenzo d'Antonio Ridolfi," in *Studi in memoria di Mario Condorelli* (Milan: Giuffrè, 1988), 3:179-200.

[2] Brucker, *Civic World*, 265; on lawyers in the regime, see ibid., 269. On Ridolfi's record in office, see David Herlihy, "The Rulers of Florence, 1282-1530," in *City States in Classical Antiquity and Medieval Italy: Athens and Rome, Florence and Venice*, ed. Anthony Molho, Kurt Raaflaub and Julia Emlen (Stuttgart: Franz Steiner, 1991), 215; repr. in *Women, Family and Society in Medieval Europe: Historical Essays, 1978-91*, ed. Anthony Molho (Providence and Oxford: Berghahn, 1995), 376. See also Martines, *Lawyers and Statecraft*, 483; Carocci, *Ridolfi di Piazza*, 28-29; Martino, "Ridolfi," 191-98; and Elio Conti, Maria Cristina Frassineti, Daniela de Rosa, Magda Cavaciocchi and Renzo Ninci, ed., *Le "Consulte" e "Pratiche" della Repubblica fiorentina nel Quattrocento*, vol. 1, 1401: *Cancellierato di Coluccio Salu-*

us with a perspective missing from Vespasiano's panegyric and that is how Ridolfi's status and career were themselves shaped by the sociopolitical terrain of late fourteenth- and early fifteenth-century Florence.

The contours of Florentine politics in this period were moulded by tension between competing models of order espoused by groups contemporaries called the *popolo* (the people) and the *grandi* (the great).[3] The conflict was inherited from the thirteenth century, when the *popolo* had subdued and disenfranchised the "magnates," the great feudal and merchant clans who had dominated the early commune.[4] By the mid-fourteenth century,

---

tati, Università degli studi di Firenze, Fonti di storia medievale e umanistica (Florence: Università di Firenze, 1981), xxxviii.

[3] On Florentine politics, see the magisterial studies of Gene A. Brucker, *Florentine Politics and Society, 1343-1378* (Princeton: Princeton University Press, 1962); and *Civic World*, which together cover the ninety years from 1343 to 1434. Marvin B. Becker examines the same period from a different perspective in *Florence in Transition*, 2 vols. (Baltimore: Johns Hopkins Press, 1967-68). For a survey of the literature, see Alison Brown, "Florence, Renaissance and Early Modern State: Reappraisals," *Journal of Modern History* 56 (1984): 285-300; repr. in *The Medici in Florence: The exercise and language of power*, Italian Medieval and Renaissance Studies, University of Western Australia, no. 3 (Florence and Perth, Australia: Leo S. Olschki and the University of Western Australia Press, 1992), 307-26. The reading of Florentine politics offered here is particularly indebted to the work of John M. Najemy; see his "Guild Republicanism in Trecento Florence: The Successes and Ultimate Failure of Corporate Politics," *American Historical Review* 84 (1979): 53-71; idem, "*Audiant Omnes Artes*: Corporate Origins of the Ciompi Revolution," in *Il Tumulto dei Ciompi: Un momento di storia fiorentina ed europea* (Florence: Leo S. Olschki, 1981), 59-93; idem, *Corporatism and Consensus in Florentine Electoral Politics, 1280-1400* (Chapel Hill: University of North Carolina Press, 1982); idem, "The Dialogue of Power in Florentine Politics," in *City States in Classical Antiquity and Medieval Italy*, 269-88; and idem, "Civic Humanism and Florentine Politics," in *Renaissance Civic Humanism*, 75-104. Like most social labels, *popolo* and *grandi* had several overlapping meanings: *popolo* sometimes meant the entire non-magnate population, enfranchised or not, while *grandi* was often restricted to magnates (see below, n. 4). Following Martines and Najemy, I use the term *popolo* to refer to enfranchised non-magnates, whatever the specific composition of this group at any given period (see Martines, *Power and Imagination*, 45-71; and Najemy, "Dialogue of Power," passim). The terms "patrician" and "patriciate" were not used by contempory Florentines, but I conform to the convention among Anglo-American Florentinists in using them to refer to the ruling elite. On the terminological problems, see the remarks of Roberto S. Lopez, *Intervista sulla città medievale*, ed. Marino Berengo (Rome: Laterza, 1984), 63-81, esp. 64.

[4] The rise of the *popolo* was not unique to Florence. The most recent survey is Philip Jones, *The Italian City-State: From Commune to Signoria* (Oxford: Clarendon Press, 1997), 485-521. See also John Kenneth Hyde, *Society and Politics in Medieval*

however, the most powerful *popolo* families had merged with the magnates to form a distinct class of patricians who stood for government by oligarchy.[5] The boundaries of this class were defined by marriage alliances, membership in the great commercial guilds and association with elite organizations, such as the merchant tribunal of the *Mercanzia* and the *Parte Guelfa* (Guelf Society), the institutional guardian of the city's papal and antidemocratic traditions.[6] The patriciate viewed with distaste the aspirations

---

Italy: The Evolution of the Civil Life, 1000-1350 (London and Basingstoke: Macmillan, 1973), 94-123; and Martines, *Power and Imagination*, 45-71. The basic study of the Florentine conflict remains Gaetano Salvemini, *Magnati e popolani in Firenze dal 1280 al 1295* (Florence: G. Carnesecchi, 1899; repr. Turin: Einaudi, 1960). Salvemini's class analysis was disputed by Nicola Ottokar in *Il comune di Firenze alla fine del Dugento* (Florence: Vallechi, 1926; repr. Turin: Einaudi, 1962). See more recently Sergio Raveggi, Massimo Tarassi, Daniela Medici and Patrizia Parenti, *Ghibellini, guelfi e popolo grasso: I detentori del potere politico a Firenze nella seconda metà del Dugento* (Florence: La Nuova Italia, 1978); Najemy, *Corporatism and Consensus*, 3-78; and Giovanni Tabacco, *Egemonie sociali e strutture del potere nel medioevo italiano* (Turin: Einaudi, 1974), 330-95. "Magnate" was essentially a legal category designating families whose wealth, prestige and propensity for factional violence were viewed as a threat to the stability of the commune; see Guidubaldo Guidi, *Il governo della città-repubblica di Firenze del primo Quattrocento*, Biblioteca storica toscana, no. 20, 3 vols. (Florence: Leo S. Olschki, 1981), 2: 121-29; and Carol Lansing, *The Florentine Magnates: Lineage and Faction in a Medieval Commune* (Princeton: Princeton University Press, 1991). For the early fourteenth century, see Marvin B. Becker, "A Study in Political Failure: The Florentine Magnates, 1280-1343," *Mediaeval Studies* 27 (1965): 246-308. On efforts by magnates to assimilate to the *popolo* in the later fourteenth century, see Christiane Klapisch-Zuber, "Ruptures de parenté et changements d'identité chez les magnats florentins du XIVe siècle," and Michel Pastoureau, "Stratégies héraldiques et changements d'armoires chez les magnats florentins du XIVe siècle," *Annales: Economies, Sociétés, Civilisations* 43 (1988): 1205-54.

[5] On the social composition of the elite, see Brucker, *Florentine Politics*, 28-40; Lansing, *Florentine Magnates*, 229-38; and Anthony Molho, *Marriage Alliance in Late Medieval Florence* (Cambridge, MA, and London: Harvard University Press, 1994), 193-214.

[6] Najemy, *Corporatism and Consensus*, 10-11. Francis W. Kent analyzes the structure of elite families in *Household and Lineage in Renaissance Florence: The Family Life of the Capponi, Ginori, and Rucellai* (Princeton: Princeton University Press, 1977). For patterns of intermarriage in the fifteenth-century ruling class, see Molho, *Marriage Alliance*, 181-348. On the *Mercanzia*, see Najemy, "Guild Republicanism," 62-63; idem, "Dialogue of Power," 284-86; and Antonella Astorri, *La Mercanzia a Firenze nella prima metà del Trecento: Il potere dei grandi mercanti*, Biblioteca storica toscana, no. 34 (Florence: Leo S. Olschki, 1998). On the Guelf Society, see Brucker, *Florentine Politics*, 99-104; and Guidi, *Il governo*, 2: 111-20.

of affluent and ambitious *arrivistes*, the so-called *gente nuova* (new men), to join their ranks, and this sentiment found expression in strategies designed to restrict the access of new men and lesser Florentines to political office and power.[7]

By the later fourteenth century, the *popolo* represented an unstable coalition of artisans and retailers from the middle strata of Florentine society allied with nonelite merchants and new men. The *popolo* advocated a more broadly based political order in which legitimate authority derived from an egalitarian federation of the city's mercantile, professional and craft guilds. This ideal had been embodied in the Ordinances of Justice of 1293, the republic's basic constitutional statute, and underlay the structure of Florentine government.[8] Not only were fully enfranchised Florentines

---

In Brucker's view, the Society's influence was in decline by the later fourteenth century, despite its importance as a focus of symbolic loyalties (*Civic World*, 18, 313-17). For a different assessment, see Alison Brown, "The Guelf Party in Fifteenth-Century Florence: The Transition from Communal to Medicean State," *Rinascimento* 20 (1980): 41-86; repr. in *Medici in Florence*, 103-50.

[7] For a study, see Najemy's *Corporatism and Consensus*. Manipulation of sortition procedures in the later fourteenth century is discussed below, pp. 20-22. Brucker defines new men as those whose families acquired political privileges after 1343 (*Florentine Politics*, 40). For discussions of the antecedents and social characteristics of this group, see ibid., 20-24, 40-45; and Marvin B. Becker, "An Essay on the *Novi Cives* and Florentine Politics, 1343-1382," *Mediaeval Studies* 24 (1962): 35-82. On the regulation of citizenship privileges, see Guidi, *Il governo*, 1: 99-138. On legal definitions and restrictions on the political privileges of new men, see Julius Kirshner, "*Civitas sibi faciat civem*: Bartolus of Sassoferrato's Doctrine on the Making of a Citizen," *Speculum* 48 (1973): 694-713; and "*Ars imitatur naturam*," 289-331.

[8] See Najemy, "Guild Republicanism," 58-60; Brucker, *Civic World*, 39-59; and Guidi, *Il governo*, 2: 73-81. The twenty-one guilds recognized by the Ordinances of Justice were divided into seven *arti maggiori* (major guilds) and fourteen *arti minori* (minor guilds). The most powerful of the major guilds were the Lana guild (wool manufacturers), Calimala (international merchants and cloth finishers), Cambio (bankers and moneychangers), Medici, speziali e merciai (physicians, apothecaries and spice importers) and Giudici e notai (lawyers and notaries). The minor guilds represented a range of skilled trades (for example, shoemakers, masons, carpenters) and small retailers (for example, butchers, vintners, bakers). For the text of the Ordinances of Justice, see the appendix to the first edition of Salvemini's *Magnati e popolani*, 384-432. Three guilds of textile workers were created in 1378; that of the carders (Ciompi) was suppressed in September 1378 and the remaining two in 1382. The basic study of the guilds remains Alfred Doren, *Le arti fiorentine*, trans. Giovanni Battista Klein, 2 vols. (Florence: Felice Le Monnier, 1940-48). On the Lana guild in particular, see Hidetoshi Hoshino, *L'arte della Lana in Firenze nel basso medioevo: Il commercio della Lana e il mercato dei panni fiorentini*

described as *popolani* and Guelfs (in distinction from magnates and Ghibellines), but matriculation into a guild was the basic condition for full participation in politics, which in practice amounted to eligibilty for the hundreds of posts that were filled every few months by lot or appointment. These included administrative jobs in the city and its dependencies, the five hundred seats on the legislative councils of the commune and the *popolo* and the leading magistracies of the republic, namely, the *Signoria*, the *Sedici Gonfalonieri* (Sixteen Ward Standard-Bearers) and the *Duodici Buonuomini* (Twelve Good Men).[9] The *Signoria*, the republic's highest office, symbolized the identification of the guilds with the commune. Composed of eight "priors of the guilds" under the chairmanship of the *Gonfaloniere della Giustizia* (Standard-Bearer of Justice) and endowed with a sacred aura expressed in elaborate civic rituals and spaces, the *Signoria* was, at least in theory, the supreme organ of the guilds themselves.[10]

In practice, however, the patriciate, concentrated in the greater guilds, monopolized power during most of the fourteenth century. Only during two periods of crisis—between 1343 and 1348 and again between 1378 and 1382—did the *popolo* succeed in displacing them.[11] The second represented the most radical challenge to elite hegemony. In July 1378, the Ciompi, disenfranchised textile workers subject to the control of the wool

nei secoli XIII-XV, Biblioteca storica toscana, no. 31 (Florence: Leo S. Olschki, 1980).

[9] The most comprehensive study of the Florentine government is Guidi, *Il governo*. On the electoral process, see ibid., 1: 149-355; and Najemy, *Corporatism and Consensus*. Offices were held for limited terms, varying from two months in the *Signoria* to six in the councils; see Guidi, *Il governo*, 2: 3-33, 49-58, 133-44. All told, Brucker counts about a thousand positions that had to be filled every year by the end of the fourteenth century (*Civic World*, 253), while Anthony Molho estimates three thousand ("Politics and the Ruling Class in Early Renaissance Florence," *Nuova rivista storica* 52 [1968]: 407). For the various offices, see Guidi, *Il governo*, 2: 199-341; 3: 167-251. The only exceptions were the permanent government secretariate and the judiciary, which were staffed by foreigners (Brucker, *Florentine Politics*," 60-64; Guidi, *Il governo*, 2: 41-48, 153-95).

[10] On the symbolic dimensions of power in this period, see Richard C. Trexler, *Public Life in Renaissance Florence* (Ithaca, NY: Cornell University Press, 1980); Nicolai Rubinstein, *The Palazzo Vecchio, 1298-1532: Government, Architecture, and Imagery in the Civic Palace of the Florentine Republic* (Oxford: Clarendon Press, 1995); Marvin Trachtenberg, *Dominion of the Eye: Urbanism, Art, and Power in Early Modern Florence* (Cambridge: Cambridge University Press, 1997); Alison Brown, "De-masking Renaissance republicanism," in *Renaissance Civic Humanism*, 179-99; and Stephen J. Milner, "Citing the *Ringhiera*: The Politics of Place and Public Address in Trecento Florence," *Italian Studies* 55 (2000): 53-82.

[11] On the *popolo* regime of 1343-48, see Brucker, *Florentine Politics*, 105-47; and Najemy, *Corporatism and Consensus*, 126-65.

manufacturers' guild, allied themselves with several minor guilds and rose in insurrection, demanding their own association and a role in government that reflected their numbers in the population.[12] The Ciompi and their organizations were suppressed within six weeks, but the regime installed by the surviving guilds in September 1378 repudiated the patrician model of government by awarding five out of nine seats in the *Signoria* to the minor guildsmen, who now included members of the two new textile workers' guilds that survived the reaction.[13]

During these struggles, the Ridolfi were squarely in the patrician camp. An old lineage that had emigrated in the late thirteenth century from Poppiano in the Val di Pesa, south of Florence, they were strongly established in the *Ferza* (Whip) ward of Santo Spirito quarter.[14] Along with the Pitti,

[12] The best recent study is Alessandro Stella, *La révolte des Ciompi: les hommes, les lieux, le travail* (Paris: L'École des hautes études en sciences sociales, 1993), 43-73. See also the classic studies of Niccolò Rodolico, *I Ciompi: Una pagina di storia del proletariato operaio*, 3rd ed. (Florence: Sansoni, 1980), 97-178; idem, *La democrazia fiorentina nel suo tramonto (1378-1382)* (Bologna: Nicola Zanichelli, 1905), 179-206; and Victor Rutenburg, *Popolo e movimenti popolari nell'Italia del '300 e '400*, trans. Gianpiero Borghini (Bologna: Mulino, 1971), 157-329. Brucker disputes the social revolutionary content of the rising in *Florentine Politics*, 336-86; and "The Ciompi Revolution," in *Florentine Studies: Politics and Society in Renaissance Florence*, ed. Nicolai Rubinstein (London: Faber and Faber, 1968), 314-56; repr. in Gene A. Brucker, *Renaissance Florence: Society, Culture, and Religion* (Goldbach: Keip, 1994), 37-79. For a review of the debate, see Volker Hunecke, "Il Tumulto dei Ciompi—600 Jahre danach: Bemerkungen zum Forschungsstand," *Quellen und Forschungen aus italienischen Archiven und Bibliotheken* 58 (1978): 360-410. For rejoinders to Brucker, see Samuel Kline Cohn, *The Laboring Classes in Renaissance Florence* (New York, London and Toronto: Academic Press, 1980), 129-54; and Richard C. Trexler, "Neighbours and Comrades: The Revolutionaries of Florence, 1378," *Social Analysis* 14 (December 1983): 53-106; idem, "Follow the flag: the Ciompi revolt seen from the streets," *Bibliothèque d'Humanisme et Renaissance* 46 (1984): 357-92; and idem, "Herald of the Ciompi: The Authorship of an Anonymous Florentine Chronicle," *Quellen und Forschungen aus italienischen Archiven und Bibliotheken* 65 (1985): 159-91. All three reprinted in *Power and Dependence in Renaissance Florence*, vol. 3, *The Workers of Florence* (Binghamton, NY: Center for Medieval and Early Renaissance Studies, 1993).

[13] Najemy, *Corporatism and Consensus*, 244-45. Elite hostility to this arrangement resulted in a decree of January 1379 awarding four seats each to the major and minor guilds and directing that the post of Standard-Bearer of Justice alternate between major and minor guildsmen (ibid., 247-50).

[14] Martino, "Ridolfi," 179; and Carocci, *Ridolfi di Piazza*, 13-15. The family retained its connections with Poppiano: according to the 1427 *catasto*, Lorenzo Ridolfi owned a house and six farms there; see ASF, Catasto 66, fols. 77r-78r. I wish to thank Luca Boschetto for sending me copies of Ridolfi's *catasto* declarations of

Corbinelli and Corsini, they dominated a district heavily populated by textile workers.[15] The Ridolfi di Piazza, as the family was called because of its association with the *piazza* and church of San Felice, were first represented in the *Signoria* in 1321.[16] Lorenzo's father, Antonio (d. 1385), was a merchant and official of the Guelf Society.[17] As a leading partisan of the society's right wing, whose campaign to purge the government of *popolo* elements and new men precipitated the troubles of 1378, he was an obvious target for the insurgents. In the riots of June and July, Antonio's *palazzo* was among those sacked and burned.[18] At the end of August, Antonio, along with several other "arch-Guelfs," was designated a magnate, stripped of political privileges and forced into exile in Viterbo.[19]

Born in 1362, Lorenzo Ridolfi inherited the oligarchic loyalties of his father along with the legal disabilities of magnate status. In the circumstances, his decision to pursue a career in canon law was a natural one given his class background and family political traditions. As Lauro Martines shows, law was a patrician monopoly largely closed to outsiders and ambitious new men. Of the two hundred lawyers who practised in Florence between 1380 and 1530, only three percent were the sons of tradesmen, while those who derived from recently enriched lineages tended to belong

---

1427, 1430 and 1433. Created in 1427, the *catasto* was a fiscal survey that provided the basis for *prestanze* assessments; on the document, see David Herlihy and Christiane Klapisch-Zuber, *Tuscans and Their Families: A Study of the Florentine Catasto of 1427* (New Haven and London: Yale University Press, 1985), 1-27. Ridolfi's *palazzo* survives, now Via Maggio 8, on the west side of the Piazza di San Felice; for its history, see Leonardo Ginori-Lisci, *I Palazzi di Firenze nella storia e nell'arte*, 2 vols. (Florence: Cassa di Risparmio di Firenze, 1972), 2: 733-34. I wish to thank Peter Kussmaul of Dalhousie University for this reference.

[15] Kent, *Household and Lineage*, 191. In 1433, there were no less than seven Ridolfi households in *Ferza* ward; see ASF, *Catasto* 437, fols. 61r-62v, 151r-152v, 250r-251v, 650r-v; and ibid., 438, fols. 152r-157v, 33r-36v, 528r-v. For a study of an adjacent Santo Spirito ward in Ridolfi's time, see Nicholas A. Eckstein, *The District of the Green Dragon: Neighbourhood Life and Social Change in Renaissance Florence*, Istituto Nazionale di Studi sul Rinascimento, Quaderni di Rinascimento, no. 22 (Florence: Leo S. Olschki, 1995).

[16] For Ridolfi priors, see Carocci, *Ridolfi di Piazza*, 28-29; Dale Kent, "The Florentine *Reggimento* in the Fifteenth Century," *RQ* 28 (1975): 630, table 2; and Najemy, *Corporatism and Consensus*, 325, table A.4; 329, table A.5. On the "di Piazza" designation, see Carocci, *Ridolfi di Piazza*, 11-12, 16-18.

[17] Martino, "Ridolfi," 179; Brucker, *Florentine Politics*, 322-23. The date of Antonio's death is recorded by Carocci, *Ridolfi di Piazza*, 69, table 1.

[18] Martino, "Ridolfi," 180; Brucker, *Florentine Politics*, 381.

[19] Martino, "Ridolfi," 180.

to the second or third generation.[20] The most prominent and influential lawyers were always from old patrician families. Among these, many, like Ridolfi and his older contemporary Lapo da Castiglionchio (d. 1381), favoured canon law, the more conservative and aristocratic of the two branches of law.[21]

The basic prerequisite for the practice of law in Florence was five years' study at the law faculty of an Italian university, most often Bologna, the biggest centre for legal studies.[22] The process was expensive, far beyond the means of all but the rich, particularly if the candidate remained for the additional two to five years required to qualify for the licentiate and doctorate in canon law, civil law or both laws.[23] Ridolfi's education was typical. In 1381, he left for Bologna, where he followed the "ordinary" (mandatory) lectures on Gratian's *Decretum*, the *Decretals* of Gregory IX and the *Liber sextus* of Boniface VIII, and the "extraordinary" (supplementary) courses on the *Constitutiones Clementinae* of Clement V.[24] According to Diplovatatius, Ridolfi's principal teachers were Johannes de Fantutiis (d. 1391) and Laurentius de Pinu (d. ca. 1398), but he also attended the lectures of John of Legnano (ca. 1320-1383) and Gasparus Calderinus (d. 1395), grandson of the famous canonist Johannes Andreae (d. 1348).[25] Ridolfi would later

[20] See *Lawyers and Statecraft*, 62-78, esp. 68-71; and the biographies at ibid., 481-509. The routine drafting and authentication of legal acts was not a function of lawyers but of notaries, who were usually of more modest social background.

[21] Ibid., 66, 74.

[22] Ibid., 31. On the curriculum and course of studies, see ibid., 80-91; Hastings Rashdall, *The Universities of Europe in the Middle Ages*, 2nd ed., ed. F. M. Powicke, 3 vols. (Oxford: Clarendon Press, 1936), 1: 216-30; and Helmut Coing, "Die juristische Fakultät und ihr Lehrprogramm," in *Handbuch der Quellen und Literatur der neueren europäischen Privatrechsgeschichte*, vol. 1, *Mittelalter (1100-1500): Die gelehrten Rechte und die Gesetzgebung*, ed. Helmut Coing (Munich: C. H. Beck'sche, 1973), 69-80.

[23] Martines, *Lawyers and Statecraft*, 81-82, 89-90. Martines estimates the average basic expenses of a law student in the early fifteenth century at twenty to thirty florins a year, roughly equivalent to the earnings of a fully employed unskilled labourer. For wage data, see Richard Goldthwaite, *The Building of Renaissance Florence: An Economic and Social History* (Baltimore and London: Johns Hopkins University Press, 1980), 436-37, appendix 3; on standards of living, see ibid., 342-50.

[24] Martino, "Ridolfi," 184. These collections are described below in the appendix on Ridolfi's authorities. For a recent introduction to medieval canon law, see James A. Brundage, *Medieval Canon Law* (London and New York: Longman, 1995).

[25] Diplovatatius, *Liber de claris iurisconsultis*, ed. Schultz et al., 343; Martino, "Ridolfi," 184. For biographical notes on these jurists, see the appendix on Ridolfi's authorities below.

draw extensively on the writings of all four for his treatise on usury.

Before completing their studies, candidates at Bologna were required to engage in a series of public disputations and *repetitiones* (expositions) of legal problems. Ridolfi presented a *repetitio* on the decretal *Cum ordinem* (X 1.3.6) in May 1386 and formally disputed with his master Laurentius de Pinu on 10 January 1387. A month later, he passed the private examination for the licentiate, which conferred the right to teach, and was immediately elected to a lectureship in the Sext and Clementines. The doctorate in canon law—after the licentiate essentially a formality, albeit an expensive one—followed in September 1387.[26]

Ridolfi stayed in Bologna for a year before returning to Florence in the summer of 1388 and a lectureship at the university to which he had been elected in May.[27] Lecturers at the University of Florence were retained on annual contracts, and the records suggest that Ridolfi was appointed yearly to an ordinary or extraordinary lectureship until 1404.[28] Public duties apparently prevented him from lecturing between 1404 and the temporary suspension of classes in 1407, but when the university reopened in 1413 he was hired to lecture on the *Decretum* and in the following year on the

[26] Martino, "Ridolfi," 184-85. On the *repetitio* genre, see below, p. 85.

[27] The election protocol is edited by Roberto Abbondanza in "Gli atti degli Ufficiali dello Studio fiorentino dal maggio al settembre 1388," *ASI* 117 (1959): 97. Founded in 1348, the university was funded largely from *monte* revenues; since military expenses took priority, it was periodically closed for lack of funds and never grew to the size of the more famous Italian schools. On the university prior to 1473, see Jonathan Davies, *Florence and its University During the Early Renaissance*, Education and Society in the Middle Ages and Renaissance, no. 8 (Leiden, Boston and Cologne: E. J. Brill, 1998). See also Rashdall, *Universities of Europe*, 2: 47-51; and Gene A. Brucker, "Florence and its University, 1348-1434," in *Action and Conviction in Early Modern Europe: Essays in Memory of E. H. Harbison*, ed. Theodore K. Rabb and Jerrold E. Seigel (Princeton: Princeton University Press, 1969), 220-36; repr. in *Society, Culture, and Religion*, 109-205. On university organization and appointment procedures, see Davies, *Florence and its University*, 9-48.

[28] Martino, "Ridolfi," 186-87. Evidence is wanting for 1399, 1400 and 1403. For 1402, see Alessandro Gherardi, ed., *Statuti della Università e Studio fiorentino dell'anno MCCCLXXXVII seguiti da un'appendice di documenti dal MCCCXX al MCCCCLXXII*, Documenti di storia italiana pubblicati a cura delle R. Deputazioni sugli studi di storia patria di Toscana, dell'Umbria e delle Marche, vol. 7 (Florence: M. Cellini, 1881; repr. Bologna: Forni, 1973), 376. Evidence for 1404 comes from the *explicit* of the *Tractatus de usuris* (3772-73). Davies observes that Ridolfi was among the lawyers most frequently retained by the university as an instructor (*Florence and its University*, 30, n. 144).

Decretals.[29] Stipends in the two law faculties varied according to the experience and distinction of teachers, but on average they were the most generous in the university, so that a lectureship provided a crucial supplement to a lawyer's professional income, particularly at the beginning of his career when he was establishing a practice.[30] Ridolfi's stipend of fifty florins in 1388 was comparable to that of other junior lecturers, such as the civil lawyer Ricciardo di Francesco del Bene (1369-1411), who was paid seventy-five florins in 1406.[31] Within ten years of his first contract, Ridolfi commanded a hundred florins, plus a thirty-florin supplement "to dispute and determine certain questions from the *Decretum*." By 1413, as an established political and professional figure, he was earning a generous 180 florins.[32]

Ridolfi's association with the university extended beyond teaching engagements. In 1418-19 and 1431 he was nominated one of the *Ufficiali dello Studio* (Officials of the University), the board of administrators appointed by the commune to hire and pay instructors.[33] He also served on the board of the *Casa della Sapienza*, a residence for poor students estab-

[29] Katherine Park, "The Readers at the Florentine Studio according to Comunal Fiscal Records (1357-1380, 1413-1446)," *Rinascimento* n.s. 20 (1980): 272-73; Gherardi, *Statuti della Università*, 389.

[30] On stipends, see Park, "Readers," 252, 270. A university appointment could be decisive. Osvaldo Cavallar suggests in a recent study that Francesco Guicciardini's (1483-1540) abandonment of law for administration was dictated partly by the difficulty of augmenting his professional fees by lecturing; see *Francesco Guicciardini giurista: I ricordi degli onorari*, Università di Firenze, Centro di studi per la storia del pensiero giuridico moderno, Biblioteca per la storia del pensiero giuridico moderno, no. 36 (Milan: Giuffrè, 1991), 204.

[31] Ridolfi's stipend is noted by Abbondanza, "Gli atti," 97. For del Bene, see Martines, *Lawyers and Statecraft*, 103. By comparison, in 1387 a fully employed skilled labourer earned about fifty-five florins (Goldthwaite, *Building of Renaissance Florence*, 437, appendix 3). The eminent canonist Franciscus de Zabarellis (ca. 1335-1417), who was retained in 1388 to lecture on the *Decretals*, received 325 florins (Abbondanza, "Gli atti," 109).

[32] Evidence for Ridolfi's stipend in the early 1390s is found in the university protocols edited by Enrico Spagnesi, *Utiliter edoceri: Atti inediti degli Ufficiali dello Studio fiorentino (1391-96)*, Università di Firenze, Pubblicazioni della facoltà di giurisprudenza, no. 34 (Milan: Giuffrè, 1979), 48-49, 125, 135, 139-40, 184, 196, 203, 216, 257, 265; references to the supplementary payments in 1395-96 are at 221, 239, 261. Ridolfi's stipend in 1413 is reported by Park, "Readers," 272-73; and Gherardi, *Statuti della Università*, 389.

[33] Gherardi, *Statuti della Università*, 198, 230; Martino, "Ridolfi," 188, nn. 55, 56; Davies, *Florence and its University*, 151, appendix 1. On the duties of the Officials, see Guidi, *Il governo*, 2: 330; and Davies, *Florence and its University*, 10-17.

lished in 1431 by a bequest of Niccolò da Uzzano.[34] Surviving records of doctorates awarded by the university show that Ridolfi was one of the most active members of the college of doctors of law, the body responsible for presenting and examining doctoral candidates. Between 1392 and 1438 he was examiner or *promotor* (sponsor) of no less than fifteen candidates for the doctorate in canon law.[35]

Vespasiano's assertion that moral scruples prevented Ridolfi from practising law reflects the eulogistic function of his sketches, for the evidence indicates that Ridolfi managed a busy and lucrative *studio* (law office).[36] What exactly did an early Renaissance lawyer do? Like all lawyers enrolled in the guild of judges and notaries, Ridolfi combined the functions of judge, advocate and counsel.[37] Among these, requests for counsel by courts, private clients, corporations and public agencies predominated. As a specialist in canon law, Ridolfi was regularly consulted on cases of contract, marriage, usury and clerics, and he was on permanent retainer as legal adviser of the Camaldolese monks.[38] His practice, however, was not restricted to ecclesiastical causes. Diplovatatius remarks that Ridolfi was also "learned in the civil law," and the registers that survive from his practice show that he was regularly engaged by the commune's executive, public officials, the university, guild officers and a range of private clients.[39]

[34] Work began in 1436 on a site near San Marco but was never completed (Davies, *Florence and its University*, 17-18). For Ridolfi's service on the board, see ibid., 18, n. 71; Martino, "Ridolfi," 188, n. 58; and Gherardi, *Statuti della Università*, 251.

[35] Davies, *Florence and its University*, 167, appendix 3. On the functions of the college, see ibid., 36-48.

[36] "Sendo singularissimo dotore in iure civili et canonica, per coscientia nolla volle exercitare, parendogli ch'ella non si potessi fare con buona coscientia" (*Le vite*, ed. Greco, 2: 131). In the light of Ridolfi's surviving *consilia*, Martines characterizes his practice as "flourishing" (*Lawyers and Statecraft*, 483).

[37] Martines, *Lawyers and Statecraft*, 33. Matriculation in the guild was a prerequisite for lawyers and notaries who wished to practise. For an account of the guild's structure and regulatory functions, see ibid., 11-61.

[38] Ibid., 92, 483.

[39] Diplovatatius, *Liber de claris iurisconsultis*, ed. Schultz et al., 342: "Iste dominus Laurentius fuit doctor et miles et doctissimus in iure civili." Ridolfi was in fact a doctor of canon law, but whatever their specialization, law students studied both systems as part of their training. On the medieval conception of canon and Roman law as complementary elements of a *ius commune* (common law), see Manlio Bellomo, *The Common Legal Past of Europe, 1000-1800*, trans. Lydia G. Cochrane, Studies in Medieval and Early Modern Canon Law, no. 4 (Washington, DC: Catholic University of America, 1995). For the range of Ridolfi's activities as a consultant, see Martino, "Ridolfi," 189-90; and Martines, *Lawyers and Statecraft*, 91, 101, 106-

Commissions for counsel usually involved the composition of a *consilium* (opinion). After summarizing the material facts of the case, the consultant adduced and analysed the relevant legal authorities on both sides of the question and then concluded with an authoritative synthesis.[40] A *consilium sapientis* (judicial opinion) replied to a question by a judge on an issue in a lawsuit or on a point of procedure; it was subscribed and sealed by the consultant (*sapiens*) and usually formed the basis of the court's sentence. Litigants also sought opinions for presentation to the court on matters arising in the course of their suits. In both cases, the lawyer was presumed to act as an impartial expert whose detachment guaranteed the legitimacy of the court's verdict. The authority attached to *consilia* was reflected in the requirement that copies of all judicial and procedural opinions presented in Florentine courts be deposited with the guild and copied

---

7, 181, 240-42, 337-38, 343, 370, 399. I am currently preparing a study of Ridolfi's practice on the basis of several hundred *consilia* preserved in the Florentine state archives and in two registers of legal opinions from the years 1388-98 and 1412-20 that survive from his law office (University of Messina, Biblioteca della facoltà di giurisprudenza A. 1; and BNF, Fondo principale II, III, 370). For an analysis of the cases and clientele of an early sixteenth-century lawyer, see Cavallar, *Francesco Guicciardini*, 47-136. A significant proportion of Guicciardini's commissions—just under a quarter—came from public bodies (ibid., 49).

[40] On the structure and typology of *consilia*, see Mario Ascheri, "Rechtsprechungs-Konsiliensammlungen-Italien," in *Handbuch der Quellen und Literatur der neueren europäischen Privatrechtsgeschichte*, vol. 2, *Neuere Zeit (1500-1800): Das Zeitalter des gemeinen Rechts*, part 2, *Gezetzgebung und Rechtssprechung*, ed. Helmut Coing (Munich: C. H. Beck'sche, 1976), 1113-1222; idem, "*Consilium sapientis*, perizia medica e *res iudicata*: Diritto dei 'dottori' e istituzioni communali," in *Proceedings of the Fifth International Congress of Medieval Canon Law, Salamanca, 21-25 September 1976*, Monumenta iuris canonici, series C: Subsidia, vol. 6, ed. Stephan Kuttner and Kenneth Pennington (Vatican City: Biblioteca Apostolica Vaticana, 1980), 533-79; Guido Rossi, *Consilium sapientis iudiciale: Studi e ricerche per la storia del processo romano-canonico*, vol. 1, *Secoli XII-XIII*, Seminario giuridico della Università di Bologna, no. 18 (Milan: Giuffrè, 1958); Cavallar, *Francesco Guicciardini*, 209-55; Julius Kirshner, "*Consilia* as Authority in Late Medieval Italy: The Case of Florence," in *Legal Consulting in the Civil Law Tradition*, ed. Mario Ascheri, Ingrid Baumgärtner and Julius Kirshner (Berkeley: The Robbins Collection, 1999), 107-40. On *consilia* as a historical source and for additional bibliography, see Ingrid Baumgärtner, "Stadtgeschichte und Consilia im italienischen Spätmittelalter: Eine Quellengattung und ihre Möglichkeiten," *Zeitschrift für historische Forschung* 17 (1990): 129-54; and idem, ed., *Consilia im späten Mittelalter: Zum historischen Aussagewert einer Quellengattung* (Sigmaringen: Jan Thorbecke, 1995). Peter Riesenberg, "The Consilia Literature: A Prospectus," *Manuscripta* 6 (1962): 3-22 remains a good introduction to the genre.

into its registers.[41] In other contexts, an opinion might take the form of a report, a treatise or an extra-judicial arbitration.[42] The pressure of work and the importance attached to *communis opinio* (consensus opinion) on complicated problems meant that *consilia* often represented collaborative efforts by two or more lawyers who jointly contributed to the composition of the opinion or endorsed the conclusions of the principal consultant.[43]

Studies of individual lawyers and the profession as a whole emphasize the importance of personal ties and public profile in constructing a successful practice.[44] In both respects Ridolfi was well placed. His membership in an old and distinguished family with close ties to other elite lineages and a network of local clients brought him many private commissions, while marriage extended his circle of connections.[45] His position as a lecturer at the university conferred public status as a legal authority, and access to government posts after 1393 increased his chances of securing public and private commissions.[46] We have no information on Ridolfi's professional

[41] See Kirshner, "*Consilia* as Authority," 107-19.

[42] A complex range of consultative activities is described by Cavallar in *Francesco Guicciardini*, 208-55, esp. 216-36. On arbitration, see Kuehn, "Law and Arbitration in Renaissance Florence," in *Law, Family, and Women*, 19-74.

[43] The practice is described by Cavallar, *Francesco Guicciardini*, 155-83, 223-31. Ridolfi wrote many of his opinions in collaboration with other jurists, among them such luminaries as Angelo degli Ubaldi, Filippo Corsini, Peter of Ancharano and Paolo di Castro (Martino, "Ridolfi," 190).

[44] See Martines, *Lawyers and Statecraft*, 106-17; and Cavallar, *Francesco Guicciardini*, 137-54.

[45] Ridolfi was married at least twice (Martino, "Ridolfi," 186, n. 43). A memorandum in his *zibaldone* (commonplace book) indicates that in 1388, while still in Bologna, he married Caterina, daughter of Angelo Barucci, by proxy (BNF, Panciatichi 147, fol. 1v). The 1427 *catasto* records a Barucci household in Santa Croce quarter whose declared weath was 8165 florins; in terms of status Molho rates the Barucci "low" (*Marriage Alliance*, 366; 379, appendix 3). A note of Ridolfi's ownership of a vernacular collection of St. Jerome's letters now preserved in the Biblioteca Riccardiana (Cod. 1667, *Vita, miracoli e transito di S. Girolamo*) indicates that he was later allied to the "high status" Guicciardini family through his marriage to Caterina di Luigi Guicciardini (Martino, "Ridolfi," 186, n. 43). According to Carocci, late in life Ridolfi married Nanna di Niccolò de' Bardi (*Ridolfi di Piazza*, 81, table 7). On neighbourhood and kinship networks, see Christiane Klapisch-Zuber, "'Kin, Friends, and Neighbors': The Urban Territory of a Merchant Family in 1400," in *Women, Family, and Ritual in Renaissance Italy*, trans. Lydia Cochrane (Chicago and London: University of Chicago Press, 1985), 68-93.

[46] On Ridolfi's admission to citizenship privileges, see below, p. 24. On the interdependence of political and professional success, see Martines, *Lawyers and Statecraft*, 107, 393-94. Ridolfi's appointment to the university in 1388 itself

income, but we know that the practice of his younger contemporary Ricciardo del Bene was worth 350 florins in 1406. As one of the small circle of leading Florentine lawyers Ridolfi probably earned considerably more, somewhere in the vicinity of five or six hundred florins a year.[47]

New conditions in Florence guaranteed Ridolfi's political rehabilitation even before his return from Bologna in 1388. Six years earlier, in 1382, the traditional elite regained power in a counterrevolutionary coup.[48] The new regime prudently discarded the policy of exclusion pursued by earlier patrician-dominated governments in favour of an expansion of the political class to accommodate the ambitions of lesser Florentines.[49] Between 1382 and 1434, the number of citizens the republic's nomination committees judged fit for public office in the periodic selection procedures called "scrutinies"

---

suggests that he was being groomed for public life; on elite control of university appointments, see ibid., 394. The close involvement of the Florentine elite in every aspect of the university is the principal theme of Davies, *Florence and its University*; on the social background of Officials of the University in the late fourteenth and early fifteenth centuries, see ibid., 49-64, esp. 51-52.

[47] Martines, *Lawyers and Statecraft*, 104. Martines discusses fees and incomes at ibid., 100-106. See also Cavallar, *Francesco Guicciardini*, 185-207. Vespasiano's portrayal of Ridolfi as "a poor man who lived on his own income" was dictated by the biographer's Roman models ("fu simile a quegli antichi Romani per la sua neteza, che si vede che volle vivere del suo, et ebbe tenuissime sustanze" [*Le Vite*, ed. Greco, 2: 131; trans. George and Waters, *Renaissance Princes, Popes and Prelates*, 316]). Ridolfi's declared wealth in the 1427 *catasto* was 7657 florins (Molho, *Marriage Alliance*, 400, appendix 3; ASF, Catasto 66, fol. 81r); the value of his net assets after deductions was 5249 florins, which placed him fifty-third out of the 150 leading taxpayers in Santo Spirito (Martines, *Social World*, 376, table 8). This considerably exceeded the average wealth of Florentine lawyers, which Herlihy and Klapisch-Zuber estimate at 1079.2 florins, and put Ridolfi in the league of the bankers and wool merchants (*Tuscans and Their Families*, 129, table 4.8). On the calculation of taxable assets in the 1427 *catasto*, see ibid., 10-17; and Elio Conti, *L'imposta diretta a Firenze nel Quattrocento (1427-1494)*, Istituto storico italiano per il Medio Evo, Studi storici, fasc. 136-39 (Rome: Istituto storico italiano per il Medio Evo, 1984), 138-49.

[48] The best account is Brucker, *Civic World*, 60-75.

[49] There is an extensive literature on the composition of the political class between 1382 and 1434. See in particular Molho, "Politics and the Ruling Class"; Ronald G. Witt, "Florentine politics and the ruling class, 1382-1407," *Journal of Medieval and Renaissance Studies* 5 (1975): 243-67; Kent, "Florentine *Reggimento*"; Brucker, *Civic World*, esp. chaps. 2, 3 and 5, 60-186, 248-318; Najemy, *Corporatism and Consensus*, chap. 8 and Epilogue, 263-317; and Herlihy, "Rulers of Florence."

almost tripled from eight hundred to over two thousand.[50] Although this pool never represented more than half the technically qualified citizens or five percent of the population as a whole, it was nevertheless bigger than under any previous regime.[51]

Viewed, however, from the perspective of class and guild affiliation, it is clear that the democratization of politics under the new regime was illusory. The two textile workers' guilds that survived from 1378 were suppressed and the minor guilds effectively marginalized.[52] The chief beneficiaries of the new policy were rich new men from the major guilds. Hundreds of citizens from families with no previous experience in politics suddenly found themselves eligible for the republic's highest posts, and those whose name tickets were actually drawn for office in the regime's first decade represented more than a third of the priors.[53] This trend was quickly reversed: the proportion of new men drawn for the priorate fell to nineteen percent between 1393 and 1400, and then to ten percent in the first decade of the fifteenth century. In the same period, families of the traditional elite appropriated a bigger share of the chief magistracy, increasing their seats from three in 1382-87 to an average of just over five in the early years of the fifteenth century.[54]

The elite maintained and extended their dominance by manipulation

[50] Kent, "Florentine *Reggimento*," 615-16; 621-23, table 1; 633, table 3. For 1382, see also Najemy, *Corporatism and Consensus*, 273, n. 31. On the scrutiny mechanism between 1382 and 1415, see Guidi, *Il governo*, 1: 203-307.

[51] On the basis of the 1427 *catasto*, Herlihy and Klapisch-Zuber estimate the population of Florence at 37,144 (*Tuscans and Their Families*, 74, table 3.4). In 1433, out of 6354 citizens nominated, 2084 were approved for office (Kent, "Florentine *Reggimento*, 621-23, table 1). Eligible officeholders therefore represented just over five percent of the urban population, which included, in addition to guildsmen who failed to meet the basic property and tax requirements, women, children, the destitute and workers lacking guild affiliation, none of whom enjoyed political privileges. For a more optimistic calculation of the size of the political class in the fifteenth century, see Molho, *Marriage Alliance*, 193-214. For comparisons with the popular regimes of 1343-48 and 1378-82, see Najemy, *Corporatism and Consensus*, 263-64, 275-76.

[52] Kent, "Florentine *Reggimento*," 633, table 3; 621-23, table 1; Najemy, *Corporatism and Consensus*, 268-79.

[53] Witt, "Florentine politics," 248, defining new men as those with no previous representation in the priorate. See also Najemy, *Corporatism and Consensus*, 292-95.

[54] Najemy, *Corporatism and Consensus*, 295-97; 320-22, table A.2; Witt, "Florentine politics," 248-50.

of the electoral process.[55] Political reform commissions in 1387 and 1393 ensured the selection of patrician candidates by altering the composition of nomination committees in favour of the elite. As an additional guarantee, the commissions supplemented the *borse* (bags) from which candidates' name tickets were randomly drawn for office with a special list of patrician candidates deposited in *borsellini* (little bags) from which a fixed proportion of names for the *Signoria* and other sensitive posts had to be taken. In other respects, they maintained the facade of open government: the pool of potential officeholders was allowed to grow and the traditional rules preventing repeated tenure of posts were strictly applied, thus averting the appearance that office was the preserve of a faction.[56] Although the number of posts actually open to new men and minor guildsmen declined in 1390s, those who succeeded in the scrutiny could still hope to be drawn for office, and the rapid turnover of personnel in the magistracies and councils meant that many were, though never in sufficient numbers to influence decisively the direction of government.[57]

In the judgement of both contemporary and modern observers, the real centre of power in this period was an oligarchy of about sixty men from a similar number of patrician families.[58] The members of this "leadership elite," as Gene Brucker calls it, were characterized by high public profile, experience in office and proven administrative competence. The elite were well represented in the magistracies and legislative councils, on embassies and on the various *balìe* (*ad hoc* commissions) struck by the government. But mainly they exerted their influence informally through the *consulte* (councils) and *pratiche* (select committees) that convened almost weekly to advise the *Signoria*.[59] As forums for sounding out public opinion or ob-

[55] For what follows, see Najemy, *Corporatism and Consensus*, 276-92; and Guidi, *Il governo*, 2: 203-307.

[56] Molho, "Politics and the Ruling Class," 411-13; Najemy, *Corporatism and Consensus*, 292-300. On the mechanism of *divieto* (disqualification), see Brucker, *Florentine Politics*, 67-69; and Guidi, *Il governo*, 1: 130-33.

[57] Najemy convincingly interprets this as a process of cooptation pursued by the elite in the 1380s, when its ascendancy was insecure, and then moderated until by 1400 there remained the appearance of broad participation but virtually nothing of its substance; see *Corporatism and Consensus*, 298-300; and below, pp. 105-7.

[58] What follows is based on Brucker's analysis of the oligarchy in 1411, *Civic World*, 262-318. See also Kent, "Florentine *Reggimento*," 265-68; and Conti, *Consulte e Pratiche, 1401*, xxxv-liv.

[59] For a discussion, see Conti, *Consulte e Pratiche, 1401*, ix-xix. The records distinguish between "closed councils," restricted to the *Signoria* and the Colleges, and "councils of the *richiesti* (summoned men)," with which we are concerned here. *Pratiche* were appointed by the *Signoria* and presented recommendations. Of *con-*

taining expert advice, such gatherings were nothing new, but under the regime of 1382-1434 they became the principal mechanism for the formulation of policy. Increasingly, the *Signoria* took no important step without summoning a council or striking a select committee, and the protocols of the counsellors' debates and recommendations provide us with an anatomy of power in early Renaissance Florence.[60]

Ridolfi's political credentials and professional expertise made him an obvious recruit to this exclusive group. As early as March 1389, the government sought his opinion in a *consulta* on the terms of a proposed league with Milan, and in 1392 he was one of five lawyers commissioned by the *Signoria* to advise on the implications of a treaty with the lord of Mantua, Francesco Gonzaga (d. 1407).[61] Despite his youth, Ridolfi could be numbered by the historian Scipione Ammirato (d. 1600) among the "capi della Repubblica" of the 1390s.[62] This assessment is confirmed by the protocols of the *consulte* and *pratiche* of 1404, the year in which Ridolfi finished the *Tractatus de usuris*, when he spoke at a total of twelve *consulte*, most of them concerned with the conduct of campaigns against Milanese strongholds in Pisa, Lombardy and the Romagna. Usually he was summoned in his personal capacity, but twice in January he spoke on behalf of the other Ward Standard-Bearers and the Twelve and twice for Santo Spirito quarter.[63] He sat on two *pratiche* and on 14 July presented the committee's recommendations on tentative negotiations to end the Great Schism.[64] Ridolfi's influential—and apparently prolix—interventions placed him in the inner circle of oligarchs who dominated debates in the first decade of the fifteenth century.[65] On the basis of the 1401 protocols, Elio Conti numbers

---

sulte and *pratiche* in the period 1343-78 Brucker notes that "rarely, if ever, did the priors flout the consensus of opinion expressed in these consultative assemblies" (*Florentine Politics*, 76).

[60] Brucker, *Civic World*, 284-85; Kent, "Florentine *Reggimento*," 601-8. On the value of these protocols as a source, see Brucker, *Florentine Politics*, 75-76; and *Civic World*, 137-38, 284-302.

[61] Martines, *Lawyers and Statecraft*, 23-24, 322.

[62] *Istorie fiorentine*, quoted by Conti, *Consulte e Pratiche, 1401*, xxxviii.

[63] Renzo Ninci, ed., *Le Consulte e Pratiche della Repubblica fiorentina (1404)*, Istituto storico italiano per il Medio Evo, Fonti per la storia d'Italia, no. 115 (Rome: Istituto storico italiano per il Medio Evo, 1991), 12, 18, 23, 45, 55, 122, 138, 159, 263, 290, 306, 340, 341.

[64] Ibid., 270.

[65] Martines quotes an undated comment of a Sienese observer that "among others Messer Lorenzo Ridolfi delivered a speech of more than an hour in the Council of the People" (*Social World*, 249, n. 36); and Brucker remarks on Ridolfi's "penchant for delivering lengthy harangues" (*Civic World*, 286).

Ridolfi among the thirteen most powerful figures in the regime, noting in addition that between 1402 and 1405 he participated in sixty-six *consulte* and *pratiche*.[66]

The political reform commission of 1393 entrenched elite dominance by admitting several magnate families to the *popolo* and the privilege of officeholding, among them the Ridolfi di Piazza.[67] In 1394, Lorenzo Ridolfi was drawn for the November-December priorate, inaugurating a career in office matched among his contemporaries only by Cosimo de' Medici (d. 1464).[68] Over the next thirty years, he served four terms in the *Signoria*, three of them in the most prestigious position, that of Standard-Bearer of Justice, which was always reserved for an elite candidate.[69] Service on the *Dieci di Balìa* (Ten of War) was almost as important as signorial office. Appointed with a year's mandate during periods of conflict, the Ten advised the *Signoria* on war aims, formulated strategy, raised voluntary war loans and recruited mercenaries to fight in the republic's armies.[70] Ridolfi was a commissioner almost continuously from 1397 to the conquest of Pisa in 1406. He was reappointed in 1409-14 during the wars with King Ladislaus of Naples (d. 1414) and again during renewed conflict with Milan in 1423-24 and 1436-40.[71] In 1406, his service was followed by appointment to the governship of the strategically important town of Vico Pisano.[72] Ridolfi was

[66] *Consulte e Pratiche, 1401*, xxvi, xxxviii, xlviii. Conti analyzes the composition of this "restricted circle of notables" or "élite dominante" at xxxv-xliv. The group roughly corresponds to the leaders of the regime in 1411 identified by Brucker, *Civic World*, 265. For Ridolfi's interventions in 1402-05, see Conti, *Consulte e Pratiche, 1401*, xlv-liv. See also the protocols of 1405-1406 recently edited by Laura De Angelis, Renzo Ninci and Paolo Pirillo, *Le Consulte e Pratiche della Repubblica fiorentina (1405-1406)*, Istituto storico italiano per il medio evo, Fonti per la storia dell'Italia Medievale, Antiquitates, no. 5 (Rome: Istituto storico italiano per il Medio Evo, 1996). Brucker counts almost a hundred speeches by Ridolfi in advisory councils beween 1403 and 1415 (*Civic World*, 265).

[67] Brucker, *Civic World*, 93; Martino, "Ridolfi," 192.

[68] Martino, "Ridolfi," 192; Herlihy, "Rulers of Florence," 377.

[69] Martino, "Ridolfi," 192, n. 81. The tickets for Standard-Bearer of Justice were drawn from a *borsellino*; see Najemy, *Corporatism and Consensus*, 161, 281; Guidi, *Il governo*, 1: 220-23; and above, p. 22.

[70] Anthony Molho, "The Florentine Oligarchy and the *Balie* of the Late Trecento," *Speculum* 43 (1968): 30-31; and Guidi, *Il governo*, 2: 203-12. The office was created in 1384. For examples of Ridolfi's interventions in *pratiche* as a spokesman for the commissioners-elect of the Ten of 1402, see Conti, *Consulte e Pratiche, 1401*, 304, 319, 330.

[71] A list of Ridolfi's service is supplied by Martino, "Ridolfi," 192, n. 81.

[72] Ibid., 196.

also active on internal judicial and quasi-judicial boards, such as the *Otto di Guardia* (Eight of Police), the *Ufficiali dell'onestà* (Officers of Decency), who regulated sodomy and prostitution, and the *Conservatori delle leggi* (Defenders of the Laws), the commission that enforced the rules on admission to public office.[73]

Martines notes that lawyers played a big role in diplomacy, where their technical and rhetorical skills could be put to good use and their status as doctors and knights enhanced the dignity of embassies.[74] Ridolfi was no exception. In November-December 1399, he was a member of a delegation to Rome entrusted with negotiating alliances with Pope Boniface IX (1389-1404) and Ladislaus of Naples against Giangaleazzo Visconti.[75] Four years later, he was sent to Rimini on a similar mission to Carlo Malatesta (d. 1429), the papal governor of the Romagna.[76] When the government became alarmed at the territorial ambitions of Filippo Maria Visconti (d. 1447) soon after ratifying a treaty with him in 1420, it was Ridolfi and Cosimo de' Medici who were despatched to Milan for talks.[77] The war that erupted four years later provided Ridolfi with his most notable diplomatic coup. Sent to Venice in the summer of 1425 to propose an alliance against Milan, he persuaded the Venetians to abandon their cherished neutrality

[73] Ridolfi was appointed to the Eight in June 1394, soon after readmission to the *popolo* (Martines, *Lawyers and Statecraft*, 332), and again in 1411 (Brucker, *Civic World*, 329). Created in 1378, the commission was responsible for the suppression of political conspiracies; see Giovanni Antonelli, "La magistratura degli Otto di Guardia a Firenze," *ASI* 92 (1954): 3-39; Guidi, *Il governo*, 2:221-27; and Andrea Zorzi, *L'amministrazione della giustizia penale nella Repubblica fiorentina: Aspetti e problemi*, Biblioteca storica toscana, no. 23 (Florence: Leo S. Olschki, 1988), 32-63, esp. 42-45, 50-53. Ridolfi's service in the Office of Decency and Defenders of the Laws is noted by Martines, *Social World*, 152, 181. On the activities of the former magistracy, established in 1403, see Guidi, *Il governo*, 2: 327; Richard Trexler, "Florentine Prostitution in the Fifteenth Century: Patrons and Clients," in *Power and Dependence*, 2: 31-65; and Michael Rocke, *Forbidden Friendships: Homosexuality and Male Culture in Renaissance Florence* (New York and Oxford: Oxford University Press, 1996), 28, 31-32, 125. On the Defenders of the Laws, see Guidi, *Il governo*, 2: 351-52; Andrea Zorzi, "I fiorentini e gli uffici pubblici nel primo Quattrocento: Concorrenza, abusi, illegalità," *Quaderni storici* 66 (1987): 725-51; and idem, *L'amministrazione*, 62-63.

[74] See *Lawyers and Statecraft*, 311-84; 283, n. 86.

[75] Ibid., 320.

[76] Ibid., 325-26.

[77] Ibid., 380.

in favour of Florence.[78]

I shall return to Ridolfi's political sentiments presently.[79] For now it is enough to note that he shared the "managerial" approach to government that Brucker attributes to the leadership as a whole.[80] His role in defining the republic's position on the Great Schism in 1408-09 provides a good illustration.[81] The issue was whether Florence should repudiate its allegiance to the Roman pope, Gregory XII (1406-15), and join those who were demanding a general council to end the schism. Opinion in Florence was divided: the leadership elite supported the conciliarists and proposed Florence itself as a venue for the council, while nonelite guildsmen were nervous about the political and religious implicatons of breaching the city's traditional Roman allegiance. It fell to Ridolfi and his fellow lawyers to rally opinion by providing a theoretical justification for the policy change. In *consulte* of January 1409, Ridolfi cited the consensus of the universities that repudiation of Gregory was consistent with both law and conscience.[82] In his view, however, the basic question was one of *Realpolitik*: what course best served the interests of Florence? On this, legal opinion was unanimous in arguing that the status and ambitions of the republic could only be enhanced by support for the council. The views of the leadership prevailed. The council met in Florentine territory, at Pisa, in March 1409 and Ridolfi himself represented the government at the assembly and on embassies to the newly-elected pope Alexander V (d. 1410).

More to our purpose here is what the incident reveals about the kind of influence Ridolfi exerted in his milieu. The quality of *vicinato*, face-to-face relations, that characterized fifteenth-century Florentine society meant

[78] Brucker, *Civic World*, 468-71; Martino, "Ridolfi," 194-95. The mission is reported at length by Vespasiano, *Le vite*, ed. Greco, 2: 132-34.

[79] See below, pp. 107-8.

[80] See *Civic World*, 367: "[The leadership] believed that the injustices and inequities stimulating civic discord could be corrected if not eliminated by legislation and administrative decisions." The term "managerial" is applied to the regime by Marvin B. Becker, "The Florentine Territorial State and Civic Humanism in the Early Renaissance," in *Florentine Studies*, 119; and by Rocke, *Forbidden Friendships*, 27.

[81] What follows is based on the accounts in Martines, *Lawyers and Statecraft*, 289-96; and Brucker, *Civic World*, 295-99.

[82] Ridolfi also composed a *consilium* in support of the council, ed. Johannes Vincke, *Beiträge zur Kirchen- und Rechtsgeschichte*, vol. 3, *Schriftstücke zum Pisaner Konzil: Ein Kampf um die öffentliche Meinung* (Bonn: Peter Hanstein, 1942), 122-34. For a discussion of academic, especially canonical, opinion in favour of the council, see Robert N. Swanson, *Universities, Academics and the Great Schism* (Cambridge: Cambridge University Press, 1979), esp. 148-74; Ridolfi's opinions are discussed at 155-56.

that men like Ridolfi, the *savvi*, prudent men "capable of shrewd and reasoned judgement, informed by worldly experience normally associated with high social standing," were easily recognized and their opinions on controversial issues treated with deference by those who lacked their prestige and technical skills.[83] Placed at the service of government, such influence was crucial in manufacturing consent to divisive policies, particularly among the nonelite elements of the enfranchised classes—the new men and lesser guildsmen—who posed the biggest potential threat to elite domination. From Vespasiano's remarks on Ridolfi's treatise on usury it is clear that this was as true of the public debt controversy as it was of the schism debate. A man of restricted learning and certainly unversed in the technical complexities of usury law, Vespasiano was nevertheless at pains to emphasize the text's authority and influence:

> The integrity of [Ridolfi's] character may be judged by his book *de usuris*, which deals with legal contracts and restitution, a book which has had great weight everywhere and has never been censured. Archbishop Antonino often quotes it in his *Summa* on contracts and restitution with full agreement; indeed, he gives it an authority almost equal to that of the Gospels. Lorenzo spent immense trouble and labour over this book, as all things are given consonant with reason and authority.[84]

In any dispute over the *monte*'s legitimacy, the knowledge that a *savvio* like Ridolfi considered its operations fully compatible with law and conscience was bound to carry considerable weight with his co-citizens.

[83] The quotation is from Athanasios Moulakis, "Civic humanism, realist constitutionalism, and Francesco Guicciardini's *Discorso di Logrogno*," in *Renaissance Civic Humanism*, 220. See also Martines, *Lawyers and Statecraft*, 106-7, 393. On *vicinato*, see Dale Kent and Francis W. Kent, *Neighbours and Neighbourhood in Renaissance Florence: The District of the Red Lion in the Fifteenth Century*, Harvard Center for Italian Renaissance Studies, no. 6 (Locust Valley, N.Y.: J. J. Augustin, 1982); Kent, *Household and Lineage*, 227-92; Klapisch-Zuber, "'Kin, Friends, and Neighbors'," in *Women, Family, and Ritual*; and Eckstein, *District of the Green Dragon*, 1-60.

[84] *Le vite*, ed. Greco, 2: 135-36; trans. George and Waters, *Renaissance Princes, Popes, and Prelates*, 318. Antoninus (Antonio di Ser Niccolò Pierozzi), an Observant Dominican, was Archbishop of Florence from 1444 until his death in 1459. On his extensive use of Ridolfi in his *Summa theologica*, a manual of moral theology, see the literature cited above p. 4, n. 5.

2
The Public Debt

The *monte comune* had existed for sixty years when Ridolfi wrote his treatise.[1] It originated as a temporary measure in response to the financial crisis

[1] On loans prior to 1345 and on the creation of the *monte*, the basic study is Bernardino Barbadoro, *Le finanze della Repubblica fiorentina: Imposta diretta e debito pubblico fino all'istituzione del Monte*, Biblioteca storica toscana, no. 5 (Florence: Leo S. Olschki, 1929). For the earliest phases of the *monte*'s history, see Marvin B. Becker, "Economic Change and the Emerging Florentine Territorial State," *Studies in the Renaissance* 13 (1966): 7-39; idem, *Florence in Transition*, 2: 151-200; Kirshner, "From Usury to Public Finance," 1-55; Richard C. Trexler, "Florence, by the grace of the Lord Pope ...," *Studies in Medieval and Renaissance History* 9 (1972): 117-215; Roberto Barducci, "Politica e speculazione finanziaria a Firenze dopo la crisi del primo Trecento (1343-1358)," *ASI* 137 (1979): 177-219; idem, "Le riforme finanziarie nel Tumulto dei Ciompi," in *Il Tumulto dei Ciompi*, 95-102; and idem, "... *Cum parva difficultate civium predictorum* ...: Spunti introduttivi per un regesto della legislazione finanziaria fiorentina del Trecento," in *Renaissance Studies in Honor of Craig Hugh Smyth*, ed. Andrew Morrogh, Fiorella Superbi Gioffredi, Piero Morselli and Eve Borsook, 2 vols. (Florence: Giunta Barbèra, 1985), 1: 3-15. For the period after 1382, see Becker, "The Florentine Territorial State"; Molho, "The Florentine Oligarchy"; idem, *Florentine Public Finances in the Early Renaissance, 1400-1433* (Cambridge, MA: Harvard University Press, 1971), 9-112; idem, "The State and Public Finance: A Hypothesis Based on the History of Late Medieval Florence," in *The Origins of the State in Italy, 1300-1600*, ed. Julius Kirshner (Chicago: University of Chicago Press, 1995), 97-135; and Conti, *L'imposta diretta*. For a comparison of the public debt regimes of Florence, Venice and Genoa, see Anthony Molho, "Tre città-stato e i loro debiti pubblici: Quesiti e ipotesi sulla storia di Firenze, Genova e Venezia," in *Italia 1350-1450: Tra crisi, trasformazione, sviluppo: tredicesimo convegno di studi, Pistoia, 10-13 maggio 1991* (Pistoia: Centro italiano di studi di storia e d'arte, 1993), 185-215. For a comparative study of the public debts of Florence, Pisa, Siena and Lucca in the thirteenth and fourteenth centuries, see Maria Ginatempo, *Prima del debito: Finanziamento della spesa pubblica e gestione del deficit nelle grandi città toscane (1200-1350 ca.)*, Biblioteca storica toscana, no. 38 (Florence: Leo S. Olschki, 2000). On the Lucchese and Sienese debts in particular, see Christine Meek, "Il debito pubblico nella storia finanziaria di Lucca nel XIV secolo," *Actum Luce* 3 (1974): 7-46; and William Caferro, *Mercenary Companies and the Decline of Siena* (Baltimore and London: Johns Hopkins University Press, 1998), 103-71.

of the mid-fourteenth century.[2] In 1343, after disastrous wars with Verona and Pisa, the commune found itself on the verge of bankruptcy, in debt for over six hundred thousand florins.[3] Its creditors included citizens who had advanced compulsory or voluntary loans and merchant banks that had guaranteed the commune's debt or made advances on their own account.[4] In better times, the banks might have absorbed these losses, but they, too, were in crisis. Three years earlier, King Edward III of England (d. 1377) had defaulted on loans he had contracted with the two biggest Florentine banks, the Peruzzi and Bardi, to finance his invasion of France. Fears of insolvency caused a run on the banks by foreign depositors, notably in Naples, with which Florence had close economic and political ties.[5] Despite the government's attempt to avert disaster by granting the banks temporary immunity from their creditors, the Peruzzi failed in 1343 and the Bardi three years later.[6] They drew in their wake half a dozen other banks and their collapse provoked a wave of bankruptcies that particularly affected the patrician class.[7]

Faced with its own insolvency, the government reacted in 1342 by suspending the republican order and nominating a *signore* (lord), the *condottiere* Walter of Brienne, titular duke of Athens (d. 1356). In an effort to stabilize the government's finances, Walter suspended all payments to creditors out of gabelle receipts and decreed an *estimo*, a survey of private assets, preparatory to direct taxes on wealth in the fall of 1342.[8] As a result of these unpopular measures, a coalition of magnates and major guildsmen

[2] See Carlo M. Cipolla, *The Monetary Policy of Fourteenth-Century Florence* (Berkeley, Los Angeles and London: University of California Press, 1982), 1-4. Recent historiography questions Barbadoro's emphasis on the *monte*'s technical modernity, stressing instead its provisional character and assimilation to the patrimonial strategies of the ruling class. See in particular Barducci, "*Cum parva difficultate*," 3-8; idem, "Le riforme finanziarie," 96; Kirshner, "Storm over the *Monte*," 238-39; and Molho, "State and Public Finance," 102-35.

[3] Barbadoro, *Le finanze della Repubblica fiorentina*, 616, 630-31; Barducci, "Politica e speculazione," 187, n. 49.

[4] Barbadoro, *Le finanze della Repubblica fiorentina*, 578-82, 617-19.

[5] Brucker, *Florentine Politics*, 7. On the interdependence of the Florentine banking sector and the economies of England and Naples, see Cipolla, *Monetary Policy*, 6-9. Edwin S. Hunt, *The Medieval Super-Companies: A study of the Peruzzi Company of Florence* (Cambridge and New York: Cambridge University Press, 1994), argues persuasively that Edward's default was only one among several factors in the collapse; see in particular 184-246.

[6] Becker, *Florence in Transition*, 1: 158-59; Cipolla, *Monetary Policy*, 8-9.

[7] Brucker, *Florentine Politics*, 16-17.

[8] Becker, *Florence in Transition*, 1: 156-60.

deposed Walter the following summer, and in December 1343 the resurrected commune ordered an inventory of its debts with a view to their systematic amortization.[9] The government decreed that all loans be recorded in a central register and income from gabelles assigned to creditors, who would receive monthly payments in proportion to the amounts they had lent. Within months, however, it became clear that the plan was unworkable because of demands on government revenue by preferred creditors, such as the papacy and other Italian powers.[10]

The government responded in two stages. In October 1344, it enacted a provision authorizing creditors to liquidate their share of the debt. Henceforth, any creditor could

> trade and transfer his rights to another Florentine; and he to whom such rights are transferred can and should be put down and inscribed by the notary for legislation or his deputy in the books of the commune of Florence, where such creditors are described as "creditors of the commune," in the place of him who alienated his rights; and [the buyer] can and should receive the same payment as would have been made to the original creditor.[11]

A second provision in February 1345 acknowledged the commune's inability to repay the principal, which would now constitute a *monte comune*, a communal "debt mountain."[12] In compensation, the government guaranteed creditors interest of five percent a year from gabelle receipts, of which 2704 florins a month were ear-marked "*in perpetuum* ... until such time as every creditor has been repaid his principal in full."[13] A provision

[9] On the developments summarized in the following section, see Barbadoro, *Le finanze della Repubblica fiorentina*, 636-44.

[10] Trexler, "Florence," 151.

[11] "Insuper quod omnes et singuli qui ab ipso communi habere vel recipere debent aliquam pecunie quantitatem vigore alicuius mutui vel assignamenti vel deputati eisdem facientis possint eisque liceat vigore et auctoritate presentis provisionis sua iura permutare et in alium florentinum transferre, et quod ille in quem translata essent talia iura, poni et scribi possit et debeat per scribam reformationum vel eius coadiutorem in libris communis Florentie ubi sunt descripti tales creditores pro creditoribus dicti communis loco illius qui talia iura transtulerit; et idem cui sic translata fuerunt fieri possit et debeat solutio prout fieri poterat dicto primo ius habenti" (ed. Kirshner, "Reading Bernardino's Sermon," 548, n. 2).

[12] "Comuni Florentie non est ad presens possibile restituere predictis ⟨creditoribus⟩ ea que recipere debent" (ed. Barbadoro, *Le finanze della Repubblica fiorentina*, 644).

[13] "... dictus redditus et proventus ... in causam et provisionem predictam sit et esse intelligatur in perpetuum deputatus ... quousque dictis creditoribus et cuilibet eorum fuerit integre de dictis eorum creditis satisfactum" (ibid.).

of June 1347 authenticating the revised *monte* registers confirmed these arrangements.[14]

The creation of the *monte* marked a departure from the traditional norms of Florentine public finance. Since the thirteenth century, as the cost of mercenaries inflated the military budget, the commune had resorted to *prestanze* and voluntary loans to offset revenue shortfalls.[15] Until the early 1340s, such loans had been repaid and creditors compensated by eight (1325) to fifteen (1336-39) percent interest.[16] Principal and interest had been secured by the binding allocation of anticipated gabelle income or liens on property forfeit to the commune.[17] But in February 1345 the government's fiscal credibility was weak. The regime that took power a few months after the expulsion of Walter of Brienne was dominated by new men and lesser guildsmen with limited experience in office.[18] Creditors,

[14] Barbadoro, *Le finanze della Repubblica fiorentina*, 649-52.

[15] On the decline of the civic militia and the commune's increasing dependence on *condottieri*, see Daniel Waley, "The Army of the Florentine Republic from the Twelfth to the Fourteenth Century," in *Florentine Studies*, 70-108; and Charles C. Bayley, *War and Society in Renaissance Florence: The 'De militia' of Leonardo Bruni* (Toronto: University of Toronto Press, 1961), 3-58. For a study of the financial impact of mercenary warfare on Siena in the second half of the fourteenth century, see Caferro, *Mercenary Companies*.

[16] For loans and rates prior to 1345, see Barbadoro, *Le finanze della Repubblica fiorentina*, 515-628.

[17] See ibid., 515-92. For additional data on gabelle assignments prior to 1345, see Charles-M. de La Roncière "Indirect Taxes or 'Gabelles' at Florence in the Fourteenth Century: The Evolution of Tariffs and Problems of Collection," trans. Janet Sondheimer in *Florentine Studies*, 144, n. 2. Until the middle of the century, gabelles were usually farmed, but with the creation of the *monte* they were increasingly administered by the commune directly (ibid., 180-85).

[18] Giovanni Villani (d. 1348) dismissed the government as one of "guildsmen, manual labourers and simpletons" claiming that "most of the twenty-one consuls of the guilds, who then controlled the commune, were common artisans from the *contado* and foreigners, who had little concern for the republic and knew less of leading it" ("E nota che fa il reggimento delle cittadi, essendone signori artefici e manuali e idioti, però che i più delle XXI capitudini dell'arti, per li quali allora si reggea il Comune, erano artefici minuti veniticci di contado e forestieri, a·ccui poco dee calere della republica, e peggio saperla guidare ..." [*Nuova Cronica* 13.43, ed. Giuseppe Porta, 3 vols. (Parma: Ugo Guanda, 1990-91), 3: 398]). Villani's characterization of the regime as significantly more inclusive than the one it supplanted has been questioned by Gene A. Brucker and Marvin B. Becker, "The *Arti Minori* in Florentine Politics, 1342-1378," *Mediaeval Studies* 18 (1956): 96-97; but now see Najemy, *Corporatism and Consensus*, 126-65, esp. 147-52, who concludes that "hitherto excluded parvenus and modest guildsmen rose in greater numbers than

most of them members of the traditional elite of merchant bankers, had little confidence that the regime's plan to fund the *monte* would not prove as abortive as the reimbursement scheme of the previous year. Moreover, gabelle receipts and property prices were depressed as a result of the crash and the banks were in no position to provide supplementary guarantees.[19] To reassure creditors, the government appended to the provision a penal clause threatening officials who tried to modify the *monte* arrangements with dismissal from office and banishment.[20] Officials were obliged to post two-thousand-florin bonds, half of which would be forfeit to the commune and half to papal treasury if they violated their oath, a measure that in effect made the pope the guarantor of the commune's debts.[21]

Despite these unusual guarantees, the reduced rate of interest—the lowest ever offered government creditors—combined with the government's admission that it was unable to redeem the loans precipitated a collapse in the debt market.[22] Credits lost three-quarters of their face value as they were dumped by nervous creditors. Snapped up by speculators prepared to assume the risk of default, discounted credits yielded a real interest rate of fifteen to twenty percent.[23] For the next century, the market price of *monte* credits would fluctuate around thirty percent of face value

---

ever before to positions of power" (149). The regime collapsed under the impact of the Black Death and was replaced by a more oligarchic government in 1348.

[19] Gate gabelles fell from 281,000 *lire* in 1337-38 to 215,000 *lire* in 1343, and in the same period retail wine gabelles declined from 183,830 *lire* to 117,900 *lire* (de La Roncière, "Indirect Taxes," 160, table 1; 176, table 2). De La Roncière concludes that "the Florentine economy, which shows signs of distress from 1339, by 1343-44 was in a state of collapse" (ibid., 171). According to Giovanni Villani, land prices fell by half in the city and by a third in the *contado*: "E nota che per li detti fallimenti delle compagnie mancarono i denari contanti in Firenze, ch'apena se ne trovavano. E·lle posessioni in città calarono a volerle vendere le due derrate per uno denaio, e in contado il terzo meno a valuta, e più calaro" (*Nuova Cronica* 12.138, ed. Porta, 3: 278).

[20] Barbadoro, *Le finanze della Repubblica fiorentina*, 645-46; Trexler, "Florence," 117-225. Trexler provides an example of the clause from a provision of 1371, ibid., 213-15.

[21] See Trexler, "Florence," 128-46. Trexler suggests that the pope had an interest in securing the fiscal viability of Florence, whose banks collected and managed almost all papal revenues. The penal clause was appended to fiscal measures until the late 1370s, even during the war with the pope between 1375 and 1378, when it was presumably unenforceable.

[22] Brucker, *Florentine Politics*, 19; Barducci, "Politica e speculazione," 188.

[23] Brucker, *Florentine Politics*, 19; Kirshner, "Storm over the *Monte*," 223.

as public confidence in the commune's fiscal stability rose and fell.[24] In fact, the government initially proved conscientious in honouring its obligations. Although interest payments were suspended between 1348 and 1351 because of the disorders caused by the Black Death, the chronicler Matteo Villani (d. 1363) later attested that although "the commune was overtaken by much ill fortune and many pressing necessities after 1345, it never broke faith, and so, because of its good faith, it always obtained *prestanze* from its citizens without complaint."[25]

In the same passage, Villani expressed approval of a new system of voluntary loans.[26] The government authorized the first in August 1345 to raise fifty thousand florins toward the purchase of Lucca from Mastino della Scala (d. 1351), lord of Verona, and was tied directly to speculation in *monte* credits. It worked like this: lenders matched the amount of their loan with an equivalent sum in credits assessed at face value; reimbursement of the total sum was guaranteed over two years, while the credits themselves were cancelled.[27] In this way, a creditor who advanced a hundred florins

[24] Kirshner, "Storm over the *Monte*," 225; idem, "From Usury to Public Finance," 24-26. Market prices are given at ibid., 25, table 2. For price data for the period 1425-75, see Conti, *L'imposta diretta*, 34, table 1. Prices peaked in 1418-1423, before the war with Filippo Maria Visconti, at sixty-one percent of face value (ibid., 32).

[25] "E cominciato questo gli anni di Cristo 1345, sopravvenendo al comune molte gravi fortune e smisurati bisogni, mai questa fide non maculò, onde avvenne che sempre a' suoi bisogni per la fede servata trovava prestanza da' suoi cittadini senza alcuno rammaricamento" (*Cronica* 3.106, ed. Ignazio Moutier, 6 vols. [Florence: Magheri, 1825-26], 2: 141-42). Villani was a scribe to the *monte* officials in the 1350s and died in the plague of 1363. On Villani and his chronicle, see Gene A. Brucker, "The Ghibelline Trial of Matteo Villani (1362)," *Medievalia et Humanistica* 13 (1960): 48-55; repr. in *Society, Culture, and Religion*, 29-36; and Louis Green, *Chronicle into History: An Essay on the Interpretation of History in Florentine Fourteenth-Century Chronicles* (Cambridge: Cambridge University Press, 1972), 44-85. On the suspension of interest payments during the plague, see Kirshner, "From Usury to Public Finance," 5-6; Becker, *Florence in Transition*, 2: 168-70; and Barducci, "Politica e speculazione," 200-201.

[26] "And [the commune] made great inroads on the *monte*; borrowing a hundred in cash and extinguishing another hundred in debt, it assigned at a fixed term two hundred from the gabelles of the commune, so that citizens made a profit of at least fifteen percent a year with the commune" ("... e molto ci si avanzava sopra il monte, accattandone contanti cento, e facendone finire al monte altri cento, a certo termine n'assegnava dugento sopra le gabelle del comune, sicchè i cittadini il meno guadagnavano col comune a ragione di quindici per centinaio l'anno" [*Cronica* 3.106, ed. Moutier, 2: 141-42]).

[27] The agreement and the loan scheme were described by Giovanni Villani:

in cash plus a hundred florins of *monte* credits bought on the market at a quarter of their face value was assured two hundred florins over two years, a net profit of sixty percent on his real investment of 125 florins.[28] The government regularly employed the scheme between 1345 and 1358 to raise about a quarter of a million florins and to extinguish a corresponding amount of debt.[29]

From 1345 to the early 1360s, the commune viewed compulsory loans as a measure of last resort to be invoked only in emergencies, as in 1355, when the emperor Charles IV (d. 1378) made his first expedition to Italy.[30] When resources were too scarce to implement the debt liquidation plan described by Villani, the government preferred to seek voluntary, short-term loans at market rates. These usually paid fifteen percent interest and were secured by the assignment of gabelles to cover principal and interest.[31] Ser Piero di Ser Grifo, the government notary in charge of drafting communal legislation, proposed an astute scheme to promote voluntary loans that was first tested in June 1358.[32] The *monte dell'uno tre*, or "three-for-one *monte*," as it was called, paid the same interest as the *monte co-*

"Provision for the said payment was immediately found in Florence through an arrangement then made by the commune, namely, that by lending an equal amount in cash a citizen could receive payment from the commune for his *monte* credits out of gabelles that would be assigned to Messer Mastino for repayment of the old and new loans within two years" ("La quale civanza del detto pagamento si trovò in Firenze di presente per uno ordine ch'allora si fece per lo Comune, che quale cittadino dovesse avere dal Comune danari per li presti vecchi, prestandone altrettanti contanti, fosse assegnato sopra le gabelle ordinate a meser Mastino infra due anni di riavere i vecchi e nuovi prestati" [*Nuova Cronica* 13.49, ed. Porta, 3: 414]). On this passage, see Barducci, "Politica e speculazione," 192-93. The agreement itself is edited by Barducci in "*Cum parva difficultate*," 9-11.

[28] Barducci, "Politica e speculazione," 190.

[29] Between 1350 and 1358, the debt was reduced from 503,864 to 270,000 florins (ibid., 193, n. 77).

[30] Ibid., 194, n. 79; Becker, *Florence in Transition*, 2: 173-74; idem, "Economic Change," 25-27.

[31] Barducci, "Politica e speculazione," 193-94. Kirshner reports rates ranging from seven percent in 1348 to 33.3 percent in 1363 ("From Usury to Public Finance," 13, table 1).

[32] Brucker, *Florentine Politics*, 60. According to Ronald G. Witt, Ser Piero was notable for his avarice as well as his fiscal ingenuity (*Hercules at the Crossroads: The Life, Works, and Thought of Coluccio Salutati*, Duke Monographs in Medieval and Renaissance Studies, no. 6 [Durham, NC: Duke University Press, 1983], 118). In 1378, the Ciompi permanently barred him from all public offices (Brucker, *Florentine Politics*, 382-83).

mune, namely, five percent, but by crediting shareholders with triple the amount actually advanced the government effectively increased the rate to fifteen percent.[33]

All of these mechanisms came into play between 1362 and 1378 as the government's imperialist policies brought it into conflict with its Tuscan neighbours and with the pope.[34] When Florence went to war with Pisa in 1362, the commune reinstated the *monte dell'uno tre*, and over two years raised sixteen new loans, this time as *prestanze*.[35] In 1368, the town of San Miniato al Tedesco rebelled against Florentine domination. The government financed its reconquest by thirteen *prestanze* at the more modest rate of ten percent, which were inscribed in a third fund, called the *monte dell' uno due* (two-for-one *monte*).[36] The war with Pope Gregory XI (d. 1378), which lasted from 1375 to 1378, cost Florence about a million florins, which were raised by a new round of voluntary and compulsory loans.[37] The government decreed twenty-two *prestanze* worth 580,000 florins in the course of the war, and two voluntary loans established in the spring of 1375 and offering ten percent interest attracted additional funds.[38]

From the beginning, the management of the debt was plagued by high levels of inefficiency, corruption and fraud that governments never managed to eliminate fully.[39] The system rested on a series of registers organ-

[33] Kirshner, "From Usury to Public Finance," 14-15; Becker, *Florence in Transition*, 2: 174-75. An extract from the provision is edited by Barducci in "*Cum parva difficultate*," 15.

[34] On the war against Pisa, see Bayley, *War and Society*, 27-35; and Brucker, *Florentine Politics*, 187-89. On the campaign against San Miniato al Tedesco and the war with the pope, see ibid., 236-38, 244-335.

[35] Becker, *Florence in Transition*, 2: 177; Kirshner, "From Usury to Public Finance," 14-15.

[36] Becker, *Florence in Transition*, 2: 177; Kirshner, "From Usury to Public Finance," 15.

[37] Barducci, "Le riforme finanziarie," 97, n.10.

[38] Kirshner, "From Usury to Public Finance," 15. The first ten percent fund was established in March and the second, the *monte libero dell'uno due*, in May. The terms of the latter were less attractive because creditors were not given a date for the reimbursement of their capital (ibid., 15, n. 69). On levies during the papal war in general, see Molho, *Florentine Public Finances*, 9, n. 1. Brucker counts sixteen *prestanze* yielding 570,000 florins (*Florentine Politics*, 315).

[39] Creditor fraud and defects in the registers inspired repeated calls for revision of the *monte*'s books; see Barducci, "Politica e speculazione," 182, n. 22. As late as 1476 and 1481, special commissions were struck to consider unpaid interest, evasion and fraud in connection with the *monte*; see Nicolai Rubinstein, *The Government of Florence Under the Medici (1434 to 1494)*, 2nd ed. (Oxford: Clarendon

ized by urban quarter in which the *monte* officials recorded credits, interest payments, transfers of title and cancellations against the names of creditors. Since creditors received no certificates, the book entries themselves had probative status in establishing claims against the commune.[40] As early as 1346, the official responsible for disbursing interest was accused of negligence, and the government ordered an overhaul of the registers with a view to cancelling credits that had been alienated or redeemed through the voluntary loan scheme.[41] There were also examples of corruption, like that of Ser Pietro di Gentile da Castelfiorentino, notary to the commission that drew up the 1343 inventory of debts. Ser Pietro accepted bribes from more than 150 creditors to inflate their claims by some seventeen thousand florins. When rumours of the fraud reached the government in 1346, it ordered an inquiry with the result that the notary was condemned to the galleys.[42]

The first revision of the books was finished in 1347, but within six years it was necessary to appoint a permanent commission, the *Ufficiali del monte* (Debt Officials), to oversee the administration of the debt and to weed out extinct and fraudulent claims.[43] Citizens discovered profiting from such claims were subject to fines, and the records of the officials testify to widespread fraud among creditors, including not only new men and prominent speculators, but members of distinguished patrician families, such as Ranieri de' Peruzzi, and even charitable and religious foundations, such as the Orsanmichele, the Misericordia and the convent of Santa Maria Novella.[44]

Press, 1997), 233-35.

[40] Julius Kirshner, "Encumbering Private Claims to Public Debt in Renaissance Florence," in *The Growth of the Bank as Institution and the Development of Money-Business Law*, ed. Vito Piergiovanni (Berlin: Duncker and Humblot, 1993), 19-20. On the legal concepts underlying transferability of credits, see ibid., 25-32. On the origins of negotiable credit instruments in general in the later Middle Ages, see John H. Munro, "The International Law Merchant and the Evolution of Negotiable Credit in Late-Medieval England and the Low Countries," in *Banchi pubblici, banchi privati e monti di pietà nell'Europa preindustriale: Amministrazione, techniche operative e ruoli economici*, Atti della società ligure di storia patria, n.s. 31, fasc. 1 (Genoa: Società ligure di storia patria, 1991), 49-80.

[41] Barducci, "Politica e speculazione," 198, n. 97. An extract from the provision is edited by Barducci in "*Cum parva difficultate*," 11-12.

[42] Barducci, "Politica e speculazione," 198-99.

[43] Kirshner, "From Usury to Public Finance," 7; Barducci, "Politica e speculazione," 199-200; Guidi, *Il governo*, 2: 266-67.

[44] Barducci, "Politica e speculazione," 200. In 1353, the captains of the confraternity of Orsanmichele were found to be profiting from extinct credits and fined 904 florins. The Misericordia and Santa Maria Novella were also fined at the same

With the proliferation of *monti* in the 1360s and the resulting growth in transactions, the status of the Debt Officials increased. By the mid-1370s, in addition to their accounting and police functions, they had acquired the trusteeship of estates bequeathed to minors and authority to execute the wills of public usurers and pawnbrokers, whose *monte* credits were forfeit to the commune.[45] Under the Medici a century later, the Debt Officials were the most important fiscal agency of the republic, dwarfing the treasury itself and disposing of virtually all communal income and expenditures.[46]

The power of the fifteenth-century officials was an index of the degree to which in a hundred years the debt had come to dominate not only the public finances of Florence but the domestic economies of propertied Florentines.[47] Income from *monte* credits and profits from speculation augmented—often supplanted—other sources of wealth for citizens and corporate bodies. Philip Jones notes, for example, that of the 162,925 florins-worth of assets that Palla Strozzi, the richest man in early fifteenth-century Florence, declared to the *catasto* officials in 1427, 54,463 represented land, 14,791 commercial investments and 94,671 public debt credits.[48] Ridolfi's holdings were perhaps more typical. The official transcript of his 1427

---

time (John Henderson, *Piety and Charity in Late Medieval Florence* [Chicago and London: University of Chicago Press, 1994], 214-15).

[45] Kirshner, "From Usury to Public Finance," 8-9. For examples, see Marvin B. Becker, "Three Cases Concerning the Restitution of Usury in Mediaeval Florence," *Journal of Economic History* 17 (1957): 447-50; idem, "Some Economic Implications of the Conflict Between Church and State in *Trecento* Florence," *Mediaeval Studies* 21 (1959): 14; and idem, "Church and State in Florence on the Eve of the Renaissance (1343-1382)," *Speculum* 37 (1962): 521-22. Ridolfi composed a *consilium* in 1396 in reply to a question from the Debt Officials on the execution of a usurer's will, ed. Federico Martino, "Un consilium inedito in materia di usura di Lorenzo Ridolfi," *Il diritto ecclesiastico* 80 (1969): 335-52.

[46] L. F. Marks, "The Financial Oligarchy in Florence under Lorenzo," in *Italian Renaissance Studies: A Tribute to Cecilia M. Ady*, ed. E. F. Jacob (London: Faber and Faber, 1960), 127-28. Marks quotes a provision of 1470 that describes the *monte* as "the heart of the body which we call the city ... every limb, large and small, must contribute to preserving this heart as the guardian fortress, immovable rock and enduring certainty of the salvation of the whole body and government of your state" (ibid., 127).

[47] For analyses of this process, see Conti, *L'imposta diretta*; and Molho, "State and Public Finance." Matteo Palmieri, *Ricordi fiscali, 1427-74*, ed. Elio Conti, Istituto storico italiano per il Medio Evo, Studi storici, fasc. 132-35 (Rome: Istituto storico italiano per il Medio Evo, 1983) illustrates the process in the private fiscal *ricordi* of the patrician and humanist Matteo Palmieri (1406-75).

[48] "Florentine Families and Florentine Diaries in the Fourteenth Century," *Papers of the British School at Rome*, n.s. 11 (1956): 190, n. 56.

catasto declaration records credits with a total face value of just over 2783 florins in several funds.[49]

Credits figured prominently in wills and gifts, where they endowed monastic and charitable foundations, dowered girls and supported widows. For example, by 1353, as a result of bequests by plague victims, the Orsanmichele was profiting from some twelve thousand florins in credits.[50] In the same period, the Franciscan convent of Santa Croce owned credits with a face value of 48,000 florins.[51] In a testament dictated a few days before his death in May 1419, the merchant and humanist Angelo Corbinelli directed that in addition to her dowry of five hundred florins his wife Filippa should enjoy the life use of 620 florins in *monte* credits if she remained in his household or five hundred florins-worth if she chose to leave. His daughters Julia and Bartolomea each received the life usufruct of three hundred florins-worth of credits in addition to cash dowries of a thousand florins

[49] The precise breakdown is as follows:

monte comune	fl.	1714	s. 4	d. 6
monte dei cinque per cento interi	fl.	716	s. 1	d. 6
monte de' prestanzoni	fl.	236	s. 7	d. 6
paghe sostenute da 1415 a 1419	fl.	43	s. 8	d. 6
paghe sostenute di monte di Pisa	fl.	11	s. 8	d. 0
paghe sostenute da 1419 a 1423	fl.	49	s. 3	d. 0
paghe sostenute da 1415 a 1416	fl.	11	s. 9	d. 6
Total	fl.	2783	s. 5	d. 10

Source: ASF, Catasto 66, fol. 80r. See also ASF, Catasto 395, fol. 245v for 1430; and ASF, Catasto 489, fol. 320v for 1433. Beginning in 1423, the expenses of the Milanese war forced the government to withhold a quarter of the interest due on *monte comune* credits, which was thus effectively reduced to 3.75 percent. The *monte dei cinque per cento interi* was created in 1424 and represented *prestanze* settled within fifteen days of imposition, on which the full five percent was paid. A *prestanzone* (literally, "big *prestanza*") was levied in March 1425 and paid a real rate of six percent (eight percent minus the twenty-five percent witheld interest). *Paghe sostenute* were the twenty-five percent of interest payments witheld from creditors of the *monte comune* and other funds, such as the *monte di Pisa*, established in 1406 to pay for the conquest of Pisa, which were counted as non-refundable credits. On the definition of these terms, see Molho, *Florentine Public Finances*, 102-03; and Conti, *L'imposta diretta*, 142. See also the examples of *monte* credits held by early fifteenth-century humanists provided by Martines in *Social World*, 85-144.

[50] Henderson, *Piety and Charity*, 188; for bequests between 1352 and 1357, see 213, table 6.2.

[51] Kirshner, "From Usury to Public Finance," 32. For other examples, see ibid., 32-34; and idem, "Reading Bernardino's Sermon," 584.

each.[52] In the same year, Ridolfi settled seventy-five florins in credits on his daughter Maddalena, whom he had placed in the convent of Santa Felicità, to revert to the family patrimony on her death.[53]

Credits also lent themselves to derivative uses. The government accepted them at face value in payment of outstanding fines, and they could serve as collateral for loans, real estate sales on credit and unpaid dowries.[54] The government encouraged such practices by creating new funds, such as the *monte delle doti* (Dowry Fund), established in 1425, in which a family could deposit money on behalf of an unmarried daughter for terms of seven and a half to fifteen years. If the girl was married at the end of the term, her husband received a cash dowry representing principal and compound interest.[55]

[52] ASF, Notarile antecosimiano 9042, fols. 70r-71r. According to a post-mortem inventory of assets drawn up by his heirs, Corbinelli's estate included credits with a face value of four thousand florins (ASF, Notarile antecosimiano 9040, 116r-v, 189v-190r). I am currently preparing an edition and study of Corbinelli's testament. Similar provisions can be found in hundreds of other Florentine testaments of the same period.

[53] ASF, Monte comune o delle Graticole 3137, fols. 186v-187r (6 May 1419): "Dominus Laurentius Antonii de Ridolfis, creditor dicti comunis in quarterio Sancti Spiritus in florenis .lxxv. de maiori summa, dictum creditum cum .x. pagis substentis et a kalendis Februarii circa permutauit a se ipso in semetipsum cum conditione quod Maddalena, et hodie uocata Bartholomea, eius filia, monialis monasterii Sancte Felicitatis de Florentia, possit, teneatur et debeat suscipere pagas dicti crediti toto tempore vite sue. Et post eius mortem dictum creditum libere pertineat ad dictum dominum Laurentium et eo defuncto ad eius heredes cum omnibus pagis. Et si casus accideret quod dicta Bartholomea decederet hinc ad .xv. annos proximos futuros allora quello tempo restasse per insino a .xv. anni le dette paghe sieno et appartenghinsi al detto munistero di Santa Felicita, et la badessa, capitolo et conuento del detto munistero le possi et debbi pigliare. Et di poi compiuti i detti .xv. anni il detto credito rimanghi libero al detto messer Lorenzo o a sue herede con tucte le paghe."

[54] For a detailed discussion, see Kirshner, "Encumbering Private Claims," 19-75. For the use of credits to pay fines and *prestanze* in arrears, see idem, "Storm over the *Monte*," 251; and idem, "'Ubi est ille?': Franco Sacchetti on the *monte comune* of Florence," *Speculum* 59 (1984): 564-65.

[55] The deposit was forfeit to the commune if the girl died before marrying (Molho, *Marriage Alliance*, 30). The commune's object was to attract funds to amortize the *monte comune* and resembled the liquidation scheme described above, pp. 33-34. On the objectives, social functions and administration of the dowry fund, see Julius Kirshner, *Pursuing Honor While Avoiding Sin: The 'Monte delle doti' of Florence*, Quaderni di Studi senesi, no. 41 (Milan: Giuffrè, 1978); Julius Kirshner and Anthony Molho, "The Dowry Fund and the Marriage Market in Early *Quattrocento* Florence," *Journal of Modern History* 50 (1978): 403-38; and Molho, *Marriage*

The foundations of these developments were laid in the mid-fourteenth century, when thousands of citizens entered the market as sellers and buyers of debt. As early as 1347, one Piero di Vannozzo Baroni became the government's biggest creditor in Santo Spirito quarter by buying up credits with a face value of sixteen thousand florins.[56] But the great boom came with the Pisan War. Between October 1365 and June 1367 there were over twenty-five hundred trades in *monte dell'uno tre* credits nominally worth almost a million florins.[57] In 1364, the wool merchant Francesco di Jacopo del Bene realized a profit of twenty-three percent from speculation in public debt in addition to the monthly interest on his credits. Over a decade, del Bene invested about five thousand florins in the *monte*, a sum that exceeded the total capitalization of his firm in 1370.[58] A contemporary observer, the chronicler Marchionne di Coppo Stefani, described fevered speculation in *monte* "futures" in 1371:

> Moreover a law was passed because many were auctioning off their *monte* interest. They would say, "Today the *monte* is worth thirty percent. Let us agree that for up to a year from today I can give you, or you give me, as much at thirty-one percent as you want. Agreed?" And so they would agree. Then the buyer waited: if prices fell, he bought, if they rose, he sold; and thus he traded his shares back and forth twenty times a year. As a result, a two percent tax was imposed on every exchange.[59]

This picture is confirmed by a survey of records from the following year revealing speculative transactions worth hundreds of thousands of florins.[60] A letter of 1375 edited by Brucker sheds light on informal networks of

Alliance, 27-178.

[56] Barducci, "Politica e speculazione," 205. For other examples of speculative investment in the first years of the *monte*'s existence, see ibid., 202-17; and Kirshner, "Storm over the *Monte*," 223-25.

[57] Kirshner, "Franco Sacchetti," 574, table 1. For a profile of Sacchetti's investments in various funds between 1362 and 1385, see ibid., 582-83, appendix.

[58] Barducci, "Le riforme finanziarie," 97-98; 99-100; Kirshner, "From Usury to Public Finance," 26.

[59] "Ancora si fece legge, conciosiacosachè molti incantavano li denari del Monte, e diceano: 'Lo monte vale 30 per centinaio questo dì; io voglio fare teco una cosa: io voglio poterti dare oggi a un anno, ovvero tu dare a me, quanto a 31 per cento che vuoi ti doni, e fa questo?' E cadeano in patto; poi stava in se. Se rinvigliavano, li comperava, e se rincaravano, li vendeva, e non promutava qua e là le scritte 20 volte l'anno. Di che vi si puose su gabella fiorini 2 per cento a ogni permuta" (*Cronica fiorentina*, ed. Niccolò Rodolico, *Rerum italicarum scriptores*, vol. 30, part 1 [Città di Castello: Lapi, 1903], rubr. 727, p. 278). On this passage, see Kirshner, "From Usury to Public Finance," 21.

[60] Barducci, "Le riforme finanziarie," 98.

information and advice on *monte* investments.[61] Gherardino di Niccolò Gherardini Giani, a member of a communal finance committee, advised a friend in Bruges, Tommaso di Piero di messer Rodolfo de' Bardi, not to sell his credits, which Gherardino was convinced would rise in value before the end of the war with the pope. He went on to suggest that Tommaso forestall an increase in his *prestanza* assessment by submitting a false declaration of assets, and offered to help by investing under his own name 350 florins Tommaso had entrusted to him.

Assessments were a frequent cause of complaint.[62] Except for brief interludes in 1325 and 1342, there had been no taxation of private property in Florence since 1315, when the practice had been abolished in favour of higher gabelles and loans.[63] The possessing classes fiercely resisted any proposal to reintroduce taxes. In 1352, for example, the commune was forced to retreat from a plan to levy a wealth tax to underwrite the war against Milan, converting payments into transferable *monte* credits, while the *estimo* compiled at this time became the basis for calculating subsequent *prestanze*.[64] Responsibility for raising loans lay with committees in the sixteen wards, who adjusted levies in accordance with wealth as reported in the *estimo*.[65] The measure of subjective authority granted the assessment committees gave rise to justifiable charges of prejudice and political partisanship, and encouraged not only evasion but scores of appeals to the communal treasury for the cancellation or reduction of levies.[66]

Despite the complaints of rich *prestanziati* (compulsory lenders) that high assessments were depleting their wealth, the system favoured those with access to liquid capital and weighed most heavily on the urban poor and subject populations in the *contado* (county) and *distretto* (district).[67]

[61] "Un documento fiorentino sulla guerra, sulla finanza e sulla amministrazione pubblica (1375)," *ASI* 115 (1957): 165-76. See also idem, *Florentine Politics*, 82.

[62] On public attitudes towards the distribution of loan burdens, see Molho, *Florentine Public Finances*, 74-87.

[63] De la Roncière, "Indirect Taxes," 143-44; Molho, *Florentine Public Finances*, 63-64; Becker, "Economic Change," 25-26.

[64] Barducci, "*Cum parva difficultate*," 7. Barducci edits an extract from the provision in ibid., 13-14. See also Brucker, *Florentine Politics*, 93, n. 151.

[65] The process was considerably more complex and arbitrary than my summary suggests. For an account of its operation in one fifteenth-century ward, see Dale Kent and Francis W. Kent, *Neighbours and Neighbourhood*, 24-47. See also Herlihy and Klapisch-Zuber, *Tuscans and Their Families*, 3-4.

[66] For example, a resident of Santo Spirito complained in 1370 that loyal Guelfs were being punished with excessive levies by enemies of the Society on the committee (Brucker, *Florentine Politics*, 201). On evasion, see ibid., 196, n. 12.

[67] See Brucker, *Florentine Politics*, 92-93; and Molho, "State and Public Fi-

Between 1384 and 1412, for example, the government tripled the basic tax rate on the *contado* from ten to forty *soldi* per *lira* of the assessed value of property.[68] Taxes on the *contado* and special imposts on the *distretto* yielded an average of just over a hundred thousand florins a year between 1402 and 1430, transfers dedicated largely to funding the *monte*.[69] The results were predictable: subject communities fell into arrears or contracted debts to Florentine banking houses and moneylenders; the regional economy stagnated; peasant sharecroppers abandoned the land; and the region was swept by tax revolts.[70]

Just as hard hit were the urban poor who owned sufficient property to be assessed but could not realize the cash necessary to meet their levies. *Miserabili* (destitute) were exempt from forced loans.[71] Nevertheless, a

---

nance," 104-110. The distinction between *contado* and *distretto* was vague, but basically the *contado* represented territory traditionally controlled by Florence, corresponding to the dioceses of Florence and Fiesole, while the *distretto* comprised towns and their *contadi* that Florence acquired by conquest, purchase or treaty from the mid-fourteenth century onward, such as Prato (1350), Pistoia (1351), Volterra (1361), San Miniato (1370), Arezzo (1384), Pisa (1406) and Livorno (1421). The distinction reflected different forms of taxation: residents of the *contado* paid direct taxes according to an *estimo*, those of the *distretto* retained their distinctive fiscal structures but paid a annual *tassa di lancie* ("lance" or military tax). The *catasto* of 1427 was the first attempt to impose a uniform system of taxation on the entire territory controlled by Florence. See Molho, *Florentine Public Finances*, 23-27; Herlihy and Klapisch-Zuber, *Tuscans and the Families*, 34-35, 39-41; and Samuel K. Cohn, *Creating the Florentine State: Peasants and Rebellion*, 1348-1434 (Cambridge: Cambridge University Press, 1999), 3, n. 9. On the administrative organization of subject territories, see Guidi, *Il governo*, 3. On the formation of the territorial state, see most recently Paolo Pirillo, *Costruzione di un contado: I fiorentini e il loro territorio nel basso Medioevo* (Florence: Le Lettere, 2001).

[68] Molho, *Florentine Public Finances*, 30-31.

[69] See Molho, *Florentine Public Finances*, 61, table 4. The data are not extant for every year. See also ibid., 28-30. On the fiscal exploitation of the territories in the late fourteenth and early fifteenth centuries in general, see Becker, "Economic Change," 31-38; idem, "Florentine Territorial State," 126-34; and Brucker, *Civic World*, 208-25.

[70] See Molho, *Florentine Public Finances*, 24-45; and Brucker, *Civic World*, 222-25. On the impoverishment of the Tuscan regional economy, see Stephan R. Epstein, "Cities, Regions and the Late Medieval Crisis: Sicily and Tuscany Compared," *Past and Present* 130 (1991): 3-50. On rural depopulation and peasant insurgencies at the beginning of the fifteenth century inspired by oppressive tax burdens, see Cohn, *Creating the Florentine State*.

[71] Brucker, *Florentine Politics*, 48; Kirshner, "From Usury to Public Finance," 10, n. 42. *Miserabili* were defined in 1342 as "those who do not own land, a house, or

growing proportion of the poor, particularly *sottoposti*, textile workers subject to the wool manufacturers' guild, were regularly assessed loans in the 1360s ranging from an average of four florins in 1362 to 1.5 in 1369.[72] The pressure on the poor increased sharply during the war with the pope as the number of households deemed to meet the minimum property requirements more than doubled between 1375 and 1378.[73] The government settled with those who were unable to pay for a fraction of the assessed amount and forfeiture of any claim to principal and future interest. Alterna-

---

assets of a hundred small florins, or practise any trade or office" ("et intelligantur pauperes et miserabiles illi qui non habent terram vel domum, nec valentiam librarum centum florenorum parvorum, nec exerceant aliquam artem vel ministerium" [ed. Barbadoro, *Le finanze della repubblica fiorentina*, 402]). Herlihy and Klapisch-Zuber note that the category comprised "the infirm, the aged, minor orphans and, above all, widows" (*Tuscans and Their Families*, 19). Stella adds casual labourers (*lavoranti*) in manufacturing and crafts who made up 40.1 percent of *miserabili* in the 1355 *estimo*, as well as a proportion of *sottoposti* and independent artisans, who together accounted for 26.9 percent (*La révolte*, 189, table 22). On the general characteristics of the poorest strata of Florentine society, often called the *popolo minuto* (little people) in contemporary sources, see Gene A. Brucker, "The Florentine *Popolo minuto* and its Political Role, 1340-1450," in *Violence and Civil Disorder in Italian Cities, 1200-1500*, UCLA Centre for Medieval and Renaissance Studies Contributions, no. 5, ed. Lauro Martines (Berkeley, Los Angeles and London: University of California Press, 1972), 155-83; repr. in *Society, Culture, and Religion*, 81-109; and Cohn, *Laboring Classes*, 65-90.

72 From figures compiled by Charles-M. de La Roncière on *sottoposti* in San Giovanni quarter in 1362, 1369 and 1378, *Prix et Salaires à Florence au XIVe Siècle (1280-1380)*, Collection de l'École française de Rome, no. 59 (Rome: École française de Rome, 1982), 374, graph 43b. For the distribution of workers in the middle and lower strata of the taxable population of San Giovanni, see ibid., 373, graph 43a, and for variations in *prestanze* assessments among *sottoposti*, ibid., 376, graph 43c. On the subsidiary processes and workers in textile manufacturing, see *Dictionary of the Middle Ages* (New York: Charles Scribner's Sons, 1988), s.v. "Textile Technology" and "Textile Workers" by John H. Munro; repr. with corrections in idem, *Textiles, Towns and Trade: Essays in the history of late-medieval England and the Low Countries* (Aldershot: Variorum, 1994), 1-35. For the classification of Florentine occupational groups in general, see Stella, *La révolte*, 154-83 and 297-350, appendices 3 and 4a-c. *Sottoposti* represented two out of five heads of fiscal households in 1352 and one out of two in 1404 (ibid., 162). On the basis of the *prestanze* records for these two years, Stella concludes that they were among the poorest groups in Florentine society: the average wealth of members of the fourteen minor guilds was twice that of typical *sottoposti* (ibid., 195-96, table 29; 196, table 30).

73 From 1148 to 2594 (Brucker, *Florentine Politics*, 316, n. 71). The average *prestanza* of *sottoposti* in San Giovanni fell to less than one florin in 1378 (de La Roncière, *Prix et Salaires*, 374, graph 43b).

tively, the poor made use of brokers, who paid the full assessment in return for a fee and title to the credit and interest. During the war, eighty percent of all *prestanziati* and some ninety percent of *sottoposti* assessed loans in Santa Maria Novella quarter paid *ad perdendum* (to be lost), a majority choosing to surrender their rights to speculators.[74] The brokers to whom the *sottoposti* turned were often their employers, whose profits from speculation were thus effectively appropriated from their employees.[75]

The burden of loans paid *ad perdendum* combined with structural inequalities built into the tax system to widen the gulf between rich and poor. Gabelles on salt, wine and other essentials constituted a highly regressive form of taxation, which had been rising since the 1360s because of increased demands on the treasury from wars and the *monti.* At the beginning of the fourteenth century, gate gabelles added 4.5 percent to the retail price of oil; by 1369-81 the surcharge had tripled. Declining real wages and rising prices caused by food shortages reinforced the effects of indirect taxes.[76] Alessandro Stella's study of textile workers illustrates how the system promoted the upward circulation of wealth.[77] Statistics derived from the *monte* records show that between 1352 and 1404 the richest two percent of households increased their share of assessable wealth from twenty-five to forty-two percent of the the total. In the same period, the poorest households subject to assessment more than tripled in number from sixteen

[74] Barducci, "Le riforme finanziarie," 98-99. See also Brucker, *Florentine Politics*, 48, 316; and idem, "Un documento," 168-69. The practice of paying *ad perdendum* was authorized with the *prestanza* of 1355 (Barducci, "Politica e speculazione," 195-96).

[75] Barducci remarks that for many *sottoposti* the result was a "financial bloodletting that by the end of the impositions exceeded three hundred *soldi*, a sum equivalent to about forty days' pay for a woolcomber and proportionately for other workers; which is to say that during the war the *sottoposti* in effect gave their labour free for a period of time to their employers, who might thus recover a portion of their investment in proportion corresponding to the level of *prestanze* imposed on workers" ("Per costoro ne derivava un salasso monetario che superava al termine delle imposizioni i 300 soldi in lire di piccoli, somma equivalente alla paga di 40 giorni circa per un pettinatore, e per gli altri in proporzione: come dire in sostanza che i sottoposti durante i conflitti prestavano mano d'opera gratuita per un certo tempo a favore dei loro padroni, i quali si riappropriavano così di una parte del compenso reale, in misura proporzionalmente crescente all'altezza delle prestanze imposte ai lavoratori" ["Le riforme finanziarie," 100]). See also Brucker, *Florentine Politics*, 316; and Kirshner, "From Usury to Public Finance," 10, 16.

[76] De La Roncière, "Indirect taxes," 186-87. Data on food prices is found in idem, *Prix et salaires*, 821-37, appendices 1-14.

[77] For Stella's classification of wealth, see *La révolte*, 184-86; the data are presented at 167, graph 5.

to fifty percent of the total, though their share of assessable wealth only rose from three to eleven percent.[78] Throughout the period, some eighty percent of assessed households fell below the average levy.[79]

The effects are illustrated in a petition poor Florentines addressed to the *Signoria* in 1369, which blamed gabelles and *prestanze* for rising levels of poverty:

> Lord priors of Florence: For the sake of your honor and that of the commune of Florence you should do something about the taxes, the forced loans, and the extra levies which the poor people of Florence must pay. If you don't do something, you will discover that no one in Florence will be able to save you. There will be an uprising if these forced loans and special levies are not reduced, for there is great privation here. People are living in misery since they earn little and prices have been so high for thirteen months and more. Just think about those who have three or four or five children, and who are assessed two or three florins, and who have to live from the labor of their hands and those of their wives. How can they stay here and live?[80]

The appeal proved to be prophetic, since the disparities aggravated by the *monte* system played a central role in the Ciompi insurrection of 1378. The petition the Ciompi presented to the government on 28 July 1378 included demands for the suspension of *prestanze*, the reintroduction of a wealth tax, the abolition of interest payments on the *monti* and the progressive elimination of the debt over twelve years.[81]

[78] Cf. Herlihy and Klapisch-Zuber's figures from the 1427 *catasto* in *Tuscans and Their Families*, 97-105; 99, figure 4.1.

[79] Stella, *La révolte*, 185. A similar picture emerges from Conti's study of the fifteenth century; see *L'imposta diretta*, 319-20; and Martines' comments in "Forced Loans," 309.

[80] Trans. Kirshner, "Franco Sacchetti," 563. See also Brucker, *Florentine Politics*, 196, n. 11; and Brucker's translation of this passage in *The Society of Renaissance Florence: A Documentary Study* (New York: Harper and Row, 1971), 233-34.

[81] Barducci, "Politica e speculazione," 216-17; idem, "Le riforme finanziarie," 100-101. The fiscal programme of the Ciompi is also discussed by Rodolico, *I Ciompi*, 184-97; idem, *La democrazia*, 255-307; and by Brucker, "The Ciompi Revolution," 341-44; repr. in *Society, Culture, and Religion*, 64-67. The role of economic grievances in the insurrection is much debated. For reviews of the historiography, see Stella, *La révolte*, 17-32; Volker Hunecke, "The Conference on the Tumulto dei Ciompi held in Florence 16-19 September 1979," *Journal of Italian History* 2 (1979): 280-92; and idem, "Il Tumulto dei Ciompi—600 Jahre danach," 395-402. Brucker observes that elements of the Ciompi programme had periodically been aired and rejected in the 1360s and 1370s (*Florentine Politics*, 94-96; idem, "The Ciompi Revolution," 353; repr. in *Society, Culture, and Religion*, 76), but, as Kirshner emphasizes, the comprehensive character of the Ciompi's demands dis-

However, the suppression of the rising at the end of August 1378 meant that the measures finally adopted fell short of the rebels' demands for radical fiscal reform, expressed in the slogan "no more *monti*, no more *prestanze*, but an *estimo*!"[82] The storm of elite protest that followed the decree of an *estimo* in 1379 forced the government to convert tax payments into interest-bearing *monte* credits, and in 1381 the experiment in direct taxation was completely abandoned.[83] In the same year, the government approved legislation reforming the debt system. Balancing elite demands that the commune keep faith with its creditors against the need to meet rising defence costs, it merged the existing *monti* into a single fund representing indebtedness of just over a million florins. Interest was fixed at the original rate of five percent and provision made for the progressive redemption of credits.[84]

The coup of January 1382 that restored patrician dominance also marked a return to the fiscal *status quo ante*. Although it retained the five percent interest rate, the government was soon contracting voluntary loans with a group of leading bankers that included the Medici, Alberti and Rinuccini, and within a decade the Debt Officials were disbursing interest on new accounts at eight, ten and twelve percent.[85] By 1388, new *prestanze* had almost doubled the debt, and hope of retiring it evaporated as diplomatic frictions with Milan developed into war in 1390.[86] Debate in the magistracies and councils now shifted to the frequency and distribution of loans and to expedients to compensate for the drain on gabelles by their allocation to the more urgent needs of defence. In July 1392, after a series of war *prestanze* totalling 1.5 million florins, the government decreed a thirty-three percent reduction of interest for three years.[87] Savings were assigned to the redemption of credits at market value, but even during the ensuing

---

tinguished them from earlier gestures by the ruling class in the direction of fiscal equity ("Franco Sacchetti," 579, n. 64).

[82] "Non più Monti, non più prestanze, ma l'estimo" (quoted by Rodolico, *I Ciompi*, 189).

[83] Brucker, *Civic World*, 54-55; Rodolico, *La democrazia*, 295-307.

[84] Brucker, *Civic World*, 53-54. For an analysis of the debates, see Rodolico, *La democrazia*, 272-82; Rodolico edits the provision of 7 December 1381 at ibid., 458-75. Revenue allocated for interest payments totalled 50,000 florins a year; for the calculation of the consolidated debt in 1380, see Molho, *Florentine Public Finances*, 65, n. 4.

[85] Becker, *Florence in Transition*, 2: 199; Molho, *Florentine Public Finances*, 70, n. 7.

[86] Interest payments had reached 79,000 florins by 1388 (Molho, *Florentine Public Finances*, 70, n. 6).

[87] Brucker, *Civic World*, 148; Molho, *Florentine Public Finances*, 10, table 1.

truce, which lasted until 1396, the government was obliged to raise an additional six hundred thousand florins by new *prestanze*.[88] Complete suspension of interest payments followed in 1395, 1397-99, 1400 and 1402.[89]

In *consulte*, speakers demanded that more revenue be squeezed out of subject territories, that "*prestanze* be abandoned and that the commune learn to live within its means."[90] As early as 1391, rifts appeared in the political class as legislative councils dominated by new men and lesser guildsmen repeatedly voted down requests for new loans put before them by the leadership elite.[91] Opposition to deficit financing of the war contributed to the constitutional crisis of 1393. Among other measures, the political reform commission created a council of eighty-one citizens (*Ottantuno*), which was authorized to bypass the councils in the imposition of new *prestanze*.[92] The distribution of *prestanze* and management of the debt remained the prerogative of the councils, where endless debates raged throughout the war over the equity of assessments and the commune's obligations to its creditors.[93] For those lower on the economic scale, the Milanese war was a replay of the 1370s as the government broadened the class of eligible *prestanziati* to include households that were unable to pay their levies or paid *ad perdendum*. The *Drago* (Dragon) ward of San Giovanni quarter provides a good illustration. In 1395, three-quarters of the 708 households assessed refused payment or settled *ad perdendum*; seven years later, ninety-six percent of 1304 households fell into these two categories.[94]

[88] Molho, *Florentine Public Finances*, 10, table 1.

[89] Idem, "Florentine Oligarchy," 42, n. 52.

[90] "... Provideatur ita quod commune sit ordinatum; et quod prestantie non imponantur post hac; sed commune vivat de suis redditibus." The opinion was expressed by Niccolò da Uzzano, a leading oligarch, in a *consulta* of 10 June 1392, quoted and trans. Brucker, *Civic World*, 145, n. 216.

[91] Brucker, *Civic World*, 145-47; Molho, "Florentine Oligarchy," 38-41.

[92] Molho, "Florentine Oligarchy," 41. The Eighty-One was given extensive jurisdiction over foreign and fiscal affairs, and the authority to convene the War Commission. For discussions, see ibid., 30-32; Brucker, *Civic World*, 147-48; and Guidi, *Il governo*, 1: 236-37. On the structural roots of tensions in the political class in this period, see Brucker, *Civic World*, 90-101; and Riccardo Fubini, "From Social to Political Representation in Renaissance Florence," in *City States in Classical Antiquity and Medieval Italy*, 227-32.

[93] Molho, "Florentine Oligarchy," 41-49.

[94] Idem, *Florentine Public Finances*, 68, table 6. The figures are even more striking if those for 1381 are included:

By September 1402, when news of the unexpected death of Giangaleazzo Visconti reached Florence, the commune had spent some five million florins on the war, of which almost three million had been borrowed from citizens in the form of *prestanze*.[95] Merchants like Francesco Datini of Prato (d. 1410), whose businesses had suffered because of blockades, were particularly bitter about the levies.[96] Between 1400 and 1402, Datini paid almost thirty-five hundred florins in forced loans.[97] Protesting what he considered punitive assessments, he moved to Bologna in 1401 to avoid further payments.[98] His decision provoked a patriotic harangue from his friend Domenico Giugni, a member of the assessment committee:

> You say that you do not intend ... to return to Florence ... because of the excessive tax burdens which have been imposed on you by the Commune, and because in your opinion, these will not be reduced.... Considering that everyone is obligated to his country, and should never abandon it, particularly in time of adversity, I tell you I am one of those who advises you not to forsake yours. If you do, you will be censured by God and by the world, because you do not have any valid reason. Those who levy taxes say that they wished to treat you equitably, and I believe that they did so, and until you have evidence to the contrary, you should not complain.[99]

But peace, and with it the financial relief Datini and others were demanding, failed to materialize.[100] The Eighty-One soon resolved to exploit the disarray of the Milanese with an offensive against Visconti possessions

	(1381)	(1395)	(1402)
ad rehabendum	397	182	51
ad perdendum	301	352	393
no payment	93	174	860
Total	791	708	1304

95 Ibid., 10, table 1.

96 For examples of Datini's views on the war drawn from his business correspondence, see Brucker, *Civic World*, 161-63; 170-71; 177, n. 361; 191. Datini was one of the richest merchants in Tuscany; for biographical information, see Iris Origo, *The Merchant of Prato: Francesco di Marco Datini* (London: The Reprint Society, 1957).

97 Molho, *Florentine Public Finances*, 96, table 7 (10 January 1400-26 August 1402).

98 Brucker, *Civic World*, 200. Brucker describes Datini's efforts to obtain relief at ibid., 282.

99 Ed. Gene A. Brucker, *Firenze nel Rinascimento* (Florence: La Nuova Italia, 1969), 285; trans. idem, *Society of Renaissance Florence*, 82-83; and quoted idem, *Civic World*, 200.

100 What follows is based on Brucker's account of the policy debates and events of 1402 to 1404 in *Civic World*, 187-208.

in Lombardy, the Romagna and Umbria. At the urging of the regime's leading spokesman, Maso degli Albizzi, and other members of the elite, among them Lorenzo Ridolfi, new *prestanze* were decreed, and by 1403 expenditures on troops had climbed to fifty thousand florins a month, a level previously seen only during the peak war years of 1390-92, 1397 and 1402.[101] Not surprisingly, the response of new men and lesser guildsmen to the policy was lukewarm. Fresh levies cost Datini an additional 2750 florins, and in a letter of 1404 to his factors in Barcelona he complained that "things here remain the same or, if anything, get worse. Nothing is done but order payments to the commune. May God soon send us peace."[102] At the same time, the reluctance of the leadership to assign troops to the capture of Milanese strongholds in Tuscany meant that commerce, cut off from the sea and deprived of the raw wool on which the textile industry depended, remained depressed.

By the beginning of 1404, it was clear that the offensive policy had failed. Alliances with the pope and Genoa had collapsed, Pisa remained in Milanese hands and discontent with the regime was growing. Former hawks, such as Mazo degli Albizzi and Lorenzo Ridolfi, began calling for peace negotiations and reduced war expenditures.[103] In April, Florence concluded treaties with Siena and Lucca by which it acquired access to the sea. Encouraged by this development, the opposition asserted itself, the legislative councils voting overwhelmingly to abolish the Eighty-One, to the satisfaction, the chronicler Giovanni Morelli (d. 1444) observed, of the *popolo* and the "fury" of the war party.[104] Further resolutions slashed subsidies to Florentine client states in Lombardy, and by late summer the government had abandoned the campaign.

[101] Molho, *Florentine Public Finances*, 61, table 4; 10, table 1. Ridolfi's support for a prolongation of hostilities is reported by Brucker, *Civic World*, 194, n. 32. Maso degli Albizzi (1343-1417) was the most powerful member of the leadership elite during the war against Milan and throughout the first decade of the fifteenth century; for a sketch, see ibid., 272-76.

[102] "Le chose di qua si stano al modo usatto e pegio se posono. Qua no' si fa nulla se no' dare ordine a paghare danari [al] Chomune. Che Dio ci mandi pacie tosto ..." (letter of 2 February 1404 quoted by Brucker, ibid., 200, n. 57). For Datini's *prestanze* payments, see Molho, *Florentine Public Finances*, 96, table 7 (3 January 1403-23 February 1405).

[103] Ridolfi recommended withdrawal of troops from Lombardy at an advisory council held in July (Brucker, *Civic World*, 197). The protocol of the *pratica* is edited by Ninci, *Consulte e pratiche, 1404*, 263.

[104] The passage is quoted and translated by Brucker, *Civic World*, 199. On Morelli's background and status, see ibid., 35-36.

In Brucker's estimate, the elite's decision to prolong the war despite its cost to the city's commercial interests never posed a grave threat to the regime, though it intensified strains in the political class that had been building for over a decade.[105] As usual, much of the tension centred on the unprecedented level of government debt. Between 1402 and 1404, expenditures on mercenaries and carrying charges on the accumulated debt exceeded the combined income from gabelles and taxes on subject territories by 1.25 million florins.[106] Although this sum was partly offset by *prestanze* that raised 950,000 florins, the new loans only had the effect of swelling the cumulative debt and magnifying carrying charges.[107] Increasingly, new men and lesser guildsmen linked complaints about the burden and unequal distribution of *prestanze* to demands for fiscal reform and the elimination of forced loans altogether.[108]

For the elite, dissatisfaction with deficit financing, the central pillar of its fiscal policy, was an uncomfortable reminder of the grievances that had inspired the Ciompi and the reforms of the guild regime the elite had overthrown only twenty years earlier.[109] Indeed, there is evidence of a patrician backlash against its critics. Following a fresh electoral scrutiny in the summer of 1404, the Eight of Police learned of a conspiracy by disaffected patricians to "restore" elite control of the commune, which they alleged was being undermined by an influx of parvenus and new men.[110] Similar

[105] In Brucker's view, the events of late 1403 and the beginning of 1404 represented at best a "minor crisis" for the regime (*Civic World*, 194). Of the leadership's change of position on further operations against the Milanese, he notes that "Maso degli Albizzi had orchestrated this *volte-face* with a minimum of public quarrelling, and with no scapegoats or blighted reputations" (ibid., 198).

[106] Molho, *Florentine Public Finances*, 61, table 4. 626,000 florins in carrying charges on the *monte* accounted for about half of this sum.

[107] For the sum of 950,000 florins, see ibid., 62, table 5. Brucker notes that a commission appointed in 1407 to investigate ways of eliminating the accumulated debt calculated the total to be 3,305,000 florins, on which 190,200 florins (roughly six percent) were owed annually in interest (*Civic World*, 210-11). By 1415 the debt had been reduced by only two hundred thousand florins to 3.1 million (Molho, *Florentine Public Finances*, 72).

[108] Such opinions were voiced, for example, in an advisory council of July 1404 (Brucker, *Civic World*, 197).

[109] The leadership's preoccupation with a possible repetition of the 1378 revolution grew more pronounced in the course of the war. An alleged conspiracy was given as a reason for the creation of the Eighty-One in 1393. Other plots were reported in 1396, 1397 and 1400 (Brucker, *Civic World*, 90-101, 171-74; see also Molho, "Politics and the Ruling Class," 412-13, 416).

[110] Brucker, *Civic World*, 199. On the 1404 scrutiny, see Guidi, *Il governo*, 1: 249-53; and Renzo Ninci, "Lo 'Squittino del Mangione': il consolidamento legale

fears underlay legislation that made citizenship privileges contingent on the payment of *prestanze*. In a provision of 7 October 1404, new men were excluded from the pool of candidates eligible for communal office unless they could show that they or their male ancestors had paid *prestanze* for a period of thirty years.[111]

The 1404 provision linking full citizenship to compulsory loans exemplifies how the political significance of the *monte comune* had been transformed during its first fifty years. At the outset, the *monte*'s chief advocates had been the new men and middling guildsmen who created it and who alone in the wake of the great bank failures disposed of the ready cash to take advantage of the market.[112] But this soon changed, particularly after 1362, as the republic's foreign policy fostered a massive expansion of the debt, on which a growing share of the possessing classes now depended for a significant proportion of their income.[113] By the mid-1360s, members of leading patrician families—Rinuccini, Sacchetti, Strozzi, Albizzi, Castiglionchio, Dietsalvi—had entered the market as speculators and investors alongside new men.[114] Elite interests guaranteed that the *monte* would survive the proletarian assault of 1378 to emerge as the central instrument of the oligarchy's fiscal regime in the next decade. When criticism of the debt erupted again in the 1390s and the first decade of the fifteenth century, the most vocal critics were not the poor, who nevertheless continued to bear

---

di un regime (1404)," *Bulletino dell'Istituto storico italiano per il Medio Evo e Archivio muratoriano* 94 (1988): 155-250.

[111] The privileges of new men were often the subject of controvery in periods of political tension; similar provisions in 1346 and 1379 disqualified those who were unable to trace native descent in the paternal line or failed to meet a thirty-year residential requirement (Brucker, *Florentine Politics*, 116-23; idem, *Civic World*, 48; see also the essays of Kirshner cited above p. 3, n. 7 and p. 10, n. 7). On the 1404 provision in particular, see Julius Kirshner, "Paolo di Castro on *Cives ex privilegio* : A Controversy over the Legal Qualifications for Public Office in Early Fifteenth-Century Florence," in *Renaissance Studies in Honor of Hans Baron*, ed. Anthony Molho and John A. Tedeschi (Dekalb: Northern Illinois University Press, 1971), 227-64; and Guidi, *Il governo*, 1: 105-07.

[112] Brucker, *Florentine Politics*, 19-21; Becker, *Florence in Transition*, 1: 218-23; Barducci, "Politica e speculazione," 206-10. See also the evidence presented by Anthony Molho, "Créanciers de Florence en 1347: Un aperçu statistique du quartier de Santo Spirito," in *La Toscane et les Toscans autour de la Renaissance: Cadres de vie, société, croyances: Mélanges offerts à Charles-M. de La Roncière* (Aix-en-Provence: L'Université de Provence, 1999), 77-93.

[113] Barducci, "Politica e speculazione," 210-17; idem, "Le riforme finanziarie," 96-97.

[114] Kirshner, "Franco Sacchetti," 574. See also Becker, "Economic Change," 30-31, esp. 31, n. 37.

the heaviest burden, but the nonelite elements of the political class itself, for whom the attractions of the *monte* were rapidly declining as levies over which they had little control drained away their resources and left them with credits of doubtful value.

3
Usury and the Public Debt Controversy

Critics began to voice doubts about the legitimacy of the *monte* within a decade of its creation.[1] Matteo Villani reported that mendicant masters disputed the moral status of government creditors in 1353-54 and the chronicler himself questioned the motivations of those who lent to the *monte dell'uno tre* a few years later. Of the latter, Villani remarked that

> in this way the commune raised the amount it needed without much difficulty, although it succeeded not because of the love or affection citizens bore towards their republic, but because of their greed for big profits. This was a far cry from the good old ways of our forefathers and drew many away from trade into usury, and so debased their consciences that even widows cared little for their souls so long as the *monte* paid well.[2]

Villani probably exaggerated citizens' enthusiasm for the new scheme, for it appears that in the summer of 1358 the uneasiness of potential investors about accusations of usury was enough to prevent the government raising what it needed by voluntary subscriptions. As a result, it was obliged to impose "compulsory" levies of fifty florins on selected citizens who, "if they were forced, ... would avoid the danger of sin."[3]

[1] The only comprehensive study of the controversy is Kirshner, "From Usury to Public Finance." Kirshner has published much of this research in "Reading Bernardino's Sermon" and in the other articles cited above and below. On the Florentine controversy in particular, see also Noonan, *Scholastic Analysis of Usury*, 121-28, 294-310; Spicciani, *Capitale e interesse*, 97-111; U. Santarelli, "'*Maxima fuit Florentiae altercatio*': L'usura e i *montes*," in *Banchi pubblici*, 81-94; Armstrong, "Politics of Usury"; and Raymond de Roover, "Il trattato di fra Santi Rucellai sul cambio, il monte comune e il monte delle doti," *ASI* 111 (1953): 3-41; text reedited by Edoardo Fumagalli, "I trattati di fra Santi Rucellai," *Aevum* 51 (1977): 289-332.

[2] "Per questa via il comune senza altra gravezza ebbe al suo bisogno soccorso; e se bene si misura, non per carità o affezione ch'avessono i cittadini alla sua repubblica, ma per la cupidigia del largo profitto; il quale fuori del buono e antico costume de' nostri maggiori molti n'ha tirati dalla mercatanzia in su l'usura, e sì ha ingrossate le coscienze, che le vedovelle poco si curano dell'anime, pur che il monte risponda bene loro" (*Cronica* 8.71, ed. Moutier, 4: 91).

[3] Quoted by Trexler, "Florence," 152. The incident is discussed at ibid., 151-53.

A similar preoccupation with usury underlay the appointment of a *syndicus ad indulgendum* (Syndic for Immunity) in June 1354, whose task was to

> pardon, limit and remit with respect to God, conscience and the world all who have hitherto received or enjoyed, or whose predecessors received or enjoyed, or who themselves or whose predecessors will in the course of the current year receive anything by way of gift, compensation, commission, usury or interest from the revenues of the commune for any money lent to the commune or advanced to it in any way; and also to make or cause to be made with regard to the said pardon, limitation and remission an instrument or instruments with all guarantees, warranties and formalities for any who desire such.[4]

The "pardon" mentioned in the provision did not refer to remission of sin, over which the commune claimed no authority, but to immunity from prosecution for restitution of interest on the grounds that the government had been the victim of usury.[5] The word was replaced after 1354 by "liberate" or "absolve," while the explicit reference to usury was dropped in 1360, after which the preferred formulas were "damages and *interesse*, return or remuneration" or, even better, "a spontaneous, free and pure gift," descriptions normally reserved for profits from legitimate private and commercial transactions.[6] By the 1370s, the government had stopped issuing certifi-

---

The text of the provision is edited by Kirshner, "Reading Bernardino's Sermon," 577, n. 107.

[4] "... ad perdonandum, finiendum, et remictendum et quoad deum et quoad conscientiam et ad mundum omnibus et singulis qui hactenus recepissent seu habuissent seu quorum predecessores habuissent seu recepissent seu qui vel quorum predecessores recipient durante tempore dicti anni aliquid de pecunia communis predicti pro dono, merito, provisione, usuris seu interesse cuiuscunque pecunie dicto communi recipienti mutuate date vel ad ipsum commune pervente quoquo modo. Et ad faciendum et fieri faciendum ad ipsa perdonantia, fine et remissione instrumentum et instrumenta cuilibet petenti, cum pattis, cautelis et solempnitatibus ..." (provision of 20 June 1354, ed. Kirshner, "Reading Bernardino's Sermon," 576, n. 104). The office was confirmed in 1357 (idem, "From Usury to Public Finance," 237), and still operative in 1367 (Trexler, "Florence," 153-54).

[5] Kirshner, "Reading Bernardino's Sermon," 575-76; idem, "From Usury to Public Finance," 238; Trexler, "Florence," 155-56.

[6] Kirshner, "Storm over the *Monte*, 225; "Reading Bernardino's Sermon," 576. The classic formula occurs in the provision of June 1383: "Quod omnem totum et quicquid quod provisum est per ordinamenta dicti communis intelligatur dari debere omnibus et singulis ... creditoribus dicti communis in quocunque monte communis predicti ad rationem quinque pro centenario annuatim pro dono, damnis et interesse seu provisione vel merito dictorum creditorum et seu sub alio quocunque

cates of immunity, incorporating blanket guarantees against restitution into the legislation authorizing *prestanze*.[7] The patrician regime that seized power in 1382 confirmed these measures in a provision of June 1383 "regarding the exoneration of the conscience of the citizens of the commune of Florence, especially with respect to the revenues of the *monte*, which are received at a rate of five percent as gift, damages and *interesse*."[8] The provision declared that

> any creditor may licitly retain as his own what he has received [from the *monte*] without any additional authorization or agreement by the commune or any official acting in the commune's name, and without any scruple of conscience or obligation to make restitution.[9]

It went on to add that whatever description might be applied to increments in future, the commune's guarantee would stand and creditors remain immune from prosecution.[10]

To what extent did these fictions reflect real moral scruples on the part of creditors? It is notable that we have no examples of compulsory restitution, though there is evidence that prior to 1383 the government was not averse to playing on lenders' consciences. Trexler, for example, detects a tendency in council debates and legislative provisions to stress creditors'

---

vocabulo similis effectus vel importantis, intelligatur dari debere et recipi et detur et recipiatur et peti, recipi possit vigore presentis provisionis pro spontaneo, libero et mero dono et donationis titulo ... " (ed. ibid., 579, n. 111). The formula is paraphrased by Ridolfi in the *thema* (introduction) to the *Questio montis* (2209-13).

7 Trexler, "Florence," 154.

8 "Circa exgravationem conscientie civium Florentinorum dicti communis et maxime in denariis montis qui recipiuntur V pro centenario pro aliquo dono, damno et interesse" (ed. Kirshner, "Reading Bernardino's Sermon," 579, n. 110). Ridolfi paraphrases the provision in the preface to the *Questio montis* (2216-21).

9 "Sed iuste illud totum petant et petere possint atque recipiant a dicto ⟨communi⟩, quod sine aliqua alia liberatione vel fine inde propterea per dictum commune et seu per aliquem sindicum nomine dicti communis fienda sine aliquo conscientie scrupulo et sine aliquo restitutionis gravamine, possit quilibet talis creditor illud quod sic receperit ut sibi vere dictum licite retinere" (ed. Kirshner, "Reading Bernardino's Sermon," 579, n. 112).

10 "Et quod idem intelligatur esse et sit dispositum de eo quod receptum fuerit in preteritum per quoscunque creditores dicti communis pro dono, damnis seu interesse, usuris vel merito aut sub alio nomine vel vocabulo huius effectus vel importantis pro aliqua vel occasione alicuius quantitatis mutuate seu deposite dicto communi aut alii pro ipso communi recipienti per aliquos de civitate, comitatu, vel districtu Florentie et seu in qua ut creditores descripti fuissent seu essent ut creditores dicti communis in aliquo monte communis predicti" (ed. Kirshner, "Reading Bernardino's Sermon," 580, n. 113).

moral obligation to restore interest they had received on their credits.[11] The Dominican master Piero degli Strozzi (1293-1362) remarked in 1353-54 that the officials of the *monte* were authorized to withhold payments from scrupulous creditors, and in 1378 Franco Sacchetti's brother Giannozzo repaid three hundred florins he had received in interest, pleading an uneasy conscience as his motive.[12] Any reservations creditors might have had were reinforced by moralists who argued that legislative subterfuges could not alter the fact that interest-bearing government loans violated the canonical usury prohibition.

A. The Usury Prohibition

Medieval canon law and theology defined usury as any predetermined charge for a loan of money or goods.[13] The prohibition of usury derived from the gospel precept to "lend, expecting nothing in return" (*Lc* 6.35: "Mutuum date, nihil inde sperantes") and the Roman law conception of a gratuitous loan (*mutuum*). *Lc* 6.35 was first linked to usury by Pope Urban III (1185-87) in the decretal *Consuluit* (X 5.19.10).[14] The citation of the precept in this context transformed it from a general injunction to charity into a specific condemnation of interest, while Roman law gave a precise

[11] Trexler, "Florence," 150-51, 154. The government did not, however, follow the example of Siena, which invoked the usury prohibition to suspend interest payments on the public debt in 1382; see Caferro, *Mercenary Companies*, 135-36.

[12] For Piero degli Strozzi, see Kirshner, "Storm over the *Monte*," 225; for Giannozzo Sacchetti, see idem, "Franco Sacchetti," 580.

[13] For a concise survey of the usury prohibition, see John Gilchrist, *The Church and Economic Activity in the Middle Ages* (London, Melbourne and Toronto: Macmillan, 1969), 62-70. The only general study remains Noonan, *Scholastic Analysis of Usury*, which must now be supplemented by Spicciani, *Capitale e interesse*; Odd Langholm, *The Aristotelian Analysis of Usury* (Bergen, Oslo, Stavanger and Tromsø: Universitetsforlaget, 1984); idem, *Economics in the Medieval Schools: Wealth, Exchange, Value, Money and Usury According to the Paris Theological Tradition, 1200-1350*, Studien und Texte zur Geistesgeschichte des Mittelalters, no. 29 (Leiden, New York and Cologne: E. J. Brill, 1992); and idem, "The Medieval Schoolmen (1200-1400)," in *Ancient and Medieval Ideas and Concepts of Social Justice*, ed. S. Todd Lowry and Barry Gordon (Leiden, New York and Cologne: Brill, 1998), 439-501. The fundamental study of the canonical doctrine is T. P. McLaughlin, "The Teaching of the Canonists on Usury (XII, XIII and XIV Centuries)," *Mediaeval Studies* 1 (1939): 81-147; 2 (1940): 1-22. See also *DDC*, s.v. "Intérêt et usure" by Auguste Dumas. Ridolfi deals with basic principles of the prohibition in Part 1, questions 1-12 (40-669). On the definition of usury, see Part 1, question 1, (40-322) and comm. nn. 40 to 318-22.

[14] The text is quoted and translated below, comm. n. 673.

meaning to the term *mutuum*.

In law, a *mutuum* was a loan of fungibles, that is, "things that are fixed by weight, number or measure, such as wine, oil, grain or cash paid in copper, silver or gold."[15] The use of such things is identical with their consumption or destruction. Because of this trait, ownership and liability passed to the borrower, who was bound to return the equivalent of the thing borrowed rather than the thing itself.[16] This contrasted with a *commodatum*, a loan for use—for example, a loan of a horse or a boat—in which the creditor retained both ownership and liability.[17] Although *commodatum* was a gratuitous contract, the creditor-owner could legitimately convert it into a contract of lease and hire (*locatio et conductio*) by charging for the use of the thing.[18] But the nature of a *mutuum* precluded charging the borrower for the use of what had become his own property. So far as the contract itself was concerned, the debtor's obligation extended only to the repayment of a thing of the same quality and quantity as the thing he was lent.

Classical Roman law circumvented this difficulty by means of a supplementary contract called *stipulatio*, which was agreed at the same time as the *mutuum* and by which the debtor promised a separate payment called *usurae* or *fenus*.[19] From patristic times, however, the church repudiated such agreements, forbidding the clergy to demand *usurae* and, in the west, extending the restriction to the laity in a series of conciliar decrees between the eighth and the twelfth centuries.[20] A flurry of anti-usury legislation towards the end of this period suggests that the church was inspired by a determination to ensure access to affordable credit at a time when the growth of the commercial economy was driving the price of money beyond

[15] "Mutui autem obligatio in his rebus consistit, quae pondere numero mensurave constant, veluti vino oleo frumento pecunia numerata aere argento auro ..." (Inst. 3.14.pr.).

[16] "... quas res aut numerando aut metiendo aut pendendo in hoc damus, ut accipientium fiant et quandoque nobis non eaedam res, sed aliae eiusdem naturae et qualitatis reddantur. Unde etiam mutuum appellatum sit, quia ita a me tibi datur, ut ex meo tuum fiat" (ibid.).

[17] Inst. 3.14.2; Dig. 13.6.5.3-5,8,9.

[18] Inst. 3.24.

[19] W. W. Buckland, *A Text-Book of Roman Law from Augustus to Justinian*, 3rd ed., rev. Peter Stein (Cambridge: Cambridge University Press, 1963), 464, n.3.

[20] Gilchrist, *Economic Activity*, 62-63. On the measures adopted by specific councils from I Nicea (325) to III Lateran (1179), see ibid., 144-49, appendix; and the translations on 155, 165, 173. *Usurae* remained legal for the laity in the Byzantine Empire (ibid., 63).

the means of small artisans, rural proprietors and peasants.[21]

The battery of patristic texts assembled by the canonist Gratian (fl. 1135-45) in the mid-twelfth century to demonstrate that "whatever is demanded beyond the principal is usury" reveals an intense suspicion of the new economic conditions. Indeed, as far as Gratian was concerned, virtually all profit was usury or *turpe lucrum* (dishonest profit).[22] In his commentary on the *Decretals* of Gregory IX, Pope Innocent IV (d. 1254) expressed fears about the destructive social effects of usury, explaining that

> usury is generally prohibited because if it were allowed all manner of evils would result, above all the abandonment by farmers of their holdings, save when they had no other choice. The result of this would be such dearth that the poor would die of starvation, for even if they had access to workable land they would be unable to obtain the livestock and tools they need to farm, since they have no money of their own and the rich would prefer to lend at usury with its higher and more secure returns than to invest their money in less profitable and riskier ventures like farming. The result would be to drive the price of food beyond the means of the poor, from which would come great danger to the faithful.... Again, it is scarcely ever the case that anyone who pays usury for very long avoids being reduced to poverty, which is a dangerous condition unless it is embraced as a gift of God.... And so it is clear that practically every evil follows from usury, and for this reason it is condemned in both the Old Testament and the New.[23]

[21] Ibid., 63-64.

[22] See, for example, Decretum Grat. C.14 q.3 dictum Grat. post c.4: "And so, it is clearly shown that whatever is demanded beyond the principal is usury" ("Ecce euidenter ostenditur, quod quicquid ultra sortem exigitur usura est"); and C.14 q.4 c.9: "He seeks dishonest profit who buys for less so that he may sell for more" ("Turpe lucrum sequitur, qui minus emit, ut plus uendat").

[23] "... ideo prohibetur ita generaliter vsura, quia si liceret eam accipere, omnia mala inde sequerentur, et maxime quia non intenderent homines culturae possessionum, nisi quando aliud non posset, et ita tanta esset caristia, quod omnes pauperes fame perirent, quia etsi possent habere terras ad colendum, non tamen possent habere animalia et instrumenta ad colendum necessaria, cum ipsi pauperes per se non haberent, et diuites tum propter lucrum, tum propter securitatem pecuniae potius in vsuras, quam in minora et minus tuta lucra ponerent pecuniam, et si aliqui ibi sua expenderent ita cara essent victualia, quod pauperes non haberent, vnde emere possent, et hoc esset maximum et summum periculum fidelibus.... Item alia causa est, quia vix potest esse, quin aliquis vsuras debens diu duret sine paupertate, quae nimis est periculosa, nisi paupertatis desiderium alicui speciali Dei dono concedatur.... et sic est inuenire fere omnia mala, quae prouenirent ex vsuris, et ideo generaliter prohibita est a domino vtroque testamento" (Innocent IV, *Commentaria super libros quinque Decretalium*, ad X 5.19 rubr. [Frankfurt: Hieronymus Feyerabendt, 1570; repr. Frankfurt: Minerva, 1968], fol. 516ra-b). For an an-

The *Decretals* themselves, published in 1234, attest to the proliferation of usurious contracts and to the development of a more precise vocabulary to describe it.[24] What Gratian condemned as mere avarice was now the *crimen usurarum* (crime of usury), a form of theft and a sin against justice or charity that could be rectified only by complete restitution.[25] It was expressed not only in loans, but in a variety of transactions that had the same effect as loans, such as simulated sale contracts, credit sales in which payment or delivery was postponed, partnerships in which the risk was unevenly shared, bills of exchange and sea loans.[26] The legislation collected

---

alysis of this passage, see Spicciani, *Capitale e interesse*, 49-64. Ridolfi summarizes Innocent's argument in Part 1, question 7 (377-96); see also comm. n. 377-96.

[24] Spicciani, *Capitale e interesse*, 20-21, 65.

[25] Cf. X 5.19.3 (=III Lateran, c. 25): "Quia in omnibus fere locis ita crimen usurarum invaluit, ut multi, aliis negotiis praetermissis, quasi licite usuras exerceant, et qualiter utriusque testamenti pagina condemnentur, nequaquam attendant ..."; X 5.19.4: "Super eo vero, respondemus, quod, quum usurarum crimen utriusque testamenti pagina detestetur ..."; and X 5.19.9: "Tua nos duxit fraternitas consulendos, quid sit de usurariorum filiis observandum, qui eis, in crimine usurarum defunctis, succedunt ..." Alexander III (1159-81) linked restitution and theft in X 5.19.5: "⟨Manifesti usurarii⟩ cogendi sunt per poenam ... eas ⟨usuras⟩ his, a quibus extorserunt, vel eorum heredibus restituere, vel, his non superstitibus, pauperibus erogare ... quum iuxta verbum B. Augustini non remittatur peccatum, nisi restituatur ablatum."

[26] X 3.17.5 describes a sale of property which was in fact a loan on security; see McLaughlin, "Teaching of the Canonists," 1: 115-17; Noonan, *Scholastic Analysis of Usury*, 95-98; and comm. n. 650-52. X 5.19.6 and 5.19.19 deal with credit sales; for discussions, see Noonan, *Scholastic Analysis of Usury*, 91-95; McLaughlin, "Teaching of the Canonists," 1: 117-120; and comm. nn. 145-64, 751-58. Risk was acknowledged as a criterion of ownership and therefore of the licitness of a contract, but X 5.19.19 condemned the sea loan or *fenus nauticum* in which the creditor assumed the risk of loss: "Naviganti vel eunti ad nundinas certam mutuans pecuniae quantitatem, pro eo, quod suscipit in se periculum, recepturus aliquid ultra sortem, usurarius est censendus." For a discussion, see Noonan, *Scholastic Analysis of Usury*, 133-53, esp. 137-39; and McLaughlin, "Teaching of the Canonists," 1: 102-5. For a translation, see Julius Kirshner and Karl F. Morrison, ed., *Medieval Europe*, vol. 4 of *University of Chicago Readings in Western Civilization*, ed. John W. Boyer and Julius Kirshner (Chicago and London: University of Chicago Press, 1986), 316-17. On the variety of new commercial instruments developed in this period, see Raymond de Roover, "The Organization of Trade," in *Cambridge Economic History of Europe*, vol. 3, *Economic Organization and Policies in the Middle Ages*, ed. M. Postan and E. Rich (Cambridge: Cambridge University Press, 1963), 46-59. On the bill of exchange, see idem, *Money, Banking and Credit in Mediaeval Bruges: Italian Merchant-Bankers, Lombards and Money-Changers, A Study in the Origins of Banking* (Cambridge, MA: Mediaeval Academy of America, 1948), 48-75; and idem, *Cam-*

in the *Liber sextus* and the *Constitutiones Clementinae* reflect a hardening of the prohibition, culminating in the declaration of the Council of Vienne (1311-12) that anyone who affirmed "that it is not a sin to practise usury" was to be "punished as a heretic."[27] The increasing severity of the legislation was matched by a theoretical critique of usury as an offence against natural justice first formulated by Thomas Aquinas (1225-74) and transmitted to the later Middle Ages by the Augustinian Gerard of Siena (d. ca. 1336), who argued that usury was "by nature vicious and bound up with malice."[28]

In the circumstances, it was difficult for theorists to accommodate novel transactions even if they were inclined to. At the procedural level, the distinction between "manifest" and "occult" usury expressed in the decrees of the Third Lateran Council (1179), the Second Council of Lyons (1274) and the Council of Vienne represented a concession to merchant bankers.[29] Manifest or "notorious" usurers were subject to the full force of

---

bium ad Venetias: Contribution to the History of Foreign Exchange," in *Business, Banking, and Economic Thought in Late Medieval and Early Modern Europe: Selected Studies of Raymond de Roover*, ed. Julius Kirshner (Chicago and London: University of Chicago Press, 1974), 239-59. Model contracts from the mid-thirteenth century can be studied in John H. Pryor, *Business Contracts of Medieval Provence: Selected "Notulae" from the Cartulary of Giraud Amalric of Marseilles, 1248*, Studies and Texts 54 (Toronto: Pontifical Institute of Mediaeval Studies, 1981).

[27] Clem. 5.5.1; see comm. n. 660-64. For translations, see Gilchrist, *Economic Activity*, 206; and Kirshner and Morrison, ed., *Medieval Europe*, 317. It was provoked by governments who openly defied the prohibition by tolerating public usurers. On the intensification of anti-usury measures in the early fourteenth century, see Spicciani, *Capitale e interesse*, 17-24. For a case study of the effect of the Vienne decree in Marseilles, see Joseph Shatzmiller, *Shylock Reconsidered: Jews, Moneylending, and Medieval Society* (Berkeley, Los Angeles and London: University of California Press, 1990).

[28] Spicciani, *Capitale e interesse*, 66-68. For Thomas' argument, see *Summa theologiae*, secunda secundae, q. 78, art. 1, in *Opera omnia*, vol. 9 (Rome: S. C. Propaganda Fide, 1897), 155-56. For a discussion, see Langholm, *Economics in the Medieval Schools*, 236-48. On Gerard of Siena, see ibid., 552-9. Gerard's text was known through a summary in Johannes Andreae's *quaestio* on VI *de reg. Iur.* 4 *Peccatum*; on the textual tradition, see comm. n. 398-406. Ridolfi summarizes Gerard's theses in Part 1, question 7 (398-460); see also comm. nn. 398-406 to 458-60.

[29] Gilchrist, *Economic Activity*, 66; McLaughlin, "Teaching of the Canonists," 2: 1-18. See also John W. Baldwin, "The Medieval Merchant before the Bar of Canon Law," *Papers of the Michigan Academy of Science, Arts and Letters* 44 (1959): 287-99; and Benjamin N. Nelson, "The Usurer and the Merchant Prince: Italian Businessmen and the Ecclesiastical Law of Restitution, 1100-1500," *Journal of Economic History*, supplement 7 (1947): 104-12.

the prohibition and required to restore their usuries under threat of excommunication and denial of burial. Such lenders were usually pawnbrokers or "public" moneylenders, who openly provided consumer credit on little or no security at rates of twenty to forty-three percent a year.[30] By contrast, the moneychangers and merchant bankers who dominated the market for commercial credit escaped these penalties because the usurious dimensions of their activities were not public but hidden or "occult." They remained under a moral obligation to make restitution, but this could be enforced only through the sacrament of penance (*iudicium animarum*) as a condition of absolution, an arrangement that clearly favoured the commercial classes.[31]

Another approach involved the elaboration of "exceptions" to the prohibition in various classes of loans or quasi-loans. In the mid-thirteenth century, the canonist Hostiensis (d. 1271) was able to identify thirteen such cases, and later jurists added to the list.[32] Some of the exceptions in-

[30] Raymond de Roover, *Money, Banking and Credit*, 127. On consumer credit in general, see ibid., chaps. 6-8, 99-167. R. H. Helmholz, "Usury and the Medieval English Church Courts," *Speculum* 61 (1986): 364-80, finds evidence only for the prosecution of manifest usurers. For a broad overview of enforcement, see Bernard Schnapper, "La répression de l'usure et l'évolution économique (XIIIe-XVIe siècles)," *Tijdschrift voor rechtsgeschiedenis* 37 (1969): 47-75.

[31] On merchant restitution, see Nelson, "Merchant Prince," 112-21; Armando Sapori, "L'interesse del denaro a Firenze nel Trecento," in *Studi di storia economica (secoli XIII, XIV, XV)*, 3rd ed., 3 vols. (Florence: Sansoni, 1955-1967), 1: 223-43; and Florence Edler, "Restitution in Renaissance Florence" in *Studi in onore di Armando Sapori*, 2 vols. (Milan: Istituto Editoriale Cisalpino, 1957), 773-80. For two thirteenth-century examples of restitution, see Robert S. Lopez and Irving W. Raymond, ed. and trans., *Medieval Trade in the Mediterranean World* (New York and London: Columbia University Press, 1955), 159-60. Raymond de Roover argues that the usury prohibition had the practical effect of focusing banking on exchange transactions; see his *The Rise and Decline of the Medici Bank, 1397-1494* (Cambridge, MA: Harvard University Press, 1963), 10-14; idem, *La Pensée économique des scolastiques: doctrine et méthodes* (Montreal and Paris: Institut d'études médiévales and J. Vrin, 1971), 76-93; and idem, "The Scholastic Attitude Towards Trade and Entrepreneurship," in *Business, Banking, and Economic Thought*, 336-45. For context, see Kirshner's introductory essay, "Raymond de Roover on Scholastic Economic Thought," 15-36, esp. 26-27. See also Francesco Galassi's evidence that the prohibition retarded the development of credit markets by channelling capital into pious bequests rather than productive investment in "Buying a Passport to Heaven: Usury, Restitution, and the Merchants of Medieval Genoa," *Religion* 22 (1992): 313-26.

[32] Gilchrist, *Economic Activity*, 67. Ridolfi lists the cases where usury is permitted in Part 1, question 8 (480-561); for discussions of the canons cited, see comm.

volved a special relationship between the parties, as, for example, when the canons allowed a son-in-law to retain the income of a pledge for an unpaid dowry rather than apply it to the extinction of his father-in-law's debt.[33] More significant for our purposes was the reception of the Roman law principle that a borrower was bound by a debt of gratitude to his creditor. Although it was not actionable and could not form part of the loan contract, a true gift (*donum*, *antidotum*) from the debtor to the lender was considered licit, indeed praiseworthy.[34]

The most important exceptions came within the category of compensation. The canon law of damages derived from Roman law, which recognized a contracting party's right to seek indemnification for losses sustained through the other party's failure to fulfil his obligations.[35] *Damnum* (damages) represented the difference (*quod interest*) between the actual condition of the injured party and the position he would have been in had the contract been properly executed. Since Roman law termed such compensation on loans *usurae*, the civilian lawyer Azo (d. 1220) coined the substantive *interesse* to distinguish such damages from illicit usury, and soon afterward Laurentius Hispanus (d. 1248) introduced the term into canon law.[36]

There was a consensus that *interesse* could be claimed under the two closely related titles of *mora* (delay) and *poena* (penalty).[37] Penal clauses,

---

nn. 481-84 to 556-61. He invokes Hostiensis' list at 533-36; I supply the text in comm. n. 533-38.

[33] X 5.19.16. See McLaughlin, "Teaching of the Canonists," 1: 131-34; Noonan, *Scholastic Analysis of Usury*, 103-04; and Arwed Blomeyer, "Aus der Consilienpraxis zum kanonischen Zinsverbot," *Zeitschrift der Savigny-Stiftung für Rechtsgeschichte, kanonistische Abteilung* 66 (1980): 317-35, esp. 327-30. Ridolfi discusses the case at 524-32; see also comm. n. 524-32.

[34] McLaughlin, "Teaching of the Canonists," 1: 143; Noonan, *Scholastic Analysis of Usury*, 104-05; comm. n. 533-38. Ridolfi treats gifts in Part 1, question 1 (107-20); see also comm. nn. 107-12 to 112-20; he discusses *antidotum* in Part 2, *oppositio* 1 (709-14); see also comm. n, 709-14. For an analysis of the function of *antidotum* in early modern economic and social thought, see Bartolomé Clavero, *Antidora: Antropología católica de la economía moderna*, Università di Firenze, Centro di studi per la storia del pensiero giuridico moderno, Biblioteca per la storia del pensiero giuridico moderno, no. 39 (Milan: Giuffrè, 1991).

[35] Dig. 17.2.60

[36] McLaughlin, "Teaching of the Canonists," 1: 141; Noonan, *Scholastic Analysis of Usury*, 106.

[37] McLaughlin, "Teaching of the Canonists," 1: 140-43; Noonan, *Scholastic Analysis of Usury*, 107-12. Ridolfi cites delay in Part 1, question 5 (368-72); see comm. n. 369-72; penalty in Part 1, question 8 (498-519; see comm. n. 498-504 to 504-19.

which encouraged adherence to the terms of an agreement, were a standard feature of medieval contracts. They were permitted in loans provided they were not *in fraudem usurarum* (in fraud of usury), that is, a form of disguised usury, which might be presumed, for example, if the penalty grossly exceeded customary damages, or if it was evident that the penalty would be deliberately incurred. Under the title of delay, the creditor claimed compensation for losses stemming from the debtor's failure to repay at the agreed time. To the extent that the parties calculated anticipated damages for delay in advance and incorporated them into the loan contract, this title was virtually the same as penalty and subject to the same criteria of licitness.[38]

If theologians and canonists generally agreed on the legitimacy of *interesse* for default and delay, the suggestion that a creditor might claim it from the beginning of the loan period for damages incurred (*damnum emergens*) or potential profits forgone (*lucrum cessans*) as a result of lending was a distinctly minority opinion.[39] *Damnum emergens* extended the concept of compensation to include payment of an indemnity to a creditor who was materially damaged by making a loan; the usual example was of a creditor who was himself forced to borrow in order to make the loan.[40] Canonists generally admitted the title but most theologians followed Thomas Aquinas in insisting that damages could not accrue during the loan period. A creditor who foresaw such damages should have abstained from lending in the first place.[41]

In his commentary on the *Decretals*, Hostiensis made a case for *lucrum cessans*, arguing that

> in that which is added to the principal, the seeking of *interesse* is not prohibited, but only shameful profit or other illicit increase .... Therefore I am of the view ... that if a merchant who frequents markets and fairs and there makes big profits should for reasons of charity lend me, who am in great need, money that he was going to employ in trade, then I am obligated to him from that moment for his *interesse*, provided nothing is done in fraud of usury ... and the said merchant is not in the habit of lending money at usury.[42]

[38] McLaughlin, "Teaching of the Canonists," 1: 140.

[39] McLaughlin, "Teaching of the Canonists," 1: 144-47; Noonan, *Scholastic Analysis of Usury*, 115-28. The best discussion of *lucrum cessans* is Spicciani, *Capitale e interesse*, 27-48.

[40] McLaughlin, "Teaching of the Canonists," 1: 145.

[41] Noonan, *Scholastic Analysis of Usury*, 118; Langholm, *Economics in the Medieval Schools*, 246, 337-38. The influential Franciscan Johns Duns Scotus (ca. 1265-1308) agreed with Thomas (ibid., 417). Among theologians, a notable exception was Scotus' confrere Peter John Olivi (1248-98) (ibid., 370).

[42] "In eo enim quod sorti accedit, non prohibetur petitio interesse, sed tantum

The Franciscan theologian Peter John Olivi came to a similar conclusion in his own discussion of this case. Defining the money in such a loan as *capitale* (capital), that is, money possessing productive capacity by virtue of being intended for trade (in contrast to money as a measure of value or money that was simply kept "in a box"), he concluded that "not only is its simple value returned but also the superadded value."[43] Both Hostiensis and Olivi imposed strict conditions on invoking the title. First, the lender had to be a merchant habitually engaged in trade; second, it was necessary that his intention was charitable; and third, the money had to have been originally destined for investment. Olivi added that the *interesse* must not be excessive but proportional to what might be expected from a typical investment over the same term.[44]

Innocent IV, however, condemned *lucrum cessans* and most authorities

---

turpis lucri, vel alterius illiciti incrementi, vt patet 14 q. iiii. *Si quis oblitus*. Ideo puto ex mente praemissorum iurium, quod si aliquis sit mercator, qui consueuit sequi mercata et nundinas, et ibi multa lucrari, mihi multum indigenti, ex charitate mutuaret pecuniam, cum qua negotiaturus erat, quod ego exinde sibi ad suum interesse remaneo obligatus, dummodo nihil fiat hic in fraudem vsurarum, vt patet in eo quod notatur supra eo. *Tuas* in fin. Et dummodo dictus mercator non consueuerit pecuniam suam taliter tradere ad vsuram" (*In Decretalium libros commentaria* ad X 5.19.16, n.4 [Venice: Iuntae, 1581; repr. Turin: Bottega D'Erasmo, 1965], V fol. 58vb-59ra). On this passage, see Spicciani, *Capitale e interesse*, 35-37.

[43] "... illud quod in firmo proposito domini sui est ordinatum ad aliquod probabile lucrum non solum habet rationem simplicis pecuniae seu rei, sed ultra hoc quamdam seminalem rationem lucrosi quam communiter capitale vocamus, et ideo non solum habet reddi simpliciter valor ipsius sed etiam valor superadiunctus" (*Tractatus de emptionibus et venditionibus, de usuris, de restitutionibus*, ed. Giacomo Todeschini, *Un trattato di economia politica francescana: il "De emptionibus et venditionibus, de usuris, de restitutionibus" di Pietro di Giovanni Olivi*, Istituto storico italiano per il Medio Evo, Studi storici, fasc. 125-26 [Rome: Istituto storico italiano per il Medio Evo, 1980], 85). Olivi's observation in fact occurs in a discussion of forced loans; he added later in connection with a commercial contract "... quia capitale, in quantum capitale, idest in quantum lucrativum est mercationibus destinatum, addit quandam lucrativam rationem supra rationem simplicis pecuniae eisudem quantitatis, quae non est sic mercationibus destinata" (ibid., 111). The case of the merchant lender is discussed at ibid., 73; and in Olivi's *Quodlibet* 1, qq. 16-17, ed. Spicciani, *Capitale e interesse*, 244-49; trans. in Kirshner and Morrison, *Medieval Europe*, 318-25). For an analysis of these passages and of Olivi's conception of capital, see Spicciani, *Capitale e interesse*, 85-96; and Julius Kirshner and Kimberly Lo Prete, "Peter John Olivi's Treatises on Contracts of Sale, Usury and Restitution: Minorite Economics or Minor Works?," *Quaderni fiorentini per la storia del pensiero giuridico moderno* 13 (1984): 266-77.

[44] Kirshner and Lo Prete, "Minorite Economics," 272.

until the seventeenth century followed him. The influential canonist Johannes Andreae maintained that it "furnishes a highway to usury."[45] The canonists Johannes Calderinus (d. 1365), Antonius de Butrio (d. 1406) and Peter of Ancharano (d. 1416) took a similar position.[46] Among theologians, Thomas Aquinas rejected *lucrum cessans* on the grounds that the creditor could not charge for a profit "he does not yet have and may in many ways be prevented from obtaining."[47] The Franciscan master Alexander Lombard (ca. 1268-1314) expressed a similar view in his treatise on usury.[48] In the wake of the Council of Vienne, several other theologians, notably the Dominican Remigio of Florence (d. 1319) and the Augustinian Gregory of Rimini (d. 1358) adopted Thomas' opinion.[49]

B. The Public Debt Controversy

A good case could be made that the operations of the *monte* violated the usury prohibition. *Prestanze* and voluntary loans were clearly *mutua* on which interest was paid from the moment the commune assumed its obligations. Could the government legitimately describe interest as a "spontaneous, free and pure gift" or as "damages and *interesse*"? Were such payments warranted under the controversial titles of *damnum emergens* and

[45] "... uerius uidetur dictum Innocentii et quod dicitur de interesse, illud locum habet post moram debitoris, et ex contrario pararetur aperta uia ad foenus" (*In quinque Decretalium libros novella commentaria*, ad X 5.19.19 [Venice: Franciscus Franciscius, 1581; repr. Turin: Bottega D'Erasmo, 1963, V fol. 77vb]). See also Spicciani, *Capitale e interesse*, 41-42.

[46] Spicciani, *Capitale e interesse*, 44.

[47] "Recompensationem vero damni quod consideratur in hoc quod de pecunia non lucratur, non potest in pactum deducere: quia non debet vendere id quod nondum habet et potest impediri multipliciter ab habendo" (*Summa theologiae*, secunda secundae, q. 78, art. 2, in *Opera omnia* 9: 159). On this passage, see Spicciani, *Capitale e interesse*, 30-31.

[48] Alexander rejected *lucrum cessans* in a discussion of Genoese forced loans: "Dices sorte quod si mutuans potest recipere aliquid ultra sortem non ratione mutui, sed propter interesse, quia mutuans de pecunia quam mutuavit communitati, fuisset lucratus. Dicendum est quod tale interesse est ab eventu, quia sicut potuit lucrari, potuit perdere et ideo in ratione talis interesse non licet aliquid accipere" (*Tractatus de usuris*, ed. A.-M. Hamelin, *Un traité de morale économique au XIVe siècle: le 'Tractatus de usuris' de maître Alexandre d'Alexandrie*, Analecta mediaevalia Namurcensia no. 14 [Louvain, Montreal, and Lille: Nauwelaerts, Librairie Franciscaine and Librairie Giard, 1962], 174).

[49] On Remigio, see Langholm, *Economics in the Medieval Schools*, 469. On Gregory, see Spicciani, *Capitale e interesse*," 40-43. Gregory made a limited exception in favour of compulsory lenders to the Venetian republic; see below, pp. 69-70.

lucrum cessans ? Could creditors accept interest in good conscience? Above all, were credits transferable, and, if so, could new creditors licitly accept interest? Such questions probably underlay the *Signoria*'s appeal in the spring of 1365 to the generals of the Dominican, Augustinian and Franciscan orders for authoritative guidance:

> Since there are manifold opinions on this practice, we wish the matter to be clarified so that all doubt may be banished from the souls of our con-citizens, and so that any directed by your judgment may be able to provide for the salvation of their souls. Therefore, in considerable distress, we ask your great reverence (which has always been circumspect in this and many greater affairs) that since masters and many learned brothers are coming together at the chapter of your order, you ask them to debate the aforesaid matters; and we ask that you send us as soon as possible letters marked with the seal of the general's office containing their decision, which, we believe, will be pleasing to God and beneficial and useful to the salvation of our souls. Thus if in fact the aforesaid practice is defiled by errors, to the detriment of souls, henceforth by that decision this practice may be avoided ....[50]

Unfortunately, the determinations of the chapters-general, if any, do not survive. Guglielmo Centueri da Cremona (d. 1402), a participant in the Franciscan chapter-general at Florence in June 1365, reported that opinion was divided.[51] A review of the opinions Ridolfi cites in his treatise leaves a similar impression of the controversy as a whole.[52] In general, however,

[50] Letter of 23 May 1365 to the generals of the Dominican and Augustinian orders, trans. Kirshner, "Reading Bernardino's Sermon," 578. Kirshner edits the text of the letter and a similar request of 25 May addresed to the Dominican provincial of Rome at ibid., 617-18, appendix 4. Unfortunately, the list of the *Signoria*'s precise questions is lost. On the communal subsidy for the Franciscan chapter-general of 1365 and the commune's sponsorship of meetings of other mendicant orders in Florence, see Julius Kirshner, "A Document of the Meeting of the Chapter General in Florence (1365)," *AFH* 62 (1969): 392-99.

[51] *De imprestitis, monte et locis Venetiarum, Florentie et Ianue*, ed. Kirshner, "Reading Bernardino's Sermon," 602-3. On Centueri's reference to the chapter-general, see ibid., 575. Centueri's comments on the *monte* were excerpted by Bernardino of Siena (1380-1444) from a commentary, now lost, on the *Sentences* of Peter Lombard. The passage was written after 1385 and possibly between 1398 and Centueri's death in 1402 (ibid., 564, esp. n. 64). Ridolfi does not appear to have been familiar with the text.

[52] In the survey that follows, I confine myself to participants in the Florentine controversy and writers cited by Ridolfi in his treatise. It should be noted, however, that the public debts of Venice and Genoa were equally controversial and generated a substantial literature of their own beginning in the later thirteenth century. For the wider Italian controversy, see Kirshner, "From Usury to Public Finance," chaps. 3 and 4, 97-233; idem, "Reading Bernardino's Sermon"; and idem, "Conscience and

disputants distinguished between lenders and speculators in debt credits and, among the former, between compulsory and voluntary lenders. Voluntary lending was uniformly denounced as a violation of the usury prohibition.[53] It was precisely to avoid incurring such censure that from the 1350s onward the government designated most loans *prestanze*, with the result that the debate focused on compulsory lenders.

Of the earlier writers cited by Ridolfi, only two, the Augustinians John Klenkock (or Clenkoh, d. 1374) and Guido de Belloreguardo (d. 1377), denied compulsory lenders any right to compensation (*damnum*). Klenkock maintained that increments should be counted as payments on the principal, adding that "it cannot be said that lenders are excused [from the charge of usury] because they lend under coercion, since it is better to endure evil than to consent to it."[54] Guido outlined his position in a *consilium* delivered at a chapter-general of the Augustinian order held in Florence in 1371.[55] In Guido's opinion, interest-bearing *prestanze* were usurious because lenders received something in excess of the principal. His main argument, however, was that the *monte* undermined the *bonum publicum* (common good) because it both impoverished the commune, which was prevented by the burden of interest payments from amortizing the principal, and fostered avarice among citizens, encouraging them to put private gain before the welfare of the community. In times of crisis, he argued, the government had the authority to demand loans from citizens without compensation. Justice demanded repayment of the sums borrowed, nothing more.

Public Finance: A *Questio disputata* of John of Legnano on the Public Debt of Genoa," in *Philosophy and Humanism: Renaissance Essays in Honor of Paul Oskar Kristeller*, ed. Edward P. Mahoney, (Leiden: E. J. Brill, 1976), 434-53.

[53] Kirshner, "Reading Bernardino's Sermon," 558.

[54] "Nec valet dicere quod creditores tales excusentur quia coacti concedunt, cum melius sit omnia mala pati quam malo consentire" (F_1 fol. 100v; *TUI* 7, fol. 49vb). Klenkock's opinion on the *monte* survives only in Ridolfi's report of it in the appendix to the *Questio montis* (F_1 fols. 100v-101r; *TUI* 7, fols. 49vb-50ra). For an analysis of the Augustinians' opinions, see Kirshner, "From Usury to Public Finance," 121-22; and idem, "Franco Sacchetti," 567.

[55] Ridolfi discusses Guido's principal theses in *Questio montis, dubium* 1 (2322-62); see also comm. nn. 2324-37 to 2349-62. He provides a summary of the *consilium* in the appendix (F_1 fols. 98r-100v; *TUI* 7, fols. 48va-49vb), where he notes its Florentine context: "Sciendum quod ... frater Guido de Belloregardo consultus in generali capitulo sui ordinis Florentie celebrato circa iamdictam materiam ..." (F_1 fol. 98r; *TUI* 7, fol. 48va). Kirshner suggests that the chapter-general was that of 24 May 1371, at which Guido was elected prior-general ("Franco Sacchetti," 567, n. 41).

The Augustinian proposal of interest-free *prestanze* was notable for its severity, but it paralleled suggestions made in government *consulte* in the early 1370s. Following the campaign against San Miniato, various ideas for reducing the debt were floated, among them the reintroduction of an *estimo* and the suggestion by a participant in a *consulta* of January 1370 that citizens be compelled to lend without compensation. The government rejected both proposals, but by March 1372 it was considering the possibility of temporarily suspending interest payments on the *monte*.[56] A few years later, the Ciompi would echo Guido's critique in their demands for the abolition of the *monte* and direct levies on the rich.[57]

In varying degrees, other writers approved compensation. Gregory of Rimini took the most restrictive position in a *quaestio disputata* on the public debt of Venice. Written between May 1357 and November 1358, when Gregory was Prior-General of the Augustinians, the *quaestio* enjoyed great authority among Florentine disputants of the later fourteenth century.[58] Gregory's analysis centred on the issue of intention. If a creditor intended to profit from his loan, he was guilty of usury. Indeed, such an intention was more reprehensible in a creditor of the republic than in an ordinary usurer, since lending to the community at usury was more wicked than usuring an individual.[59] But the government's intention was also significant. If it offered profit in return for a loan and creditors understood this to be the case, or even if they mistakenly believed it to be so, they were guilty of

[56] Becker, *Florence in Transition*, 2: 180.

[57] See above, pp. 45-46.

[58] For the dating of the text, see Kirshner, "From Usury to Public Finance," 117. I am grateful to Professor Kirshner for providing me with a copy of his unpublished critical edition of the *quaestio*, which I used as a control on the early printed text I consulted (*Tractatus de imprestantiis Venetorum et de usura* [Reggio Emilia: Ludovicus de Mazalis, 1508]). Because Kirshner's text remains unpublished, reference is to the 1508 edition alone. For a detailed discussion of Gregory's opinions on compensation, see Kirshner, "From Usury to Public Finance," 117-21. Lapo da Castiglionchio cited Gregory's *quaestio* in a *repetitio* of the 1370s on the debt (see below, pp. 81-82). It also dominates Ridolfi's treatment of the *monte*: *Questio montis*, *dubium* 2 (2459-2998) is largely dedicated to refuting Gregory's account of compensation, while *dubia* 4, 5 and 6 (3030-3408) dispute his analysis of the credit market. For a discussion, see below, pp. 86-87, 89-91, 93-96.

[59] "Quin etiam magis peccare videtur quis fenerando communitati quam fenerando personae singulari, quia cum bonum gentis et ciuitatis sit melius et divinius, ut dicit Philosophus .i. Ethicorum, et ut dicit Augustinus: 'Caritas communia propriis, non propria communibus anteponit'" (*Tractatus*, art. 3 [ed. cit. fol. B6v]). Cf. *Questio montis*, *dubium* 2 (2490-93). See also comm. n. 2467-93.

usury and bound to make restitution.[60] Profit was licit only when creditors were guided by patriotic motives and the government by "some honest and reasonable cause," such as liberality or a desire to compensate creditors for real damages they incurred by their obligation to lend.[61]

Gregory distinguished between ordinary damages or *diminutio prehabiti* (diminution of property) and *lucrum cessans*, which he defined as the "non-acquisition of a possible or anticipated profit" (*non acquisitio lucri possibilis vel etiam sperati*).[62] The latter could be claimed only by merchants who would otherwise have invested their money in commerce, while in both cases compensation had to be individually adjusted to reflect real losses.[63] Similarly, if payments were considered a gift, justice demanded that they

[60] "Nam vel illud statuit dari communitas ipsa ratione mutui sive recepti sive recipiendi sive ulterius retinendi, vel non ratione mutui sed alia ratione vel causa. Si ratione mutui ... qui huiusmodi lucrum recipiunt eam esse intentionem communitatis sciunt vel credunt, quia sic datum lucrum recipientes dantis communitatis intentioni consentiunt, iam ipsi ratione mutui et propter mutuum lucrum recipiunt ac per hoc ex mutuo lucrum intendunt. Ex quo ulterius sequitur quod illud perceptum usura est et cetera, quae dicta sunt de peccato et obligatione ad restituendum.... Quin etiam dico quod si communitas non propter mutuum dedisset et tamen isti putarent eam dedisse propter mutuum, procul dubio peccarent non restituendo si possent" (*Tractatus*, art. 3 [ed. cit. fols. B6v-B7r]). Cf. *Questio montis*, *dubium* 2 (3323-62). See also comm. n. 3323-73.

[61] "Demum nec in recipientibus ulla esset intentio lucri neque propter mutuum lucrum dat ipsa communitas sed aliqua alia causa honesta et rationabili, ut puta propter restaurationem damni quod forte mutuantes inde perpessi sunt, vel propter remunerationem benivolentiae quam ipsi mutuando se habere ad communitatem probauerunt, vel ex mera liberalitate ipsius communitatis, dico tale lucrum non esse usuram, cum in nullo predictorum casuum sit lucrum intentum ex mutuo aut etiam pro mutuo vel propter mutuum datum" (*Tractatus*, art. 3 [ed. cit. fol. B7v]). Cf. *Questio montis*, *dubium* 2 (2532-50). See also comm. n. 2532-50.

[62] *Tractatus*, art. 4 (ed. cit. fol. C1v).

[63] "... dico quod in isto casu mutuantes coacti et ex mutuatione impediti a lucro quod licite vel negotiando vel alio modo acquisivissent licite possunt exigere recompensationem sui damni, secundum discretum iudicium prudentis viri considerantis simul quantum eodem tempore alii similem negotionem vel artem exercentes cum equali pecunia communiter vel plures lucrati sunt, ut secundum hoc arbitretur utrum isti fuissent non mutuando sed aliud agendo lucrati vel non.... Et quia contingit non semper equale lucrum acquiri sed quandoque maius, quandoque minus, interdum autem nullum sed damnum potius sustineri, ideo non videtur mihi tutum secundum conscientiam ut pro recompensatione huiusmodi semper una et eadem quantitas lucri taxanda sit; sed quolibet anno esset taxanda secundum arbitrium sapientum et expertorum" (*Tractatus*, art. 4 [ed. cit. fols. C2v-C3r]). Cf. *Questio montis*, *dubium* 2 (2551-72). See also comm. n. 2551-72.

reflect the degree of patriotic self-sacrifice exhibited by the lender, so that, for example, a poor man who lent a hundred was rewarded more generously than his rich neighbour who advanced a thousand at no particular inconvenience to himself.[64] In neither case could interest payments be made before the principal had been repaid.[65] Since the public debt of Venice, like the Florentine *monte*, paid a uniform rate of interest on largely unamortized principal, it fell short of the stringent conditions laid down by Gregory, who warned Venetians, in the words of the apostle Paul, that "God is not mocked" (*Gal* 6.7).[66]

Other writers were more accommodating. In his *Questio de monte*, written in 1353-54, the Franciscan Francesco da Empoli (d. 1370) did not dispute the right of Florentine *prestanziati* to receive *interesse* at a rate of five percent, which he characterized as an "approximation of the damages" they incurred by lending.[67] The Dominicans Piero degli Strozzi and Domenico

[64] "Item causa remunerationis mutuantium dari non apparet, propterea quia si propter illam daretur, plus daretur ei in quo maior affectus benivolentiae probaretur. Et quia potest contingere quod ex maiori affectu unus mutuet centum quam alius mille, ut puta si quis mutuans mille sit in centuplo ditior et quasi invitus mutuet, qui vero centum mutuat libenter plus mutuaturus si posset plus, certe plus deberet dari ultra sortem ei qui mutuavit centum quam ei qui mille, et ita daretur si propter dictam causam daretur; et tamen oppositum contingit" (*Tractatus*, art. 3 [ed. cit. fol. B7v]). Cf. *Questio montis, dubium* 2 (2594-2603). See also comm. n. 2585-2610.

[65] Gregory considered the fact that this was not the case conclusive evidence of the corrupt intentions of the government and creditors: "Ad quod etiam accedit quod illud lucrum datur non quando soluta est sors et communitas a debito liberata est" (*Tractatus*, art. 3 [ed. cit. fol. B7v-B8r]). Cf. *Questio montis, dubium* 2 (2607-10). See also comm. n. 2585-2610.

[66] *Tractatus*, art. 3 (ed. cit. fol. B8r). Cf. *Questio montis, dubium* 2 (2622). See also comm. n. 2611-22.

[67] On Francesco's life and career, see *Dizionario biografico degli Italiani*, vol. 49 (Rome: Istituto della Enciclopedia italiana, 1997), s.v. "Francesco da Empoli" by Julius Kirshner. Francesco dealt with the issue of the original creditors succinctly: "Respondeo in hoc casu proposito sunt duo puncta. Primum est si Petrus licite possit recipere illos .5. annuatim pro eo quod coactus fuit prestare. Et quantum ad hoc supponatur pro certo quod sic, quia ratione interesse potest quis licite recipere aliquid ultra sortem in casu proposito" (*Questio de monte*, ed. Armstrong, "Politics of Usury," 28). Later he notes: "Que est causa quare primus potest recipere licite .5. annuatim pro .c.? Quia coactus fuit a comunitate prestare .c., quod quidem est sibi dampnum, pro cuius dampni extimatione accipit illud interesse" (ibid., 36). For a discussion, see ibid., 5-7. A similar line was taken in the 1380s by Guglielmo Centueri, who referred explicitly to the losses incurred by merchants (ed. Kirshner, "Reading Bernardino's Sermon," 593).

Pantaleoni (d. 1376) agreed, though they viewed payments as gifts rather than compensation.[68] Pantaleoni emphasized that the compulsory character of *prestanze* distinguished them from ordinary loans: interest that might be illicit under normal circumstances was justified by the commune's pressing need, a conclusion neatly expressed in the legal maxim "necessity knows no law."[69]

Most subsequent writers adopted a similar line. Near the end of the fourteenth century, the Dominican Nicholas de Anglia (fl. 1402), whose *quaestio disputata* on the Venetian debt Ridolfi knew by hearsay, maintained that "a citizen who lends to the commune and accepts profit is excused from usury by coercion, as well as by the fact that the profit is given spontaneously and freely."[70] Peter of Ancharano spoke for most canonists when he argued in a *quaestio disputata* of 1398 that governments levied compulsory loans out of necessity and under these circumstances citizens were justified in accepting interest payments.[71]

[68] Kirshner, "Storm over the *Monte*," 239; idem, "Franco Sacchetti," 561. Strozzi wrote in 1353-54 and Pantaleoni between 1362 and 1376. Strozzi's *Tractatus super casu de monte communi* was known to Ridolfi, who included it in the appendix to the *Questio montis* (F_1 fols. 91r-98r; *TUI* 7, fols. 44vb-48va) as the work of an anonymous Dominican master ("Cunctorum scripta rimatus et alium reperio de ordine predicatorum, cuius nomen ignoro" [F_1 fol. 91r; *TUI* 7, fol. 44vb]). The text has been edited from F_1 and its authorship established by Kirshner, "Storm over the *Monte*," 258-76. Pantaleoni's tract was attributed in the fifteenth century to the Sienese canonist Fredericus Petruccius (fl. 1322-43) and appears in printed editions of the jurist's *consilia*. The attribution of this text has been corrected by Julius Kirshner, "A Note on the Authorship of Domenico Pantaleoni's Tract on the *Monte Comune* of Florence," *AFP* 43 (1973): 73-81. Ridolfi does not appear to have known Pantaleoni's tract either directly or under Petruccius' name. For a discussion of both texts, see Kirshner, "Storm over the *Monte*," 247-257.

[69] "Quod non est licitum lege, necessitas facit licitum" (X 5.41.4). On the use of the tag in this context, see Kirshner, "From Usury to Public Finance," 113.

[70] "Ad quintum dicendum quod non sola coactio excusat ab usura civem dantem mutuum communitati et recipientem lucrum ab eadem, sed quia lucrum illud grate et sponte datum est nullo pacto precedente unde et poterit non dari" (*Questio disputata de imprestitis Venetorum*, ed. Julius Kirshner, "The Moral Theology of Public Finance: A Study and Edition of Nicholas de Anglia's *Quaestio disputata* on the Public Debt of Venice" *AFP* 40 [1970], 72). On the authorship and dating of this text, see ibid., 49-51; for Nicholas' views on compensation, see 54-57. Ridolfi refers to Nicholas as "a certain English master" (*quidam magister Anglicus*) who, he had heard, approved payments on the grounds of *interesse* (2634-36).

[71] "... sed causa et origo istorum imprestitorum est iustissima et fundata super bono rei publice nam, ut dicitur in themate, coguntur ciues subuenire ciuitati in necessitatibus, necessitas enim etiam iure diuino prohibita facit licita" (*Quaestio*

If a majority of writers accepted the right of compulsory lenders to receive compensation, no similar consensus emerged on the issue of speculation. According to Matteo Villani, the Florentine controversy originated in 1353-54 when

> many questions arose: whether the purchase [of Monte credits] was licit without making restitution; also, whether buyers could make purchases in order to have the profits which the commune had assigned to its creditors; and whether one hundred florins lent to the commune by the original creditor could be purchased for twenty-five florins or more or less according to their value in the market. The opinions of the theologians and legists in many disputations were varied: one held that the contract was illicit and required restitution, the other not; and the friars preached about it in diverse ways: those of the order of Saint Dominic say that it cannot be made licitly and the Augustinians agree with them; and the Franciscans preach that it can be made licitly.[72]

The chief protagonists were the leading Franciscan and Dominican masters in Florence, Francesco da Empoli and Piero degli Strozzi. Francesco had been a lecturer in theology at Oxford in the 1340s and served as vicar of the Franciscan convent of Santa Croce in Florence in 1347.[73] A member of a distinguished patrician family, Piero degli Strozzi had studied theology in Paris, served as prior of Santa Maria Novella in the 1330s and 1340s, and by 1353 was provincial minister of the Dominican province of Rome.[74] Both subsequently occupied chairs of theology in the University of Florence: Strozzi in 1358 and Francesco in the following year.[75] Of the two, Villani wrote,

---

disputata de monte Venetorum vel Florentinorum, BNF, Magliabechiano xxix, 179, fol. 281r-v). Ridolfi admits that he had not read the *quaestio* but states that he had it on the authority of a trustworthy source that Peter defended public creditors' right to receive five percent interest (3381-85). Peter's authorship of this text, sometimes attributed to the civilian jurist Bartolus of Sassoferrato (ca. 1313-57), has been established by Julius Kirshner, "A *Quaestio de usuris* Falsely Attributed to Bartolus of Sassoferrato," *RQ* 22 (1969): 256-61. According to the *explicit* of the Florentine manuscript (MS cit. fol. 288r), Peter publicly disputed the question in 1398, when he was lecturing in Bologna. On the dating and Peter's academic career, see idem, "Reading Bernardino's Sermon," 614-15. For the argument of the *quaestio*, see ibid., 565-72; and idem, "From Usury to Public Finance," 139, 194-200. For the opinions of other lawyers at the beginning of the fifteenth century, see ibid., 123-25. The civilian Baldus de Ubaldis (ca. 1327-1400) was apparently exceptional in censuring the compensation of compulsory lenders (ibid., 124).

72 *Cronica* 3.106, ed. Moutier, 2: 142-43; trans. Kirshner, "Franco Sacchetti," 558.

73 Kirshner, "Storm over the *Monte*," 231; and idem, "Francesco da Empoli."

74 Idem, "Storm over the *Monte*," 219-20.

75 Ibid., 219-20, 231.

> Master Piero says that it is not a licit contract and preached about it without offering clear arguments. On the other hand, master Francesco, who with great care and complete clarity had already participated in many disputations on this with other masters in theology and doctors of law and of the decretals, held and preached and wrote that [this contract] was licit and without the obligation to make restitution, and that those who undertook such a contract could do so without acting against the dictates of their conscience. The reason why he wrote with such complete command is that he was prepared to uphold what he preached and wrote.... many were in evident agreement with the arguments of master Francesco, and thus without pangs of conscience they sold and bought [credits], trading with one another as they would merchandise.[76]

Neverthless, the chronicler added, "many people remained in doubt."[77] He reproached the Dominicans for creating a climate of uncertainty without offering a definitive response to Francesco:

> If the contract is able to be proven usurious, those who preach have an obligation to lead people away from error by reproving those who defend a contrary position. If the contract can be made licitly, considering that men are eager for profit, it is evil to cast suspicion upon them through preaching which lacks prudence and to defile the consciences of those who act lawfully.[78]

Francesco devoted most of his *quaestio* to defence of the debt market.[79] His basic contention was that the contract between "John," the buyer of a credit, and "Peter," the original lender, was licit because it was not a loan but a sale in which John bought Peter's *ius* (right) to principal and *interesse*.[80] The relationship between John and the commune was not a loan because John lent nothing to the commune; since usury occurred only in

[76] *Cronica* 3.106, ed. Moutier, 2:143; trans. Kirshner, "Franco Sacchetti," 559.
[77] Ibid.
[78] Ibid.

[79] For a detailed analysis of Francesco's arguments, see Armstrong, "Politics of Usury," 7-14. For different readings, see Kirshner, "Storm over the *Monte*," 240-46; idem, "Reading Bernardino's Sermon," 587; idem, "From Usury to Public Finance," 175-82; and Spicciani, *Capitale e interesse*, 103-6.

[80] "Quantum ad secundum, utrum scilicet Johannes possit emere illud ius percipiendi capitale et interesse sequens, respondeo quod sic, quia hic contractus nullo iure prohibetur nec diuino nec humano, ergo licite potest fieri" (*Questio de monte* [ed. cit. 28]). The argument did not originate with Francesco: another Franciscan, Astesanus (d. ca. 1330), had proposed a similar analysis of the Genoese debt in his influential manual for confessors, and the Dominican Bartolomeo da San Concordio (d. 1347) had denied that purchasers of credits were lenders, arguing that they acquired a *ius* to principal and interest (Kirshner, "Moral Theology of Public Finance," 53; see also Armstrong, "Politics of Usury," 6).

loans, John should not be considered a usurer. To the objection that John in effect became the creditor of the commune, Francesco responded that the commune remained obligated as debtor to Peter; John merely became the owner of an action (*actio*) to enforce Peter's claims.[81] The fact that the commune registered the credit transfer did not mean that John actually became the commune's creditor: the government's intervention merely witnessed and recorded the agreement between John and Peter.[82]

Francesco denied that the speculative purchase of a *monte* credit was in fraud of usury, for the discounted price reflected uncertainty about the credit's future value. For the same reason, a purchase price of twenty-five percent of the credit's face value did not violate the rules on just pricing.[83]

[81] "Preterea in contractu emptionis iuris inter istos duos effectus eius quod agitur est ut commoditas et utilitas crediti et actionis que est ex parte creditoris in me transeat. Et ex hoc non attingitur uinculum consistens ex parte debitoris, nec etiam uinculum obligationis ex parte creditoris transit de eo in emptorem, set exercitium sue actionis accom⟨m⟩odatur emptori ut ad suam utilitatem exigat quod debetur uenditori. Preterea, facto contractu uenditionis, sors non est debita emptori a communitate uirtute emptionis, ⟨et⟩ maxime proprie, set uenditori" (*Questio de monte* [ed. cit. 30]).

[82] "... dico quod sindicus non est factus ad faciendum contractum aliquem inter communitatem et emptorem, set solum ad faciendum firmum esse contractum inter emptorem et uenditorem ut, ipso facto etiam inuito uenditore, emptor habeat ius suum quod emit ab eo. Et ad hoc sunt omnes scripture que fiunt super hoc et non ad faciendum nouum contractum cum communitate" (ibid., 43).

[83] "Istud autem quod iste habet recipere a communitate est coniunctum cum alico dubio tam ex parte sortis quam ex parte interesse; nam si nullum dubium esset annexum, quis dubitat quod nullus daret .c. et id interesse pro .xxv.? Et patet etiam dubium quia scio quod de facto multi dimiserunt emere propter dubium tantum. Modo ergo primus propter dubium quod habet non est certus quid habebit, computato capitali ac etiam interesse, propter pericula que possunt interuenire, et idcirco conuenit cum secundo per istum modum dicens: 'nescio quid habebo a communitate propter dubium; quidquid habebo dabo tibi si dederis mihi .30. florenos uel .25. modo; et si nichil habebo, nichil tibi dabo" (ibid., 33). Medieval theorists understood the just price of a thing to be its current market or lawfully regulated price; see John W. Baldwin, *The Medieval Theories of the Just Price: Romanists, Canonists, and Theologians in the Twelfth and Thirteenth Centuries*, Transactions of the American Philosophical Society, n.s. 49, part 4 (Philadelphia: American Philosophical Society, 1959), 20-21, 28-29, 54; and Langholm, *Economics in the Medieval Schools*, 44-45. Moral theology, in accordance with the Aristotelian doctrine of commutative justice, insisted on equality in exchange (Baldwin, *Medieval Theories*, 68-80). Canon law, on the other hand, permitted variations in what was given or received of up to half the just price (ibid., 22-27, 42-46). Ridolfi discusses just price in Part 2, *oppositiones* 6 and 7 (835-67), and Part 2, question 16 (1945-86); see also comm. nn. 836-40 to 867 and 1945-46 to 1970-86.

The seller received a just price if he received the market price of his credit at the time of selling. "The right," Francesco observed, "to a hundred florins and a hundred florins in cash are not the same thing, since one can exist without the other and one is of greater value than the other."[84] The potential risks attached to holding *monte* credits justified discounts, for it was common knowledge that the commune might be unable or unwilling to meet its obligations. In this respect there was an analogy between the buyer of a *monte* credit and an insurer of commercial cargo who charged a premium of ten or twenty percent but assumed the whole risk of loss.[85]

In his response, Strozzi reminded Florentines of the moral risks they ran by speculating in debt: "we ought to beware lest under the sway of words good citizens be made usurers and led by avarice to desire profits from which they should be restrained."[86] The Dominican emphasized the donative character of the interest paid to *prestanziati*. He conceded that Peter might legitimately sell the principal of his loan to John, but denied that this was true of the gift a grateful government had conferred on him, for a gift did not constitute an alienable right.[87] That speculators understood themselves to be buying rights to both principal and interest did not alter the fact that communal legislation could at most authorize only the transfer of a claim to principal. Strozzi rejected as sophistry Francesco's

[84] "Est tertio considerare quomodo distinguntur ius exigendi .c. florenos et .c. floreni, quia non sunt idem, cum unum sit sine alio, et unum est maioris ualoris alio, ex quo soluuntur ⟨argumenta⟩ tertio arguentium" (*Questio de monte* [ed. cit. 44]).

[85] "Preterea probatur propositum per simile de dubio, quia possum licite securare mercationes tuas usque Ianuam recipiendo super me dubium et uolendo .x. uel .xx. pro .c. secundum quod michi plus uel minus uidetur graue illud periculum recipere super me, ergo et in eo quod habes a communitate recipere possum te securare de dubio quod ibi habes uolendo a te recipere tantum quantum michi est graue te super hoc securare. Sic in proposito, quia totum dubium quod tu habes super me recipio dando tibi .25. quia ex tunc, si nichil unquam reciperes, esset dampnum meum, non tuum. Si tamen reciperes siue paruum siue multum, totum erit meum" (ibid., 34).

[86] "Considerandum est ergo, ne sub verboso regimento liciti cives efficiantur usurarii et inducantur ad lucra ex avaritia a quibus sunt retrahendi" (*Tractatus super casu de monte communi*, ed. Kirshner, "Storm over the *Monte*," 275). For a detailed discussion of Strozzi's arguments, see ibid., 247-51.

[87] "Illud quod communitas dono confert emptori, ut dicit, non venditur ei nec vendi potest per venditorem iuris sortis, sed communitas confert dono, ut dicitur in scriptura, predicto emptori predictum interesse, ergo non venditur, nec vendi potest ab ipso venditore sortis. Maior patet cum donum sit libera datio ... Minor probatur, quia scribitur in statuto communitatis quod camerarius ... teneatur dare et solvere cuilibet creditorum pro dono et cetera" (*Tractatus*, ed. cit., 259).

denial of a legal relationship between the commune and John, maintaining that by virtue of his purchase John became a "true creditor of the commune and the commune ... his debtor, since this is acknowledged by both parties in words, documents and deeds."[88]

In practice, of course, buyers of credits received the same interest payments as the original creditors. What, in Strozzi's judgement, was the status of these new creditors? His answer was unambiguous: according to *Lc* 6.35, their intentions were usurious, for their sole object was profit.[89] This was in contrast to the original lenders, who acted under coercion or from patriotic motives and were rewarded by the commune's gift. These extenuating conditions did not apply to speculators, who made themselves voluntary creditors of the government. Strozzi considered Francesco's analogy to maritime insurance inapplicable to the debt market: the merchant who bought insurance did not transfer his cargo to the insurer but simply paid a fee for a service, whereas the speculator appropriated all profit from the credits he bought and this not as a fee from the seller, whom he was allegedly securing, but from the commune. Indeed, if anything, the seller incurred damages, since he lost three-quarters of the value of his principal plus any potential profit, while the discount served to secure the speculator against losses in the event of the commune's default.[90] Nor could the speculator ap-

[88] "Et certe negari non potest quod emptor non sit vere creditor et commune debitor, cum hoc utraque pars verbis et scriptis et factis confiteatur, nec videtur iustum sub verbis se abscondere, ubi de re est manifestum" (ibid., 266; trans. 248).

[89] "Ultimo superest ut de quinta conclusione tractemus, que habet quod lucrum, quod habent predicti emptores a communitate, eo modo quo habent est inlicitum et sapit usuram. Hanc sic probat, quia credere et concedere sortem sub ratione crediti vel capitalis alicui sola spe et intentione lucri habendi est inlicitum et sapit usuram. Sed predicti emptores concedunt et credunt sortem seu capitale communitati sola spe et intentione lucri habendi. Ergo illud lucrum est inlicitum et sapit usuram. Maior est c. *Consuluit, de usuris*. Minor probatur, spes enim et intentio ad voluntatem pertinent. Illud ergo quod solum movet voluntatem ad predictam concessionem et credentiam sortis et cetera, est speratum, ergo. Maior istius pro simili est nota cum finis intentus sit movens agentem ad actum. Minor probatur, quia illud est causa, quo posito vel ammoto res vel actus ponitur vel ammovetur. Sed illo lucro posito vel ammoto, ponitur vel ammovetur prefata concessio: ergo illud lucrum est sola et tota causa" (*Tractatus*, ed. cit., 266). The speculator is said to "lend" and "concede" principal to the commune because in Strozzi's view he has substituted for the original creditor.

[90] "Item ille securator mercationum querit pretium suum ab eo, cuius bona super se recipit cum periculo. Emptor vero de quo loquimur, non querit nec habet lucrum ab eo, cuius periculum super se recipit ... sed expectat, recipit et habet a communitate pro sorte ei credita et sibi ab ea debita. Item videamus quem securat iste emptor, non communitatem, quia non indiget, non venditorem, immo infert

peal to risk to justify his profit, for any loan made with the intention to profit was usurious, regardless of the debtor's reliability. But in practice, Strozzi maintained, profits on government debt were more secure than commercial investments

> since there is more doubt about merchants who have frequently failed and do fail than there is about the commune, which has never failed to give profit once it began; and if sometimes the commune deferred payments, it made them up later.[91]

Strozzi explained variations in the price of *monte* credits by the availability of liquid capital at any moment, but he was clear that ultimately the market served the interests of the political bosses:

> I say that the guarantee of the validity and security of the aforesaid [payments is] the will and power of ruling citizens who have money invested in the commune and seek a profit. And it would be very difficult to change this and to take money against their will from those whom God knows if they would willingly forgo both principal and *interesse*.[92]

As Julius Kirshner argues, Strozzi's "ruling citizens" with money tied up in the commune were not the possessing class as a whole, but the segment of it that was in a position to exploit the market in public debt.[93] This minority was enriched at the expense of the community as a whole, for

> it ought to be considered that out of the twenty-four thousand florins a year

---

ei dampnum de tribus partibus sortis cuius ius emit et de toto lucro, de quibus si venditor iam incurrit periculum, nunc evasit" (ibid., 268-69).

[91] "Item si hoc dubium communitatis excusat lucrum illud, videtur quod possimus ponere pecuniam apud mercatores et recipere lucrum, cum plus sit dubium apud mercatores qui frequenter defecerunt et deficiunt, quam communitatem que ex quo cepit dare predictum lucrum nunquam subtraxit, et si aliquando distulit, postea supplevit" (ibid., 272). Strozzi added later that he had it "ab his mercatoribus qui ista tractant, ex quo prefata provisio vel lucrum dari cepit per communitatem civibus, nunquam defecit, et si aliquando dilata est, suppleta est" (ibid., 273).

[92] My reading of the manuscript departs slightly from that of Kirshner at this point (ibid., 274). I read: "Catenas autem firmitatis et securitatis de predictis dixi voluntatem et potentiam civium regentium, qui habent pecunias in communitate et querunt lucrum; et minus difficile esset ista mutare et subtrahere eis invitis, qui si libenter perderent sortem et lucrum, deus novit" (F_1 fol. 97r). At *minus* a marginal corrector's note reads "alia littera 'nimis'," suggesting an emendation of the text to "et nimis difficile esset ista mutare." Not only does *nimis* make more sense, but it seems likely that the *minus* in the copy Ridolfi had before him was a corruption of *nimis*, an easy mistake to make, since the two words have almost the same number of minims. I have adopted *nimis* in the translation.

[93] "Storm over the *Monte*," 250.

> given to the said citizens as profit could eventually be repaid the entire principal of the original creditors ... Again, it should be noted that the amount paid out in profits is obtained from gabelles, which both poor and rich citizens pay at grave inconvenience; and so the losses of the many are turned to the profit of the few.[94]

In the early 1350s, the "few" were the new men who had forced their way into the political class in the fiscal and political turmoil of the previous decade. Strozzi's condemnation of the *monte* and its chief beneficiaries mirrored the political struggle between the new men and the old elite. As played out in the arena of ethics and law, it pitted Strozzi, a representative of old patrician wealth and lineage, against Francesco da Empoli, who spoke for the new men and lesser guildsmen.[95]

Pantaleoni, himself a member of an old patrician family, modelled his tract on that of Strozzi, who had been his religious superior at Santa Maria Novella.[96] Although it was written at least a decade after the original controversy, the tract was framed as a detailed refutation of Francesco da Empoli's *quaestio*.[97] Pantaleoni agreed with Francesco that title to compensation was vendible, but he maintained that the effect of regular interest payments had been to indemnify creditors fully, so that they had nothing to sell.[98] He supported this argument—which would appear to apply only to *prestanziati* who had held five-percent credits for twenty years—by

[94] "Item considerandum est quod de xxiiii^m florenorum qui annuatim dantur civibus pro lucro predicto possent paulatim solvi sortes primorum creditorum integre et qui primi subvenerunt communitati, non perderent sortes suas vel tres partes. Item considerandum est, quod prefata quantitas que transit in lucrum civium colligitur ex gabellis, quas solvunt cives pauperes et divites cum gravamine suo, et sic dampnum multorum transit in lucra aliorum" (*Tractatus*, ed. cit., 275).

[95] Kirshner, "Storm over the *Monte*," 238-39; Armstrong, "Politics of Usury," 19-21. On the substantial *monte* holdings of the Strozzi and Pantaleoni families, and on the participation of mendicant houses in the market, see Kirshner, "Storm over the *Monte*," 231-33, esp. nn. 48-52. The best account of the conflict between new men and the traditional elite between 1343 and 1378 is Brucker, *Politics and Society*; for the early 1350s, see esp. chaps. 3-4, 105-93. The alignment of the controversialists reflected the social composition of Florentine mendicant convents: the Franciscans recruited mainly new men and lesser guildsmen, while the Dominicans attracted entrants from the traditional elite; see Daniel R. Lesnick, *Preaching in Medieval Florence: The Social World of Franciscan and Dominican Spirituality* (Athens, GA, and London: University of Georgia Press, 1989), 40-85, 185-212.

[96] Kirshner, "Domenico Pantaleoni's Tract," 79.

[97] For the dating, see ibid., 78-79. For a detailed discussion, see "Storm over the *Monte*," 252-56; and idem, "From Usury to Public Finance," 181-85.

[98] Kirshner, "From Usury to Public Finance," 252-53.

invoking Thomas Aquinas' argument against *lucrum cessans* and Strozzi's observations on *monte* interest as a gift.[99] As I noted above, Pantaleoni considered the original lender immune from the accusation of usury because of the coercive circumstances of his loan.[100] But this immunity was not transferable and therefore Francesco's account of credit sales was no more than a legal fiction, for "here there is no *commodatum*, or lease and hire, simply the purchase of certain loans."[101] In Pantaleoni's view, the market in debt credits was in fraud of usury and speculators were usurers who, even if they could not be prosecuted in an ecclesiastical court, were guilty before God in the penitential forum.[102]

Gregory of Rimini, Guido de Belloreguardo and John Klenkock made similar criticisms of the debt market.[103] Like Pantaleoni, Gregory and Klenkock held that compulsory lenders were fully compensated when they had accumulated interest equivalent to their principal and therefore had nothing to sell. Gregory, however, allowed the creditor to sell his right to any principal that remained after the deduction of interest payments; if he had received no interest he could sell his claim to the whole principal, but if payments had exceeded the principal, he was obliged to restore the difference to the commune.[104] All three theologians condemned speculators. Guido compared them to simoniacs or buyers of ecclesiastical office and denounced them for buying at less than the just price.[105] Gregory argued

[99] Ibid., 253. See above, pp. 65, 70-71.

[100] See above, p. 71.

[101] "Non enim est hic accomodatio seu conductio sive locatio, sed simpliciter emptio quorundam mutu⟨or⟩um" (ed. Kirshner, "Storm over the *Monte*," 255, n. 111). Francesco did not in fact regard the contractual relationship between the original creditor and the speculative buyer as *commodatum*; on this, see Armstrong, "Politics of Usury," 9, n. 32.

[102] Kirshner, "Storm over the *Monte*," 256.

[103] For a full discussion, see Kirshner, "From Usury to Public Finance," 188-89.

[104] "Si receperunt tantum quantum fuit mutuum suum, dicendum quod ipsi non possunt prima prestita nec in toto nec in parte licite. Ratio ad hoc est quia iam recepere totum quod recipere debent, et sic eis a communitate sufficienter satisfactum est; igitur ex mutuo prius facto nullum ius habent in ipsam communitatem quod cuiquam de iure vendere possint.... Si vero non tantum sed minus receperunt, tantum et non plus licite vendere possunt, quantum sors ipsa ad id vel ultra quod receperunt se extendit.... Si autem plus acceperunt, non solum non possunt licite vendere, sed etiam id quod plus sorte receperunt communitati tenentur restituere" (*Tractatus*, art. 3, [ed. cit. fol. B8r-v]). Cf. *Questio montis, dubium* 4 (3035-44). See also comm. n. 3035-44.

[105] "Primo quia isti bonum quod aliis faciunt et illam caritatem quam eis impendunt in mutuando, ipsi ab eis emunt et lucrum inde recipiunt et sic simoniam

that they were usurers if their object was profit, for they either contracted a loan or agreed to postpone settlement of a debt in return for interest. In support of his contention, he alleged the decretal *Consuluit* (X 5.19.10), which condemned as usurers lenders who refused to prolong the repayment term without an implicit promise by the debtor to pay more than the principal. Buyers whose intentions were pure could buy the rights to principal, but on no account could they claim damages, which were due only to compulsory lenders.[106]

Despite the Augustinians' unanimous rejection of the debt market, the opinions of theologians did not correspond to "official" positions of the various mendicant orders.[107] Indeed, at least among Dominicans and Franciscans, members of the same order often held different views. Guglielmo Centueri, a Franciscan, denied the legitimacy of the market and attacked the propositions of his confrere Francesco da Empoli.[108] Despite Strozzi's and Pantaleoni's censure of the market, the Dominican Nicholas de Anglia approved the trade in discounted credits in terms of purchase-sale.[109] In his question on the Venetian *monte*, he argued that discounts reflected uncertainty about the future value of credits: to sellers discounts represented a

---

aliqualiter commictunt cum usura .... Ex istis verbis apparet quod caritatem proximo impendere, ad quam obligamur iuxta preceptum diuinum, uel aliquod aliud beneficium spirituale, et postea illam caritatem uel illud beneficum emant uel uendant, et lucrum inde recipiant uel intendant, tales gratiam et rem spiritualem emptioni et uenditioni submictunt, et per consequens simoniam commictunt; ideo eiciendi essent de templo militantis ecclesie .... Quia emit mutuatum in dampnum proximi, ergo illum decipit. Antecedens patet quia centum consequitur pro .xxviii. et sic iniusto pretio, et sic defraudatur" (F_1 fol. 99r-v; *TUI* 7, 49rb).

[106] "... inquirendum est de intentione ipsorum, quoniam emunt vel intentione lucri percipiendi a communi, et sic emendo peccant et crimen usurarum incurrunt; nam ex tunc mutuum dant in dati dilatione solutionis, intentione lucri. Et hoc bene probatur ex eo quod habetur in titulo *de usuris* c. *Consuluit* ... Vel non intentione lucri percipiendi emunt huiusmodi prestita. Et sic dico quod nisi prava intentio vel mala circumstantia reddat emptorem inordinatum, licite emunt .... Item in casu in quo isti damnum incurrerent emptione talium prestitorum, non sic possent consulere sibi de lucro a communitate recepto ut primi, quia sui damni non apparet communitatem causam dedisse ... sed ex se et propria cupiditate se ingesserunt ad tale commercium" (*Tractatus*, art. 3 [ed. cit. fols. B8v-C1r]). Cf. *Questio montis, dubium* 5 (3055-67). See also comm. n. 3055-67.

[107] See Kirshner, "Storm over the *Monte*," 228-31.

[108] Idem, "Reading Bernardino's Sermon," 573, 586-87. In this, Centueri was closely followed thirty years later by the Franciscan Bernardino of Siena (ibid., 573-89).

[109] For a detailed discussion, see idem, "Moral Theology of Public Finance," 57-61.

preference for cash in the present over doubtful future returns; to buyers, the actual or potential damages they incurred by relieving sellers of their credits.[110] Since sellers licitly accepted interest, it could also be accepted by buyers, who succeeded to all the sellers' rights in a legitimate purchase contract.[111] Indeed, Nicholas added, such agreements were similar to the purchase of an annuity or *redditus* (rent), a legitimate contract in which the buyer obtained rights to income in return for an immediate cash payment.[112]

As a group, lawyers favoured the market in public debt and the assimilation of the agreement between the creditor and the speculator to purchase-sale.[113] This was the position of Lapo da Castiglionchio, who composed a *repetitio* on the decretal *In civitate* (X 5.19.6) some time between 1369 and 1378 in which he defended the legitimacy of the debt market against Gregory of Rimini.[114] The *repetitio* is noteworthy as the only surviving canonistic treatment of the *monte dell'uno tre* and *dell'uno due*, though Lapo's analysis was equally applicable to the traffic in ordinary *monte* credits, and for this reason Ridolfi drew extensively on it for his own

[110] "Potest enim contingere quod pretium datum est magis utile vendenti quam res vendita, licet res vendita plus valeat in se, propter quod vendens potest rationabiliter propter utilitatem pretii dati vel benivolentiam ad ementem libere dare ementi quod superest de valore in re vendita ultra tantum pretium. Secundo, contractus potest iustificari ex parte ementis si ipse dampnificetur de dato pretio et nichilominus vult per commutationem subvenire proximo tali pretio indigenti" (ed. cit., 69).

[111] "Videtur enim emi ius in .c. libras quod habuit venditor et illud ius statim soluto pretio est translatum et ita plenariam et perfectam possessionem habet illius iuris, sicut venditor prius habuit" (ibid., 72).

[112] "Talis contractus poterit excusari, si secundum communem commutationem emptionis et venditionis maioris pretii non taxetur, licet in se sit maioris valoris; tantum enim valet res quantum secundum communem cursum commutationis vendi potest, sicut redditus annuus .c. librarum vendatur pro perpetuo .m. libris licitus est contractus, si secundum communem commutationem venditionis et emptionis pretium tanti redditus communiter sic taxetur. Et non est dubium quin in se plus valeat, quia 10 annis emptor recipit integrum pretium datum et residuum erit perpetuum sibi lucrum" (ibid., 70).

[113] Kirshner, "Reading Bernardino's Sermon," 563.

[114] *Allegationes*, allegatio 137 (Venice: Johannes Variscus, 1571, fols. 162va-164vb). The *terminus a quo* for the composition of the text is 1369 when the *monte dell'uno due* was created, and the *terminus ad quem* 1381, when Lapo died, although it probably dates from before 1378, when the jurist was exiled by the Ciompi (Brucker, *Politics and Society*, 370). For a discussion of Lapo's theses, see Kirshner, "From Usury to Public Finance," 191-94. On the *repetitio* genre, see below, p. 85.

treatment of the reformed *monte* of 1381.[115] In Lapo's opinion, the central issue was not whether speculators licitly bought debt credits but whether the original creditors licitly sold them. If sellers charged no more than the principal, or at least no more than they were legally entitled to, the contract was licit, and buyers succeeded to all the benefits enjoyed by sellers. Secondly, he maintained, since the transaction was not a loan but a contract of purchase-sale (*emptio venditio*) buyers might legitimately be motivated by a desire for profit.[116]

In his *quaestio disputata* on the Venetian and Florentine debts, Peter of Ancharano adopted Nicholas de Anglia's analysis of the market in terms of purchase-sale and annuity, while criticizing the theologian for failing to acknowledge the legal authorities on which his case rested.[117] Peter identified Nicholas' *redditus* as a *census* contract, in which a purchaser bought the right (*ius*) to an annual return from productive, usually agricultural, property.[118] The contract was unknown to Roman law, but Innocent IV, Hostiensis and Johannes Andreae considered it licit. All agreed that a *census* founded on existing income and tied to real property, such as a house or a possession, or to a revenue-producing person, such as a serf or a freedman, was licit. Returns could be guaranteed—for example, ten percent a year—or dependent on productivity—for example, a quarter of the crop. The term could vary: various legal writers approved life, perpetual and fixed-term *census*.

[115] See below, pp. 87, 93-95. On Lapo's analysis of shares in the *monte dell'uno tre* and *monte dell'uno due* as transferable life annuities (*census*), see below, pp. 98-99.

[116] "Casus autem in quo dicti mutuantes licite uendunt esse potest, uel quia ultra sortem nil receperunt uel receperunt sed in casu licito, secundum praemissa, quibus casibus licite uendere possunt. Nec in hoc uidentur ipsi emptores habere inordinatum intentionem. Nec est uerum dicto casu quod ipsi ementes ex tunc mutuum dent; nam est contractus emptionis et non mutui. Nec est uerum quod dent dilationem sed expectant dilationem datam authori suo. Nec uidetur uerum quod si dicto casu emunt intentione lucri, quod sic emendo peccent, quia in contractu emptionis non est reprobata spes lucri" (*Allegatio* 137, n. 12 [ed. cit. fol. 163vb]). Cf. *Questio montis, dubia* 5 and 6 (3068-81 and 3338-56). See also comm. nn. 3068-81 and 3338-56.

[117] "Reperio super hoc tres disputationes magistrorum sacre theologie absque ullis allegationibus decretorum vel iuris divini, canonici vel civilis ex quo potest clare percipi quod supra in solutione questionis premisi" (MS cit. fol. 287r). For a discussion, see Kirshner, "Reading Bernardino's Sermon," 565-72; and idem, "From Usury to Public Finance," 194-200.

[118] Noonan, *Scholastic Analysis of Usury*, 154-70. For Peter's discussion of *census*, see MS cit. fols. 283r-285r. It is parallel to Ridolfi's account of *census* in Part 2, question 11 (1652-1785). See also comm. n. 1652-53 to 1778-85.

Census contracts were lawful purchase-sales because they comprised a price, a specific quantity of money and *merces* (merchandise) in the form of a return in cash or produce. Since *census* were not loans, buyers could legitimately receive more than they originally paid. Similarly, in acquiring debt credits, the buyer licitly paid a price for a right to income proportional to the principal of the original loan.[119] In Peter's opinion not only was the transaction clearly a purchase-sale, but since the principal would never be repaid, the subject of the transaction—the credit—could not be considered a loan or a loan surrogate. It is notable, however, that Peter was reluctant to endorse a market in which there was a rapid turnover of credits. He considered the profits accruing to speculators under such conditions excessive and preferred arrangements similar to life annuities at a fixed rate.[120]

An important element of Peter's defence of the debt market was his argument from long custom. Christened by Kirshner the "incredibility thesis," it contended that it was unthinkable that the traffic in public debt shares should have survived so long uncensured if it was really illicit.[121] Peter noted that the market had never been condemned by church authorities, including the pope: indeed, he observed, many princes of the church and other ecclesiastical dignitaries owned shares in the public debt of Venice, which they would hardly do if they believed the practice to be usurious.[122] Writing more than forty years after the eruption of the Florentine

[119] "Secundo, ut dixi, hoc probat nature diversitas utriusque contractus, nam ad substantiam contractus emptionis et venditionis requiritur res et precium ... sed in mutuo est sola pecunia ... In ista autem emptione inprestitorum reperitur res que venditur, hoc est ipsum ius exigendi annuum redditum, quod est ius incorporale, sicut ususfructus, ius decimandi, et alie servitutes que adherent quandoque rebus corporalibus quandoque non ... Item est precium ex parte emptoris; ex quibus patet quod iste non debet censeri contractus mutui sed emptionis et venditionis" (MS cit. fol. 281r).

[120] In illustration, Peter cited the case of the Archbishop of Rheims, who purchased from the monastery of St. Denis for the price of two thousand *livres* a life annuity of four hundred *livres*. After twenty years, the monastery attempted to withdraw from the agreement on the grounds that it was usurious. The contract was, however, upheld as a licit *census* by Oldradus de Ponte (d. after 1337) in a *consilium* that Petrus appears to be citing here (MS cit. fols. 286r-287r; cf. Kirshner, "Reading Bernardino's Sermon," 570, n. 78). Oldradus' opinion is also cited by Ridolfi in Part 2, question 18 (2030-38). For a summary, see comm. n. 2030-38.

[121] "Reading Bernardino's Sermon," 572.

[122] "Preterea ab illo tempore citra fuerunt multi sancti patres et eciam episcopi in illa civitate, insuper et romani pontifices, iusti viri et sancti, qui consuetudines pernici⟨os⟩as locorum per suas constitutiones reprobarunt ... Istam autem consuetudinem de istis inprestitis nunquam reprobarunt, nec potest dici quod eam ignoraverint, cum apud omnes principes christianitatis et civitates nota sit, et

controversy, Peter argued that official silence and tradition created a presumption of legitimacy, remarking in a passage that inverted Matteo Villani's criticism of investors' greed, that

> *imprestita* [forced loans] have existed in Venice from time immemorial, and moderns should not believe that their forebears, who were devout Catholics —which is obvious from the sacred relics and the magnificently decorated monasteries and churches there—would have instituted them recklessly or inadvisedly. Nor should it be thought that they would buy and sell credits heedlessly, without believing that the practice was both licit and permissible.[123]

habeant ibi dicta inprestita et eciam cardinales et alii curiales; non est ergo credendum eos sub dissimulatione dissimulasse, si intellexissent hec sapere usuram" (MS cit. fol. 283r). See the examples given above pp. 38-39, 78 n. 95. In 1432 Pope Eugenius IV became one of the principal creditors of the Florentine *monte*, acquiring credits with a face value of a hundred thousand florins; see Julius Kirshner, "Papa Eugenio IV e il monte comune: documenti su investimento e speculazione nel debito pubblico di Firenze," *ASI* 127 (1969): 339-82.

[123] "Sed a tempore cuius contrarii memoria non existit fuerunt creata ista inprestita in Veneciis et credere debent homines moderni temporis eorum antiquos, qui fuerunt Catholici viri devoti, ut testantur ibi corpora sanctorum et multitudo ⟨mona⟩st⟨eri⟩orum et ecclesiarum et eorum magnifica ornamenta, ista inprestita non instituisse sine magna prudencia et concilio; nec eciam credendum quod indifferenter omnes emerent et venderent nisi firmiter crederent hoc esse licitum et permissum" (MS cit. fol. 282v). The argument did not go unchallenged: both Centueri and Bernardino attacked it in their writings (Kirshner, "Reading Bernardino's Sermon," 573-85). It is notable that Ridolfi did not invoke this argument.

4
Ridolfi on the Public Debt

A. The Criterion of Intention

In the prologue to the *Tractatus de usuris*, Ridolfi remarks that as a way of organizing his discussion he "decided to take as the basis of a *repetitio* the decretal *Consuluit* in the title *de usuris* (X 5.19.10)" (19-20). A form peculiar to the law faculties, the *repetitio* allowed a master to present a systematic treatment of themes raised by a single decretal or *lex*. Along with the *quaestio disputata*, another instructional form used in the university, it was the genre preferred by Ridolfi.[1] His choice of *Consuluit* as the subject of his *repetitio* is significant not only because the decretal's citation of *Lc* 6.35 placed it at the heart of the usury debate, but also because it dealt with cases of occult usury. When asked to rule on the licitness of three transactions in which there was no express but merely an implicit agreement to repay more than the principal, Pope Urban III condemned them all, declaring the creditors "quasi-usurers" who "should be considered evil-doers on account of their intention to profit and effectively compelled in the penitential forum to restore what they have received."[2]

Commentators on *Consuluit* explained that although occult or quasi-usury could not be censured on formal grounds, the lender's immoral intentions could be probed and punished in the sacrament of penance. Therefore, according to the *glossa ordinaria* (ordinary gloss),

> although the church may not judge [a lender] a usurer on the basis of the contract's form, nevertheless God will punish him as a usurer by reason of intention unless he makes restitution. In this way a person might be usurer in the

[1] Martino, "Ridolfi," 186-87. On the *repetitio* genre, see *DDC*, s.v. *Répétition* by N. Naz; and Bellomo, *Common Legal Past*, 137-39. Contemporaries viewed Ridolfi's treatise as a vast *repetitio* on X 5.19.10; see an anonymous treatise on exchange from the late fifteenth century preserved in the Archivio di Stato di Firenze, whose author cites Ridolfi: "... ut dicebat dominus Laurentius de Ridolfis in sua magna repetitione c. *Consuluit, de usuris* post dominum Antonium de Butrio" (ASF, Carte Strozziane, Terza Serie, 41/13, fol. 256vb). On the *quaestio disputata* genre, see Bellomo, *Common Legal Past*, 139-43.

[2] The text is cited in full and translated below, comm. n. 673.

eyes of God but not in the eyes of the church.[3]

By focusing on *Consuluit*, Ridolfi signals that he is not solely concerned with the "notorious" usury of moneylenders and pawnbrokers, but also with transactions such as commercial credit agreements and *prestanze*, whose legitimacy was ultimately contingent on the inner dispositions of creditors.

Ridolfi formulates his account of intention in the course of defining usury in the opening question of the treatise.[4] Since his conclusions underlie his assessment of the *monte*, it is useful to begin by outlining them. He notes first that according to the authoritative definition of Hostiensis usury is "anything added to the repayment of a lent thing for the use of that thing by agreement or intention at the time of the contract or by exaction afterwards" (48-51).[5] On the authority of Gottofredo da Trani (d. 1245), however, Hostiensis permitted the lender to entertain a secondary expectation of profit in the form of a gift, so long as his primary motive remained charitable, the test of which was that he would lend even in the absence of a gift. This was also the opinion of the gloss.[6] Ridolfi summarizes the principle in his own formula: "usury is profit from a loan principally intended as such" (54-55).

Gregory of Rimini rejected the canonistic distinction between primary and secondary intention, arguing that usury was any "intentional profit from a loan" (51-54).[7] While he condoned a gift of gratitude to the creditor, he maintained that if the latter knew or believed the gift to be contingent on the loan it represented usury (132-231).[8] In Ridolfi's view, Gregory's opinion "presses too hard," and he meets it by an appeal to the "consensus (*communis opinio*) of the glosses and our doctors [that is, the canonists], which I regard as more consonant with the law" (234-35). From this perspective, Gregory's conclusion holds only if a desire for profit in the form of a gift supplants the creditor's primary, charitable intention during the term of the loan. If the debtor is not constrained to give a gift and the

[3] "Nota quod quicquid recipitur ultra sortem: licet ex forma contractus non sit usurarius quoad ecclesiam iudicandus, propter intentionem tamen quoad Deum tanquam vsurarius punietur nisi restituerit; et sic aliquis non est usurarius quoad ecclesiam, sed quoad Deum" (gl. ord. ad X 5.19.10, casus [ed. Lyons 1584, col. 1739]). Ridolfi cites this gloss in Part 2, question 3 (1049).

[4] Part 1, question 1 (40-322).

[5] Cf. Hostiensis, *Summa aurea*, X 5.19 *de usuris*, n.1 (Venice 1574; repr. Turin, 1963, cols. 1612-13).

[6] Part 2, *oppositio* 1 (704-9). For the text of the gloss, see comm. n. 698-709.

[7] Cf. Gregory of Rimini, *Tractatus*, art. 1 (ed. cit. fol. A7r).

[8] Cf. ibid. (ed. cit. fols. A6r-B1v).

creditor's primary motivation remains charitable, the creditor's recognition that the gift is an acknowledgement of his generosity neither precludes a subordinate desire for it nor renders him a usurer (240-317). Indeed, debtors are under a natural obligation to make an *antidotum* (return-gift) to their benefactors, although such an obligation may not be expressed formally in the contract (107-32).[9]

B. Compulsory Loans

For his discussion of the *monte* and its operations, Ridolfi did not draw on the contemporary accounts of Peter of Ancharano, Nicholas de Anglia or Guglielmo Centueri, although, as I noted above, he was familiar with the first two by hearsay.[10] Instead, he looked to the previous generation of writers, especially Gregory of Rimini and the Florentine controversialists of 1353-78, Francesco da Empoli, Piero degli Strozzi, Guido de Belloreguardo and Lapo da Castiglionchio, from whose analyses he took the structure and many of the specific arguments of the *Questio montis*. Lapo's *repetitio*, augmented by supplementary questions, furnished the basic plan of the *questio*. Ridolfi constructed his defence of *prestanziati* and their right to accept compensation as a detailed response to the Augustinian critique of lenders' intentions and his exoneration of the market in *monte* credits as a refinement of the purchase-sale analysis first advanced by Francesco da Empoli and elaborated by Lapo.[11]

The first three *dubia* (sub-questions) of the *Questio montis* examine the moral dispositions of compulsory creditors and government legislators. Ridolfi starts by dismissing the objection that because only the emperor may impose general levies *prestanze* are *de facto* illegitimate. He appeals to the authority of Bartolus of Sassoferrato, who argued that cities and corporations could require extraordinary contributions called *collecta* from their memberships on the grounds of "necessity" (2270-94). It was a juristic commonplace that necessity and *utilitas rei publicae* (public utility) were sufficient cause for public authorities to override property rights guaranteed by the *ius commune*.[12] In a parenthetical digression, also deriving from Barto-

[9] See above, p. 62; Part 2, *oppositiones* 1-2 (696-742); and comm. nn. 696-97 to 740-42.

[10] See above, pp. 71-72, nn. 70, 71.

[11] For additional discussions of Ridolfi's analysis of the *monte*, see Noonan, *Scholastic Analysis of Usury*, 122-25; Kirshner, "From Usury to Public Finance," 125-31, 200-201; and idem, "Reading Bernardino's Sermon," 554-55, 571-72, 590.

[12] For a recent discussion of *utilitas rei publicae*, see Kenneth Pennington, *The Prince and the Law, 1200-1600: Sovereignty and Rights in the Western Legal Tradition*

lus, Ridolfi underscores the point, arguing that urgent public necessity justifies even the seizure of citizens' goods and their sale at less than market prices (2281-89).

The significance of the argument from necessity lay in the fact that it provided a conceptual basis for distinguishing compulsory from voluntary loans. Laws authorizing *prestanze* from the 1360s onward incorporated similar justifications. In his summary of communal legislation in the *thema* to the *Questio montis*, Ridolfi notes that "when the commune of Florence needs money it imposes on its citizens obligations that are commonly called *prestanze*" (2195-97). A provision from early in the Milanese war was even more explicit, stating that "after due consideration, it is necessary to impose four *prestanze* in the city of Florence to meet an emergency and to preserve the freedom of the said commune."[13]

At an earlier phase of the Florentine controversy, Domenico Pantaleoni had advanced the argument from necessity to justify interest paid on compulsory loans.[14] Guido de Belloreguardo, however, challenged this rationale, arguing that interest payments weakened the fiscal health of the commune and implicated public creditors in sin, proposing instead a regime of interest-free loans.[15] In *dubium* 1, Ridolfi rejects Guido's arguments, maintaining that such a method of raising money is a political, if not a theoretical, impossibility:

> I reply that ... even if the commune is able to compel citizens to lend without legislating that they receive something beyond the principal, nevertheless not every possibility is desirable; for we can do any number of things from which, for the good of the republic and to avoid scandal, we rightly abstain (2370-74).

(Berkeley, Los Angeles and London: University of California Press, 1993), 232-34. On the genealogy of the concept, see Gaines Post, *Studies in Medieval Legal Thought: Public Law and the State, 1100-1322* (Princeton: Princeton University Press, 1964), 241-309, esp. 269-90. For a discussion of necessity in the context of government loans, see Kirshner, "From Usury to Public Finance," 98-108; and idem, "Reading Bernardino's Sermon," 553-61.

[13] Provision of 14 July 1391: "Attendentes consideratione solerti quod pro nonnullis emergentibus causis et pro conservatione libertatis dicti communis necessarium est imponere in civitate Florentie quattuor prestantias ..." (ed. Kirshner, "Reading Bernardino's Sermon," 555, n. 27).

[14] See above, p. 71. By the end of the fourteenth century, the argument had become the stock defence of payments to public creditors; it was also used by Nicholas de Anglia, Antonius de Butrio and Peter of Ancharano (Kirshner, "From Usury to Public Finance," 99; idem, "Reading Bernardino's Sermon," 553-55; and idem, "Moral Theology of Public Finance," 54-55).

[15] See above, pp. 67-68.

The degree of compulsion involved would render such levies insupportable and give rise to factional strife, for

> on the evidence of our own eyes, how many citizens do we not daily see damaged by *prestanze*—indeed how many do we not see destroyed and reduced to extreme penury—whom annual interest payments of five percent in some small measure relieve, refresh and console? If it were not for this, they might be driven in their desperation to plot against the republic, at grave risk to their souls and peril to the republic (2379-84).

Clearly, then, it is in the interests of the government to indemnify citizens, for in this way it not only guarantees itself a reservoir of solvent lenders in the future but secures their loyalty in the present. According to a popular proverb, "his regime is safest who is loved by his subjects." Indeed, Ridolfi adds, "it is better for a republic to have the citizens' love than their money alone; for, as another proverb says, 'good the *soldo* that is better than a florin'" (2396-97).[16] That is, in terms of public utility, a *soldo* willingly paid by a citizen assured of interest is preferable to a florin extorted from him against his will.

Interest payments should be seen, Ridolfi maintains, as a sort of reward for citizens' contributions to the common good rather than as usury paid on a loan. Nor should the government be classified as an ordinary debtor, for what a popular religious tract says about God himself might also be applied to the commune: "Who has anything that is not yours? You pay debts, but owe nothing; forgive debts, but lose nothing" (2399-2400).[17] Moreover, Ridolfi asks, how can it be said that the government fosters avarice by offering *prestanziati* five percent a year? They could expect greater and more secure returns from legitimate commercial or property investments, while the principal of *prestanze*, by contrast, is irrecoverable and interest payments often haphazard (2299-2305). And whereas money spent buying a field can be recovered by selling it, *monte* credits are worth only a fraction of their nominal value (2434-49).

Gregory of Rimini, however, offered a more penetrating critique of lenders' motivations.[18] Ridolfi meets it by deploying the canonists' distinc-

[16] For parallels to the first proverb in Cicero and Petrarch, see Kirshner, "Reading Bernardino's Sermon," 557, n. 38. I supply the texts at comm. n. 2389-97.

[17] The source of this passage is discussed in comm. n. 2397-2400. Ridolfi had an elevated conception of government, declaring at a *consulta* of 1429 that "just as we should adore one God, so you, Lord Priors, are to be venerated above all citizens, and those who look to others are setting up idols, and are to be condemned" (quoted by Kent, "Florentine *Reggimento*," 580).

[18] *Questio montis, dubium* 2 (2459-2998). Gregory's views are discussed above, pp. 68-70.

tion between primary and secondary intention:

> I believe that, other things being equal, such lenders—not only if they are forced to lend, but even if they lend willingly—are immune from the sin and vice of usury and from any obligation to make restitution, always provided that they lend primarily from charity and not from hope of profit or increase; although they may entertain a secondary hope of such profit (2638-42).

What appears to be an endorsement of voluntary loans is not as extraordinary as it first appears: later in the *Questio montis* Ridolfi maintains that in practice nobody willingly lends to the government (2765-76). Here he is silently invoking the concept of *lucrum cessans*, which Gregory himself had utilized, while stripping it of Gregory's restrictive conditions. Later he will advance it directly (2768), but at this stage his purpose is simply to assimilate the patriotic common good to charity so that although creditors are forced to lend they willingly accept the need to do so from love of the republic, knowing that "after God, they are more obligated to [the commune] than to any other" (2655-57). The unspoken assumption, of course, is that creditors would otherwise invest the principal of their loans more profitably in licit enterprises.

Ridolfi considers in turn the three principal signs of usury that Gregory detected in government loans: that the government does not pay interest freely but under compulsion; that the interest is incommensurate with real damages sustained by the lenders; and that the citizens who legislate compulsory loans and interest are also the chief beneficiaries of the public debt (2638-2905).

The first objection holds only if the commune is in fact an unwilling debtor and creditors understand this to be so. Ridolfi considers both ideas absurd. The commune cannot be constrained by its own citizens and, moreover, in its own legislation it declares the interest a gift. To the objection that because the gift is contingent on a loan it must be usury, Ridolfi responds that

> this does not always follow. I say that sometimes profit on a loan is given as usury, sometimes not, but rather as a gratuitous gift whose cause lies not in the loan itself, but arises from the service, advantage or profit accruing to the debtor, or from a certain nobility of spirit, as in one who is aware that he is under a natural obligation to make a return-gift ... or because he knows that his creditor has been injured by lending (2734-41).

To Gregory's contention that truly donative interest payments would vary in proportion to the degree of self-sacrifice exhibited by lenders, Ridolfi replies that it is not only impractical but undesirable to assess individual loss and generosity. Unequal treatment would foster conscientious scruples in some and envy in others. Therefore the commune has resolved to treat everyone equally and to "temper the strict truth of justice" in the interests of peace, order and good government (2750-55). In a similar way, Ridolfi observes, status distinctions between members of corporate bodies, such as universities, are not necessarily based on merit but on extrinsic qualities such as seniority, and in illustration he asks, "how often do we not see a doctor or master given precedence over others whose shoe-latchet he is not worthy to unloose?" (2759-60)

In the case of government creditors, it is enough that everyone is compensated at the modest, essentially token, rate of five percent, which roughly corresponds to the return that might be expected on land.[19] In Ridolfi's estimate, this practice at least has the advantage of rewarding unworthy and grasping creditors no more than they merit. In fact, he maintains, all government creditors are injured by reason of profits forgone (*lucrum cessans*) and therefore "there is no creditor who should not seek indemnities as *interesse* and who if *interesse* is offered should not accept it" (2765-72). Given the variety and extent of the miseries caused by *prestanze* —miseries that can be fully known only to God and not to any earthly agency—it is not surprising that the commune ties compensation to sums actually lent rather than to individual losses (2791-2801).

This argument, however, appears to be undermined by Gregory's observation that the lawmakers who decree rates of compensation are themselves the government's biggest creditors, a fact that reveals the purely fictional character of the statutory rhetoric of gift and reward. Ridolfi admits the force of the argument, conceding that legislators and creditors are effectively the same people. He rejects the obvious solution that a citizen might function in several distinct capacities, so that "he gives or legislates compensation in his capacity as a magistrate or public person, but receives it in his capacity as a private person," since officials who have the authority to prohibit illicit contracts are morally bound to exercise it (2823-26). Instead, in accordance with his distinction between primary and secondary intention, Ridolfi argues that those who legislate *any* rate of compensation from motives of self-interest are guilty of usury in the forum of conscience and bound to make restitution.[20] In his judgement, however, legislators who act primarily in the public interest may in good conscience authorize and receive "customary and fitting" compensation (*consuetum lucrum et condecens*) at five percent (2853-60).

[19] Kirshner notes that when interest was paid regularly, credits yielding five per cent were comparable to investments in land and commerce, which fluctuated between four and six per cent in the fourteenth and fifteenth centuries ("From Usury to Public Finance," 27).

[20] *Questio montis, dubium* 3 (2999-3029).

Periodically, however, circumstances compel the commune to resort to loans paying rates of eight or ten percent, called *prestanzoni* and *accatti* to distinguish them from five-percent *prestanze* (2835-52).[21] In Ridolfi's view, such loans are probably illicit regardless of the legislators' intentions because they provide prospective lenders with a temptation to profit that is absent from the "customary and fitting" rate. Moreover, it is difficult to construe the more advantageous rates as an expression of benevolence on the part of the commune rather than an inducement to lending. Nevertheless, he argues, some creditors might be able to demonstrate that they have incurred losses that correspond to the higher rates of compensation. In such cases, the interest may be considered licit under the title of *lucrum cessans*, and the same would hold true if in a period of frequent *prestanze* the commune decided that citizens in general were suffering excessive losses and legislated correspondingly higher rates of compensation for everyone. Ridolfi, however, cautions that citizens profiting from these extraordinary levies should examine their real motivations and consider whether they have succumbed to avarice (2861-89).[22]

A related (*incidens*) question arose "daily" from the practice of offering a premium for early payment of *prestanze* (2906-98).[23] Ridolfi gives two examples. In the first, the city decrees a forced loan bearing interest of five percent to be received only by citizens who pay by a certain deadline; those who fail to do so will receive nothing. Are citizens who pay by the deadline in order to obtain interest guilty of usury? In the second case, a loan is decreed in November. Those who pay within a month will begin to receive interest on 1 January; those who miss the deadline must wait until 1 September. Do the former sin? In Ridolfi's judgement, the loan that constitutes the underlying subject (*subiectum*) of these cases is not itself usurious, for the lenders are not guided by a primary intention to profit but by patriotic motives. Moreover, in both of the proposed cases they will be compelled to lend, even without profit. By extension, therefore, it is wrong to suggest that a purely secondary quality—the desire to secure a premium for lending—is corrupt, for "if the profit is licit, it is licit to seek it" (2960-61).

Ridolfi proposes an analogy. The government decrees conscription and

[21] See above, pp. 46-47. Francesco Datini, for example, paid eight forced loans at eight to ten percent interest between May 1402 and July 1403 (Molho, *Florentine Public Finances*, 96, table 7).

[22] By the mid-1420s, Ridolfi had either revised his opinion on *prestanzoni* or concluded that the circumstances of the war with Milan met the conditions he lays down here, since his *catasto* declaration of 1427 shows him holding 236 florins-worth of *prestanzoni* credits; see above p. 38, n. 49.

[23] An example is the *monte dei cinque per cento interi* of 1424 (see above, p. 38, n. 49), though similar devices had presumably been employed earlier.

offers me a bounty of a thousand *lire* if I join the army within a month; otherwise I get nothing, though I still must serve. Or it offers me a thousand *lire* in six months if I join within a month; otherwise five hundred or a thousand *lire*, but only after a year. In Ridolfi's opinion, anyone who joins by the deadline in order to obtain the premium cannot be accused of immorality, since he would be conscripted in any case. The analogy is complete if we consider that in Ridolfi's view the profit paid on *prestanze* is not usury but either a gift or compensation for the performance of a civic duty comparable to military service. If it is licit to seek an enlistment bounty, it is equally licit to seek a premium by meeting the deadline for *prestanze*.

Noonan considers Ridolfi's endorsement of *prestanze* premiums a radical innovation, arguing that it is

> an astonishing departure from earlier writers and from [Ridolfi's] own teaching everywhere else. It meant that interest might be sought for its own sake, without any immediate compulsion or charitable motive inspiring the loan.... Laurentius' advocacy of it may be seen either as a lack of consistent principle, or as a brilliant foreshadowing of the future.[24]

In my view, Noonan reads too much into the text. The burden of Ridolfi's argument in *dubium* 2 is to distinguish between the "customary and reasonable" rate of five percent and excessive rates of compensation. Excessive rates are justifiable only on an individual basis or under unusual conditions; but rates of five percent, which he specifies in the cases he discusses here, may be presumed to meet all the criteria of licitness. The commune's offer of premiums does nothing to alter the fundamental characteristics of *prestanze*. Nor do premiums furnish an inducement to lending in the way that higher rates of interest might, since citizens in the present case will eventually be compelled to lend anyway. At best, it could be said that premiums create conditions under which citizens are penalized for dilatory payment. Ridolfi may be probing the limits of his doctrine of intention, but the context of the opinion suggests, as Kirshner has remarked, that "the issue is not a matter of principle, but of opportunity" and therefore morally neutral.[25]

C. The Public Debt Market

Ridolfi's opinions on the market in debt credits conform broadly to those of Francesco da Empoli and Lapo da Castiglionchio.[26] His analysis, how-

[24] *Scholastic Analysis of Usury*, 125.

[25] Kirshner, "Reading Bernardino's Sermon," 559, n.43; idem, "From Usury to Public Finance," 129.

[26] See above, pp. 73-75, 81-82.

ever, displays greater conceptual sophistication and a more explicit acknowledgement of actual market practice. He clarifies Francesco's rather muddled account of the transaction between the original creditor and the speculator and faults Lapo for conceding too much ground to critics such as Gregory of Rimini. At the same time, he distinguishes between the simple sale of credits and the more questionable activities of brokers who paid the assessments of distressed *prestanziati* in return for title to their credits.[27]

In *dubium* 4 (3030-53), Ridolfi reports Gregory of Rimini's opinion that a creditor may sell the right to any principal that remains after the deduction of the interest he has received, noting that this opinion was received by Lapo da Castiglionchio. Ridolfi agrees that creditors can alienate "any claim they have in or over the *monte*" (3045-47), but argues in *dubium* 5 (3054-3318) that their rights are considerably more extensive than either Gregory or Lapo allowed, since, as he established in *dubia* 1 and 2, interest payments are not in fact a way to liquidate the principal of forced loans but a reward for citizens' patriotism. At the same time, he criticizes Lapo's response to the central thrust of Gregory's critique of the market as too shallow. He remarks rather sententiously that canonists as much as theologians must be careful to look beyond the "outer husk of words and contractual formulae ... especially in questions that touch the soul" (3091-93). Since, in Gregory's view, the original creditors are usurers in virtually every instance, buyers, who become their proxies, are usurers as well. Indeed, they are usurers even within the terms outlined by Ridolfi in the first two *dubia*, for they cannot claim to be acting under duress or from motives other than profit (3055-3107). Is the transaction between creditor and speculator merely a fiction disguising an agreement whereby the latter replaces the former as the commune's creditor? If so, it is a form of "fraud from contract to contract" (*fraus de contractu ad contractum*), in which a legal agreement conceals an illegal transaction and is therefore void by reason of the parties' corrupt intentions (3108-18).

In Ridolfi's judgement, however, sales of debt credits are not fraudulent but legitimate purchase-sale agreements in which there is no contradiction between the intentions of the parties and their words (3119-87). The contract is a real sale because it comprises both a price and a vendible thing, namely, the right (*ius*) to the seller's principal in the *monte* and any action arising from it. The fact that debt credits represent rights and not corporeal things does not constitute an objection, since rights are themselves vendible.[28] Purchasers of debt credits, then, cannot be accused of usury, even

[27] See above, p . 44.

[28] In Part 2, question 12, *census* is analyzed as a vendible right comparable to

though they are motivated by a desire for profit, since the profit on credits is itself legitimate and in a contract of purchase-sale, unlike a loan, a primary intention to profit is perfectly licit (3188-3225).

Like Francesco da Empoli, Ridolfi viewed the relationship between the buyer of a credit and the commune as qualitatively different from that between the original lender and the commune.[29] Although the buyer seeks the same benefit he would have sought as a lender, because he lends the commune nothing, it cannot be maintained that he stands to it as creditor to debtor. In other words, he does not replace the primary creditor as creditor but simply succeeds to the primary creditor's rights by virtue of his purchase. Turning the argument from fraud on its head, Ridolfi maintains that the same end might be sought through different contracts, one of which is licit, the other illicit, for identity of goal does not render the two effectively the same transaction.[30] Moreover, it does not necessarily follow that one who seeks profit by means of buying debt credits (a licit transaction) would do so by way of a loan to the government (an illicit transaction if undertaken freely), for, according to a maxim of Gratian, "no one is presumed to be indifferent to his own salvation" (3215-16).[31]

Ridolfi entertains a potential objection based on the fact that credits are discounted by up to seventy percent of their face value "in accordance with changing circumstances" (*secundum temporum diuersitatem*) (3226-3318). Three decretals, *In civitate* (X 5.19.6), *Naviganti* (X 5.19.19) and *Consuluit*, discuss commodity sales in which the seller charges a premium in return for deferring payment or, conversely, asks less than the market price in exchange for delayed delivery. Unless there is uncertainty about the future value of the commodity, such agreements amounted to disguised loans and usurious "sales of time" (3232-37).[32] Ridolfi responds that since no time elapses between payment for and delivery of a *monte* credit, there is no sale of time and therefore the decretals do not apply (3237-42). Moreover, the rules on exchange permit variations in what is given or received of up to

---

an inheritance, which represents "all the rights which the dead man possessed" (Dig. 50.16.24) and not just his real property; see 1802-7 and comm. n. 1802-7.

[29] See above, pp. 73-74.

[30] Francesco da Empoli made the same argument; see *Questio de monte*, ed. cit. 36-38; for a discussion, see ibid., 12-13.

[31] Decretum Grat. C.1 q.7 c.26

[32] The argument that usury is the illicit sale of time, which is common to all and therefore non-vendible, first appeared in the writings of the theologian Peter the Chanter (d. 1197) and subsequently became a commonplace of usury analysis (Langholm, *Economics in the Medieval Schools*, 57, n. 78). It was adopted as a subsidiary argument against usury by Innocent IV (Noonan, *Scholastic Analysis of Usury*, 50).

half the just price, while the prices paid for *monte* credits reflect their real market value.[33] He notes that the subject of the sale is not the sum of money that was originally lent to the government but a right or title to this money. The uncertainty of ever recovering it is a liability that substantially reduces the value of the title. If the principal were recoverable, the market value of the credit would be enhanced in the same way that a house subject to a temporary servitude (*servitus*) or lien is worth more than one burdened with a perpetual servitude (3259-67).[34]

Granted, then, that purchasers legitimately buy credits, can they also legitimately accept interest payments?[35] Ridolfi reports Gregory of Rimini's wholesale condemnation of speculators:

> It is his meaning, as is clear from the foregoing, that in every case in which purchasers intend to receive profit arising from money lent to the commune by the original creditors in virtue of money that they have paid the same original creditors, they commit usury, just as the original creditors, for whom they voluntarily substitute, committed usury if they lent to the commune with the same intention (3359-64).

But, as Ridolfi points out, the issue of intention is irrelevant in a contract of purchase-sale, such as the agreement between buyers and sellers of *monte* shares, and therefore

> I say that in every case in which the original creditor licitly receives something from the commune, he may licitly sell it, and that it may licitly be bought and received, whether it is the principal, or some increase or profit, or whatever else you want to call it (3376-79).

Ridolfi maintains that this position is defensible on moral grounds. By restricting the ethical choices open to speculators, critics of the *monte* achieve the opposite of their intention and induce a state of indifference expressed in a popular saying: "Since I can't do business without endangering my soul, I'd rather ride to hell than walk" (3390-92). The law, Ridolfi observes, aims at equity rather than rigour for its own sake, for souls, like foals, do not benefit from excessive harshness (3401-6).

The status of brokers presented a more complex problem, for they obtained title to credits from citizens who had been assessed loans but had not paid them.[36] Should brokers be classed as ordinary buyers of credits when in fact they pay their clients' assessments directly? Or should the

[33] See above, pp. 74-75, n. 83.

[34] Ridolfi's source here was probably Francesco da Empoli. See *Questio de monte*, ed. cit. 36, 42-43.

[35] *Questio montis, dubium* 6 (3319-3408).

[36] *Questio montis, dubium* 7 (3409-3667).

transaction be regarded as a fiction in which a broker ("Martin") is deemed to lend his client ("Peter") the assessed sum of, say, ten florins, after which Peter sells Martin his rights in the *monte* for half of that amount? Ridolfi doubts that the contract is a purchase-sale, since Peter has no rights to sell until he has paid his *prestanza*. Moreover, it might be objected that, if anything, the transaction is a loan because Martin, not Peter, is described as the lender in the *monte* registers. For the sake of the fee he receives from Peter and anticipated interest profit, Martin makes himself a voluntary creditor of the commune at an effective rate of ten percent (3416-79).

In Ridolfi's view, the transaction is neither a strict purchase-sale nor a loan, but the innominate contract called *do ut facias*, "I give something that you may do something" (3480-3505). From this perspective, Peter gives Martin five so that Martin might pay the other five on his behalf for a total of the ten for which Peter is obligated to the government. On his side, Martin enters into an agreement to absolve Peter of his obligation to the government and, having done so, is appropriately described as the commune's creditor in place of Peter. The contract nevertheless approximates a licit purchase-sale, since at the moment Peter pays Martin the latter acquires Peter's claim over the *monte* plus any anticipated profit, and once the transaction has been concluded neither party has any further obligations towards the other. Finally, the parties to the contract are commonly referred to as "buyers" and "sellers," a semantic point that reinforces the legal parallel between this agreement and purchase-sale (3506-13).

But is it possible to sell an anticipated right? And if so, does the original creditor's anticipated right to profit represent a temptation to illicit gain (3514-71)? Ridolfi argues that an "anticipated right grounded in immediately subsisting circumstances" (3521) is analogous to other incorporeal rights. It is in this sense, for example, that a cleric who possesses a papal *litera expectatiua* (letter of expectancy) is said to have an immediate ground for his anticipation of a benefice. Like other incorporeal rights, anticipated rights can be alienated. Ridolfi denies, however, that in the present case the anticipated right furnishes a primary hope of profit, for the original creditor lent under compulsion, knowing that ultimately "compulsion and payment are certain" (3640-43). The broker's desire for profit, of course, may be excused by the nature of the contract, though Ridolfi notes that if he is content to lend to the commune directly or, indeed, if he intends to evade the appearance of usury by means of the agreement, he is guilty of usury, for intention remains the criterion of licitness in all cases (3572-3667).

D. GOVERNMENT ANNUITIES

The last problem Ridolfi considers is whether the government can raise money by selling annuities (*census*) for the life of a creditor or a beneficiary nominated by him at rates corresponding to those paid *monte* creditors.[37] Lapo da Castiglionchio had discussed the issue in connection with the *monte dell'uno tre* and *monte dell'uno due*, noting that "this question sails on high, stormy seas, which are not clearly charted."[38] Lapo nevertheless concluded on the authority of Innocent IV and Hostiensis that such contracts were legitimate provided there was no fraud or deception beyond half the just price. The fact, however, that the agreement did not specify the age of the beneficiaries, who if young might conceivably earn excessive profits, gave Lapo pause, as did a provision that allowed the commune to redeem the *census* at a fraction of the purchase price.

Ridolfi dissents from Lapo's opinion to the extent that he considers the contract open to fraud unless carefully circumscribed (3705-24). Although canonical *communis opinio* approved *census* based on existing income from land or servile labour, *census* created for the sake of specific credit requirements were more controversial.[39] For example, Innocent IV and Hostiensis accepted them but Johannes Andreae did not. Ridolfi follows the last in regarding such agreements as usually in fraud of usury, particularly when the term and the return are guaranteed or when the *census* is based on the person or labour of the seller, for such an agreement approximates a loan.[40] On the other hand, *census* based on the totality of the seller's real property and rights are licit, provided they are not simply a way to evade the usury prohibition by creating a personal obligation.[41] Conditions, however, whereby the seller can rescind a *census* by repaying the original sum or a part of it will usually create a presumption of fraud.[42]

Ridolfi considers government *census* licit if they pay a "modest" (*conueniens*) annuity (presumably five percent) derived from the existing property and revenues of the commune (3725-71). The *census* should not be redeemable at a discount unless participation in the fund is open to all citi-

[37] *Questio montis, dubium* 8 (3668-3771).

[38] "Et haec quaestio nauigat alto mari turbido, id est, non clare difinito" (*Allegationes*, allegatio 137, n.15, fol. 164rb). The burden of Lapo's discussion is at ibid., fol. 164rb-vb. See also above, pp. 81-82.

[39] See above, pp. 82-83.

[40] See Part 2, questions 11 and 12 (1652-1839); and comm. nn. 1652-53 to 1816-39.

[41] Part 2, question 13 (1840-78); and comm. nn. 1840-43 to 1860-78.

[42] Part 2, question 18 (2001-2182, esp. 2081-2182); and comm. nn. 2004-13 to 2165-82.

zens without distinction. A redemption clause in an agreement with an individual citizen—and *a fortiori* with one who is a notorious usurer—is to be presumed fraudulent. The possibility that profits might exceed the original investment is not an objection to the contract, for profit is legitimate in purchase-sale agreements. Like Peter of Ancharano, however, Ridolfi favours a perpetual or life *census* over short-term annuities, since the former are more subject to risk and therefore less likely to be fraudulent than the latter.[43]

It is worth noting that despite the reservations of Ridolfi and other theorists *census* represented the solution to the problem of usury and public debt ultimately favoured by the church authorities and most early-modern regimes.[44] In a bull of 1425 responding to a question of the bishop of Wratislaw, Pope Martin V (1368-1431) ruled that redeemable *census* based on the seller's total property and commonly resorted to by secular authorities, churches and monasteries to raise funds were licit purchase-sale agreements rather than loans and therefore exempt from the usury prohibition.[45] A bull that Pope Nicholas V (1397-1455) addressed in 1452 to the king of Aragon and a response from Pope Callistus III (1378-1458) to a question from the south German bishops in 1455 confirmed this position.[46] By the sixteenth century, annuities, or *rentes* as they are known to economic historians, had become the standard mechanism for raising public funds.[47]

[43] For Peter of Ancharano's opinion, see above, pp. 82-83.

[44] For the various opinions, see Noonan, *Scholastic Analysis of Usury*, 154-70.

[45] Extrav. comm. 3.5.1.

[46] Noonan summarizes Nicholas V's bull in *Scholastic Analysis of Usury*, 160-61. For Callistus III's bull, see Extrav. comm. 3.5.2. See also Herman van der Wee, "Monetary, Credit and Banking Systems" in *Cambridge Economic History of Europe*, vol. 5, *The Economic Organization of Early Modern Europe*, ed. E. E. Rich and C. H. Wilson (Cambridge: Cambridge University Press, 1977), 303-04.

[47] For discussions, see van der Wee, "Monetary, Credit and Banking Systems"; James D. Tracy, *A Financial Revolution in the Hapsburg Netherlands: Renten and Renteniers in the County of Holland, 1515-1565* (Berkeley and London: University of California Press, 1985), esp. 7-70; and John Munro's review of Tracy in *American Historical Review* 92 (1987): 434-35. See also John Munro, "The 'New Institutional Economics' and the Changing Fortunes of Fairs in Medieval and Early Modern Europe: The Textile Trades, Warfare, and Transaction Costs," forthcoming in *Vierteljahrschrift für Sozial- und Wirtschaftsgeschichte* 88 (2001). The Consolidated Stock of the Nation, created by the consolidation of the outstanding British public debt in 1747-49 and still traded on the British Stock Exchange, were defined as annuities. I wish to thank John Munro for these references.

5
Law, Politics and Public Debt

Dubium 2 of the *Questio montis* includes a dramatic account of the privations endured by government creditors. "How many citizens," Ridolfi asks,

> do we ourselves not see virtually perishing of hunger because of heavy *prestanze*; how many houses and contents sold up; how many citizens reduced from riches to penury, even beggary; how many citizens, reputed rich and secure, are not unjustly assessed, indeed crushed, by their enemies' hatred, so that the very bread is snatched from their mouths and their children torn from the breast? How many orphans, widows and wards do we not see whose wealth is left undefended? Is it then remarkable that the commune decrees the payment of compensation in proportion to the amount lent? (2791-99)

Prestanze undoubtedly represented a heavy, often intolerable, burden, and until a more transparent system was (temporarily) introduced with the *catasto* of 1427 the assessment procedure supplied political rivals with a convenient weapon.[1] Nor is the reference to widows, orphans and debtors just a pious *topos*: the poorest Florentines, many of whom bore the double burden of gabelles and *prestanze*, found themselves in exactly the predicament Ridolfi describes. Ridolfi's target, however, was not the social inequalities magnified by the *monte* system. The poor, who paid their assessments *ad perdendum* or sold their credits to speculators, were ineligible to collect interest. Ridolfi's concern was with the possessing classes, above all with the tiny minority who owned the bulk of credits. By 1427, eighty-six percent of *monte* credits were owned by the richest ten percent of Florentine households, while seventy-one percent of households owned none at all.[2] Ridolfi's defence of the compensation paid to government creditors, like his overall emphasis on occult usury, served the interests of the rich.

[1] On this, see Molho, *Florentine Public Finances*, 79-87; and above pp. 41-42.

[2] Kirshner, "Reading Bernardino's Sermon," 556-57, esp. n. 34. The figures are derived from the *catasto* records by David Herlihy, "Family and Property in Renaissance Florence," in *The Medieval City*, ed. Harry A. Miskimin, David Herlihy and Abraham L. Udovitch (New Haven and London: Yale University Press, 1977), 8, table 1.2. See also Herlihy and Klapisch-Zuber, *Tuscans and Their Families*, 99, fig. 4.1.

Ridolfi was not alone in his solicitude for the material security of the possessing classes. His insistence that government creditors suffered a depletion of their patrimonies and therefore merited "relief, refreshment and consolation" (2381-82) rested on a conception of poverty he shared with most other contemporary lawyers, preachers and moralists. In this view, the poor were not only the destitute—properly described as *miserabiles*—but the clergy, especially members of religious orders, and people of substance threatened by a diminution of status because of material adversity, the *poveri vergognosi* (shamed poor), so called because they could not beg without dishonouring themselves.[3] Welfare assistance for *miserabiles* was derisory, except during famines and epidemics, when it served to avert social revolt.[4] By contrast, more respectable indigents could count on range of measures that included special testamentary arrangements, the provision of dowries and discreet assistance by confraternities such as the Orsanmichele.[5] Charity in Renaissance Florence served to maintain the social order and the dominance of the ruling class. The government's allocation of interest to distressed creditors performed a similar function and was dictated by the same class considerations.

[3] On poverty in medieval Florence, see Henderson, *Piety and Charity*. On medieval and modern categories of poverty, see ibid., 241-58; Richard C. Trexler, "Charity and the Defense of Urban Elites in the Italian Communes," in *The Rich, the Well Born and the Powerful: Elites and Upper Classes in History*, ed. Frederic Cople Jaher (Urbana, Chicago and London: University of Illinois Press, 1973), 64-74; and Michel Mollat, *The Poor in the Middle Ages: An Essay in Social History*, trans. Arthur Goldhammer (New Haven and London: Yale University Press, 1986).

[4] Henderson calculates the general, "city-wide" monthly subsidy offered by the Orsanmichele to the destitute in the first half of the fourteenth century at five *soldi*, a sum sufficient to feed a family for a day (*Piety and Charity*, 253). Despite a rising cost of living, the subsidy was the same in the 1350s (ibid., 323). On the government's provision of subsidized grain during famines leading up to the Black Death, see ibid., 273-92. Of the policy, Henderson remarks that "it would be misleading to present a cozy picture of a beneficent commune simply tending to the needs of the poor from a sense of Christian charity. Behind this policy lay the desire to minimize the spectre of popular disorder, which raised its head during every period of shortage" (ibid., 243).

[5] See Trexler, "Charity," 75-105. Trexler notes that distressed merchants were sometimes granted episcopal exemption from the obligation to retore usury in their wills (ibid., 78). On the importance of an adequate dowry in maintaining family honour, see Kirshner, *Pursuing Honor*, 4-15. For illustrations, see Molho, *Marriage Alliance*, 128-78; and Henderson, *Piety and Charity*, 307-9, 316-21, 337. On the charitable activities of the Osanmichele in the fourteenth century, see ibid., 241-353. On the criteria for and distribution of *limosine suggellate* (sealed alms), see ibid., 253-54, 257-58, 313-21.

The possessing classes, however, were not only the chief beneficiaries of Ridolfi's vindication of the *monte*, but also its principal audience. As I noted earlier, consent to the fiscal policies of the patrician elite was threatened by the disaffection of new men and middling Florentines who by the end of the fourteenth century were resisting the conscription of their capital through war *prestanze* and whose commitment to the regime was historically less fervent than that of the highest ranks of Florentine society.[6] In these circumstances, what the elite needed was not simply a defence of the debt against conventional criticisms derived from the usury prohibition, but a positive identification of the *monte* and its institutions with the interests of enfranchised Florentines in general.

It is from this perspective that we should interpret Ridolfi's warnings that alternative methods of procuring revenue would result in factionalism and strife as desperate creditors sought to recoup their losses by seizing control of the republic.[7] The spectre of disorder ruled out the uncompensated levies proposed by Augustinian critics of the debt and even more so direct taxes on property. "It is better," Ridolfi remarks in *dubium* 2, "that the commune provide for its needs with the consent and approval of citizens than by exactions and unrestricted violations of this sort" (2376-78). Indeed, conventional wisdom enjoined the republic to seek the love of citizens, not their enmity.[8] Nevertheless, the argument from expediency and utility remained essentially negative, for the best loved republic would presumably make no demands at all on private property. Given that this course was ruled out by the "imminent necessity" threatening the very existence of the republic, how could the *monte* system to be presented as the object of public "consent and approval"?

Ridolfi's solution was to shift the burden of his argument from necessity as cause to a more positive account in which the public utility served by the debt approximated contemporary ideas of "public good" (*bonum publicum*), which was not only "juxtaposed to discord, party factionalism, and strife, but was also defined as the collective good of society."[9] On the authority

[6] See above, pp. 46-52.

[7] See above, pp. 88-89. For the views of other writers on this theme, see John Kenneth Hyde, "Contemporary Views on Faction and Civil Strife in Thirteenth- and Fourteenth-Century Italy," in *Violence and Civil Disorder*, 273-307; and Lauro Martines, "Political Conflict in the Italian City States," *Government and Opposition* 3 (1968): 69-91.

[8] See above, p. 89.

[9] Pennington, *Prince and the Law*, 236. Pennington is particularly concerned to show how *bonum publicum* could provide a theoretical basis for the limitation of princely prerogative and he detects the earliest juridical use of the concept in this way in the commentaries of a younger contemporary of Ridolfi, Nicholas de Tude-

of Aristotle and Augustine, who held that the common good should be placed before private interest, Ridolfi represented monetary contributions to the public good as an exercise in Christian charity.[10] While the formally coercive dimensions of *prestanze* absolved creditors of the charge of usury, Ridolfi's equation of public good with charity elevated participation in the *monte* into the fulfilment of an evangelical counsel.[11] A similar sentiment may underlie Masaccio's (1401-28) interpretation of the payment of the tribute money (*Mt* 17.23-26) in the Brancacci chapel of Santa Maria del Carmine. Painted between 1423 and 1428 during a period of heavy taxation and forced loans, the fresco represents Jesus and Peter as willingly complying with government levies.[12]

---

schis (1386-1445). However, in a more general sense, the notion of *bonum publicum* or *bonum commune* as the collective social good in contrast to a state of division and faction had antecedents among non-legal writers of the thirteenth and fourteenth centuries, notably Thomas Aquinas and Remigio of Florence, and was popular among the humanists of the early fifteenth century. According to A. Black, "In Italian city-states, 'common good (*bonum commune*)' was sometimes equated with 'the good of the commune (*bonum Comunis*),' meaning ... political conditions under which men could live amicably—notably legal, and fiscal impartiality" ("The Individual and Society," in *The Cambridge History of Medieval Political Thought, c. 350-c. 1450*, ed. James H. Burns, [Cambridge: Cambridge University Press, 1988], 596). Ridolfi uses the term or a variant three times in *dubia* 1 and 2 of the *Questio montis:* 2350; 2332-33, 2857 (*bonum publicum*); 2373 (*bonum rei publice)*. In each case it is contrasted to private interest (*priuatum bonum, priuatum commodum*).

[10] For Augustine and Aristotle, see above, p. 68, n. 59, and comm. n. 2467-93. These texts were cited by Gregory of Rimini, who, of course, used them as ammunition *against* government creditors. Ridolfi repeatedly emphasized that lenders "are moved by the charity by which they are bound to the republic" (2728-29). See also ed. lin. 2639, 2655, 2948. For examples of the same sentiment in Peter of Ancharano, Nicholas de Anglia, Antonius de Butrio and Bernardino of Siena, see Kirshner, "Reading Bernardino's Sermon," 557-61.

[11] On the association of *bonum publicum* or *buon comune* with the virtue of charity, see Henderson, *Piety and Charity*, 16-20.

[12] See the detail reproduced as the frontispiece to this volume. Anthony Molho, "The Brancacci Chapel: Studies in its Iconography and History," *Journal of the Warburg and Courtauld Institutes* 40 (1977): 62-67, links the fresco to debates over clerical taxation in the 1420s. Others detect an allusion to the *catasto* of 1427; see Steffi Roettgen, *Wandmalerei der Frührenaissance in Italien,* vol. 1, *Anfänge und Entfaltung 1400-1470* (Munich: Hirmer, 1996), 94. Medieval commentators often conflated *Mt* 17.23-26 with *Mt* 22.21: "Render therefore to Caesar the things that are Caesar's, and to God the things that are God's" (Molho, "Brancacci Chapel," 62). Ridolfi was associated with the Carmine and figured, along with other *oltrarno* notables, in a (now lost) fresco by Masaccio celebrating the consecration of the church in 1422 (Eckstein, *District of the Green Dragon*, 102-03).

In Ridolfi's opinion, citizens who responded to the government's need and were moved to lend exhibited a high degree of virtue, for is not the fatherland second only to God in the moral economy (2655-57)? Indeed, was the commune not comparable to God himself in its claims over citizens and their wealth?[13] Lovers of the common good were therefore justly compensated for their sacrifices. It was wrong to compare lenders unfavourably to the biblical patriarchs, who, according to Guido de Belloreguardo, "although they had many enemies and fought many wars, never resorted to such contracts [as *prestanze*], which are offensive to God" (2360-62). A better standard of comparison, Ridolfi insisted, were the patriots of ancient Rome. Did not Livy, Valerius Maximus and other Roman historians all testify "that our forefathers, the Romans, though under no obligation to do so, nevertheless rewarded citizens for generous and selfless deeds?" (2412-15).[14]

Ridolfi's emphasis on the common good and his appeal to classical antiquity had affinities with the contemporary political ideology Hans Baron labelled "civic humanism" (*Bürgerhumanismus*).[15] According to Baron, the confrontation between republican Florence and signorial Milan crystallized a new political consciousness that found expression at the beginning of the fifteenth century in the writings of Coluccio Salutati (1331-1406), chancellor of the republic from 1375 to 1406, and his disciple Leonardo Bruni (1370-1444). Civic humanism exalted the republican origins and traditions of Florence, which Salutati and Bruni portrayed as a bulwark of liberty against the tyrannical traditions personified by Julius Caesar and, more recently, Giangaleazzo Visconti. According to the civic humanists, Florentine

[13] See above, p. 89.

[14] For examples from Livy and Valerius Maximus, see comm. n. 2412-15.

[15] The term is Baron's, coined during his research on Leonardo Bruni in the 1920s. He discusses the concept most fully in *Crisis of the Early Italian Renaissance*. Additional studies are collected in idem, *Humanistic and Political Literature in Florence and Venice at the Beginning of the Quattrocento: Studies in Criticism and Chronology* (Cambridge, MA: Harvard University Press, 1955); idem, *From Petrarch to Leonardo Bruni: Studies in Humanistic and Political Literature* (Chicago and London: University of Chicago Press, 1968); and idem, *In Search of Florentine Civic Humanism: Essays on the Transition from Medieval to Modern Thought*, 2 vols. (Princeton: Princeton University Press, 1988). For positive assessments of Baron's contribution to the historiography, see Riccardo Fubini, "Renaissance Historian: the Career of Hans Baron," *Journal of Modern History* 64 (1992): 541-74; John M. Najemy, review of *In Search of Florentine Civic Humanism*, *RQ* 45 (1992): 340-50; and Ronald G. Witt, "The Crisis after Forty Years," *American Historical Review* 101 (1996): 110-18. For more critical perspectives, see Hankins, "The 'Baron Thesis'," 309-38; and the essays collected in idem, ed., *Renaissance Civic Humanism*.

political institutions nourished a spirit of republicanism and broad citizen engagement in public life. For example, in 1391, when the Sienese compared Florence to Athens under the Thirty Tyrants, Salutati responded that "as you know, not only do thirty men not tyrannize our people, they don't even rule them.... There are thousands of men who administer our republic."[16] Bruni's panegyric of Florence, written in 1403-04 in the wake of Visconti's death and the collapse of the Milanese campaign, made similar claims:

> Florence thinks that what concerns many ought to be decided by the action of the whole citizen-body acting according to the law and legal procedure. In this way liberty flourishes and justice is preserved in this most holy city. In this system nothing can be resolved by the caprice of any single man acting in opposition to the judgment of so many men.[17]

Critics of the Baron thesis have questioned the humanists' commitment to the ideals they espoused rhetorically and pointed to the contradictions between civic humanism's claims and the realities of Florentine politics between 1382 and 1434.[18] As I noted above, despite a large pool of citizens formally eligible for office, a restricted elite effectively monopolized power,

[16] Quoted by Conti, *Consulte e Pratiche, 1401,* xxxv; trans. Alison Brown, "Florence, Renaissance and Early Modern State: Reappraisals," *Journal of Modern History* 56 (1984): 290; repr. in *The Medici in Florence*, 303. On Salutati's propaganda efforts during the Milanese war, see Witt, *Hercules at the Crossroads*, 147-77.

[17] *Laudatio florentinae urbis*, ed. Baron in *From Petrarch to Leonardo Bruni*, 260; trans. Benjamin G. Kohl in *The Earthly Republic: Italian Humanists on Government and Society*, ed. Benjamin G. Kohl and Ronald G. Witt (Philadelphia: University of Pennsylvania Press, 1978), 170. For Baron's dating of the *Laudatio*, see *Crisis of the Early Italian Renaissance*, 216-24.

[18] See in particular Charles Trinkaus, "Hans Baron's Two Works on Quattrocento Humanism," *Journal of the History of Ideas* 17 (1956): 426-32; Peter Herde, "Politik und Rhetorik in Florenz am Vorabend der Renaissance: Die ideologische Rechtfertigung der Florentiner Aussenpolitik durch Coluccio Salutati," *Archiv für Kulturgeschichte* 47 (1965): 141-220; idem, "Politische Verhaltensweisen der Florentiner Oligarchie 1382-1402," in *Geschichte und Verfassungsgefüge: Frankfurter Festgabe für Walter Schlesinger* (Wiesbaden: Steiner, 1973), 156-249; Philip Jones, "Communes and Despots: The City State in Late Medieval Italy," *Transactions of the Royal Historical Society*, 5th series, 15 (1965): 71-96; and Jerrold Seigel, "Civic Humanism or Ciceronian Rhetoric?" *Past and Present* 34 (1966): 3-48. For Baron's response to Seigel, see "Leonardo Bruni: 'Professional Rhetorician' or 'Civic Humanist'?" *Past and Present* 36 (1967): 21-37. For a review of the controversy, see Hankins, "The 'Baron Thesis'," 314-18. Most recently see Najemy, "Civic Humanism and Florentine Politics"; Mikael Hörnqvist, "The two myths of civic humanism," in *Renaissance Civic Humanism*, 105-42; and James Hankins, "Rhetoric, history, and ideology: the civic panegyrics of Leonardo Bruni," in ibid., 143-78.

from which they excluded new men and middling Florentines.[19] Conti's analysis of participation in the *consulte* of 1401 illustrates how this process worked in the republic's most influential policy forums.[20] Out of 170 citizens the *Signoria* summoned at least once that year, only eleven were drawn from the minor guilds, while the overwhelming majority had already held office in one of the three leading magistracies and could be classified as members of the oligarchy.[21] Among the latter, an inner circle of thirteen largely monopolized discussion.[22] Conti also detects a further restriction of access to *consulte* in the opening years of the fifteenth century. Extending his survey to the middle of the decade, he shows that the number of fresh advisers summoned fell from just over forty percent in 1401 to nineteen in 1405.[23]

A way of bridging the gulf between civic humanist theory, which attributed power to the many, and republican practice, which restricted it to the few, is suggested by Gramsci's concept of "hegemony."[24] According to Gramsci, ruling classes rule through a combination of force and consent; only the weakest regimes rely exclusively on violence. A stable and durable regime must elicit at least a modicum of consent from those it dominates, and it is in this consensual realm that hegemony operates. Hegemony comprises the ensemble of cultural strategies, discourses and ideologies through which a dominant social group represents its own interests as those of a wider range of groups whose acquiescence is necessary for its peaceful enjoyment of power. The forging of successful hegemony is not, however, entirely one-sided: it may, indeed generally will, involve "selec-

[19] See above, pp. 20-23.

[20] *Consulte e pratiche, 1401*, xxi-xliv.

[21] Ibid., xxiv.

[22] See above, pp. 23-24, n. 66.

[23] *Consulte e pratiche, 1401*, xlv-xlviii. See also Brown, "Reappraisals," 291-92; repr. in *The Medici in Florence*, 315-16.

[24] See Antonio Gramsci, *Quaderni del Carcere*, ed. Valentino Gerratana, 4 vols. (Turin: Einaudi, 1977), 3: 1513-20, 2010-12. Hegemony is the subject of an extensive literature on its relationship to classical Marxist theories of ideology. For useful discussions, see Terry Eagleton, *Ideology: An Introduction* (London and New York: Verso, 1991), 112-23; Robert Bocock, *Hegemony* (London and New York: Tavistock Publications, 1986); T. J. Jackson Lears, "The Concept of Cultural Hegemony: Problems and Possibilities," *American Historical Review* 90 (1985): 567-93; and Harvey J. Kaye, "Political Theory and History: Antonio Gramsci and the British Marxist Historians," in *The Education of Desire: Marxists and the Writing of History* (New York and London: Routledge, 1992), 9-30. I want to thank Tina Loo for introducing me to this literature and to the critical legal studies school (see below, p. 109, n. 37).

tive accommodation to the desires of subordinate groups," to the extent necessary to persuade subordinates that their submission to the dominant group is natural and in their own best interests.[25]

John Najemy's account of the role of civic humanism in what he calls the "consensus" politics of the period after 1382 is consistent with this model.[26] The relative stability of the regime over a period of fifty years is evidence of the elite's success in persuading nonelite elements of the political class that restricted access to power under its supervision was a satisfactory object of political ambition. Civic humanism functioned in this process as an ideological complement to the institutional controls described earlier.[27] Humanist appeals to the city's republican traditions and evocations of the patriotism and civic loyalty displayed by citizens' Roman ancestors mobilized consent to the regime and reinforced the illusion of open government.[28]

Ridolfi belonged to Salutati's circle and certainly shared its ideological objectives. In his *zibaldone*, he recorded his early attachment to Salutati, "that illustrious man or, better, seer," whose house he frequented and from whom he absorbed the new classical learning popularized by Petrarch (d. 1374) and Boccaccio (d. 1375).[29] To this period, prior to Ridolfi's legal

[25] Lears, "Cultural Hegemony," 571.

[26] The manufacture of consent among nonelite fractions of the political class is the theme of the last section of Najemy's *Corporatism and Consensus*, 263-300, esp. 298-300. On the relationship between consensus and civic humanism, see ibid., 301-17. See also the essays listed above, p. 8, n. 3, particularly "Dialogue of Power" and "Civic Humanism and Politics," where Najemy employs a more explicit class analysis than he does in his earlier publications. On problems with translating the Latin *consensus* as "consensus," see Brown "Reappraisals," 289-90; repr. in *The Medici in Florence*, 312-13.

[27] See above, pp. 20-22.

[28] For a discussion of humanism as an ideological programme in the service of urban elites, see also Martines, *Power and Imagination*, 191-217. On the role of humanism in the transition to the Medici ascendancy, see Mark Jurdjevic, "Civic Humanism and the Rise of the Medici," *RQ* 52 (1999): 994-1020.

[29] On Salutati's private library, the meeting-place of his disciples, see Witt, *Hercules at the Crossroads*, 183. The first entry in Ridolfi's *zibaldone* records the birth of a son, Antonio, on 1 May 1381 "clarissimo viro et, ut rectius dicam, vati, Coluccio Pyerio" (MS cit. fol. 1r; quoted by Martino, "Ridolfi," 182, n. 18). Ridolfi was a sponsor at the baptism. The *zibaldone* also contains a copy of a letter dated Bologna, 24 December 1381, in which Ridolfi addresses Salutati in terms of affection, describing himself as the "disciple" of "that most reverend man and illustrious poet, Coluccio, son of Piero, chancellor of the commune of Florence, my father and particular master" ("Laurentius de Ridolfis de Florentia reuerendissimo viro, imo poete, clarissimo, domino Coluccio Pierio, cancellario Comunis Florentiae, patri et

studies in Bologna, belong a number of short treatises on classical prosody, logic and rhetoric composed under Salutati's guidance.[30] The association was resumed when Ridolfi returned to Florence in 1388, and in 1392 the chancellor appealed to his disciple, then on an embassy to the pope, to sponsor a petition to the curia on behalf of his nephew.[31]

Brucker links the emphasis on unity and consent that ran through Ridolfi's interventions in *consulte* to civic humanism, characterizing Ridolfi as "probably the strongest advocate, in the inner circle, of a *governo largo*, a regime with a broad popular base."[32] Indeed, a better expression of the regime's hegemonic strategy could hardly be found than Ridolfi's advocacy in 1416, at a time of renewed tension and factionalism, of an expansion of advisory committees to embrace a broader cross-section of opinion "so that all might speak with one tongue, and so that greater unity will be achieved among the *popolo*."[33] Two years earlier, in the wake of an alleged plot against the leadership, he had urged conciliation, asserting that "a city is the unity of its citizens, and where there is not unity, there is no city, but a fortress."[34] Ridolfi's recognition of strains within the political class was evident in 1412, when he argued for the swift resolution of an unpopular war with Genoa on the grounds that "the war is not being waged solely by the priors and colleges, but also by the masses (*multitudine*)" who paid for it by their *prestanze* and heavier gabelles.[35]

---

domino suo singularissimo" [MS cit. fol. 18v; quoted by Martino, "Ridolfi," 182, n. 18]).

[30] For a discussion, see Martino, "Ridolfi," 181-83. The treatises are contained in the *zibaldone* (MS cit. fols. 2r-3v, 20r-37v).

[31] Martino, "Ridolfi," 182, n. 18; Witt, *Hercules at the Crossroads*, 283-84.

[32] *Civic World*, 367. See also Martino, "Ridolfi," 191-98. On the penetration of public discourse by civic humanist concepts, see Gene A. Brucker, "Humanism, Politics and the Social Order in Early Renaissance Florence," in *Florence and Venice: Comparisons and Relations*, vol. 1, *Quattrocento*, ed. Christine Smith and Salvatore Camporeale (Florence: La Nuova Italia, 1979), 3-11; repr. in *Society, Culture, and Religion*, 237-45.

[33] Cited and trans. Brucker, *Civic World*, 307.

[34] Cited and trans. ibid., 399.

[35] Cited and trans. ibid., 349. Comparable examples of Ridolfi's sentiments in 1402-04, when he was writing the *Tractatus de usuris*, are unfortunately wanting because the protocols of *consulte* and *pratiche* kept by Salutati in his capacity as chancellor provide little indication of a speaker's arguments, but merely summarize his conclusions and positive recommendations (cf. Conti, *Consulte e pratiche, 1401*, passim). On changes in the format of the protocols after Salutati's death in 1406, see Brucker, *Civic World*, 285-86; and idem, "Humanism, Politics and the Social Order," 9; repr. in *Society, Culture, and Religion*, 243.

Did Ridolfi's legal vindication of the *monte* perform a legitimating function on behalf of the elite analogous to that of civic humanism? Or is such an interpretation ruled out by lawyers' own understanding of themselves as exponents of a science that transcended sectional and class interests?[36] The concept of hegemony is helpful here as well. Recent studies inspired by Gramsci emphasize law's vital role as a form of ideology that generates consent in civil society.[37] In this view, law enjoys "relative autonomy": it reflects the power relations of society, but does not reproduce them directly. Instead, it obscures inequalities by presenting itself as a system of universal rules at a remove from society. At the same time, law's abstract character has the effect of making the conclusions reached by its application to specific problems predictable only within broad limits.[38] The relative autonomy of the law ensures broad assent to its authority and renders it a powerful ideological tool.[39]

The usury ban in general and the *monte* controversy in particular illustrate the ideological character of law. Theology and law represented the usury prohibition as a deduction from divine law and the legal definition of a loan, but this formulation obscured the fact that it originally served to reinforce a traditional, land-based order that was threatened by new commercial forms of economic activity.[40] The result was that even in communities such as Florence where commerce achieved dominance, the usury ban and its characterization of profit as shameful continued to command assent and made necessary the various accommodations described earlier.[41] Ridol-

[36] For discussions, see above, p. 3, n. 7. Julius Kirshner, however, has more recently argued for the autonomy of lawyers in the face of political pressure; see "Citizen Cain of Florence," in *La Toscane et les Toscans*, 175-89; and "*Consilia* as Authority," 130-38.

[37] For a nuanced application of Gramsci's ideas to law, see Hugh Collins, *Marxism and Law* (Oxford and New York: Oxford University Press, 1982), 35-76. My views have also been influenced by Alan Hunt, *Explorations in Law and Society: Toward a Constitutive Theory of Law* (New York and London: Routledge, 1993), 17-57, 117-38. See also ibid., 249-66, where Hunt argues more generally for a materialist reading of law that locates it in the context of historically specific social and economic relations.

[38] On relative autonomy and the limits of the concept, see Hunt, *Explorations*, 139-81, esp. 165-69.

[39] For an elegant treatment along these lines, see Douglas Hay, "Property, Authority and the Criminal Law," in *Albion's Fatal Tree: Crime and Society in Eighteenth-Century England*, ed. Douglas Hay, Peter Linebaugh, John G. Rule, Edward P. Thompson and Cal Winslow (Harmondsworth: Penguin, 1977), 17-63.

[40] See above, pp. 57-58.

[41] See above, pp. 60-65.

fi himself felt obliged to conclude his vindication of the debt market with a typically aristocratic and tutiorist reservation:

> Nevertheless, in doubtful cases the safer way should always be chosen, and therefore I recommend that those who can do so should abstain [from the market] ... as indeed I myself have always done (3406-8).

Both advocates and opponents of the *monte* appealed to a shared fund of "objective" legal concepts and in so doing obscured the essentially political interests at stake in the controversy. Kirshner, for example, suggests that the debate between Francesco da Empoli and Piero degli Strozzi in 1353-54 illustrates

> how a common arsenal of legal weapons was targeted in support or denial of particular ends; how willful political assertions were presented in guise of an omniscient neutral theology and jural determinism.... these texts were not merely bulletins advising that traffic in *monte* credits was or was not hazardous to one's spiritual health, but were also political texts aimed in support or denial of the *Monte Comune*'s legitimacy.[42]

Ridolfi himself was fully aware of the intimate connection between the *monte* debate and political interests. In *dubium* 2, he admits that perhaps more than any other factor, the identity of the legislators and beneficiaries of *monte* interest caused him to question the legitimacy of the system (2810-34). The task of the lawyer, however, is to allay such doubts in the interests of political order by the deployment of appropriate legal concepts, in this case, careful distinctions regarding the psychology of legislators.[43]

Writing about the ideological function of criminal law in eighteenth-century England, Douglas Hay observes that "loyalties do not grow simply in complex societies: they are twisted, invoked and often consciously created."[44] The oligarchic elite of fifteenth-century Florence manufactured consent to its dominance in various ways, rhetorical, institutional, legal. Ridolfi's vindication of the *monte*, like the republican rhetoric of civic humanism, was part of this process. Through his apology for the central but increasingly controversial mechanism of public finance, Ridolfi represented the interests of the patrician elite as the interests of enfranchised Florentines in general, particularly dissenting elements of this group whose consent and acquiescence were necessary for the stability of the regime.

[42] "Storm over the *Monte Comune*," 238. See also Armstrong, "Politics of Usury," 15-24. For an analogous example, see Kirshner's discussion of the controversy over Florentine citizenship in "*Ars imitatur naturam*" and "Paolo de Castro on *Cives ex privilegio*."

[43] See above, p. 91.

[44] "Property, Authority and the Criminal Law," 62.

Was Ridolfi successful? One measure is the authority he enjoyed among later writers who treated the debt question in Florence and elsewhere. The Franciscan preacher Bernardino of Siena and the Dominican moralist Antonino of Florence both reproduced Ridolfi's analysis in their own treatments of the *monte*.[45] By the middle of the fifteenth century, the jurists Ambrosius de Vignate (fl. 1460-70) and Alexander de Tartagnis (d. 1477) could declare the debate effectively closed largely on the authority of Ridolfi.[46] The influence of the treatise on Ridolfi's fellow citizens, who, he claims, "assailed my ears with their eloquence" (6) in their appeals for guidance is, of course, more difficult to assess. We can only point to the unprecedented durability of the regime Ridolfi served and to the opinion of at least one Florentine, Vespasiano da Bisticci, who assured his readers that "no one writes more forcibly or more reasonably concerning the *monte* at Florence" than Messer Lorenzo.[47]

[45] See the literature cited above in n. p. 3, n. 5.

[46] For Ambrosius de Vignate, see Kirshner, "Storm over the *Monte*," 257. For the opinion of Alexander de Tartagnis, see *Consilia*, consilium 245 (Venice: Bernardinus de Benalis, 1499, vol. 2, fols. 96r-97v).

[47] "Del Monte di Firenze non c'è ignuno che ne iscriva con più ragione et più sodamente et non se ne inganna, come fanno i più" (*Le vite*, ed. Greco, 2: 135-36; trans. George and Waters in *Renaissance Princes, Popes, and Prelates*, 318). It is worth noting, however, that the collapse of the patrician regime in the early 1430s was precipitated in part by internal divisions over debt and taxation; see Molho, *Florentine Public Finances*, 113-92; and Dale Kent, *The Rise of the Medici: Faction in Florence, 1426-1434* (Oxford: Oxford University Press, 1978), 211-351.

6
The Edition

The edition that follows is based exclusively on Florence, Biblioteca Nazionale Centrale, Fondo principale II, III, 366 (formerly Magliabechiano xxix, 184). I shall refer to this manuscript by the siglum F_1.

A. Description of F_1

(1) Paper 295 x 220 mm.
(2) i + 102 + i leaves, now foliated 1-101.
(3) Collation: i^4 (catchword missing), ii^{10} (*irritandum*), iii^{10} (*puta quia*), iv^{10} (*mandatum*), v^{10} (*nostro*), vi^{10} (*potest per solutionem*), vii^{10} (*tunc distribuetur*), viii^8 (*Vltimo*), ix^{10} (*antecedens patet ex se*), x^{10} (*libris de quibus*), xi^{10}.
(4) Written space ruled with a plummet, one column 210 x 115 mm exclusive of marginalia and glosses.
(5) Italian *littera cursiva* hand, s. xv, autograph of Lorenzo di Antonio Ridolfi.
(6) Titles, rubrics, versals and paragraph marks in red and/or blue, with the exception of the *Questio montis* (Part 3, question 5), where colour is used only on fols. 73r-v and 83r. A red running title in Arabic numerals at the top centre of rectos indicates the *particula*. See also Giuseppe Mazzatinti, *Inventari dei manoscritti delle biblioteche d'Italia*, vol. 10 (Forli: Luigi Bordandini, 1900; repr. Florence: Leo S. Olschki, 1955), 49.

B. Contents of F_1

F_1 contains only the *Tractatus de usuris*, which is distributed as follows:
(1) fols. 1r-4r. "Tabula super secunda particula" (table of the 8 *oppositiones* and 154 *quaestiones* of Part 2).
(2) fols. 5r-10v. "Prima particula" (Part 1: 12 *quaestiones*).
(3) fols. 10r-68r. "Secunda particula" (Part 2: 8 *oppositiones* and 154 *quaestiones*).
(4) fols. 69r-72r. "Tertia particula" (Part 3: 4 *quaestiones*).
(5) fols. 73r-87v. "Questio montis" (=Part 3, question 5).

(6) fols. 87v-101v. "Dicta plurium doctorum in materia montis et glose Laurentii super illis, seu additiones et responsiones ad illa" (appendix reporting and glossing the opinions of five earlier *monte* disputants).
(7) fol. 101v. Colophon.

C. The Status of F_1

F_1 is Ridolfi's autograph. On the assumption that it reflects the author's intentions better than any copy, I have decided against a critical edition that takes into account the readings of the other extant manuscripts. Instead, I have treated F_1 as if it were a *codex unicus*. Such a procedure requires justification.

In the discussion that follows, I refer to extant manuscripts of Ridolfi's works by the following sigla:

C3 = Lorenzo Ridolfi, *Consiliorum liber tertius*. BNF, Fondo principale II, III, 370 (formerly Magliabechiano xxix, 185).[1]

RJ = Lorenzo Ridolfi, *Repertorium iuris*. BNF, Magliabechiano xxix, 171.[2]

Z = Lorenzo Ridolfi, *Zibaldone*. BNF, Panciatichi 147.[3]

Manuscripts of Lorenzo Ridolfi, *Tractatus de usuris*:

A = Augsburg, Staats- und Stadtbibliothek, 2° Cod. Aug. 388, fols. 6r-87r.[4]

F_2 = Florence, Biblioteca Nazionale Centrale, Conventi soppressi 1721, fols. 1ra-102vb.[5]

[1] Description in Mazzatinti, *Inventari* 10: 49.

[2] The hand is a *littera cursiva*, s. xv. See Martino, "Ridolfi," 184, n. 33.

[3] Description in *Indici e Cataloghi*, VII: I *Codici Panciatichiani della r. Biblioteca Nazionale Centrale di Firenze*, vol. 1, fasc. 3 (Rome: Ministero della Pubblica Istruzione, 1891), 229-32.

[4] The hand is a *littera cursiva*, s. xv^2 or xvi^1. See Paul Oskar Kristeller, *Iter Italicum: A Finding List of Uncatalogued or Incompletely Catalogued Humanistic Manuscripts of the Renaissance in Italian and Other Libraries*, vol. 3 (Leiden: E. J. Brill, 1983), 457b.

[5] The hand is a humanist minuscule, s. xv. Provenance: monastery of Santissima Annunziata, Florence. See the manuscript catalogues: *Catalogo dei mss. dei conventi soppressi*, 139; and *Indice dei Manoscritti scelti nelle Bibioteche Monastiche del dipartimento dell'Arno dalla Commissione degli Ogetti d'Arti e Scienze, e dalla medesima rilasciati alla Pubblica Libreria Magliabechiana*, 4.

F_3 = Florence, Biblioteca Medicea Laurenziana, Conventi soppressi 264, fols. 56ra-118vb.[6]

L = Lucca, Biblioteca Capitolare Feliniana, 311, fols. 193ra-249vb.[7]

M_1 = Munich, Bayerische Staatsbibliothek, Clm 7580, fols. 216r-293r.[8]

M_2 = Munich, Bayerische Staatsbibliothek, Clm 26669, fols. 1r-84v.[9]

P = Paris, Bibliothèque nationale, Nouvelles acquisitions latines 1802, fols. 1ra-88rb.[10]

R_1 = Vatican City, Biblioteca Apostolica Vaticana, Palatino lat. 788, fols. 61r-115r.[11]

R_2 = Vatican City, Biblioteca Apostolica Vaticana, Ottoboniano 3335, fols. i-iv, 1r-120v.[12]

R_3 = Vatican City, Biblioteca Apostolica Vaticana, Rossiano 685, fols. 272r-315v.[13]

[6] The hand is a humanist minuscule, s. xv. Provenance: Badia monastery, Florence. See the manuscript catalogue of Franciscus de Furia, *Supplementum alterum ad Catalogum codicum Graecorum, Latinorum, Italicorum etc. Bibliothecae Mediceae Laurentianae*, 1: 1064-65.

[7] The hand is a *littera textualis*, s. xv. The manuscript was copied in Basel in 1438 by Laurentius Zorus de Russia. See the manuscript catalogue of Bernardinus Baronius, *Catalogus antiquae Bibliothecae Illustrissimorum et Reverendissimorum DD. Maioris Lucanae Ecclesiae Canonicorum* (1757), 202-203.

[8] The hand is a *littera cursiva*, s. xv. The manuscript was copied in 1450 by Johannes Franz de Leppheim. Description in Carolus Halm, Georgius Thomas and Gulielmus Meyer, *Catalogus Codicum Latinorum Bibliothecae Regiae Monacensis*, vol. 3, part 3 (Munich: Biblioteca Regia, 1873), 174, entry 1377.

[9] The hand is a *littera cursiva*, s. xv. The manuscript was copied in 1437 by Petrus Hamebach de Nurmberga. Description in Carolus Halm and Gulielmus Meyer, *Catalogus Codicum Latinorum Bibliothecae Regiae Monacensis*, vol. 4, part 4 (Munich: Biblioteca Regia, 1881; repr. Wiesbaden: Otto Harrassowitz, 1969), 201, entry 2192.

[10] The hand is a *littera cursiva*, s. xv. See Kristeller, *Iter Italicum* 3: 275a.

[11] The hand is a *littera textualis*, s. xv. Description in Henry Stevenson and Giovanni Battista de Rossi, *Codices Palatini latini Bibliothecae Vaticanae*, vol. 1 (Vatican City: Typographeum Vaticanum, 1886), 281.

[12] The hand is an Italian *littera cursiva*, s. xv^1. See Martino, "Ridolfi," 187, n. 52.

[13] Two *littera cursiva* hands, s. xv. See Kristeller, *Iter Italicum*, vol. 2 (Leiden: E. J. Brill, 1967), 466b.

R_4 = Vatican City, Biblioteca Apostolica Vaticana, Rossiano 1038, fols. 308r-368r.[14]

W = Vienna, Österreichische Nationalbibliothek, 4139, fols. 71r-172r.[15]

Kristeller reports a fourteenth manuscript of the *Tractatus de usuris* in the library of the Padri Redentoristi of Santa Maria della Fava, Venice, but the inventory kindly sent to me in June 1998 by the superior, Don Luigi Aroffo, does not show a copy of the treatise currently in the collection.[16]

My assessment of F_1's status as the autograph is based on its provenance and on the hand.[17]

The provenance of F_1 provides an important circumstantial argument for its authority. F_1 dates from the early fifteenth century and has been transmitted along with two other manuscripts that originated in Ridolfi's law office: *C3*, a *minutare*, a "minute-book" or register of legal opinions, drafted between 1412 and 1420 and *RJ*, an alphabetical glossary of legal terms entitled *Repertorium iuris*. By the later fifteenth century, all three were part of a collection of legal manuscripts assembled by the Florentine civilian Antonio di Vanni di Francesco Strozzi (1451-1523). Another twenty codices from the collection are preserved in the *Carte Strozziane fondo* of the Archivio di Stato di Firenze.[18] By the seventeenth century, the collection had passed to Carlo di Tommaso Strozzi (1587-1670), whose owner-

[14] The hand is a *littera cursiva*, s. xv. See Kristeller, *Iter Italicum* 2: 467b-468a.

[15] The hand is a *littera cursiva*, s. xv. Provenance: Augustinian convent of Saint George, Hertzberg (?). Description in *Tabulae codicum manu scriptorum praeter graecos et orientales in Bibliotheca palatina Vindobonensi asservatorum*, vol. 3 (Vienna: Caroli Geroldi Filius, 1869; repr. Graz: Akademische Druck- u. Verlagsanstalt, 1965), 178-80.

[16] *Iter Italicum* 2: 291b.

[17] Kirshner ("Reading Bernardino's Sermon," 551, n. 10) and Martino ("Ridolfi," 187, n. 52) both consider F_1 to be the autograph. Martino regards the colophon of F_1 as particularly decisive. The colophon reports the date on which Ridolfi finished the treatise, a dedication to his patron saints and conventional apologies for prolixity (3772-86). It is missing from the other two Florentine manuscripts (F_2 and F_3). An examination of the remaining ten manuscripts, however, reveals that the colophon is attested in three witnesses: *P*, R_2 and *W*. It does not therefore represent decisive evidence for the autographic status of F_1.

[18] ASF, Carte Strozziane, Terza serie, 41/1-20. See *Guida generale degli Archivi di Stato italiani*, vol. 2 (Rome: Ministero per i Beni Culturali e Ambientali, Ufficio Centrale per i Beni Archivistici, 1983), 167-68; and *Le carte Strozziane del r. Archivio di Stato in Firenze, Inventario*, 3 vols. (Florence: Ministero dell'Interno, 1884-91), 3: 168-73. For a discussion of Antonio Strozzi's collection, see Martines, *Lawyers and Statecraft*, 451.

ship is noted on the fly leaf of all three volumes.[19] The association of F_1 with two of Ridolfi's other law books strongly suggests proximity to the author himself, even if it does not prove that it is an autograph.

The argument for the status of F_1 ultimately rests on an evaluation of the hand, which I consider to be identical to that of *C3*, the other roughly contemporary manuscript we know to be in the hand of Ridolfi himself. As Vincenzo Colli observes in his recent essay on the typology of *consilia* collections, *C3* is an autograph minute-book in which we can observe the jurist himself drafting his opinions directly on the page rather than an amanuensis writing to dictation or registering copies of drafts.[20] The typical features of *C3*'s hand can all be observed in the hand of F_1.

What are these features? The hand of both manuscripts is a practised one, accustomed to writing quickly and accurately, but lacking the highly cursive traits seen in most notarial scripts. In general, it exhibits the standard characteristics of an Italian *littera cursiva* of the fourteenth or early fifteenth century: *s* and *f* descend well below the line; the hasts of *b* and *d* are often looped (*l* and *h* usually only in combinations like *ch*, *cl*, *pl*); *a* is written with a single compartment and *g* with an open tail; *e* is written with two strokes and lacks a compartment; terminal *m* often takes the *3* shape and *r* the *2* form. Uncial *m* is common, especially at the beginnings and ends of words, but often in the middle as well. Though rare, the letter *z* (as in *prestanzonibus*) resembles *c*-cedilla (*ç*). Ligatures are common: *dc* (for

[19] F_1, *RJ* and *C3* are listed in the eighteenth-century manuscript inventory by Ferdinando Fossi, *Catalogo dei codici della Libreria Strozziana comparati dopo la morte di Alessandro Strozzi da S.A.R. Pietro Leopoldo Granduca di Toscana e passati alla Pubblica Libreria Magliabechiana* (1789), fols. 18v and 23v. For a description of other volumes from the Strozzi collection now in the BNF, see Martines, *Lawyers and Statecraft*, 451-54. Two miscellanies in the BNF contain legal and diplomatic material by Ridolfi: a collection of model orations, Magliabechiano vi, 134 (formerly Strozzi 185); and a *consilia* collection by various jurists: Magliabechiano xxix, 172 (formerly Strozzi 84).

[20] "*I libri consiliorum*: Note sulla formazione e diffusione delle raccolte di *consilia* dei giuristi dei secoli XIV-XV," in *Consilia im späten Mittelalter*, 228. Mazzatinti also considers *C3* autographic; see *Inventari* 10: 49. As Colli shows, autograph *consilia* are not unknown; for examples, see "I *libri consiliorum*," 227-28. See also the autograph *consilium* of Baldus edited by Julius Kirshner in "Baldus de Ubaldis on Disinheritance: Contexts, Controversies, *Consilia*," *Ius Commune: Zeitschrift für Europäische Rechtsgeschichte* 27 (2000): 186-87; and the manuscripts discussed by Mario Ascheri in "Analecta manoscritta consiliare (1285-1354)," *Bulletin of Medieval Canon Law* 15 (1985): 61-94. Although the hand that I identify as that of Ridolfi predominates, it should be noted that *C3* contains several *consilia* in other hands (see for example, fols. 15r-18v, 34r-39r, 56r-60v, 84r-86r). These are usually annotated by the Ridolfi hand.

example, in the abbreviated form of *dictorum*), *de* and *do* are written with two strokes and are indistinguishable except that the shoulders of *c* and *e* are slightly concave. The letters in the combinations *cr*, *co*, *cu* and *ti* often share a common stroke.

Capitals are more distinctive: *A* is always written with two strokes and resembles a rustic Latin *A* or a Greek lambda (*Λ*); *D*, *E* and *H* have uncial forms; *N* is similar to the Latin *H*, though the connecting bar descends slightly to the right; *I* is always *longa* with a stroke to the left or looped.

Signes de renvoi, marks that indicate where material written in the margin is to be inserted into the text, are common in F_1 and even more so in *C3*, which, as might be expected, includes substantial marginal interpolations and corrections. Ridolfi's *signes de renvoi* are conventional and occur in other medieval manuscripts, but it is notable that he consistently favoured combinations of dots and horizontal strokes, the latter sometimes terminating in bulbs or circles, over the *X* or cross forms and their variations.

The same traits can be observed in *RJ*, which was begun no earlier than 1399.[21] Ridolfi's autograph *zibaldone* (*Z*) contains dated entries from 1379 to 1388, but most were written between 1379 and 1382, when Ridolfi was a student in Florence and Bologna. When allowance is made for the time that separates the manuscripts, the hand, particularly in the capitals, is recognizably that of F_1, while Ridolfi's *ricordi* of his doctorate and first marriage at *Z*, fol. 1r-v, written no earlier than 1388, are identical to the mature hand of F_1 and *RJ*.

A possible objection to my assessment of F_1 is suggested by several errors that we might not expect in an author's own work. These occur most frequently in citations of legal authorities. At twelve places in the sections of the text edited below, Ridolfi offers a corrupt *incipit* (1270, 1499, 1634-35, 2100, 2285-86, 2289, 2464, 3117), refers to the wrong fragment (776, 1859) or even to the wrong compilation (1507, 2283). In my experience, however, such errors are not uncommon in late medieval legal texts, which often contain hundreds of references, many of them cited from memory or

[21] *RJ* opens with an invocation of Christ, the Virgin and "the blessed Jerome, Lawrence, Bernard and Catherine, my patrons, and of all the heavenly court" ("In nomine Yhesu Christi eiusque matris viriginis gloriose, beatorum Jeronimi, Laurentii, Bernardi et Caterine patronorum meorum totiusque celestis curie. Amen" [fol. 1r]). Bernard and Catherine were not Ridolfi's own patron saints, but those of his wife and eldest son Bernardo, who was born in 1399 or 1400. According to Ridolfi's *catasto* declaration of 31 May 1433, Bernardo was then thirty-three (ASF, Catasto 438, fol. 157r), so that he must have been born between 31 May 1399 and 30 May 1400.

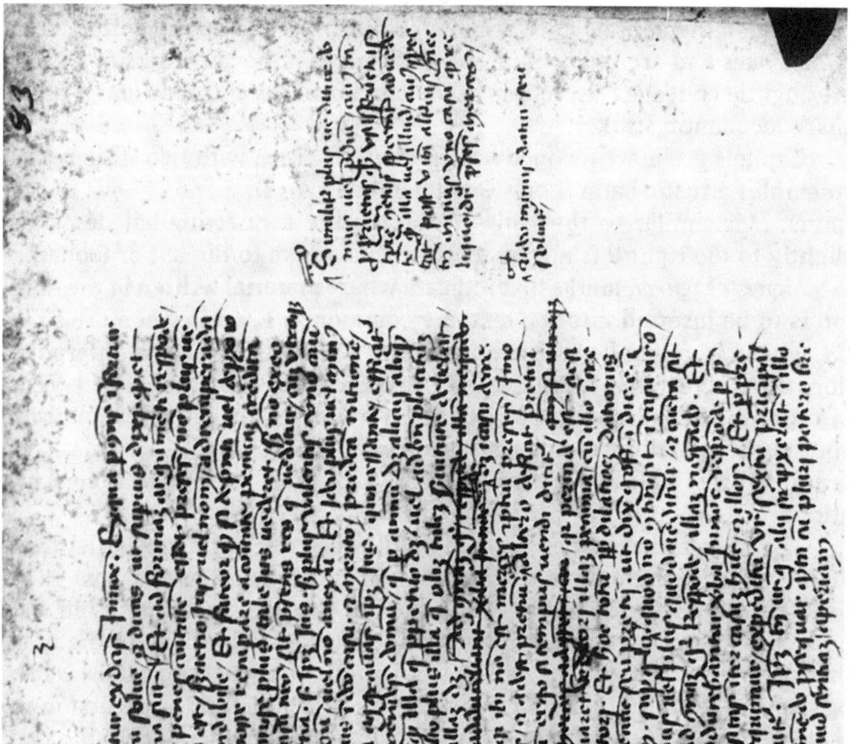

BNF, Fondo principale II, III, 366 (Lorenzo Ridolfi, *Tractatus de usuris*), fol. 83r–detail. (Reproduced with the permission of the Ministero per i Beni e le Attività Culturali della Repubblica Italiana.)

BNF, Fondo principale II, III, 370 (Lorenzo Ridolfi, *Consiliorum liber tertius*), fol. 233r–detail. (Reproduced with the permission of the Ministero per i Beni e le Attività Culturali della Repubblica Italiana.)

at second hand.[22] It is perhaps noteworthy that two-thirds of the citation errors involve Roman law references. For example, at 1499 Ridolfi cites Dig. 2.14.27(28).4 as "Cum unus." A marginal correction in a second hand reads: "alia littera 'Si unus,'" which is, in fact, the correct lemma. However, if the sixteenth-century edition of the text Ridolfi summarizes here is any indication, the corruption may have originated with his source.[23] By contrast, mistakes in citing the canons, with which Ridolfi was presumably more familiar, are relatively trivial.

A more serious objection is presented by apparent examples of homoeoteleuta (1236, 2407, 2572, 2575, 3165, 3297, 3360, 3461). Homoeoteleuton occurs when a copyist reads the second occurrence of a word or phrase in his exemplar as the first, with the result that he omits what comes between.[24] None of these passages, however, can be construed as a true homoeoteleuton since none displays the double occurrence of words or phrases that would mislead a copyist. Instead, they reflect expansions or clarifications on the part of the author as he wrote. A typical example occurs at 3297. At 3281-97, Ridolfi replies to the objection that the sale of *monte* credits resembles the sale of goods on credit by proposing a different analogy. He then begins a dismissal of the critics' conclusion ("Ad consequentiam igitur responde ... "), but decides instead to elaborate on his argument (3300-11). Subsequently, he thinks of yet another analogy, which he writes in the margin with a *signe de renvoi* indicating that it should be inserted after *debet* (3297). Only at 3312 does he pick up his original train of argument and his earlier phrase in order to conclude the *dubium*.[25]

D. The Manuscript Tradition

In my opinion, the identification of F_1 as Ridolfi's autograph is secure, but I have taken the precaution of examining the other twelve extant manuscripts of the *Tractatus de usuris*.

Three copies lack all or part of Part 3: R_3 contains only Parts 1 and 2, while M_1 and M_2 omit the *Questio montis*, Ridolfi's appendix of earlier writers on the *monte* and the colophon. The remaining six manuscripts contain Parts 1-3, but three (A, F_2 and F_3) omit the colophon and all or part of Ridolfi's glosses in the appendix. Only three manuscripts, P, R_2 and W, contain all the elements of the treatise found in F_1.

[22] On the role of memory, see Brundage, *Medieval Canon Law*, 52-53. On the oral character of university law instruction, see Bellomo, *Common Legal Past*, 126-29.

[23] See comm. n. 1499.

[24] For a discussion, see Martin L. West, *Textual Criticism and Editorial Technique* (Stuttgart: E. B. Teubner, 1973), 24-25.

[25] Many similar examples can be found in *C3*: see, for example, 6r, 9r, 12r etc.

Sample collations of Part 1 and the *Questio montis* in F_1 against the other manuscripts do not yield a stemma, but only groups of manuscripts. Of all the manuscripts, R_2 is closest to F_1, indeed, it is almost certainly a copy, as indicated by the scribe's introduction of two marginal corrector's annotations in F_1 into the text itself and by his slavish reproduction of one of F_1's deletions.[26] Neither of the compound readings occurs in the other manuscripts, thus ruling out R_2 as a conduit for the later tradition.

F_2 and F_3 share not only a similarity of hand and Florentine provenance, but a close common ancestor, as indicated by a similar but not identical pattern of errors. Identical structure and distinctive errors, such as "Matheus de Empoli" (or even "Matheus de Neapoli" in R_1) for "Francischus de Empuli," show that *L*, R_1 and R_4 descend from a common ancestor dating from at least 1438, when *L* was copied in Basel. Similarly, an identical structure and common errors show that M_1, datable to 1450, is a copy of M_2, which was itself copied in 1437. The remaining manuscripts cannot be linked directly to any of the other groups: *P* and R_3 appear to stand alone, though *W* and *A* may share a distant common ancestor, indicated by some common errors.

The confusion in the textual tradition suggests that there was extensive contamination at an early stage.

E. Orthography and Format

Because of F_1's authority, I have emended the text only in cases of obvious error. All emendations are noted in the *apparatus criticus*. In the text, angle brackets (⟨ ⟩) indicate an editorial addition and square brackets ([ ]) material that should be suppressed. Punctuation, capitalization and paragraph divisions are editorial.

I have retained F_1's orthography: *e* for the diphthongs *ae* and *oe* the occasional use of *y* for *i* (as in *symilibus*, *archydiaconus*), *comune* and *comunitas* for the classical Latin *commune* and *communitas*, *litera* (*littera*), *glosa* (*glossa*), *michi* (*mihi*), *nichil* (*nihil*), *Francischus* (*Franciscus*), *schandala* (*scandala*), *inhiri* (*iniri*), *contraenda* (*contrahenda*), *prolissum* (*prolixum*), *prontus* (*promptus*) and several cases where classical orthography would lead us to expect an *s*: *scripxi* (*scripsi*), *prescripxit* (*prescripsit*), *exto*

[26] R_2, fol. 16r, reads: ". . .quia tunc non ualet, ut l. alias si unus cum unus § Pacta que turpem . . ." On this marginal notation, see above, p. 120; and comm. n. 1499. At fol. 116r, R_2 has: ". . . minus uel nimis difficile esset ista mutare et subtrahere . . . " This passage, which is not included in the edition, is discussed above, p. 77, n. 92. At 2458, F_1 deletes the words "super sexto dubio principali" after "Clenkoh," all of which R_2 faithfully reproduces (fol. 87r).

(*esto*), *iuxte* (*iuste*), *extimari* (*estimari*) and *extimatio* (*estimatio*).[27] Ridolfi spells the ablative of attributive present participles inconsistently: there are examples such as *in militante iudicio* (*militanti*), *in articulo precedente* (*precedenti*), *ex pacto interueniente* (*interuenienti*), *sine causa subsistente* (*subsistenti*), *de actione competente tibi* (for *competenti*), as well as *in sequenti parte*, *in questione incidenti* or *in dubio sequenti*. I have not corrected or harmonized his usage. I have reproduced the manuscript's ordinal and cardinal numerals, which alternate between Roman and Arabic forms. Some rather eccentric spellings are frequent: *opportet* and *opporteat* (for *oportet*, *oporteat*), *diggeret* (*digeret*), the double *d* and single *m* of *quoddamodo* (*quodammodo*), the pleonastic forms *quicdquam* for *quicquam* and *quidquam*, and *contracxisset* for *contraxisset*. *Tamtum* occurs three times, but the more usual *tantum* is also spelled out in three places: I have chosen to expand the standard abbreviations as *tantum*. I have departed from F_1's orthography in the case of terminal *i longa* (*j*, as in *dispensarj*), which I have transcribed as *i*, and in that of *u* and *v*, which I have rendered as lowercase *u* and uppercase *V*.

I have silently expanded abbreviations in accordance with Ridolfi's normal usage. I make an exception in the case of legal citations, where I follow the prevailing convention among editors of legal texts and leave the sigla and titles of the canon and civil law collections in their abbreviated forms.[28] I have, however, italicized legal titles and lemmata in order to distinguish them from the surrounding text and to prevent confusion. The legal abbreviations *ar.* (*argumentum*, *argumento*, etc.), *R.* (*responsum*, *respondeo*, etc.) and *v.* (*versiculum*, *versiculo*, *verbo*, etc.) have been silently expanded as seemed appropriate in the context. It should be noted that the citation is given in the ablative case (in the sense of "at" or "in"), unless dependent on a previous ablative, when it is read as a genitive.[29] In other respects, Ridolfi's usage and syntax are typical of medieval, particularly scholastic, texts.[30]

[27] Similar examples can be found in other contemporary Latin manuscripts of Italian origin. On spelling in the circle of Salutati and Bruni at the beginning of the fifteenth century, see Baron's introduction to his edition of Bruni's *Laudatio florentinae urbis*, in *From Petrarch to Leonardo Bruni*, 219-23.

[28] Stephan Kuttner, "Notes on the Presentation of Text and Apparatus in Editing Works of the Decretists and Decretalists," *Traditio* 15 (1959): 457.

[29] On this, see Hermann Kantorowicz, "Citations in the Later Middle Ages (1935)," trans. W. H. Bryson, in *Dictionary of Sigla and Abbreviations to and in Law Books Before 1607*, ed. W. H. Bryson (Charlottesville: University Press of Virginia, 1975), 3-16, esp. 5-6.

[30] On usage and sentence structure in medieval Latin, see A. George Rigg, "Morphology and Syntax," in *Medieval Latin: An Introduction and Bibliographical*

The headings in angle brackets at the beginnings of the various subdivisions of the text are derived as follows: for Part 1, from the list of *quaestiones* at F_1 fol. 5r (32-39); for Part 2, from the table of *oppositiones* and *quaestiones* at F_1, fols. 1r-4r; for the *Questio montis* from the list of *dubia* at F_1, fol. 73v (2246-63).

F. UNEDITED QUESTIONS

As I remarked earlier, Ridolfi conceived of the *Tractatus de usuris* as a comprehensive digest of legal opinion on usury.[31] Of the 179 *quaestiones* and *oppositiones* into which he divided the treatise, the present edition includes only thirty-nine: I have omitted the remaining 140 *quaestiones* of Parts 2 and 3 because they have no direct relevance to the *monte* controversy. Though beyond the scope of the present study, this material is nevertheless of interest to students of the usury prohibition in general and a complete edition of it is desirable. In the meantime, a brief description of the unedited material is in order if only to clarify the nature of the broader project Ridolfi set himself.

In the prologue to the treatise, Ridolfi indicates that Part 2 deals with "the matter of usury in general" (27-28), revisiting several topics raised in a preliminary way in Part 1. The organization of Part 2 is not entirely systematic, which is due to the fact that the material and indeed many of the questions themselves—as the portions edited below (670-2182) indicate—are largely derived from earlier authors. Ridolfi's usual procedure is to review the opinions on a given topic and where there is no consensus to indicate his preferred solution.

Ridolfi dedicates several questions and sequences of questions to usurious or potentially usurious contracts. Qq. 19-20 examine commercial partnerships. Agreements that may conceal usury are reviewed in qq. 21-23 (agricultural contracts), qq. 27-31 and 45-46 (speculative sales and loans). Q. 24 examines whether a merchant may claim compensation under the title of *lucrum cessans*. Q. 25 asks whether it is usurious to charge for transporting specie, and q. 26 whether a moneychanger may licitly charge a percentage on exchange transactions. Qq. 32-33 distinguish between renting and lending money. Qq. 34-42 review loans in which a favour of some sort is a condition of credit.[32] Q. 43 considers whether it is licit to buy cheap and sell dear. Qq. 47-48 ask whether the guarantor of a debtor or a citizen seized by a foreign city because of his government's debt can sue for

---

Guide, ed. Frank A. C. Mantello and A. George Rigg (Washington, DC: Catholic University of America Press, 1996), 83-92.

[31] See above, p. 1.

[32] On q. 35, see comm. n. 740-42.

usury paid on money borrowed to settle such obligations.[33] Two sequences of questions, 49-54, 64-66, review exceptions to the rule that the fruits of pledges must be applied to the reduction of the principal.[34] Q. 55 reviews opinions on the licitness of usuring an enemy.[35] Qq. 60-61 consider when compulsory resale clauses and q. 67 when penal clauses are presumed to be in fraud of usury.[36] Q. 119 asks whether a seller in delay is responsible for usury paid by the buyer.

Restitution is a major theme of Part 2. Q. 44 asks whether a usurer must restore not only usuries themselves but profits he acquired by means of them. Qq. 56-59 consider the liability of corporate bodies, factors, notaries and usurers' families for the restitution of usury.[37] Ten questions, 68-77, examine whether a usurers' property, that of his heirs or those who otherwise come into possession of it is exposed to suits for restitution of usury by the usurer's debtors. Q. 78 asks if a debtor can release his creditor from the obligation to make restitution, and q. 80 if a general acquittance of obligations includes the obligation to restore usury.[38] Qq. 79, 82-88, 116-118 and 120 discuss standards of proof in actions for restitution brought against usurers or their heirs.

A related topic is that of usurers' testaments. The Second Council of Lyons ruled that even if a usurer provided for restitution in his testament, he would be denied burial until his heirs made satisfaction or unless he himself had previously furnished guarantees of full restitution. Qq. 89-100 review the formalities that must accompany the redaction of a usurer's will and the reception of guarantees, and qq. 103 and 106 deal with the validity of the testaments of relapsed usurers. Qq. 101, 107-109 and 115 discuss the disposal of compensation intended for a usurer's unknown victims (*incerti*), qq. 110-113 whether restitution is due to foreigners or enemies. Qq. 102 and 104-105 discuss the burial of occult and notorious usurers. Q. 121 asks whether a usurer's pious legacies are invalid.

Usurers often required debtors to swear not to seek restitution or to denounce them as usurers, topics dealt with in qq. 62, 63, 81, 122-129 and 136-137.[39] Q. 114 considers the proper judicial venue for usury cases, and qq. 130-131 and 133-135 judicial interventions in actions involving usury,

[33] On q. 47, see comm. n. 490-94.

[34] On qq. 49-50, see comm. n. 485-89; on 51-54, see comm. nn. 524-32 and 3172-76.

[35] On q. 55, see comm. n. 638-40.

[36] On q. 60, see comm. n. 1816-39.

[37] On q. 56, see comm. n. 2810-34.

[38] On q. 78, see comm. n. 1627-39.

[39] On q. 62, see comm. n. 994-97; on q. 81, see comm. n. 1502-13.

such as the execution of a usurer's will in a secular court. X 5.19.14 forbade a usurer to sue a creditor for restitution unless he himself first repaid money he extorted from his own debtors; qq. 132 and 138-147 review the procedural issues. Q. 148 considers whether governments who authorize public usurers to charge minimal rates of interest fall under the prohibition of the Council of Vienne. Qq. 149-153 discuss the powers of a court to compel a usurer or a suspected usurer to open his books to inspection. Q. 154 asks whether a usurer may witness a testament.

If Part 2 examines usury in general, Part 3 reviews five "special" (*in specie* 28) cases of particular relevance to the Florentine merchant and banking sectors. Of these, the public debt receives the most elaborate treatment in the *Questio montis*, which is the fifth and final question of Part 3.

In the first of the remaining questions of Part 3, Ridolfi examined *cambium ad Venetias*, or "dry exchange," a short-term speculative deposit in which the lender's profit depended on the prevailing rate of exchange between Florence and Venice at maturity. The contract was cast as a bill of exchange, though no funds were actually transferred. Since exchange rates generally favoured the lender, he could anticipate a profit of about seven percent. Ridolfi concluded that the transaction was not a loan in the strict sense but nevertheless cautioned against it.[40]

The second question discusses *retrangula* or *baroccolum*, a three-cornered transaction involving one or possibly two loans. In Ridolfi's example, a *retrangulator* bought cloth on credit from a merchant for five hundred florins payable in a year. The *retrangulator* in turn lent 450 florins to a third party who agreed to settle the *retrangulator*'s debt of five hundred with the merchant at term. The difference of ten percent represented the *retrangulator*'s profit. Ridolfi considered the contract usurious, at least as far as the *retrangulator* was concerned. Whether the transaction was illicit on the part of the merchant depended on whether there was doubt about the future value of the cloth.[41]

Ridolfi devoted the third question of Part 3 to *securitas*, which denoted either a loan guarantee for which the guarantor charged a percentage of the debt or an agreement insuring commercial cargo, in which the insurer assumed the risk for a percentage of the cargo's value. Ridolfi considered

[40] On the contract, see de Roover, "*Cambium ad Venetias*," 239-59. De Roover discusses the judgements of the lawyers and theologians at 250-57, and Ridolfi's views at 252-53.

[41] The contract was also scrutinized by the *Offitiales super illicitis contractibus*, a commission of the *Mercanzia* established by a communal provision of 27 August 1414; see ASF, Provvisioni, Registri 103, fols. 50v-51v; and ASF, Mercanzia 19, fols. 1r-4v. I wish to thank Luca Boschetto for bringing this material to my attention.

both contracts licit because neither was a loan and because in each case the guarantor assumed the risk of loss or default.

The fourth question considers the activities of *accaffinantes*, who appear to have been brokers who recruited mercenaries (*stipendiarii*) on behalf of the government. Ridolfi considered the fee *accaffinantes* charged per lance (*lancea*) legitimate compensation for their labour, but not the expense advances they often supplied to the mercenaries, which took the form of ordinary loans at interest.

The last element of the treatise that I have excluded from the edition is the appendix of earlier *monte* disputants Ridolfi appends to the *Questio montis*. Ridolfi summarizes and glosses five texts: the *Questio de monte* of Francesco da Empoli, *consilia* on the debt by Guido de Belloreguardo and John Klenkock, an anonymous *Tractatus super casu de monte communi* and a *quaestio disputata* on the Sienese public debt by an anonymous canonist. As was noted earlier, two of these have been edited: the *Tractatus super casu de monte communi* has been edited from this manuscript and attributed to Piero degli Strozzi by Julius Kirshner, and I have recently published a critical edition of Francesco da Empoli based on independent witnesses.[42] The three remaining texts are of interest because of the light they shed on the fourteenth-century debt controversy. Ridolfi cites Guido de Belloreguardo's *consilium* extensively, and I have summarized it above and in the commentary. It is to be hoped that independent manuscript witnesses of Guido's *consilium* and that of Klenkock can be located and critically edited. I have unfortunately been unable to attribute the remaining *quaestio*.

G. The Venice Edition of 1584

The *Tractatus de usuris* was printed several times in the late fifteenth and sixteenth centuries.[43] Of these editions, the one most widely cited by scholars is that included in the *Tractatus universi iuris* printed in Venice in 1584.[44] The portions of Ridolfi's text edited below correspond to fols. 15ra-21va and 38va-43rb of this edition.

There are several reasons for replacing the Venice edition with a modern one. One is accessibility. Like most early-modern editions of scholastic texts, the Venice edition uses many abbreviations and lacks an *apparatus fontium* in the modern fashion, features that make the text difficult for non-specialists to use.

But the most compelling rationale for a new edition is accuracy. Early-modern publishers rarely had the resources or the inclination to obtain the

[42] See above, pp. 70-71, nn. 67, 68.

[43] For a list of editions before 1500, see Martino, "Ridolfi," 187, n. 52.

[44] *Tractatus universi iuris* (Venice, 1584), vol. 7, fols. 15ra-50rb.

best exemplars of the texts they printed with the result that their editions are often marred by omissions, errors and mistaken conjectures. The Venice edition is no exception. It is unclear what manuscripts or editions the printer depended on, but even a superficial reading of the text reveals that it is marred by many errors. As is usually the case, some, such as minor changes of tense or mood, or the substitution of a more commonly used word for an exotic one, are relatively trivial and do not critically affect the interpretation of the text. Others, however, seriously obscure Ridolfi's meaning. As the autograph, F_1 obviously represents a superior version.

A few examples of the different kinds of error in the Venice 1584 edition drawn from Part 1 and the *Questio montis* will illustrate the superiority of F_1.[45] The lemma followed by a square bracket represents F_1's reading.

6 pulsatus] pulsantes
7-8 animarum] animorum
8 comuni ... conscientie] communique et conscientiae
11 ineuntur] iniungitur
15 intrare] intentare
16 disposui] dispositioni
16 usurarum] usurariorum
27 .cliiii.^{or}] 155
48 uero] notat
66 usurarius] usura
78 *Debitores*] *Creditores*
84 resonat] reformata
87 species] spes
104 aliquando^1] ad invicem
116 mutuaturus] mutuatus
116 dilectione] dilatione
142 ductus] dicturus
158 cum ... finali] *om.*
162 tamquam ... mutuo] *om.*
175 profecto] perfecto
189 futurum] facturum
193 uolitio] *om.*
212 patri] patris
224 preintentum] propter intentionem
243 magister] magistri
248 mutuaui] mutuanti
274 stricte] obscure
280 mutuaturus] mutuatur
302 contrarium] contrariorum
305 gratis] gratia
320 genitum] gentium
321 gignitur] speratur
321 prauam] paruam
370 uel quasi mora] *om.*
378-79 et Ostiensis ... rubrica] *om.*
385 securitatem] caritatem
386 minora] timore
399 de sui natura] *om.*
402 euagemur] euagemus
409 idcirco] ideo cito
429 extrinsecis] intrinsecis
432 ualorem] uigorem
450 locabilibus] localibus
462 disputantem] disputationem
481 permicatatur] mittatur
483 dicebat] inducebat

[45] For a complete collation of my edition against the Venice 1584 text, see Lawrin Armstrong, "The *Tractatus de materia montis* of Lorenzo Ridolfi: Edited from Florence, Biblioteca Nazionale Centrale, Fondo Principale II, III, 366" (PhD thesis, University of Toronto, 1996), 509-40, appendix 2.

567 subuentio] subuentionis
578 *Mouet*] *Monet*
597 ecclesiam] ecclesiasticam
601 pro parum] perperam
603 trutinandum] aestimandum
607 misterio] ministerio
614 uolentem] valentem
616 conseruas] confirmas
617 aufers] auferes

2192-93 egregius decretorum] Gregorius de Cremona
2198 cuilibet] quilibet
2203-4 aliquando non in totum] *om.*
2211 dampnis] damni
2218 teneatur] teneantur
2224 renouata] reuocatum
2225 singulorum] singulis
2237 alienare] alienari
2245 schaturiunt] oriuntur
2246 indici] induci
2303 dari] denari
2305-6 uerisimile] uerissime
2345 pecuniarium] pecuniarum
2345 personale] personarum
2377 conscito] constituto
2379 media] medici
2439 offenditur] ostenditur
2441 media] medica
2492 Augustinus] Ange.
2496 statuit] statuti
2571 prelibatis pensatis] praelibati census
2597 affectus] effectus
2598 affectu] effectu
2602 remunerationis] remuneratio
2604 impenditur] impeditur
2612 comunitas] communitatis
2641 fore] forte
2648 motus] mutuans
2655 amore] morte
2674 omnitenus] omittemus
2714 accattonibus] taxationibus
2755 ueritati] seueritati
2759 doctior] deterior
2823 concernens] concurrentes
2827 *Postulastis*] *Pastoralis*
2838 prestanzonibus] protestationibus
2839 ullatenus] nullatenus
2848 uiolentata] uiolentia
2886 augmenti] argumenti
2914 respectu] respecti
2985 conscientiam] conscientia
2985 infirmitas] infirmatur
3007-8 contritione] conditione
3078 auctori suo] suo creditori
3103 mouentur] mutuantur
3122 scit] sic
3177 tollitur] colligitur
3210 causatum] causam
3332 huius] istud
3337 tormentum] incrementum
3343-4 examinatio ... nec] *om.*
3353 a parte comunitatis quam] *om.*
3379 nuncupare] *om.*
3513 cedo] credo
3556 subsistentis] subsequentis
3566 Archydiaconum] Areti.
3714 resolutorium] resultorium

Lorenzo Ridolfi

Tractatus de usuris

Florence, Biblioteca Nazionale Centrale
Fondo Principale II, III, 366
fols. 5r-23r, 73r-87v, 101v

⟨TRACTATUS DE USURIS⟩

5r Prima particula

Tractatus de usuris editus a Laurentio de Ridolfis de Florentia incipit in nomine Iesu Christi eiusque matris dulcissime uirginis gloriose beatorumque Ieronimi et Laurentii. Amen.

Plurimorum aures crebro pulsatus eloquio atque, ut inter beniuolos fieri adsolet, importuna deuictus instantia, quatenus pro conciuium animarum salute comuni, que iuri, que conscientie consona ⟨sunt⟩ in materia montis comunitatis nostre atque, ut illorum uerbo utar, cambia, securitates, accaffinitates, retrangulas et baroccola, que per quosdam cotidie ineuntur, aperire deberem, en colla, ut decet, subire decreui illorumque potius uoluntatibus non sine tremore atque timore rationabili annuere, attenta materie grauitate uiriumque mearum imbecillitate, quam cum pertinacia resistere, nam etsi hoc securius, illud urbanius. Et ex quo talem opportet intrare materiam ad saturitatem est animus sicque disposui omnia occurrentia circa usurarum uoraginem explanare ut sic in modum summe hac tota conglutinata materia huc ualeam, cum dabitur, habere recursum.

Pro cuius quidem expeditione, deliberaui michi in repetitionem pro fundamento assummere decretalem *Consuluit, de usuris*.[1] Descendamus ergo ad illam et quantum pertinet ad eius intellectum dumtaxat tamquam preambulam ad infra principaliter dicenda cum aliquibus textualibus una cum apparatu suo simpliciter expediamus; deinde ad uniuersalem usurarum materiam descendemus. Et in tres particulas tractatum nostrum diuidemus, quarum una duodecim continens questiones in modum summe applicabitur rubro, due alie nigro. Sed harum prima octo continens oppositiones et .cliiii.^{or} questiones tractabit usurarum materiam in genere; secunda uero in spetie quinque principales diggeret questiones quantum pertinet ad cambia, securitates, accaffinitates, retrangulas et baroccola montisque materiam, quam quidem .viii. principalibus dubiis explicabo.

1 TRACTATUS DE USURIS *ed.*
28 in spetie *in marg. sin. add.*

[1] X 5.19.10

Prius igitur circa rubricam de aliquibus uideamus iuxta promissa. Et primo, quid sit usura? Secundo, unde dicatur. .3.º, in quibus commictatur. .4.º quot sint eius speties. .v.º, ex quibus causis ueniat. .vi.º, qualiter petatur. .vii.º, quare prohibeatur et utrum sit naturaliter uitiosa. .viii.º, utrum ullo casu permictatur. .ix.º, utrum mutuo recipere ad usuram sit peccatum. .x.º, utrum dispensari possit ut quis sine peccato ualeat fenerari. .xi.º, quomodo quis usurarius detegatur. .xii.º, que sit eorum pena.

.i. questio ⟨Quid sit usura?⟩

Ad primum dic quod usura est lucrum ex mutuo pacto debitum uel exactum; ita describit Innocentius in c. .i. infra eodem[2] et Iohannes Andree ibidem[3] et in questione posita super regula *Peccatum, de reg. iuris* li. .vi.[4] Alii dicunt quod usura est "quicquid sorti accedit." Hec ponitur in textu in c. *Plerique* .xiiii. q. .iii.[5] et repetitur in dicta regula *Peccatum*. Sed quia ista descriptio nimis nuda uidetur, ideo dixit Gofredus[6] quod tu debes addere hec uerba, scilicet "intentione precedente uel pacto." Ostiensis uero in summa eodem titulo § .i.[7] dicit quod usura est "quodcumque solutioni rei mutuate accedit ipsius rei usus gratia pactione interposita
5v / uel hac intentione habita in contractu uel exactione habita ex post facto." Alii dicunt, scilicet reuerendus pater frater Gregorius de Arimino, sacre theologie magister summus et ordinis sui heremitarum prior generalis, in questione per eum formata super monte comunitatis Venetiarum,[8] quod "usura est lucrum ex mutuo intentum." Alii quod usura est

32 Notantur questiones prime particule *in marg. sin. not. al. man.*
40 .i. questio *in marg. sin.*
50 in contractu uel exactione habita *in marg. add.*

[2] Innocent IV (Sinibaldus Fliscus), *Commentaria super libros quinque Decretalium*, ad X 5.19.1, n.1 (ed. Frankfurt 1570, repr. 1968, fol. 516rb).

[3] Johannes Andreae, *In quinque Decretalium libros novella commentaria*, ad X 5.19.1, n.2 (ed. Venice 1581, repr. 1963, V fol. 72rb).

[4] Idem, *In titulum de regulis iuris novella commentaria* (=*Quaestiones mercuriales*), ad VI *de reg. iur.* 4, *Peccatum*, n.7 (ed. Venice 1581, repr. 1963, fol. 62va-b).

[5] Decretum Grat. C.14 q.3 c.3

[6] Gottofredo da Trani (Goffredus Tranensis), *Summa super titulis Decretalium*, X 5.19 *de usuris*, n.1 (ed. Lyons 1519, repr. Darmstadt 1968, p. 438b).

[7] Hostiensis (Henricus de Segusio), *Summa aurea*, X 5.19 *de usuris*, n.1 (ed. Venice 1574, repr. 1963, cols. 1612-13).

[8] Gregory of Rimini, *Tractatus de imprestantiis Venetorum et de usura*, art.1 (ed. Reggio Emilia 1508, fol. A7r).

lucrum ex mutuo principaliter intentum. Et sic habemus sex descriptiones. Nunc uideamus quenam melior.

Et dico quod licet aliqui reprobent primam et potissimum dictus magister Gregorius ex eo quia non conuenit omni contento subdiffinito quia, absque omni pactione uel exactione lucri exterius expressa, per solam intentionem uel spem lucri ex mutuo usura contrahitur et ad restitutionem obligatio. Nichilominus puto quod unaqueque sane intelligendo saluari possit, et sic dicere urbanius est, nec est credendum tot et tantos doctores illam hactenus sequutos tantum errasse. Vnde dico quod Innocentius et alii sic describentes habuerunt respectum ad usuram ueram siue propriam, non autem ad quasi usuram, sicut appellatur mentalis, ut patet in hac decretali *Consuluit*,[9] ibi "quasi usurarius" et cetera. Quod equidem ex ipsorum uerbis colligitur manifeste cum post dictam descriptionem subdidit idem Innocentius[10] et cum eo ibidem Iohannes Andree[11] et dominus meus Iohannes de Lignano,[12] sic: "nam si gratis aliquid detur, non est usura nisi spes adsit" et cetera. Et clarius id explicat dictus dominus meus in c. finali infra eodem titulo.[13]

Posset etiam dici quod includit etiam mentalem usuram talis descriptio, late et generaliter intelligendo uerbum illud "exactum" in descriptione positum ut dicas "exactum," scilicet ore uel corde. Et similiter dici posset de debito ex pacto. Et non intelligas ideo dici "debitum" quia efficaciter sit debitum nam, etsi obligatio oriatur, est tamen exceptione elidibilis, nisi interueniat iuramentum, *de iureiuran.*, *Ad nostram* .i.[14] et c. *Debitores*.[15] Quod prosequere ut in c. finali per dominum meum.

Secunda descriptio, etsi sit clarior ex additis per Gofredum, tamen ea intentione ipsam formatam fuisse per gloriosum Ambrosium credendum est, cui concordat quod in c. et in § finali eiusdem questionis dicitur.[16] Quam prosequere una cum tertia ut scribit Gofredus in summa eodem titulo circa principium.[17]

.4.ª descriptio, que fuit Ostiensis in idem, resonat cum precedente, de cuius intellectu uideamus pro ipsius et aliarum introductione

[9] X 5.19.10

[10] Innocent IV, *Commentaria*, ad X 5.19.1, n.1 (ed. cit. fol. 516rb).

[11] Johannes Andreae, *Novella*, ad X 5.19.1, n.2 (ed. cit. V fol. 72rb).

[12] John of Legnano, *Commentaria in Decretales*, ad X 5.19.1 (Florence, Biblioteca Medicea-Laurenziana, Edili 54, fol. 95r).

[13] Ibid., ad X 5.19.19 (MS cit. fol. 99v).

[14] X 2.24.7

[15] X 2.24.6

[16] Decretum Grat. C.14 q.3 c.4 et dictum Grat. post c.4

[17] Gottofredo da Trani, *Summa*, X 5.19 *de usuris*, n.1 (ed. cit. pp. 438b-439a).

pleniori.[18] "Quodcumque" ergo ideo in illa dicitur quia siue sit pecunia siue species siue fructus siue quoduis aliud ex quo ultra sortem exigis usura est, .xiiii. q. .iii. *Vsura*[19] et c. *Plerique.*[20] "Solutioni rei mutuate" ideo subditur quia in contractu mutui tantum locum habet secundum Gofredum[21] et Raymundum[22] et omnes. Sed tu iunge secundum Ostiensem "regulariter," est enim dare casus in quibus auctoritate legis usure prestantur, licet nullum mutuum sit contractum secundum Ostiensem, qui hoc prosequitur in summa eodem titulo § .i. et § *Pro quibus.*[23] "Ipsius rei usus gratia" ideo annectitur quia si non gratia usus, id est consumptionis, sed loco pene apponeretur sine fraude aliud esset, ut patet supra *de arbi., Dilecti*[24] et .xii. q. .ii. *Fraternitas*[25] secundum Ostiensem,[26] secundum quem inter usuram et penam talis est differentia, quoniam usura prestatur ratione spatii temporis, C. eodem aut. *Ad hec,*[27] sed pena non prestatur secundum spatium alicuius temporis sed secundum quod inter partes conuentum est et ut pactum seruetur, infra *de penis, Constitutus.*[28] Vel sic pena prestatur, quia non fit quod conuenit uel quia non soluitur quod debetur, supra *de arbi., Dilecti.*[29] Sed usura prestatur ut sors non
6r soluatur / sed sortis solutio differatur, infra eodem *Consuluit.*[30] Vnde usura et pena aliquando uidentur contrarie, immo aliquando usura excludit penam, C. *de iur. do. impe.* l. .ii.,[31] quandoque ipsum debitum, ff. *depositi, Si hominem* § *Quotiens*[32] secundum Gofredum[33] et Ostiensem in

[18] Hostiensis, *Summa*, X 5.19 *de usuris*, n.1 (ed. cit. cols. 1613-14).

[19] Decretum Grat. C.14 q.3 c.4

[20] Decretum Grat. C.14 q.3 c.3

[21] Gottofredo da Trani, *Summa*, X 5.19 *de usuris*, n.2 (ed. cit p. 439b).

[22] Raymond of Penyafort, *Summa de poenitentia et matrimonio cum glossis Ioannis de Friburgo (recte* Guillelmi Redonensis), 2.7 *de usuris* n.1 (ed. Rome 1603, repr. Farnborough 1967, p. 227b).

[23] Hostiensis, *Summa*, X 5.19 *de usuris*, nn.1 et 4 (ed. cit. cols. 1613, 1615).

[24] X 1.43.4

[25] Decretum Grat. C.12 q.2 c.11

[26] Hostiensis, *Summa*, X 5.19 *de usuris*, n.1 (ed. cit. col. 1613).

[27] Excerptum Nov. 34.1 = Auth. 36 coll. 4.5 post C. 4.32.16.

[28] X 5.37.7

[29] X 1.43.4

[30] X 5.19.10

[31] C. 8.33(34).2

[32] Dig. 16.3.7.2

[33] Gottofredo da Trani, *Summa*, X 5.19 *de usuris*, n.2 (ed. cit. p. 439b).

summa eodem titulo.[34] "Pactione interposita uel hac intentione habita in contractu uel exactione habita ex post facto" ideo concluditur quia si, nullo pacto ab initio interueniente nec exactione ex post facto habita, debitor aliquid gratis offerret, recipi posset sine aliquo peccato, dummodo mala intentione ab initio caruisset; nullam enim maculam oblatio suscipienti ingerit et cetera, .i. q. .ii. *Sicut episcopum*.[35] Quod intellige: si hac intentione principaliter ductus est mutuans ad mutuandum, aliter non mutuaturus, quo casu etsi non in militante saltem in triumphante iudicio censendus est usurarius in effectu et induci debet ad restitutionem. Exto quod non sic si aliter mutuaturus ex dilectione uel caritate secundario spero aliquam retributionem, secundum Ostiensem ubi supra, cui etiam concordat Gofredus, de quo infra latius dicam.[36] Ideo bene dixit sexto et ultimo describens quod usura est "lucrum ex mutuo principaliter intentum," quasi dicat secus si secundario intendatur.[37]

Nolo tamen sub silentio preterire quod ubi supra post Ostiensem dixi quod non commictitur usura ubi nullum pactum uel exactio interuenit, dummodo mala intentione ab initio caruerit mutuans.[38] Ego firmiter assero quod etiam si ab initio mala caruit intentione sed illam habuit ex post facto, quod idem erit acsi illam ab initio habuisset. Et hoc idem puto fuisse de mente Ostiensis et credo quod intellexerit de mala intentione ab initio, hoc est que fuit primaria causa mutuandi, ut sic differat a secundaria, quam supra dixit non esse peccatum,[39] non autem quod uoluerit notare differentiam inter spem malam habitam tempore mutui et spem malam habitam post mutuum factum, penitendo de bona quam habuit tempore mutui, proponendo in corde suo nunc quod non mutuaret nec mutuum consistere pateretur nisi speraret usuram. Pro quo que super uerbo "intentum" scripxit dictus reuerendus magister Gregorius in dicta sua questione,[40] ubi uidetur his concordare et statim ponam. Sed in quibusdam nimis late loquitur. Vnde sciendum quod dictus reuerendus magister Gregorius indistincte firmat usuram commicti siue quis primario, hoc est aliter non mutuaturus, siue secundario, hoc est aliter nichilominus ex caritate mutuaturus ducatur ad mutuandum sub spe aliqua lucri, contra comunem opinionem glosarum et doctorum, de qua supra dixi et infra repetam in prima oppositione ad textum.[41] Et quia hec

[34] Hostiensis, *Summa*, X 5.19 *de usuris*, n.1 (ed. cit. col. 1613).
[35] Decretum Grat. C.1 q.2 c.4
[36] See below, 696-714.
[37] See above, 54-55.
[38] See above, 107-20.
[39] See above, 108-12.
[40] Gregory of Rimini, *Tractatus*, art. 1 (ed. cit. fols. A6r-B1v).
[41] See above, 61-63; see below, 696-714.

medullam tangunt decretalis nostre ⟨*Consuluit*⟩[42] et eorum propter que principaliter ductus sum ad scribendum, non sit labos in his paulisper insistere. Videamus ergo dicta et rationes quibus mouetur et expediamus suam descriptionem, que fuit penultima in ordine.

Dicebat ergo dictus magister quod "usura est lucrum ex mutuo intentum." "Lucrum" ideo dicitur quia lucrum proprie dicitur superhabundantia siue incrementum quod quis habet ex uoluntaria commutatione ultra ea que prius sua erant, iuxta ea que scribit Philosophus ⟨libro⟩ .v. *Ethycarum* capitulo .vii.[43] Et ita ponitur in proposito, scilicet pro genere et quatenus genus est, quia omnis usura lucrum est sed non conuertitur, quia non omne lucrum est usura. Primum patet, si enim quis tantumdem recipiat et non plus, sicut non recipit lucrum, sic neque usuram. Rursus, si plus quis recipiat quam mutuauerit, si tamen tale receptum non sit ei lucrum, utputa quia aliter erat ipsius recipientis, pone depositarius, raptor uel aliter debitor mutuantis, recepto prius mutuo, reddit cum mutuo depositum uel rem raptam aut aliter debitam, etiam non aliter, nisi ille mutuasset redditurus, non equidem dicendus est usuram recipere. Ad
6v hoc *de usuris* c. .i. in fine cum ibi notatis in glosa finali;[44] / et uide quod infra dicam parte .ii. questione .xlii.[45] Secundum etiam clare patet quia in contractu uenditionis, locationis et conductionis et similibus est dare lucrum et non tamen est usura. Ideo in diffinitione subditur "ex mutuo" tamquam differentia distinguens usuram a lucris que non ex mutuo acquiruntur, nam ille proprie loquendo non dicuntur usure, iuxta notata in c. *In ciuitate* eodem titulo.[46] Similiter, si pure et gratis aliquid donetur, usura non commictitur.

Circa quod quero hic incidenter utrum possit sine uitio usurarum ex mutuo lucrum percipi seu quid est necessarium ad hoc ut non dicatur quis aliquid recipiens ultra sortem mutuatam usuram commictere et sic tale lucrum non esse usuram.

Respondeo quod ⟨si⟩ pure, gratis, sine ulla pactione, intentione ac expectatione lucri quis mutuet et quod dans, licet propter mutuum sibi

159 parte ii. *in marg. add.*
166 Incidens questio *in marg. sin. not.*

[42] X 5.19.10

[43] Aristotle, *Ethica Nicomachea* 5.4.1132b10-15, translatio Roberti Grosseteste, recensio recognita, ed. Renatus Antonius Gauthier in *Aristoteles Latinus*, vol. XXVI, fasc. 4 (Leiden and Brussels, 1973), 461.

[44] X 5.19.1; gl. ord. ad X 5.19.1, v. *Beneficium* (ed. Lyons 1584, col. 1733).

[45] F_1 fols. 29v-30v; *TUI* 7, fol. 24ra.

[46] Gl. ord. ad X 5.19.6, v. *Ex tali forma* (ed. cit. cols. 1736-37).

factum det, aliter non daturus, pretendat non consideratione mutui sed ex amicitia tantum se dare et liberaliter donare, et qui mutuauit credat ipsum simpliciter donare et datum uelut simpliciter donatum recipiat, his profecto concurrentibus, lucrum ex mutuo sine usura percipitur nec ad illius restitutionem quis tenetur, quamdiu stat in eo talis credulitas nec apparet unde oppositum rationabiliter ipse credere debeat. Ideo in descriptione sequitur "intentum," ad hoc enim ut lucrum ex mutuo sit usura requiritur quod mutuans intendat illud lucrum ex mutuo recipere, quam intentionem siue antecedenter habuerit, quia uidelicet quando mutuauit, siue postea ante receptionem lucri spem uel intentionem lucri percipiendi ex mutuo habuit, siue concomitanter et simul habeat intentionem recipiendi lucrum ex suo mutuo. Cum tale lucrum sibi datur, profecto tale lucrum usura est et talis usurarius est censendus in animarum iudicio. Et quod predicta sint uera, scilicet quod habens ante receptionem talem intentionem, si lucrum deinde percipiat sit usurarius, et idem similiter, si nulla talis precessit intentio, adfuit tamen dum lucrum receptum est declaro. Pone nullum intendebat mutuans creditor lucrum ex mutuo futurum gratis mutuauit, sed debitor postea creditori propter mutuum sibi factum et in recompensationem ipsius lucrum aliquod exhibet, et illud creditor etiam propter mutuum a se factum et in recompensationem recipit. Quod talis assistens et concomitans de presenti intentio et uolitio lucri ratione mutui prius facti reddat mutuantem usurarium seu reum criminis usurarum probatur, quia hoc facit intentio talis pro futuro tempore, ergo et similis intentio pro presenti.

Antecedens supra probatum est.[47] Consequentia tenet et patet quia similis culpe esse uidetur uelle habere cras lucrum pro mutuo quod nunc facit, uel pro eius usu futuro et aut pro eius usu preterito uelle habere nunc lucrum pro mutuo quod heri uel ante fecit. Vtrumque enim uelle est uelle eiusdem iniuste commutationis, qua scilicet acceptum preualet dato, siue in qua pro minori quod datur maius uel pro pauciori quod recipitur plus.

Confirmatur quia omnis ratio qua probatur mutuationem usurariam esse de se malam similiter probat siue precedat siue concomitetur intentio lucri, ut patet diligenter intuenti. Declaratur etiam propositum quia si aliquis mutuet prorsus gratis sine exactione et intentione quacumque lucri percipiendi, postea uero in successu temporis uelit et exigat sortem et aliquid plus sibi dari propter mutuum factum, et quod exigit recipiat, procul dubio usuras recepisse dicetur et ad restitutionem obligatur. Immo non solum uerum est hoc quando idem qui prius mutuauit gratis postea lucrum petit sed etiam in eo qui in ius mutui mutuanti succedit, sicut filius heres patri. Sed cum exactio exterior non requiratur ad rati-
7r onem culpe usurarie, quinimo absque omni exteriori / petitione, per so-

[47] See above, 170-85.

lam intentionem, quis usurariam contrahat culpam, ut ex superioribus patet, sequitur quod per solam intentionem presentem, ubi etiam nulla talis precessit, iudicabitur mutuans usurarius in iudicio animarum.[48]

Hoc quoque sequitur ex dicto Raimundi in summa[49] dicentis quod si creditor mutuat propter Deum tantum sine intentione lucri, debitor tamen propter mutuum acceptum uel ulterius retinendum ei dederit, restituere tenetur. Constat autem quod si tenetur et non restituit, peccat, et non propter aliud nisi quia iam uult habere lucrum illud pro mutuo a se facto, sicut et propter illud mutuum debitor lucrum dedit. Illud autem peccatum non est nisi peccatum usurarium iudicandum, ergo non solum illud lucrum ex mutuo usura est quod fuit preintentum siue intentum propter spem uel expectationem, sed et illud quod intentum per acceptationem et uolitionem presentem secundum modum premissum. Et uidetur hec sententia iuuari ex uerbo Ieronimi .xiiii. q. .3. *Putant*,[50] qui dicit "scripturam appellare usuram omnem superabundantiam et quicquid illud est si ab eo quid dederint plus receperint"; et tu subintellige, "propter mutuum quod dederunt." Et sic colligendo partes diffinitionis patet hanc esse diffinitionem usure: "lucrum ex mutuo intentum."

Hec sunt in effectu uerba dicti magistri, ex quibus recte intuenti clare patet ipsum sentire quod supra dixi in uersiculo "unde sciendum" et cetera.[51] Sed quia in contrarium est comunis glosarum et doctorum nostrorum opinio, quam magis iuri consonam arbitror, et aliud asseuerare est sanguinem elicere, sicut in simili scripxit Archydiaconus et Iohannes Andree post eum in c. *Quamquam* infra eodem li. .vi. in principio super uersiculo "de usuris,"[52] uideamus quomodo respondeatur rationibus magistri.

Et ad primam dico quod ubi dicit magister quod "hoc facit intentio pro futuro tempore,"[53] quod istud est uerum si principalis causa mutui ex hoc, non ex dilectione et caritate, processit, et tunc bene fateor consequentiam quam facit magister. Sed ubi principalis causa et intentio fuit ex dilectione, secundario tamen spem posuit, etiam in eodem instanti, etiam in lucro futuro, ut sic, etsi nullum lucrum perciperet, nichilominus erat mutuare paratus, tunc nego antecedens. Fateor bene tamen, ut

[48] See above, 167-209.

[49] Guillelmus Redonensis, *Apparatus in Summam Raymundi*, 2.7 *de usuris*, n.4, v. *Intentio corrupta* (ed. cit. pp. 229b-230a).

[50] Decretum Grat. C.14 q.3 c.2

[51] See above, 135-65.

[52] Johannes Andreae, *In sextum Decretalium novella commentaria*, ad VI 5.5.2, n.2 (ed. Venice 1581, repr. 1963, fol. 145rb); Guido de Baysio, *In sextum Decretalium commentaria*, ad VI 5.5.2, n.1 (ed. Venice 1606, fol. 118va).

[53] See above, 194-95.

supra dixi circa finem descriptionis domini Ostiensis,[54] quod etiam si ab initio, cum mutuaui, intentio principalis fuit a caritate causata, sed postea in progressu illam mutaui et in corde proposui pro principali talis mutui causa non caritatem sed lucrum et superabundantiam in tantum quod nisi illud sperarem pro posse mutuum retractarem, quod tunc, quicquid inde percipio et, tali uolito, confertur, restitutioni obnoxium est in animarum iudicio, pro quo que scripxit Iohannes Andree in decretali *Nobis* super glosa secunda *de symo.*[55] Et eo casu bene procedunt tam predicta ratio prima domini magistri quam secunda et tertia statim sequentes et sic intelligendo eius dictum non discordaret a dictis aliorum; aliter autem non procedunt rationes sue, ut clare patet intuenti.

Ad dictum Raimundi[56] respondetur quod ueritate caret si prima mutuantis intentio fuit ex caritate, spem tamen secundario posuit in lucro, mutuaturus nichilominus omni casu, ut sepius dictum est supra. Quod intellige: nisi angelus bonus in malum se conuerterit,[57] id est nisi bona spes in malam deinde se transformauerit, iuxta statim dicta, et dummodo turbata non fuerit dantis debitoris intentio nec illam turbatam credidit ipse creditor, iuxta ea que infra dicam in questione .ix. in sequenti parte et statim etiam tangam ad finem huius questionis.[58] Quo casu posset procedere dictum Raimundi et sic, credo, intellexerit ipse Raymundus. Nec mirum quia per talem scientiam et consensum in recipiendo quod datur a debitore, animo turbato, et sic ut usuram, creditor mutat intentionem, et sic tunc turbatur etiam intentio creditoris.

7v Ad uerbum Ieronimi in c. *Putant*[59] responde / quod intelligitur secundum superius lucidata, et ita intelligit Iohannes Andree in mercuriali posita super dicta regula *Peccatum* in secunda columpna uersiculo “Occurrit tamen dubium” et cetera.[60]

Et ex predictis infertur quod nimis stricte locutus est etiam idem magister supra ponendo necessaria ad hoc ut non dicatur recipiens aliquid ultra sortem usurarum uitio inuolui, de quo super uersiculo “ex mutuo” supra in questione incidenti tactum est.[61] Vnde dico quod etsi mutuans

263 fuerit dantis *in marg. dex. add.*

[54] See above, 112-20.

[55] Johannes Andreae, *Novella*, ad X 5.3.27, n.5 (ed. cit. V fol. 28ra).

[56] See above, 217-31.

[57] Cf. 2 *Cor* 11.14.

[58] See below, 1514-1600, 274-89.

[59] Decretum Grat. C.14 q.3 c.2; see above, 226-31.

[60] Johannes Andreae, *Novella*, ad VI *de reg. iur.* 4, *Peccatum*, n.8 (ed. cit. fol. 62vb).

[61] See above, 161-231.

intentionem habeat recipiendi aliquid ultra sortem, dummodo non sit sua primaria intentio propter quam inductus est ad mutuandum sed amor proximi, mutuaturus etiam si nil sibi ultra sortem daretur, sperat tamen etiam quod seruitium attendet et eius ratione gratus erit in eum si sibi uisum fuerit, non commictit peccatum uel usuram, quia nec ut usura, eo sciente, soluitur nec ut usura recipitur, cum talis non precesserit uel adsit etiam intentio de presenti, et sic extra descriptionem usure. Et sic tollitur quod obici posset de c. *Tua nos, de sy.*[62] cum symilibus. Et similiter si expectet, dummodo secundario, non primario. Et hoc dico, cessantibus pactionibus uel turbatis exactionibus, quia tunc secus presummitur, iuxta notata in c. *Nobis, de symo.* in glosa secunda[63] et super ea per Iohannem Andree[64] post alios.

Insuper dico quod etsi debitor ex sua liberalitate, etiam habito respectu ad seruitium mutui sibi ex caritate impensi, tamquam qui gratus esse uult de beneficio mutui sibi liberaliter facti, ut est animi nobilis et peregrini, aliquid conferat mutuanti, quantumcumque ex hoc respectu id sibi sic collatum credat uel firmiter sciat mutuans, nichilominus licite recipit quia ex quo sua primaria intentio a caritate causata est et illi cotidie inheret, non recipit ut usuram nec ille soluit ut usuram. Si enim reciperet ut usuram credens ut usuram solui, tunc secus, quod dic ut infra in questionibus .vi. et .vii. super textu,[65] et facit quod infra dixi in questionibus .ix. et .x. etiam super textu.[66] Et tunc procederet quod dixit idem magister in responsionibus suis in principio[67] per c. *Tua nos, de sy.*[68] et alia similia.

Premissorum tamen contrarium ubi supra uisus est sentire iamdictus magister et repetit etiam in tertio articulo eiusdem prime questionis post principium,[69] nisi iam tu dicas eum intellexisse quando non ex tali liberalitate et gratis sed ut usuram ultra sortem soluit mutuanti et ut talem recepit creditor ipse mutuans. Pro quo facit quod ipse idem post predicta in eodem articulo subdit ultra medium et in fine. Et uide quod

284 etiam *in marg. dex. add.*
299 ix. et *in marg. sin. add.*
302 ubi supra *in marg. dex. add.*

[62] X 5.3.34; cf. Gregory of Rimini, *Tractatus*, art. 4 (ed. cit. fol. C1r).
[63] Gl. ord. ad X 5.3.27, v. *Interueniente* (ed. cit. col. 1623).
[64] Johannes Andreae, *Novella*, ad X 5.3.27, n.5 (ed. cit. V fol. 28ra).
[65] See below, 1205-1473.
[66] See below, 1514-1651.
[67] Gregory of Rimini, *Tractatus*, art. 4 (ed. cit. fol. C1r).
[68] X 5.3.34
[69] Gregory of Rimini, *Tractatus*, art. 3 (ed. cit. fols. B6r-C1r).

infra dicam in ultima questione tertie partis, scilicet in questione montis, dubio secundo.[70] Et facit ad predicta quod infra dicam super textu in .viii. oppositione et in .iii.ª et .ix.ª questionibus.[71] Facit etiam ad materiam pro et contra quod scripxit Iohannes Andree post Innocentium et Ostiensem in decretali .i. *de symo.*[72] et eodem titulo *Cum in ecclesie* in uerbo "Requiratur"[73] et in c. *Cum sit* in glosa prima[74] et super ea et in c. *Ad nostram.*[75] Et omnino uidendum quod notat eodem titulo *Non satis* super uerbo "Recepit,"[76] et quod legitur et notat⟨ur⟩ in c. *Dilectus* .ii. in fine,[77] et eodem titulo *Ad apostolicam* super uerbo "Immutare" in nouella et super glosa tertia.[78]

Sed uideamus modo quid est formale et quid materiale in descriptione usure. Respondeo: qualitercumque accipiatur quod materiale est lucrum proueniens et genitum materialiter ex mutuo. Formale uero quod gignitur ex mutuo tali modo uel per solam prauam intentionem uel per pactum et exactionem.[79]

.2. questio ⟨Vnde dicatur.⟩

Ad secundum principale responde quod usura dicitur quasi "usus rei," quia ob usum rei datur, id est, pecunie. Vel dicitur usura quasi "usurea," id est, "usus eris," id est, pecunie. In idem tamen recidit cum priori secundum Gofredum[80] et Ostiensem.[81]

308 scilicet m *post* questione¹ *del.*
310-17 Facit ... glosa tertia *in marg. sin. add.*
323 .2. questio *in marg. sin.*

[70] See below, 2459-2998.

[71] See below, 868-1002, 1021-1142, 1514-1600.

[72] Johannes Andreae, *Novella*, ad X 5.3.1, n.7 (ed. cit. V fol. 21va-b); Innocent IV, *Commentaria*, ad X 5.3.1 (ed. cit. fol. 498rb); Hostiensis, *Commentaria*, ad X 5.3.1 (ed. Venice 1581, repr. 1965, V fol. 14vb).

[73] Johannes Andreae, *Novella*, ad X 5.3.9, n.2 (ed. cit. V fol. 23ra).

[74] Gl. ord. ad X 5.3.10, v. *Procurationem* (ed. cit. cols. 1609-10).

[75] Johannes Andreae, *Novella*, ad X 5.3.21, n.2 (ed. cit. V fol. 26va).

[76] Ibid., ad X 5.3.8, n.4 (ed. cit. V fol. 22vb).

[77] Ibid., ad X 5.3.30, n.4 (ed. cit. V fol. 28vb).

[78] Ibid., ad X 5.3.42, n.5 (ed. cit. V fol. 35ra-b).

[79] Cf. Johannes Andreae, *Novella*, ad VI *de reg. iur.* 4, *Peccatum*, n.9 (ed. cit. fol. 63ra).

[80] Gottofredo da Trani, *Summa*, X 5.19 *de usuris*, n.2 (ed. cit. p. 439b).

[81] Hostiensis, *Summa*, X 5.19 *de usuris*, n.2 (ed. cit. col. 1614).

.3. questio ⟨In quibus commictatur.⟩

Ad tertium principale dicas quod usura non commictitur nisi in contractu mutui secundum Gofredum[82] et Raymundum[83] in summis eodem titulo. Sed dicit Ostiensis:[84] iunge tu scilicet "regulariter." Hoc pro tanto dicit quia in casibus auctoritate legis usure prestantur, licet nullum mutuum sit contractum, quos uide per eum in summa eodem titulo § *Pro quibus*.[85]

Ex predictis ergo infertur quod usura commictitur regulariter in his tantum que consistunt in numero, pondere uel mensura. Patet consequentia quia mutuum, in quo consistit usura, ut predicitur, contrahitur in his tantum que consistunt in numero, pondere uel mensura.

Sed oppone de c. *Plerique*[86] et sequenti .xiiii. q. .iii.[87] Huius timore dixit Gofredus in summa huius tituli § *Sed usura*[88] quod etiam preter res 8r / predictas usura commictitur, nam si tibi mutuem aliquid ex his que consistunt in numero, pondere uel mensura, et tu michi conuenias pro usura equum uel uestem siue predium uel quicquid aliud, quodcumque ei nomen imponas, usura est, ut dictis iuribus in contrarium allegatis. Vnde non placet sibi quod notat frater Raymundus in summa sua hoc eodem titulo,[89] qui dixit non dici commicti usuram nisi in his rebus tantum circa quas consistit mutuum, scilicet que consistunt in numero, pondere uel mensura, *Insti., Quibus mo. re. contrahi. obli.* circa principium.[90] Hoc idem in effectu dixit Ostiensis in summa sua eodem titulo circa principium[91] non dampnans dictum Raymundi sed illud saluans, dicens illud debere intelligi quoad contractum quia, ut supra dictum est, in aliquo contractu dicitur regulariter commicti usura, porro quoad usuram aliud est, "nam si tibi mutuo" et cetera, ut supra dixit Gofredus.[92] Dominus meus in c. finali infra eodem titulo[93] per alia uerba idem dicebat quod Ostiensis et sic quia si ponderatur datum, illud potest esse aliud,

328 .3. questio *in marg. sin.*

[82] Gottofedo da Trani, *Summa*, X 5.19 *de usuris*, n.3 (ed. cit. p. 439b).
[83] Raymond of Penyafort, *Summa*, 2.7 *de usuris*, n.1 (ed. cit. p. 227b).
[84] Hostiensis, *Summa*, X 5.19 *de usuris*, n.1 (ed. cit. col. 1613).
[85] Ibid., n.4 (ed. cit. col. 1615).
[86] Decretum Grat. C.14 q.3 c.3
[87] Decretum Grat. C.14 q.3 c.4
[88] Gottofredo da Trani, *Summa*, X 5.19 *de usuris*, n.3 (ed. cit. p. 439b).
[89] Raymond of Penyafort, *Summa*, 2.7 *de usuris*, n.1 (ed. cit. p. 227b).
[90] Inst. 3.14.pr.
[91] Hostiensis, *Summa*, X 5.19 *de usuris*, n.1 (ed. cit. col. 1613).
[92] See above, 339-44.
[93] John of Legnano, *Commentaria*, ad X 5.19.19 (MS cit. fol. 99v).

sed si ponderatur illud quod mutuo prestatur cui accedit usura, illud semper consistit in numero, pondere uel mensura; et ista fuit intentio Raimundi. Quod etiam clarius prosequitur Iohannes Andree in mercuriali super regula *Peccatum* in .3. columpna uersiculo "Sed si queratur,"[94] ubi etiam reperies tactum quare mutuum solum consistit circa illa tria; item quare usura commictitur solum in illis rebus circa quas consistit mutuum, et illuc omnino recurre.

.4.ª questio ⟨Quot sint eius speties.⟩

Ad quartum principale respondetur quod due sunt speties usurarum, nam una est spiritualis et equa, secunda corporalis et iniqua. Quod prosequere ut per Gofredum in summa eodem titulo § *Due*[95] et per Ostiensem in ⟨summa eodem titulo⟩ § *Quot sunt eius speties.*[96]

.5.ª questio ⟨Ex quibus causis ueniat.⟩

Ad quintum principale dicas quod ueniunt ex pacto; item ex mora uel quasi mora et cetera. Quod prosequere ut per Gofredum in summa eodem titulo § *Veniunt*[97] et plenius per Ostiensem in ⟨summa eodem titulo⟩ § *Ex quibus causis.*[98]

.6.ª questio ⟨Qualiter petatur.⟩

Ad sextum dic ut plene per Ostiensem in summa eodem titulo § *Qualiter petantur.*[99]

.7.ª questio ⟨Quare prohibeatur et utrum sit naturaliter uitiosa.⟩

Ad septimum sciendum quod diuersi diuersas rationes assignauerunt. Innocentius super hac rubrica et Ostiensis infra eodem c. .ii., et post eos Iohannes Andree super ipsa rubrica,[1] reddebant tales rationes:

356 et *post* usura *del.*
363 .4.ª questio *in marg. sin.*
368 .5.ª questio *in marg. sin.*
373 .6.ª questio *in marg. sin.*
376 .7.ª questio *in marg. sin.*

[94] Johannes Andreae, *Novella*, ad VI *de reg. iur.* 4, *Peccatum*, nn.10-11 (ed. cit. fol. 63ra-b).

[95] Gottofredo da Trani, *Summa*, X 5.19 *de usuris*, nn.4-5 (ed. cit. p. 440a).

[96] Hostiensis, *Summa*, X 5.19 *de usuris*, n.3 (ed. cit. cols. 1614-15).

[97] Gottofredo da Trani, *Summa*, X 5.19 *de usuris*, n.5 (ed. cit. p. 440a-b).

[98] Hostiensis, *Summa*, X 5.19 *de usuris*, nn.5-6 (ed. cit. cols. 1615-17).

[99] Ibid., n.7 (ed. cit. cols. 1617-19).

[1] Johannes Andreae, *Novella*, ad X 5.19 rubr., n.2 (ed. cit. fol. 72ra); Innocent IV, *Commentaria*, ad X 5.19 rubr. (ed. cit. fol. 516ra-b); Hostiensis,

quia si fenerari liceret, fere exinde omnia mala sequerentur, maxime quia non intenderent homines agriculture nisi quando aliud non possent, per quod tanta insurgeret caristia quod omnes pauperes fame perirent nam, etsi habere possent terram ad colendum, non possent habere animalia et alia instrumenta necessaria ad colendum nam a se non quia pauperes, a diuitibus non quia propter lucrum et securitatem pecunie potius eas ponent in usuras quam in minora et minus cauta lucra. Et dato quod aliqui in his expenderent, ita cara essent uictualia quod pauperes non haberent unde uiuerent, ex quo periculum maximum esset fidelibus. Alia ratio quia uix potest esse quin diu debens usuras depauperetur. Paupertas uero periculosa, nisi cui ex spetiali Dei dono conceditur. Alia ratio quia uix in diligendo pecuniam euitatur ydolatria, .xlvii. di. *Sicut*[2] et c. *Omnes*.[3] Item quia ex ea omnia fere mala prouenirent. Alii dicunt potius illam prohibitam quia est contra pietatem et caritatem qua tenetur quis proximo subuenire quam propter mala que ex illa sequuntur, pro hoc quia uidemus multos contractus ex quibus possent mala sequi non prohibitos. Et idem in effectu sentire uidentur Guiglelmus et Genzellinus in clementina unica infra eodem titulo.[4]

Sed aduertendum quod licet rationes predicte inferant usuram debuisse prohiberi, non tamen plene probant quod usura de sui natura sit uitiosa et malitia conuoluta, quia et in multis aliis non prohibitis uel saltem certis casibus permissis per approbationem posset locum habere. Sed quia hoc utile et pulcrum est uidere, paulisper in eo euagemur. Vnde aduertendum quod uenerabilis pater frater Gherardus ordinis heremitarum[5] notabiliter hunc passum tetigit, qui pro indubitato ponens illam de sui natura uitiosam et malitia conuolutam dumtaxat institit in assignan-
8v do talis conclusionis / rationes. Et quia eius uerba ab⟨b⟩reuiando tamen posuit Iohannes Andree in dicta questione mercuriali super regula *Peccatum*,[6] ubi omnium tam theologorum quam iuristarum opiniones recitantur, idcirco me expediam cum remissionibus ponendo solum (ut fecit in simili etiam Iohannes Calderinus, qui hunc passum tetigit in repetitione

406 ab⟨b⟩reuiando: F_1 abreuiando

Commentaria, ad X 5.19.2, nn.1-3 (ed. cit. V fol. 56ra).

[2] Decretum Grat. D.47 c.8

[3] Decretum Grat. D.47 c.3.

[4] *Locum non inveni*. Cf. Gl. ord. ad Clem. 5.5.1, v. *Proximi* (ed. Lyons 1559, col. 256).

[5] Gerard of Siena, *Tractatus de usuris et de prescriptionibus*, q.1, art.2 (Rome, Biblioteca Angelica, 625, fols. 210va-212rb).

[6] Johannes Andreae, *Novella*, ad VI *de reg. iur.* 4, *Peccatum*, nn. 12-16 (ed. cit., fols. 63rb-64ra).

dicti c. finalis infra eodem titulo)[7] rationes eiusdem, que sunt quactuor. Prima, quia facit rem naturalem supernaturalem sue nature et rem artificialem sue arti et maxime contra naturam. Secunda, quia facit quod res que non parit fructum generat lucrum, quod est contra naturam. .3.ª, quia facit quod ea que habent omnino eundem ualorem unum eorum excrescit in ualore per alterum, quod est contra naturam. .4.ª, quia facit quod res mutuata per abusum trahatur ad aliquid ad quod non est ordinata principaliter nec consequenter, quod etiam est similiter contra naturam.

Prima ratio sic declaratur. Consistentia in numero, pondere uel mensura habent determinatum ualorem a natura uel arte unde eorum ualor determinate pensatur ex numero quantum ad numerabiles, ex pondere quantum ad ponderabiles, ex mensura quantum ad mensurabiles, nec quamdiu persistunt in eodem numero, pondere uel mensura augentur uel minuuntur in sui ualore. Et si aliquando augeri uel minui uideantur, hoc non est propter augmentum uel minutionem ualoris sed illarum rerum in quas commutantur. In aliis autem rebus uel naturalibus uel artificialibus non est sic, quia earum ualor non pensatur ab aliquo intrinseco necessario sed ex causis extrinsecis contingentibus ex loco, ex tempore et conditionibus personarum aliisque pluribus et uariis circumstantiis. Agit ergo usurarius exigens ultra mutuatum numerum, pondus uel mensuram contra naturam, hoc est contra naturalem ualorem a natura uel ab arte secundum naturam determinatum. Dicit ibi Iohannes Andree[8] quod de plano concedit quod facilior est harum extimatio et maxime tempore quo contrahitur restringendo ad illud, sed non capit quomodo sit uerum dicere quod a natura habeant certum et determinatum ualorem, durante pondere, numero uel mensura, non alterandum in plus uel minus; et recte et optime iudicio meo.

Secunda ratio declaratur sic.[9] Vsura facit germinare contra naturam rem de sui natura ingerminabilem, igitur et cetera. Patet antecedens quia cum res numerabiles, ponderabiles uel mensurabiles habeant, ut predixi, certum et determinatum ualorem a natura institutum, ergo ultra germinare non possunt, cuius contrarium facit usurarius, ergo contra naturam.

421 eorum *scripsi:* F_1 earum

[7] Johannes et Gaspar Calderinus, *Repetitiones et distinctiones in decretales*, in X 5.19.19 (Vatican City, Biblioteca Apostolica Vaticana, Vat. lat. 2652, fols. 283v-284r).

[8] Johannes Andreae, *Novella*, ad VI *de reg. iur*. 4, *Peccatum*, n.13 (ed. cit. fol. 63vb).

[9] Ibid., n.14 (ed. cit. fol. 63vb).

Ad hoc quod dicit canon quod "usure arte nequissima ex auro aurum nascitur," .xlvii. di. *Sicut hi.*[10]

.3.ª declaratur sic.[11] Dicebam quod duorum, id est rei et usus eius, que habent omnino eundem ualorem, usura facit quod unum per alterum excrescat in ualore. Hoc patet discurrendo per singulas res mutuabiles, ipse enim et ipsarum usus una consumptione consumuntur, nec unum sine altero consumi potest, quod in aliis rebus locabilibus dici non potest, in quibus rei usus habet distinctum ualorem a re et potest alienari solus usus, ut in domo uel equo, et sola proprietas, retento ad tempus usu. Cum ergo contractus usurarius faciat rem mutuatam excrescere in ualore per suum usum cum tamen ipsorum coniunctorum idem sit ualor, patet id contra naturam rei attentari et sic uitiosum.

Ex predictis infertur declaratio quarte rationis, scilicet quod usurarius utitur rebus ad alium usum quam ad illum ad quem a natura uel ab arte fuerunt ordinate, contra id quod habetur .xxii. q. .ii. *Is autem,*[12] supra *de reli. do.*, *De senodochiis,*[13] et *de religi. do.*, *Quia contingit* in clementinis.[14]

Quam tamen latius ibi prosequitur post dictum fratrem Gherardum disputantem ipse Iohannes Andree,[15] ubi omnino uide, et per Iohannem Calderinum[16] et dominum meum infra eodem c. finali[17] et per reuerendum magistrum Gregorium de Arimino in dicta sua questione, articulo secundo, conclusione tertia.[18] Aliquid scripxit Baldus in l. .i. C. *de sum. tri. et fi. ca.*[19] Subtiliter et eleganter scripxit dictus uenerabilis frater ⟨Gherardus⟩, secundum quem in hoc assignare rationem siue causam sufficientem non est omnino facile. Tamen michi uidetur quod transire possimus cum comuni iuristarum opinione que ponitur in c. .i. .xiiii. q.

465-66 Aliquid ... et fi. ca. *in marg. sin. add.*

[10] Decretum Grat. D.47 c.8

[11] Johannes Andreae, *Novella*, ad VI *de reg. iur.* 4, *Peccatum*, n.15 (ed. cit. fol. 63vb).

[12] Decretum Grat. C.22 q.2 c.4

[13] X 3.36.3

[14] Clem. 3.11.2

[15] Johannes Andreae, *Novella*, ad VI *de reg. iur.* 4, *Peccatum*, nn.12-16 (ed. cit. fols. 63rb-64ra).

[16] Johannes et Gaspar Calderinus, *Repetitiones*, in X 5.19.19 (MS cit. fol. 284r).

[17] John of Legnano, *Commentaria*, ad X 5.19.19 (MS cit. fols. 99v-100r).

[18] Gregory of Rimini, *Tractatus*, art. 2 (ed. cit. fols. B2r-B5r).

[19] Baldus de Ubaldis, *In Codicis libros commentaria*, in C.1.1(4).1, nn. 36-37 (ed. Venice 1615, VI fol. 6va-b).

.iii. in glosa[20] et per eundem repetitur super dicta regula *Peccatum*,[21] scilicet quod in contractu usurario recipit creditor lucrum de eo quod non est suum, immo transit in dominium ipsius debitoris quia mutuum est 9r "quod / de meo fit tuum."[22] Quam rationem, licet impugnet dictus frater Gherardus ibidem, tamen Iohannes Andree illam defendit una cum ratione confirmatiua que ibi sequitur, scilicet quia pecunia mutuata transit cum suo periculo in debitorem et ideo iniustum uidetur quod de ea grauetur amplius ultra sortem. Ibi omnino uide et per dominum meum in dicto c. finali[23] et per Baldum de Perusio in l. *Cunctos populos C. de sum. tri. et fi. ca.* in .i. questione in principio.[24]

.viii.ª questio ⟨Vtrum ullo casu permictatur.⟩

Ad .viii.^{m}, cum querebatur utrum ullo casu permictatur usura, respondeo indubitanter quod non. Gofredus tamen in summa eodem titulo § *Sed numquid*[25] dicebat quod in .vii. casibus usura licite petitur secundum iura canonica.

Primus, cum laico beneficium assignatur et laicus male tenet. Potest enim tunc ecclesia uel persona ecclesiastica illud in pignus recipere, non computatis fructibus in sortem, infra eodem titulo c. .i.[26] et c. *Conquestus*.[27] Numquid autem idem in laico, item numquid in emphyteosi et in usufructu, infra tangam in questionibus .49. et .50., parte secunda.[28]

Secundus, cum fideiussor soluit debitum et usuras, forte quia iurauit, tunc exiget a debitore, ut supra *de fideius.*, *Constitutus*[29] secundum Gofredum. Sed tu de hoc dic ut per Iohannem Andree in questione mercuriali super regula *Dampnum* infra *de regulis iuris* li. .vi.,[30] cuius conclu-

480 .viii.ª questio *in marg. sin.*

[20] Gl. ord. ad Decretum Grat. C.14 q.3. c.1, v. *Plus quam* (ed. Paris 1561, col. 1095).

[21] Johannes Andreae, *Novella*, ad VI *de reg. iur.* 4, *Peccatum*, n.12 (ed. cit. fol. 63rb).

[22] Dig. 12.1.2.2; Inst. 3.14.pr.

[23] John of Legnano, *Commentaria*, ad X 5.19.19 (MS cit. fol. 99v).

[24] Baldus de Ubaldis, *Commentaria*, in C. 1.1(4).1, nn.30-31 (ed. cit. VI fol. 6va).

[25] Gottofredo da Trani, *Summa*, X 5.19 *de usuris*, n.6 (ed. cit. pp. 440b-441a).

[26] X 5.19.1

[27] X 5.19.8

[28] F_1 fol. 36v; *TUI* 7, fol. 26rb.

[29] X 3.22.3

[30] Johannes Andreae, *Novella*, ad VI *de reg. iur.* 86, *Damnum*, nn.3-16 (ed. cit. fol. 16rb-vb).

sionem infra ponam in questionibus super nigro, questione .47.[31]

.3.us casus, secundum Gofredum, cum petitur usura canonica, hoc est, pena a canone inflicta, que potest exigi ultra sortem, .xii. q. .ii. *In legibus.*[32]

.4.us, cum petitur usura non tamquam usura sed tamquam interesse, ut in contractibus bone fidei, et tunc non petitur quasi usura sed quod intersit moram adhibitam non fuisse, ut ff. *Pro socio* l. *Socium.*[33] Quod intellige cum interesse est intra rem, uel cum petitur causa dampni uitandi, non lucri captandi, ut ff. *de actio. emp. et uen.* l. *Si sterilis* § *Cum per uenditorem,*[34] et ideo caute canon dixit incrementa susceperit, .xiiii. q. .iiii. *Si quis oblitus.*[35] Ad predicta facit quod notabiliter scripxit glosator in l. *Cum allegas* C. eodem titulo,[36] que uult quod pena quatenus interest possit peti in quocumque contractu de mundo. Et si dicatur quomodo hoc, cum sit interesse extra rem, respondeo: aut loqueris in pecunia in qua non cadit nisi interesse extra rem et tunc potest peti ex conuentione, secundum Bartolum, qui ita notat in l. *Si penam* ff. *de uerb. obl.,*[37] et Baldum in dicta l. *Cum allegas,*[38] aut in aliis rebus, et tunc secus. Et quia supra exemplificaui de contractibus bone fidei tantum, dicas idem in contractibus stricti iuris, si loquamur de interesse conuento, iuxta notata in c. *Cum uen., de excep.* in glosa *Que sint.*[39] Hinc etiam dixit Baldus de Perusio in l. *Acceptam* C. *de usuris* in .xviii. questione[40] quod comune et equum interesse uenit in omni contractu, si loquamur de conuento. Si autem loquamur de interesse non conuento, uenit solum in contractibus bone fidei, non autem stricti iuris, ut etiam notat C. eodem titulo in dicta

502 emp. *post* de *del.*

[31] F_1 fols. 33r-34r; *TUI* 7, fol. 25ra-va.

[32] Decretum Grat. C.12 q.2 c.10

[33] Dig. 17.2.60(61)

[34] Dig. 19.1.21(22).3

[35] Decretum Grat. C.14 q.4 c.4

[36] Gl. ord. ad C. 4.32.15, v. *Vltra* (ed. Geneva 1625, col. 959).

[37] Bartolus of Sassoferrato, *Commentaria,* in Dig. 45.1.68, nn.1-2 (ed. Venice 1602-1603, VI fol. 24rb).

[38] Baldus de Ubaldis, *Commentaria,* in C. 4.32.15, n.26 (ed. cit. VII fol. 90ra).

[39] Gl. ord. ad X 2.25.6, v. *Bona fidei* (ed. cit. col. 841).

[40] Baldus de Ubaldis, *Commentaria,* in C. 4.32.19, nn.47-49 (ed. cit. VII fol. 93vb).

l. *Cum allegas.*[41] Et uide ad materiam infra parte secunda questione .119.[42]

Quintus, in contractu locationis, in quo licite percipitur aliquid ultra sortem, id est ultra id quod datur. Et quare aliud in contractu locationis quam in contractu mutui infra tangetur.[43]

.vi.[us], ratione incertitudinis, ut infra c. *In ciuitate.*[44]

.vii.[us], cum possessiones a socero sunt pro numerata dote genero pignori obligate, nam tunc fructus non computantur in sortem, ut infra eodem titulo *Salubriter.*[45] Quid autem si, soluto matrimonio, mulier recipit in pignus possessionem pro dotibus ab heredibus mariti infra tangam in questionibus.[46] An autem in casibus in quibus fructus sunt in sor-
9v tem computandi debeant computari non tantum / percepti sed etiam hi qui percipi potuerunt, uide per Ostiensem in summa *de pigno.* § *Quando efficaciter* uersiculo "Sed numquid creditori"[47] et per Iohannem Andree in c. .i. infra eodem titulo, scilicet *de usuris.*[48]

Ostiensis uero in summa eodem titulo § *An aliquo casu* dicebat regulariter et firmissime tenendum quod non licet ultra sortem aliquid exigere, fallit tamen in .xiii. casibus quos ibi enumerat, et illuc recurre pro eis.[49] Glosa summe .xiiii. q. .iii.[50] et in c. *Conquestus* infra eodem titulo[51] idem in effectu sentiebant et ibi uide etiam per doctores et per Baldum de Perusio in l. *Cunctos C. de sum. tri. et fi. catho.* in .i. questione.[52] Sed rectius loquutus est Ostiensis[53] et etiam dicta glosa quam fecerit Gofre-

524 mutuata dote *post* pro *del.*
539 dicta *scripsi*: F_1 dicte

[41] Ibid., in C. 4.32.15, n.21 (ed. cit. VII fol. 90ra).
[42] F_1 fol. 56v; *TUI* 7, fol. 33rb.
[43] Secunda particula, q. 33 (F_1 fol. 27v; *TUI* 7, fol. 23ra).
[44] X 5.19.6
[45] X 5.19.16
[46] Secunda particula, qq. 51-54 (F_1 fols. 36v-37v; *TUI* 7, fol. 26rb-va).
[47] Hostiensis, *Summa*, X 3.21 *de pignoribus*, n.9 (ed. cit. col. 992).
[48] Johannes Andreae, *Novella*, ad X 5.19.1, n.5 (ed. cit. V fol. 72rb).
[49] Hostiensis, *Summa*, X 5.19 *de usuris*, n.8 (ed. cit. col. 1623).
[50] Gl. ord. ad Decretum Grat. C.14 q.3 dictum Grat. ante c.1, v. *Quod autem* (ed. cit. cols. 1094-95).
[51] Gl. ord. ad X 5.19.8, v. *De feudo* (ed. cit. cols. 1737-38).
[52] Baldus de Ubaldis, *Commentaria*, in C. 1.1(4).1, nn.31-36 (ed. cit. VI fol. 6va).
[53] Hostiensis, *Summa*, X 5.19 *de usuris*, n.8 (ed. cit. col. 1619).

dus[54] quia nullo casu est uerum dicere quod usura sit permissa. Et hoc est quod dicebat Iohannes Andree in .4. articulo dicte questionis mercurialis super dicta regula *Peccatum*,[55] ubi hunc articulum disputauit et dicit improprie dici hoc uel illo casu usuram permissam, cum nullo casu sit permissa; et ideo quando aliqui casus a iuristis excipiuntur, non est intelligendum quod in dictis casibus usura permictatur sed quia in eis est prima facie aliquid simile usure usura uidetur. Ibi uide.

Et in articulo precedente[56] tractatur etiam utrum iura debeant concedere contractum usurarium propter aliquod bonum quod inde oriatur uel propter aliquod malum quod inde uitetur, quod ibidem notabiliter prosequutus est disputans. Et licet primo distinguat inter ius naturale, canonicum et ciuile, ostendendo etiam quomodo tribus modis accipi potest concessio uel permissio, et quomodo duabus de causis malum potest permicti, finaliter tamen concludit in articulo quod contractus usurarius nullo modo est permissibilis siue propter bonum quod posset exinde oriri siue propter malum quod posset exinde uitari. Ibi uide.

Tractat etiam ibidem in ultimo articulo[57] satis diffuse utrum eo ipso quod contractus usurarius est prohibitus in iure canonico sit necessario prohibitus in iure ciuili; de quibus omnibus etiam tractauit dominus meus in dicto c. finali infra eodem[58] et supra eodem c. .i.,[59] ubi etiam per Iohannem Andree.[60] Et quia plene et abunde per predictos tactum est, ideo sub silentio preteribo.

.9.ª questio ⟨Vtrum mutuo recipere ad usuram sit peccatum.⟩

Ad nonum, cum queritur utrum mutuo recipere ad usuram sit peccatum, sciendum quod prout refert Archydiaconus in c. *Mouet* .xxii. q. .i.,[61] Huguccio et Thomas[62] argumento illius textus dixerunt quod non,

562 .9.ª questio *in marg. sin.*

[54] Gottofredo da Trani, *Apparatus in Decretales Gregorii IX*, ad X 5.19.8, v. *Clericorum* (Paris, Bibliothèque Nationale, lat. 15402, fol. 162va).

[55] Johannes Andreae, *Novella*, ad VI *de reg. iur.* 4, *Peccatum*, n.23 (ed. cit. fol. 64va).

[56] Ibid., nn.17-22 (ed. cit. fol. 64ra-va).

[57] Ibid., nn.24-30 (ed. cit. fols. 64va-65rb)

[58] John of Legnano, *Commentaria*, ad X 5.19.19 (MS cit. fol. 100r).

[59] Ibid., ad X 5.19.1 (MS cit. fol. 95v).

[60] Johannes Andreae, *Novella*, ad X 5.19 rubr., n.2 (ed. cit V fol. 72ra).

[61] Guido de Baysio, *Rosarium*, ad Decretum Grat. C.22 q.1 c.16, n.1 (ed. Lyons 1516, fol. 247va).

[62] Thomas Aquinas, *Summa theologiae*, secunda secundae, q.78, art.4 (ed. Rome 1897, vol. 9, pp. 165-66).

si recipiatur ab illo qui usuram exercet et paratus est facere, et hoc si accipit propter aliquod bonum quod est subuentio sue necessitatis uel alterius, sicut etiam licet ei qui incidit in latrones manifestare bona que habet, que latrones diripiendo peccant, ad hoc quod non occidatur, exemplo decem uirorum qui dixerunt ad Ysmael: "Noli occidere nos, quia habemus ⟨thesaurum⟩ in agro," Iere. .xli.[63] Et subdit quod alii dicunt quod non solum in necessitate sed etiam pro utilitate quam quis consequitur agendo negotia sua hoc licet; sed istis cessantibus, dicunt eum qui accipit pecuniam ad usuram peccare mortaliter.

Sed Bernardus Yspanus, ut refert idem Archydiaconus in c. *Si quis usuram* .14. q. .4.,[64] distinguit sic: aut recipiens ad usuram prestat causam aut prestat occasionem tantum. Primo casu peccat, secundo non, argumento dicti c. *Mouet*[65] et .xxiii[i.] q. .v. *De occidendis*[66] et c. *Cum homines*.[67] Exemplum in primo casu pone aliquem ad fenerandum inducit qui tale propositum non habebat. Exemplum in secundo pone ⟨quem⟩ induxit ad fenerandum qui hoc facere prius habebat in animo.

Iohannes Andree hunc passum examinat in c. *Super eo* supra eodem titulo[68] ubi refert quosdam indistincte tenere id esse peccatum, pro quibus facit illa decretalis in fine, que dicit "inuoluatur," scilicet una cum usurario qui pecuniam dat, si enim non esset qui reciperet, non esset qui daret. Ad quod uide quod scripxit Iohannes Andree *de sy., Non satis* in glosa *Si non esset*,[69] et "qui occasionem dampni dat, dampnum dedisse uidetur," *de iniuri.* c. finali.[70] Sed secundum Osti-
10r ensem ibi,[71] nimis est rigida / talis opinio. Item si uera esset, iuramentum in hoc non obligaret quod tamen obligat, ut supra *de iureiuran.* c. .i.[72] et c. *Debitores*.[73] Damasus in questione .i. *de iureiuran.*[74] dixit non esse peccatum, quasi sit uexationis redemptio. Ad hoc, supra

[63] *Ier* 41.8

[64] Guido de Baysio, *Rosarium*, ad Decretum Grat. C.14 q.4 c.10, n.1 (ed. cit. fol. 208rb).

[65] Decretum Grat. C.22 q.1 c.16

[66] Decretum Grat. C.23 q.5 c.8

[67] Decretum Grat. C.23 q.5 c.19

[68] Johannes Andreae, *Novella*, ad X 5.19.4, n.2 (ed. cit. V fol. 73ra).

[69] Ibid., ad X 5.3.8, n.4 (ed. cit. V fol. 22vb).

[70] X 5.36.9

[71] Hostiensis, *Commentaria*, ad X 5.19.4, n.5 (ed. cit. V fol. 56va).

[72] X 2.24.1

[73] X 2.24.6

[74] Damasus, *Quaestiones, de iureiurando* (Vatican City, Biblioteca Apostolica Vaticana, Borghese 261, fol. 30rb)

de symo., Dilectus .i.[75]

Innocentius et Iohannes Andree[76] post eum ibidem recitant plures opiniones. Vna habet quod cuique id licet pro opere uirtuoso, ut si uelit inde facere elemosinam, ecclesiam uel aliud opus pium. Sed propter luxuriam uel lasciuiam, id non licet.

Secunda habet quod etiam nec semper id licet pro opere uirtutis quoniam etsi opus misericordie et liberalitatis sit pascere pauperes non tamen pro parum uel nullo modo egentibus pascendis licet recipere mutuo ad usuram. Sed consideranda sunt tempus, locus similesque circunstantie et trutinandum bonum quod sequitur si mutuo accipiatur ex opere uirtutis cum illo quod sequitur si mutuo non accipiatur. Exemplum: ex uno lancis latere pone quod bonum quod sequitur si mutuo accipiatur ex opere uirtutis sit quod pascentur pauperes, edificabitur bassilica, ementur ornamenta diuino misterio deputanda; ex alio latere bonum quod sequitur si dimictatur et non accipiatur mutuo est quod creditor non mutuabit ad usuram tibi, mutuauit tamen quantum in eo fuit, quia dispositus erat ad mutuandum et alius est qui paratus est accipere. Equidem maius bonum est accipere quam non accipere, quinimo tunc licitum erit etiam rogare ut mutuet, quia licet omni casu peccet ipse mutuans, minus tamen cum in bonum opus. Sed si ex hoc alio lancis latere bonum quod sequeretur in non accipiendo foret quod uolentem non mutuare amplius ad usuram uel uolentem mutuare et modum non habentem quia non est qui accipiat, tu conseruas in suo bono proposito uel aufers illi non accipiendo facultatem mutuandi, certe isto casu hoc ultimum bonum preponderabit primo. Melius est ergo a tali mutuo abstinere quam quoduis opus facere uirtuosum, non enim propter bonum opus faciendum peccare debeo.

Alia et tertia opinio habet quod cum quis paratus est ad usuram dare et alius recipere, michi licitum est indifferenter recipere, dummodo non pro causa inlicita, quia tunc peccarem et in recipiendo et etiam in suadendo quod pro tali inlicita causa mutuaret.

Vltimo dicit Innocentius plus uideri, uidelicet quod si ex omissione alimonie pauperum uel alterius pii operis magna pericula corporum uel animarum timentur, tunc si uenerit habens pecuniam, granum uel aliud illi operi necessarium et rogatus dare nolit uel mutuare suaderi potest quod aliam spetiem mutuet sub usuris, quia minus in hoc peccabit quam faceret in tanta necessitate illam abscondendo, argumento quia inter duo mala suadendum est quod uitetur maius. Ita dixit dominus Innocentius

[75] X 5.3.28

[76] Johannes Andreae, *Novella*, ad X 5.19.4, n.2 (ed. cit. V fol. 73ra-b); Innocent IV, *Commentaria*, ad X 5.19.4, nn.1-2 (ed. cit. fols. 516va-517ra).

et ponit Iohannes Andree et dominus meus ibidem;[77] et uide super regula *Peccatum* in questione.[78]

.x. questio ⟨Vtrum dispensari possit ut quis sine peccato ualeat fenerari.⟩

Ad decimum, cum queritur utrum dispensari possit ut quis sine peccato ualeat fenerari, textus uidetur aperte cantare quod non in dicto c. *Super eo*.[79] Iohannes Andree ibidem[80] dicit hoc uerum, saluo quod dicitur secundum unum modum legendi in c. *Ab illo* .14. q. .4.,[81] de quo infra uidebis in questione .55.[82] Sed in iam commisso crimine remictendo bene posset dispensari secundum Gofredum ibidem,[83] et facit quod notatur supra eodem *Preterea* in glosa secunda.[84] Idem concludit ibidem dominus meus.[85] Et uide per Archydiaconum ad materiam generalius in c. finali .14. q. .5.[86] cum remissionibus suis. Et uide plenissime per Iohannem Andree in dicta regula *Peccatum* in .3.º membro questionis.[87]

.xi. questio ⟨Quomodo quis usurarius detegatur.⟩

Ad undecimum, cum queritur qualiter contractus usurarius detegatur, dic ut plene per Ostiensem in summa sua eodem titulo § *Qualiter*

632 -tur *post* uide *expunc. et del.*
634 .x. questio *in marg. sin.*
636-37 queritur ... pec(-cato) *sup. lin. add.*
647 .xi. questio *in marg. sin.*

[77] John of Legnano, *Commentaria*, ad X 5.19.5 (MS cit. fol. 96r-v).

[78] Johannes Andreae, *Novella*, ad VI *de reg. iur.* 4, *Peccatum*, nn. 18-22 (ed. cit. fol. 64ra-vb).

[79] X 5.19.4

[80] Johannes Andreae, *Novella*, ad X 5.19.4, n.3 (ed. cit. V fol. 73rb).

[81] Decretum Grat. C.14 q.4 c.12

[82] F_1 fols. 37v-38v; *TUI* 7, fol. 26va-b.

[83] Gottofredo da Trani, *Summa*, X 5.19 *de usuris*, n.7 (ed. cit. p. 441a-b); idem, *Apparatus*, ad X 5.19.7, v. *Excommunicationis* (MS cit. fol. 163rb).

[84] Gl. ord. ad X 5.19.7, v. *Suspendas* (ed. cit. col. 1737).

[85] John of Legnano, *Commentaria*, ad X 5.19.5 (MS cit. fol. 96v).

[86] Guido de Baysio, *Rosarium*, ad Decretum Grat. C.14 q.5. c.15, n.4 (ed. cit. fol. 209va).

[87] Johannes Andreae, *Novella*, ad VI *de reg. iur.* 4, *Peccatum*, nn. 17-22 (ed. cit. fol. 64ra-va).

contractus[88] cum suis remissionibus, et per ea que leguntur et notantur *de emp. et uen.*, *Ad nostram*,[89] et *de pigno.*, *Illo uos*,[90] et supra *de iureiuran.*, *Ex litteris*,[91] et infra eodem *Cum in diocesi*,[92] et per Baldum in l. *Cum allegas* C. *de usuris*,[93] de quibus magis specifice patebit infra in questionibus super nigro.[94]

10v / .xii. questio ⟨Que sit eorum pena.⟩

Ad duodecimum et ultimum, cum queritur que sit usurariorum pena, dic ut plene per Gofredum in summa sua eodem titulo § *Compelluntur*,[95] plenius per Ostiensem in ⟨summa⟩ sua eodem titulo § *Que pena.*[96]

Additur et hodie alia pena, scilicet que introducta est per decretalem .ii. infra eodem li. .vi.[97] Posset dici etiam alia introducta, scilicet per c. .i. infra eodem libro et titulo.[98] Item et alia per clementinam .i. *de sepul.*[99] Item et alia per clementinam unicam infra eodem titulo,[1] de quibus insuper magis specifice, Deo dante, tractabitur ut occurret.

An autem notarii conficientes instrumenta super usuris uel prelati subscribentes et sigillantes aliqua pena plectantur, tractauit Ostiensis in summa eodem titulo § *An aliquo* ad finem,[2] et infra dicam.[3]

Et hec de prima parte sic dicta sufficiant.

Sequitur secunda particula.

655 .xii. questio *in marg. sin.*

[88] Hostiensis, *Summa*, X 5.19 *de usuris*, n.9 (ed. cit. cols. 1627-28).

[89] X 3.17.5; gl. ord. ad X 3.17.5, v. *Dimidiam* (ed. cit. col. 1126).

[90] X 3.21.4; gl. ord. ad X 3.21.4, v. *Consueuerit* (ed. cit. col. 1144).

[91] X 2.24.32; gl. ord. ad X 2.24.32, v. *Ex fama* (ed. cit. col. 829).

[92] X 5.19.15; gl. ord. ad X 5.19.15, v. *Manifestos* (ed. cit. col. 1742).

[93] Baldus de Ubaldis, *Commentaria*, in C. 4.32.15, nn.12-28 (ed. cit. VI fols. 89va-90rb).

[94] Secunda particula, passim (670-2182 and F_1 fols. 23r-68v; *TUI* 7, fols. 17rb-37rb).

[95] Gottofredo da Trani, *Summa*, X 5.19 *de usuris*, n.7 (ed. cit. p. 441a-b).

[96] Hostiensis, *Summa*, X 5.19 *de usuris*, n.10 (ed. cit. cols. 1628-30).

[97] VI 5.5.2

[98] VI 5.5.1

[99] Clem. 3.7.1

[1] Clem. 5.5.1

[2] Hostiensis, *Summa*, X 5.19 *de usuris*, n.8 (ed. cit. col. 1627).

[3] Secunda particula, q. 58 (F_1 fol. 39r; *TUI* 7, fol. 27ra).

⟨Secunda particula⟩

Nunc expeditis ad sufficientiam que circa rubricam cadunt, descendamus ad nigrum, quod pro secunda particula designaui.

Consuluit.[1] Casus.[2] Mutuans ea mente ut plus sorte percipiat, non dans parabolam iuramenti nisi aliquid inde percipiat, uendens rem plus debito quia solutionem pretii differt tenentur ex his in iudicio animarum. Hec dicit.

Diuiditur in duas, quia in prima ponitur consultatio tria dubia continens, in secunda ad omnia simul responsio. Secunda ibi, "uerum."

Iterum, prima potest subdiuidi in tres, sicut tres sunt consultationes, que de se patent. "Quasi usurarius" bene querit, quia usurarius non est proprie. "Et utrum," secunda questio. "Inuoluatur," supra eodem *Super eo* in fine.[3] "Parabolam" Lombardus fuit, secundum Ostiensem; aliter parabola dicitur quasi umbra et prohemium ueritatis, ut scribit deuotus meus ad Algasiam, questione .vi.[4] "Et an negotiator," .3.ª questio. Luce .vi.º capitulo.[5] "In lege" Deuteronomii .xxiii. capitulo,[6] et Ezechielis .xviii. ⟨capitulo⟩.[7] "Taliter," id est, "tali intentione."

Collige pro notabili primo quod habes in summario. .2.º quod usurarius mentalis non dicitur proprie usurarius sed quasi usurarius. .3.º ex uerbo "uulgo," quod licite arguimus a uulgaribus prouerbiis; concordat supra *de Iude, Etsi Iudeos*.[8] .4.º nota inspiciendam ⟨esse⟩ consuetudinem patris familias, ff. *de usu., Qui semisses,*[9] ff. *de pigno. ac.* l. *Vel uniuersorum,*[10] .xlvii. di. *Quoniam,*[11] et bene facit *de confirm. uti. uel inuti., Ad nostram.*[12] Item nota quinto quod quicquid accedit sorti usura est, .xiiii. q. .iii. per totum.[13] Vltimo nota quod inter iudicium fori et iudicium

[1] X 5.19.10

[2] Cf. Johannes Andreae, *Novella*, ad X 5.19.10, nn.1-4 (ed. cit. V fol. 75rb); Hostiensis, *Commentaria*, ad X 5.19.10 (ed. cit. V fol. 57va-b).

[3] X 5.19.4

[4] Jerome *Epistola* 121.6 (*PL* 22.1019).

[5] *Lc* 6.35

[6] *Dt* 23.19-20

[7] *Ez* 18.8-17

[8] X 5.6.13

[9] Dig. 22.1.13

[10] Dig. 13.7.12

[11] Decretum Grat. D.47 c.2

[12] X 2.30.5

[13] Decretum Grat. C.14 q.3

poli magna est differentia, de quo infra dicam.[14]

.i. oppositio ⟨Vtrum spem lucri secundario tantum in mutuo ponere usuram inducat uel peccatum.⟩

Oppone ad responsum prime et secunde questionis sic: "qui nimis emungit sanguinem elicit," Prouerbiorum .30. capitulo in fine, supra *de renump.*, *Nisi cum pridem.*[15] Sed in proposito ita facere uidetur Vrbanus, igitur et cetera. Probo minorem, nam si dare mutuo teneor sine ulla spe remunerationis, aliter iudicandus sum male agere, ergo nec etiam sperare possum quod in necessitatibus meis hic michi subueniat.

Solutio: secundum glosam[16] intellige quod hic dicitur cum quis mutuans principaliter spem ponit in lucro et de tali querebatur hic, ut patet in principio. Sperare enim aliquid secundario, quodcumque illud sit, non est malum, argumento .lxi. di. *Quid proderit,*[17] .lix. di. *Si officia.*[18] Et similiter nec etiam ex tali spe secundaria aliquid recipere, argumento .i.
11r q. .ii. *Quam pio.*[19] Imo naturaliter debitor est tali mu/tuanti obligatus ad antidotum, ut supra *de testa.*, *Cum in offitiis*[20] et l. *Sed ⟨et⟩ si lege* § *Consuluit* ff. *de peti. here*[21] secundum glosam que fuit Alani, cui concordat Gofredus,[22] qui rationem supradictam tenebat quod iudex principaliter ponens spem in remuneratione iustitiam uendere uidetur, .xi. q. .iii. *Qui recte*[23] et idem in ordinante .i. q. .i. *Ordinationes.*[24]

.2. oppositio ⟨Vtrum naturalis obligatio antidoti possit deduci in ciuilem siue in pactum in contractu mutui.⟩

Oppone secundo: si debitor tenetur creditori in tantum quod illi est ad antidotum obligatus, ergo uidetur quod ipsa naturalis obligatio possit

696 .i. oppositio *in marg. sin.*
706 quodcumque illud *in marg. sin. add.*
715 .2. oppositio *in marg. sin.*

[14] Cf. gl. ord. ad X 5.19.10, casus (ed. cit. col. 1739); see below, 835-61.

[15] X 1.9.10 (*Prv* 30.33)

[16] Gl. ord. ad X 5.19.10, v. *Sperantes* (ed. cit. col. 1739).

[17] Decretum Grat. D.61 c.7

[18] Decretum Grat. D.59 c.2

[19] Decretum Grat. C.1 q.2 c.2

[20] X 3.26.7

[21] Dig. 5.3.25(28).11

[22] Gottofredo da Trani, *Apparatus glossarum in Decretales Gregorii IX*, ad X 5.19.10, v. *Sperantes* et v. *Intentione* (MS cit. fol. 163rb).

[23] Decretum Grat. C.11 q.3 c.66

[24] Decretum Grat. C.1 q.1 c.113

deduci in ciuilem et pactum interuenire, ad hoc *de preben.*, *Significatum*[25] et *de elec.*, *Significasti*[26] cum symilibus, cuius contrarium sentit decretalis uestra ⟨*Consuluit*⟩.

Solutio: dicas quod non sequitur est naturaliter ad antidotum obligatus, ergo potest deduci in ciuilem uel in pactum, ut notatur in c. .i. .xiiii. q. .iii. in glosa secunda,[27] et Gofredo hic[28] et per Ostiensem in summa eodem titulo § finali uersiculo "Quid si tibi"[29] ubi, licet conetur defendere contrarium (quod etiam sentire uidetur glosa .i. in fine in dicto c. .i. .14. q. .3.[30] secundum unam lecturam), tamen concludit quod predixi, quod etiam tenet Raymundus in summa eodem titulo,[31] et idem glosa super uerbo "Onera" in clementina una eodem titulo[32] et ibidem Stephanus prouincialis.[33] Et est ratio, ut dicit Gofredus, quia deducere in pactum sapit spem lucri.

Archydiaconus autem in dicto c. .i.[34] recitans uerba Petri clarius exprimit et reddit pro ratione quare naturalem obligationem antidoti non licet in pactum deducere: quia antidotum non est debitum simpliciter et ideo cum deducitur in pactum nascitur obligatio et ita plus promictitur. Est ergo post pactum debitor qui prius non erat ex antidoto debitor et sic esset usura ex quo plus promictitur. Non sic in casu decretalium *Significatum* et *Significasti* et similium iurium, quia ista onera, ista debita, insunt ex sua natura rei et ex onere sibi iniuncto. Cum ergo deducuntur in pactum, non est nisi declarare quod prius inerat. Et uide per Iohannem Calderinum infra eodem c. finali in .v. questione,[35] et quod infra dicam in .35. questione.[36]

[25] X 3.5.11

[26] X 1.6.4

[27] Gl. ord. ad Decretum Grat. C.14 q.3 c.1, v. *Expectes* (ed. cit. cols. 1095-96).

[28] Gottofredo da Trani, *Apparatus*, ad X 5.19.10, v. *Sperantes* (MS cit. fol. 163rb).

[29] Hostiensis, *Summa*, X 5.19 *de usuris*, n.12 (ed. cit. col. 1633).

[30] Gl. ord. ad Decretum Grat. C.14 q.3 c.1, v. *Plus quam* (ed. cit. col. 1095).

[31] Raymond of Penyafort, *Summa* 2.7 *de usuris*, n.4 (ed. cit. pp. 230b-231a).

[32] Gl. ord. ad Clem. 5.5.1, v. *Onera* (ed. cit. col. 256).

[33] *Locum non inveni.*

[34] Guido de Baysio, *Rosarium*, ad Decretum Grat. C.14 q.3 c.1, n.6 (ed. cit. fol. 207va).

[35] Johannes et Gaspar Calderinus, *Repetitiones*, in X 5.19.19 (MS cit. fols. 285r-286r).

[36] F_1 fol. 28r-v; *TUI* 7, fol. 23rb-va.

.3. oppositio ⟨Vtrum creditor possit etiam ex pacto interueniente in contractu mutui cum uniuersitate celebrati euitare collectas ad quas uniuersitati interim tenebatur.⟩

Oppone .3.° de notatis per Guillelmum in *Speculo* eodem titulo in fine,[37] ubi firmat quod euitare posset creditor, etiam ex pacto interueniente in contractu mutui inito cum uniuersitate, collectas ad quas interim uniuersitati tenebatur. Hic autem uidetur contrarium aperte sentire textus ibi "nichil inde sperantes,"[38] ergo et cetera.

Solutio: huius timore dicunt hic doctores quod debemus intelligere "nichil inde sperantes," scilicet "lucri." Sed dicit hic Iohannes Andree[39] et dominus meus Iohannes de Lignano post eum[40] quod predicta procedunt si nulle certe collecte statute sunt, secus autem in certis, argumento eorum que infra notantur eodem titulo c. finali,[41] et uide per dictum dominum meum etiam supra eodem *In ciuitate*.[42] Et hoc dictum Iohannis Andree approbat etiam Iohannes Calderinus in repetitione c. finalis infra eodem titulo, ubi uide in .4. questione ad finem.[43]

.4. oppositio ⟨Vtrum extra contractum mutui possit usura commicti. Et utrum dispositio decretalis *In ciuitate* procedat in his que non consistunt in numero, pondere uel mensura.⟩

Oppone .4.° ad solutionem tertie questionis textus tui de c. *In ciuitate* supra eodem titulo.[44]

Solutio: illud intelligitur quantum ad iudicium ecclesie quod ratione etiam dubii excusatur, istud autem de iudicio anime, et sic sunt casus diuersi, non aduersi, secundum glosam.[45] Vel aliter secundum eam dicas quod aliud est querere utrum ex forma contractus quis dicatur usurarius, quo casu loquitur decretalis *In ciuitate*, et aliud utrum ex intentione de-

743 .3. oppositio *in marg. sin.*
759 .4. oppositio *in marg. sin.*

[37] William Durant, *Speculum iuris*, 4.4 *de usuris*, n.6 (ed. Venice 1576, II p. 502a-b).

[38] X 5.19.10 (*Lc* 6.35)

[39] Johannes Andreae, *Novella*, ad X 5.19.10, n.3 (ed. cit. V fol. 75rb).

[40] John of Legnano, *Commentaria*, ad X 5.19.10 (MS cit. fol. 97v).

[41] Johannes Andreae, *Novella*, ad X 5.19.19, n.6 (ed. cit. V fols. 77vb-78ra).

[42] John of Legnano, *Commentaria*, ad X 5.19.10 (MS cit. fol. 97v).

[43] Johannes et Gaspar Calderinus, *Repetitiones*, in X 5.19.19 (MS cit. fol. 285r).

[44] X 5.19.6

[45] Gl. ord. ad X 5.19.10, v. *Male agere* (ed. cit. col. 1739).

prauata quis dicatur in iudicio anime male agere, quo casu loquitur decretalis ista. Nec habet obstare si dicatur quod cum forma sit que dat esse rei, quod non possit per consequens usurarius censeri quia, ut dicit glosa .3. supra eodem *In ciuitate*,[46] istud non procedit semper in isto casu. Vt enim dicit ibidem glosa .v.ª:[47] "licet ex sui forma non sit contractus usurarius, potest tamen fieri in fraudem usurarum, unde eque tenentur, *de pigno., Illo uos*,[48] et 'quodcumque ei nomen imponas, usura
11v est,' .14. q. .3. c. .i. et .ii."[49] Et, / ut statim dicam in oppositione sequenti,[50] iuris fictione et tacite dicitur etiam in tali contractu mutuum interuenisse ratione intentionis, et hinc insurrexit cotidiana pratica totius orbis que habet non solum instrumenta cantantia in contractu uenditionis sed etiam lauda et sententias omneque aliud genus contractuum, sub quacumque uerborum forma conceptorum, coram ecclesiastico iudice impugnari de usuraria prauitate, mentem facti et rei ueritatem proponendo et dicendo tales contractus celebratos in fraudem usurarum. Et probatur talis pratica *de iureiuran., Ad nostram*,[51] *de emp. et uen., Ad nostram*,[52] *de pigno., Illo uos*[53] et capitulo *Cum contra*[54] cum notatis in illis per doctores.

Ego non recte concipio quomodo decretalis illa *In ciuitate* faciat contra hanc, nam sicut hic dicitur male agere qui rem plus debito uendit eo quod differt solutionem pretii, ita et ibi peccare dicitur qui uendit rem plus quam ualeat eo quod differt pretii solutionem. Et licet ibi dicatur quod ex forma contractus non possit dici usurarius, hic tamen non dicitur contrarium. Videtur tamen illa decretalis ex alio capite facere contra istam, scilicet ex eo quod ibi dicit textus in fine et hoc, puto, considerauerit glosa.[55] Sed limita hunc textum secundum illum et utrumque secundum textum decretalis finalis in fine infra eodem titulo, ut etiam utrobique glosa dixit.[56]

Aliam limitationem dabat etiam dominus Baldus de Perusio. Dixit

[46] Gl. ord. ad X 5.19.6, v. *Ex tali forma* (ed. cit. col. 1737).

[47] Ibid., v. *Venditores* (ed. cit. col. 1737).

[48] X 3.21.4

[49] Decretum Grat. C.14 q.3 c.1-2 (*recte* c.3).

[50] See below, 823-34.

[51] X 2.24.7; gl. ord. ad X 2.24.7, v. *Ad restituendum* (ed. cit. col. 801).

[52] X 3.17.5; gl. ord. ad X 3.17.5, v. *Emptionis* (ed. cit. col. 1126).

[53] X 3.21.4; gl. ord. ad X 3.21.4, v. *Obligatis* (ed. cit. col. 1143).

[54] X 3.21.6; gl. ord. ad X 3.21.6, v. *Extenuassent* (ed. cit. cols. 1145-46).

[55] Gl. ord. ad X 5.19.6, v. *Vsurarum* (ed. cit. col. 1737).

[56] Ibid., v. *Venditores* (ed. cit. col. 1737); ad X 5.19.19, v. *Tempore non fuerat venditurus* (col. 1745).

enim C. eodem titulo super rubrica[57] quod tunc est locus ei quod disponitur in ipsa decretali *In ciuitate* et huic quando res que uenditur consistit in pondere, numero uel mensura, quia in his tantum usura commictitur. Secus si uendatur domus uel predium, presertim cum emptor interim percipit utilitatem, C. *de ac. emp.* l. *Curabit.*[58] Baldus.

Hoc dictum non uidetur uerum, nam etsi usura consistat in his que consistunt in numero et cetera, quia in mutuo tamen hoc est uerum quoad sui formam, ut supra eodem *In ciuitate*, sed tamen potest etiam commicti in fraudem, forma non seruata, ut supra statim dixi et hic et supra in dicto c. *In ciuitate* est casus, pro quo que ibi scripxit Gofredus[59] et statim dicam in sequenti oppositione. Eque enim contrahitur ex mente mutuum cum uenditur fundus secundum casum nostrum et dicti c. *In ciuitate* sicut quando uenditur res consistens in pondere, numero uel mensura, ut de se patet, nam ita uno casu sicut reliquo fingitur pretium ab emptore traditum uenditori et sibi postea mutuatum cum lucro. Si tamen uerbum "presertim," quo usus est dominus Baldus improprie, hoc est pro "tantum" summeretur, tunc posset procedere dictum suum iuxta notata in c. *Conquestus* supra eodem[60] et per Ostiensem in summa eodem titulo § *Ex quibus* uersiculo "Ex quasi" et § *An aliquo* uersiculo .vii.,[61] ubi uide. Quod etiam non fateor indistincte, licet indistincte sic firmet glosa in dicta l. *Curabit*[62] et in l. *Iulianus* § *Papinianus* ff. *de actio. emp. et uen.*[63] et ibi Bartolus.[64] Posset enim esse quantitas quam plus petit ratione dilationis solutionis tanta et in tantum excedens ipsos fructus, quod de facili fraudulentam iudicarem. Via ergo media eligatur. Ad hoc quod infra dicam in .15. et .16. et .18. questionibus.[65]

.v.ª oppositio ⟨Ad idem.⟩

Oppone .v.º ad idem: papa pro fundamento responsionis sue ad un-

823 .v.ª oppositio *in marg. sin.*

[57] Baldus de Ubaldis, *Commentaria*, in C. 4.32.rubr., nn.11-12 (ed. cit. VII fols. 87vb-88ra).

[58] C. 4.49.5

[59] Gottofredo da Trani, *Apparatus*, ad X 5.19.6, v. *Nisi dubium sit* (MS cit. fol. 163ra).

[60] Gl. ord. ad X 5.19.8, v. *De feudo* (ed. cit. cols. 1737-38).

[61] Hostiensis, *Summa*, X 5.19 *de usuris*, n.6 (ed. cit. col. 1617); n.7 (col. 1622).

[62] Gl. ord. ad C. 4.49.5, v. *Ratio* (ed. cit. col. 1035).

[63] Gl. ord. ad Dig. 19.1.13(14).26, v. *Excedit* (ed. cit. I p. 966b).

[64] Bartolus of Sassoferrato, *Commentaria*, in Dig. 19.1.13(14).26, n.2 (ed. cit. II fol. 118vb).

[65] See below, 1895-1986, 2001-2182.

umquodque de tribus prelibatis quesitis adducit auctoritatem euuangelii "date mutuum" et cetera.[66] Sed cum in .3.º quesito non mutuum sed uenditio interueniat, ergo sequitur quod inepte et inconuenienter ad responsum et decisionem illius adduxerit auctoritatem suprafatam.

Solutio: potest dici quod attento quod ratione dilationis solutionis faciende pretium augmentatur, perinde censendum est acsi pretium ueri ualoris tempore uenditionis uenditor recepisset et emptori mutuasset sub illo pluri usurarum nomine, et licet non quoad formam, tamen ex mente. Ad hoc que notat post Gofredum Iohannes Andree supra eodem c. *In ciuitate* super glosa antepenultima.[67]

.vi.ª oppositio ⟨Ad idem.⟩

Oppone .vi.º ad idem quod iuris dispositione permictente attentatur non est iudicandum male agi. Sed iuris dispositione permissum est contrahentibus se decipere usque ad dimidiam iusti pretii, supra *de emp. et uen., Cum dilecti*[68] et c. penultimo[69] et C. *de rescin. uendi.* l. .ii.[70] et finali,[71] ergo et cetera.

Solutio: Innocentius in c. *In ciuitate* supra eodem in quadam sua additione,[72] ut refert etiam Iohannes Calderinus in c. finali infra eodem in
12r .3. oppositione,[73] / et dominus meus ibidem[74] dicebant quod illud habet locum iure fori, non iure poli, pro quo facit ista decretalis *Consuluit* cum sua glosa finali.[75]

Sed dicit ipse Iohannes Calderinus quod istud non uidetur bene dictum, quoniam non est dubium quod idem in iudiciali foro cum in eo de hoc constaret. Propter quod, secundum eum, dicendum est quod contraria locuntur in uera uenditione si tamen dolus non dedit causam con-

835 .vi.ª oppositio *in marg. sin.*
836 di *post* quod *del.*

[66] *Lc* 6.35

[67] Gottofredo da Trani, *Apparatus*, ad X 5.19.6, v. *Nisi dubium sit* (MS cit. fol. 163ra); Johannes Andreae, *Novella*, ad X 5.19.6, n.6 (ed. cit. V fol. 74rb).

[68] X 3.17.3

[69] X 3.17.6

[70] C. 4.44.2

[71] C. 4.44.18

[72] Innocent IV, *Commentaria*, ad X 5.19.6, n.1 (ed. cit. fol. 517ra-b).

[73] Johannes et Gaspar Calderinus, *Repetitiones*, in X 5.19.19 (MS cit. fols. 281v-282r).

[74] John of Legnano, *Commentaria*, ad X 5.19.19 (MS cit. fol. 99v).

[75] X 5.19.10; gl. ord. ad X 5.19.10, v. *Male agere* (ed. cit. col. 1739).

tractui nec incidit in contractu, sed fuit deceptio in re ipsa quia credebat uenditor rem minus ualere uel emptor plus ualere: non enim est credendum quod ius canonicum, quod a spiritu sancto processit, .l. di. *Si quis diaconus*,[76] deceptionem uel dolum approbaret. Sed hic uterque, et emptor et uenditor, sciebant quantum res ualebat iusto pretio, unde hic non fuit ulla deceptio in re ipsa. Item hic non erat uera uenditio, considerato quod ipsius pecunie solutio expectatur, quod habet rationem mutui quia ultra iustum pretium pro huius expectatione exigitur et hoc pertinet ad rationem usure, secundum Iohannem Calderinum. Pro prima solutione sua facit glosa prima supra eodem *In ciuitate*;[77] pro secunda uero glosa .iii. in decretali *Ad nostram, de emp. et uen.*[78] et finis glose secunde dicte decretalis *In ciuitate.*[79]

.vii.ª oppositio ⟨Ad idem.⟩

Oppone .vii.º ad idem: "tantum res ualet quantum uendi potest, ff. *Ad Trebellia.* l. .i. § *Si heres*,[80] ff. *ad legem Falci., Querebatur*,[81] ff. *de fur., Si quis uxori* § ultimo.[82]"[83] Si sic relinquitur ergo impossibile fore quod casus interuenerit quod ultra ualorem debitum merces uendita fuerit.

Solue ut supra eodem titulo *In ciuitate* in glosa secunda.[84]

.viii.ª oppositio ⟨Vtrum recipere aliquid ultra sortem a soluere seu dare uolente sit peccatum uel usura. Et si sic, quare sic. Et utrum creditoris uel debitoris uoluntas sit in talibus attendenda, et cetera.⟩

Oppone .viii.º ad primum et ultimum responsum et supradicta post glosam et doctores. Et uidetur quod immo nec sit peccatum nec ad restitutionem quis teneatur de receptis in primo uel ultimo casu. Proba: quod quis licite recipit non cadit in peccato uel restitutione. Sed tale est hoc, igitur et cetera. Maior est notissima et probatur .xiiii. q. .v. *Non sane*,[85]

852 a papa *post* quod *del.*
862 .vii.ª oppositio *in marg. sin.*
868 .viii.ª oppositio *in marg. sin.*

[76] Decretum Grat. D.50 c.29
[77] Gl. ord. ad X 5.19.6, v. *Comparant* (ed. cit. col. 1736).
[78] Gl. ord. ad X 3.17.5, v. *Patet* (ed. cit. col. 1126).
[79] Gl. ord. ad X 5.19.6, v. *Non valent* (ed. cit. col. 1736).
[80] Dig. 36.1.1.16
[81] Dig. 35.2.82(81)
[82] Dig. 47.2.52(53).29
[83] Gl. ord. ad X 5.19.6, v. *Non valent* (ed. cit. col. 1736).
[84] Ibid.
[85] Decretum Grat. C.14 q.5 c.15

supra *de censi., Cum apostolus,*[86] *Sopite,*[87] *Procurationes,*[88] infra *de sen. ex., Cum uoluntate*[89] cum symilibus. Minor probatur ex eo quod quisque licite recipit quod sibi uoluntarie datur, .xviii. di. *De eulogiis,*[90] .i. q. .ii. *Placuit,*[91] supra *de sy., Dilectus* .ii.[92] Accedant notata in regula *Peccatum, de reg. iuris* li. .vi.[93] Sed in proposito nedum uoluntarie sed quinimo forte ipso dante rogante et instante, et sic nec dolus nec iniuria poterit recipienti adscribi, ff. *de condi. inde.* l. .i.,[94] ff. *de reg. iuris, Cuius per errorem*[95] infra eodem titulo *Scienti* li. .vi.[96] Accedat ad hoc uerbum illud Vallerii Maximi sic dicentis "perquam stultum esse argumentando a quibus bona precamur, ab his porrigentibus nolle assummere."[97] Et si dicatur, dans substinet dampnum et nemo debet cum alterius iactura ditari, responde: hoc procedit ex uoluntate sua, et sic, si culpa est, sua est, sibique debet et non alteri imputari, ut in regula *Dampnum, de reg. iuris* li. .vi.,[98] et ff. *de nego. ge., Si quis negotia*[99] cum symilibus.

Solutio: est dare quedam que de sui natura non sunt inlicita et in his procedunt supradicta. Est et dare quedam que de sui natura, ratione pacti uel contractus, sunt inlicita, ut in usuris. Vnde contrahentes non possunt facere licitum quod de sui natura est inlicitum, secundum Iohannem Calderinum infra eodem c. finali,[1] qui allegat in argumentum supra *de foro compe., Si diligenti,*[2] infra *de sen. ex., Contingit* .i.[3] Et posuit etiam

[86] X 3.39.6

[87] X 3.39.14

[88] X 3.39.23

[89] X 5.39.54; cf. gl. ord. ad X 5.39.54, v. *Vel alio* et v. *Quasi gerunt causam eorum* (ed. cit. col. 1927).

[90] Decretum Grat. D.18 c.8

[91] Decretum Grat. C.1 q.2 c.1

[92] X 5.3.30

[93] Gl. ord. ad VI *de reg. iur.* 4, *Peccatum*, v. *Restituatur* (ed. cit. col. 719).

[94] Dig. 12.6.1

[95] Dig. 50.17.53(54)

[96] VI *de reg. iur.* 27, *Scienti*

[97] Valerius Maximus, *Factorum et dictorum memorabilium* 1.1, ext. 3, ed. Carolus Kempf (Stuttgart, 1966), 12. Cf. Cicero, *De natura deorum* 3.84, ed. Arthur Stanley Pease, 2 vols. (Cambridge, MA, 1955-58), 2: 1198.

[98] VI *de reg. iur.* 86, *Damnum*

[99] Dig. 3.5.22(24)

[1] Johannes et Gaspar Calderinus, *Repetitiones*, in X 5.19.19 (MS cit. fols. 282r-283r).

[2] X 2.2.12

[3] X 5.39.36

effectiue Iohannes Andree in dicta questione super regula *Peccatum* in principio,[4] et dominus meus in c. *Nauiganti* infra eodem in ultima oppositione,[5] ubi uide, et magister Gregorius de Arimino in tractatu suo montis in .3. parte, scilicet in responsionibus ad argumenta in principio;[6] sunt enim multi casus in quibus etiam a uolente non licet, secundum eum, recipere.

Et si dicatur, in primo casu decretalis nostre nulla interuenit pactio, fateor aperta sed celata sic ex parte mutuantis, etsi non dantis, ex quo 12v / ea intentione ductus est mutuans ut aliquid reciperet ultra sortem, aliter non mutuaturus. Item sola spes sine pactione inducit usuram, ut hic est casus et infra et supra tangitur. Et ut dicebat Iohannes Calderinus in dicto c. finali infra eodem,[7] interdum uoluntas uel consensus dantis in talibus modicum operatur; nam et ab inuito interdum aliquid aufertur sine dolo uel iniuria, interdum etiam a uolente aliquid summitur scelerate, ut ab eo qui uoluntarie dat iudici ut etiam iustam ferat sententiam, ut hec omnia habentur in predicto c. *Non sane* .xiiii. q. .v.[8] Ad idem .i. q. .i. *Eos*,[9] et *de rescrip.*, *Statutum* uersiculo "Si quid autem" li. .vi.,[10] et *de censi.*, *Exigit* ad finem eodem libro,[11] et in clementina *de hereti.*, *Nolentes* uersiculo "Quodsi."[12] Hinc dicebat deuotus Bernardus quod "usura est legalis latro predicens quod intendit."[13]

Potest etiam dici quod neutro casu est libera uoluntas, cum debitor in primo soluere, emptor in secundo consentire presummantur propter eorum indigentiam. Est ergo eorum uoluntas turbata et quoddamodo uiolentata, iuxta ea que in simili scripxit Iohannes Calderinus in dicto c.

900 licet *post* non *del.*

[4] Johannes Andreae, *Novella*, ad VI *de reg. iur.* 4 *Peccatum*, n.4 (ed. cit. fol. 62rb).

[5] John of Legnano, *Commentaria*, ad X 5.19.19 (MS cit. fol. 99r-v).

[6] Gregory of Rimini, *Tractatus*, art. 4 (ed. cit. fol. C1r-v).

[7] Johannes et Gaspar Calderinus, *Repetitiones*, in X 5.19.19 (MS cit. fol. 282v).

[8] Decretum Grat. C.14 q.5 c.15

[9] Decretum Grat. C.1 q.1 c.21

[10] VI 1.3.11

[11] VI 3.20.2

[12] Clem. 5.3.2

[13] Pseudo-Bernard of Clairvaux, *Epistola ad Raymundum dominum Castri Ambruosii* (*PL* 182.650); Johannes Andreae, *Novella*, ad VI *de reg. iur.* 4, *Peccatum*, n.7 (ed. cit. fol. 62vb).

finali,[14] qui pro simili allegat c. *Matheus* supra *de symo.*[15]

Sed oppone contra hanc ultimam solutionem: licet enim propter indigentiam presummatur quis non uoluntarie sed coacte soluere aliquid ultra sortem quando interuenit pactio, non tamen quando non interuenit, cum non ualeat compelli.

Solutio: subest timor ne repetat capitale de presenti non sine magno forsan incommodo debitoris, iuxta ea que leguntur ff. *de condi. indebi.* l. *Si non sortem* § *Si quis falso* in glosa[16] et facit quod notatur in c. *Debitores* supra *de iureiuran.*[17] Vel si non est locus repetitioni capitalis, eo quod iam restituit, ne, si quid non soluerit ultra, reputetur ita indiscretus quod aliter non reperiat mutuantem et in suis necessitatibus sibi subuenientem, argumento eorum que notantur .x. q. .ii. *Hoc ius* in glosa *Sed numquid creditor* et cetera[18] et per Iohannem Andree in questione super regula *Dampnum* in .3.° argumento prime partis et in solutione questionis in quarto membro in uersiculo "Et dico cum Gofredo,"[19] ubi hoc satis aperte comprobari uidetur. Et uide quod infra dicam questione .47., conclusione .vii.ª.[20]

Sed ratio prelibata concludit quem usurarium ⟨esse qui⟩, etiam si non primario sed secundario spem habens uel etiam nullo modo illam habens, aliquid ultra sortem a debitore recepit. Sed non est ita, sola enim eo modo coacta debitoris uoluntas: si pactio non interuenit nec corrupta creditoris spes uel intentio, non inducit peccatum uel usuram in creditore; sed altero ex predictis interueniente, bene. Nec corrupta dici potest si non primario, etsi secundario, interueniat, iuxta supra notata in .i. oppositione.[21] Et ita intelligo rationem Calderini,[22] quia et sic ipse intellexit, ut patet aperte cum se referat ad casum dicte decretalis finalis. Consideramus etenim in hoc animum recipientis potius quam dantis, hinc uidemus quod etsi libera foret debitoris uoluntas in dando ultra sortem, ita tamen quod ad mutuum respectum habuerit, nichilominus creditor recipiens illud ultra ⟨sortem⟩ secundum suam depra-

[14] Johannes et Gaspar Calderinus, *Repetitiones*, in X 5.19.19 (MS cit. fol. 282v).

[15] X 5.3.23

[16] Gl. ord. ad Dig. 12.6.26.2, v. *Indebitum* (ed. cit. I p. 701a).

[17] Gl. ord. ad X 2.24.6, v. *Cogendi sunt* (ed. cit. cols. 799-800).

[18] Gl. ord. ad Decretum Grat. C.10 q.2 c.2, v. *Probat* (ed. cit. col. 929).

[19] Johannes Andreae, *Novella*, ad VI *de reg. iur*. 86, *Damnum*, n.4 (ed. cit. fol. 16rb); n.13 (fol. 16vb).

[20] F_1 fols. 33v-34r; *TUI* 7, fol. 25rb.

[21] See above, 696-714.

[22] Johannes et Gaspar Calderinus, *Repetitiones*, in X 5.19.19 (MS cit. fol. 282v).

uatam intentionem tenetur ad restitutionem si uult penitentiam agere de peccato, ut infra tangetur in .3. questione,[23] quod sane intelligo et secundum limitationem quam infra dabo in .vi. et .vii. questionibus[24] ad finem et uide omnino etiam questionem .ix.[25]

Item plus dico quod etsi animum debitoris considerare debemus (quod tamen non semper est uerum, ut infra tangam in .ix. questione),[26] non tamen eum ex quouis leui uel minimo iudicare compulsum, "ne si nimia subtilitate" in his utamur "eis in pernitiem uertatur," C. *Ad Trebell.* l. penultima in principio,[27] C. *de uer. si.* l. .iii⟨i⟩. in fine,[28] et quod notatur .x. q. .ii. *Hoc ius* in glosa preallegata ad finem.[29] Et sic non debemus di-
13r cere eum compulsum semper presummi tamquam nolentem / indiscretum reputari, dummodo sit facta restitutio capitalis, quoniam eadem ratione idem diceremus in fine seu liberatione facta per creditorem usurarum usurario, non obstante quod capitalis restitutio facta foret, cum tamen contrarium comuniter asseramus; et si non sic, cum ipsius capitalis restitutio non est facta. Ad hoc quod scripxit Fredericus de Senis in opere suo consilio .xviii. in principio solutionis, ibi "etiam precibus uel seruitiorum exhibitione inductus" et cetera.[30]

Preterea, ut scribit Iohannes Andree post disputantem super dicta regula *Peccatum* in secunda columpna,[31] donatio uel oblatio quam non preuenit petitio uel obligans pactio presummitur esse grata et libera, ac per consequens illius oblati licita est receptio, secundum eundem. Item nec debemus, uidere meo, circumscriptis dictis disputantis, semper eum coactum iudicare seu presummere. Hoc dico loquens ab experto, uidi enim plures soluere ultra sortem nulla prorsus intranea uel extranea coactione ducti sed quinimo laudabili discretione, quoniam cum tali pecunia sic mutuo accepta uiderunt se lucrari duplum eius quod soluunt pro centenario suo creditori. Vnde dico discreti iudicis in hoc multum exuberare arbitrium ita tamen quod semper in tutiorem partem declinet et

958 iii⟨i⟩.: F_1 iii.

[23] See below, 1021-1142.
[24] See below, 1205-1473.
[25] See below, 1514-1600.
[26] See below, 1524-59.
[27] C. 6.49(48).7.pr.
[28] C. 6.38.4
[29] Gl. ord. ad Decretum Grat. C.10 q.2 c.2, v. *Probat* (ed. cit. col. 929).
[30] Fredericus Petruccius, *Consilia et questiones*, quaestio 18 (ed. Venice 1508, fols. 13vb-14ra).
[31] Johannes Andreae, *Novella*, ad VI *de reg. iur.* 4. *Peccatum*, n.7 (ed. cit. fol. 62va).

quatenus anime salus tangitur. Veniet ergo in hoc arbitrio considerare personam dantis: an sit discreta uel canina ut sic presummatur ex discretione et sic uoluntarie, an ex necessitate et sic coacte, dare; ex exterioribus namque de interioribus presummimus, *de presump.*, *Ex studiis*[32] cum symilibus. Item an sibi ab aliis sic consueuerit fieri et ipse aliis, an non. Item an multum aut parum aut nichil lucratus fuerit cum iamdicta pecunia mutuo accepta. Item utrum sine illa ualeat sua mercimonia exercere uel sua alia explicare negotia, quisquis fuerit, sine magno incommodo; an e contra. Item an consueuerit creditor a non dante ultra sortem aliquid suam pecuniam reuelle siue repetere. Item an sit homo multe discretionis et honestatis, an uorax et auarus, an consanguineus uel affinis uel intimus debitoris amicus. Et sic de similibus ex quibus coniecturare ualeat et arbitrari uir bonus an coacta uerisimiliter presummi debeat talis datio, an ex liberalitatis riuulo schaturire; ex preteritis namque presummimus circa futura, .xxiii. q. .v. *Si apud*,[33] *de presump.*, *Mandata*[34] et c. *Scribam*.[35] Accedant ad predicta in argumento que scripxit Ostiensis et post eum Iohannes Andree in decretalibus *Ex literis*, *de iureiuran.*[36] et *de emp. et uen.*, *Ad nostram*.[37] Et uide omnino infra in .x.[38] et .lxii. questionibus.[39]

Sed quid concludimus tandem? Estne uerum quod turbata debitoris uoluntas, si pura est intentio creditoris, non inducat peccatum uel usuram in creditore? Credo quod sic sed non indistincte uel semper, sed cum limitatione quam infra dabo in .9. questione.[40] Ad quod bene facit quod scribit Augustinus libro .i. *de ciuitate Dei* capitulo .xvi.º.[41]

.i. questio

Modo ad questiones descendens, primo quero pro declaratione tex-

987 a *interlin.*
1003 .i. questio *in marg. sin.*

[32] X 2.23.3; cf. gl. ord. ad X 2.23.3, v. *Intelligitur* (ed. cit. col. 786).

[33] Decretum Grat. C.23 q.5 c.24

[34] X 2.23.6

[35] X 2.23.9

[36] Johannes Andreae, *Novella*, ad X 2.24.32, n.4 (ed. cit. II fol. 199vb); Hostiensis, *Commentaria*, ad X 2.24.32, n.1 (ed. cit. II fol. 137va).

[37] Johannes Andreae, *Novella*, ad X 3.17.5, nn.3-5 (ed. cit. III fols. 80vb-81ra); Hostiensis, *Commentaria*, ad X 3.17.5, nn.1-3 (ed. cit. III fol. 58va).

[38] See below, 1601-51.

[39] F_1 fol. 40r-v; *TUI* 7, fol. 27va-b.

[40] See below, 1524-31, 1592-1600.

[41] Augustine, *De ciuitate Dei* 1.16, ed. Bernardus Dombart, 4th ed. rev. Alphonsus Kalb (Leipzig, 1928-29); repr. in *CCSL* 47 (Turnhout, 1955), 18.

tus circa secundam consultationem decretalis huius ⟨*Consuluit*⟩:[42] que fuit consulentis intentio in illa?

Respondeo quod ⟨fuit⟩ talis: cum enim instaret finis termini quo debitor tenebatur per iuramentum soluere creditori et non uolens soluere postulabat termini prorogationem; obaudiebat creditor; nil tamen uerbo petebat. Id tamen ea intentione denegabat ut a debitore sibi aliquid solueretur, uel forte erat iuramento adstrictus debitor creditori ne ullatenus sine libera ipsius licentia se posset absentare, quam eadem intentione sibi creditor denegabat, propter quod sciens debitor se aliter incassum procul dubio laborare aliquid offert suo creditori, queritur modo et cetera.

.2.ª questio

Secundo quero an uerbum illud "date mutuum"[43] et cetera sit in precepto?

13v Solutio: / secundum Gofredum,[44] sic, in casu necessitatis, quo omnia sunt comunicanda, .xlvii. di. *Sicut hi*,[45] .xii. q. .i. *Dilectissimis*.[46]

.3.ª questio ⟨Vtrum usurarius intentionalis teneatur ad restitutionem recepti ultra sortem.⟩

.3.º quero: bene uideo quod mutuans et non habens primario sed secundario dumtaxat spem ad lucrum non peccat nec tenetur ad restitutionem, ut hic in glosa secunda[47] et dixi supra in .i. oppositione,[48] et firmabant etiam Gofredus hic[49] et Ostiensis in summa huius tituli post principium,[50] de quo hic per Iohannem Andree[51] et per eundem plenius in mercuriali posita super regula *Peccatum*, *de reg. iuris*. li. .vi. in .i. articulo

1013 debitor *scripsi:* F_1 creditor
1016 .2.ª questio *in marg. sin.*
1021 .3.ª questio *in marg. sin.*

[42] X 5.19.10

[43] *Lc* 6.35 (X 5.19.10)

[44] Gottofredo da Trani, *Apparatus*, ad X 5.19.10, v. *Date mutuum* (MS cit. fol. 163rb).

[45] Decretum Grat. D.47 c.8

[46] Decretum Grat. C.12 q.1 c.2

[47] Gl. ord. ad X 5.19.10, v. *Sperantes* (ed. cit. col. 1739).

[48] See above, 696-714.

[49] Gottofredo da Trani, *Apparatus*, ad X 5.19.10, v. *Sperantes* (MS cit. fol. 163rb).

[50] Hostiensis, *Summa*, X 5.19 *de usuris*, n.1 (ed. cit. col. 1613).

[51] Johannes Andreae, *Novella*, ad X 5.19.10, n.4 (ed. cit. V fol. 75rb).

questionis,[52] quo casu non loquitur decretalis nostra ⟨*Consuluit*⟩.[53]

Sed quid de casu quo loquitur decretalis nostra, scilicet de illo qui principaliter spe ductus usure mutuo dedit pecuniam suam, id tamen non deduxit in pactum? Si nichil recepit ultra sortem mutuo datam, non est questio: agat penitentiam de peccato. Sed si aliquid secundum spem suam a debitore recepit, teneturne ad restitutionem? Dixerunt quidam[54] quod non, nisi aliquid fecerit propter quod debitor aliquid dare necessario compellatur, puta negando terminum, recipiendo cautiones maioris summe uel denegando relaxationem iuramenti ei qui se iurauit non absentaturum et cetera uel his similia. Non enim refert quid ex equipollentibus fiat et an uerbo uel demonstratione seu circumlocutione aliquid ostendatur, *de testi., Licet* .ii.,[55] *de consan. et affi., Tua nos,*[56] ff. *si cer. pe.* l. *Certum est,*[57] ff. *de rei uen., Si in rem* in fine[58] cum symilibus, et sic, secundum istos, sicut non nocet simonia mentalis quoad restitutionem sed per penitentiam aboletur,[59] ita nec usura mentalis.

Alii dicunt, et est tutius secundum Innocentium,[60] immo uerissimum secundum Ostiensem,[61] quod semper tenetur restituere ex quo principaliter illa intentione ductus est, quod etiam placuit Raymundo in summa huius tituli, uersiculo "Sed numquid uoluntas,"[62] et Archydiacono in c. .i. .xiiii. q. .iii.[63] Et hec quoad iudicium anime et ita firmant hic Iohannes Andree[64] et dominus meus[65] et etiam glosa,[66] si recte ponderas, et notauit etiam dominus meus in c. finali infra eodem[67] et in c. finali supra *de*

[52] Johannes Andreae, *Novella*, ad VI *de reg. iur.* 4, *Peccatum*, nn.7-8 (ed. cit. fol. 62va-b).

[53] X 5.19.10

[54] Innocent IV, *Commentaria*, ad X 5.19.10 (ed. cit. fol. 517vb).

[55] X 2.20.47

[56] X 4.14.7

[57] Dig. 12.1.6

[58] Dig. 6.1.6

[59] Cf. X 5.3.46

[60] Innocent IV, *Commentaria*, ad X. 5.19.10 (ed. cit. fol. 517vb).

[61] Hostiensis, *Commentaria*, ad X 5.19.10, n.3 (ed. cit. V fol. 57vb).

[62] Raymond of Penyafort, *Summa* 2.7 *de usuris*, n.4 (ed. cit. pp. 229b-230a).

[63] Guido de Baysio, *Rosarium*, ad Decretum Grat. C.14. q.3 c.1, n.3 (ed. cit. fol. 207va).

[64] Johannes Andreae, *Novella*, ad X 5.19.10, n.4 (ed. cit. V fol. 75rb).

[65] John of Legnano, *Commentaria*, ad X 5.19.10 (MS cit. fol. 97r).

[66] Gl. ord. ad X 5.19.10, casus (ed. cit. col. 1739).

[67] John of Legnano, *Commentaria*, ad X 5.19.19 (MS cit. fol. 99v).

sy.,[68] et ipse Iohannes Andree in mercuriali posita super regula *Peccatum* in secunda columpna,[69] licet aliud senserit disputans ibidem (cui concordat Paulus ⟨de Liazariis⟩ in clementina .i. *de usu.*),[70] qui uoluit id locum habere et sic intelligit hanc decretalem cum corrupta creditoris intentio innotuit debitori, quasi uideatur tunc quoddam pactum implicitum quod habet uim expliciti. Est enim, secundum eum, usura duplex, quarum una simpliciter est mentalis et solum uitians sed non obligans ad restituendum, ex eo quod fit sine omni exactione et pacto explicito uel implicito. Alia uero est uitians et obligans ad restituendum, ex eo quod fit cum exactione et pacto explicite uel implicite intellecto. Si ergo fiat cum implicito, est usura mentalis; si cum explicito, est usura uocalis. Et sic ex predictis infertur in proposito nostro quod in casu quo non innotuit debitori corrupta creditoris intentio, exto quod ea intentione principaliter ductus sit, non obligatur ad restitutionem. Et hanc partem, ut dixi, tenebat dictus disputans.

Et quia propter inferius tangenda hoc scire per principalius est necessarium, discutiamus plenius hunc passum.[71] Vnde sciendum quod disputans hic pro hac sua opinione adducebat tales rationes. Prima, quia cum formale in usura sit exactio ex pacto obligante uel aliquid aliud equipollens, ergo sequitur quod ubi non est talis exactio uel aliud equipollens, ibi non cadit usura ad restitutionem obligans, quamuis bene usura uitians. Confirmatur quia aliud dicendo non saluaretur descriptio usure, que habet quod usura est lucrum ex mutuo pacto debitum uel exactum. .2.ª ratio est quia sicut in furto dicimus quod si aliquis gratis et
14r liberaliter in dono recipit quod furari intendebat et affectabat, / quamuis sit fur mente, non tamen in opere ita quod ad restitutionem teneatur, ergo a simili, si quis lucrari intendit ex mutuo quod concedit et tamen a suo debitore nichil exigit nec ipsum per aliquod pactum compellit, sed gratis et liberaliter ab eo aliquid recipit, quamuis sit usurarius mente, non tamen est censendus usurarius in opere ut ad restitutionem teneatur. .3.ª ratio est quia tota ratio quare usurarius tenetur ad restitutionem

1052-53 cui concordat ... de usu. *in marg. dex. add.*
1064 est *post* ductus *del.*
1074 si *interlin.*

[68] Ibid., ad X 5.3.46 (MS cit. fol. 73v).

[69] Johannes Andreae, *Novella*, ad VI *de reg. iur.* 4, *Peccatum*, nn.8-9 (ed. cit. fol. 62vb-63ra).

[70] Paulus de Liazariis, *Lectura in Clementinas*, in Clem. 5.5.1, v. *Solvantur usurae* (Vatican City, Biblioteca Apostolica Vaticana, Vat. lat. 1452, fol. 240rb-va).

[71] Johannes Andreae, *Novella*, ad VI *de reg. iur.* 4, *Peccatum*, n.8 (fols. 62vb-63ra).

usurarum est quia illud quod recipit ultra sortem non fuit ei gratis et liberaliter donatum sed cum quadam exactione et pacto indebite usurpatum. Vbi ergo est sola spes lucri et intentio corrupta ex parte recipientis, dummodo illa non sit nota debitori, ibi quicquid debitor donat, gratis et libere donat, et per consequens nichil est indebite usurpatum et ideo ipse recipiens, quamuis fuerit in intentione deprauatus, non tamen uidetur teneri ad restitutionem. Hec ille.

Sed tu per ordinem responde ad has rationes secundum Iohannem Andree. Et ad primam dicas quod nec ipse disputans saluat prelibatam descriptionem usure dicendo de intentione nota debitori quod sufficiat ad introducendum effectum restitutionis fiende, quasi dicat Iohannes Andree quod etsi debitori sit nota intentio creditoris, non tamen pactum seu exactio ex pacto, quod tu asseris formale in usura, interuenit. Item dicit Iohannes Andree tenendo contrarium et distinguendo inter principalem et secundariam intentionem, tu saluabis auctoritatem illam euangelicam "date mutuum" et cetera, et satis eius rigorem temperaueris sic distinguendo.

Non uidetur plene responsum, quia etsi non interuenerit pactum explicitum, tamen interuenit implicitum et sic aliquid pacto equipollens, quod sufficere uidetur. Sed dicas quod immo, quia etsi pactum implicitum interuenerit, non tamen exactio ex pacto obligante locum habere potest uel aliud equipollens. Vbi enim quod exigere possit creditor a debitore usuras mentales tamquam ex pacto etiam implicito debitas, exto quod mens et intentio corrupta in eius notitiam deuenerit? Non ergo sit diuersum debitorem sciuisse uel nesciuisse intentionem creditoris. Item dico descriptionem predictam non fore plenam, nisi uelimus eam ampliare etiam ad casum nostrum secundum quod feci in .i. questione supra posita super rubrica[72] et faciat ad predicta quod statim tangam in ultima responsione.[73]

Ad secundam rationem respondet Iohannes Andree quod inter casum illum furti et nostrum est maxima dissimilitudo quoniam licet donatarius in casu furti habuerit intentionem corruptam ad furandum, non tamen donatio causatur ab eius facto nec est annexa illi intentioni corrupte, cuius contrarium in mutuo quod, cum ex bono caritatis deberet fieri gratis, fiebat principaliter ex spe lucri, quod etiam ipse disputans concedit esse uitiosum, cuius spei uitiose sequitur effectus consequendo lucrum, secundum Iohannem Andree, quod statim tibi latius dilucidabo.[74]

Sed uenio ad respondendum tertie rationi. Et dico primo quod ubi dixit disputans quod "tota ratio quare usurarius tenetur ad restitutionem usurarum est" et cetera, ego nego quod sit tota. Et dico quod spes cre-

[72] See above, 84-120.

[73] See below, 1119-31.

[74] See below, 1134-42.

ditoris prohibita est et hoc de significatione uerbi non requirit alterius notitiam. Ex quo igitur contra bonum caritatis, nequaquam aliter mutuaturus fuisset creditor, quod per debitorem, aliter non donaturum donari uidetur, accedit huic spei uitiose, ergo adstrictum est uitio et restitutioni, secundum Iohannem Andree ubi supra. Hec opinio, quam sequitur Iohannes Andree, michi placet, quam multum coadiuuant que scripxit in questione montis magister Gregorius de Arimino, cuius dicta infra ponam in questione montis[75] et partim supra posui in questione .i. super rubrica,[76] que tamen non aliter approbo quam, ut ibi uidebis, quia "nimis emunsit," uidere meo.

14v Quare autem / aliud in simonia mentali notant Archydiaconus in dicto c. .i.[77] et Iohannes Andree[78] et dominus meus[79] in c. finali *de sy.* Sed aduertatur: si remictat qui soluit ultra sortem, liberabitur, sicut liberaretur si fieret remissio usure ex pacto solute, de quo infra dicam.[80] Immo etsi non remictat sed donet spem et intentionem deprauatam habenti, non habito respectu ad mutuum sibi factum, sicut dicimus in furante; aliter idem dicendum foret in furante. Hec patent ex statim dictis post Iohannem Andree et bene facit in argumento *de sepul., De his,*[81] *de testa., Requisisti,*[82] cuius tamen contrarium sentit magister Gregorius in .3.º articulo, uersiculo "Quinimmo,"[83] sed non placet, ut infra dicam in iamdicta questione.[84]

.4. questio ⟨Vtrum possit in foro contentioso condempnari et compelli ad restitutionem usurarum usurarius intentionalis.⟩

Sed quere quarto: quid si is contra quem agitur in hoc iudicio contentioso confiteatur suam prauam intentionem?

Respondet Ostiensis[85] quod si petebatur ut uere usurarium, propter

1132 dis *post* in[2] *del.*
1143 .4. questio *in marg. sin.*

[75] See below, 2467-2629.

[76] See above, 51-71, 132-322.

[77] Guido de Baysio, *Rosarium*, ad Decretum Grat. C.14 q.3 c.1, n.3 (ed. cit. fol. 207va).

[78] Johannes Andreae, *Novella*, ad X 5.3.46, n.6 (ed. cit. V fol. 36va).

[79] John of Legnano, *Commentaria*, ad X 5.3.46 (MS cit. fol. 73v).

[80] See below, *secunda particula*, q. 7 (1260-1473).

[81] X 3.28.4

[82] X 3.26.15

[83] Gregory of Rimini, *Tractatus*, art. 3 (ed. cit. fol. B7r-v).

[84] See below, *Questio montis, dubium* 2 (2494-2531, 2694-2744).

[85] Hostiensis, *Commentaria*, ad X 5.19.10, n.4 (ed. cit. V fol. 57vb).

iniustam petitionem absoluetur reus, nisi dicatur hic aliquid speciale propter periculum animarum, allegans *de iudi., Dilecti,*[86] *de cogna. spi., Tua.*[87] Sed si petebatur ut quasi usurarium iniuste et contra salutem anime receptum, fit condempnatio secundum eum, et ponit etiam Iohannes Andree[88] et dominus meus.[89]

Aduerte quia in contrarium uidetur facere glosa finalis in fine istius decretalis ⟨*Consuluit*⟩[90] in eo quod dicit quod intentio cum effectu facit hominem usurarium. Ad idem quod hic dixerunt Tancredus et Vincentius,[91] qui dicunt quod isti non inducerentur ad restitutionem receptorum nisi esset usura.

Preterea sicut de occultis solus Deus iudicat[92] et eius ministri in animarum iudicio, publicata autem per confessionem uel aliter iudicant ipsi ministri in iudicio contentioso et publico, ut probatur .xxxii. *Erubescant,*[93] .ii. q. .i. *Vnus,*[94] eadem causa et q. .v. *Consuluisti,*[95] .xxxii. di. q. .v. *Christiana,*[96] *de offi. ordi., Si sacerdos,*[97] ita dicam in proposito quod licet antequam publicaretur intentio huius mutuantis in foro contentioso solum esset in animarum iudicio inducendus ad restitutionem, tamquam in illo tantum usurarius, nunc ex quo publicata est compelli debet in ipso foro contentioso, tamquam in ipso usurarius; ex ipsa enim intentione factus est usurarius. Ideo dicebat hic glosa nostri capituli[98] quod quoad Deum reuera usurarii uidentur, quia restituere tenentur sic recepta. Si reuera igitur usurarii sunt quoad Deum ante publicationem, ergo et etiam quoad e C.14 q.3 cclesiam militantem post publicationem.

Preterea simplicitatem, puritatem et rei ueritatem amplectitur

1169 et *post* publicationem *canc.*

[86] X 2.1.6

[87] X 4.11.7

[88] Johannes Andreae, *Novella*, ad X 5.19.10, n.7 (ed. cit. V fol. 75va).

[89] John of Legnano, *Commentaria*, ad X 5.19.10 (MS cit. fol. 97r).

[90] Gl. ord. ad X 5.19.10, v. *Male agere* (ed. cit. col. 1739).

[91] Vincentius Hispanus (Tancredus), *Apparatus ad Decretales Gregorii IX*, ad X 5.19.10, v. *Inducendi* (Paris, Bibliothèque Nationale, lat. 3968, fol. 158v).

[92] Cf. *Rm* 2.16

[93] Decretum Grat. D.32 c.11

[94] Decretum Grat. C.2 q.1 c.6

[95] Decretum Grat. C.2 q.5 c.20

[96] Decretum Grat. C.32 q.5 c.23

[97] X 1.31.2

[98] Gl. ord. ad X 5.19.10, v. *Male agere* (ed. cit. col. 1739).

ecclesia, subtilitatem autem respuit, ut supra *de procu., Petitio,*[99] *de iudi., Dilecti.*[1] Siue ergo ut usurarium siue ut quasi usurarium petatur, non uidetur quoad ecclesiam curandum, ex quo de intentione constat, cui uerba deseruiunt, non econtra. Nichil enim habet obstare narrandi diuersitas, ubi eadem dicuntur, infra *de uer. si., Intelligentia,*[2] nichil preterea in his.

Preterea incorporalia non possidentur sed quasi possidentur et nichilominus si iura discurras reperies sepe unum pro altero poni, ut est uidere *de iudi., Examinata,*[3] *de re iudi., Cum Bertoldus* uersiculo "Licet autem,"[4] *de iur. pa., Consultationibus,*[5] *de reli. do., Constitutus,*[6] *de insti., Cum uenissent,*[7] *de resti. spo., Ad decimas* li. .vi.[8] cum symilibus. Bene facit quod in dicta decretali *Cum Bertoldus* notat Iohannes Andree post Innocentium et Ostiensem super uerbo "Memorato" in nouella[9] et quod notat post Ostiensem in c. *Consuluit* super glosa .i. in fine *de app.*[10] Ad idem *de app., Ad audientiam*[11] et alia multa iura eiusdem tituli, in quibus prouocationis uerbum quod extraiudiciali proprie adaptatur pro appellatione ponitur quod iudiciali conuenit, et econuerso. Quare puto, maxime ut animarum periculis occurramus, id tamquam tutius esse tenendum. Pro hoc quod scribitur post Ostiensem per Iohannem Andree in dicta decre-
15r tali *Cum Bertoldus* super uerbo / "Irritandam" ad finem decretalis in no-

1188 conuenit *interlin.*

[99] X 1.38.9

[1] X 2.1.6

[2] X 5.40.6

[3] X 2.1.15

[4] X 2.27.18

[5] X 3.38.19

[6] X 3.36.6

[7] X 3.7.6

[8] VI 2.5.2

[9] Johannes Andreae, *Novella*, ad X 2.27.18, n.13 (ed. cit. II fol. 238ra); Innocent IV, *Commentaria*, ad X 2.27.18, n.4 (ed. cit. fol. 311vb); Hostiensis, *Commentaria*, ad X 2.27.18, n.19 (ed. cit. II fol. 165vb).

[10] Johannes Andreae, *Novella*, ad X 2.28.18, n.5 (ed. cit. II fol. 256ra); Hostiensis, *Commentaria*, ad X 2.28.18, nn.3-4 (ed. cit. II fol. 176ra).

[11] X 2.28.34

uella.[12] Paulus ⟨de Liazariis⟩ tamen in clementina una eodem titulo[13] firmat opinionem Ostiensis.

.5. questio ⟨Vtrum contra usurarium intentionalem possit agi conditione ex decretali *Consuluit, de usur.*⟩

Sed quere quinto successiue: potestne agi contra hos usurarios mentales, de quibus nostra loquitur decretalis ⟨*Consuluit*⟩,[14] conditione ex hac decretali?

Respondeo: Innocentius[15] hic tangebat sed non soluebat. Sed Iohannes Andree hic[16] dicit quod ex his que ponit hic glosa finalis et ipse super ea, hoc potes colligere, quasi dicat, potes, si confiteantur uel aliter publicetur intentio sua, dummodo apte petas, iuxta statim post Ostiensem dicta in questione precedente, cuius uerba ipse Iohannes Andree posuit super dicta glosa finali, ad que se refert.

.vi.ª questio ⟨Vtrum ad restitutionem teneatur recepti ultra sortem is qui sine ulla conuentione mutuauit, spe tamen ductus principaliter lucri, posito quod debitor ratione mutui illud ultra sortem libere donauerit et ex laudabili discretione, aliter non donaturus, et hoc siue spes creditoris fuerit mala siue bona, et sic illi declarauit.⟩

.vi.º quere: mutuasti michi .c. sine ulla pactione, principalis tamen tua huius mutui causa fuit eo quod sperabas ex eo lucrum. Deinde, ego ultra sortem tibi .x. donaui, habito respectu ad mutuum quod si non interuenisset illa .x. nullatenus donassem, et insuper cum intentione, libere et ex laudabili discretione ex dicto seruitio michi facto, donandi, siue ea spe primario siue secundario, siue nec primario nec secundario sed ex solo caritatis fonte ductus fueris ad michi mutuandum et ita tibi declaraui tuque, hoc cognito, hanc donationem accceptasti. Esne restitutioni obnoxius?

Videtur primo quod sic, cum hic concurrat intentio praua et quod ratione dumtaxat recepti mutui, aliter non donaturus, donaui, quod quidem donatum accedit huic intentioni siue spei praue, que quidem

1194 .5. questio *in marg. sin.*
1205 .vi.ª questio *in marg. sin.*

[12] Johannes Andreae, *Novella*, ad X 2.27.18, n.12 (ed. cit. II fol. 237vb-238ra); Hostiensis, *Commentaria*, ad X 2.27.18, nn. 17-19 (ed. cit. II fol. 165vb).

[13] Paulus de Liazariis, *Lectura*, in Clem. 5.5.1, v. *Solvantur usurae* (MS cit. fol. 240rb-va).

[14] X 5.19.10

[15] Innocent IV, *Commentaria*, ad X 5.19.10 (ed. cit. fol. 517vb).

[16] Johannes Andreae, *Novella*, ad X 5.19.10, n.7 (ed. cit. V fol. 75va).

spes praua totam massam inficit,[17] non habita consideratione ad liberum donantis animum, ex quo se retulit ad mutuum. Ad hoc notata per Iohannem Andree super dicta regula *Peccatum*[18] et tibi recitaui supra in .3. questione ante finem.[19]

In contrarium facit quia ex quo tibi libere et uere donaui tuque hoc nosti et ut sic donatum acceptasti, uideris licite potuisse recipere, quia non ut usuram sed ut gratuitum donum acceptasti, non obstante quod prius etiam ut usuram fuerit animus recipiendi, ex quo peccatum exortum est, quod sola contritione delebitur. Non obstat quod dicebat Iohannes Andree quoniam licet aliter ad restitutionem quis teneatur quando non est sibi facta remissio, tamen non sic cum est facta. Sed in proposito nostro uidetur facta, ex quo omni casu tibi donaui libere, etsi ratione recepti mutui, et tu libere acceptasti, sciens aliter te teneri ad restitutionem.

Videtur quod si tu, continuata spe tua uitiosa quam a principio habuisti cum mutuasti, gerebas in mente recipere et non restituere, etiam si aliter non libere donassem uel remisissem, tenearis ad restitutionem, cum tunc tale donatum, respectu habito ad dictum mutuum, accedat, ut dicebat ubi supra Iohannes Andree, spei tue uitiose. Sed ubi aliter, non obstante quod habueris spem uitiosam a principio, meliori ductus consilio illoque mutato et fermento ueteri expurgato, spem illam deposuisti et nouus homo factus mutuum ex caritate[20] apud debitorem uis permanere, et insuper incrementum nunc geras in mente non recipere, nisi iam gratis et libere donauerim, non tenearis ad restitutionem, et maxime si hoc in notitiam donantis deuenerit ante donationem. Ad hoc .l. di. *Ferrum*[21] et quod notat Iohannes Andree post Innocentium in decretali *Mandatum* in principio *de rescrip.*[22] cum similibus. Et idem dico si, non mutato consilio, gerebas in mente recipere sed demum si non remicteret, restituere. Et hoc si debitori sit animus nolle recipere, etiam si uellet usurarius restituere sed tamquam pure donatum, penes usurarium remanere; perinde enim est acsi restituisset et ille post restitutionem donasset siue uolenti et parato restituere remisisset, ut de se patet et

1237 gerebas in mente recipere *post* tu *del. Vid. inf.* 1249.

[17] Cf. 1 *Cor* 5.6

[18] Johannes Andreae, *Novella*, ad VI *de reg. iur.* 4, *Peccatum*, n.8 (ed. cit. fol. 62vb).

[19] See above, 1111-31.

[20] Cf. 1 *Cor* 5.6-8

[21] Decretum Grat. D.50 c.18

[22] Johannes Andreae, *Novella*, ad X 1.3.38, nn.3-12 (ed. cit. I fol. 48va-b); Innocent IV, *Commentaria*, ad X 1.3.38, n.1 (ed. cit. fol. 26va-b).

faciunt infra notata in questione sequente post Dynum, et melius notata post Iohannem Andree et post Fredericum.[23] Et hec dico sequendo opi-
15v nionem Iohannis Andree circa usurarum remissionem / de qua infra latius tangam statim. Sed sequendo opinionem domini Frederici, de qua ibi dicam, uideretur indistincte non teneri, etiam si gereret in mente non restituere si remissio non fieret.

.vii.ª questio ⟨Vtrum sufficiat usurario in foro conscientie remissio sibi facta ab his qui debent usuras recipere sine reali et actuali restitutione.⟩

Pro quorum quidem declaratione septimo quero utrum sufficiat usurario in foro conscientie remissio sibi facta ab his qui debent usuras recipere sine reali et actuali restitutione.

Vbi sciendum quod glosa secunda in regula *Peccatum* in principio[24] tenet quod sic. Dynus ibidem[25] contra, nisi cum res est restitutioni parata, quia tunc quoddamodo fingitur restituta et postea restituenti donata, argumento ff. *de dona. inter ui. et uxo.* l. .iii. in fine,[26] *de iur. do.* l. *Vir ab eo,*[27] *si cer. pe., Singularia* circa finem,[28] *de solu.* l. *Proculo.*[29]

Fuit theologorum quorundam opinio quod non sufficit quod res sit parata restitutioni sed quod offeratur opus est, etiam si pars iam foret restituta. Iohannes Andree ibidem super glosa[30] demum assummit uiam mediam, quia aut gerit in mente usurarius restituere, et tunc remissio sufficiat, aut non, et tunc secus. Et uide quod scripxit in additione *Speculo* eodem titulo ad finem questionis ibi formate quam cum suo consuluit adoptiuo.[31] Fredericus de Senis in opere suo consiliis .xviii.º et .xxii.º,[32] ubi hunc passum disputauit, firmat indistincte opinionem dicte glose sic

1260 .vii.ª questio *in marg. sin.*

[23] See below, 1260-1473.

[24] Gl. ord. ad VI *de reg. iur.* 4, *Peccatum*, v. *Restituatur* (ed. cit. col. 719).

[25] Dino of Mugello, *Commentaria in regulas iuris*, in 4, *Peccatum*, nn.5-7 (ed. Venice 1570, p. 60).

[26] Dig. 24.1.3.12

[27] Dig. 23.3.49(50)

[28] Dig. 12.1.15

[29] Dig. 46.3.79 (*recte* Pecuniam)

[30] Johannes Andreae, *Novella*, ad VI *de reg. iur.* 4, *Peccatum*, n.3 (ed. cit. fol. 62rb).

[31] Idem, *Additiones in Speculum iuris*, in 4.4 *de usuris*, v. *Libellus concipitur* (ed. cit., II pp. 501a-502a).

[32] Fredericus Petruccius, *Consilia et questiones*, quaestio 18 (ed. cit. fols. 13va-14ra); quaestio 22 (fols. 17vb-18rb).

dicens quod si is cui debet restitui pecunia usuraria uel male ablata non coactus, non deceptus uel circumuentus, et omni dolo et calliditate, ui et metu cessantibus, etiam precibus uel seruitiorum exhibitione inductus, pecuniam sibi debitam, non oblatam nec restitutioni paratam, usurario dimictat, liberatus est usurarius a restitutione, non tamen a peccato quod contracxit exercendo usuras, nisi et de illo peccato penitentiam agat; concludens finaliter posse dici quod si usurario perseueranti in crimine et non disposito ad aliquam restitutionem is qui debet recipere usuras remictat illas motu proprio uel ad petitionem usurarii, liberatus est usurarius a restitutione rei, non, dico, a peccato quod contracxit usurarius fenerando, nam in re male ablata obligatur quis pene eterne per peccatum mortale quod contracxit auferendo rem a proximo inlicite, et obligatur eidem ad restitutionem ipsius rei. Sicut enim duos offendit, scilicet Deum et proximum, sic duobus satisfacere tenetur, *de usur., Cum tu,*[33] *de homici., Sicut dignum* § *Eos.*[34] Hanc opinionem uidentur etiam firmare Ostiensis in summa *de usur.* § *Que pena* uersiculo "Quid si fenerator" et uersiculo "Dicendum est igitur."[35] Ad hoc *de pigne. ac.* l. *Si rem* § *Omnis* uersiculo "Satisfactum,"[36] et Archydiaconus *de usu.* c. .ii. li. .vi. ubi super uerbo "Satisfactum"[37] dicit "satisfactum accipimus quomodocumque uoluntati creditoris satisfaciat." Idem Lapus de Castiglonchio in c. *In ciuitate* eodem titulo.[38]

Quid tenendum? Dico quod ad hoc, ut omnis tollatur dubitatio an sit uel non sit liber animus remictentis et per consequens clara conscientia usurarii, item ut inducantur facilius ad contritionem et de cetero sibi a talibus abstineant, cum de salute anime uel eius periculo disceptetur et ideo cautius agendum, .xlii. di. *Quiescamus,*[39] *de elec., Vbi periculum* li. .vi.,[40] cautum est predicare quod nisi se disponant ad restituendum, si non fiat remissio, quod remissio non sufficiat, iuxta doctrinam Iohannis Andree; et cautius quod esse debeat pecunia restitutioni parata, iuxta illam Dini; et magis cautum quod offeratur iuxta illam theologorum; et cautissimum quod actualiter restituatur et in soluentis manibus reponatur, iuxta illam aliorum quorundam.

Sed de iure, etiam in foro conscientie, puto illam ⟨opinionem⟩ glose

[33] X 5.19.5

[34] X 5.12.6

[35] Hostiensis, *Summa*, X 5.19 *de usuris*, n.12 (ed. cit. cols. 1633-34).

[36] Dig. 13.7.9.3

[37] Guido de Baysio, *Commentaria*, ad VI 5.5.2, n.1 (ed. cit. fol. 118va).

[38] Lapo da Castiglionchio, *Allegationes*, allegatio 137, n.14 (ed. Venice 1571, fols. 163vb-164rb).

[39] Decretum Grat. D.42 c.2

[40] VI 1.6.3

quam sequitur Fredericus indubitanter uerissimam que, quia ad supradicta et infra dicenda multum operatur, utile est quod clarius ostendatur. 16r Et quod sit uera probatur primo / ex rationibus Frederici, quarum prima hec est. In maioribus criminibus, sicut est in crimine furti seu uiolentie uel rapine, re furtiua uel rapta apud furem uel raptorem remanente de uoluntate domini, purgatur uitium furti seu rapine sine aliqua restitutione, ut l. *Si fur.* ff. *de usuca.* in principio[41] et ff. *de preca.* l. *Certe* § *Julianus*,[42] ergo in usura, que est minus. Quod autem illa sint maiora patet ex maioritate pene, siue enim de his agatur ciuiliter siue criminaliter, maior pena infertur quam usurariis, siue manifestum sit furtum siue non, siue uiolentia uel rapina sit publica siue priuata, ut patet C. et ff. *de fur.*,[43] et *de ui pu. uel pri.*,[44] et *de ui et ui ar.* l. .i.[45] Et non est dubium id esse grauius admissum quod est grauius uindicandum, xxiiii. q. .ii. *Non afferamus.*[46] Secunda eius ratio: in crimine usurarum et in aliis etiam maioribus, sufficit condignam facere satisfactionem uel emendationem, ut in c. .ii. *de rap.*,[47] ut quis sit liberatus a peccato, ut patet *de usur.*, *Quanto*[48] et eodem titulo c. .ii. in principio li. .vi.,[49] et *de sepul.* c. ultimo,[50] et *de rapto.*, *In literis*[51] cum symilibus. Sed satisfactum intelligitur quomodocumque desiderium creditoris adimpleatur, etiam si pecunia non soluatur, ut ff. *Qui satis. coga.* l. .i.[52] et *de pi. ac.* l. *Si rem.* § *Satisfactum autem accipimus* et cetera.[53] Si enim creditor remictit actionem sibi competentem, ex quo hoc sponte facit, sibi satisfactum intelligitur. .3.ª ratio: qui potest donare quod est plus, ut notatur *de rescrip.*, *Statutum* li. .vi.[54] ad finem, potest remictere uel qui potest unum, potest

1316 dominum *post* apud *del. et expunc.*

[41] Dig. 41.3.32.pr.
[42] Dig. 43.26(25).6.3
[43] C. 6.2; Dig. 47.2
[44] C. 9.12
[45] Dig. 43.16.1
[46] Decretum Grat. C.24 q.1 c.21
[47] X 5.17.2
[48] X 5.19.18
[49] VI 5.5.2
[50] X 3.28.14
[51] X 5.17.5
[52] Dig. 2.8.1
[53] Dig. 13.7.9.3
[54] VI 1.3.11

aliud, quia quasi pro eodem reputantur, supra *de testi., Veniens* .i.[55] et ff. *de calump., Quin etiam.*[56] Sed certum est quod si usurarius restituisset pecuniam debitori eidemque creditori, ipse posset illam donare usurario, ergo eodem modo potest remictere. .4.ª ratio, que secundum eum uidetur insolubilis: quidam sunt speciales casus in quibus obligatis ad restitutionem non sufficit remissio, *de rescrip., Statutum* ad finem li. .vi.,[57] et eodem libro *de censi., Exigit,*[58] et ibi de hoc, ergo in aliis stabit regula quod sufficiat remissio, ut notatur *de cle. non resi.* c. i. ad finem,[59] *de reg. iuris, Peccatum* li. .vi.[60]

Sed quia opposita iuxta se posita magis elucescunt, ueniamus ad contraria que formauit, quorum primum est hoc. A significatione uerbi seu uocabuli non est recedendum, nisi constet de mente contraria, ff. *de le.* .iii. l. *Non aliter,*[61] et notatur infra *de uer. signi., Propterea.*[62] Sed cum beatus Augustinus dixerit "non dimictitur peccatum nisi restituatur ablatum," .14. q. .vi[i]. *Si res*[63] et *de reg. iuris, Peccatum,*[64] et aliud est restituere, aliud remictere, l. *Plus*, l. *Cum pretor* et l. *Restituere* ff. *de uer. si.*,[65] patet per consequens quod non est satisfactum regule per remissionem sed opus est ut realis sit restitutio, cum restituere sit in pristinum statum reponere, ut in predictis legibus et *de usur.* l. *Videamus,*[66] sicut in aliis restitutionibus dicitur, C. *de repu.* l. .i.[67] et *de sen. pas.* l. .i.,[68] et maxime cum hic tractetur de peccato, ubi tutior uia est eligenda. Secunda ratio: exto quod pactum fiat de non petendo usuras, nichilominus repeti possunt, ut *de iureiuran., Ad nostram* .ii.[69] Ergo licet fiat remissio, nichilominus peti poterunt; ergo non recta conscientia retinentur etiam post remissionem. Tertia ratio: qui soluit indebitum scienter donat, ff. *de con-*

[55] X 2.20.10
[56] Dig. 3.6.2
[57] VI 1.3.11
[58] VI 3.20.2
[59] Gl. ord. ad VI 3.3.1, v. *Vtilitas* (ed. cit. cols. 384-85).
[60] Gl. ord. ad VI *de reg. iur.* 4, *Peccatum*, v. *Restituatur* (ed. cit. col. 719).
[61] Dig. 32.1.69(67)
[62] X 5.40.8
[63] Decretum Grat. C.14 q.6 c.1
[64] VI *de reg. iur.* 4, *Peccatum*
[65] Dig. 50.16.22, 81, 75
[66] Dig. 22.1.38.4
[67] C. 2.47(48).1.pr.
[68] C. 9.51.1
[69] X 2.24.20

di. indebiti l. .i.,[70] et tamen qui soluit usuras scienter nichilominus repetit, non obstante quod uideatur donasse. Ergo si donatio non ualet, quomodo ualebit remissio? Sed dicit ipse Fredericus: solue hanc ultimam per c. *Debitores* et eius glosam *de iureiuran*.[71] Ibi uide. Ad secundam rationem non respondet ibi sed alibi, ut infra tangam.[72] Sed ad primam bene respondet, dicens quod non obstat significatio uerbi "restituere," nam 16v Augustinus, ex cuius uerbis sumpta est regula prelibata, non / habuit respectum ad strictam significationem uerbi sed mens sua, que uerbis est preferenda, ut legitur et notatur *de uer. si., Propterea,*[73] fuit quod si tu offendisti proximum rapiendo et subtrahendo uel usuras extorquendo, quod reconcilies te cum ipso. Et quia comuniter homines non iactant pecunias suas, ut in l. *Cum de indebito,*[74] et uolunt sibi restitui res ablatas, ideo retulit se ad uerbum restitutionis. Quod autem sic intellexerit Augustinus patet multipliciter, nam Augustinus in uerbis suis non posuit "restituere" sed "reddere," .xiiii. q. .vi. c. .i. in principio,[75] et inter reddere et restituere aliqua datur differentia, ff. *de uer. signi.* l. *Verbum reddere*.[76] Preterea Romani pontifices, quorum auctoritas in decisionibus preferenda est aliorum dictis, etiam sanctorum, ut .xx. di. in summa,[77] utuntur uerbo "satisfacere" et "emendare," ut patet *de rap*. c. .ii.[78] et *de fur*. c. finali.[79] Preterea si sic in uerbis iudicare deberemus, multe sequerentur absurditates. Proba: pone quod dedi tibi dampnum, nichil tamen tibi abstuli uel ad me peruenit. Hic non potest fieri restitutio proprie sumpto uocabulo; sufficiet satisfactio et tamen grosso modo loquendo diceremus iste non potest saluari, nisi dampnum, id est, extimationem restituat. Item pone ⟨quod⟩ debeo tibi .c. ex causa usuraria. Rogo te ut possim illa .c. tenere cum conscientia bona quia uolo assummere comunionem in paschate, et obligo me tibi per instrumentum in .c. ex causa mutui uel depositi et ad certum terminum, et tu es contentus. Numquid ero tutus? Vtique. Satisfactum enim intelligitur, et cetera. Hec dixit Fredericus.

1376 si *post* l. *canc.*

[70] Dig. 12.6.1
[71] Gl. ord. ad X 2.24.6, v. *Cogendi sunt* (ed. cit. cols. 799-800).
[72] See below, 1443-73.
[73] X 5.40.8; gl. ord. ad X 5.40.8, v. *Proprietas* (ed. cit. col. 1934).
[74] Dig. 22.3.25.pr.
[75] Decretum Grat. C.14 q.6 c.1
[76] Dig. 50.16.94 (*recte* Verbum reddendi)
[77] Decretum Grat. D.20 dictum Grat. ante c.1
[78] X 5.17.2
[79] X 5.18.5

Sed cum reuerentia, hec ultima ratio non probat dictum suum principale, quia hic satisfit restitutio et constat de animo usurarii quod uult restituere ex quo sic se obligat. Et si dicatur, nonne prius etiam erat obligatus ante hanc obligationem quam modo facit ex causa mutui, respondeo: utique. Sed forte deficiebant probationes creditori usurarum. Item forte est usura mentalis, de qua non constat, nisi in animarum iudicio. Nunc autem constabit etiam in contentioso, quantum ad effectum solutionis, uigore dicte noue obligationis.

Sed contra rationes Frederici facere uidetur, et primo contra primam, quod scripxit Iohannes Andree in dicta regula *Peccatum*[80] et posui supra in .3. questione[81] et dominus meus repetit infra eodem c. finali,[82] nam, ut ibi dictum est, longa est differentia inter donationem uel remissionem factam de furto, per quam res furata sine uitio remanet penes furem, et donationem usure, cum in primo casu non accedat donatio intentioni corrupte furantis sed bene in secundo intentioni corrupte usuram recipientis. Sed tu solue quod etsi cum debitor usurario mentali (quo casu loquitur Iohannes Andree) aliquid soluit, quia solutum, considerato animo uitioso recipientis, rei uitiose accedit, non liberet a restitutione recipientem, eo quod non gratis et ut donum recipit sed ut usuram, licet alius fuerit soluentis animus, quia liber, qui tamen non constabat recipienti et de illo poterat uerisimiliter dubitare, argumento decretalis *Super eo* supra *de renump.*,[83] *de presump., Quia uerisimile*,[84] ff. *de proba., Cum de indebito.*[85] Secus tamen in casu nostro, scilicet quando post factam solutionem (quo casu loquimur) illam confirmat, puta donando quod repetere potest uel remictendo, quia tunc presummitur penitus libera, alio non dato; ad id. C. *ad Vell.* aut. *Siue a me.*[86] Et ipse recipiens tunc non ut usuram sed ut donum recipit siue retinet quod prius receperat ut usuram; bene facit l. *Quedam mulier* cum sua glosa finali ff. *de rei uendi.*[87] et quod notat Bartolus in l. *Cum solus* in fine ff. *de usuca.*[88]

1396-97 Nunc autem ... obligationis *in marg. dex. add.*

[80] Johannes Andreae, *Novella*, ad VI *de reg. iur*. 4, *Peccatum*, n.8 (ed. cit. fol. 62vb).

[81] See above, 1111-18.

[82] John of Legnano, *Commentaria*, ad X 5.19.19 (MS cit. fol. 99v).

[83] X 1.9.5

[84] X 2.23.10

[85] Dig. 22.3.25.pr.

[86] Excerptum Nov. 61.1 = Auth. 62 coll. 5.14 post C.4.29.21.

[87] Dig. 6.1.77; gl. ord. ad Dig. 6.1.77, v. *Sufficiebat* (ed. cit. I p. 440a).

[88] Bartolus of Sassoferrato, *Commentaria*, in Dig. 41.3.29, n.4 (ed. cit. V fol. 99va-b).

Immo plus, quia etiam in usurario mentali forte, si tempore solutionis posset sibi clare constare quomodo dans omnino uult donare ex mera liberalitate, licet accedat rei uitiose, attento animo primo creditoris, nichilominus non tenebitur ad restitutionem aliam. Ex quo enim sibi constitit 17r quomodo non dabat ut usuram sed libere donabat, et ut / libere donatum, non ut usuram, recepit, non uidetur inlicitum recepisse nec rei accedere uitiose, uel uerius, saltem quantum pertinet ad restitutionem (non dico quantum pertinet ad peccati abolitionem, ubi contritio requiritur), ex quo sic clare constiterit de intentione debitoris, fingitur restituisse et sibi gratis deinde donatum fuisse, ut supra dixi in questione .vi.[89] Et sic que prius erat penes creditorem uitiosa modo erit penitus absque uitio, et sic idem quod in furto.

Immo etiam in usurario conuentionali idem dicere possumus. Nec obstat quod notant in c. *Preterea* supra eodem Iohannes Andree[90] et dominus meus[91] per c. .i. .47. di.,[92] quia fateor quod a uoluntarie soluentibus usuras ut usuras non possum recipere. Nec obstat quod notatur in c. *Nobis, de sy.* in glosa secunda[93] et super ea per Iohannem Andree post alios,[94] quia non nego interuenisse hic usuram nec restitutionem fiendam, sed dico illam factam et hoc si in tali uoluntate perdurauerit ipse debitor. Quia tamen non uideo quomodo clare predicta constare possint nisi per ipsius debitoris assertionem liberam, de raro poterunt occurrere memorata et maxime quia id deinde asserendo et in illa perseuerando tunc expresse remictit. Securius tamen esset restituere et iterato recipere uel expressam habere remissionem.

Contra secundam insuper rationem Frederici faciunt notata per Iohannem Andree et me ubi supra.[95] Licet enim creditori remictendo actionem sibi competentem sponte satisfactum intelligatur, non sic tamen in casu nostro, cum ipsa remissio accedat rei uitiose, quod non contingit in illo. Sed solue ut in precedente. Sed obicies: posito quod usurarius teneatur satisfacere Deo et proximo, sicut Deum et proximum offendit, dicas michi pro Deo: exto quod proximo, ex quo donauit uel remisit,

1429 modo *post* sic *del.*
1434 absque uitio *post* recipere *del.*
1434-42 Nec ... remissionem *in marg. dex. add.*

[89] See above, 1205-59.
[90] Johannes Andreae, *Novella*, ad X 5.19.7, n.1 (ed. cit. V fol. 74va).
[91] John of Legnano, *Commentaria*, ad X 5.19.7 (MS cit. fol. 97v).
[92] Decretum Grat. D.47 c.1.
[93] Gl. ord. ad X 5.3.27, v. *Interveniente* (ed. cit. col. 1623).
[94] Johannes Andreae, *Novella*, ad X 5.3.27, n.5 (ed. cit. V fol. 28rb).
[95] See above, 1398-1430.

satisfecerit, ut sic repetere non ualeat in iudicio, quomodo potest Deo satisfacere si corde indurato in mente gerit non restituere, si non remictatur? Sed responde tu michi et uidebis solutionem. Pone quod creditor malegratibus tuis te inuitum et renitentem compulit ad usurarum restitutionem auctoritate iudicis, deinde uero usuras illas tibi donat: numquid poteris satisfacere Deo absque alia restitutione illasque tenere ut tuas? Vtique. Et tamen quantum fuit in te, non restituisti. Cur ergo non idem si facta est tibi remissio qui, ut dixi, non eras restituere paratus, attento quod perinde est acsi creditori satisfactum fuisset ex quo sponte remisit, ut in iuribus superius allegatis? Taciti siquidem et expressi equa est conditio neque refert quid ex equipollentibus faciamus. Ex quo enim ad duo tenebaris in satisfaciendo Deo, scilicet ad contritionem et ad restitutionem, cum ultima per remissionem sit sublata, remanet sola prima, sicut in fure dicimus cui facta est remissio uel donatio rei furtiue, qui licet ante donationem non solum contritionem habendo sed rem restituendo, ueram et salutarem poterat agere penitentiam et non aliter, modo tamen per penitentiam siue contritionem id efficiet. Sed aduertendum quod non solum contritionem habere debet de peccato quod perpetrauit in eo quod ad usuram mutuauit sed etiam de eo quod in peccato corde faraonico perseuerando proponebat in mente non restituere, "tanto" enim "grauiora sunt crimina" et cetera, *de consue.* c. finali[96] cum concordantiis. Et insuper, si uult ueram habere contritionem in corde suo, debet firmiter nunc proponere quod sibi precauebit a talibus in futurum.

.viii.ª questio ⟨Quare si fiat pactum uel iuretur de non petendo usuras, nichilominus peti poterunt, et non sic si fiat liberatio. Et utrum idem sit in pacto quod in liberatione, quando fit postquam usure deberi incipiunt.⟩

Sed quere .viii.º successiue: quare si fiat pactum uel iuretur de non petendo usuras, nichilominus peti poterunt, ut probari uidetur *de iureiuran., Ad nostram* .ii.,[97] et non sic si fiat remissio uel liberatio?

Respondeo: hunc passum tetigit Fredericus in opere suo consilio .clxxix.,[98] dicens quod ista sunt satis diuersa et ideo non mirum si diuersa est iuris dispositio. Qui enim remictit ius crediti transfert aliquid in debitorem et quoddamodo a se abdicat actionem sibi competentem et pro tanto satisfacere et soluere, id est dissoluere, obligationem dicitur,

1474 .viii.ª questio *in marg. sin.*

[96] X 1.4.11

[97] X 2.24.20

[98] Fredericus Petruccius, *Consilia et questiones*, consilium 184 (ed. cit. fol. 74rb-va).

argumento ff. *de solu.* l. *Solutionis uerbum*[99] et ff. *de uer. si.* l. *Solutionis.*[1] At qui paciscitur de non petendo non agit contra obligationis substantiam, id est non dissoluit obligationem sed obligatur ad non petendum. 17v / Verum, quia huiusmodi pactum est nudum, non datur ex tali nudo pacto actio sed exceptio, ut l. *Iurisgentium* § *Sed cum nulla.*[2] Qui ergo paciscitur non petere usuras, si remoueatur exceptione, replicabit de improbo pacto, quasi non potuerit obligari et sic ope replicationis consequetur usuras, saltem per modum siue medium c. *Ad nostram* superius allegati.[3] Sed non sic consequi poterit illas qui remictit, quasi sit pinguius remictere quam pacisci, licet utraque tollatur obligatio naturalis, ut l. *Sticum* § *Naturalis* ff. *de solu.*[4]

Tandem in eodem consilio concluditur quod etsi predicta procedant que de pacto dicta sunt quando pactum interponitur antequam incipiant deberi usure, quia tunc non ualet, ut l. *Cum unus* § *Pacta que turpem.* ff. *de pac.*,[5] ne homines inuitentur ad delinquendum, ut l. *Promictendo* ff. *de iure do.*,[6] tamen non sic quando pactum de non petendo usuras postquam deberi incipiunt factum est liberaliter a soluente. Immo ita liberabit sicut remissio uel donatio quantum ad securitatem excipiendi si petantur, et repetendi si restituantur per facti uel iuris errorem. Ratio assignatur ibidem: quia incipiunt esse post pactum indebite naturaliter et sola ciuilis obligatio remanet, ut l. *Sticum* § *Naturalis* ff. *de solu.*[7] et l. *Si non sortem* § *Indebitum* ff. de *condi. inde.*[8] et notatur in l. *Cum quis* C. *de iure et fac. igno.*[9] Ad decretalem *Ad nostram* respondet quod non obstat quia ibi testator retulit se ad factum, non ad ius, iussit enim usuras restitui his qui eas probarent soluisse, quod perpetuo durat, etiam post remissionem, non autem iussit eas restitui his quibus eas debebat, quia tunc nil redderetur ab heredibus. Vide quod infra dicam circa hoc ultimum in questione .lxxxi.[10]

1499 Cum unus: *in marg. sin. alia man. corr.*: alia littera Si unus.
1507 C. *scripsi*: F_1 ff.

[99] Dig. 46.3.54
[1] Dig. 50.16.176
[2] Dig. 2.14.7.4
[3] X 2.24.20
[4] Dig. 46.3.95.4
[5] Dig. 2.14.27(28).4 (*recte* Si unus)
[6] Dig. 23.3.41(42)
[7] Dig. 46.3.95.4
[8] Dig. 12.6.26.3
[9] Gl. ord. ad C. 1.18(21).10, v. *Cum quis* (ed. cit. cols. 255-56).
[10] F_1 fol. 45v; *TUI* 7, fol. 29va.

.ix. questio ⟨Vtrum creditor, cui ex caritate mutuanti debitor aliquid ultra sortem contulit, non uoluntarie sed quasi coacte, puta dubitans ne aliter indiscretus reputaretur in tantum quod alium uel hunc de cetero non inueniret mutuantem uel alia quauis simili causa, teneatur ad restitutionem.⟩

Nono quero utrum creditor, cui ex caritate mutuanti debitor aliquid ultra sortem contulit, non uoluntarie sed quasi coacte, puta dubitans ne aliter indiscretus reputaretur in tantum quod alium uel hunc de cetero non inueniret mutuantem uel quauis alia simili causa, teneatur ad restitutionem?

Hunc passum tetigi supra in .viii.[a] oppositione,[11] et licet tutius sit restituere, tamen puto quod si tempore quo recepit pure recepit, credens dantem liberaliter et animo donandi discretione ductum et non ut usuram, nec aliter coacte dare, quod non teneatur ad restitutionem, etiam si postea sciat non liberaliter dedisse, nisi eum aliter remorderet conscientia illamque nequiret iuri conformare. Quod tamen scrupulosum est potius quam laudabile ex quo timetur non timendum, ut in simili dixit Ostiensis.[12]

Patent predicta; ex quo enim tempore dationis et receptionis bonam fidem habuit, licite recepit et illius dominium licite in ipsum transiit, non obstante dubitatione tua qua ductus es ad dandum illi (horum penitus inscio), nec aliquid attemptanti ex quo in tale dubium et ad tale quid dandum te adduxerit, quo casu secus, ut in secundo responso decretalis nostre ⟨*Consuluit*⟩.[13]

Ad predicta quod legitur et notatur in regula *Factum legiptime, de reg. iuris* li. .vi.[14] Pro hoc quod supra post Ostiensem scripxi super rubrica in .i. questione circa diffinitionem usure et etiam quod post Gofredum ibidem.[15] Si enim, secundum ipsum Gofredum, usura est "quicquid sorti accedit intentione precedente uel pacto," et in casu nostro nulla talis precessit intentio uel pactum, nec insuper receptionis tempore pullulat, sed pura est et omni turpitudine munda, igitur et cetera. Nec obstant notata per dictum magistrum Gregorium, ut supra late scripxi in dicta questione

1514 .ix. questio *in marg. sin.*

[11] See above, 868-1002.

[12] Hostiensis, *Summa*, X 2.26 *de praescriptionibus*, rubricella *de praescriptione rerum immobilium*, n.3 (ed. cit. col. 726).

[13] X 5.19.10

[14] VI *de reg. iur.* 73, *Factum legitime*; gl. ord. ad VI *de reg. iur.* 73, *Factum legitime*, v. *Factum legitime* (ed. cit. cols. 776-777).

[15] See above, 44-51, 79-144.

.i. ultra medium[16] et infra tangam in ultima questione tertie partis in secundo dubio.[17] Sed uidetur obstare quod post Ostiensem scripxit Iohannes Andree in decretali finali in principio super uerbo "Qui" *de re-*
18r *scrip.*,[18] ubi dicit quod recipiens ab / impetrante rescriptum sub simili nomine sui nominis ignoranter, licet euitet penam condempnationis expensarum, de qua ibi loquitur textus in fine, tamen si, scita fraude, prosequitur et utitur literis dictis, ex rati habitione tenetur. Sed dic quod ibi loquitur in facto nondum consumato, hic in facto consumato et perfecto, unde sicut hic dico quod si sciuisset ante receptionem iste creditor uoluntatem debitoris et sic ante actum perfectum, non reciperet sana conscientia; secus autem si post. Ita in proposito, scita fraude ante finem et perfectionem, usus literarum incidit in penam expensarum; secus autem si sciret postquam literis illis usus fuisset, quia non teneretur ad expensas factas.

Pro et contra facit quod notatur in c. .i. .xiiii .q. .vi. in glosa .i.[19] et in c. *Si uirgo* .xxxiiii. q. .ii.[20] et in c. *Vigilanti, de prescrip.*[21] et eodem titulo c. finali[22] et in c. *Possessor, de re. iuris* li. .vi.[23] Sed michi semper placuit opinio glose in dicto c. *Si res* et in dicto c. *Vigilanti* et in c. finali eodem titulo, scilicet, quod mala fides superueniens prescriptioni complete non faciat quem obnoxium restitutioni. Cum enim dicitur quod "possessor male fidei ullo tempore non prescribit," utique uerissimum est, quia dum est in cursu prescribendi semper requiritur bona fides; sed qui prescripxit iam non prescribit, igitur non requiritur bona fides. (Potest siquidem lex de meo facere tuum, iuxta notata per Innocentium et alios supra *de*

1551 Sed *post* fine *del.*
1554 debitor *post* iste *del.*
1558 literis illis *scripsi*: F_1 literas illas

[16] See above, 164-231.

[17] See below, 2459-2622.

[18] Johannes Andreae, *Novella*, ad X 1.3.43, n.4 (ed. cit. I fol. 53ra-b); Hostiensis, *Commentaria*, ad X 1.3.43, n.3 (ed. cit. I fol. 28rb).

[19] Gl. ord. ad Decretum Grat. C.14 q.6 c.1, v. *Nisi restituatur* (ed. cit. col. 1106).

[20] Decretum Grat. C.34 q.2 c.5; gl. ord. ad Decretum Grat. C.34 q.2 c.5, v. *Possidere* (ed. cit. col. 1919).

[21] X 2.26.5; gl. ord. ad X 2.26.5, v. *Nouerit* (ed. cit. col. 856).

[22] X 2.26.20; gl. ord. ad X 2.26.20, v. *Nulla temporis* (ed. cit. cols. 875-876).

[23] VI *de reg. iur.* 2, *Possessor*; gl. ord. ad VI *de reg. iur.* 2, *Possessor*, v. *Possessor* (ed. cit. cols. 713-715).

consti., Que in ecclesiarum[24] et infra *de iniuri., In nostra*[25] et notat etiam glosa in dictis c. *Vigilanti* et finali. Ad idem quod notant glosa et Bartolus super prohemio ff. ueteris[26] et in l. *Item si uerberatum* ff. *de rei uendi.*[27] et in l. *Antiochensium* ff. *de priuile. credi.*,[28] et quod notari consueuit in l. *Bene a Zenone* C. *de quadri. prescrip.*,[29] et glosa et Archydiaconus in c. *Per principalem* .ix. q. .iii.[30] et in § *Quamuis* .xxiii. q. .viii.,[31] ubi omnino uide quod scribit ipse Archydiaconus, et in questionibus Oldradi consilio .223.)[32] Quam opinionem circa prescriptionem sequuntur etiam Iohannes, Gofredus, Vincentius, Innocentius et Ostiensis.[33] (Qui Ostiensis tamen dicit quod si pur sua conscientia remaneret lesa, debet satisfacere conscientie, licet potius sit scrupulosa quam theolog⟨ic⟩a, ex quo timet ubi non est timendum, *de sy., Etsi questiones*,[34] de quo remictit ad summam *de prescrip.* sub rubrica *de prescrip. rerum immobilium* § *Que exi-*

1570 et infra ... In nostra *in marg. sin. add.*
1580 theolog⟨ic⟩a: F_1 theologa

[24] Innocent IV, *Commentaria,* ad X 1.2.7, nn.2-4 (ed. cit. fol. 3va-b).

[25] Ibid. ad X 5.36.8 (ed. cit. fol. 541rb).

[26] Gl. ord. ad Dig. Prooem. II, const. *Omnem*, v. *Sanctionem* (ed. cit. I pp. 1b-2a); Bartolus of Sassoferrato, *Commentaria,* in Dig. Prooem. II, const. *Omnem*, nn.3-6 (ed. cit. I fol. 4ra-vb).

[27] Bartolus of Sassoferrato, *Commentaria,* in Dig. 6.1.15, n.1 (ed. cit. I fol. 171ra).

[28] Gl. ord. ad Dig. 42.5(6).37(21), v. *Sua* (ed. cit. III p. 325a); Bartolus of Sassoferrato, *Commentaria,* in Dig. 42.5(6).37(21), n.1 (ed. cit. V fol. 128ra).

[29] Gl. ord. ad C. 7.37.3, v. *Omnia principis* (ed. cit. col. 1867).

[30] Gl. ord. ad Decretum Grat. C.9 q.3 c.21, v. *Ad nos* (ed. cit. col. 920); Guido de Baysio, *Rosarium*, ad Decretum Grat. C.9 q.3 c.21, n.1 (ed. cit. fol. 170rb).

[31] Gl. ord. ad Decretum Grat. C.23 q.8 c.22, v. *Emeret* (ed. cit. cols. 1436-37); Guido de Baysio, *Rosarium,* ad Decretum Grat. C.23 q.8 dictum Grat. post c.22, n.5-6 (ed. cit. fol. 267ra).

[32] Oldradus de Ponte, *Consilia et quaestiones,* consilium 223 (ed. Rome, 1472), fols. 170ra-b, 172vb-173ra

[33] Johannes Andreae, *Novella,* ad VI *de reg. iur.* 2, *Possessor*, nn.41-42 (ed. cit. fol. 61va); Gottofredo da Trani, *Summa,* X 2.26 *de prescriptionibus*, n.7 (ed. cit. p. 235a-b); Vincentius Hispanus, *Apparatus*, ad X 2.26.5, v. *Postquam* (MS cit. 87ra); Innocent IV, *Commentaria,* ad X 2.26.20, n.1 (ed. cit. fol. 303vb); Hostiensis, *Summa,* X 2.26 *de praescriptionibus*, rubricella *de praescriptione rerum immobilium*, n.3 (ed. cit. cols. 725-29).

[34] X 5.3.18

gantur sub § *Verum quicquid.*)[35] Et, ut dicit dominus meus,[36] hec est comunis canonistarum opinio. Hanc etiam reperio in c. *Si uirgo* prealegato[37] tenuisse Huguccionem, etsi in c. *Vigilanti* referat Iohannes Andree[38] eum sensisse contrarium. Or quia hunc passum plene examinat Iohannes Andree in mercuriali posita super dicta regula *Possessor* in ultimo articulo,[39] ultra non prosequor sed illuc remicto, ubi omnium ponuntur opiniones habunde, et ibi firmat Iohannes Andree hanc opinionem limitatam secundum quod supra dixi post Ostiensem. Et hanc tene, et uide omnino ibi scripta.

Et que supra primo loco in decisione questionis dixi,[40] uera intelligo, nisi iam talis credulitas foret crassa uel supina quod ex his que supra dixi in ultima oppositione[41] et statim dicam in sequenti questione[42] bonus uir poterit arbitrari. Contra determinationem tamen prelibatam sentit magister Gregorius de Arimino, ut patet ex his que post eum infra dicam in questione montis, dubio secundo, parum post principium.[43] Vt dixi, tutius est sed non credo necessarium. Tene quod uis. Pro et contra facit quod notatur in glosa penultima in c. *Si diligenti, de prescrip.*[44] et in c. *Abbate sanc., de re iudi.* in glosa tertia circa medium li. .vi.[45]

.x.ª questio ⟨Vtrum dans aliquid ultra sortem ubi nulla pactio interuenit presummatur gratis et liberaliter dare. Item numquid recipiens presummatur recta conscientia et non deprauata recipere?⟩

.x.º quero utrum dans aliquid ultra sortem ubi nulla pactio interuenit presummatur gratis et liberaliter dare. Item numquid recipiens presummatur recta conscientia et non deprauata recipere?

1599-1600 de prescrip. ... li. vi. *in marg. dex. add.*
1601 .x.ª questio *in marg. sin*

[35] Hostiensis, *Summa,* X 2.26 *de praescriptionibus*, rubricella *de praescriptione rerum immobilium*, n.3 (ed. cit. cols. 725-29).

[36] John of Legnano, *Commentaria*, ad X 2.26.20 (Munich, Bayerische Staatsbibliothek, Clm 8786, fol. 235 va-b).

[37] Gl. ord. ad Decretum Grat. C.34 q.2 c.5, v. *Possidere* (ed. cit. col. 1919).

[38] Johannes Andreae, *Novella,* ad X 2.26.5, n.6 (ed. cit. II fol. 217rb).

[39] Idem, *Novella,* ad VI *de reg. iur.* 2, *Possessor*, nn.39-45 (ed. cit. fols. 61rb-62ra).

[40] See above, 1514-59.

[41] See above, 868-1002.

[42] See below, 1601-51.

[43] See below, 2467-2531.

[44] Gl. ord. ad X 2.26.17, v. *Bona fides* (ed. cit. col. 869).

[45] Gl. ord. ad VI 2.14.3, v. *Dominii vel quasi* (ed. cit. cols. 344-346).

Ad primum membrum, etsi aliquid supra dixerim in ultima oppositione,[46] respondeo et uidetur primo quod non, quia nemo presummitur iactare suum siue donare in dubio, ff. *de proba.* l. *Cum de indebito* § i.,[47] 18v *de renump., Super hoc,*[48] *de resti. spo., Sollicite,*[49] *de presump., Quia / uerisimile.*[50] In contrarium facit quod notat Iohannes Andree super regula *Peccatum* in questione mercuriali in secunda columpna,[51] ubi hoc expresse firmat disputans. Preterea cum debitor sciat se naturaliter ad antidotum obligatum, *de testa., Cum in officiis,*[52] *de dona.* c. .i.,[53] ff. *de peti. here.* l. *Sed et si lege* § *Consuluit,*[54] ergo uidetur potius gratis quam coactus et inuitus dare, et hoc potissimum cum ex tali pecunia sic gratis et sine omni pactione mutuata multum lucratus est, ut sepe contingit.

Solutio: si tempore quo aliquid ultra sortem soluitur debitum sortis extinctum erat, alio non dato, presummitur gratis dare, sed si durabat, presummetur metu repetitionis sortis id actum, argumento eorum que notatantur in glosa in l. *Si non sortem* § *Si quis falso* ff. *de condi. indebi.*[55] et supra *de iureiuran., Debitores.*[56] Possent tamen tot et talia concurrere quod presumptio talis cessaret iuxta supra notata in ultima oppositione circa finem.[57] Presumptio namque presumptione tunditur, *de presump., Illud*[58] et c. *Literas*[59] cum symilibus, et multo fortius si scriptura donantis cantaret quod libere soluit et non coactus, cum tunc non sit locus coniecturis, ff. *de uer.* l. *Continuus* § *Cum ita.*[60] Et ita iam uidi consultum per multos doctores famosissimos, sed ego id uerum intelligo nisi per creditorem usurarum probaretur in contrarium tale quid per quod de fraude

1618 Solutio *in marg. sin. add.*

[46] See above, 937-1002.

[47] Dig. 22.3.25.pr.

[48] X 1.9.5

[49] X 2.13.2

[50] X 2.23.10

[51] Johannes *Andreae, Novella,* ad VI *de reg. iur.* 4, *Peccatum*, n.8 (ed. cit. fol. 62vb).

[52] X 3.26.7

[53] X 3.24.1

[54] Dig. 5.3.25(28).11

[55] Gl. ord. ad Dig. 12.6.26.2, v. *Indebitum* (ed. cit. I p. 701a).

[56] Gl. ord. ad X 2.24.6, v. *Cogendi sunt* (ed. cit. cols. 799-800).

[57] See above, 968-97.

[58] X 2.23.11

[59] X 2.23.14

[60] Dig. 45.1.137.2

constaret, iuxta ea que leguntur et notantur *de renump*. c. .ii. li. .vi.[61] Videmus enim sepe per experientiam quod accipientes mutuo pecuniam sunt in tanta et tali egestate quod quicquid uolent creditores facient ut dilationem habeant in restitutione sortis, et quicquid uolent scribent et confitebuntur. Ad hoc quod notat Iohannes Andree *de emp. et uen., Ad audientiam nostram*.[62] Hec tamen uerba ipsa liberalitatem sapientia operabuntur, quod in aduersarium transfundent onus probandi contrarium et interim illis stabitur, *ut ec. bene., Vt nostrum*.[63] Ad idem quod scripxit glosator in clementina *Literis, de proba*.[64] et uide infra in questione .78.[65]

Ad secundum membrum respondeo quod sic, quia quilibet presummitur bonus, alio non dato, *de scrup*. c. uno,[66] et sue salutis memor, .i. q. .vii. *Sancimus*,[67] *de homici., Significasti* .ii.[68] et quod notatur *de peni*. di. .vi. *Placuit*[69] et in clementina prima *de priuil*. in glosa ordinaria.[70] Talia tamen possent in contrarium probari ex quibus aliud diceretur.

Accedat ad utrumque membrum quod scribit Iohannes Andree in *Speculo, de usur*. super prima forma libelli[71] et quod infra dicam in questione .lxii.[72] Pone enim quod probetur quod talis consueuit ad usuras mutuare; item quod consueuit quotiescumque uidebat sibi nil dari ultra sortem, mutuum uel depositum repetere, et alteri qui consueuit dare aliquid ultra sortem mutuare uel penes illum deponere. Quid iudicabis de tali nisi malum? In condempnando tamen non sit iudex prontus.

1635 Hec *scripsi*: F_1 Hoc

[61] VI 1.7.2; gl. ord. ad VI 1.7.2, v. *Coniecturas* (ed. cit. col. 184).

[62] Johannes Andreae, *Novella,* ad X 3.17.5 (*recte Ad nostram noueris audientiam*), nn.3-5 (ed. cit. III fols. 80vb-81ra).

[63] X 3.12.1

[64] Gl. ord. ad Clem. 2.7.1, v. *Fecisse narramus* (ed. cit. col. 104).

[65] F_1 fols. 44v-45r; *TUI* 7, fol. 29ra-b.

[66] X 1.12.1

[67] Decretum Grat. C.1 q.7 c.26

[68] X 5.12.18

[69] Gl. ord. ad Decretum Grat. D.6 de poen. c.3, v. *Pro ignorantia* (ed. cit. col. 1897).

[70] Gl. ord. ad Clem. 5.7.1, v. *Non habita* (ed. cit. col. 263).

[71] Johannes Andreae, *Additiones in Speculum iuris*, in 4.4 *de usuris*, v. *Libellus concipitur* (ed. cit. II pp. 501a-502a).

[72] F_1 fol. 40r-v; *TUI* 7, fol. 27va-b.

.xi.ª questio ⟨Vtrum emens redditus alicuius castri ad uitam uel aliud certum tempus licite emat.⟩

.xi.º quere: quid si quis emit redditus alicuius castri ad uitam suam uel suam et heredum uel aliud certum tempus tenendos: censebiturne talis contractus usurarius?

Respondeo: Innocentius supra eodem *In ciuitate*[73] tetigit hunc passum et recitat opiniones quorundam, quorum aliqui dixerunt quod si redditus comuni extimatione non excedit annuatim redditum quem de tanta pecunia in terra empta potuisset habere, licitus est contractus; si uero excedat comuniter, est inlicitus. Allegat in argumento istud c. *Consuluit*[74] sed non uideo quomodo faciat. Alii dixerunt quod quando in perpetuum emit, semper licitus est contractus, cum sit licitum contrahentibus se in pretio decipere, l. *In cause* .ii. [§ *Quod serui.*] ff. *de mino.*[75] Alii dicunt, et forte bene secundum Innocentium, quod si redditus constituantur ante contractum uel uenditam actionem, siue fuerit constiutus in re, puta in domo uel possessione uel aliis huius⟨modi⟩, siue in persona, puta serui, liberti uel rustici, uel actione uel nomine. Item siue /
19r sint certi redditus, puta quia reddit .x., siue incerti, puta quia reddit quartam fructuum qui percipiuntur de aliqua domo de operis alicuius persone. Item siue sit contractus perpetuus, puta quia extenditur ad heredes alterius contrahentium, siue sit ad uitam hominis, siue ad certum tempus, puta usque ad .v. annos. Item siue redditus sint in pecunia siue in aliis rebus siue in facto reputant tales contractus licitos. Ibi enim est licitus et purus contractus uenditionis: est namque pretium, scilicet certe pecunie quantitas, et est merces, scilicet certus redditus, uel canon uel annona, C. *de sacrosanc. ec.* l. *Iubemus* in principio,[76] in auth. *de rebus ec. non alie.* § *Ab Anastasio,*[77] C. *de here. uel ac. uen.* per totum,[78] secundum Innocentium.

Ostiensis uero, ut refert Iohannes Andree in dicto c. *In ciuitate,*[79] simpliciter dixit tenendum quod huiusmodi contractus, siue sint in perpetuum siue ad tempus, et siue ad certum censum siue sine, regulariter sunt permissi, dummodo neuter ultra dimidiam decipiatur et dummodo

1652 .xi.ª questio *in marg. sin.*
1667 huius⟨modi⟩: huius F_1

[73] Innocent IV, *Commentaria,* ad X 5.19.6, n.2 (ed. cit. fol. 517rb-vb).
[74] X 5.19.10
[75] Dig. 4.4.16(17).4
[76] C. 1.2(5).10
[77] Excerptum Nov. 7.pr = Auth. 7 coll. 2.1 post C. 4.35.23.
[78] C. 4.39
[79] Johannes Andreae, *Novella,* ad X 5.19.6, n.2 (ed. cit. V fol. 74ra-b); Hostiensis, *Commentaria,* ad X 5.19.6, n.7 (ed. cit. V fol. 57ra-b).

non celebrentur in fraudem usurarum, aliter autem secus, *de emp. et uen., Ad nostram,*[80] ff. *de actio. emp. et uen., Julianus* § *Idem Papinianus,*[81] C. *de usur., Eos qui,*[82] et quod notatur infra eodem *Tuas,*[83] ad quod accedat C. *de pac. inter emp. et uendi.* l. .ii. et l. *Cum te fundum.*[84]

Sed oppone predictis de decretali predicta *In ciuitate* et de c. *Nauiganti* infra eodem § finali[85] et de c. isto *Consuluit* in ultimo responso.[86] Nulli nempe uenit in dubium quod usque ad illud tempus saltem longum plus percipiet de redditu quam sit pretium.

Soluit Innocentius[87] quod licet certum sit nunc quod usque ad .xx., .xxx., .xl. uel .l. annos uel ulteriores plus acciperet de redditu quam sit pretium quod dat, tamen hec certitudo non facit inlicitum contractum uenditionis, cum et hoc idem sit dare in uenditione alicuius possessionis, ubi certum est secundum inferiores causas quod plus acciperetur de certis fructibus eius quam sit pretium quod pro ea datur, et sine expensis uel labore, dando ad affictum certum uel emphyteosim. Non obstant iura predicta, in illis enim reprehenditur tantum quando carius uenditur merces propter terminum quem dat prolissum emptori ad soluendam pecuniam, uel quia pro minori emit mercem, quia statim dat pecuniam et per prolixius tempus expectat mercem, que penitus sunt inlicita, de quo omnino uide quod infra dicam post Baldum in questione .43. parum post principium,[88] quia hic solummodo uendit tempus pro illa pecunia que uenit et iustum pretium excedit, quod patet ex eo quia si utraque parata essent, et pretium et merces, pro minori fieret. Sed in casu nostro omnia sunt presentia quia nec tempus uenditur, quia res ipse de quibus diximus, scilicet redditus uel actio, tantum ualebit uel ad minus creditur ualere subsequentibus temporibus quantum modo ualet, uel saltem est dubium et hoc sufficit ad hoc ut contractus sit licitus, ut dicto c. *In ciuitate.*

Est ergo conclusio Innocentii quod tunc demum predicta procedant quando redditus constituti sunt ante contractum uel uenditam actionem.

1704 uendit: uendidit F_1 *per dittogr.*; -di- *expunc.*

[80] X 3.17.5
[81] Dig. 19.1.13(14).26
[82] C. 4.32.26
[83] X 5.19.13; gl. ord. ad X 5.19.13, casus (ed. cit. col. 1740).
[84] C. 4.54.2,6
[85] X 5.19.19
[86] X 5.19.10
[87] Innocent IV, *Commentaria,* ad X 5.19.6, n.2 (ed. cit. fol. 517va).
[88] F_1 fol. 30v-31v; *TUI* 7, fol. 24ra-va.

Quid ergo si post? Solutio: dicit Innocentius[89] quod quidam dicunt idem, etiamsi redditus uel nomen propter hoc de nouo constituantur in rebus uel personis aliis a contrahentibus, puta quia dicit emptor, "tu constitues tales redditus in tali possessione uel seruo," uel "facies quod talis confitebitur se debere tibi mille usque ad annum et ego de illis mille, uel magis de actione pro illis mille competente tibi, dabo quingenta." Hos enim contractus licitos asseuerant, quia non est hic mutuum sed emptio. Item multi casus possunt interuenire quod iste emptor amicteret in hoc contractu, puta si inops fieret nomen. Et hoc uidetur sentire Innocentius et ita firmat in dicto c. *In ciuitate* dominus meus[90] sentire ipsum Inno-
19v centium. Hoc etiam firmare, secundum / quosdam, uidetur dominus Iohannes Andree in additionibus ad *Speculum* super hac rubrica.[91] Hoc idem Lapus de Castiglonchio in dicto c. *In ciuitate* in secunda questione principali,[92] scilicet quod omnes tales contractus sint liciti, dummodo cessent fraus et deceptio. Subdit ibi tamen Innocentius nichilominus quod cunctis est consulendum fidelibus quod a tali contractu se abstineant, scilicet quod de nouo propter hoc constitutum redditum uel actionem emant.

Ego autem uix uideo quomodo sine fraude hoc fieri possit. Non dico tamen quin possit sed de facili contrarium presummam, in quo plurima uenient consideranda, ut infra dicam in questione sequenti et in questionibus .18.[93] et .60.[94] Immo plus quia michi uidetur quod Innocentius potius sentiat quod consulit quam quod refert et idem Iohannes Andree in ipso c. *In ciuitate*, nec reperio quod in additionibus *Speculo* aliud teneat. Quinimmo si, ut quidam uolunt, predicta ultimo loco notata in dicto c. *In ciuitate* procedunt quando tempus certum et redditus certus de nouo constitutus in contractu inseruntur et non aliter (prout quemdam famosissimum doctorem disputando terminasse audio), pro quo etiam facit quod infra dicam, tunc apertius uidetur ibi hoc ipsum sentire quod in dicto c. *In ciuitate*, quoniam ibi dicit quod quando fructus essent certi, puta censuales redditus non submissi fortune et tempori fortuito, sed similiter etiam tempus certum, quod tunc hunc contractum plus traheret ad usuram. Immo sunt qui dicunt ipsum Iohannem Andree ibi intellexisse predicta etiam in redditu constituto ab antiquo, pro quo facit quia

[89] Innocent IV, *Commentaria,* ad X 5.19.6, n.2 (ed. cit. fol. 517va-b).

[90] John of Legnano, *Commentaria,* ad X 5.19.10 (Florence, Biblioteca Medicea-Laurenziana, Edili 54, fol. 97r).

[91] Johannes Andreae, *Additiones in Speculum iuris,* in 4.4 *de usuris,* super rubr. (ed. cit. II pp. 500b-501a).

[92] Lapo da Castiglionchio, *Allegationes*, allegatio 137, n.15 (ed. cit. fol. 164rb).

[93] See below, 2001-2182.

[94] F_1 fols. 39r-40r; *TUI* 7, fol. 27rb-va.

generaliter loquitur. Sed contrarium sentiunt quoad redditum constitutum ab antiquo in dicto c. *In ciuitate* Innocentius et Ostiensis et post eos ipse Iohannes Andree dummodo cessent fraus et deceptio. Et quod idem senserit etiam in additionibus *Speculo* (quicquid illi dicant) uidetur quia remictit ad notata in dicto c. *In ciuitate*. Que quidem remissio facit etiam pro opinione disputantis de qua supra premisi. Que quidem opinio forte non est simpliciter uera nec ex uerbis Innocentii colligitur, sed potius contrarium, ut ibi patet, quoniam eius dictum est generale et indistinctum et in exemplo reddituum possessionum uel serui, etsi ponat certitudinem in redditibus, non tamen quicdquam dicit de tempore. Item, ut supra dixi,[95] de facili, cum de nouo propter hoc redditus constituitur, fraus presummitur, maxime aliis interuenientibus que in hoc ueniunt consideranda. Illud autem bene sanctius et uerius reputo quod etiam in redditu constituto ab antiquo, ubi tam in eo quam in tempore omnimoda certitudo concurrit, ut quia censum annuum florenorum centum uendit pro sexcentis ad tempus .viii. uel .x. annorum, dicamus usuram presummi, et maxime aliis concurrentibus que talem coadiuuent presumptionem, inter quas illa erit potissima si fenerari consueuit, argumento c. *Illo uos, de pigno.*[96] et que notat Iohannes Andree in *Speculo* super dicta rubrica in fine.[97] Nec id est contrarium supra notatis per Innocentium et Ostiensem, immo consonum. Quisnam etenim hic fraudem non presummat? Est ergo quandoque dare redditum certum et tempus certum et prefinitum, quandoque utrumque incertum, quandoque redditum incertum et tempus certum, quandoque tempus incertum et redditum certum, quandoque redditum certum et tempus infinitum. Item est dare quod quandoque de nouo constituitur ipse redditus, quandoque ab antiquo extitit constitutus. In quibus omnibus membris quid sit concludendum satis aperte patet ex supradictis et infra dicendis in sequentibus questionibus, et maxime usque ad .18. inclusiue et in questione montis,[98] et ex his que scribit Iohannes Andree in additionibus *Speculo* super rubrica sepius memorata. Istud autem bene fatendum est penitus inlicitum (reuertendo ad uerba Innocentii) quod ipse idem qui dicitur emptor in se constituat redditum uel actionem qua se obliget ad plus dandum uel in pecunia uel in specie quam acceperit, secundum Innocentium, cuius uerba ponit etiam in iamdicto c. Iohannes Andree[99] et

[95] See above, 1732-35.

[96] X 3.21.4

[97] Johannes Andreae, *Additiones in Speculum iuris,* in 4.4 *de usuris*, super rubr. (ed. cit. II p. 501a).

[98] See below, 3668-3772.

[99] Johannes Andreae, *Novella,* ad X 5.19.6, n.2 (ed. cit. V fol. 74rb).

dominus meus,[1] qui tamen ibidem etiam aliam questionem formabat, predictam etiam in uentre tenentem, quam quidem non intendo sub silentio preterire.

20r / **.12. questio ⟨Constituit quis censum unius floreni in domo. Vendidit illum pro .x. cum pacto quod liceat illum redimere pro dictis x. Valebat tamen census ille .xx. si uero pretio et sine tali pacto uenderetur. Estne licitus?⟩**

Quero igitur et .12.º: constituit quis censum unius floreni in domo. Vendidit talem censum pro .x. florenis, adiecto pacto quod liceret illi redimere pro illis .x. florenis. Valebat tamen census ille .xx. si uero pretio sine pacto libere uenderetur. Estne inlicitus uel usurarius talis contractus?

Arguit ubi supra dominus meus[2] ad partes. Et primo ad affirmatiuam: pecunia, que non debet uendi, hic uenditur, igitur contractus inlicitus, ff. *de fideius.* l. *Si ita*[3] et l. i. ff. *de contraem. emp.*,[4] quia omnium rerum est extimatio. Item uenditur usus rei inseparabilis a re. Item ratione pacti cuius interuentu pro minori uenditus est. Item accedit aliquid pecunie, ergo inlicita surgit presumptio usuram concludens, *de emp. et uen., Ad nostram,*[5] *de pigno., Illo uos.*[6]

In contrarium, hic non est mutuum ad quod accedat usura, .xiiii. q. .iii. c. .i.[7] Item licet contrahentibus se decipere, dummodo non ultra dimidiam, *de emp. et uendi., Cum dilecti.*[8] Item non uitiatur emptio si emptor plus pretio recipiat. Item uenditur ius uendibile, quia ius et iura uenduntur, ff. *de here. uel ac. uen.* per totum,[9] ff. *de contrahen. emp., Qui tabernas.*[10]

Soluit quod si census constituatur non habita relatione ad rem ut quia obligo me tibi ad unum florenum quia michi decem das et uendo tibi hoc ius percipiendi non relatum ad rem, et tunc inlicita est talis uenditio, quia non uenditur ius, immo tunc de nouo oritur, feneratorius

1786 .12. questio *in marg. sin.*

[1] John of Legnano, *Commentaria,* ad X 5.19.10 (MS cit. fol. 97r).
[2] Ibid. (fol. 97r-v).
[3] Dig. 46.1.42(43)
[4] Dig. 18.1.1
[5] X 3.17.5
[6] X 3.21.4
[7] Decretum Grat. C.14 q.3 c.1
[8] X 3.17.3
[9] Dig. 18.4
[10] Dig. 18.1.32

contractus est ergo, .xiiii. q. .iii. *Plerique*[11] et c. *Quicquid.*[12] Sed aliquando constituitur census in re et uenditur: tunc contractus talis est ualidus et licitus, quia hic ius uendibile, hic pretium. Quod intellige nisi dolus uel deceptio ultra dimidiam interueniat, ff. *de mino.* l. *In cause,*[13] *de emp. et uendi., Cum dilecti*[14] et c. *Cum causa.*[15] Sed aliquando constituitur iste census tempore uenditionis et uenditur post, et tunc aliquando census non posset aliter haberi de re, aliquando posset haberi ut quia constituo censum domui de decem, cum non posset conduci nisi pro .v., tunc credit hunc contractum fraudolosum ex quo census ille aliter de re non posset haberi, quia tunc surgit obligatio personalis, *de pigno., Illo uos,*[16] *de emp. et uen., Ad nostram.*[17] Sed si potest census haberi de re, tunc credit illum licitum. Et hoc tunc tantum procedit quando non est adiectum pactum de retrouendendo. Si enim adiectum foret, tunc dicas quod si pro minori pretio debet retrouendi, cum tunc implicetur quod census perceptus computetur in sortem; tunc credit talem contractum usurarium, ut dictis c. *Ad nostram* et *Illo uos*. Sed si pro maiori pretio, idem. Si uero pro eodem pretio, tunc credit illum licitum. Prosequere ut ibidem per eum et uide quod statim dicam in questione sequente et in questione .18.,[18] ubi per notata ibidem post eundem dominum meum in consilio per eum reddito una cum domino Laurentio de Pinu. Idem uidetur dicendum etiam in casu quo pro eodem pretio. Nec habet obstare quod ibi loquitur in censu personali et non constituto in re, quia quoad fraudem de contractu ad contractum ex illo resolutionis capite nulla est diuersitas inter contractum census personalis et contractum census realis, siue in re, constituti. Posset tamen dici quod ideo forte est diuersitas, quia plura concurrebant quam hic fraudis presumptionem afferentia; et uide quod ibi dicam in fine et infra in questione .lx. huius partis[19] et in questione finali in ultimo membro tertie partis.[20]

[11] Decretum Grat. C. 14 q.3 c.3
[12] Decretum Grat. C.12 q.2 c.36
[13] Dig. 4.4.16(17).4
[14] X 3.17.3
[15] X 3.17.6
[16] X 3.21.4
[17] X 3.17.5
[18] See below, 1840-78, 2001-2182.
[19] F_1 fols. 39r-40r; *TUI* 7, fol. 27rb-va.
[20] See below, 3668-3772.

.13. questio ⟨Vtrum sit usura si emi ab habente possessiones censum .x. corbium frumenti pro pretio pro quo haberentur possessiones ex quibus haberentur uerisimiliter dicte .x. corbe, adiecto quod de omnibus bonis suis indifferenter soluere teneatur.⟩

Sed quere .xiii.º: emi ab habente possessiones censum .x. corbium frumenti pro pretio pro quo haberentur possessiones ex quibus haberentur uerisimiliter dicte .x. corbe, adiecto quod de omnibus bonis suis in-
20v differenter soluat. / Numquid est usura?

Dubium facit quia non emo frumentum certi predii et sic potius uidetur obligatio personalis, et sic non est locus supradictis et notatis per Innocentium in dicto c. *In ciuitate* supra eodem. Item hic non emitur certum ius reale.

Soluit dominus meus infra eodem c. finali in .i. questione[21] dici posse quod si census constituitur in bonis et ad bona fiat relatio, non est censendus contractus usurarius, cum hic merces, hic pretium, et talia iura realia licitum est uendere, ff. *de here. uel ac. uen.* per totum.[22] Et maxime procedunt predicta cum legiptimum est pretium et ad obiectum census relatum. Caueat tamen contrahens ab intentione deprauata, dampnate namque intentionis solus Deus cognitor est, supra eodem *Cum tu* in fine.[23]

Non recte concipio quomodo in casu proposito census ille constituatur in bonis, etiam dato quod propter hoc omnia sua bona obliget. Non nego tamen quin posset illum constituere in bonis suis et illum uendere nec ullam differentiam facio siue consistat in pecunia siue in rebus, puta in grano, uino uel oleo et cetera, argumento .xiiii. q. .iii. *Plerique*[24] et uide infra in questione sequente et in dicta questione .18.[25] et quod notat ⟨Iohannes de Lignano⟩ post Innocentium in dicto c. *In ciuitate*. Et ita credo dominum meum intellexisse. Ad predicta bene facit quod in questione illius qui uendidit fructus domus pro .c. annis scripxit Bartolus in l. .ii. § *Instituto* ff. *de le.* .ii.[26] dicens quod aut uendidit fructus constituendo ius ususfructus in re ipsi ementi et tunc est alienatio, ut l. finali

1840 .13. questio *in marg. sin.*

[21] John of Legnano, *Commentaria,* ad X 5.19.19 (MS cit. fol. 99v).

[22] Dig. 18.4

[23] X 5.19.5 (*recte* X 5.19.6; cf. gl. ord. ad X 5.19.6, v. *Occultari* [ed. cit. col. 1737]).

[24] Decretum Grat. C.14 q.3 c.3

[25] See below, 1879-94, 2001-2182.

[26] Bartolus of Sassoferrato, *Commentaria,* in Dig. 31.1.88(91).15, nn.3-4 (ed. cit. IV fol. 46va).

C. *de rebus alie. non alie.*,[27] aut non constituendo sed obligando se actione personali ad dandos fructus et tunc non est alienatio, ut l. finali ff. *de contraenda emptione*;[28] et facit l. *Liberto* in principio ff. *de annu. lega.*[29] Et qualiter perpendatur an constituat ius ususfructus in re uel ne notatur ff. *de usufruc.* in l. *Si ⟨quis⟩ ita.*[30] Ad idem quod scripxit dominus meus Iohannes de Fantutiis de Bononia in clementina .i. *de rebus ec. non alie.*[31] et quod ego scripxi in tractatu alienationis in questione .28. quem posui super c. *Sine exceptione* .xii. q. .ii. in repetitione.[32]

.14. questio ⟨Habet statutum uel consuetudo quod rectores uendant de pecunia ciuitatis alicui et suis heredibus .v. uel .x. annuatim pro .c., quam pecuniam conuertit ciuitas in utilitatem suam. Estne usura?⟩

.xiiii.° quero: habet statutum uel consuetudo ciuitatis quod rectores uendant de pecunia ciuitatis alicui et suis heredibus quinque florenos uel .x. annuatim pro .c., quam pecuniam conuertit ciuitas in utilitatem suam. Estne usura?

Solutio: dominus meus in c. finali infra eodem[33] dicit quod cum pecunia sit mensura aliarum rerum, ff. *de fideius.* l. *Si ita*,[34] ff. *de contrahen. emp.* l. .i.,[35] talis contractus non erit licitus peccantque rectores sed non singulares, nisi consequantur bursale commodum. Posset tamen secundum eundem talis contractus defendi ubi ciuitas constitueret censum quinque uel .x. florenorum qui concerneret bona ciuitatis, non autem quantitatem. Hoc uerum intelligo nisi id fieret in fraudem, et uide quod infra dicam in questione montis in ultimo dubio.[36]

1871 non[1] *interlin.*
1879 .14. questio *in marg. sin.*

[27] C. 4.51.7

[28] Dig. 18.1.81.1

[29] Dig. 33.1.21.pr.

[30] Dig. 7.1.20(24); gl. ord. ad Dig. 7.1.20(24), v. *Legatus esset* (ed. cit. I p. 456b).

[31] *Locum non inveni.*

[32] Lorenzo Ridolfi, *Repetitio in Decretum Grat.* C.12 q.2 c.52 (Messina, Biblioteca della Facoltà di Giurisprudenza A. 1, fols. 75r-84r). Reference from Martino, "Ridolfi," 186, n. 47.

[33] John of Legnano, *Commentaria,* ad X 5.19.19 (MS cit. fol. 99v).

[34] Dig. 46.1.42(43)

[35] Dig. 18.1.1

[36] See below, 3668-3771.

.15. questio ⟨Emit Titius ab ecclesia possessiones pro certa pecunie quantitate ad uitam suam tenendas. Estne licitus?⟩

Ad hec .xv.° quero: emit Titius ab ecclesia quadam certas possessiones pro certa pecunie quantitate tenendas toto tempore uite sue ita ut post mortem suam ad ecclesiam redeant. Eritne licitus talis contractus?

Respondeo: Raymundus et Gofredus in summis eodem titulo[37] iudicauerunt talem contractum usurarium eo quod homines sperant uiuere et sic sperant se amplius percepturos de prouentibus possessionum quam sit pecunia quam dederunt, et sola spe usura contrahitur. Fatentur bene tamen quod si quis receperit unam possessionem ecclesie et dederit eidem aliam equiualentem, immo etiam si illa quam recepit ab ecclesia sit in duplo ualens quam illa sua quam confert cum pacto quod in uita sua
21r utraque fruatur et, adueniente morte, ambe / ad ecclesiam cum pleno dominio reuertantur, quod contractus talis est licitus, est enim contractus precariarum, qui a iure approbatur. Immo plus quia si suam uelit de presenti in ecclesiam transferre ita quod ipse ea non utatur et fruatur poterit ab ecclesia recipere possessionem in triplo ualentem, ut .x. q. .ii. *Precarie*, ubi de hoc per Archydiaconum[38] post Huguccionem. Sed Ostiensis, in summa eodem titulo § *An aliquo* ad finem uersiculo "Quid de his,"[39] dampnat tale primo dictum, dicens neutro casu usuram commicti, nam ita homines possunt sperare lucrum in contractu secundo, scilicet precariarum, sicut in primo, scilicet emptionis et uenditionis; non ergo est dare causam quare primus non sit licitus sicut hic ultimus, dummodo non fiat in fraudem usurarum, secundum eum. Et hoc placet Iohanni Andree, qui hoc pulcre examinat in additionibus ad *Speculum* super hac rubrica,[40] ubi omnino uide, quod etiam sentit Archydiaconus in c. *Quicumque* .14. q. .iiii.[41] Cynus, in l. *Si pater* C. *de inoffi. te.*,[42] tenet idem, dummodo talis emens ad uitam dederit pretium secundum quod uerisimile est quod uiuere possit: aliter si iuuenis homo emeret mille

1895 .15. questio *in marg. sin.*

[37] Raymond of Penyafort, *Summa* 2.7 *de usuris*, n.8 (ed. cit. pp. 233b-235b); Gottofredo da Trani, *Summa*, X 5.19 *de usuris*, n.12 (ed. cit. p. 444a-b).

[38] Guido de Baysio, *Rosarium*, ad Decretum Grat. C.10 q.2 c.4 (ed. cit. fol. 173va)

[39] Hostiensis, *Summa*, X 5.19 *de usuris*, n.8 (ed. cit. col. 1626).

[40] Johannes Andreae, *Additiones in Speculum iuris*, in 4.4 *de usuris*, super rubr. (ed. cit. II pp. 500b-501a).

[41] Guido de Baysio, *Rosarium*, ad Decretum Grat. C.14 q.4 c.9, n.3 (ed. cit. fol. 208rb).

[42] Cino of Pistoia, *In codicem commentaria*, in C. 3.28.12, n.1 (ed. Frankfurt 1578, repr. 1964, I fol. 154rb)

libras pro .c. libris, non procederet secure talis contractus sed debet taxari secundum etates, ut ff. *ad l. Fal.* l. *Hereditatem.*[43] Hoc idem approbat ibi Baldus,[44] qui allegat c. *Nauiganti* infra eodem titulo.[45]

Sed ego id non sic simpliciter affirmo, quinimmo satis erit quod non interueniat deceptio ultra dimidiam iusti pretii, que qualiter cognoscatur in casu isto discutietur in questione sequenti. Et pro hoc quod scripxit Iohannes Andree post Innocentium et Ostiensem in dicto c. *In ciuitate,*[46] ubi talis contractus non reprobatur ex eo quod sit emptor plus percepturus sed ex eo quod interuenit deceptio ultra dimidiam iusti pretii, dato etiam quod nil fiat in fraudem usurarum. Ad predicta insuper adduci posset decretalis *Ad nostram, de rebus ec. non alie.,*[47] ubi papa contractum illum rescindit, non ex eo quod amplius sit percepturus sed ratione lesionis contingentis ex eo, quod nimis ultra modum ledebatur et cetera. Quod dic ut ibi.

Quid autem de ementibus fructus sub certo pretio ad uitam? Vide per eum ⟨Baldum⟩ in l. *Si ea* C. *de usur.,*[48] ubi cum Petro tenet inspici debere personarum qualitatem et etatem et tunc arbitrari iustum uel iniustum, de quo per Ostiensem in summa *de usur.* § *An aliquo casu* uersiculo .xii.[49] et per Archydiaconum in dicto c. *Quicumque* .xiiii. q. .iiii.[50] Et uide infra questiones .17. et .18.[51] et quod supra dixi in questione .xi.[52] post Innocentium et Ostiensem.

1939 de *post* Si *del.*

[43] Dig. 35.2.68

[44] Baldus de Ubaldis, *Commentaria,* in C. 3.28.12, n.2 (ed. cit. VI fol. 196va).

[45] X 5.19.19

[46] Johannes Andreae, *Novella,* ad X 5.19.6, n.2 (ed. cit. V fol. 74ra); Innocent IV, *Commentaria,* ad X 5.19.6, n.2 (ed. cit. fol. 517rb-va); Hostiensis, *Commentaria,* ad X 5.19.6, n.7 (ed. cit. V fol. 57ra-b).

[47] X 3.13.11

[48] Baldus de Ubaldis, *Commentaria,* in C. 4.32.14, n.1 (ed. cit. VII fol. 89rb).

[49] Hostiensis, *Summa,* X 5.19 *de usuris,* n.8 (ed. cit. cols. 1622-23).

[50] Guido de Baysio, *Rosarium,* ad Decretum Grat. C.14 q.4 c.9, n.2 (ed. cit. fol. 208ra-b).

[51] See below, 1987-2182.

[52] See above, 1657-1785.

.16. questio ⟨Que et quando dicatur interuenire seu possit dici deceptio ultra dimidiam iusti pretii in contractu precedente?⟩

Sed quia comuniter dicunt scribentes predictam conclusionem Ostiensis ueram nisi ultra dimidiam iusti pretii interueniat deceptio, quod est regulare in quacumque uenditione, *de emp. et uen., Cum dilecti*[53] et c. finali,[54] et facit quod statim dixi post Cynum,[55] uideamus .xvi.º quando seu que in talibus contractibus possit dici deceptio ultra dimidiam.

Vbi sciendum quod istum passum reperio tetigisse in c. *In ciuitate* supra eodem dominum Lapum de Castiglonchio.[56] Et dicit quod quia tales contractus fiunt ad uitam, aliquando unius, aliquando duorum uel plurium, aliquando iuuenum, aliquando senium, ideo difficile est diffinire. Iura tamen ciuilia et canonica uidentur uoluisse hoc taxare, nam l. .i. C. *de sacrosanc. ec.*, canonizata .x. q. .ii. *Si yconomus*[57] dicit quod si tu uelis dare rem tuam ecclesie et recipere ad uitam tuam aliam rem ecclesie, potes recipere duplo ualentem. Canon uero [*Si*] *precarie* eadem questione[58] uidetur dicere de triplo, et glosa in ipso c.,[59] uolens ad concordiam reducere, dat intellectum canoni, qui de triplo loquitur, scilicet quod uendicet sibi locum cum debilis uel senex est qui rem ecclesie recipit. Et Huguccio et Laurentius ibi[60] dicunt quod ad filios uel heredes tale ius non transmictitur, sed tantum in diebus uite accipientis. Item dictus canon dicit quod si dono ecclesie proprietatem rei mee sed tamen usum retineo, eo casu non triplum sed duplum tantum ab ecclesia recipio. Ex quibus iustus iudex instrui posset et formare animi sui motum et
21v discernere quando in huiusmodi / contractibus esset deceptio ultra dimidiam. Hec dictus Lapus.

1945 .16. questio *in marg. sin.*

[53] X 3.17.3

[54] X 3.17.7

[55] See above, 1921-26.

[56] Lapo da Castiglionchio, *Allegationes*, allegatio 137, n.15 (ed. cit. fol. 164rb-vb).

[57] Decretum Grat. C.10 q.2 c.2.11 et c.3 (*est lex canonizata* C. 1.2.14.5)

[58] Decretum Grat. C.10 q.2 c.4

[59] Gl. ord. ad Decretum Grat. C.10 q.2 c.4, v. *Duplum* (ed. cit. col. 933).

[60] Huguccio, *Summa decretorum*, ad C.10 q.2 c.4, v. *Tantum in suo nomine* (Lons-le-Saunier, Archives départementales du Jura, 16, fol. 206r); Laurentius Hispanus, *Apparatus in Decretum*, ad C.10 q.2 c.4, v. *Tantum in suo nomine* (Vatican City, Biblioteca Apostolica Vaticana, Palatino lat. 658, fol. 45r).

Quod clarius exprimens dico argumento supradictorum que clarius post Huguccionem exprimit Archydiaconus in dicto c. *Precarie*[61] et satis etiam ex uerbis Gofredi, de quibus in questione precedente, quod si emo ab ecclesia possessionem pro certo pretio tradendo ipsi ecclesie post mortem meam, tunc si possessio ualet ultra duplum eius quod me soluturum post mortem constitui, dicitur interuenire deceptio ultra dimidiam iusti pretii. Si autem pecuniam soluo tempore contractus, tunc dicitur interuenire deceptio ultra dimidiam quando talis possessio ualet ultra triplum. Posset insuper conditio contrahentis cum ecclesia esse nature tam debilis etatisque tam decrepite quod in eo casu ultra uendere quam duplum uel triplum non esset peccare in spiritum sanctum, argumento eorum que in glosa dicti c. *Precarie* notat Iohannes ⟨Teutonicus⟩,[62] cui etiam applaudet Iohannes Fauentinus,[63] quoniam in eo ecclesie meliora prospicimus, si recte intueamur. Id tamen non audeo constanter affirmare cum de triplo tantum ad plus canones attestentur. Facit tamen pro hoc quod supra scripxi post Cynum in questione precedente.[64] Cogita.

.17. questio ⟨Vendit quis fructus predii ad tempus, puta .x. annorum pro mille, cum fructus illius predii annuatim ualeant .cl. Estne licitus ex parte emptoris huiusmodi contractus?⟩

.xvii.°, quid de tali questione: uendit quis fructus predii ad tempus, puta .x. annorum, pro mille, cum fructus illius predii comuniter annuatim ualeant .cl. Estne licitus talis contractus ex parte emptoris?

Refert Iohannes Andree in additionibus ad *Speculum* super hac rubrica[65] hanc questionem fuisse sibi formatam in quodam monasterio. Et pro emptore facit quod illa mille submictit fortuito casui, ex quo nullos casus excipit hostilitatis, sterilitatis uel alios. Item dato quod cesset omnis sterilitas in capite decem annorum, non haberet nisi quingentas libras de fructu uel lucro, et certe plus habuisset comuniter in redditu ueram emptionem faciendo de mille, scilicet ultra .l. annuatim. Quod prosequere ut ibi per eum, qui sentit talem contractum licitum.

1987 .17. questio *in marg. sin.*

[61] Guido de Baysio, *Rosarium,* ad Decretum Grat. C.10 q.2 c.4 (ed. cit. fol. 173va).

[62] Gl. ord. ad Decretum Grat. C.10 q.2 c.4, v. *Duplum* (ed. cit. col. 933).

[63] Johannes Faventinus, *Summa decretorum*, ad C.10 q.2 c.4 (Klosterneuburg, Stiftsbibliothek 655, fol. 82r).

[64] See above, 1921-26.

[65] Johannes Andreae, *Additiones in Speculum iuris*, in 4.4 *de usuris*, super rubr. (ed. cit. II p. 500b).

.18. questio ⟨Vtrum contractus ubbie sit licitus, puta cum dantur .c. ecclesie cum pacto quod certo tempore habeat annuatim a tali .x. et cetera.⟩

Sed quid .xviii.º de tali contractu quem ubbiam uocant quemque pridie inter monasterium quoddam ex una parte et religiosos quosdam et quamdam dominam ex alia celebratum uidi? Ecce dant quidam prout fecerant illi cuidam monasterio centum cum pacto quod ad uitam suam et cuiuscumque ex eis ecclesia talis det eis quolibet anno .xvi. dictaque .c. sua sint, hoc adiecto, quod si durante uita talium ecclesia uoluerit contractum rescindere et dicta .c. restituere, optionem habeat et tunc a dicta annua solutione illorum .xvi. liberetur, et propter hoc omnia et singula sua bona eisdem dicta ecclesia obligauit. Quid iuris? Estne licitus talis contractus?

Videtur quod sic, quoniam ista est quedam emptio illius annualis redditus: hic interuenit pretium, hic interuenit merces, scilicet certus redditus, igitur et cetera. Pro hoc quod notant Innocentius et Ostiensis et post eos Iohannes Andree supra eodem *In ciuitate*[66] et tibi notaui supra questione .xi. huius partis. Hoc idem uidetur sentire in simili in dicto c. *In ciuitate* in determinatione secunde questionis principalis dictus dominus Lapus[67] ubi determinat quod comune Florentie potest sibi nouos creare creditores, uidelicet uendere redditum annuum ad rationem qua respondet creditoribus montium ad uitam ementis et alterius nominandi ab eo, cum pacto quod superuiuenti remaneat dictum creditum, et cum pacto quod post mortem utriusque totaliter sit extinctum pro tempore sequuturo, et cum pacto quod liceat dicte comunitati redimere dictum debitum soluendum creditori pro pretio et redemptione dicti iuris ad rationem .xxviii. pro .c. et quod talis creditor teneatur ad dictam rationem reuendere dicto comuni ad omnem eius uoluntatem,
22r de quo infra / in questione montis in ultimo dubio[68] latius dicam.

Preterea hic soluens .c. numquam est rehabiturus illa, quod non contingit in mutuo. Pro hac parte facit quod scripxit Oldradus in questionibus suis, questione .207.,[69] ubi tenet contractum quo abbas et conuen-

2001 .18. questio *in marg. sin.*
2018 huius partis *in marg. sin. add.*

[66] Johannes Andreae, *Novella,* ad X 5.19.6, n.2 (ed. cit. V fol. 74ra-b); Innocent IV, *Commentaria,* ad X 5.19.6, n.2 (ed. cit. fol. 517rb-vb); Hostiensis, *Commentaria,* ad X 5.19.6, n.7 (ed. cit. V fol. 57ra-b).

[67] Lapo da Castiglionchio, *Allegationes*, allegatio 137, n.15 (ed. cit. fol. 164vb).

[68] See below, 2668-3771.

[69] Oldradus de Ponte, *Consilia seu responsa*, consilium 207 (ed. Frankfurt 1576, fol. 107ra-vb).

tus sancti Dyonisii uendiderunt archiepiscopo Bremensi annuam pensionem siue redditum .400. librarum annuatim percipiendum in dicto monasterio quamdiu uixerit pro pretio duarum milium et quadringentarum librarum de iure licitum. Ibi uide. Pro et contra facit quod notatur infra in questione .53.[70] Omnino uide quod infra subd⟨i⟩tur in uersiculo "possent quidem" parum ante consilium.[71]

Credo in questione proposita contractum inlicitum in casu quo ultra illa .c. aliquid habeatur illudque restitutioni obnoxium. Vt enim uides, redditus non constituitur in re nec ad rem fit relatio sed ad personam contrahentem, licet bona pro obseruatione contractus obligentur et sic non uenditur ius, immo nunc de nouo oritur et uenditur quid inuendibile, scilicet pecunia, que inuendibilis est quia nulla rerum extimatio, ff. *de fideius.* l. *Si ita.*[72] Seu uerius contractus innominatus celebratur "do ut facias," in quo fraus uidetur interuenire de contractu ad contractum, maxime attenta incrementi maxima quantitate et adiectione pacti de rescindendo cum uoluerit, ex quibus perinde uidetur acsi mutuum contracxisset in effectu. Coadiuuat etiam, licet sola de per se non sit efficax ratio, ratione incertitudinis quod in paucis annis totum capitale rehabebit nec est uerisimile quod in breui omnes moriantur. Ad predicta facit quod supra scripxi in hac secunda parte questione .12. cum quinque immediate sequentibus,[73] et uide quod infra dicam in fine, scilicet in dicto uersiculo "possent quidem," erat enim finis ante appositionem consilii quod ibi statim sequitur. Et sic non obstant supra allegata et per Innocentium notata et etiam per Ostiensem et alios in c. *In ciuitate,*[74] quia loquuntur in alio casu, scilicet cum constituuntur in re, actione uel nomine, uel in personis aliis a contrahentibus, ut ibidem exemplificatur, et fraude circumscripta, que hic manifeste presummitur. Et ita possent intelligi etiam notata per Lapum ibidem in iamdicta questione[75] ubi dicam quid credo qui per illa mouetur. Pro hoc quod scripxit dominus meus ibidem et posui in dictis questionibus .xii.[a] et .xiii.[a] et .xiiii.[a][76] ubi

2037-38 Omnino ... consilium *in marg. dex. add.*
2053-55 scilicet ... sequitur. *in marg. dex. add.*

[70] F_1 fol. 37r; *TUI* 7, fol. 26rb.

[71] See below, 2069-80.

[72] Dig. 46.1.42(43)

[73] See above, 1786-2000.

[74] Innocent IV, *Commentaria,* ad X 5.19.6, n.2 (ed. cit. fol. 517rb-vb); Hostiensis, *Commentaria,* ad X 5.19.6, n.7 (ed. cit. V fol. 57ra-b); Johannes Andreae, *Novella,* ad X 5.19.6, n.2 (ed. cit. V fol. 74ra-b).

[75] See below, 3668-3771.

[76] See above, 1786-1894.

horum uidetur esse decisio. Sint ergo cauti contractus tales ineuntes ut redditum constituant in re seu ad rem referant, non autem ad personam uendentis et multo minus ementis. Hoc dico propter notata per Innocentium in c. *In ciuitate* in fine et que supra dixi in questione .12. post dominum meum.[77] Caueant sibi tamen etiam sic contrahentes ne legi fraudem faciant, quia non alios sed proprias animas decipient.

Possent quidem talia in his contractibus ubbie interuenire, ut iam pluries uidi et potest colligi ex notatis supra in .vi. questionibus immediate precedentibus, ex quibus eos licitos reputarem. Indubitatum est enim quod ratio quare extra contractum mutui quandoque usura commictitur est quia in fraudem celebrari presummitur et presumptio est quod in effectu sit mutuum, iuxta notata supra eodem *In ciuitate* post Gofredum.[78] Vnde non dico semper contractum ubbie reprobatum, quem diuersimode celebrari uidi. Ad hoc autem, ut fraus presummatur uel non, multa uenient consideranda: quantitas, res, etas et alia similia. Ad hoc notata per Iohannem Andree in c. *Ad nostram*[79] et in additionibus *Speculo* hoc titulo *de usuris*[80] et quod supra scripxi in quactuor precedentibus questionibus.

Post supra scripta nunc nunc ad manus meas uenit quoddam consilium dominorum meorum Iohannis de Lignano et Laurentii de Pinu de Bononia[81] directe propositam questionem nostram concernens, immo illam continens, cuius quidem tale est thema: abbas, capitulum et conuentus monasterii sancte Marie a conuentu sancti G. ordinis mendicantium recepit donationis titulo inreuocabiliter et inter uiuos ducatos .cc. cum pactis et conditionibus infrascriptis, uidelicet quod abbas et conuentus monasterii sancte Marie teneatur dare et soluere ipsi conuentui sancti G. quolibet anno in perpetuum quinque pro .c. et liceat ipsi abbati 22v et conuentui monasterii sancte Marie / dictam annualem solutionem redimere a dicto conuentu sancti G. restituendo eidem integram summam .cc. ducatorum primo receptam, quam summam idem conuentus sancti

2080 Omnino ad materiam uidendum quod scripxi in quodam meo consilio quod habetur in .v.° volumine et carta 179. Laurentius de Ridolfis. *in marg. sin. add. postea.*

2081 Consilium Iohannis de Lignano et Laurentii de Pinu *in marg. dex. add.*

[77] See above, 1786-1839.

[78] Johannes Andreae, *Novella,* ad X 5.19.6, n.6 (ed. cit. V fol. 74rb); Gottofredo da Trani, *Apparatus*, ad X 5.19.6, v. *Forma* (MS cit. fol. 163ra).

[79] Johannes Andreae, *Novella,* ad X 3.17.5, n.4 (ed. cit. V fols. 80vb-81ra).

[80] Idem, *Additiones in Speculum iuris*, in 4.4 *de usuris*, v. *Libellus concipitur* (ed. cit. II p. 501b).

[81] *Locum non inveni.*

G. recipere tenetur quandocumque monasterium sancte Marie restituere uoluerit, qua restitutione facta ipsum monasterium sancte Marie ipsi conuentui sancti G. in nullo amplius teneatur.

Concludunt quod etsi ex sui forma non sit contractus usurarius directo, quia est donatio inreuocabilis inter uiuos et non mutuum, quod est uerum obiectum usure, tamen dicendum est eum fore confectum in fraudem usurarum et factam fraudem de contractu ad contractum, iuxta notata .xiiii. q. .iii. *Plerique*,[82] ff. *de legi.* l. *Qui contra*.[83] Quod probat aperte relatio pacti in continenti appositi ad contractum predictum, ex qua relatione oritur contractus innominatus "do ut facias" et nascitur actio prescriptis uerbis ad obseruantiam pacti, iuxta notata in l. *Petens* C. *de pac.*[84] Exponendo igitur contractum istum formaliter erit talis, uidelicet "dono tibi .cc. ut perpetuo singulis annis prestes .v. pro .c." Aut ergo ista prestatio deducta in pactum, si licita diceretur, diceretur licita ut fructus pecunie donate aut propter usum pecunie donate qua utitur donatarius. Sed neutrum dici potest. Non primum quia repugnat nature pecunie germinare fructum et sic principiis naturalibus rerum, propter quod reprobatur contractus usurarius. Non secundum quia similiter et illud foret contra naturam et principia rerum, nam paciscendo pro usu pecunie donate sibi dari pecuniam nil aliud est quam usum pecunie inseparabilem a pecunia, cum usus pecunie sit consumptio, l. *Non omnis* ff. *Si cer. pe.* et l. *Rogasti* eodem titulo[85] et notatis in regula *Peccatum* li. .vi.,[86] separare ab ea. Non enim pecunia sine ipsius usu nec ipsius usus sine ipsa consumi potest quia una consumptione utrumque consumitur, quod non euenit in aliis non consistentibus in numero, pondere uel mensura, in quibus usus habet distinctum ualorem a re ipsa et potest alienari solus usus et etiam sola proprietas, usu retento, ut in fundo uel uinea, que sunt species fructuum germinatiue, C. *de dona.* l. *Quisquis*,[87] .xii. q. .ii. *Precarie*.[88] Et idem in specie artificiata que usu deterioratur et regulariter inde pensio trahitur, ut in domo et similibus. In quibus omnibus ideo secus foret dicendum si donarentur sub pacto de quo in questione proposita.

Demonstrat et insuper hanc fraudem, secundum eos, secundum

[82] Gl. ord. ad Decretum Grat. C.14 q.3 c.3, v. *Praecepta* (ed. cit. col. 1096).

[83] Dig. 1.3.30(29) (*recte* Fraus)

[84] Gl. ord. ad C. 2.3.27, casus (ed. cit. cols. 344-45).

[85] Dig. 12.1.19, 11

[86] Johannes Andreae, *Novella*, ad VI *de reg. iur.* 4, *Peccatum*, n.12 (ed. cit. fol. 63rb-va).

[87] C. 8.53(54).28

[88] Decretum Grat. C.12 q.2 c.44

pactum quo conceditur donatario facultas resoluendi obligationem annue prestationis soluendo illa .cc. donata integraliter, non computatis annuis prestationibus. Repugnat enim nature perfecte donationis inreuocabilis, ut l. *Perfecta C. de dona. que sub modo fiunt,*[89] non enim potest reuocari perfecta donatio, nisi in casibus a iure expressis, *de dona.* c. finali.[90] Infertur ergo quod pactum hic appositum resolutionis ex pacto donatarii iunctum cum pacto annue prestationis necessario inferunt donationem illam factam in fraudem usurarum; faciant notata in c. *Illo uos, de pigno.*[91] et c. *Ad nostram, de emp. et uen.*[92] et *de usur.* in c. *In ciuitate*[93] et c. *Consuluit*[94] et .xiiii. q. .iii. *Plerique,*[95] secundum eos.

Hic nulla per donatorem fit reuocatio sed datur facultas et optio donatario, et istud non repugnat nature donationis. Item ista non est proprie donatio, de cuius natura est quod sit gratuita, imo contractus "do ut facias," ut supra dixistis. Videtur ergo melior ratio quam facere tacite uidentur per c. prealligata,[96] hoc est, quod ratione talis facultatis resoluendi et liberationis annue prestationis uideatur effectiue contractus mutui, licet in sui figura et in fraudem fuerit celebratus contractus donationis et sic facta est fraus de contractu ad contractum. Et quod ista sit etiam
23r predictorum intentio patet quia ponunt / in hac fraude illa similia que posuit glosa .i.ª in c. *Plerique* .14 q. .3.[97]

Et tandem in hec uerba concludunt, uidelicet: concluditur ergo his premissis, relatione habita pactorum ad donationem precedentem, presummi uehementer illa adiecta in fraudem usurarum, maxime cum per pactum secundum sit concessa facultas donatario resoluendi obligationem annue prestationis, soluta tota summa integraliter, nulla computatione facta illius annue prestationis solute. Et maxime in religiosis talia pacta reprobanda sunt, qui debent esse predicatores uerbi et facti, ne

2126-27 pensionis *post* annue *del.*
2142 mutui *post* contractus *del.*

[89] C. 8.54(55).4
[90] X 3.24.10
[91] Gl. ord. ad X 3.21.4, v. *Obligatis* (ed. cit. col. 1143).
[92] Gl. ord. ad X 3.17.5, v. *Emptionis* (ed. cit. col. 1126).
[93] Gl. ord. ad X 5.19.6, v. *Ex tali forma* (ed. cit. cols. 1736-37).
[94] Gl. ord. ad X 5.19.10, casus (ed. cit. col. 1739).
[95] Gl. ord. ad Decretum Grat. C.14 q.3 c.3, v. *Praecepta* (ed. cit. col. 1096).
[96] X 3.24.10
[97] Gl. ord. ad Decretum Grat. C.14 q.3 c.3, v. *Praecepta* (ed. cit. col. 1096).

rubentibus buccis, ut dicit canon, ieiunia predicent.[98] Et ex his, secundum eos, patet quid dicendum in questionibus ex themate elicitis, scilicet primo, quod contractus non est licitus; secundo, quod per talem contractum non est abbas uel monasterium efficaciter obligatum; .3.°, quod successor potest petere rescissionem talis contractus et ab ipsa prestatione annua cessare; .4.°, quod annua prestatio computatur in sorte. Iohannes de Lignano et Laurentius de Pinu.

Aduertatis, licet in hoc themate non appareat quod donatarius pro annua prestatione fienda in genere obligauerit omnia bona sua, quod euenit in casu nostro, tamen non dico hunc casum diuersum ex hoc a nostro, et hoc propter ea que post dictum dominum meum et alios scripxi supra in questione .13. et supra hac eadem questione .xviii.[99]

Sed unum non obmictam, uidelicet quod contra illud quod ipsi dicunt de secundo pacto, quo donatario conceditur facultas resoluendi et cetera, quod per id fraus detegatur, fortiter obstat quod legitur et notatur in dicta decretali *Illo uos, de pigno* in glosa.[1] Hoc uidetur et in glosa penultima[2] et super ea per Iohannem Andree[3] et ipsum dominum meum Iohannem de Lignano[4] cum legibus ibidem allegatis. Nam rem uendere cum pacto de ea rescindenda seu resoluenda si displiceat non reprobatur et facit emptor omnino fructus interim perceptos suos nec in sortem computare tenetur, quia ad restitutionem non obligatur. Si sic, ergo in proposito nostro nulla presummi debet fraus, etsi non computentur in quantitate ducentorum restituenda ipse annue prestationes percepte. Immo dico plus quod si de eis computandis factum fuisset pactum, ex eo presummeretur contractus mutui, ut ibi est casus, quia repugnat nature contractus ipsum tale pactum. Sed forte dictum memoratum dictorum consulentium uendicat sibi locum quando tale pactum interuenit in casu quo ius ipsum siue redditus de nouo constituuntur tempore ipsius contractus, quo magis presummitur fraus quam in prius constitutis, ut scripxi supra questionibus .xi. et .xii. huius partis.[5]

[98] Cf. Decretum Grat. D.35 c.4

[99] See above, 1840-78, 2001-2080.

[1] X 3.21.4; gl. ord. ad X 3.21.4, v. *Proximos annos* (ed. cit. col. 1143).

[2] Gl. ord. ad X 3.21.4, v. *Praesumitur* (ed. cit. col. 1143).

[3] Johannes Andreae, *Novella,* ad X 3.21.4, n.6 (ed. cit. III fol. 90ra).

[4] John of Legnano, *Commentaria,* ad X 3.21.4, v. *Conditio* (Munich, Bayerische Staatsbibliothek, Clm 8787, fol. 46va).

[5] See above, 1652-1839.

73r ⟨Tertia particula⟩

.5. questio. Questio montis.

Vltimo superest ut montis materiam explicemus, in qua instare paulisper intendo. Et pro euidentia premicto quod in hac materia scripxerunt, ut audio, unus tamen altero diffusius, plures reuerendi sacre pagine professores. Et inter alios, latius et altius frater magister Gregorius de Arimino, generalis prior sui ordinis heremitarum sancti Augustini,[1] ac, ut nouiter post plura infrascripta reperio, magister frater Francischus de Empuli ordinis minorum;[2] et in multis aduersa⟨tur⟩. Deinde commentando decretalem *In ciuitate* supra eodem copiose satis scripxit egregius decretorum doctor dominus Lapus de Castiglonchio.[3] Quorum dicta inferius ut dabitur recitabo.

Facti prius igitur seriem explicando, dico quod florentina comunitas pecunia indigens ciuibus suis onera imponit, que uulgari sermone "prestantias" appellamus, ad quas soluendas quilibet inuitus compellitur statuitque cuilibet quousque restituat capitale siue sortem .v. dandos pro centenario et aliquando plures ultra sortem. Et ita de facto a diu obseruauit obseruatque cotidie appellanturque tales "creditores montis." Et contingit aliquando quod dictis creditoribus uel ab eis iura habentibus fuit tamtum responsum de accessione predicta uere sortis et per tantum tempus, quod aliquando accessio adequata est sorti, aliquando non in totum, aliquando excedit sortem.

Et insuper, maxime ad omnem dubitationem tollendam et exonerationem conscientie cuiuscumque, et ut tollatur omnis nexus quo quicumque de ciuitate uel comitatu Florentie pro infrascriptis uel eorum occasione ligatus uel adstrictus quomodolibet diceretur quoad Deum, conscientiam uel ad mundum, statuit quod quicquid prouisum est per ordinamenta dicti comunis dari debere talibus mutuantibus ad dictam rationem pro dono, dampnis et interesse seu prouisione uel merito dictorum creditorum, intelligatur dari debere et recipi et detur et recipiatur et peti

2183 Tertia particula *ed.*
2184 .5. questio *in marg. sin.*
2188 magister *in marg. dex. add.*
2190 magister *in marg. dex. add.*
2191 aduersa⟨tur⟩: F_1 aduersa

[1] Gregory of Rimini, *Tractactus* (ed. cit.).

[2] Francesco da Empoli, *Questio de monte*, ed. Armstrong, in "Politics of Usury," 28-44. See also Ridolfi's summary of the *questio* at F_1 fols. 87v-91r; *TUI* 7, fols. 43rb-44vb.

[3] Lapo da Castiglionchio, *Allegationes*, allegatio 137 (ed. cit. fols. 162va-164vb).

et recipi possit pro spontaneo, libero et mero dono et donationis titulo et taliter recipiat et recipere intelligatur quilibet talis creditor a comuni predicto, et nichilominus etiam pro dampnis et uero interesse et pro aliquali remuneratione et ut benefacientibus bene fiat. Et ita et taliter illud totum recipiat unusquisque talis creditor sicque petere et exigere ualeat, quod nullatenus ad restitutionem aliquam teneatur etiam quoad conscientiam uel ad Deum illudque sic receptum absque alia liberatione uel fine per dictum comune fienda, absque ullo conscientie scrupulo uel restitutionis grauamine, ut sibi uere donatum licite ualeat retinere.

Et quod presens prouisio et omnia et singula in ea contenta in fauorem dictorum creditorum singulis diebus pro futuro tempore donec per comune predictum fuerint renouata intelligatur singulis diebus et horis singulorum dierum renouari et de nouo condi et renouata et de nouo condita. Et sic effectum suum singulis dictis horis et temporibus sortiatur et semper lex presens loquatur acsi singulis uicibus et temporibus condita esset extendendo eas ad quantitates in preteritum receptas per quoscumque creditores dicti comunis ex causis memoratis.

Et quod sibi solum locum uendicet in ciuibus, comitatinis uel districtualibus suis.

Et quod per hoc non preiudicetur comuni iamdicto in aliquo iure sibi quesito uel querendo in posterum uigore alicuius ultime uoluntatis facte uel fiende, ut hec omnia clare patent in quadam reformatione que incipit "Maxime ad omnem" et cetera, ut supra.

Sanciuit et insuper ipsa comunitas huiusmodi talia credita cum iure percipiendi huiusmodi accessiones alienare posse in alios, cum hoc tamen pacto, quod ipsi comunitati redimere liceat dictum debitum creditori soluendum pro pretio et redemptione dicti iuris ad rationem .xxviii. pro .c. Et quod talis creditor teneatur ad dictam rationem reuendere dicto comuni ad omnem eius uoluntatem, remanente dicto uenditori lucro facto usque ad tempus dicte reuenditionis.

Et insuper sepesepius sindicum constituit ad liberandum et per illum liberantur omnes et cetera.

Modo hinc plurima schaturiunt dubia: /

73v Primo, utrum recta conscientia talia possint onera indici et ad illorum solutionem compelli cum assignatione incrementi prelibati.

.2.º, utrum dicti soluentes onera memorata licite tale percipiant incrementum.

.3.º, posito quod non, utrum uigore donationis, remissionis et liberationis supradicte excusentur a restitutione et liberentur a peccato.

.4.º, an dicti soluentes licite uendant ius quod habent in dicto monte uigore talis crediti.

.v.º, utrum alii illud ab eis licite emant.

2254 illud *interlin.*

.vi.º, posito quod sic, utrum licite percipiant incrementum quod prius percipiebant ipsi uenditores.

.vii.º, quid de his qui pro aliis, a quibus quandoque certam quotam pro quolibet floreno, quandoque nichil percipiunt, soluunt prestantias et in illorum loco quoad tale creditum describuntur?

.viii.º, quid si comunitas sic sibi nouos constituat creditores, puta quia uendit annuum redditum ad rationem qua respondet creditoribus montis sui ad uitam ementis et alterius ab eo nominandi cum pactis, de quibus scilicet in themate ad finem?

De quibus omnibus et per ordinem uideamus.

⟨Primum principale dubium. Vtrum recta conscientia talia possint onera indici et ad illorum solutionem compelli cum assignatione incrementi prelibati.⟩

Ad primum igitur dico ex duplici capite uideri dicta onera sic indici non posse.

Primo quia sine principis permissu indici nequeunt, ut l. .i. C. *de exac. tribu.* li. .x.[4] et eodem libro, *de excu. mu.* l. *Placet*.[5]

Secundo quia assignatione dicti incrementi inuitantur ciues ad delinquendum, de quo uidetur esse casus in c. *Super eo* supra eodem titulo,[6] ubi de hoc.

In contrarium facit quoad primam rationem quoniam etsi generalem collectam camere fiscali applicandam nemo possit imponere sine permissu principis, ut in prealligata lege, tamen collectam spetialem unaqueque ciuitas seu uniuersitas pro necessitate sibi incumbente indicere potest, ut l. *Omnes* .ii. C. *de ope. pu.*,[7] de quo est dare glosam notabilem in l. .i. § *Quod si nemo* super uerbo "Proconsul" ff. *quod cuiusque uni. no.*[8] (Et ista ueritas et sic poterit a sibi subditis extorquere licite ex hoc capite; ad idem ff. *de pigno. ac.* l. finali § finali,[9] ubi uidetur esse casus, et facit ff. *de peri. et commo. rei uendi.* l. *Lectos*.[10] Nec mirum certe quoniam uidemus ob easdem necessitates eos compelli posse ad res eorum uendendas pretio uiliori, ff. *de usufruc.* l. *Si pendentes* § *Si quid coa-*

2283 ff. *scripsi*: F_1 C.

[4] C. 10.19.1
[5] C. 10.48(47).8(9)
[6] X 5.19.4
[7] C. 8.11(12).12(11)
[8] Gl. ord. ad Dig. 3.4.1.2, v. *Proconsul* (ed. cit. I p. 193a).
[9] Dig. 13.7.43.1
[10] Dig. 18.6.13(12)

dunari.[11] Possunt etiam ob eandem causam urgueri ad deputandum eorum nemora uel molendinos seu alia similia usui publico, recepta tamen competenti mercede, ut l. *Venditor* § *Si constat* ff. *comunia predi.*,[12] et facit ff. *de rei uen.* l. *Item si uerberato.*)[13] Ad propositum insuper l. *Rescripto* § finali *de mune. et ho.*,[14] et in corpore *Qui. mo. naturales effi. sui* § *Si uero nec ciuis* et ibi glosa notabilis.[15] Ad idem quod scripxit Innocentius *de sen. ex., Graue.*[16] et Guilelmus in *Speculo, de sen.* § *Sequitur* uersiculo "Quid si uniuersitas"[17] et Bartolus in l. .iiii. § *Actor* ff. *de re. iud.*[18] et in consilio suo quod incipit "Si aliqua possessio"[19] et cetera.

Contra secundam rationem uero facit quod scripxit Damasus in questione .i. *de iureiuran.*[20] ubi determinat non esse peccatum mutuo ad usuram recipere. Preterea, ut ex infra dicendis apparebit, non semper est usura in hoc casu, nedum ex parte comunitatis sed nec etiam ex parte mutuantium. Nec etiam est uerum quod ex hoc inuitentur ad peccandum, considerato siquidem quod si inlicite quis uellet suam pecuniam uti siue trafficare, longe plus lucraretur, immo et in licitis etiam, quinimmo et in possessionibus, que magis secure sunt quam comunitati mutuare, non est dicendum quod per hoc, quod quinque dari statuuntur, inuitentur ad usurarie mutuandum; maxime cum dubium sit nedum de
74r lucro sed etiam de sorte principali, ne / perdatur capitale. Sed cum uerisimile sit non debere perdi, etsi procedat iamdicta ratio tempore isto et tempore montis ueteris, quo statutum de .v. pro lucro dandis disponit, tamen non sic forte olim, tempore quo prius .xv. et postea .x. dari statutum fuerat. Fuit enim dare tempus quo .v. tantum dabantur pro lucro et hic appellabatur mons uetus. Secundo fuit dare tempus quo dabantur .xv. et credo ⟨quod⟩ fuerit tempore guerre Pisanorum et qua-

2290 h *post* mune. *canc.*

[11] Dig. 7.1.27(34).3 (*recte* Si quid cloacarii)
[12] Dig. 8.4.13(14).1
[13] Dig. 6.1.15.2 (*recte* Item si uerberatum)
[14] Dig. 50.4.6.5
[15] Excerptum Nov. 89.2 = Auth. 7.1 coll. 2.1; gl. ord. ad excerptum Nov. 89.2 = Auth. 7.1 coll. 2.1, v. *Persoluat* (ed. Venice 1492, fols. 67vb-68ra).
[16] Innocent IV, *Commentaria*, ad X 5.39.53, n.2 (ed. cit. fol. 559rb-va).
[17] William Durant, *Speculum iuris*, 2.3 *de executione sententiae*, n.5 (ed. cit. I p. 823b).
[18] Bartolus of Sassoferrato, *Commentaria*, in Dig. 42.1.4.2, nn.1-4 (ed. cit. V fol. 106va).
[19] Idem, *Consilia, quaestiones et tractatus*, consilium 180, nn.1-2 (ed. cit. X fol. 43ra).
[20] Damasus, *Quaestiones, de iureiurando* (MS cit. fol. 30r).

rumdam aliarum guerrarum. Et postmodum .xv. redacta sunt ad .x. et hic appellatur mons nouus. Deinde circa annum domini .1380. statutum est quod fiat mons nouissimus et dentur tantum .v. Cum enim tantum dari, scilicet .x. uel .xv., sit nimis excessiuum et ad mutuandum allectiuum, ideo forte tunc aliter concludendum, nisi iam natura seu conditio temporis aliud induceret, ut quia in maximo foret comunitas constituta peric⟨u⟩lo, ex quo tunc et de sorte posset uerisimiliter dubitari. Sed ubi pur usuram presupponere uelimus omni casu, tunc passus iste decidendus esset secundum ea que supra diffuse scripxi super rubrica in .ix. questione.[21]

Sciendum tamen quod, ut nouissime comperii, reuerendus sacre pagine magister et ordinis heremitarum prior generalis, frater Guido de Belloregardo consultus[22] respondit indistincte quod lex statuens tale lucrum non est licite instituta et ideo non est obseruanda sed abolenda. Probat quia in diminutionem rei publice et eius lesionem et per consequens mala. Patet antecedens quia iam comunitas finaliter soluit duplum pecunie, quia per multiplicationem quinque et quinque soluitur usque ad summam sortis et tandem debet solui sors principalis, allegata .iii. distinctione § *Officium* cum c. sequenti.[23] Item quia per ipsam non refrenatur nocendi cupiditas, immo potius augetur. Item non est iusta nec utilis ex quo continet plus priuatum bonum singularium personarum quam publicum ipsius comunitatis. Vltimo adducit dictam secundam rationem quam supra feci,[24] scilicet quod inuitat homines ad peccandum, quia inducit eos ad recipiendum plus quam dederint et ultra sortem, que consuetudo est mala, immo forsitan quasi usuraria, saltem ex parte recipientis.

Et si dicatur quod considerato quod lex talis est instituta propter bonum ciuitatis custodiendum et protegendum ad habendum pecunias multas pro gentibus armorum in custodiam et protectionem ciuitatis, et sic non mala sed bona est et sic non obstant supradicta, respondit idem magister quod, his non obstantibus, firme manent rationes supra posite, eo quod aliter et sine peccato potest comunitas defensari, eo quod, subsistente necessitate, potest a sibi suppositis, etiam inuitis, iuxte exigere auxilium tam pecuniarium quam personale et ipsi ad illud prestandum obligantur, et quantum prestant tamtum secundum regulam iustitie et non ultra rehabere debent; et sic faciendo, minus in expensis grauabitur ipsa comunitas, quod est propositum.

2318 peric⟨u⟩lo: F_1 periclo

[21] See above, 562-633.

[22] F_1 fols. 98r-100v; *TUI* 7, fols. 48va-49vb.

[23] Decretum Grat. D.3 dictum Grat. post c.3; c.4

[24] See above, 2272-74.

Secundo, quod non procedat talis responsio probat per rationem: nam si ita esset quod propter bonum comune defensandum talis contractus uel lex, uidelicet ut quinque uel ultra dentur pro centenario, licitus seu licita et rationabilis diceretur, sequeretur per consequens quod contractus usurarius permicteretur, quod repugnat legi diuine et canonice. Patet consequentia quia per contractum usurarium potest haberi tanta pecunia quod per illam poterit res publica defensari et custodiri, ergo qua ratione licitum asseritur dare .v. uel ultra pro centenario ut ciuitas defensetur? Eadem concluditur licitum fore contractum usurarium celebrari, cum per illum similiter, ut dictum est, ciuitas defensetur.
74v At istud / est absurdum, ergo et illud. Pro hoc facit quod legitur de patribus ueteris testamenti, qui quamuis multos haberent aduersarios et multa bella, nichilominus tales contractus, ex quibus Deus offendi poterat, minime celebrantur. Guido.

Quid dicendum? Ego, non obstantibus predictis, non recedo a prius supra per me dictis. Et dico quod optime procedit responsio superius posita in uersiculo "Et si dicatur"[25] ad rationes ipsius magistri, saluo quam ad ultimam in qua dicendum est ut supra premisi et scripxi super rubrica in .ix. questione.[26]

Ad responsiones autem quas idem magister supra fecit uolendo ostendere quod dicta responsio posita in dicto uersiculo "Et si dicatur" et cetera non sit bona, respondeo et primo ad primam quod etsi ciues ad mutuandum compellere ualeat ⟨comune⟩ absque eo quod statuat aliquid dari ultra sortem, tamen non omne possibile debet esse uolibile, sepe namque multa possumus que pro bono rei publice et pro fugiendo scandalo non facimus et merito, argumento c. *Imprimis* .ii. q. .i.[27] cum symilibus, coactiones siquidem difficiles frequenter consueuerunt exitus habere, *de sponsa., Requisiuit*[28] cum concordantiis. Et melius est cum aliquali conscito et pace ciuium suis necessitatibus prouidere quam per huiusmodi coactiones et uiolentias absolutas, non sine forte graui scandalo, quot siquidem ex hoc enormiter experientia media dampnificari cotidie cernimus, immo et multos funditus destrui et ad extremam pauperiem deduci, qui ex hoc saltem aliqualiter subleuantur, refrigerantur et consolantur quod dicta quinque percipiunt annuatim? Et nisi hoc esset in desperationem forsitan ducerentur et in rem publicam machinarentur in

2362 Guido *in marg. dex. add.*
2376 cum symilibus *post* Requisiuit *del.*
2378 absolutas *in marg. sin. add.*

[25] See above, 2338-48.
[26] See above, 562-633.
[27] Gl. ord. ad Decretum Grat. C.2 q.1 c.7, v. *In primis* (ed. cit. col. 644).
[28] X 4.1.17

graue anime et corporis sui dispendium et rei publice periculum. Et si dicatur, talibus et non aliis si lex prouideat bene est, respondeo quod lex debet esse comunis pro rei publice utilitate, ne alii scrupuloso corde moueantur, ut infra latius explicabo,[29] et durum foret atque difficile distinguere unum ab alio.

Preterea interest rei publice erga suos ciues se taliter habere quod non deducantur in pauperiem ut cum aliter opus fuerit sibi ualeant subuenire. Si ergo in dampni restaurationem uel ex liberalitate, ut alliciantur ad bene se habendum erga rem publicam, aliquid gratis donat et sic indubie utilitas rei publice procuratur, quare id improbandum? Vulgatum est prouerbium quod "illius regimen tutum est qui subditorum suorum corda possidet."[30] Et plus facit pro re publica amorem ciuium habere quam solam pecuniam. Et dicit aliud prouerbium: "buono e quel soldo che meglora il fiorino." (Dici profecto potest in proposito de comunitate quod in libello de stimulo amoris, parum post principium, de Deo deuote inquiit Bernardus: "Et quis habet quicdquam non tuum? Reddis debita nulli debens, donas debita nichil perdens.")[31] Pro hoc optime facit textus in decretali ultima *de peculio cleri.*[32] Constat enim clericos teneri bona et possessiones ecclesie pro posse manutenere et de bono in melius illa conducere, et tamen ibi premiantur per papam hoc facientes cum etiam postquam illam ecclesiam dimiserint fructus percipiant terre ad culturam reducte uel uineate toto tempore uite sue, etiam si aliter propter crimen ab illa remoti fuerint, secundum unam lecturam quam ibi ponunt Innocentius et Ostiensis et Iohannes Andree.[33] Ad idem

2391 ut *interlin.*
2397-2400 Dici ... perdens *in marg. sin. add.*
2407 Ad secundam rationem responde negando consequentiam. Et ad consequentie probationem dicas *post* Andree *del. Vid. inf.* 2416-17.

[29] See below, 2647-74, 2745-56.

[30] Cf. Cicero, *Oratio Philippica* 2.44.112, ed. Albert Curtis Clark (Oxford, 1918); Francesco Petrarca, *Rerum Senilium liber XIIII. Ad magnificum Franciscum de Carraria Padue dominum. Epistola I. Qualis esse debeat qui rem publicam regit,* ed. Vincenzo Ussani (Padua, 1922), 8. References from Kirshner, "Reading Bernardino's Sermon," 557, n.38.

[31] Cf. Augustine, *Confessionum libri XIII* 1.4, ed. Martinus Skutella, rev. Lucas Verheijen in CC*SL* 27 (Turnhout, 1981), 3.

[32] X 3.25.5

[33] Innocent IV, *Commentaria,* ad X 3.25.5 (ed. cit. fol. 400rb); Hostiensis, *Commentaria,* ad X 3.25.5, n.1 (ed. cit. III fol. 72vb); Johannes Andreae, *Novella,* ad X 3.25.5, n.1 (ed. cit. III fol. 105ra).

facit, immo est textus, in l. *Si quando*, § *Illud* C. *de inoffi. testa.*,[34] ubi commendatur filios premiis ad paterna obsequia prouocari. Ad idem quod scribit magister Gregorius[35] et infra dicam in dubio sequenti in uersiculo "Et subdit ad predicta"[36] et cetera.

Quid ultra? Nonne et patres nostros Romanos ciues suos ob utiliter et prospere gesta remunerasse legimus ad que nichilominus tenebantur? Que longum nimis reserare foret sed ad Titum Liuium,[37] Vallerium Maximum[38] et alios hystoriographos recurramus.

75r Ad secundam rationem responde / negando consequentiam. Et ad consequentie probationem dicas quod non omne illud per quod potest pecunia haberi pro defensione ciuitatis permictitur. Proba quia multis modis potest haberi pecunia, potest namque ex uectigalibus et aliis rei publice redditibus, puta tributis, censibus et ceteris. Potest insuper haberi ex rapina, depredationibus et extorsionibus et similibus. Sed etsi dummodo pecunia habeatur res publica ualeat defensari, non tamen sequitur quod modus omnis approbetur sed licitus dumtaxat et rationi se conformans, sicut est primus et non secundus. Sicut in simili hominem occidi utile est rei publice[39] sed non omnem hominem et omni casu, nam malefactorem occidi utile est rei publice, ne crimina remaneant impunita et alii horum timore perterriti se abstineant; sed innocentem occidi non est utile sed dampnosum. Sic ad propositum: etsi utile sit rei publice pecuniam habere, non tamen per uiam usurariam, quantum est ad hoc quod ipsa comunitas suam pecuniam mutuet ad usuram nec quantum est ad hoc ut etiam illam alteri soluat in casu quo et in ipsa soluente sit dare peccatum. Quod distingue iuxta supra notata et super rubrica in .ix. questione.[40]

Et si dicatur sic in nostro contingere proposito, id penitus denegatur, quando non exceditur in eo quod dari statuitur, nec etiam in illo casu semper, ut superius est ostensum et plenius ostendetur in his que in sequenti dubio latissime disserentur. Et sic tollitur etiam quod supra adducebatur de patribus nostris ueteris testamenti, quoniam in nullo, quantum est ex parte comunitatis eo casu, Deus offenditur, quinimo regulariter nec ex parte mutuantium. Quisnam rogo (michi dicas), experientia

[34] C. 3.28.35.1

[35] Gregory of Rimini, *Tractactus*, art. 3 (ed. cit. fols. B6r-C1r).

[36] See below, 2611-22.

[37] Cf. Livy, *Ab urbe condita* 4.59.11-60.2, ed. R. S. Conway and C. F. Walters (Oxford, 1914).

[38] Cf. Valerius Maximus, *Factorum et dictorum memorabilium* 2.8.3, 4.4.1 (ed. cit. pp. 95, 188).

[39] Cf. *Io* 11.50; 18.14

[40] See above, 562-633.

media omnium magistra, *de elec., Quam sit* li. .vi.,[41] ut supra dixi,[42] spe adductus primaria lucri quinque florenorum pro centenario comunitati mutuaret, considerato quod longe plus licite perciperet ex tali pecunia ipsam in alios usus, nedum inlicitos sed etiam licitos et longe tutiores, conuertendo? Obmictamus alia lucra maiora que cotidie licite fieri conspicimus. Nonne si in terra talem pecuniam conuertam quinque uel ultra percipiam? Et si centum expendi in ipsius emptione, si uolam reuendere centum comuniter rehabebo? Vtique. Et tamen si uolam uendere centum comuni mutuata, non centum sed .xxv. uel .xxx. tantum rehabebo.

Hec procedunt tenendo quod dixi. Sed ubi tu presupponas indistincte quod inuitentur ad peccandum per talem legem, prout presupposuit magister prelibatus (quod, ut predixi, non fateor) omni casu, tunc bene assentio illationi sue, quia etiam propter utilitatem rei publice absit ut in peccatum incidere debeamus. Debemus enim potius omnia mala pati quam malo consentire et animam corpori tamquam pretiosiorem preferre, *de peni. et remis., Cum infirmitas*.[43] Perprius enim Deo quam patrie obligamur; et hic uide quod infra dicam post magistrum Iohannem Clenkoh.[44]

.ii.ᵐ principale dubium ⟨Vtrum dicti soluentes onera memorata licite tale percipiant incrementum.⟩

Videamus nunc de secundo dubio principali, circa quod sciendum quod magister Gregorius prelibatus[45] pro parte affirmatiua sex inducebat que quia contrarium determinat apponere non curaui. Pro negatiua autem allegat c. *Plerumque* .xiiii. q. .iii.[46] Tandem soluendo effectiue determinat quod predixi. Verum quia ego aliter infra dicam, uideamus motiua
75v sua suamque conclusionem magis specifice, ut ueritas / clarius elucescat.

Dicit[47] igitur pro solutione ipsius questionis inquirendum de intentione mutuantium, nam cum intentio lucri faciat quem usurarium, etiam

2450 quod in *post* presupponas *del.*
2454 argumento de tempo. or. Ad aures et ibi notatorum *post* debeamus *del.*
2458 super sexto dubio principali *post* Clenkoh *del.*
2459 .ii.ᵐ principale dubium *in marg. sin.* Secundum principale dubium *in marg. dex. add. al. man.*

[41] VI 1.6.6
[42] See above, 2299-2305.
[43] X 5.38.13
[44] F_1 fols. 100v-101r; *TUI* 7, fols. 49vb-50ra.
[45] Gregory of Rimini, *Tractactus, proemium* (ed. cit. fols. A5v-A6r).
[46] Decretum Grat. C.14 q.3 c.3 (*recte* Plerique)
[47] Gregory of Rimini, *Tractactus*, art. 3 (ed. cit. fol. B6r-v).

si nulla pactio exterius intercedat, ergo dicendum quod aut huius mutuantes et tale lucrum recipientes aliquam intentionem lucri habuerunt aut nullam. Si aliquam, et tunc dicas tale lucrum fore usuram et sic mutuantes et recipientes teneri ad illius restitutionem si possunt, et si non possunt, peccare mortaliter si non habent animum restituendi cum poterunt. Et hoc siue talem intentionem lucrum recipiendi habuerint tempore facti mutui, scilicet quia cum mutuant, mutuant propter lucrum percipiendum, siue tempore tantum quo lucrum recipiunt, puta quia cum recipiunt, illud recipiunt propter mutuum prius factum; et idem si post quandocumque, ut infra patebit.[48] Et ponit etiam ipse idem in primo articulo in descriptione super uerbo "intentum"[49] et supra etiam recitaui super rubrica in .i. questione.[50]

Probat[51] hoc sic: omne lucrum ex mutuo intentum est usura, ut patet in sua diffinitione. Sed illud lucrum est lucrum ex mutuo intentum, ergo est usura. Probat hoc idem secundo sic: predicta uendicant sibi locum cum priuata uel singularis persona mutuat alteri persone singulari uel priuate certam pecunie quantitatem ex iamdicta intentione, ergo et cum mutuat comunitati. Patet consequentia quia in mutuo facto comunitati eque bene concurrunt quecumque pertinent ad usuram, malitiam, culpam et obligationem ad restituendum, sicut in illo quod factum extitit singulari uel priuate persone, ut clarum est, igitur ⟨et cetera⟩.

Preterea magis uidetur quis peccare fenerando comunitati, cui magis obligatur, quam alteri, cum bonum gentis et ciuitatis sit melius dominium, ut dicit Phylosophus ⟨libro⟩ .i. *Ethycarum*.[52] Et Augustinus inquiit: "comunia propriis et non propria comunibus antepone."[53]

Sed si queratur quomodo deprehendetur talium mutuantium intentio, respondeo secundum eum[54] inquirendo de intentione comunitatis tale lucrum dantis uel dare statuentis, quoniam aut dat uel dare statuit ratione mutui recepti siue recipiendi siue ulterius retinendi, aut non ratione mutui sed alia ratione uel causa.

Primo casu, si ipsi mutuantes talem intentionem sciunt uel credunt, usura est et ad peccatum et ad restitutionem tenentur; consentiunt enim

2484 dispon *post* cum *del.*

[48] See below, 2499-2510.

[49] Gregory of Rimini, *Tractactus*, art. 1 (ed. cit. fols. A7v-A8v).

[50] See above, 132-44, 177-231.

[51] Gregory of Rimini, *Tractactus*, art. 3 (ed. cit. fol. B6r-v).

[52] Aristotle, *Ethica Nicomachea* 1.2.1094b6-10 (ed. cit. p. 376).

[53] Augustine, *Epistula* 211.12, ed. Albertus Goldbacher, in *CSEL* 57 (Vienna and Leipzig, 1911), 366.

[54] Gregory of Rimini, *Tractactus*, art. 3 (ed. cit. fol. B7r-v).

sic recipiendo intentioni comunitatis dantis et iam ipsi ratione mutui et propter lucrum mutuum recipiunt ac per hoc ex mutuo lucrum intendunt. Immo plus quia etsi tunc non haberent huiusmodi credulitatem uel scientiam habent tamen postea post receptionem in successu temporis, nichilominus ad restituendum illa prius habita obligantur, nam ex quo propter mutuum comunitas dedit, aliter non datura, non est iuxte acquisitum recipientibus nec in eos translatum est dominium dicti lucri, ut patet ex dictis per eundem in primo articulo in descriptione super uerbo "intentum" et in secundo ad finem.[55] Et est contra illud quod supra dixi in secunda parte in .ix. questione.[56]

Quinimmo et ultra dicendum, secundum eum,[57] uidelicet quod si comunitas non propter mutuum dedisset et tamen ipsi putarent eam propter mutuum dedisse procul dubio peccarent non restituendo si possent, cum sic putantes et tamen retinendo utique uolunt retinere alienum. Immo plus quia si nec ante nec tunc nec postea talem habent scientiam uel credulitatem de intentione comunitatis, nichilominus si ex aliquibus inditiis potest eis innotescere intentio comunitatis, ut forte ex
76r eo quod mutuantibus statuit dare tale lucrum / et plus mutuantibus plus dari, et non obstante quod alii ciues similia uel maiora beneficia comunitati contulerint, id tamen in eis non statuitur nec aliquam remunerationem similem consecuntur uel ex probabilibus aliis argumentis que cum possunt nolunt aduertere uel inquirere, huiusmodi tales minime sunt non obnoxii, cum affectata ignorantia non excuset. Si uero isto uel alio casu recipiens nullam penitus lucri haberet intentionem neque intentio dantis propter mutuum ullo modo posset ex exterioribus inditiis apparere siue comprehendi et dans diceret se prorsus non propter mutuum sed ex mera liberalitate dare, quia in recipiente nulla uidetur esse corrupta intentio nec taliter recipiens absque culpa sua sciret intentionem dantis et ipse absque omni intentione lucri pro mutuo esset immunis, utique immunis esset etiam a peccato ipse recipiens et retinens et tale lucrum usura non est quia non fuit nec est intentum ex mutuo.

In secundo autem principali membro, scilicet quando nullam intentionem lucri habuerunt dicti mutuantes et recipientes, dic secundum eum ut supra[58] quod si prorsus nec ante nec tunc nec postea illam habu-

2523 non[1] *interlin.*
2528 igno *post* sua *del.*
2530 ipse recipiens et retinens *post* peccato *del.*
2533 ip *post* habuerunt *del.*

[55] Ibid., art. 1, 2 (ed. cit. fols. A7v-A8v, B5r-B6r).
[56] See above, 1514-1600.
[57] Gregory of Rimini, *Tractactus*, art. 3 (ed. cit. fol. B7r-v).
[58] Ibid.

erunt nec insuper ullo tempore sciuerunt uel crediderunt comunitatem propter mutuum lucrum aliquod dare uelle neque intentio comunitatis dantis propter mutuum dare fuit nec ex ullis potest inditiis exterioribus apparere quod propter illud dederit, et dans diceret se prorsus non propter mutuum sed ex aliqua rationabili causa dare, utputa propter restaurationem dampni quod forsitan mutuantes inde perpessi sunt uel propter beniuolentiam quam ipsi mutuantes in mutuando comunitati ostenderunt uel etiam ex mera liberalitate comunitatis, tunc nullam commicterent usuram uel peccatum nec ad ullam restitutionem tenentur; non enim hic est dare ⟨lucrum⟩ intentum ex mutuo. Non enim in primo casu lucrum censeri debet sed potius quedam dampni restauratio, ad quam de iure tenetur ipsa comunitas que fuit ipsius causa compellendo illos ad mutuum propter quod ipsi dampnum passi sunt, allegato c. *Peruenit, de fideius.*,[59] et hoc si ex illa causa tantum tale dampnum incurrerunt, aliter secus, nam scribitur *de reg. iur.* quod "dampnum quod quisque sentit"[60] et cetera.

Et intelligit, ut patet ex his que ibidem et clarius in responsionibus ad argumenta seu rationes prime questionis scribit,[61] ubi ad secundam rationem respondet de dampno quod consistit in diminutione prehabiti, licet et in dampno quod consistit in non acquisitione lucri polliciti uel sperati posset etiam sibi locum uendicare quoad inuite et coacte mutuantes, ut dicamus quod tales sic coacte mutuantes et ex tali mutuatione a lucro impediti quod licite negotiando uel alio licito modo acquisiuissent, licite possunt exigere seu recipere recompensationem sui dampni secundum discretum iudicium prudentis uiri considerantis si uel quantum eo tempore alii similem negotiationem uel artem exercentes cum equali pecunia comuniter lucrati sunt, ut secundum hoc arbitretur utrum isti fuissent non mutuando sed aliquid agendo lucrati uel non; et si sic, quantum. Dicit tamen quod non credit tantumdem debere eis recompensari et hoc propter personales labores quos non adhibent et pericula que non substinent iminentia circa lucrum negotiationis uel aliud quod intendebant, sed secundum hoc et alia consideranda taxanda
76v esset quantitas recompensationis / huius. Et quia contingit non semper equale lucrum acquiri sed quandoque minus quandoque maius, interdum autem nullum sed dampnum potius substineri, non credit quod una et eadem uniformis debeat esse quolibet anno taxatio sed quinimo quolibet anno de nouo sit fienda taxatio, prelibatis pensatis secundum arbi-

[59] X 3.22.2

[60] VI *de reg. iur.* 86, *Damnum*

[61] Gregory of Rimini, *Tractactus*, art. 4 (ed. cit. fols. C1v-C3r).

trium sapientis.

Sentit ex supradictis magister reuerendus, si recte percipio, quod dampnificatus ex tali mutuo licite petere possit emendam seu restaurationem tamquam interesse, quod equidem in non supposito uel in supposito et non subsistente necessitatis causa procedere posset. Sed in supposito et subsistente dicta causa, cum ad id ex debito teneatur, ut supra tactum fuit in primo principali dubio,[62] non uideo quomodo id petere possit. Dico a domino inuito, non tamen dico quod domino sup⟨p⟩licare ut uelit compati dampnis suis non ualeat, quia immo et illo aliquid dante ob dictam causam licite recipere poterit, sicut et posset si, ex eo quod condempnationem pecuniariam debite soluit, dampnificatus est et a domino cui sup⟨p⟩licasset consequeretur pecuniam condempnationis et id in quo dampnificatus fuisset propter illius solutionem.

Sed quid dicemus? Rebus sic stantibus, ut cotidie cernimus, numquid presummendum est in casu nostro quod pro restauratione dampni comunitas dictum lucrum impendat? Equidem dicit idem magister in dicta .i. questione articulo tertio[63] quod non sed immo propter mutuum, quod probat ex eo quod omnibus mutuantibus datur nec est uerisimile quod omnes dampnum patiantur ex mutuo a se facto. Secundo quia si aliqui dampnificantur, non tamen est uerisimile quod equaliter: imo satis est possibile quod qui minus mutuauerunt maius dampnum passi sunt et tamen minus datur eis, quod nequaquam contingeret si propter restaurationem dampni daretur. Similiter non uidetur quod ex beniuolentia dari presummatur seu causa remunerationis beniuolentie quam sic mutuantes in mutuando ostenderunt comunitati, quia si propter illam daretur, certe plus daretur ei in quo maior affectus beniuolentie probaretur. Sed contingere potest quod ex maiori affectu unus mutuet .c. quam alter mille, qui est in centuplo ditior. Potest enim contingere quod qui centum mutuat, libenter mutuat et libentius plus, si posset, mutuaret, qui autem mille mutuat, inuitus mutuat. Ex quo sequitur quod plus, attenta beniuolentia, deberetur remunerationis ei qui centum quam ei qui mille mutuauit, et tamen, ut uidemus, oppositum seruatur. Igitur

2572 Sed quid dicemus? Rebus sic stantibus, ut cotidie cernimus, numquid presummendum est quod pro restauratione dampni comunitas dictum lucrum impendat? *post* sapientis *del. Vid. Inf.* 2585-87.
2575 procedere posset *post* supposito[1] *del. Vid. Inf.* 2576.
2578 membro *post* principali *expunc. et del.*: dubio *in marg. dex. add.*
2579 sup⟨p⟩licare: F_1 suplicare
2583 sup⟨p⟩licasset: F_1 suplicasset
2602 daretur *post* beniuolentia *del.*

[62] See above, 2338-48.

[63] Gregory of Rimini, *Tractactus*, art. 3 (ed. cit. fols. B7v-B8r).

concluditur quod non propter dictam causam impenditur: ex quo enim non nisi secundum proportionem quantitatum pecuniarum datur mutuantibus, satis probabiliter iudicari potest quod non ex mera liberalitate detur. Ad hoc etiam facit quod illud lucrum non datur quando est soluta sors et comunitas est debito liberata, quo tempore magis posset liberalitas extimari, sed quando adhuc debitum manet, ex quo satis presummi potest quod propter mutuum tribuatur.

Et subdit ad predicta quod si tamen secundum ueritatem propter remunerandam beniuolentiam comunitas illud daret, laudabiliter ageret, nam beneficium laudabilissime fit ad amicos, ut dicit Phylosophus ⟨libro⟩ .viii. *Ethicorum* capitulo .i.,[64] et licite etiam quibus daretur reciperent, sicut licite amicus beneficium recipit ab amico. Ex quo enim licitum fuis-
77r set antequam mutuauerint recipere, / igitur et longe fortius postea, cum propter mutuum et gratiam comunitati factam non debeant fieri peioris conditionis. Tandem concludens et admonens quod non uelint errare et se ipsos decipere qui ultra sortem recipiunt sed intus inspiciant quam habent intentionem, et secundum premissa inditia et alia similia quibus possunt studeant uidere qua intentione huius⟨modi⟩ lucrum comunitas dare decreuerit, scientes quod, ut dicit Apostolus, "non irridetur Deus."[65]

Ex quibus omnibus satis euidenter colligitur iamdictum reuerendum magistrum sentire quod predixi, hoc est quod minus licite dicti primi creditores tale recipiant incrementum et ad restitutionem teneantur. Que conclusio et determinatio egregio canonum doctori domino Lapo de Castiglonchio in repetitione dicti c. *In ciuitate*[66] iusta uidetur et equa et rationibus comprobata. Et hanc plures in sacra pagina professores sequutos audio, quorum dicta nondum uidere potui.

Contrarium tamen, ut nouissime comperii, scripxit alius reuerendus sacre theologie magister prefatus, scilicet frater Francischus de Empoli ordinis minorum, in questione seu tractatu montis, id pro indubitato ponens ea sola ratione quod quis potest licite aliquid recipere ratione interesse ultra sortem, quod in casu nostro contingere asseuerat.[67] Et hanc disputando, inter alios, firmasse audio quendam magistrum Anglicum de

2618 et admonens *in marg. dex. add.*
2621 huius⟨modi⟩: F_1 huius
2623 Conclusio Gregorii *in marg. dex. add.*

[64] Aristotle, *Ethica Nicomachea* 8.1.1155a5-10 (ed. cit. p. 520).

[65] *Gal* 6.7

[66] Lapo da Castiglionchio, *Allegationes*, allegatio 137, n.10 (ed. cit. fol. 163va).

[67] Francesco da Empoli, *Questio de monte* (ed. cit. p. 28); F_1 fol. 87v; *TUI* 7, fol. 43rb.

ordine predicatorum[68] et plurimos iuris professores cum sigillo consuluisse. Horum tamen dicta non uidi, ideo non firmiter assero.

Quid dicendum? Credo, alio non dato, tales mutuantes, nedum si coacte sed etiam si uoluntarie mutuant, dummodo ex caritate non autem spem in lucro seu incremento primario, etsi bene secundario, ponendo mutuent, immunes esse a peccato et usurarum uitio nec ulle fore restitutioni obnoxios. Que quidem conclusio apertissime comprobatur ex supra notatis super rubrica in questione .i.[69] et super nigro in .i. et .viii. oppositionibus[70] et in .iii., .vi., .vii., .viiii. questionibus,[71] ex quibus apparebit contrariorum solutio, sed declarando deducamus illa latius et spetialius.

Tunc quis usuram commictit ultra sortem quicdquam recipiendo quando spe lucri motus principaliter mutuat, non autem quando non spe lucri principaliter, etsi secundario, nisi iam debitor coactus incrementum solueret uel inuitus solutionisque tempore uel prius id in notitiam deuenisset creditoris, ut ex notatis in iamdictis locis et potissimum in .i. oppositione et in .iii. et .ix. questionibus[72] manifestissime comprobatur. Sed in casu nostro, non spe lucri principaliter quis motus comunitati mutuat, immo ut imperanti comunitati pareat penasque inflictas effugiat, uel caritate et amore ut illi in suis necessitatibus subueniat, sciens se illi post Deum, teste Ambrosio,[73] secundo loco magis quam cuilibet alteri obnoxium. Vtroque casu aliter nequaquam mutuaturus et merito, cum in aliis pecuniam illam exponendo, ut sepius supra dictum est, longe plus uerisimiliter lucraretur, et magis liberum plurisque ualoris foret ipsum capitale. Nec coacta quia cogi non potest a suppositis uel inuita

2638 Conclusio auctoris *in marg. dex. add.* Quid uelint ista uerba "alio non dato," uide infra eadem in carta iii.[a] in uersiculo "Ex quibus concluditur" et cetera *in marg. sin. add. al. man.*
2639 in *post* autem *del. et expunc.*
2654 e *post* penasque *canc.*
2657 et *post* obnoxium *canc.*
2659 et tutius *post* plus *del.*
2659-60 et magis ... capitale *in marg. sin. add.*

[68] Nicholas de Anglia, *Questio disputata de imprestitis Venetorum*, ed. Kirshner in "Moral Theology of Public Finance," 66-72.

[69] See above, 54-56, 232-301.

[70] See above, 696-714, 868-1002.

[71] See above, 1021-1142, 1205-1513.

[72] See above, 696-714, 1021-1142, 1514-1600.

[73] Ambrose, *De Tobia* 3.9, ed. Carolus Shenkl in *CSEL* 32 (Leipzig, 1887), 522.

soluit ipsa comunitas sed ex sua spontanea uoluntate, iusta, honesta et rationabili causa regulata, ut in reformatione, de qua in themate supra fit mentio,[74] apertissime demonstratur. Quin etiam etsi inuite solueret, id tamen creditoribus non constat maxime, cum contrarium in iamdicta reformatione ipsa comunitas asseueret, et in incertis, non in certis, locus 77v est coniecturis, ff. *de uer. o.* l. *Continuus* / § *Cum ita*[75] cum concordantiis, per que tollitur quod obici posset per supra notata in questione .x.[76]

Ergo concluditur quod predixi, de quo tamen infra latius disseram spetialiter nos ad factum referendo et iamdictam conclusionem declarando et limitando et ideo dixi in illa "alio non dato."[77] Aduertas tamen, si huiusmodi creditores in oppositum conscientia remorderet illamque deponere ac iuri conformare nequirent, etsi, ut in simili inquiit Ostiensis, et ego post eum supra in iamdicta .ix. questione,[78] scrupulosa sit potius quam theologica, satisfaciant omnitenus conscientie.

Superest modo ut ad rationes dicti reuerendi magistri acutissimas equidem responsum demus. Ad primam igitur dicas destruendo probationem suam quod maior non est indistincte uera secundum canonistas, quia non est uerum quod omne lucrum ex mutuo intentum indistincte sit usura. Tolle instantiam quod sufficit, ut .i. q. .i. *Sicut urgueri.*[79] Lucrum enim ex mutuo secundario intentum non est usura regulariter, ut supra dixi[80] et etiam in .i. oppositione et in .3. questione super textu,[81] et uide etiam omnino in .i. questione super rubrica ad finem in uersiculo "Ex quibus recte"[82] et cetera. "Regulariter" dixi propter supradicta per notata supra in .ix. questione super textu.[83]

Eodem modo potest responderi ad secundam negando antecedens in ponente spem in lucro secundario, nisi iam, ut notatur in dicta .ix. questione et supra dixi, inuite uel coacte solueret debitor idque sciret uel etiam crederet ipse creditor, quod negatur, ut dixi, in nostro contingere casu.[84]

2662 .x. *post* in *del.*

[74] See above, 2205-21.
[75] Dig. 45.1.137.2
[76] See above, 1601-51.
[77] See above, 2638-42.
[78] See above, 1514-1600.
[79] Decretum Grat. C.1 q.1 c.47
[80] See above, 2638-42.
[81] See above, 696-714, 1021-43.
[82] See above, 232-39.
[83] See above, 1514-1600.
[84] See above, 2647-74.

Sed nunc aliquantisper latius, ut spopondi, uideamus in facto, ne nos ipsos decipiamus ex quo quidem facto ius oritur, utrum in nobis mutuantibus talis, qualem predixi, sit intentio. Per que etiam discutiemus an uera sint que in hoc scripxit magister Gregorius.

Et primo uidetur per ea que supra post eum scripxi in uersiculo "Sed si queratur"[85] quod non. Nam si uerum est dicere quod mutuantium intentio deprehendatur ex intentione comunitatis dantis uel dare statuentis et si illa est deprauata, erit et illa mutuantium id scientium uel credentium quandocumque, tamquam que illi concomunicat et commiscetur per mutuum consensum, sequitur quod predixi. Patet istud quia et talis uidetur comunitatis intentio et talis uidetur scientia uel credulitas mutuantibus inesse. Probantur predicta ex his que supra recitaui in uersiculo "Imo plus, quia si nec ante"[86] et cetera, et in uersiculo "Sed quid dicemus? Rebus sic stantibus"[87] et cetera, et sequenti. Nec obstat quod comunitas non potest cogi sed bene cogere et sic non presummitur inuita soluere, quia etsi non possit cogi directe, potest tamen indirecte, quoniam forte dubitans ne tam libenter et pronte sibi mutuent sui ciues, quos etiam nollet habere aspere compellere, ex quo plurima posset incurrere dispendia ut ad subueniendum alliciantur et prontiores efficiantur et quoddamodo uoluntarii dabit lucrum, aliter non datura, his cessantibus. Quod uidemus per experientiam, cum enim indiget comunitas pronta pecunia, lucrum augmentat, et nos insuper, quanto prontiores sumus ad soluendum, cum scimus lucrum augmentatum, ut contingit cum .viii. uel .x. pro centenario dare constituit, ut diebus istis est in prestanzonibus uel accattonibus uidere? Et per conuersum cum nullum uel modicum indicte prestantie fit assignamentum? Nec hec nos ignorare possumus ullatenus affirmare, eo quod nos ipsi horum auctores et promulgatores existimus, argumento decretalis *Ab excommunicato, de re-*
78r *scrip.*[88] et regule *Eum, qui certus* li. .vi.o[89] / cum concordantiis, idque cotidie in nobis et aliis cernimus experientia mediante. Concluditur ergo in facto taliter quod de iure quod ex illo oritur. Concludendum uidetur dictum lucrum usuram fore, cum nec nos ad mutuandum nec comunitas ad dandum iamdicto animo moueatur, vel si nos iamdicto animo moueamur, non sic ipsa comunitas, cuius animus nobis notus est et cui per

2690 uideamus: uideas F_1, -mu- *interlin.*
2713 his *post* ut *del.*

[85] See above, 2494-2510.
[86] See above, 2515-31.
[87] See above, 2585-2610.
[88] X 1.3.41
[89] VI *de reg. iur.* 31, *Eum, qui certus*

consequens noster concomunicat, et de uno transit in alium et incipit esse quod non erat, argumento .l. di. *Ferrum*[90] cum symilibus.

Hic attendendum quod non omnes pariter ac eadem unanimitate mouentur. Sunt namque forsitan qui ex causa lucri, quod intendunt primo loco, ad sic mutuandum mouentur et de his nulla dubitatio. Sunt et qui primo loco mouentur ex caritate qua afficiuntur rei publice uel quia coacti aliud facere nequeunt et de his sermo noster est, et hi non uidentur peccare. Nec obstat quod intentio nostra regulatur ex intentione comunitatis, que nobis non potest non esse nota quia, eo dato, negatur tamen quod intentio comunitatis sit deprauata. Et cum dicitur quod ex quo propter mutuum datur, ergo est usura, dico id non semper sequi. Vnde dico quod propter mutuum aliquando potest dari ut usura et aliquando non ut usura sed ut donum gratuitum causatum non ex ipso mutuo sed ex seruitio sibi impenso et commodo exinde percepto uel lucro consecuto uel ex animi nobilitate quadam, tamquam qui scit se ad antidotum naturaliter obligatum et nisi in beneficiis suis creuerit nil se prestitisse putet, *de dona.* c. primo,[91] *de testa. Cum in officiis*[92] cum symilibus, uel quia scit eum dampnificatum qui mutuauit, ut supra dixi in .i. questione ad finem super rubrica,[93] ubi omnino uide. Et si sic dari sciat uel credat recipiens, non peccat. Et an sic credere teneatur, uide supra parte secunda in decima questione.[94]

Et cum dicitur quod ista non uidetur fuisse intentio comunitatis, quia si hoc esset uerum plus daret illi qui maiorem quam qui minorem beniuolentiam ostentasset erga comunitatem, non habita consideratione ad quantitatem pecunie sed beniuolentie, cuius oppositum seruatur de facto, et similiter plus illi qui ex tali mutuo plus dampnificatus fuisset quam illi qui minus, respondeo quod equum foret sed cum hec non possint de facili in notitiam comunitatis deduci et ne alii scrupuloso corde moueantur et schandala atque liuores inuidie oriantur si ad imparia iudicaremur, ideo sic pariliter et ex memoratis causis mota ⟨comunitas⟩ omnes tractare decreuit et bene, argumento *de consti., Cum omnes* cum

2726 sunt *post* attendendum *del.*
2741 uel quia ... mutuauit *in marg. sin. add.*
2743-44 Et an ... questione *in marg. dex. add.*
2749 plus[2] *interlin.*

[90] Decretum Grat. D.50 c.18
[91] X 3.24.1
[92] X 3.26.7
[93] See above, 240-317.
[94] See above, 1601-51.

ibi notatis,[95] et iustitie ueritati detrahere, .l. di. *Vt constitueretur*[96] et quod notatur *de regulis iuris, Qui schandalizauerit* in glosa,[97] sicut in simili uidemus quod in collegio magistrorum et ordinatorum, qui prior est in tempore, prior est in sede et aliis, non habita distinctione an primus sit secundo doctior. Quotiens etenim uidemus precedere doctorem uel magistrum qui non esset dignus soluere corigiam calciamenti sequentium?[98] Et probantur etiam prelibata per iura, *de maio. et obe.* c. .i.[99] et c. *Statuimus*[1] et utrobique concordantie infinite.

Preterea satis est quod donum est moderatum et non excessiuum et quale quicumque minus merens mereretur, sicut est dare .v. pro centenario et sic tamtum quantum comuniter respondet in terra. Dico "satis est" quantum ad hoc quod excusetur minus merens tantum recipiens quantum plus merens, non enim inficiari possumus, quin saltem ratione lucri cessantis unusquisque ciuis dampnificetur et cum quilibet compellatur ad soluendum (quia experientia media nemo libenter mutuat) et talibus secundum dicta ipsius magistri sit fienda etiam talis dampni restauratio, ergo concluditur quod nemo est qui non debeat tale lucrum ut interesse consequi et licite, si datur, recipere possit. Nec plus merentibus querele locus est contra minus merentes quod ipsi minus merentes eis
78v percipiunt tantum quantum ipsi, ex quo / debitum percipiunt ipsi minus illis merentes. Sed si qua est querelandi causa contra comunitatem est que non restaurat eos in eo pluri quod pre illis merentur.

Nec insuper obstat quod comunitas postquam soluta est uera sors et debito liberata non confert tale lucrum, quia licet ultra non conferat, non sequitur ergo ut usuram tribuebat. Cessat enim tunc dampnum in mutuante, cessat commodum in comunitate et satis ex impenso seruitio remuneratus est mutuans. Aliter diceretur in simili usuram commictere is qui liberaliter mutuauit mille florenos michi mercatori sine ulla, saltem primaria, spe remunerationis, et ego, qui illos tenui per .x. annos, ex quibus lucratus sum .xx. in licitis mercantiis pro quolibet centenario annuatim, ex liberalitate et optima ductus discretione, uidens quod ex illis lucratus fui tantum sibi quolibet anno dictorum .x. annorum donaui octo pro quolibet centenario, quos non donaui in anno .xi.º quia mille, cum quibus lucrari consueui, iamiam restitueram; cuius contrarium est ipsa uer-

2755-56 et iustitie ... in glosa *in marg. dex. add.*

[95] X 1.2.6; gl. ord. ad X 1.2.6, v. *Constitutum* (ed. cit. col. 18).

[96] Decretum Grat. D.50 c.25

[97] Gl. ord. ad X 5.41.3, v. *Veritas* (ed. cit. col. 1963).

[98] Cf. *Io* 1.27; *Mc* 1.7

[99] X 1.33.1

[1] X 1.33.15

itas, ut supra tetigi. Faciat ad predicta quod supra scripxi in .x. questione.[2]

Quot insuper per experientiam uidemus fame quasi mori (ut sic loquar) propter prestantiarum onera, quot mobilia et immobilia sua cuncta distrahere, quot de ditissimis pauperrimos factos, quinimmo quoddamodo ad mendicitatem deductos, quot reputatos habundantes et diuites et propterea ultra debitum oneratos, quot ex inimicitia indicentium grauatos ultra posse, quibus panis ex ore et lac ex infantium labiis tollitur, quot orphanos, uiduas et pupillos in his suam exposuisse substantiam? Mirandumne igitur si ipsa comunitas in genere statuit per respectum ad quantitatem mutuate pecunie certam quotam dari? Cui omnia esse nota nequeunt, cum id solius sit diuinitatis, ut in c. *Vt nostrum, ut ec. bene.*[3] cum concordantiis?

Nec insuper uerum est dicere quod ipsa comunitas non remuneret suos ciues ex aliis collatis beneficiis: sepe, siquidem sine recitatione, id factum uidimus diebus nostris.

Preterea in incertis, non in certis, locus est coniecturis, ut dicta l. *Continuus* § *Cum ita* ff. *de uerbis obli.*[4] cum symilibus. Sed cum ipsa comunitas declarauerit ex qua causa tale tribuat incrementum, ut patet ex tenore reformationis,[5] non opportet ad presumptiones, uerisimilitudines coniecturasque recurri.

Ad ultimum quod supra iungebam in uersiculo "nec obstat quod comunitas non potest cogi"[6] et cetera dico quod hoc est quod plus me semper in dubitationem adduxit una cum eo quod infra tangam. Et si dicatur quod solutio facilis sit, cum non sit uerum quod inuita hoc statuat ipsa comunitas–cum non sit credendum quod, cum aliter facere possit, uelit in tantum suos dampnificare ciues et, ut sic loquar, lac de infantium attrahere labiis, quod aliter sequeretur iuxta proxime dicta nec legem nisi generalem ex suprascripta causa statuere potest et gratis et libere quoad omnes promulgat, sicut qui ad antidotum obligatus est si, ut est de lege liberalitatis, in beneficiis crescit, ut in c. .i. *de donatio.*,[7] non dicitur coactus facere et nichilominus stimulis dicte legis punctus id facit, aliter non facturus–respondeatur michi: quomodo hoc procedere potest cum recta conscientia statuentium quoad commodum et incrementum ipsos

2817 nisi generalem *post* generalem *del.*

[2] See above, 1601-51.
[3] X 3.12.1
[4] Dig. 45.1.137.2
[5] See above, 2205-21.
[6] See above, 2703-25.
[7] X 3.24.1

eosdem statuentes concernens? Nonne effectiue eadem est persona dans seu dare statuens et recipiens? "Effectiue" ideo dixi ut tollam quod obici posset in contrarium: quod dans seu dare statuens dat seu dare statuit 79r ut persona magistralis et publica et recipit ut priuata, / ut in simili legitur *de conces. preben., Postulastis*[8] et *de ap.* c. penultima li. .vi.,[9] et notatur *de elec., Cum inter uniuersas*[10] et c. *Cum inter canonicos* et ibi textus et glosa,[11] et facit *de priuile., Cum cappella*[12] cum symilibus. Licet enim a iure alia persona censeatur in nostro proposito ratione diuersorum respectuum, cum tamen conscientia sit eadem et unica, que illarum iudici non potest non esse nota, ergo quatenus de illa tractamus et illa considerata, erit in effectu eadem reputanda; et uide quod supra scripxi in secunda parte, questione .56.[13]

Secundo respondeatur: etsi quoad .v. pro .c. dari consueta procedere possit responsio tua, quod non presummatur inuita uel compulsa ipsa comunitas, etiam indirecte, quoad statuta uel decreta dari ultra consuetum, prout est, ut dixi, uidere in prestanzonibus uel accattis, quomodo id ullatenus dici potest? Quenam tunc rogo, dicas, uersus comunitatem maior in mutuante munificentia uel beniuolentia in his quam in prestantiis? Quenam maior dampni consecutio, maxime in his in quibus factum est assignamentum pro rehabendo capitale infra annum uel biennium uel circa, ut est de more comuniter in talibus? Quenam in comunitate dante ratio maioris gratitudinis et liberalitatis? Et si dicatur quod ratio sit quia maius fuit seruitium ratione maioris ingruentis necessitatis, respondebo id falsum, quoniam imo fuit, ni falli uolumus, ut tamquam que in maiori erat necessitate constituta, sibi faciliorem et prontiorem constitueret subuentorem et sic uiolentata ex ipsa necessitate quoddamodo, que quidem uiolentia uel coactio non potest non esse nobis nota, ut supra dixi, et quanto in maiori est necessitate et anxietate constituta, tanto magis illi compati et subuenire debemus et ex debito obligamur tantoque minus habet quod nobis tribuat incrementi.

2843 ut ... talibus *in marg. dex. add.*
2850 ut supra dixi *in marg. dex. add.*
2851-52 et ex debito obligamur *in marg. sin. add.*
2852 ut nobis tribuat *post* habet *del.*

[8] X 3.8.15

[9] VI 2.15.11

[10] Gl. ord. ad X 1.6.18, v. *Regia* (ed. Lyons 1496-1509, fol. 23rb).

[11] X 1.6.21; gl. ord. ad X 1.6.21, v. *Confirmauit* (ed. Lyons 1584, cols. 135-36).

[12] X 5.33.16

[13] F_1 fol. 38v; *TUI* 7, fol. 26vb.

Ex quibus concluditur quod etiam quoad lucrum condecens et consuetum dari, scilicet .v. pro .c., si tali statuto annuentes omnes uel aliqui tantum ad suum priuatum commodum respexerunt, usuram in foro conscientie commictunt tales, scilicet annuentes ex tali respectu. Etiam si non ex tali respectu annuentes sed aliter propter bonum publicum, sine illis sufficerent ad sic statuendum. Alii autem non statuentes quoad tale consuetum lucrum et condecens, non; nec etiam ipsi statuentes qui ad publicum commodum dumtaxat respectum habuerunt.

Quo autem ad lucrum inusitatum et inconueniens, quatenus est dare excessum, scilicet .viii. uel .x. pro centenario, in quo non liberalitas uel dampni restauratio sed compulsa et necessitata uoluntas interuenire presummitur, indistincte forte dicendum est quod quilibet peccet et usurarum uitio recipiendo inuoluatur, nisi iam quis tantum et tale dampnum incurrisset quod adscenderet ad illud plus statutum dari ultra consuetum, quod etsi in aliquibus contingere possit, non tamen in omnibus, ut uidemus experientia mediante. In quibus ergo non contingit, stet regula supra posita, cum nec liberalitas nec dampnificatio seu interesse ratione dampni hoc casu concurrant et sic nequeunt iuuari ratione legis, que debet esse comunis et cetera, ut supra dixi in alio casu.[14] In quibus autem tale dampnum contingit, procedat exceptio.

Et si dicatur quod etsi tales dampnificentur, tamen non habent actionem ad repetendum et paria sunt non dare et inuite dare sed coacte quoad peccatum uel uitium usurarum, dic quod immo quoad istos non est presummendum quod in comunitate fuerit coactio uel noluntas et satisfit regule iustitie secundum eius debitam et regulatam uoluntatem. Fallit etiam dicta regula si aliter constare posset quod ipsa comunitas dictum augmentum ultra consuetum statuit, uolens liberaliter donare omnibus illud ultra uel quia uidit ciues suos ex nimia iteratione mutui dampnificari et ultra solitum uoluit eos in compensationem de illo ultra restaurari. Habenti enim in bonis duo milia, si quingentos mutuet comunitati, pro quibus percipit ad rationem quinque, restant mille quingenti, de
79v quorum traffico in suis mercimoniis / habebit forte .x. uel .xii. Si ergo et illa etiam comunitati mutuet, nimis dampnificabitur; nimirum ergo si in

2853 Conclusio limitans suprascriptam *in marg. dex. not.*
2854 scilicet .v. pro .c. *in marg. sin. add.*
2857 annu non ex *post* respectu *del.*
2858 non *interlin.*
2861 Notata de prouisione ultra v. *in marg. dex. al. man. not.*
2863 dampni *interlin.*
2877 regule *in marg. dex. add.*
2877 debitam et regulatam *in marg. sin. add.*

[14] See above, 2384-88.

tali dampno prouidere uoluerit ipsa comunitas. Sed an augmenti causa sit hec uel illa de qua supra sepius dixi, uideant ipsi ciues, qui cordis sui archana nouerunt[15] et sibi caueant ne se ipsos decipiant auaritia blandiente.

Et si queratur circa primum dictum nostre conclusionis, cur si aliorum consensus sufficiunt sine suo id sic supra asseris, respondebo quia satis aperte eius intentio demonstratur cur mutuauit uel saltem quod sit mutata de bona in malam et sic perinde acsi a principio mala fuisset, iuxta supra notata in .i. questione super rubrica.[16] Et hoc uerum puto indistincte quoad maculam peccati, non autem quoad aliam restitutionem, unde dico quod quatenus de ulteriori restitutione talis incrementi tractamus. Aliud est cum aliorum consensus sufficiunt, quo casu si receptum fuit tale incrementum forte non est necessario iterum restituendum, considerato eo quod disponitur in reformatione de qua supra in themate. Pro quo que supra scripxi in .vi. questione secunde partis in fine et in .vii.[a] ⟨questione⟩ eiusdem partis ad finem.[17] Secus uero cum aliorum consensus non sufficiunt et in primo etiam casu, si aliud sibi dictat conscientia, satisfaciat illi, quod etiam tutius est omni casu. Imo, circumscripta dicta reformatione, ubi alias aliter non apparet de uoluntate comunis, nedum tutius sed necessarium foret.

Incidens dubium

Sed incidit circa predicta dubium facti et cotidianum. Pone quod indicitur onus prestantie uel accatti cum incremento siue lucro condecenti et consueto, scilicet .v. pro .c. annuatim, percipiendo dumtaxat per illos qui infra certum tempus soluerint: numquid soluentes infra dictum tempus, qui aliter infra illud non soluissent, peccant in tantum quod ad restitutionem teneantur eius quod perceperint ad rationem memoratam? Et intelligo ut dubium procedat de talibus qui non statuerunt nec statui procurarunt uel saltem non respectu sui priuati commodi et qui aliter licite tale lucrum perciperent.

2895 quoad aliam: -ad *post* quo *del. et expunc.*; -ad aliam *interlin.*
2896 ulteriori *in marg. dex. add.*
2898 non *post* incrementum *del.*
2898 forte non *in marg. dex. add.*
2898 iterum *in marg. sin. add.*
2902 di *post* aliud *del.*
2903-2905 illi, quod etiam ... foret *in marg. dex. add.*: quod *interlin.*
2906 Incidens dubium *in marg. sin.*
2914 respectu sui p *post* non *del.*

[15] Cf. *Ps* 43.22; 1 *Cor* 14.25.

[16] See above, 258-69.

[17] See above, 1236-59, 1390-1473.

Alud incidens dubium

Similiter pone, ut cotidie fieri uidemus, de Nouembre indicitur onus et statuitur quod his qui soluerint infra mensem incipiat dictum lucrum in kalendis Ianuarii; qui uero soluerint post mensem incipiat in kalendis Septembris. Peccantne et cetera soluentes infra mensem qui aliter infra illum non soluissent? Videtur quod sic utroque casu, sicut etenim si ea spe uel intentione ducti primario mutuassent, aliter non mutuaturi, ut tale lucrum perciperent ex pecunia mutuata usuram commicterent et ad restitutionem tenerentur, sic si ea intentione primario ducti ad soluendum infra mensem ut citius dictum lucrum percipiant uel aliter non percepturi si infra mensem non soluerint, ad hoc, ut percipiant soluerint infra mensem, aliter infra illum non soluturi, argumento sumpto a simili quod ualidissimum est in iure, *de consti., Translato*[18] cum concordantiis. Et patet ipsa similitudo, quia sicut primaria intentio in primo casu reprobatur, sic et in secundo per consequens reprobetur, cum utrobique eadem uidetur ratio subesse.

In contrarium facit quia alia ratio uidetur uno casu quam altero pactum reformare, ergo alia debet esse iuris dispositio. Deducitur antecedens quia quotiescumque fundamentum malum est, omne corruit hedificium, .i. q. .i. *Cum Paulus.*[19] Et si non tenet principale nec accessorium, quod illius sequitur naturam, ut in c. *Si super gratia, de offi. dele.*[20] et in regula *Accessorium, de regulis iuris* li. .vi.[21] cum concordantiis; sed non sic e conuerso. Item sepe quid permictitur accessorie quod principaliter reprobatur, *Ne sede ua.* c. .i. cum materia sua,[22] *de elec., Dudum* .ii. cum ibi notatis,[23] *de preben., Super eo*[24] et c. *Quia sepe* li. .vi.[25] et eodem titulo in clementina *Per literas* coniuncta glosa sua.[26] Ad idem ff. *de serui. ru. predio.* l. *Vna est uia*[27] et l. *Si comunem.* ff. *quemadmo. serui. admic.*[28] cum symilibus. Preterea etsi qualitas conrumpatur, non tamen subiectum;
80r qualitas enim potest adesse / et abesse preter subiecti corruptionem.

2916 Aliud incidens dubium *in marg. sin.*

[18] X 1.2.3; cf. glo. ord. ad X 1.2.3, v. *Quod de uno* (ed. cit. col. 16).

[19] Decretum Grat. C.1 q.1 c.26 (1 *Cor* 3.11)

[20] VI 1.14.9

[21] VI de reg. iur. 42, *Accessorium*

[22] X 3.9.1; gl. ord. ad X 3.9.1, v. *Sede vacante* (ed. cit. col. 1089).

[23] X 1.6.54; gl. ord. ad X 1.6.54, v. *Intitulatum* (ed. cit. cols. 201-202).

[24] VI 3.4.6

[25] VI 3.4.15

[26] Clem. 3.2.2; gl. ord. ad Clem. 3.2.2, v. *Ecclesias* (ed. cit. cols. 150-51).

[27] Dig. 8.3.18

[28] Dig. 8.6.10

Nunc ad propositum: ex quo mutuum, quod est fundamentum, quod est principale, quod est subiectum, non est corruptum, quia ad mutuandum non sunt tales inducti sub spe uel intentione primaria dicti lucri uel incrementi sed ex caritate qua rei publice afficiuntur uel quia coacti, quod patet quia etiam sine illo lucro mutuarent, absit ut corrumpatur (ex eo quod corruptum asseratur hedificium) accessorium uel qualitas, sicut est illud prius, scilicet infra mensem ad mutuandum siue ad mutuum prestandum induci ut percipiat uel citius percipiat lucrum memoratum.

Preterea absit ut corruptum sit hedificium siue accessorium uel qualitas antedicta, nedum fundamentum principale uel subiectum. Istud patet ad sensum, nam ex quo intentio comunitatis lucrum dantis et dare statuentis non est corrupta nec etiam in ipsa mutuatione intentio mutuantis, ex quo non spe lucri primario ad mutuandum inducitur, ut supra clare ostendidi, et sic superest quod non est usura tale lucrum, ergo, licet ad citius prestandum quis inducatur ut illud percipiat uel citius percipiat, non est usura. Probatur consequentia quia ex quo tale lucrum licitum est, ergo non est malum illud appetere. Patet istud per simile, verbi gratia, donat michi comunitas mille si infra mensem ad exercitum migrauero, aliter nichil, uel donat michi mille infra semestre percipienda si infra mensem ad exercitum migrauero; si autem post mensem quingenta tantum uel mille sed infra annum percipienda tantum. Vtique si, ut illa citius consequar uel ut illa, aliter non consecuturus, consequar, infra mensem migrauero, nulla est usura uel peccatum. Nec obstat si dicatur: hic non est mutuum sicut in casu nostro, quia ex quo, ut predixi, lucrum est licitum illo casu, quia non tamquam usura et incrementum ultra sortem soluitur uel recipitur sed ut uerum et liberale donum uel ut interesse, ergo non est ulla diuersitatis ratio inter hunc et illum et sic ergo nulla in iuris dispositione alteratio.

Et si dicatur: immo quia sepe quod in se bonum est alteratur ex qualitatum adiectione (exemplum: elemosinam facere in se bonum et meritorium est, etsi ad superbiam, ostentationem uel ad pompam fiat, alteratur et melius esset abstinere, quia nulla caritas ubi superbia uel inanis gloria dominatur, ergo nullum meritum, teste Apostolo .i. ad Corinthios .xiii. capitulo ibi "Si habuero"[29] et cetera, et *de pe.* di. .iii. *Si quis*[30] et *De conse.* di. .4. *Solet*,[31] et concordat deuotus meus Ieronymus super epistola

2968 ut *post* quia *del.*
2970-71 uel ut interesse *in marg. sin. add.*

[29] 1 *Cor* 13.2-3
[30] Decretum Grat. D.3 de poen. c.49
[31] Decretum Grat. D.4 de cons. c.31

ad Galathas.[32] Similiter episcopatum desiderare bonum est[33] sed ex ambitione pessimum, ut in c. *Qui episcopatum* .viii. q. .i.[34] et *de preben., Quamuis* .i. li. .vi.[35] cum concordantiis. Similiter mutuare et cum mutuo proximo subuenire meritorium est sed si auaritie causa id fiat malum est et sic de similibus discurrendo. Ita siquidem infirmitas per peccatum conscientiam maculat et alterat, sicut infirmitas per febrim corpus), respondeatur quod etsi predicta uerissima sint ratione finis ad quem tenditur et quem considerare debemus, quia, attestante Philosopho, cuius finis bonus est ipsum quoque bonum est,[36] et poeta "exitus acta probat" et cetera,[37] nostrum tamen casum non contingunt, cuius finis in bonum dirigitur uel saltem non in malum, quia, ut dixi, nullum peccatum est desiderare et pro posse consequi quod gratis et liberaliter confertur et similiter recipitur. Et sic nulla infirmitas per peccatum occurrit que habeat maculare ex caritate uel aliter sine peccati macula factum. Accedant que supra post Fredericum scripxi in .vii. questione secunde partis.[38] Et hoc credo de iure uerius, nisi iam lucis angelus in tenebrarum angelum se transformet. Facit tamen in contrarium quod notatum in c. uno infra *de cleri. non resi.* li. .vi. in glosa penultima[39] et quod scripxit Archydiaconus .i. q. .ii. *Sacerdos.*[40]

80v **/ .iii.^{m} principale dubium ⟨Posito quod non, utrum uigore donationis, remissionis et liberationis supradicte excusentur a restitutione et liberentur a peccato.⟩**

Nunc de tertio principali dubio uideamus utrum scilicet uigore donationis, remissionis et liberationis excusentur inlicite recipientes a restitutione et liberentur a peccato.

Hic passus uidetur satis expeditus per supra notata super textu in

2982 li. .v. *post* Quamuis *del.*
2991 seu ratione dampni *in marg. sin. add. al. man. post* liberaliter
2999 .iii. ^{m} principale dubium *in marg. sin.*

[32] Jerome, *Commentarius in epistolam ad Galatas* 3, in *Gal* 5.26 (*PL* 26.452); cf. ibid., in *Gal* 5.14 (*PL* 26.438) (=Decretum Grat. C.1 q.1 c.65).

[33] Cf. 1 *Tim* 3.1

[34] Decretum Grat. C.8 q.1 c.11

[35] VI 3.4.4

[36] Cf. Aristotle, *Ethica Nicomachea* 1.7.1097a18-23 (ed. cit. p. 382).

[37] Ovid, *Heroides* 2.85, ed. Henricus Dörrie (Berlin, 1971), p. 59.

[38] See above, 1260-1473

[39] Gl. ord. ad VI 3.3.1, v. *Receperit* (ed. cit. col. 385).

[40] Guido de Baysio, *Rosarium*, ad Decretum Grat. C.1 q.2 c.9, n.5 (ed. cit. fol. 106rb).

questione .vii.[41] per que respondendum uidetur quod per illam liberentur a restitutione sed non a peccato. Ad hoc enim, ut illud tollatur, contritione opus est cum penitentia salutari, que quidem penitentia fieri poterit absque alia restitutione, quia restitutum censetur ablatum uirtute remissionis antedicte. Et sic non obstat dictum Augustini quod ponitur in decretali *Cum tu*[42] et in regula iuris *Peccatum*[43] cum concordantiis; quod dic ut plene supra scripxi in dicta .vii. questione in fine. Et hanc conclusionem amplectitur etiam dominus Lapus prelibatus in repetitione dicte decretalis *In civitate.* [44]

Sed ego dubito an sibi locum uendicet iamdicta conclusio in eo qui statuit uel decreuit una cum aliis de populo talem remissionem uel liberationem fieri et illam fecit. Et credo quod non in foro conscientie si habuit respectum ad commodum uel interesse suum et hoc si aliorum consensus sine suo non sufficiebant; alioquin secus quoad restitutionem. Sed aget penitentiam eo casu, contritione precedente, non solum de peccato quod commisit ad usuram mutuando, quod non tollitur per solam remissionem, quinimo nec per restitutionem actualem sed etiam de eo quod non erat paratus restituere, si remissio facta non foret sed in peccato perseuerare, ex quo peccatum augetur, *de consue.* c. finali [45] cum concordantiis, quod presummitur ex predictis, cum per exteriora de interioribus presummatur, *de presump., Ex studiis* [46] cum symilibus. Re autem aliter se habente, penitentiam agat de primo tantum et in hoc sue conscientie relinquatur: res enim sua agitur. Et accedat ad predicta quod supra scripxi post Fredericum in .vii. questione secunde partis. [47]

.iiii.[m] principale dubium ⟨An dicti soluentes licite uendant ius quod habent in dicto monte uigore talis crediti.⟩

Ad quartum igitur principale dubium transeamus: an uidelicet dicti soluentes licite uendant ius quod habent in dicto monte uigore talis crediti.

3019 quoad restitutionem *in marg. sin. add.*
3030 .iiii.[m] principale dubium *in marg. sin.*

[41] See above, 1260-1473.
[42] X 5.19.5
[43] VI *de reg. iur.* 4, *Peccatum*
[44] Lapo da Castiglionchio, *Allegationes*, allegatio 137, n.14 (ed. cit. fols. 163vb-164rb).
[45] X 1.4.11
[46] X 2.23.3
[47] See above, 1260-1473.

Ad quod respondendum est secundum dictum magistrum Gregorium in dicto suo tractatu in secunda questione principali[48] quod si tantum quantum mutuauerunt perceperunt, in eo etiam lucro quod a comunitate inlicite perceperunt computato non possunt, quoniam iam exinanita est uera sors, ad quod allegat c. .i. supra eodem titulo.[49] Sed si non tantum sed minus, tunc uendere possunt quantum superest, et sic si totum superest, quia nichil perceperunt uel si aliquid non propter mutuum sed aliter licite, iuxta supradicta post eum, totum uendere possunt. Et idem in dicto c. *In civitate* in secundo quesito prime principalis questionis firmat dominus Lapus de Castiglonchio predictus.[50]

Et ego idem dico in genere; fateor siquidem quod quicquid iuris habent in dicto mutuo uel ad dictum mutuum super dicto monte licite uendere possunt. Ad spetiem autem descendendo, dico quod plus iuris habent super dicto monte ex dicto mutuo quam predicti senserint, quia quod inlicitum reputant in quibusdam licitum affirmaui, ut clare patet ex his que supra diffuse scripxi in secundo dubio principali,[51] et sic plus uendere possunt quam ipsi senserint. Et procedit dubium prelibatum, circumscripta remissione, de qua in dubio proxime precedenti, illa siquidem operatur quod in nullo sors extenuatur ex lucro.

.v.^{m} dubium principale ⟨Vtrum alii illud ab eis licite emant.⟩

Ad quintum quo queritur utrum alii ab eis licite emant tale ius sciendum quod magister Gregorius ubi supra in secunda questione principali[52]
81r sic / dixit uidelicet quod inquirendum est de intentione eorum, quoniam aut emunt intentione percipiendi lucrum a comunitate aut non. Primo casu sic emendo peccant et usuram commictunt, quoniam ex tunc ipsi mutuum dant siue dant dilationem solutionis intentione lucri. Pro hoc casus in hac nostra decretali *Consuluit* in secunda consultatione;[53] est etenim ibi secunda consultatio utrum reatu criminis usurarii inuoluatur qui, ut uulgo dicitur, non aliter parabolam iuramenti concedit, id est, dilationem solutionis admictit, donec, quamuis sine exactione, emolumentum aliquod inde percipiat: cui ibidem respondetur quod sic. In

3038 inlicite *interlin.*
3054 .v.^{m} dubium principale *in marg. sin.*

[48] Gregory of Rimini, *Tractatus*, art. 3 (ed. cit. fol. B8r-v).
[49] X 5.19.1
[50] Lapo da Castiglionchio, *Allegationes*, allegatio 137, n.11 (ed. cit. fol. 163va).
[51] See above, 2459-2905.
[52] Gregory of Rimini, *Tractatus*, art. 3 (ed. cit. fols. B8r-C1r).
[53] X 5.19.10

secundo uero casu secus, nisi alia praua intentio uel mala circumstantia reddat eorum intentionem inordinatam, secundum eum.

Dictam conclusionem dampnat dominus Lapus[54] quia cum querat idem magister an licite ematur a primis creditoribus, opportet intelligi questionem eo casu quo ipsi uenditores licite uendunt, qui quando non licite uendunt nec alii ab eis licite emunt. Sed quando dicti mutuantes licite uendunt, ut quia nil ultra sortem receperunt, uel receperunt sed in casu licito iuxta premissa certe emere poterunt alii ab eisdem nec in hoc aliquam inordinatam intentionem habere uidentur, secundum eum. Nec, secundum eum respondendo ad rationes magistri, uerum est dicere quod ex tunc mutuent, non enim mutui sed emptionis contractum ineunt. Nec etiam est uerum quod dent dilationem solutionis sed expectant dilationem datam a comuni auctori suo. Nec insuper uerum uidetur quod si dicto casu emunt intentione lucri, quod sic emendo peccent, quia in contractu emptionis non est reprobata spes lucri, *de emp. et ven., Cum dilecti*[55] et c. *Cum causam* cum ibi notatis.[56] Lapus de Castiglonchio.

Iuri consona uidetur conclusio domini Lapi. Illa tamen magistri pro tanto fomentum habere uidetur quia cum secundum eius opinionem supra notatam[57] inlicite tale lucrum percipiant comuniter ipsi mutuantes et qui tale ius mutui siue crediti propter mutuum factum emunt se in locum mutuantium subrogant, superest ut sicut illi peccarunt si spem percipiendi mutuando habuerunt tunc uel postea, sic et isti, quoniam licet in sui figura sit contractus emptionis inter creditores comunitatis uendentes et hos ementes, tamen inter ipsos ementes et ipsam comunitatem est effectiue contractus mutui, sicut prius erat inter ipsam et illos primo mutuantes. Quem quidem effectum et non uerborum corticem uel contractus formulam considerat teologus et considerare debet etiam canonista, argumento decretalis *Dilecti* supra *de iudi.*[58] cum concordantiis, in his potissimum quibus anima regulatur naturaliter, siquidem subrogati eodem iure iudicantur quo et hi quibus subrogantur, .xviii. q. .ii. *Eleutherius,*[59] *de iudi., Quia V.,*[60] *de fo. compe., Dilecti,*[61] *de resti. spo.,*

[54] Lapo da Castiglionchio, *Allegationes*, allegatio 137, n.12 (ed. cit. fol. 163va-b).

[55] X 3.17.3; gl. ord. ad X 3.17.3, v. *Deceptione* (ed. cit. col. 1124).

[56] X 3.17.6; gl. ord. ad X 3.17.6, v. *Dimidiam* (ed. cit. col. 1126).

[57] See above, 2467-2531.

[58] X 2.1.6

[59] Decretum Grat. C.18 q.2 c.30

[60] X 2.1.11

[61] X 2.2.17

Sepe;[62] sufficiat regula *Is, qui in ius* cum concordantiis ibi positis in glosa *de regulis iuris* li. .vi.[63]

Et ex predictis inferri uidetur quod nedum secundum opinionem magistri circa perceptionem talis lucri sed etiam secundum opinionem aliorum et meam, de qua supra, maxime in secundo principali dubio[64] latissime scripxi, emptio huiusmodi reprobetur. Quod patet quia dicti primo loco mutuantes mouentur uel ex caritate qua rei publice afficiuntur uel ex coactione que eis ab illa infertur et sic nulla intentio lucri primarie. Sed isti ementes quoad formam contractus et quoad uendentes, sed mutuantes quoad ueritatem et quoad comunitatem, primarie moueri ui-
81v dentur ex intentione lucri, ergo / usurarii.

Preterea ubicumque fit fraus de contractu ad contractum iudicamus talem contractum non ut sonat eius forma sed ut iacet rei ueritas. Sed sic contingit in proposito, ergo et cetera. Maior probatur per c. *Ad nostram* supra *de emp. et uendi.*,[65] *de pigno.*, *Illo uos*[66] et c. *Cum contra*,[67] *de iureiuran.*, *Ad nostram*[68] cum ibi notatis. Ad idem supra c. *In ciuitate* cum ibi notatis in glosa .iii.[69] Ad idem C. *Plus ualere quod agitur quam quod simulate concipitur* in rubro et nigro per totum[70] et quod supra scripxi in .iiii.ª principali oppositione ad textum.[71] Ad idem ff. *de dona. inter ui. et uxo.*, *Si sponsus* § *Circa*[72] *et ff. ad Velle.* l. *Quamuis*.[73] Faciant notata .xiiii. q. .iii. *Plerique*[74] et l. *Qui contra* ff. *de legi.*[75] Minor probari uidetur ex notatis supra in questione .18.[76] post dominum meum.

Sed huic uidetur de facili responderi quia hic nulla fit fraus de contractu ad contractum, celebrat enim contractum emptionis et uenditionis

[62] X 2.13.18

[63] VI *de reg. iur.* 46, *Is, qui in ius*; gl. ord. ad VI *de reg. iur.* 46, *Is, qui in ius,* casus (ed. cit. col. 756).

[64] See above, 2459-2905.

[65] X 3.17.5; gl. ord. ad X 3.17.5, v. *Emptionis* (ed. cit. col. 1126).

[66] X 3.21.4; gl. ord. ad X 3.21.4, v. *Obligatis* (ed. cit. col. 1143).

[67] X 3.21.6; gl. ord. ad X 3.21.6, v. *Extenuassent* (ed. cit. cols. 1145-46).

[68] X 2.24.7; gl. ord. ad X 2.24.7, v. *Ad restituendum* (ed. cit. col. 801).

[69] X 5.19.6; gl. ord. ad X 5.19.6, v. *Ex tali forma* (ed. cit. cols. 1736-37).

[70] C. 4.22

[71] See above, 759-822.

[72] Dig. 24.1.5.5

[73] Dig. 16.1.8.8

[74] Gl. ord. ad Decretum Grat. C.14 q.3 c.3, v. *Praecepta* (ed. cit. col. 1096).

[75] Gl. ord. ad Dig. 1.3.29(28) (*recte* Contra), v. *Prohibet* (ed. cit. I p. 22).

[76] See above, 2081-2182.

hic emens, qui non celebraret contractum mutui. Ex quo enim nouit quod tu primo mutuans licite percipis illud lucrum, scit per consequens quod licite et illud ipse percipiet emendo a te ius uel actionem ad illud. Nullam ergo adhibet fraudem nec contractum simulat, imo palam contrahit et ita contrahit in medulla sicut in cortice, quia uere facit quod uerborum cortex intonat et sic est sua intentio, ut etiam statim declarabitur. Si enim secus esset, secus dicerem; et hec faciunt etiam ad statim dicenda in sequenti questione.[77]

Credo dictum domini Lapi uerum quoad emptionem iuris quod habet uendens pro uera sorte, de quo intelligitur dubium propositum. Hec enim mercimonii species est, hic etenim interuenit pecunia et res que uenditur et que uendibilis est; ius enim et iura uenduntur, ff. *de here. uel ac. uen.* per totum[78] et notaui tibi supra in .xii. questione secunde partis.[79] Emunt enim comuniter centum pro .50. uel .40. uel .30. secundum temporum diuersitatem et sic lucrantur, ut uides, et tale lucrum sperare in emptione, aliis circumstantiis non interuenientibus talem contractum habentibus deprauare, non est improbatum. Nec obstat quod improbatur contractus ex quo minus iusto pretio, saltem infra dimidiam, emitur, quia negatur quod minus iusto pretio sit emptum; quia immo tantum uenditur quantum ualet.[80] Si ergo in hoc tantum spes et intentio uersata est ementis, nulla est usura.

Sed si ultra progressa est, scilicet ad lucrum ex sorte proueniens, quod est quod queritur in dubio sequenti, tunc michi dubium est et eo casu procedere uidentur rationes et intentio magistri, pro cuius conclusione multum faciunt que supra declarando deduxi.[81] Sed in contrarium facit quia cum in casu quo lucrum a comunitate statutum et preordinatum licite et ordinate statuatur et preordinetur, illud primo loco mutuans licite recipiat certis casibus, secundum eum (immo secundum alios et me omni casu, paucis exceptis iuxta superius adnotata,[82] et de hoc de-

3121 hic pri *post* nouit *del.*
3130 de quo ... propositum *in marg. sin. add.*
3143 quod est ... sequenti *in marg. sin. add.*

[77] See below, 3319-3408.
[78] Dig. 18.4
[79] See above, 1786-1839.
[80] Gl. ord. ad X 5.19.6, v. *Non valent* (ed. cit. col. 1736). See above, 862-67.
[81] See above, 3055-67.
[82] See above, 2861-2905.

beat formatum dubium intelligi, ut etiam dixit ipse dominus Lapus),[83] concluditur quod illud tale lucrum a comunitate preordinatum non est inlicitum uel usura, et per consequens quod sicut illud, de quo dixi in membro precedenti,[84] sperare uel appetere ordinate non est usura uel peccatum eo quod licitum et non improbatum lucrum est, sic et istud, ex quo licitum similiter est et minime reprobatum, sperare uel appetere non est usura uel peccatum.

Tolle exemplum: utique predium in pignus recipere pro centum et fructus uelle lucrari usura est et a iure regulariter improbatum, *de emp. et uen.*, *Ad nostram*,[85] *de pigno.*, *Illo uos*,[86] supra hoc eodem titulo *de usuris* c. .i.[87] cum symilibus, et similiter si ego in locum tui me subrogo, usurarius ero. Sed pone quod tu fructus illos ordinate appetas liciteque percipias ut quia de pignoratitio in emptitium contractum transeas, equidem si et ego a te illud emens in tui locum me subrogo sub spe non tam lucrum percipiendi ex uero capitali, de quo sine fraude et dolo tamen minus do quam sit ipsum capitale sed insuper lucrum percipiendi et ex
82r fructibus, iam non / commicto usuram.

Vel pone quod magis nostro congruit proposito in genero qui predium recepit a socero in pignus pro dotibus, qui licite fructus percipit nec in sortem computat,[88] equidem si uendat omne ius alteri quod habet in dicto predio, licite percipiet, ut credo, hic alter fructus ex tali predio, sicut et ipse percipiebat. Et tamen si hic alter in pignus recepisset ab illius socero dictum predium, computaret fructus in sortem. Nec obstat quod scripxit Baldus C. *de usuris* super rubrica[89] et notaui supra questione .54. parte secunda,[90] quia loquitur non cum uendidit sed cum pignorauit. Quo casu etiam non sic simpliciter scripxit Collectarius ut scripxi in iamdicta questione post dominum meum.[91]

3165 iam non *post* capitale *del. Vid. inf.* 3166.

[83] Lapo da Castiglionchio, *Allegationes*, allegatio 137, n.12 (ed. cit. fol. 163va-b).

[84] See above, 3119-25.

[85] X 3.17.5

[86] X 3.21.4

[87] X 5.19.1

[88] Cf. X 5.19.16

[89] Baldus de Ubaldis, *Commentaria*, in C. 4.32.rubr., n.13 (ed. cit. VII fol. 88ra).

[90] F_1 fol. 37r-v; *TUI* 7, fol. 26rb-va.

[91] Ibid.

Et per predicta tollitur ratio quam supra iungebam illationi facte ex rationibus magistri in uersiculo "Et ex predictis inferri"[92] et cetera, quoniam etsi isti ementes moueantur sub spe lucri percipiendi, non tamen usuram conmictunt, quia mouentur sub spe lucri, scilicet liciti, quale est hoc, ut predixi. Illa autem ratio procederet quando sub spe lucri inliciti mouerentur, sicut facerent mutuantes qui primo loco ad mutuandum mouerentur sub spe lucri et per consequens sub spe lucri inliciti. Et est diuersitatis ratio clara ex supradictis, spes enim talis primaria, etsi in mutuo reprobetur, que non potest non esse mala, secus in contractu emptionis et uenditionis in quo talis spes, dummodo ordinata, nullatenus reprobatur, quia tendit in licitum, non autem in inlicitum.

Nec obstat quod supra dicebam,[93] quod iste contractus, etsi in sui figura sit emptionis et uenditionis, tamen uirtualiter est contractus mutui inter comunitatem et ipsum ementem, quia istud ego nego quod ullus sit contractus mutui inter ementem et comunitatem. Nec ualet consequentia–idem commodum consequitur emens quod fuisset consecutus mutuans si non uendidisset seu ipse emens si a principio comunitati mutuasset, ergo effectiue mutuum contrahit–quoniam sepe contingit quod ex diuersis contractibus, quorum unus est licitus, alter inlicitus, quis eundem effectum consequitur et tamen falsum est quod unus sit alius effectiue, nisi per respectum ad factum, quod quidem factum non est simpliciter attendendum, sed una cum eius qualitate, que habet eius naturam alterare.[94] Quod patet per exemplum supra positum, nam ita effectiue consequitur quis fructus ex contractu emptitio et uendititio sicut ex pignoratitio et tamen unus approbatur et alter reprobatur. Considerat enim Deus aduerbia et non uerba, hoc est, non quid fiat sed an bene uel male fiat. Ad hoc que supra in simili scripxi super primo et secundo dubio principali.[95]

Que ad propositum reducendo, dico quod etsi effectiue idem commodum consequatur hic emens quod consequeretur si a principio mutuasset comunitati, tamen non sequitur quod cum illa mutuum contrahat, quia non per uiam mutui sed per uiam emptionis uere et sine fraude uel dolo consequitur tale commodum. Et non surrogatur mutuanti ut mutuans sed ut emens ius illud a mutuo uendentis causatum; ut enim surrogatum sapiat naturam eius cui surrogatur quoad omnia, opportet quod quoad omnia et uniformiter surrogetur, quod non contingit in proposito nostro. Et si dicatur sicut facit hunc contractum cum isto per uiam istam emptionis, ita credendum est quod faceret per uiam mutui cum comu-

[92] See above, 3099-3107.

[93] See above, 3082-98.

[94] Cf. Francesco da Empoli, *Questio de monte* (ed. cit. pp. 37-39); F_1 fols. 89v-90r; *TUI* 7, fol. 44rb.

[95] See above, 2416-33, 2450-58, 2973-98.

nitate, negatur, quia de nemine presummendum est malum ⟨et inmemor⟩ sue salutis, .i. q. .vii. *Sancimus*.[96]

Tolle in simili, ut aliquando contingere uidi: emerem libenter a te predium mille ualens pro mille et tamen si michi uelles pignori obligare, non facerem; et tamen utroque casu idem consequerer. Scis quare: quia unum licet, alterum non. Quia ergo scit hic emens in casu nostro quod licite emit, ideo emit. Si pur tamen talis haberet talem intentionem de-
82v prauatam / et ideo facit cum isto quod similiter faceret cum comunitate ad finem ne possit usurarius conuinci (quod tamen, alio non dato, non presummam), tunc secus. Et sic intelligo limitari sequentia; et uide infra in .vii.° membro principali.[97]

Sed inquies: nonne in contrarium est casus in decretali nostra *Consuluit*[98] in ultimo responso et supra eodem *In ciuitate*[99] et infra eodem *Nauiganti*[1] in ultimo responso? Pro quo etiam optime facit quod scripxit Iohannes Andree post Gofredum in dicta decretali *In ciuitate* super glosa antepenultima[2] et ego supra scripxi in .v. principali oppositione ad textum nostre decretalis.[3]

Respondeo non, dico enim quod hic alia ratio reformat pactum. Ibi namque ideo uitiosus est contractus emptionis et uenditionis et equipollet contractui mutui, quia is qui aliter erat rem uenditurus pro .x., si tunc data fuisset pecunia uoluit .xii. propter dilationem solutionis et sic est perinde acsi illa .x. sibi mutuasset pro duobus pro illo tempore; et sic tempus uendidit. Sed in casu nostro non sic, quoniam uendens tale ius quod habet pro pecunia mutuata uendit illud quantum tunc comuniter ualet et ius ipsum tribuit emptori in continenti, et etiam in continenti pretium recipit ipsius rei uendite. Nec hic ulla interuenit ex parte contrahentium dilatio seu propter dilationem uel anticipationem maior uel minor quantitas et sic non uenditur tempus.

3216 i. q. .vii. Sancimus *in marg. dex. add.*: (.v)-ii. *interlin.*
3217 ut aliquando contingere uidi *in marg. sin. add.*
3218 pro totidem *post* si *del.*; michi *interlin.*
3219 et tamen eodem casu, idem consequerer *post* consequerer *del.*
3240 ipsius *interlin.*

[96] Decretum Grat. C.1 q.7 c.26
[97] See below, 3649-67.
[98] X 5.19.10
[99] X 5.19.6
[1] X 5.19.19
[2] Johannes Andreae, *Novella*, ad X 5.19.6, n.6 (ed. cit. V fol. 74rb); Gottofredo da Trani, *Apparatus*, ad X 5.19.6, v. *Alias merces* (MS cit. fol. 163ra).
[3] See above, 823-34.

Quod auctoritate probo et declaro quia, ut dixit Innocentius supra eodem *In ciuitate*,[4] contractus de quo ibi et in c. isto *Consuluit*[5] et in c. *Nauiganti*[6] tunc reprobatur quando carius uenditur merces propter terminum quem dat prolixum emptori ad soluendam pecuniam uel pro minori emit mercem, quia statim dat pecuniam et per prolixius tempus expectat mercem, que penitus sunt inlicita, quia eo casu solummodo uenditur tempus pro illa pecunia que iustum pretium excedit, quod patet ex eo quia si utraque parata essent, et pretium et merces, pro minori fieret. Sed in casu quo omnia sunt presentia, scilicet merces et pretium, tunc secus, quia tempus tunc non uenditur, quia res ipse de quibus supra dictum est, scilicet redditus, actio uel ius tantum ualebunt uel ad minus ualere creduntur subsequentibus temporibus quantum modo ualent, uel saltem est dubium. Et hoc sufficit ad hoc ut contractus sit licitus, ut in c. *In ciuitate*, secundum Innocentium.

Hoc ultimo dictum de dubio non procederet in aliter uenditura, si essemus in casu ipsius decretalis *In ciuitate*,[7] ut in c. *Nauiganti*[8] eodem titulo in fine. Operatur bene tamen, fateor, tale dubium quod ipsum ius minus ualet et minus uenditur. Est enim dubium an et quando rehabiturus sis et propter hoc non est liberum sed tali circumstantia aggrauatum ipsum ius quod uenditur et ideo minus uenditur quam si esset clarum et liberum. Minus enim uenditur res onerata quam libera, ut de se patet: si enim domus uel terra debet alicui seruitutem aliquam, certe minus uenditur quam libera. Item minus uenditur res pro qua non datur bona satisdatio quam illa pro qua datur bona et de qua per consequens in tuto uiuis.[9]

Sed inquiet quis forte: ex codicibus tuis te ipsum dampnas. Tu allegas uerba Innocentii in decretali *In ciuitate*,[10] ubi dicit in illo casu ideo contractum ipsum prohiberi quia uenditur tempus pro illa pecunia que excedit iustum pretium, quod dicit ex eo patere quia si utraque parata essent, scilicet merces et pretium, pro minori fieret. Sed tunc sic, nulli dubium quod si merces, hoc est pecunia comunitati mutuata, foret presens sicut est presens pecunia que datur per emptorem uenditori pro

3243 auctoritate *in marg. sin. add.*
3267 uiu *post* tuto *del.*

[4] Innocent IV, *Commentaria*, ad X 5.19.6, n.2 (ed. cit. fol. 517va).
[5] X 5.19.10
[6] X 5.19.19
[7] X 5.19.6
[8] X 5.19.19
[9] Cf. Francesco da Empoli, *Questio de monte* (ed. cit. p. 36); F_1 fol. 89v; *TUI* 7, fol. 44ra.
[10] Innocent IV, *Commentaria*, ad X 5.19.6, n.1 (ed. cit. fol. 517ra-b).

pretio iuris ad dictam pecuniam mutuatam uenditi, multo plus uenderetur quam uendatur. Ergo si minus uenditur, procedit ex tempore, quo differt emptor habere ipsam pecuniam, cuius ius uenditur et quod succedit loco mercis. / 83r Antecedens patet ex se. Consequentia probatur ex dictis Innocentii, ex qua per consequens infertur quod usura commictitur.

Sed tu solue et dicas ut superius dixi[11] quod et merces et pretium presentia sunt. Et ad formam argumenti responde primo quod si pecunia, que est penes comunitatem, esset presens, non plus uenderetur quia inuendibilis est, sed actio, ius uel nomen ad recuperandam pecuniam bene est uendibile.[12] Et fateor quod si de presenti uel de proximo quis certus foret se posse recuperare a comunitate pecuniam creditam ad quam ius competit, quod longe plus tale ius uenderet sed non ex eo quod magis eo casu quam in casu nostro sit presens res que uenditur, cum utroque casu sit dare rei presentiam, scilicet ipsum ius, sed plus ualentis uno casu quam alio propter onus annexum uel non a⟨n⟩nexum et ideo plus uel minus uenditur. Venditur enim plus in dicto casu et merito predicta ratione, quia tunc cessat circumstantia aggrauans ipsum ius, qua cessante, efficitur liberum, sicut in simili uendens domum que per annum debet alicui aliquam seruitutem plus uendetur quam illa que perpetuo debet uel ad beneplacitum illius cui illam debet et multo plus illa que olim talem seruitutem debebat et hodie libera est et nullam debet. Similiter plus uenditur domus uel predium cuius tam proprietas quam ususfructus tempore contractus spectant ad uendentem quam illa uel illud cuius spectant post uitam alterius. Nec tamen minus uno casu quam reliquo dicitur presens merces. Sed in casu decretalis illius et similium, de quarum dispositione fatur Innocentius, non sic, quia ibi non est merces et pretium presens, imo uno casu deficit merces et adest pretium et ideo minus datur seu soluitur, altero deficit pretium sed adest merces et ideo pretium augmentatur. Nimirum ergo si tempus uendi

3290 a⟨n⟩nexum: F_1 anexum
3297 Ad consequentiam igitur responde illam negando. Et cum ad eius probationem adducebantur uerba Innocentii *post* debet *del. Vid. inf.* 3312-13
3297-3300 Similiter plus ... presens merces *in marg. dex. add.*
3301 de quarum ... Innocentius *in marg. sin. add.*
3303 et ideo ... soluitur *in marg. dex. add.*
3304 et ideo pretium augmentatur *in marg. sin. add.*

[11] See above, 3243-56.

[12] Cf. Francesco da Empoli, *Questio de monte* (ed. cit. p. 32); F_1 fol. 88v; *TUI* 7, fol. 43vb.

dicitur, quia perinde est acsi emens primo casu mutuaret uenditori illam pecuniam cum illo incremento et in secundo uendens emptori et hoc totum propter dilationem dationis mercis uel solutionis pecunie seu pretii, ut dixit Gofredus in dicto c. *In ciuitate* et post eum Iohannes Andree super glosa antepenultima.[13] Quod non contingit in casu nostro, cum tunc non ualeat minus uel plus quod uenditur et cuncta sint presentia, ut predixi.

Ad consequentiam igitur responde illam negando. Et cum ad eius probationem adducebantur uerba Innocentii, responde per predicta quod longa est diuersitas inter casum hunc et illos. Et per predicta, si hanc conclusionem sequimur, expeditum uidetur sextum principale dubium quod statim sequitur. Ipsum tamen, ut que alii scripxerunt in illo tradam distinctim, reassummendo prosequar quanta cum pluri potero breuitate et ibi clarius quid sentiam aperiam.

.vi.^{m} principale dubium ⟨Posito quod sic, utrum licite percipiant incrementum quod prius percipiebant ipsi uenditores.⟩

Rursus igitur quero pro clariori expeditione sexti dubii principalis, posito quod licite dictum ius quod habent in dicto monte soluentes uendant et ementes emant, utrum licite percipiant ipsi ementes incrementum illud quod prius ipsi uenditores percipiebant.

In quo sciendum quod iamdictus magister, qui, ut uidistis,[14] tenebat quod ementes inlicite emebant ius soluentium si lucri intentione ducebantur a comunitate percipiendi, se per infrascripta uerba formaliter expediebat, dicens sic, uidelicet ad secundam uero partem questionis,[15] utrum scilicet licite emptores lucrum recipiant a comunitate, illud per omnia dicendum est quod dictum est de primis mutuantibus, nisi quod in eo casu in quo tam isti quam illi peccarent, isti magis peccarent quia ultro se ingerunt ad huius exercitium usurarum, illi uero requisiti et aliquo modo forte coacti. Item in eodem casu quo isti dampnum incurrerent ex emptione talium prestitorum, non sic possent consulere sibi de lucro a comunitate recepto ut primi, quia suo dampno non apparet causam dedisse ex se, eo quod non ad illius instantiam sed propria cupidi-
83v tate se ingesserunt ad tale / tormentum. Gregorius.

3305 quoniam si utroque tali casu, tam pretium quam merces ad ipsemet in cer *post* dicitur *del.*
3309 antepenultima *in marg. sin. add.*
3319 .vi.^{m} principale dubium *in marg. sin.*
3326-27 si lucri ... percipiendi *in marg. dex. add.*

[13] Gottofredo da Trani, *Apparatus*, ad X 5.19.6, v. *Alias merces* (MS cit. fol. 163ra); Johannes Andreae, *Novella*, ad X 5.19.6, n.6 (ed. cit. V fol. 74rb).
[14] See above, 3055-67.
[15] Gregory of Rimini, *Tractatus*, art. 3 (ed. cit. fol. C1r).

His addit dominus Lapus[16] sepedictus, sic dicens: hec uerba magistri sunt michi dubia, nec bene concipio quid sibi uelit dum dicit "illud per omnia dicendum" esse quod dictum est de primis mutuantibus. Nam si intelligit in eis examinandum de ipsorum intentione ea que supra examinanda sunt de intentione mutuantium, istud non congruit, ut de se patet, tum quia quoad istos non cadit examinatio intentionis comunitatis nec examinatio intentionis uendentis, ut de se patet. Item in casu quo ipsi uendentes minus licite uendunt, ut supra expeditum est, quia ipsi emptores emere non possunt. Si autem intelligit dum dicit "illud per omnia dicendum" esse quod dictum est de primis mutuantibus, id est quia eo casu dicti etiam emptores dictum lucrum licite recipiant, tunc esset sopita antiqua questio eorum qui dicebant quod licet primi mutuantes licite reciperent, non tamen ementes ab eis, quod dictum non uidetur ratione fulciri. Nam cum tunc demum secundum premissa primi mutuantes licite recipiant quando sine pactione, sine spe uel intentione lucri, tam a parte comunitatis quam a parte mutuantium, dono puro, beniuolentia, restitutione dampni, aliquid recipiunt, quare tam iustum debitum uendere non possunt et alius ab eis licite emere non apparet. An tamen dictus magister sic intellexerit per alia sua dicta satis dubito.

Ego autem non dubito quod non sic intellexit, ut satis euidenter colligitur ex hic et in questione proxime precedente per eum notatis.[17] Est ergo eius intentio, ut ex precedentibus colligitur, quod omni casu quo isti intelligunt recipere lucrum proueniens ex pecunia mutuata comunitati per primos creditores propter pecuniam per eos solutam primis creditoribus usuram commictunt sicut et ipsam commicterent ipsi primi creditores, in quorum loco se uoluntarie ponunt, si ea intentione comunitati soluissent.

Sed aduertendum quod alius sacre theologie magister, cuius dicta, ut predixi, nouiter comperii, uidelicet frater Francischus de Empuli,[18] simul in effectu hanc cum duabus proxime precedentibus questionibus tractans et pro indubitato ponens primo quod supra in secundo prin-

3349 si *post* esset *del.*
3360 propter pecuniam per eos solutam primis creditoribus *post* lucrum *del. Vid. inf.* 3361-62.
3362 credito *post* ipsi *del.*
3366 de *post* Empuli *del.*
3367 duabus *scripsi*: F_1 duobus
3368 in pr *post* supra *canc.*

[16] Lapo da Castiglionchio, *Allegationes*, allegatio 137, n.13 (ed. cit. fol. 163vb).

[17] See above, 3055-3107.

[18] Francesco da Empoli, *Questio de monte* (ed. cit. pp. 28-44); F_1 fols. 87v-91r; *TUI* 7, fols. 43rb-44vb.

cipali dubio[19] trutinaui oppositum concludebat eius quod primus. Et cum eo multi sunt. Sed alii plures, quorum dicta nouissime comperii, tenuerunt contrarium, quorum rationes et motiua inferius secundo loco latius explicabo. Sed quod uerum credo primo ponere est animus, ut nolentes laborare in uidendo per alios diffuse scripta infra posita sciant quid sentio.

Conclusio

Dico igitur quod omni casu quo primo loco mutuans aliquid licite a comunitate percipit, illud idem licite uendit illudque licite emitur et percipitur, siue sit sors siue accessio siue lucrum uel quouis nomine uelis nuncupare. Et hoc sane intelligo, scilicet circumscripta fraude et intentione deprauata, ut infra dicam in decisione sequentis membri in fine, ubi omnino uide.[20] (Vt michi fertur per fidedignum, qui de proprio auditu loquitur, egregius utriusque iuris doctor dominus Petrus de Ancharano[21] disputauit hanc questionem in imprestitis Venetiarum et tenuit ciues soluentes coacte licite recipere illa .v. pro centenario et similiter emptores talis crediti. Eius dicta tamen nondum habere potui).

Et istud dicere credo etiam magis faciat pro salute animarum nostrarum. Non equidem tutum arbitror uel utile tam strictis passibus incedere tamque seuere scribere in hac materia, ut quidam fecerunt, hoc enim nil aliud est quam inducere plurimos in uiam perditionis, iuxta illud dictum quo utuntur, licet non laudabiliter, multi sic dicentes: "ex quo non possum sine anime periculo meam trafficare pecuniam, uolo ire ad inferos eques et non pedes." "Medium tenuere beati,"[22] *de offi. custo.* c. .i.,[23] qui enim "nimis emungit, sanguinem elicit," *de renump.*, *Nisi cum pridem*.[24] Sepe enim, scriptum est, multa pereunt et in pernitiem reuer-
84r tuntur quando in eis nimia subtilitate / utimur, C. *de uer. si.*, *Cum quidam* circa finem[25] et C. *ad Trebelli.* l. penultima,[26] et notatis .x. q. .ii. *Hoc*

3373 infra *post* uidendo *del.*
3375 Conclusio *in marg. sin.*
3381-85 Vt michi ... potui *in marg. sin. add.*

[19] See above, 2630-2905.

[20] See below, 3649-67.

[21] Peter of Ancharano, *Quaestio disputata de imprestitis Venetiarum* (BNF, Magliabechiano xxix, 179, fols. 278v-288r).

[22] Hans Walter, ed., *Proverbia sententiaeque latinitatis medii aevi* (Göttingen, 1964), 2.2, no. 14571, p. 849.

[23] X 1.27.1; gl. ord. ad X 1.27.1, v. *Modum* (ed. Lyons 1496-1509, fol. 56ra).

[24] X 1.9.10

[25] C. 6.38.4.1

[26] C. 6.49(48).7

ius[27] et in c. *Nichil est, de elec.* in glosa.[28] Ad idem *de iudi., Dilecti* cum ibi notatis in glosa[29] et super ea. Et facit quod scripxit in simili Archydiaconus et Iohannes Andree *de usuris, Quamquam* li. .vi. super uersiculo "de usuris."[30]

Non dico tamen quod sinistra fiat iurium interpretatio et tam dulcis quod fetorem pariat animabus sed quinimo dextera uera et qualis est fienda, sed non ultra debitum amara, ut quidam faciunt, uolentes plus sapere quam oporteat, *de re. iudi., Abbate* li. .vi. ad finem,[31] et credentes ex asperando proficere animabus, cuius contrarium, sicut in puledris, sepe contingit, argumento *de iudi., Dilecti.*[32] Quia tamen in dubio uia tutior est eligenda, consulo quod abstineant qui aliud facere possunt, argumento supra eodem *In ciuitate*, ut et ego hucusque feci.

.vii.^{m} principale dubium ⟨Quid de his qui pro aliis, a quibus quandoque certam quotam pro quolibet floreno, quandoque nichil percipiunt, soluunt prestantias et in illorum loco quoad tale creditum describuntur?⟩

Querebam .vii.°: quid de his qui pro aliis, a quibus quandoque certam quotam pro quolibet floreno, quandoque nichil percipiunt, soluunt prestantias et in illorum loco quoad tale creditum describuntur?

Reperio quod hanc questionem quidam tractantes[33] non querebant utrum isti tales pro aliis soluentes licite faciant sed utrum teneantur ad restituendum dictam quotam illis a quibus recipiunt et pro quibus prestantias soluunt. Et ad negatiuam assignant talem rationem: quia dantes illam quotam soluentibus prestantias pro eis redimunt dampnum et incommodum quod incurrissent prestando comuni cum illa certa quota quam tribuunt soluentibus pro eis. Puta tenebantur comuni ad .x.: quota est .v. quam soluentibus tribuunt et sic dampnum et incommodum .x. redimunt cum .v.

Contrarium determinant quod dicunt patere tali ratione: quia ponamus quod comprestans sit Martinus et is pro quo prestatur sit Petrus; certe sicut ipse Martinus teneretur Petro in .v. si prestitisset sibi .x. et

3401 interpretatio *scripsi*: F_1 interpetratio
3409 .vii.^{m} principale dubium *in marg. sin.*

[27] Gl. ord. ad Decretum Grat. C.10 q.2 c.2, v. *Probat* (ed. cit. col. 929).
[28] Gl. ord. ad X 1.6.44, v. *Administrent* (ed. Lyons 1584, col. 185).
[29] X 2.1.6; gl. ord. ad X 2.1.6, v. *Subtiliter* (ed. cit. col. 527).
[30] Guido de Baysio, *Commentaria*, ad VI 5.5.2, n.1 (ed. cit. fol. 118va); Johannes Andreae, *Novella*, ad VI 5.5.2, n.2 (ed. cit. fol. 145rb).
[31] VI 2.14.3
[32] X 2.1.6
[33] Cf. Guido de Belloregardo, *Consilium de monte* (F_1 fol. 99v; *TUI* 7, fol. 49ra-va).

dedisset uel prouidisset de .v., sic in casu isto. Ad argumentum factum in oppositum dicendum quod Petrus redemit dampnum suum, quia potius uult pati dampnum suum .v. florenorum quam .x. Sed licet hoc sit possibile, tamen non potest licite petere .v. de illis uel pro illis .x. quos prestat, sicut usurarius non licite recipit .x. pro .c. quos prestitit, secundum eos.

Examinemus hunc articulum primo. Secundo uidebimus id quod principaliter querebamus. Pro quorum duorum expeditione, uidetur michi examinari debere utrum talis contractus sit contractus emptionis et uenditionis uel mutui uel qualis.

Et uidetur primo quod emptionis et uenditionis ⟨est⟩, quoniam uendit ius sibi competiturum, facta solutione, cum omni suo onere et emolumento. Patet istud nam si cum teneretur Petrus pro suis prestantiis soluere .x. comunitati, tu Martinus soluis pro eo dictas prestantias comunitati et soluis de tuo proprio quinque et alia quinque recipis ab ipso Petro, perinde est acsi Petrus soluisset illa .x. et deinde ius sibi competens ad illa .x. tibi Martino uendidisset pro .v. Sic enim faciendo iam liberatur ipse Petrus ab onere memorato sibi indicto et perinde habebitur acsi soluisset et sicut si Petrus omnia illa .x. realiter et uere soluisset, licite tibi uendere posset et tu emere. Et non mutui sed emptionis et uenditionis contractus censeretur, ut supra uidistis in examinatione dubii precedentis.[34] Sic dicamus ante factum, frustra enim fit per plura quod potest fieri per pauciora, *de rescrip.*, *Auditor* in clementinis[35] cum concordantiis.

Preterea dato etiam quod ab ipso principio diceretur quoad illa .v.
84v que Martinus soluit / pro Petro mutuum, nonne ex quo conuenerunt simul quod commodum et incommodum, utile et onus foret totius quantitatis, scilicet decem, ipsius Martini est perinde acsi Petrus restituisset illa .v. sibi mutuata ipsi Martino et deinde pro pretio iuris sibi Petro pro illis .x. competentis contra comunitatem ipsi Martino uenditi illa .v. recepisset a Martino? Videtur profecto quod sic, cum par hinc inde sequatur effectus nec refert quid ex equipollentibus fiat, *de testi.*, *Licet ex quadam*,[36] ff. *Si cer. pe.* l. *Certum* et notatis,[37] *de rescrip.*, *Cum in multis* li. .vi.[38] Nec si ipsa .x. soluisset a principio ipse Petrus et deinde ius sibi ad illa competens uendere uellet plus quam .v. dumtaxat reperiret, ut

3461 In contrarium, quod immo sit contractus mutui *post* .vi. *del. Vid. inf.* 3465.

[34] See above, 3119-76.

[35] Clem. 1.2.3; gl. ord. ad Clem. 1.2.3, casus (ed. cit. col. 24).

[36] X 2.20.47

[37] Dig. 12.1.6; gl. ord. ad Dig. 12.1.6, v. *An uocabulis* (ed. cit. I p. 648b).

[38] VI 1.3.2

per experientiam cotidie cernimus, nulla ergo in ipso contractu interuenit deceptio in casu nostro.

In contrarium, quod immo sit contractus mutui, uidetur tali ratione: quia non describitur ut mutuans ipse Petrus in libro montium sed immo ipse Martinus et non ut emens sed ut mutuans ab ipso principio.

Item ante factam solutionem prestantie sibi Petro indicte, nullum competit ius et nulla actio ipsi Petro aduersus comunitatem, ergo illam non potest uendere uel cedere Martino. Conuentio igitur inter eos celebrata non potest sapere contractum emptionis et uenditionis quoad illa .v. que pro eo soluit ipse Martinus nec quoad alia .v. que eidem Martino dedit ipse Petrus nec quoad omnia .x. simul comunitati soluta, sed quinimo omni casu contractum mutui; soluendo etenim .x. comunitati ipse Martinus pro Petro et se ponendo in eius locum uoluntarie, hoc facit pro illis .v. que percipit a Petro et pro lucro quod consequetur a comunitate de totis .x., soluendo solum .v. de suis propriis. Et sic perinde est acsi mutuaret ipsi Petro illa .v. pro quinque et ipsi comunitati illa .x. ad rationem .v. pro centenario.

Soluendo dico quod nec est contractus emptionis et uenditionis nec contractus mutui sed, relatione facta pacti ad contractum, pro quo, ut pactum seruetur, nascitur actio prescriptis uerbis, resultat unus contractus qui appellatur contractus innominatus "do ut facias": do tibi .v. ut pro me soluas alia .v. et sic in totum .x. ad que sum comunitati obnoxius et a tali obligatione me liberes, ut l. *Petens* C. *de pac.*[39] Qui quidem contractus in presenti accedere uidetur ad naturam emptionis et uenditionis, ex eo quod dat Petrus .v. Martino ut soluat comunitati pro eo illa .x., pro quibus et omni lucro exinde uenturo, et quod, facta solutione, sperari potest, ius sit et esse intelligatur ipsius Martini et ad ipsum pertineat. Et sic est perinde acsi pro .v. uenderet ius illud speratum ipse Petrus ipsi Martino, non solum de tota sorte, scilicet .x., sed etiam omnis lucri futuri, si quod erit dare. Patet etiam quia secundum huiusmodi contractus naturam et usum ipse Martinus nec illa .v. nec etiam lucrum illud quod a comunitate est percepturus tenetur Petro restituere, nec Petrus ipsi Martino illa .v. que soluit pro eius liberatione ipsi comunitati. Consequitur ergo Petrus liberationem ab obligatione qua tenebatur pro prestantia sibi indicta ipsi comunitati ex ipsa solutione Martini et ipse Martinus consequitur ius crediti ad omnia .x. soluta comunitati et ad lucrum exinde speratum et constitutum, prout est de natura contractus
85r emptionis et uenditionis / et non sic de natura contractus mutui, in quo debitor obligatur ad restituendum tantundem in numero, pondere uel

3473 Martinus *post* ipse *del.*
3475 ipse Martinus *scripsi*: F_1 ipsum Martinum

[39] C. 2.3.27

mensura suo creditori. Et si recte consideras nec Petrus minus consequitur nec Martinus plus hoc casu quam si primo loco soluens totius quantitatis fuisset ipse Petrus et post ipsam factam solutionem ius talis crediti uendidisset ipsi Martino; ut recte calculanti clare patet.

Preterea arguendo ab allusione uocabuli, argumento *de preben.*, *Cum secundum*[40] cum concordantiis, hoc idem probatur, nam uulgo tales dicuntur "emptores" et illi "uenditores." Vel retento, ut est ueritas, quod sit contractus innominatus "do ut facias," dici potest quod erit sensus talis contractus: talis scilicet ut tu soluas pro me .x. comuni pro prestantia michi indicta et me liberes, dono tibi .v. et omne ius quod spero a comunitate pro dono uel interesse ipsorum .x. et etiam ad ipsa .x. tibi cedo.

Nec obstat quod supra dicebam[41] quod ante solutionem nullum ius competit Petro, ergo non potest cedi uel uendi, quia immo tale ius competit quod uendi potest, scilicet ius quod sperat habere facta solutione, ad quam ex indictione prestantie iam facta obligatur. Et sic est ius speratum ex causa subsistente de presenti, maxime ex quo decretum est interesse per legem comunitatis et talis spes potest cedi et uendi, ut l. *Spem C. de dona.*[42] Vnde aduertendum quod aliquando est dare ius quod quis habere sperat ex aliqua causa subsistente de presenti, ad hoc ff. *de condi. ob. causam* l. *Quod Seruius*,[43] et tale ius seu talis spes potest cedi uel uendi, ut dicta l. *Spem*. Aliquando est dare ius quod quis sperat sed non ex aliqua causa subsistente de presenti et tunc secus. Hinc est quod etsi dicatur statuliber qui habet spem libertatis, ut ff. *de sta. li.* l. .i..[44] nichilominus non omnis libertatem sperans dicitur statuliber ut sic ueniat sub uerbo statuliberi. Nam etsi sperare libertatem omnis seruus possit, etiam si nulla subsistat causa huius spei de presenti et hoc respectu possit quilibet dici statuliber largo modo, tamen quoad propositum non sic, sed qui potest libertatem sperare ex aliqua causa subsistente de presenti, talis enim proprie dicitur statuliber, ut ff. *de statulibe.* l. .ii.[45]

Similiter si est dare quod frater fratri succedat et diuidantur, certe per talem diuisionem non uidetur transactum de tali iure nec a tali iure recessum. Ratio: quia tempore transactionis non erat debita fratri transigenti illa hereditas re nec spe ex aliqua causa de presenti subsistente.

3514 Notantur de spe *in marg. dex. not.*

[40] X 3.5.16
[41] See above, 3468-79.
[42] C. 8.53(54).3
[43] Dig. 12.4.8
[44] Dig. 40.7.1
[45] Dig. 40.7.2

Casus est, si recte inspiciatur, ff. *de liber. le.*, *Post emancipationem* coniuncta glosa sua.;[46] Sed si est dare quod frater fratri succedat iure fideicommissi, tunc uidetur transactum de tali iure et a tali iure recessum per diuisionem, quia est fratri transigenti tunc debita spe et tali spe que habet causam subsistentem de presenti, scilicet ius fideicommissi. Et idem si sibi sit debita ex ui substitutionis pupillaris, ut l. .ii. ff. *de statuli.*[47] et notatis Bartolo in l. *Qui Rome* § *Duo fratres* ff. *de uer. obli.* ubi uide in .i. oppositione et in .vi.[a] questione.[48]

Potest dari et tale simile canonicum, nam quilibet clericus potest dici expectans in ecclesia florentina. Nam quilibet sperare et expectare potest in illa prebendam, et nichilominus sub expectantis nomine non ueniet nisi qui habet spem ex causa de presenti subsistentem, ut quia literas optinuit expectatiuas, *de preben.*, *Dilectus*[49] *de offi. dele.*, *Ex parte* .i.,[50] *de*
85v *rescrip.*, *Eam te*,[51] *Constitutus*,[52] *Capitulum*,[53] / *Mandatum*,[54] *Literis*,[55] *Abbatem*,[56] eodem titulo *Tibi qui* cum duobus sequentibus li. .vi.[57] et eodem libro *de preben.*, *Si postquam* et per totum[58] et eodem libro *de conces. preben.* c. .i. et per totum.[59]

Potest insuper et dari secundum. Nam si quis spem habeat ad aliquod beneficium, curatum uel dignitatem uirtute alicuius cause de presenti subsistentis, ut puta quia gratiam habet expectatiuam ad illa, certe si aliud simile deinde consequatur illi quod prius in spe habebat uirtute talis gratie renumptiare intelligitur, et tamen si nullam habet gratiam sed solam spem in genere, non intelligitur renumptiare, ut in clementina *Gratie, de rescrip.*[60]

Preterea tolle aliud. Nouitius ante professionem non dicitur perfecte religiosus et tamen ratione spei habentis causam subsistentem de pre-

[46] Dig. 34.3.6(7); gl. ord. ad Dig. 34.3.6(7), v. *Ius eius* (ed. cit. III p. 693b).

[47] Dig. 40.7.2

[48] Bartolus of Sassoferrato, *Commentaria*, in Dig. 45.1.122.6, nn.4, 19 (ed. cit. VI fols. 44vb-45ra, 46rb-va).

[49] X 3.5.19

[50] X 1.29.12

[51] X 1.3.7

[52] X 1.3.19

[53] X 1.3.30

[54] X 1.3.38

[55] X 1.3.39

[56] X 1.3.40

[57] VI 1.3.12-14

[58] VI 3.4.13; 1-41

[59] VI 3.7.1-8

[60] Clem. 1.2.4

senti gaudet priuilegio immunitatis, *de sen. ex.*, *Religioso* li. .vi.[61] Item efficitur de foro ecclesiastico, ut scripxit Iohannes Andree de regula *Beneficium* eodem libro super glosa magna,[62] ubi uide, et in dicto c. *Religioso* post Archydiaconum.[63] Et tamen non sic de habente spem profitendi sine dicta causa de presenti subsistente, ut patet in eo qui appetit uel sperat profiteri et nondum est religionem ingressus. Ad predicta insuper bene facit dicta decretalis *Beneficium* in uersiculo "Aut constet quod uitam"[64] et cetera. Item facit quod legitur in clementina finali *de rescrip.* in glosa magna in principio.[65]

Ad aliud quod primo dicebatur, quod non describitur "ut emens sed ut mutuans"[66] et cetera, respondeo quod ut proprie emens non potest describi nec ut mutuans sed ut inhiens contractum innominatum sic tamquam qui pro tali obligato comunitati ad soluendum soluit. Ex qua solutione illius obligati liberatio sequitur et sic effectiue describitur creditor ratione iamdicti celebrati innominati contractus qui, ut dixi, accedit ad naturam contractus emptionis et uenditionis. Et istud credo de iure uerissimum.

Ex quo satis clare apparet quid in utroque sit articulo concludendum, uidelicet quod in primo dictus Martinus non teneatur ad restituendum Petro illa .v. In secundo uero, quod fuit principale dubium, licet comuniter contrarium per uulgares affirmetur, quod ipse Martinus licite talem contractum celebret et sic eque percipiat sortem et lucrum hoc casu, sicut in casu proxime precedentis dubii principalis.[67] Patet istud quia si effectiue talis contractus sapit naturam contractus emptionis et uenditionis, ergo secundum illum iudicandus est et sic per consequens quecumque in illo dicta in hoc repetita intelligantur. Ex quibus satis patet contrariorum solutio.

Sed quoad primum articulum, specifice soluendo contrarium supra factum per aliter concludentes, dico etiam plus, scilicet quod si ratio per eos facta concluderet, sequeretur quod etiam in contractu quorumlibet iurium uenditorum, quinimmo et etiam corporalium, idem foret per omnia concludendum. Probo: nam cum hic contractus accedat ad naturam contractus emptionis et uenditionis, ut dictum est, ergo qua ratione tu dicis in proposito quod perinde censeri debet, acsi Petrus mutuasset Martino .x. et rehabuisset sola .v. et per consequens teneatur ipsi Petro ad alia .v.? Eadem ratione opportebit te dicere quod si heri emisses

[61] VI 5.11.21

[62] Johannes Andreae, *Novella*, ad VI 3.14.4 (ed. cit. fol. 122vb).

[63] Ibid., ad VI 5.11.21, n.2 (ed. cit. fol. 169vb); Guido de Baysio, *Commentaria*, ad VI 5.11.21, n.1 (ed. cit. fol. 131a).

[64] VI 3.14.4

[65] Gl. ord. ad Clem. 1.2.5, casus et v. *Post datam* (ed. cit. cols. 26-27).

[66] See above, 3465-67.

[67] See above, 3375-3400.

86r aliquod ius incorporale uel etiam corporale, pone predium ualens / tunc centum et hodie quinquaginta tantum, et hodie uendas Martino pro illis quinquaginta quos ualet et non ultra, quod perinde erit acsi Martino mutuasses centum et rehabuisses sola quinquaginta et sic tibi ad alia quinquaginta teneatur; quod quidem prorsus est absonum. Nec ualet si dicas quod in casu nostro nulla occurrit temporum diuersitas ex qua ius ipsum sic debeat alterari et in pretio minorari, quia in nullo tibi dico quod alteratur ualor ipsius iuris. Licet enim opporteat te .x. soluere comunitati, tamen ius ipsum quod tibi partum est prius spe et postmodum tibi uel habenti causam a te re non ualuit nec ualet nisi illa .v. tantum, quod quidem operatur dubium restitutionis fiende per comunitatem, ut supra dictum est in alio dubio principali.[68] Item dico quod ex tali alteratione uel non alteratione nulla tamen sequitur iuris diuersitas.

Sed ut omnis tollatur dubietas, ponamus aliud simile. Opportuit ex aliqua causa me emere predium uel aliquod ius uel nomen pro centum, uel forte michi pro centum computare ab aliquo meo malo debitore. In continenti idem predium, ius uel nomen tibi uendo pro .50., quia nec plus ualuit uel ualet. Equidem secundum illorum rationem teneberis michi in aliis .l. Sed absit. Stet ergo conclusio supra posita.

Sed contra conclusionem principalis dubii iterum sic opponitur: si hic uenditur spes seu ius speratum ex causa subsistente de presenti, ut supra dictum est, ergo concluditur quid inlicitum et usurarium in ipso uendente quoad id quod comunitati mutuatur. Patet consequentia quia sperare lucrum ex mutuo est usura, ut in isto c. *Consuluit*.[69] Sed tunc ultra, si inlicitum fuit in uendente, ergo et in emente. Patet consequentia ex his que supra conclusa sunt in determinatione proxime precedentis dubii principalis.[70]

Solue quod aliud est sperare ex aliquo actu uel ministerio precedente aliquid, ut in proposito, aliud est mutuare ex illa spe tantum. Quid uolo dicere? Ista stant simul quod quis non mutuet ex spe lucri preordinati et tamen spem habeat in lucro seu habere possit ratione ⟨lucri⟩ preordinati, quod est de facili uidere per ea que in precedentibus fuerunt sepius repetita. Qui enim inuitus uel coactus, ut in casu nostro, mutuat, iam non mutuat principaliter ob spem lucri: imo quia aliud facere nequit, quod patet quia dampnum est sibi, non lucrum, et ad id compellitur. Si ergo lucrum sperat, hoc est illa .v. pro centenario, hoc non est prima causa sui mutui sed secunda. Immo uerius dici posset quod nec etiam est secunda, quia lucrum tale non est causa mutui huius etsi postquam malegratibus suis opportuit mutuare, immo uerius soluere, spem possit habere, quod est sibi aliquale refrigerium coactionis in lucro preordinato.

[68] See above, 3257-3318.
[69] X 5.19.10
[70] See above, 3357-64.

Et predicta spes, etiam si esset secunda causa mutui memorati non uitiat contractum, ut supra sepius dictum est. Nec obstat quod prius spem habuit quam soluerit, quia ex quo indictio facta est, coactio et solutio est certa, maxime ex preteritis, ex quibus certi reddimur de presentibus et futuris, *de presump.*, *Mandata celestia*[71] et c. *Scribam*[72] cum concordantiis ibi positis in glosa. Vnde quoad hoc est acsi soluerit, experientia media omnium magistra, *de elec.*, *Quam sit* li. .vi.,[73] est enim dare causam subsistentem de presenti, sicut dicitur statuliber qui libertatem sperat ex causa subsistente de presenti, ut supra dixi.[74] In intentione namque spes sequitur, non precedit, solutionem.

Sit igitur inlibata conclusio prelibata, saluo nisi iam fieret fraus in intentione de contractu ad contractum argumento eorum que scribuntur in glosa et super ea .14. q. .3. *Plerique*[75] et supra in questione ubbie, que
86v est questio .xviii.[a][76] / Puta si Martinus emens dictum ius speratum aliter foret libenter mutuaturus ipsi comunitati uel ipsi Petro illa .v. pro aliis .v. cum dicto lucro, et uolens effugere ne posset de prauitate usuraria conuinci ficte transiuit ad contractum memoratum cum Petro, ex intentione namque iudicamur, *de rescrip.*, *Mandatum*,[77] *de elec.*, *Dudum* .ii. in fine,[78] *de procura.*, *Petitio*,[79] *de iureiuran.*, *Veniens*[80] et c. *Quanto*[81] et c. *Quemadmodum*,[82] *de preben.*, *Cum causam*[83] et c. finali[84] cum symilibus. Et specialius ad propositum c. *Ad nostram*[85] et c. *Illo uos*[86] sepius allegata, et c. *In ciuitate*,[87] *Consuluit*[88] et *Nauiganti*.[89]

Hoc autem qualiter perpendatur: quoad triumphantem eius conscientie relinquo; quoad militantem uero, dico quod ex adiacentiis iuxta

[71] X 2.23.6
[72] X 2.23.9
[73] VI 1.6.6
[74] See above, 3520-32.
[75] Gl. ord. ad Decretum Grat. C.14 q.3 c.3, v. *Praecepta* (ed. cit. col. 1096).
[76] See above, 2001-2182.
[77] X 1.3.38
[78] X 1.6.54
[79] X 1.38.9
[80] X 2.24.16
[81] X 2.24.18
[82] X 2.24.25
[83] X 3.5.36
[84] X 3.5.38
[85] X 3.17.5
[86] X 3.21.4
[87] X 5.19.6
[88] X 5.19.10
[89] X 5.19.19

ea que supra scripxi in simili in .x. questione secunde partis.[90] Et hec limitatio repetita intelligatur etiam in decisione duorum proxime precedentium principalium dubiorum, scilicet quinti et sexti,[91] fraus enim nemini patrocinari debet, maxime in his que animam concernunt. Vbi fraudans fraudatur, iura sunt uulgaria.

.viii.^{m} dubium principale ⟨Quid si comunitas sic sibi nouos constituat creditores, puta quia uendit annuum redditum ad rationem qua respondet creditoribus montis sui ad uitam ementis et alterius ab eo nominandi?⟩

Transeamus nunc ad .viii.^{m} et ultimum dubium principale quo querebam: quid si comunitas sic sibi nouos constituat creditores, puta quia uendit annuum redditum ad rationem qua respondet creditoribus montis sui ad uitam ementis et alterius ab eo nominandi cum pactis de quibus supra dixi in themate?[92]

Et in hoc sciendum quod dominus Lapus de Castiglonchio, doctor eximius, in dicta decretali *In ciuitate*[93] hunc passum examinans et recitans circa eum notata per Innocentium, Ostiensem et alios[94] in dicta decretali *In ciuitate* finaliter concludit per ibi notata quod dicta comunitas potest nouos creare creditores et uendere annuum redditum et quod ab utraque parte potest super hoc talis contractus licite inhiri cum pactis et modis memoratis. Quod intelligo, ut etiam ipse sentire uidetur, dummodo in fraudem usurarum nil fiat et dummodo non interueniat deceptio ultra dimidiam iusti pretii, ut etiam in eadem decretali *In ciuitate* scripxit Ostiensis, cuius et aliorum in materia uerba posui supra in .xi. questione.[95]

Sed stat dubium generale: quando seu que in talibus possit dici deceptio ultra dimidiam iusti pretii, quod ipse ibidem examinat, sed ego tibi plene dixi supra in questione .16.[96]

Item stat dubium spetiale: utrum per constitutionem talium reddituum, de quibus queritur in proposito et de quibus supra in themate, sci-

3668 .viii.^{m} dubium principale *in marg. sin.*
3682 contractus *in marg. dex. add.*

[90] See above, 1601-51.

[91] See above, 3108-28, 3157-66, 3205-16, 3375-3400.

[92] See above, 2236-42.

[93] Lapo da Castiglionchio, *Allegationes*, allegatio 137, n.15 (ed. cit. fol. 164rb-vb).

[94] Innocent IV, *Commentaria*, ad X 5.19.6, n.2 (ed. cit. fol. 517rb-vb); Hostiensis, *Commentaria*, ad X 5.19.6, n.7 (ed. cit. V fol. 57ra-b); Johannes Andreae, *Novella*, ad X 5.19.6, n.2 (ed. cit. V fol. 74ra).

[95] See above, 1657-1785.

[96] See above, 1945-86.

licet .xv. pro centenario ad uitam duorum cuiuscumque etatis possit dici deceptio ultra dimidiam iusti pretii. Hoc etiam tetigit et indecisum reliquit dictus dominus Lapus. Arguebat tamen ad affirmatiuam per iura allegata in questione dubii immediate tacti, que minorem taxam fecerunt in huiusmodi lucris, ut est uidere in l. .i. C. *de sacrosanc. ecclesia* canonizata .x. q. .2. *Si iconomus,*[97] que uidetur loqui et permictere duplum, et in canone *Precarie* eadem causa et questione,[98] qui canon uidetur permictere triplum.

Pro negatiua adducebat pactum in dicta uenditione de qua queritur appositum, uidelicet quod dicta comunitas possit se liberare redimendo dictos redditus constitutos. In quo pacto, si bene aduertatur, magnum commodum et prerogatiua ipsi comunitati relinquitur.

Michi stat tertium dubium, quod non est aliud quam ipsum principale quesitum, uidelicet utrum in casu quesito possit dici fraudem interuenisse. Hoc dico per ea que supra scripxi in questione .18.[99] post do-
87r minum meum, per que / uidetur quod sic. Ad idem quod supra scripxi in questionibus .13. et .14.,[1] ubi omnino uide. Et si diceretur quod redditus iste concernit bona ciuitatis et sic est realis, hoc male uideo. Item eo dato, per quod tolleretur quod scribitur in dictis questionibus .13. et .14., nichilominus non uideo quomodo tollatur quod scribitur in dicta questione .18. Stant enim adhuc circumstantie illis similes et maxime pactum rescissorium seu resolutorium cum cessatione annue prestationis. Nec obstat quod ibi loquitur in donatione, hic in uenditione, quia ita uno casu sicut reliquo potest fraus fieri de contractu ad contractum. Item contractus ille, qui est innominatus, sapit et accedit ad naturam uenditionis. Item etsi ex illo capite fraus tol⟨l⟩eretur, quod tamen non uidetur, saltem non tol⟨l⟩itur ipsa fraus seu fraudis presumptio ex alio capite, uidelicet quod pro minori pretio se potest liberare uenditor. Ad hoc supra notata in secunda parte in questione .xii.[2] ad finem post dominum meum, ubi omnino uide.

Quibus omnibus pensatis, cum reuerentia tanti patris talem contractum non puto sic simpliciter et indistincte tutum uel approbandum.

Ad hoc igitur ut ualeat et fraudis presumptio cesset, opus esse credo primo ut redditus ipse non excessiuus sed conueniens constituatur; secundo quod in rebus comunitatis; .3.° quod nulla detur facultas contractum resoluendi pro maiori uel minori pretio; .4.° quod contraens

3728 contraens *scripsi*: F_1 contraems

[97] Decretum Grat. C.10 q.2 c.2.11 et c. 3 (*est lex canonizata* C. 1.2.14.5)
[98] Decretum Grat. C.10 q.2 c.4
[99] See above, 2001-2182.
[1] See above, 1840-94.
[2] See above, 1786-1839.

cum comunitate non consueuerit fenerari, ut sic omnis cesset presumptio fraudis de contractu ad contractum, ut hec omnia probantur ex notatis in iamdictis questionibus et iuribus ibidem allegatis.

Ex his igitur dico quod si comunitas absque fraude legem facit per quam constituit in bonis suis certos redditus, deputans iuxta morem officiales ad illos uendendos ad uitam alicuius uel sui et alterius uel ad aliud indefinitum tempus ad rationem illam ad quam respondet creditoribus montis nec istud facit ad petitionem alicuius id procurantis et cum ea contrahere uolentis sed in genere, non habito respectu ad aliquem in spetie, quod tunc talis contractus erit licitus si inter eam et aliquem iniatur, etiam si sit pactum de resoluendo et etiam pro minori pretio. Et eo casu potest sibi locum uendicare dictum domini Lapi,[3] quia ante contractum erat constitutus redditus et in rebus et ad tempus incertum, et sic nulla fraus presummitur iuxta supra notata in .xi. et in .xii. et in .xviii. questionibus.[4]

Sed si id fiat de nouo ad petitionem alicuius in specie et interueniat inter hunc et illam tale pactum, tunc secus, alio non dato quod fraudem cessare faciat, quia tunc constituitur in contractu ipse redditus, ubi fraus magis presummitur et maxime si talis consueuit fenerari, iuxta supra notata in dictis questionibus et in precedenti et in .xviii. Vbi uero redditus non constituerentur in bonis comunitatis sed fieret relatio solum ad personam comunitatis, tunc omnino presummeretur inlicitus talis contractus qui deinde fieret, ut patet ex ibidem notatis.

Aduertendum etiam quod non sine ministerio dixi in primo casu quem licitum asseueraui de uenditione ad uitam uel ad aliud indeffinitum tempus, hoc est, perpetuum, quia si tam redditus quam tempus certa forent, tunc fraus presummeretur, ubi maior esset certa quantitas quam in certo tempore perciperet quis a comunitate annuatim quam illa quam daret comunitati in presenti. Puta si .c. daret comunitati et comunitas pro determinato tempore .xv. annorum daret huic tali annua .x., quod quidem usuram sapit, iuxta ea que scripxi supra in secunda parte .xi.[a] questione.[5]

Et si dicatur quare aliud cum tempus est certum et finitum quam quando certum et infinitum seu indefinitum, cum utroque casu nulla
87v uersetur incer/titudo que habeat iustificare contractum et ab usura excusare, respondetur quia cum utrumque certum et determinatum est uidetur magis sapere naturam mutui quam emptionis, cum de proximo,

3761 quam *post* finitum *canc.*

[3] Lapo da Castiglionchio, *Allegationes*, allegatio 137, n.15 (ed. cit. fol. 164rb).

[4] See above, 1652-1839, 2001-2182.

[5] See above, 1652-1785.

hoc est tempore certo et determinato, sit ad fictum uenditorem reuersurus et sic fraus presummitur, et non immerito ex quo certitudinaliter habetur quod soluens .c. de presenti habebit .cl. in capite .xv. annorum et non ultra. Sed in casu quoad tempus certum sed perpetuum et indeffinitum seu infinitum non sic, hoc enim est de natura emptionis, quod in perpetuum rem habeat emptor et pecuniam uenditor.

101v / Hoc opusculum perfeci ego, Laurentius de Ridolfis, doctor minimus actu legens ordinarie in nostro generali studio florentino die .xiiii.ª Februarii anno dominice incarnationis m.°cccc.°iii.° Sit ergo laus omnipotenti Deo eiusque matri dulcissime uirgini gloriose beatisque Ieronimo et Laurentio patronis meis totique celesti curie triumphanti. Amen.

Et si quid in eo nequaquam iuri consonum reperiri contingat, omnes, precor, liment, corrigant et emendent prout uiderint oportunum idque non michi, non fidei sed inscitie mee potius, immo prorsus, adscribant. Nec quod prolixitate nimia usus uidear mordeant etiam supplico id namque profecto confiteor, sed huius potissima fuit causa, ut satisfacerem librorum copia carentibus, qui aliter ex hoc parum consequerentur utilitatis si sola remissione usus fuissem uel plurima nota doctoribus et prouectis scolasticis autem incognita. Sub silentio pertransissem his doctus que post Ostiensem et alios scripxit Iohannes Andree in decretali unica *Vt ecclesiastica be.* super uerbo "profutura" in nouella.[6]

[6] Johannes Andreae, *Novella*, ad X 3.12.1, n.4 (ed. cit. III fol. 68vb); Hostiensis, *Commentaria*, ad X 3.12.1, n.7 (ed. cit. III fol. 50va).

Commentary: Part 1

Unless otherwise noted, all translations are my own. All translations of the Digest are from *The Digest of Justinian*, ed. and trans. Alan Watson et al., 4 vols. (Philadelphia: University of Pennsylvania Press, 1985).

PROEMIUM

3-5 **Tractatus ... Amen:** It was customary to introduce legal treatises, *consilia* and public acts with an invocation of God and the saints. The form Ridolfi uses here can also be seen in several of his extant *consilia*. For examples, see ASF, Arte dei giudici e notai o proconsolo 670, where Ridolfi begins a *consilium* requested by the proconsul of the guild of judges and notaries in 1393 with the form: "In nomine Yesu Christi eiusque matris virginis gloriose beatorumque Ieronimi et Laurentii totiusque celestis curie triumphantis ..." (fol. 49v); and another of 1410: "Iesu Christi nomine repetito eiusque matris virginis gloriose beatorumque Ieronimi Laurentii suffragiis humiliter imploratis, dico et consulo ..." (fol. 114v). Ridolfi concludes the *Tractatus de usuris* with an act of thanks along similar lines (3774-76). Lawrence was, of course, Ridolfi's patron, a status he also accords the bible translator and exegete Jerome, whom he often refers to as *deuotus meus*. Here he was probably imitating the great Bolognese canonist Johannes Andreae, who also had a particular devotion to Jerome (see Stephan Kuttner, Introduction to Johannes Andreae, *In quinque Decretalium libros novella commentaria* [Venice, 1581; Turin, 1963], vol. 1, xiii). In his biographical sketch, Vespasiano claims that Ridolfi "greatly admired S. Jerome and made a collection of his Epistles larger than any other in Italy or elsewhere. It contains some on the interpretation of the Psalter, and differences of translation, and many Greek and Hebrew texts. This shows him to be not only a jurist and a canonist, but also a profound scholar in sacred learning. The book of the Epistles of S. Jerome in one volume he gave to the Church of Santo Spirito for the library, for the use of all who might wish to consult it" (*Le vite*, ed. Greco, 2: 136; trans. George and Waters, *Renaissance Princes, Popes, and Prelates*, 318-19).

6-18 **Plurimorum ... recursum:** Ridolfi gives the *proemium* a formal air by employing the so-called Roman, or papal, *cursus* at periods and minor pauses. The cadences "pulsatus eloquio," "fieri adsolet," "diuictus instantia" and "illud urbanius" are examples of the *tardus* rhythm; "salute comuni," "aperire deberem" and "habere recursum" of *planus*. For an introduction to *cursus* and bibliography, see Terence O. Tunberg, "Prose Styles and *Cursus*," in *Medieval Latin*, 111-21. In the remainder of the treatise, Ridolfi's prose reflects the less elaborate style typical of scholastic and dialectical writing.

6-14 Plurimorum ... urbanius: Ridolfi's affectation of modesty ("attenta materie grauitate uiriumque mearum imbecillitate") and reluctant acquiescence to the requests of his fellow citizens for guidance ("plurimorum aures crebro pulsatus eloquio atque ... importuna deuictus instantia") are conventional *exordium topoi* (see Ernst Robert Curtius, *European Literature and the Latin Middle Ages*, trans. William R. Trask, Bollingen Series no. 36 [Princeton: Princeton University Press, 1953], 83-89). Vespasiano informs us that "his opinions were sound and much sought, both in the city and without" and that "he never considered his own interest, always setting the service of God and the world at large before his personal advantage" (*Le vite*, ed. Greco, 2: 131, 135; trans. George and Waters, *Renaissance Princes, Popes, and Prelates*, 316, 318).

6 aures: An accusative of specification: "repeatedly assailed with respect to my ears by the eloquence of many."

14-18 Et ex ... recursum: Ridolfi entitles his work *tractatus*, that is, a treatise devoted exclusively to a single topic. As a comprehensive digest of legal opinion on usury setting "forth everything connected with the abyss of usury," the treatise takes on the character of a *summa* or compendium proceeding by means of the dialectical method of the *quaestio*. On the genre of the canonistic *summa*, see *DDC*, s.v. *Somme* by Raoul Naz.

19-31 Pro cuius ... explicabo: See Introduction, pp. 85-86, 123-26. Ridolfi declares that the twelve questions of Part 1 are dedicated to the rubric, or title, *de usuris*; Parts 2 and 3 and their subdivisions to "the black," that is, to the constituent fragments of the title, in particular the canon *Consuluit* (X 5.19.10). He further specifies that Part 2 is dedicated to the subject of usury "in general," Part 3 to five "special" cases.

32-39 Prius ... pena: Ridolfi's selection of topics is traditional and modelled on Raymond of Penyafort (*Summa*, X 5.19 *de usuris* [ed. cit. p. 227a]) and Hostiensis (*Summa*, X 5.19 *de usuris*, n.1 [ed. cit. col. 1612]). Questions 7 ("why usury is prohibited and whether it is by nature vicious"), 9 ("is it a sin to accept a loan at usury?") and 10 ("whether one may be dispensed from the sin of lending at usury") derive from Johannes Andreae's *quaestio* on the rule *Peccatum* in the *Liber sextus* (*Novella*, ad VI *de reg. iur.* 4, *Peccatum*, n.6 [ed. cit. fol. 62va]).

PART 1, QUESTION 1

40 Quid sit vsura: "What is usury?"

41-44 Ad primum ... li. .vi.: In his commentary on X 5.19.1, Innocent IV, and Johannes Andreae after him, says that "usury is profit owed or exacted in a loan contract (*mutuum*)."

44-45 Alii ... *Peccatum*: Citing Ambrose, Gratian defines usury as "anything that accedes to the principal [in a loan]": "Esca usura est, et uestis usura est, et quodcumque sorti accidit usura est; et quodcumque uelis ei nomen inponas, usura est" (Decretum Grat. C.14 q.3 c.3).

45-47 Sed quia ... pacto: Gottofredo da Trani restricts the definition of Decretum Grat. C.14 q.3 c.3 to cases in which the increment is the result of a "preceding intention or agreement."

47-51 Ostiensis ... facto: In his *summa* on the title *de usuris* of the decretals, Hostiensis defines usury as "anything added to the repayment of a thing lent for the use of the thing by agreement or intention at the time of the contract or by exaction afterwards."

51-54 Alii ... intentum: In article 1 of his *quaestio disputata* on the public debt of Venice, Gregory of Rimini defines usury as "any intentional profit from a loan."

54-56 Alii ... melior: Ridolfi prefers the definition, "usury is profit from a loan principally intended as such."

57-63 Et dico ... errasse: Gregory of Rimini objects to Innocent's definition of usury as "profit owed or exacted in a loan" because it includes only formal, contractual usury, glossing over the potentially usurious intentions of the lender.

63-71 Vnde dico ... titulo: In support of his contention, Gregory cites X 5.19.10, which states that a lender whose willingness to lend depends on his expectation of profit is to be judged "as if he was a usurer" (*quasi usurarius*). On the authority of John of Legnano's commentary on X 5.19.19, Ridolfi maintains that there is no contradiction because Innocent's definition applies only to formal usury (*usura propria*), not to the mental or quasi-usury that is the subject of X 5.19.10. Gregory's objection is met by the qualification that Innocent appended to his own definition, namely, that "what is offered freely is not usury unless it is hoped for."

For the text and a discussion of X 5.19.10, see Part 2, *casus* and *oppositiones* 1 to 8 (nn. 673 to 998-1002).

72-74 Posset ... corde: Even without qualifications, Innocent's definition can be read as comprehending the notion of mental usury if the term "exacted" is understood as "exacted by word or intention."

74-78 Et similiter ... meum: The same qualification applies to the word "owed," for even if there is an agreement (*pactum*) creating an obligation on the part of the debtor, he cannot be compelled to pay usury unless he has sworn an oath to do so. This *exceptio* is provided by X 2.24.6: "Debtors should not be forced to pay usury to which they have obligated themselves. But if they have sworn an oath to pay, they are obliged by the Lord to fulfil their oath" ("Debitores ad soluendas usuras, in quibus se obligaverant, cogi non debent. Si vero de ipsarum solutione iuraverint cogendi sunt Domino reddere iuramentum"). X 2.24.7 holds debtors to their oaths not to seek repossession of their pledges until the debt has been repaid; the lender, however, is ordered to apply the fruits of the pledges to the reduction of the principal.

79-83 Secunda ... principium: Ambrose intended the remark reproduced at Decretum Grat. C.14 q.3 c.3 to be understood in its obvious sense, that is, that anything added to the principal is usury. This is the doctrine of the Council of Nijmegen cited at Decretum Grat. C.14 q.3 c.4 and the opinion of Gratian himself: "behold, it is clearly demonstrated that anything demanded beyond the pricipal is usury" ("ecce euidenter ostenditur, quod quicquid ultra sortem exigitur usura est" [Decretum Grat. C.14 q.3 dictum Grat. post c.4]). Gottofredo limits the canon's application to a "preceding intention or agreement" because usury consists in hope or expectation of profit. This allows him to introduce a distinction between the primary and secondary intention of the lender: "I understand this to be true when the principal cause of the loan lies in the lender's hope or expectation of profit or gain; but if he is not principally motivated by such hope, but rather by charity and love, and only secondarily hopes for a reward, this I do not consider wicked" ("quod intelligo verum esse cum causa mutuandi principaliter ponitur in spe vel expectatione lucri siue emolumenti; aliter, si non principaliter propter hoc moueatur mutuator ad mutuandum, sed ob charitatem et dilectionem, secundario autem sperat de aliqua retributione, non puto hoc vitiosus" [*Summa*, X 5.19 *de usuris*, n.1 (ed. cit. p. 438b-39a)]).

84-120 **.4.ª descriptio ... intendatur**: A summary of Hostiensis' analysis of his own definition of usury as "anything added to the repayment of a thing lent for the use of the thing by agreement or intention at the time of the contract or by exaction afterwards."

86-88 **Quodcumque ...** ***Plerique***: See nn. 44-45 and 79-83.

88-90 **Solutioni ... omnes**: All authorities agree that the *locus* of usury is a loan contract (*mutuum*).

90-93 **Sed tu ...** ***quibus***: Hostiensis adds that usury is usually committed in a loan, for there are three cases in which Roman law permits the payment of usury where there is no loan. At Dig. 5.3.51.1, Papinian says that a possessor owes *usurae* on fruits or income derived from an inheritance before the heir instituted an action for possession. He adds at Dig. 22.1.3.4 that if an heir delays delivering things left by way of *fideicommissum*, preferring to convert them to cash, he owes *usurae* for the delay. At Dig. 22.1.17.8, the jurist Paul says that if a testator bequeathed money for the erection of public statues or images and the heirs delay setting them up beyond the deadline established by the governor, they owe the republic *usurae* of four percent for the delay.

93-107 **Ipsius ... titulo**: Hostiensis adds the qualification "for the use of the thing" in order to distinguish usury from penalty, for something may be added to the principal as a penalty provided this is done without fraud. X 1.43.4 states that penalties accepted by contracting parties are licit and may be enforced, but, according to Decretum Grat. C.12 q.2 c.11, it is illicit to seek profit from damages: "Absit ut ecclesia ... lucra de dampnis querere."

A penalty may be distinguished from usury because the latter is charged on the passage of time, as in the Authentic *Ad haec*, which describes an agricultural loan in which at the end of a year the creditor receives a full bushel for the loan of a half or its equivalent in cash. By contrast, a penalty derives its force from the agreement of the parties. X 5.37.7 describes a contract in which the parties mutually agree to a penalty for default. In X 1.43.4, a penalty is imposed on the party to an arbitration who refuses to accept the arbitrator's judgement. Usury, on the other hand, is offered in order to defer payment of the principal, as in X 5.19.10, where a merchant sells on credit for a higher price than he would receive if the price were paid immediately. Here the "penalty" is in fact a charge for delayed payment. For the text of X 5.19.10, see n. 673.

Not only are penalty and usury not equivalent, but they are sometimes mutually exclusive, as at C. 8.33.2, where a creditor who accepts usury for a year after petitioning for possession of a pledge is deemed to have foregone the privilege sought. Dig. 16.3.7.2 notes that when a moneylender goes bankrupt, depositors are compensated before those who have money at interest with him. According to Gottofredo and Hostiensis, usury precludes the recovery of the principal in this case.

107-12 **Pactione ... *episcopum***: A debtor may offer his creditor a gift out of gratitude and the latter may licitly accept it, provided such a gift is not incorporated into the contract or demanded afterward, and so long as the creditor's intentions are pure from the outset. Decretum Grat. C.1 q.2 c.4 states that ordination may not be sold, but a thank-offering may be accepted "because an offering that does not proceed from the request of the recipient is without stain of guilt" ("quia eius oblatio nullam culpae maculam ingerit, quae non ex ambientis petitione processit").

112-20 **Quod intellige ... intendatur**: If the lender is motivated primarily by his desire for a gift–and the proof of this is that he would not otherwise be willing to lend–he will be censured in the judgement of heaven as a usurer in effect, even though he cannot be condemned in an earthly court and compelled to make restitution. The corollary drawn by both Gottofredo and Hostiensis is that if the lender is motivated primarily by love of his neighbour–and the proof of this is that he would be willing to lend even in the absence of a gift–he may licitly entertain a secondary hope for a gift, a view expressed in Ridolfi's definition of usury as "profit from a loan principally intended as such."

121-32 **Nolo ... usuram**: Hostiensis' suggestion that a lender may licitly accept a gift, provided his intentions are pure "from the outset," that is, from the moment of the loan agreement, must not be understood to permit the formation of such intentions subsequently.

132-44 **Pro quo ... ordine**: Gregory of Rimini rejects the canonists' distinction between primary and secondary expectation of profit in determining whether the lender's intention is usurious.

145-231 **Dicebat ... intentum**: A summary of article 1 of Gregory of Rimini's *quaestio*, in the course of which he arrives at a definition of usury as "any intentional profit from a loan."

145-64 **Dicebat ... titulo**: Gregory appeals to Aristotle's analysis of exchange for a definition of profit: "These names, both loss and gain, have come from voluntary exchange; for to have more than one's own is called gaining, and to have less than one's original share is called losing, e.g., in buying and selling and in all other matters in which the law has left people free to make their own terms; but when they get neither more nor less but just what belongs to themselves, they say that they have their own and that they neither lose nor gain" (*Ethics* 5.4.1132b10-15, trans. W. D. Ross [Random House: New York, 1941], 1009-10). For a discussion of this passage, see Baldwin, *Medieval Theories*, 10-12, 62-65.

Gregory observes, however, that although all usury is profit, not all profit is usury. In support of the first observation, he notes that one who gets back as much as he lent or something that is already his own is not a usurer. X 5.19.1 forbids clerics to retain the fruits of pledges on loans without applying them to the reduction of the principal, unless the pledge is an ecclesiastical benefice wrongfully possessed by a layman. The gloss extends this privilege to laymen recovering property wrongfully held by their debtors: "I understand the same of a layman, namely, that in this way he may recover possession from an unjust possessor. But he could not recover the possession of somebody else, because the fruits are not his own, and so if he retains them, it would be usury" ("Idem intelligo de laico, quod hoc modo sibi licet redimere possessionem de manu iniusti detentoris; alienam tamen possessionem taliter redimere non posset quia fructus illi non sunt sui, vnde si illos retineret, vsura esset" [gl. ord. ad X 5.19.1., v. *Beneficium* (ed. cit. col. 1733)]).

The second proposition is proved because profit is licit in contracts of sale and rent. The distinction is clear in X 5.19.6, which deals with the case of someone who sells on credit merchandise worth, say, five pounds, extracting from the purchaser a promise to pay six at the end of a certain period. Though not formally usurious, such a contract is nevertheless illicit: "although such a contract cannot be formally censured as usurious, nevertheless the sellers are guilty of sin, unless there is uncertainty about the value of the merchandise at the time of payment" ("licet autem contractus huiusmodi ex tali forma non possit censeri nomine usurarum, nihilominus tamen venditores peccatum incurrunt, nisi dubium sit, merces illas plus minusve solutionis tempore valituras"). The gloss notes that the form of the contract must be considered before condemning a transaction as usurious, since "everything is from a form" ("quia omne esse est ex forma"), that is, a profit may not properly be called usury unless it is obtained in a *mutuum* (gl. ord. ad X 5.19.6, v. *Ex tali forma* [ed. cit. col. 1737]). It adds, however, that the contrary argument can be found at X 5.19.10 and concludes that "although the contract is not formally usurious, it can be made in fraud of usury" ("licet enim ex forma non sit contractus usurarius, potest tamen fieri in fraudem usurarum" [ibid., v. *Vsurarum*]).

164-231 Similiter ... intentum: May a lender accept a gift from his debtor without being guilty of usury? Gregory replies that he may, provided he lends without any expectation of such profit and believes that the debtor is acting purely from motives of friendship, though in reality he may be offering the gift on account of the loan. For this reason, Gregory's definition qualifies the *lucrum* as "intentional." But if at any point before, during or after extending the loan the lender develops a desire for profit, he is guilty of usury. So, for example, if the creditor knows or comes to know that the debtor is offering a gift in compensation for the loan he received, he is guilty of usury by intention.

In support of his conclusion, Gregory cites William of Rennes' gloss on the *Summa* of Raymond of Penyafort: "What if a debtor makes a gift to his creditor on account of the loan he has received or will receive: assuming the intention of the creditor is just, is he bound to make restitution? Response: I do not think he is with respect to a gift consumed in good faith nor indeed with respect to anything remaining, so long as he thinks it likely that his debtor was acting from gratitude. But if he thinks or suspects that the gift is motivated by the loan, he is so bound" ("Quid si non sit corrupta intentio creditoris, vbi debitor propter creditum acceptum, vel vlterius retinendum dat ei aliquid, numquid creditor tenetur ei restituere illud? Responsio: credo quod non tenetur bona fide de consumptis, nec etiam de extantibus, quamdiu probabiliter credit, quod ex sola dilectione gratis ei seruierit; si autem credit, vel probabiliter dubitat, quod propter mutuum receptum vel vlterius retinendum ei seruierit, restituere tenetur" [*Apparatus in Summam Raymundi*, 2.7 *de usuris*, n.4, v. *Intentio corrupta* (ed. cit. p. 229b-30a)]). In Decretum Grat. C.14 q.3 c.2, Jerome writes that "scripture calls usury an excess, that is, anything they receive in addition to what they gave" ("diuina scriptura omnis rei superhabundantiam aufert, ut plus non recipias quam dedisti. Alii pro pecunia fenerata solent munuscula diuersi generis accipere, et non intelligunt scripturam usuram appellare et superhabundantiam quicquid illud est, si ab eo, quod dederint, plus acciperint"; Gregory adds "on account of the loan that they made."

232-39 **Hec sunt ... magistri**: "To say otherwise is to draw blood." The maxim, from *Prv* 30.33 via Decretum Grat. D.4 c.6 ("qui multum emungit, elicit sanguinem"), is cited by Guido de Baysio (d. 1313) and Johannes Andreae to argue that a usurer is bound to restore only his usuries, not any additional profits he has acquired by means of them. Ridolfi maintains that Gregory's opinion, which contradicts the canonical consensus, also "presses too hard" and must be qualified.

240-57 **Et ad primam ... intuenti**: Ridolfi accepts Gregory's conclusion (n. 164-231) that a creditor who receives a gift as recompense for making a loan, even if he did not lend with the expectation of such a gift, is to be considered a usurer, but only if such an expectation was or subsequently became his primary motivation, since, in the canonists' view, the lender may at any stage entertain a secondary desire for profit. In support of his conclusion, Ridolfi cites Johannes Andreae's comments on X 5.3.27, which describes the case of a candidate elected to a vacant benefice after the chapter, without the candidate's knowledge, had been promised a bribe to elect him. The pope concludes that the election must be presumed simoniacal. The gloss asks whether the election is valid if the chapter was not swayed by the promise of money but would have elected the candidate in any event. It concludes that if the promise of a bribe intervened in the process, the presumption must be that the intentions of the electors were corrupt. Commenting on the gloss, Johannes Andreae notes that since "no one is a proper witness in his own case," the electors' claims of impartiality must be dismissed. But what if, prior to the offer of the bribe, an elector made his intention to elect the candidate known to another party who could then serve as a witness? The jurist replies that perhaps the elector was lying or perhaps he would subsequently have changed his mind if the bribe had not been offered: "hoc teneas, maxime quia non video quomodo probari possit ista intentio eligentis, nisi per ipsum, cui ut soli et criminoso et deponenti in facto suo non crederetur. Et secundum hoc facile esset cuique, qui per pecuniam eligit, dicere se alias fuisse electum. Sed dices: imo poterit hoc probare per alios cum quibus dixerat prius se uelle illum eligere. Respondeo: forte falsum tunc dicebat ... uel pone quod uerum; potuisset tamen animum mutasse, si pecunia data non fuisset" (*Novella*, ad X 5.3.27, n.5 [ed. cit. V fol. 28ra]).

258-69 **Ad dictum ... creditoris**: Ridolfi denies that the case from William of Rennes (n. 164-231) is pertinent unless the lender's primary intention underwent a change from charity to anticipation of profit or unless the debtor was constrained by some external consideration so that he did not give freely and this factor was known to the lender (see also Part 2, question 9, nn. 1514-18 to 1592-1600).

270-73 **Ad verbum ... et cetera**: In reply to the passage from Jerome cited by Gregory, Ridolfi adduces Johannes Andreae, who reads Decretum Grat. C.14 q.3 c.2 as condemning a primary intention to profit: "But a question arises concerning what has just been said, namely, whether the intention or expectation of profit alone makes a person a usurer in the absence of an explicit agreement. On this, all jurists appear to agree that where the intention and expectation of profit alone provide the principal motivation for lending, this renders the lender a usurer and obliges him to make restitution in the presence of God in the penitential forum. And this conclusion is confirmed by X 5.19.10, which I cited above, and by the text from *Lc* 6 mentioned there–'Lend, expecting nothing in return'–and by the opinions of the saints Augustine, Ambrose and Jerome cited at Decretum Grat. C.14 q.3, where they all appear to agree that when a lender expects something more than what he lent he commits usury and is obliged to make restitution" ("Occurrit tamen dubium de eo quod dictum est statim, scilicet vtrum sola intentio siue spes lucri constituat hominem vsurarium, non interueniente ibi aliquo pacto obligante. Ad hoc tamen videntur communiter respondere omnes iurisperiti quia vbi sola intentio et sola spes lucri est principalis causa mutui, ibi ex sola intentione et spe lucri constituitur homo vsurarius et tenetur ad restitutionem in foro poenitentiae coram Deo; et firmatur per illam decretalem superius allegatam *de usuris Consuluit* vbi scripsi et super illud ibi inductum Luce .vi. 'mutuum date, nihil inde sperantes,' et super auctoritatibus sanctorum Augustini et Ambrosii et Hieronymi quae ponuntur xiiii. q. iii, et videntur omnes in hoc concordare quod vbi mutuans expectat aliquid vltra illud quod dedit, vsuram committit et per consequens ad restituendum tenetur" [*Novella*, ad VI *de reg. iur.* 4, *Peccatum*, n.8 (ed. cit. fol. 62vb)]).

274-89 **Et ex predictis ... alios**: A lender is allowed to have a secondary expectation of profit provided his primary motivation is charity–and the proof of this is that he would lend even if his debtor failed to offer him a gift–since in this case there is no preceding or concurrent intention to profit. However, in article 4 of his *quaestio*, Gregory cites X 5.3.34, which seems to undermine this conclusion. The decretal states that if a cleric confers his goods on a church in return for a prebend on the explicit understanding that he will continue to enjoy his goods in the form of a prebend, he is a simoniac; but if he offers his property without a formal agreement or conditions, and if the chapter agrees, he may be admitted to a canonry and allowed to enjoy his goods as a prebend without scruple. It is noted, however, that if the cleric intended to obtain spiritual office by means of his temporal goods or if the chapter admitted him for the sake of these goods–that is, if they would not have accepted him without his gift–they will be judged culpable by God, if not in the forum of the church. Ridolfi replies that this case is not analogous to that of a lender whose primary intention is not profit, since he would have lent regardless of profit. For the gloss to X 5.3.27 and Johannes Andreae's comments on it, see n. 240-57.

290-301 **Insuper ... similia**: Ridolfi maintains, moreover, that even if the debtor's gift is in recognition of the benefit freely conferred on him by the creditor and the creditor is aware of this, so long as the creditor's primary intention remains charitable, the gift is neither given nor received as usury. Gregory's citation of X 5.3.34 is relevant only if both parties consider the gift a form of disguised usury.

The intentions of the creditor and debtor are more fully discussed in Part 2, questions 6 and 7 (nn. 1210-18 to 1447-73) and touched on in Part 2, questions 9 and 10 (nn. 1514-18 to 1645-51).

302-310 **Premissorum ... questionibus**: For Ridolfi's analysis of article 3 of Gregory's *quaestio*, see *dubium* 2 of the *Questio montis* (nn. 2459-60 to 2996-98). For Part 2, *oppositio* 8, see nn. 868-70 to 998-1008; for question 3, nn. 1021-22 to

1134-42; and for question 9, nn. 1514-18 to 1592-1600.

310-17 **Facit ... tertia:** X 5.3.1 forbids a bishop and his staff (deacon, notary and so on) to exact anything for conferring orders. In his comments on the gloss, Johannes Andreae cites Innocent IV and Hostiensis. Innocent maintains that the decretal applies only to those whose services are essential for the canonical validity of the ordination. Moreover, if gifts are customary and freely offered, they do not constitute simony. Hostiensis adds that if the notary is retained especially for the occasion, he may licitly receive compensation, as may the ordinary office-holder, provided there is no prior agreement or exaction after the fact.

X 5.3.9 prohibits charges for ordination and other rites: "horribile nimis est ... vt pro ... sacramentis aliquid requiratur." Glossing the canon, Johannes Andreae notes Innocent IV's opinion that the decree does not prohibit free offerings. X 5.3.10 forbids a bishop to exact more than his expenses for consecrating a church. Bernard of Parma (d. 1266) notes in the gloss that if a church is poor, the bishop should consecrate it at his own expense. X 5.3.21 forbids charging for the exercise of a church ministry. Johannes Andreae notes that the decretal does not forbid voluntary offerings: "*Exigatis* uiolentiam notat; aliud ergo si gratis offeratur" (*Novella*, ad X 5.3.21, n.2 [ed. cit. V fol. 26va]). X 5.3.8 states that he who offers money for a religious rite is as guilty of simony as he who accepts it. Johannes Andreae notes that if there were no givers of simoniacal bribes there would be no takers and vice versa. By the same argument, debtors who pay usury are as guilty as the creditors who receive it. But the two cases are not really similar and "the reason for the difference is that here the giver [that is, the simonist] is not constrained by necessity and is really a corruptor ... but in the second case he who obliges himself sought a loan from his neighbour, although it is written 'lend freely expecting nothing in return' [*Lc* 6.35] ... and so there is sin if the lender does not extend the loan without a charge. It is enough to be sure that the debtor does not voluntarily oblige himself to usury but is impelled by necessity, which excuses him of theft" ("ratio diuersitatis quia hic dans et offerens nulla necessitate trahitur et est principaliter corruptor ... in secunda uero is qui se obligat a proximo debitum exigit, cum sit scriptum 'date mutuum nihil' et cetera ... in qua ergo culpa est, si fenerator non uult debitum reddere, nisi uendatur; satis constat quod non uoluntarie se obligat debitor ad usuras sed impellit ipsum necessitas, que excusat etiam a furto" [*Novella*, ad X 5.3.8, n.4 (ed. cit. V fol. 22vb)]).

X 5.3.30: what has been freely offered for a sacrament without an agreement may be received without sin: "Illud tamen gratanter recipi poterit, quod fuerit sine taxatione gratis oblatum." Johannes Andreae observes that receiving as a result of an agreement is disapproved, but not gifts: "*Recipi*: recipere ergo non reprobatur, sed ex pacto recipere" (*Novella*, ad X 5.3.30, n.4 [ed. cit. V fol. 28vb]). X 5.3.42 directs that sacraments are to be conferred for free, but that the bishop may compel laymen to observe customary offerings for services: "sed per episcopum loci veritate cognita compescantur, qui malitiose nituntur laudabilem consuetudinem immutare." Johannes Andreae, following Innocent IV, notes that the decretal is directed against those who want to abolish the custom whereby a gift is offered for burial and similar rites. Such customs are permissible provided there is no compulsion before the fact; otherwise it is simony. Commenting on Bernard of Parma's gloss on this canon, Johannes Andreae, following Hostiensis, notes that although they may not require anything for performing a sacrament, clerics may seek their customary dues by suing in the bishop's court.

318-22 **Sed uideamus ... exactionem:** Usury has two elements, one material, the other formal. The material element is profit arising from a loan, the formal the intention to make such a profit in itself or expressed externally through an agreement or demand. The observation is from Gerard of Siena via Johannes Andreae's *quaestio disputata* on the rule *Peccatum* of the Sext.

Part 1, Question 2

323 **Vnde dicatur:** "Why it is called 'usury'"

324-27 **Ad secundum ... Ostiensem:** The word *usura* comes from *usus rei* because something is given for the use of a thing, or from *usus aeris*, that is, the "use of money" (*aes* = copper = money). According to Gottofredo and Hostiensis, the two derivations amount to same thing.

Part 1, Question 3

328 **In quibus commictatur:** "In what contracts usury is committed."

329-34 **Ad tertium ... *quibus*:** According to Gottofredo and Raymond of Penyafort, usury is committed only in a loan contract (*mutuum*), though Hostiensis provides examples from Roman law in which usury was paid in other contracts (see n. 90-93).

335-48 **Ex predictis ... principium:** Following Raymond, Gottofredo observes that usury is committed only in fungibles, that is, things that according to the *Institutiones* of Justinian (527-65) may be weighed, measured or numbered and are the proper subjects of loans (see Introduction, p. 57). But out of deference to Decretum Grat. C.14 q.3 c.3 and c.4 (see nn. 44-45 and 79-83), Gottofredo adds that usury may be committed in things that fall outside this class, giving as examples a horse or clothing that is promised in repayment of a loan but is of greater value than the principal (see nn. 145-64 and 420-38).

349-53 **Hoc idem ... Gofredus:** Hostiensis reconciles Raymond and Gottofredo by suggesting that Raymond spoke only with respect to the contract, because usury is usually committed in a loan. Gottofredo, however, is correct with respect to usury as profit rather than in terms of the object lent, since the former may consist in something that is not a fungible.

353-58 **Dominus ... Raimundi:** John of Legnano says that if you consider only what is given in a usurious contract (that is, the profit), it may fall outside the Roman law definition, since it may not be measurable, but if you consider that to which profit accrues (the thing lent), it is always a fungible: "Sed aduerte, si ponderatur datum illud potest, quia forte datur quid immensurabile et ibi vsura, sed si ponderatur quod prestatur mutuo cui accedat vsura illud semper consistit in numero, pondere uel mensura" (*Commentaria*, ad X 5.19.19 [MS cit. fol. 99v]).

358-62 **Quod etiam ... recurre:** In his *quaestio* on *Peccatum*, Johannes Andreae explains why loans consist in fungibles: "I say that in a loan the debtor is not bound to restore the thing lent in its very substance, since this is often impossible and was not the point of the loan in the first place .... But he is obliged to restore a thing of the same and equal value if real justice is to be maintained between lender and borrower. But certainty about the value of a thing is not intrinsic except in things whose value can be numbered, weighed or measured" ("Dico quod in mutuo non tenetur debitor restituere rem mutuatam sub identitate substantiae, quia hoc est saepius impossibile, nec ad istum finem recipitur ... sed tenetur eam restituere sub certitudine eiusdem valoris siue aequalis valoris, si debeat saluari vera iustitia inter mutuantem et illum cui fit mutuum. Certitudo autem aequalis valoris non inuenitur ex natura rei, nisi in illis tribus, quarum valor pensatur ex numero, pondere vel mensura" [*Novella*, ad VI *de reg. iur.* 4, *Peccatum*, n.11 (ed. cit. fol. 63ra)]).

PART 1, QUESTION 4

363 Quot sint eius speties: "How many kinds of usury there are."

364-67 Ad quartum ... *speties*: There are two kinds: spiritual and corporeal, the former just, the latter unjust. According to Gottofredo, citing Decretum Grat. D.46 c.10, spiritual usury is the manifold reward we may expect from God if we behave mercifully in life. Hostiensis, citing Augustine, adds "'in return for one we shall receive a hundredfold and have eternal life': O wretched man, why do you lend to man? Lend to God and you will receive a hundredfold and have eternal life!" ("nam pro vno centuplum accipiemus et vitam aeternam possidebimus, Augustinus. Homo miser, cur foeneraris homini? Foenerare Deo et centuplum accipies et vitam aeternam possidebis!" [*Summa*, X 5.19 *de usuris*, n.3 (ed. cit. col. 1615)]). According to Gottofredo, corporeal usury can be divided into (1) usury on a loan (*foenus sortis*) and (2) compound interest (*foenus foeneris*). The latter was condemned even in Roman law, but canon law condemns both.

PART 1, QUESTION 5

368 Ex quibus causis ueniat: "What are the causes of usury?"

369-72 Ad quintum ... *causis*: Usury is demanded on the basis of an agreement (*pactum*) or because of delay (*mora*) or its equivalent (*quasi mora*) in repaying the principal.

Hostiensis observes that in Roman law usury was owed on the basis of an agreement concluded separately from the loan, usually a *stipulatio*, though in contracts based on good faith (*bona fides*) a simple agreement (*nudum pactum*) sufficed: "Et quidem secundum leges antiquas ex stipulationibus habitis inter partes vel pacto nudo in contractu bonae fidei in continenti apposito" (*Summa*, X 5.19 *de usuris*, n.5 [ed. cit. col. 1615]). According to Dig. 22.2.5, usury was also payable by agreement on *fenora nautica*, "transmarine loans" to purchase cargo for transport by sea, and in other loans in which the creditor assumed the risk of loss: "In exchange for bearing a risk, a person may recover what he has given and something else besides money, even if no penal clause is fulfilled, provided the transaction is not a gamble. Examples from which *condictiones* arise are 'if you do not manumit,' 'if you do not do so and so,' 'if I do not get well,' and so forth. No doubt also if I give a large sum to a fisherman who wants to buy tackle on terms that he repays me if he makes a catch or to an athlete to enable him to support himself and compete on terms that if he wins, he repays me. In all these cases, a pact can increase the obligation without a stipulation."

Both Hostiensis and Gottofredo, following the civilian jurist Azo, note that usury is due in delay. Delay occurs when someone is prevented from fulfilling an obligation at the proper place and time, for, as Dig. 46.3.85 says, "full performance is made only both in quantity and on time" so that, for example, if I arrange to receive ownership of land on a given day and this does not happen due to the owner's negligence, I am owed damages for delay (Dig. 45.1.114). A debtor is guilty of delay when he "ought to have realized that he was under an obligation to deliver" (Dig. 12.1.5), but the case is otherwise if he has not been properly notified (Dig. 22.1.32.1). Indeed "cases in which there is a good reason for putting off payment are not cases of 'delay'" (Dig. 22.1.21). On default in fulfilment of contracts of good faith "interest is payable from the date of delay" (Dig. 22.1.32.2), as it is in failure to fulfil a *fideicommissum* (Dig. 31.84). Gottofredo notes that these examples hold good in canon law unless they are used to conceal usury.

Hostiensis adds that the defaulter is responsible for fruits of which the creditor has been deprived by his delay (Dig. 22.1.2; 22.1.38.7, 8, 10). Moreover, the thing owed is at the debtor's risk and he is liable for damage or destruction that can be shown to have resulted from the delay (Dig. 30.47.6; 6.1.15.3). Usury is due in delay particularly in cases of possession in bad faith, such as when a possessor knows or ought to know that an inheritance belongs to someone else (Dig. 5.3.20.11). Delay is purged–liability ended–through the transformation of the obligation into a new one (*novatio*) (Dig. 46.3.72.1), the payment of the debt (*oblatio*) or the deposit (*depositio*) owed in a place designated by a public official.

Usury is demanded in cases "like delay" (*quasi mora*) when, for example, a buyer has not paid for a thing delivered (C. 4.49.5), when a creditor receives more than he is owed in the sale of a pledge (Dig. 13.7.6, 7) or when a procurator profits from his principal's money (Dig. 17.1.10.3). Hostiensis notes in conclusion that in a loan usury is owed in delay not as usury but as interest or damages: "Sed et si foenerauerit, dixerunt quidam, quod tenetur quasi ex mora, sed Azo dixit quod conuenitur sicut de sorte. Item si adhibuit moram, conuenitur non tamquam ad vsuram, sed ad interesse" (*Summa*, X 5.19 *de usuris*, n.6 [ed. cit. col. 1617]). He cites Dig. 17.2.60.pr.: "where a partner delays paying in profits made and spends the money on his own account, he is obliged to pay interest as well; not technically as interest but as compensation for the interest not received through delay."

PART 1, QUESTION 6

373 Qualiter petatur: "How usury is sought."

374-75 Ad sextum ... *petantur*: Hostiensis notes that *stipulatio* and *pactum* provided the creditor with an action for recovery of the agreed sum or quantity (*condictio certi*) (C. 8.37.1). Payment of interest over a long period could be invoked to establish the existence of a *stipulatio* (Dig. 22.1.6). Usury owed in delay could be sought in an action along with the principal obligation, provided the latter remained actionable, and was awarded at the discretion of the court.

The rates of legal usury (*usurae legitimae*) were fixed by Justinian on a scale dictated by the status of the creditor: *illustres*, the highest imperial officials, could charge four percent, merchants eight, others six (C. 4.32.26.2). Justinian set the rate of interest on transmarine loans at twelve percent (*centesimum*). Hostiensis understands the latter rate to be monthly, so that interest on a transmarine loan would equal (in fact, exceed) the principal in a year–"in traiecticia autem pecunia licet stipulari usque ad centesimum usuram, quae aequiparatur sorti in anno" (*Summa*, X 5.19 *de usuris*, n.7 [ed. cit. col. 1618])–though historically the rate probably represented one percent a month or twelve a year (Berger, *Encyclopedic Dictionary*, s.v. *Centesima*). It was forbidden, even on the grounds of local custom, to exceed these rates.

Hostiensis concludes by citing the opinion of Azo that such measures of human law were dictated by "worldly necessity" in the light of which the emperor could not completely forbid usury but only moderate it. Usury is forbidden in both testaments; and since the law of an inferior cannot derogate from that of his superior and since, according to Justinian himself in Nov. 83.1 (Auth. 6.11) and Nov. 6.1 (Auth. 1.6), the laws should imitate the canons, measures permitting usury are invalid.

Part 1, Question 7

376 Quare ... vitiosa: "Why usury is prohibited and whether it is by nature vicious."

377-96 Ad septimum ... prohibitos: For the text of Innocent IV's judgement on usury, see Introduction, p. 58. He adds that the avarice generated by usury is a form of idolatry. Decretum Grat. D.47 c.8, extracted from a sermon of Ambrose on *Lc* 12.16 ("The land of a rich man brought forth plentifully"), observes that even the prayers of the avaricious are concerned with riches. Decretum Grat. D.47 c.3, from the *Moralia* of Gregory the Great, contrasts lovers of this world with the soldiers of Christ: "all lovers of the world are strong in earthly things but weak in those of heaven. For the sake of earthly glory they are prepared to exert themselves even to the point of death; for eternal hope they will do nothing. For earthly riches they will endure any injury; for heavenly riches they refuse to bear even the slightest reproach. For earthly praise they will labour the whole day, but are wearied by a moment of prayer to the Lord" ("Omnes huius seculi dilectores in terrenis rebus fortes sunt, in celestibus debiles. Nam pro temporali gloria usque ad mortem desudare appetunt, et pro spe perpetua nec parum quidem in labore subsistunt; pro terrenis lucris quaslibet iniurias tollerant, et pro celesti mercede uel tenuissimi uerbi contumelias recusant; terreno iudici toto etiam die assistere fortes sunt, in oratione uero coram Domino uel unius horae momento lassantur"). Innocent also remarks that some prefer to condemn usury as a violation of the principle of charity by which we are obliged to help our neighbour rather than because of its attendant evils, since there are many licit contracts that can produce ill effects.

Innocent's account of the rationale for the usury prohibition is cited verbatim by Hostiensis and Johannes Andreae in their commentaries on the decretals. The argument is discussed by Noonan, *Scholastic Analysis of Usury*, 49-50; McLaughlin, "Teaching of the Canonists," 1: 110-11; and, most recently, Spicciani, *Capitale e interesse*, 49-83, who situates the passage in its wider intellectual context and traces its fate in the later literature. Spicciani notes that Innocent and Hostiensis were exceptional in maintaining that usury was prohibited not because it was an offence against natural law, but because it violated divine positive law and because of its moral and social effects. Although Innocent's argument continued to be cited in the fourteenth century, particularly by canonists, the competing thesis increasingly came to dominate the debate, a development reflected by Ridolfi, who notes but then ignores Innocent's argument from positive law, remarking that "although the foregoing reasons show that usury ought to be prohibited, they nevertheless do not prove that usury by its very nature is vicious and bound up with malice, since they can be applied to many other cases that are licit or at least approved. But since it is both useful and excellent to see that this is so, we shall linger for a while over it" (398-402).

396-97 **Et idem ... titulo:** I have not been able to consult a manuscript of Guillelmus and Jesselinus de Cassanis (d. 1334/35) on Clem. 5.5.1. The ordinary gloss to Clem. 5.5.1, however, passes over Innocent's arguments and "in effect" endorses the notion that usury is prohibited because it is an offence against charity.

398-406 **Sed aduertendum ... rationes:** The Augustinian friar and theologian Gerard of Siena advanced a natural law argument against usury, namely, that it is "by nature vicious and bound up with malice," in question 1, article 2 of his *Tractatus de usuris et de praescriptionibus* (for a summary and discussion of the argument as it appears in Gerard's treatise, see Langholm, *Economics in the Medieval Schools*, 552-9). The history of the treatise is complex. It survives in a single manuscript in the Biblioteca Angelica, Rome (cod. 625; see H. Narducci, *Catalogus codicum manuscriptorum praeter Graecos et orientales in Bibliotheca Angelica*, vol. 1 [Rome, 1893], 259-60) and was printed once in the seventeenth century (Cesena, 1630). Gerard's treatise was, however, reported and analyzed by Johannes Andreae in his *quaestio* on *Peccatum*. Because of its association with the more famous jurist and the scarcity of Gerard's own text, the analysis has sometimes been attributed to Johannes Andreae himself, for example, by Noonan, *Scholastic Analysis of Usury*, 67, where it is incorrectly described as the "Andrean argument"; on the correct attribution, see Langholm, *Economics in the Medieval Schools*, 556-7. Although Ridolfi has the argument via Johannes Andreae and Johannes Calderinus, he is clear about its authorship.

406-19 **Et quia ... naturam:** Following the example of Johannes Calderinus in his *repetitio* on X 5.19.19, Ridolfi refers the reader to Johannes Andreae's report of Gerard's treatise and proposes to reproduce only Gerard's four central theses as they are presented by Johannes Andreae. These are (1) that usury makes a natural thing exceed its nature and an artificial thing its art; (2) that it causes a naturally unfruitful thing to bear fruit; (3) that it makes a fungible increase in value through its use; and (4) that it uses a thing for a purpose different from that to which it was ordained.

420-38 **Prima ratio ... meo:** "Usury makes a natural thing exceed its nature and an artificial thing its art." As noted above (n. 335-48), loans (*mutua*) are contracted only in fungibles because the debtor does not repay the loan with the identical substance he borrowed but with an equivalent amount. Fungibles may be divided into natural (for example, wine, grain, oil, gold or silver bullion) and artificial fungibles (for example, money, that is, specie, or, to give a modern example, paper clips). According to Gerard, fungibles of both classes derive from their measure a fixed and determinate value that remains constant provided the measure remains unchanged. If they appear to increase or decrease in value, it is not because of any change in their intrinsic value expressed in number, weight or measure, but because of an increase or decrease in the value of the things for which they may be exchanged. For example, a bushel of wheat is always worth a bushel of wheat of the same quality, but in terms of another substance, for example, money or goats, it might, because of scarcity, be worth more in February than in August.

Natural and artificial nonfungibles (for example, vineyards, houses, horses), by contrast, derive their value from external and contingent variables, such as time, place and condition; for this reason they are not comparable to one another and cannot be the subjects of *mutua*. Contingent variables do not affect the value of fungibles: in terms of number, weight or measure, a fungible is never worth more than itself (a bushel of wheat is always worth a bushel of wheat, not a bushel and a half; ten florins are always worth ten florins, not twelve). By demanding more than the amount lent, the usurer contradicts the intrinsic value of a fungible determined and fixed by its nature or art.

Noonan describes this analysis as a theory of "the fixed value of fungibles" (*Scholastic Analysis of Usury*, 67), while Langholm suggests that "the self-valuation of fungibles" is a more accurate description, since the theory does not fix the value of fungibles in terms of other substances (*Economics in the Medieval Schools*, 557). It is clear, however, from both Johannes Andreae's *quaestio* and Ridolfi's summary of it that Johannes had reservations about the theory as it stood: while readily conceding that the valuation of fungibles in terms of number, weight and measure is a convenience, particularly when making a contract, he does not understand why it is true to say that such things have a determinate value in such terms by nature. Ridolfi agrees. What is the point of the jurists' objection? The text makes it clear that they do not understand Gerard to be arguing that the value of fungibles cannot fluctuate in terms of other commodities. Langholm argues that Johannes Andreae misunderstands or simply rejects the argument (*Economics in the Medieval Schools*, 557). Neither is in fact true: the jurists accept Gerard's argument in general, but question the proposition that the categories of number, weight and measure derive from nature. As applied to fungibles, they are in fact legal categories or constructs that have meaning only in a contractual context and, more specifically, in the context of a loan. The value of a fungible is fixed and determined by the terms of the contract–not by nature–and once the agreement has been concluded the value of the fungible cannot fluctuate in terms of number, measure and weight. With this reservation, however, the remainder of Gerard's argument holds good.

439-45 Secunda ratio ... *Sicut hi*: "Usury causes a thing that by its nature is unfruitful to bear fruit contrary to its nature." As reported by Johannes Andreae, the argument runs as follows. Things that bear fruit increase in value along with the fruit. Lendable things, however, have a fixed and determinate value in terms of number, weight or measure and therefore they cannot increase in value and cannot bear fruit. A usurer makes a lendable thing bear fruit, therefore he acts contrary to its nature. In confirmation, Johannes Andreae cites Decretum Grat. D.47 c.8: "by the detestable art of usury gold gives birth to gold" ("usurae arte nequissima ex ipso auro aurum nascitur"). Gerard's argument is designed to show that all fungibles, not just money, are sterile by nature or in terms of their purpose.

446-55 .3.ª declaratur ... uitiosum: "Though a fungible and its use have the same value, usury causes the one to increase by means of the other." This passage represents a highly compressed version of Gerard's correction of Thomas Aquinas' argument from consumptibility. Thomas' argument in *Summa theologiae*, secunda secundae, q. 78, art. 1 runs as follows: there are certain things (fungibles) whose proper use is their consumption; for example, to use wine is to drink it, to use money is to spend it in exchange for goods. In the case of such things, use cannot be separated from the thing itself and therefore to grant the use of it is also to grant the ownership of it. For this reason, in a loan of fungibles, ownership of the thing lent passes to the borrower, as in the Roman law definition of a loan. But the usurer wishes to sell the thing and its use separately and therefore sells the same thing twice or sells something that does not exist. Gerard objects that a fungible and its use are indeed separable, if only logically, but because a fungible has a fixed and determinate value that cannot increase or decrease whatever use it is put to, the two (thing and use) have the same value and are consumed or alienated together. This is in contrast to a rentable or nonfungible thing, for which rent represents the difference between the value of the thing itself and the additional value that derives from its use. In this case, the use may be sold and ownership retained or vice versa. A usurer, then, causes a fungible to increase in value through its use, though the two share a single constant value and in so doing he acts against nature. On the significance of this argument in late medieval analyses of usury, see Langholm, *Economics in the Medieval Schools*, 559-60; and *Aristotelian Analysis*, 89-90, 124-26. See also n. 466-73.

456-58 Ex predictis ... ordinate: "The usurer uses things for a purpose different from that to which they were ordained by nature or art." Citing Aristotle's *Politics* (1.9.1257a-b), Johannes Andreae gives the examples of wine and money. The primary purpose of wine is drinking, but it may also legitimately be exchanged for money or something else. Likewise, the principal purpose of money is exchange for goods, but it may be used secondarily for exchanging currencies. But when a usurer, motivated by greed, delivers a sum of money in order to receive a greater sum in return, he violates the purpose of money.

458-60 contra ... clementinis: Ridolfi takes the citations from Johannes Calderinus' *repetitio* on X 5.19.19. In Decretum Grat. C.22 q.2 c.4, Augustine notes that language was instituted so that people might understand one another's thought, not that they might deceive one another. Therefore, to employ words for deceit is a sin. X 3.36.3 requires bishops to ensure that alms-houses and similar institutions fulfil the purposes for which they were founded and Clem. 3.11.2 extends this to the rectors of such institutions.

461-66 Quam tamen ... *fi. ca*: Johannes Calderinus notes that, according to Gratian, what is positively condemned in the scripture is thereby also contrary to natural law and proceeds to add that usury holds God, scripture and the laws in contempt: "And so from the foregoing it follows that usury is prohibited because it is vicious in itself and not vicious because it is condemned .... And this is also clear because it is prohibited in the old and new testaments .... and things so prohibited are contrary to natural law, as in Decretum Grat. D.1 dictum Grat. ante c.1 .... And on reflection, the crime of the usurer is even greater, for he shows more contempt for God than other sinners, since a man is ashamed of other sins, but not this one .... Again, the usurer abuses nature more overtly than other sinners, as was proven earlier. Again, he rejects scripture more completely than others, for if he truly believed scripture it is unlikely that he would openly and shamelessly attack it .... Again, he despises the laws, for often he perseveres in danger of death, notwithstanding the laws' prohibition .... And so, in Decretum Grat. D. 88. c. 11 *palea Eieciens* cited above, John Chysostom says that of all merchants the usurer is the most accursed" ("Ex predictis etiam sequitur quod vsura ideo prohibita quia in se vitiosa, non vitiosa quia prohibita ... Quod etiam apparet ex eo quia prohibita est ex ueteri et nouo testamento ... talia autem sic prohibita sunt contra ius naturale, ut in primo decretorum *Humanum genus* etc.... Et inspecto facto exagerandum fuit huius crimen nam vsurarius deum contemnit audacius quam alii peccatores, cum de aliis peccatis erubescat homo sed de isto minime.... Item naturam eludit expressius, ut probatum est supra. Item scripturam respuit deterius, nam si perfecte crederet scripture non est verisimile quod sit aperte et impudenter contra ipsam attemptaret ... Item iura spernit diutius, nam sepissime usque ad mortis periculum perseuerat, non obstante iurium prohibitione ... Vnde ergo dicit Iohannes Crisostimus quod vsurarius super omnes mercatores plus est maledictus in preallegata palea 88 di. *Eieciens*" [*Repetitiones*, in X 5.19.19 (MS cit. fol. 284r)]).

In his commentary on X 5.19.19, John of Legnano offers a version of the preceding argument, combined with Thomas' consumptibility argument: "Another reason [usury is condemned] is that the lender sells the use inseparable from the thing itself, for the use of money is its consumption ... therefore this contract is contrary to natural principles. The argument is confirmed because one who seeks fruit from money seeks fruit from a thing not designed to give birth ... Again, with respect to its intrinsic character, money is always of the same value, and so a sum worth twenty today is worth the same tomorrow. Therefore anyone who wants twelve for ten acts in violation of natural principles by selling the use" ("Tolle aliam rationem, quia mutuans vendit usum inseparabilem a re ipsa, quia usus pecunie est ipsius consumptio ... ergo contrahere repugnat principiis naturalibus. Confirma: querens fructum de pecunia querit fructum de re non apta ad producendum partum .... Item, pecunia, actenta bonitate intrinseca, semper est eiusdem valoris, quia tantum valent odie x. quantum cras; iste ergo qui uult xii. pro x. facit contra principium naturale valere rem, vsus vendens" [*Commentaria*, ad X 5.19.19 (MS cit. fols. 99v-100r)]).

In the second article of his *quaestio*, Gregory of Rimini argues that usury is sinful intrinsically and not simply because it is forbidden. He advances three reasons from Aristotle to prove this: (1) usury violates the principle of equality in exchange; (2) the usurer claims payment for something that is not his own, namely, the use or fruit of the principal; and (3) usury is illiberal. In support of (1), Gregory cites *Ethics* 5.4.1131b25-1132b20 to the effect that commutative justice requires an equality between things given and received in exchange. Usury violates this principle because the usurer receives not only the original sum lent but also a profit. It might be objected, however, that in the original agreement the usurer delivered not only the money but its utility and that it is for the latter that he receives an increment on the principal. One might argue, then, that the equality rule is observed only in a usurious contract and conversely that any agreement whereby the debtor repays only the principal is unjust. Gregory replies that this reasoning is both faulty and absurd, for when the debtor repays the principal he also returns the ownership of its use, so that the creditor gets back what he lent; but if the debtor is required to pay usury as well, he unjustly repays more than he received. Argument (2) is a version of Thomas' consumptibility argument: a usurer receives usury either for the principal or for the use the borrower makes of the principal. In either case, he acts unjustly by receiving what is not his own; for in a loan not only does ownership of the money pass to the borrower, but also ownership of the use, which Gregory defines in Aristotelian terms as exchange for necessities (*Politics* 1.9.1257b). The same holds true for other fungibles, whose proper use involves their consumption. Since ownership and use both pass to the borrower, the lender has no claim over them. Argument (3), Gregory notes, "proceeds from authority," for at *Ethics* 4.1.1121b, Aristotle numbers usurers among those who violate the principal of liberality–earlier defined as a mean between prodigality and meanness–because they "take from the wrong sources more than they ought."

In reply to the question of whether civil law permits usury, Baldus refers the reader to Johannes Andreae's comments on *Peccatum*, noting that "the usury prohibition is the same in every forum; for what things are by nature is the same everywhere, just as a stone everywhere falls, and fire everywhere rises and creates warmth, as Aristotle says" ("Item dic quod prohibitio vsurarum in omni foro est eadem. Nam quae naturalia sunt, in omni loco eadem sunt, sicut lapis vbique descendit et ignis vbique ascendit et calefacit, secundum Aristotelem" [*Commentaria*, in C.1.1.1, nn.36-37 (ed. cit. VI fol. 6va-b)]).

466-73 **Subtiliter ... tuum:** Gerard observes that "it is not altogether easy to assign a reason or a sufficient cause [for the usury prohibition]." But Ridolfi, along with Johannes Andreae, affirms the sufficiency of the "common opinion of the jurists," namely, that usury is forbidden because in a loan "what was mine becomes yours." The maxim is from the Roman jurists Paul (Dig. 12.1.2.2) and Gaius (Inst. 3.14.pr.) and refers to the fact that in a loan of fungibles ownership (*dominium*) passes from the lender to the creditor. This conception lies behind the gloss to Decretum Grat. C.14 q.3 c.1: "*More than*: supply, 'in things that consist in weight, number and measure.' It is otherwise in the case of a horse or a house, because there it is licit to receive both principal and interest. And this is the reason: because in the said things that consist in weight, number and measure ownership is transferred, since that is what a loan is" ("*Plus quam*: supple, quod consistit in pondere, numero et mensura, sed in equo et domo aliud est, quia ibi licitum est recipere sortem et lucrum, et est ea ratio, quia in predictis quae consistunt in pondere, numero et mensura transfertur dominium, cum illud sit mutuum" [gl. ord. ad Decretum Grat. C.14 q.3 c.1, v. *Plus quam* (ed. cit. col. 1095)]). The ownership argument also figures in Thomas' critique of usury (see n. 446-55).

473-77 **Quam ... sortem:** As reported by Johannes Andreae, Gerard objects to this argument because it can be maintained that ownership passes to the debtor only with respect to the substance of the money (or other fungible) lent, while the creditor retains ownership of the value of the principal. In response, Johannes Andreae denies that the creditor retains ownership in any form. Instead, his rights are exercised through an *actio principalis* or an *actio directa* that lies against a defaulting debtor: "You should say that here the disputant [Gerard] is mistaken, for if the debtor had a box of coins, that does not mean that the creditor is creditor of one of them; rather, he has an *actio principalis* against the debtor" ("Tu dic quod non bene aduertit hic disputans, quia si debitor haberet vnum scrinium nummorum, non est dare quod creditor vnius ex illis sit dominus; habet autem principalem actionem contra debitorem" [*Novella*, ad VI *de reg. iur.* 4. *Peccatum*, n.12 (ed. cit. fol. 63rb)]).

Moreover, risk follows ownership and therefore it is unjust to burden a debtor with charges beyond the principal. Gerard, however, also considers the criterion of risk questionable because (1) other things (for example, a horse or a boat) may be lent for a profit, though they are at the borrower's risk, and (2) it seems reasonable that in addition to assuming the risk, the debtor should pay something for the service done him by the creditor. To argument (1) Johannes Andreae replies that this reasoning confuses loans of nonfungibles–*commodatum* if gratuitous, *locatio* if there is a charge–and fungibles (*mutuum*) on precisely the point that distinguishes them, namely, risk, which does not pass to the borrower in either *commodatum* or *locatio*. To argument (2) he replies that Gerard seems here to separate the elements in a loan that he argues elsewhere are inseparable (see n. 446-55).

477-79 **Ibi omnino ... principio:** In his comments on X 5.19.19, John of Legnano notes the ownership argument and suggests a possible objection: the usury demanded in a loan does not arise from the money lent, but from an obligation to seek profit: "Again, in a loan contract one seeks profit from what is no longer one's own, which is contrary to nature. Lent money belongs to the one who accepts it, therefore [the creditor] seeks profit from something that is not his own. This reasoning can be attacked thus: [the creditor] seeks profit not from the money lent but from an obligation by which he is bound to seek his own profit. This [argument] may be dismissed because what the obligation concerns is what has been handed over and nothing else" ("Item, in contractu mutui querit quis lucrum de non suo, quod repugnat nature actus. Pecunia vero mutuata est illius qui recipit, ergo de re non sua querit aliter lucrum. Sed hec ratio calumpniatur sic, quia iste non ex mutuata pecunia, sed ex obligatione qua tenetur aliter queret sibi lucrum. Tollitur istud quia in obligatione venit quod est deductum, non aliud" [*Commentaria*, ad X 5.19.19 (MS cit. fol. 99v)]).

Baldus says that usury is prohibited because it is "a form without matter, substance or cause," arguing that since ownership of the thing lent passes to the creditor, a charge for the use of it can correspond only to a period of time, which cannot be the basis of an obligation: "First I ask why usury is prohibited? I reply that in usury there is a form without matter, substance or cause. Hence it has the form of a substance but no substance, because there is no corresponding cause. By way of demonstration, I propose several considerations. First, every payment–with the exception of a gift–must be proportionate to something. Second, when the use of a thing is transferred along with ownership in such a way that ownership must be returned, usury cannot correspond to anything but time. Third, time does not provide a proper measure, since it is common, like air and the sun. From these points it follows that the payment of usury has no cause, because an obligation cannot be founded on time alone, [as in] Dig. 44.7.44.1 ['it is accepted that an obligation until a certain date can be constituted no more than such a legacy can; for what starts as a debt to someone ceases to be a debt in definite ways only']" ("Quaero primo quare vsurae sunt prohibitae? Respondeo quia in eis est figura sine materia et sine substantia et sine causa. Vnde est ibi figura substantiae, sed non substantia, quia non est ibi congrua causa. Ad hoc ostendendum pono quasdam considerationes. Et prima consideratio, quod omnis praestatio, excepta donatione, debet proportionari ad aliquid. Secundo considero quod quando transfertur vsus rei cum dominio, ita quod dominium debet reddi, ibi vsura non potest proportionare, nisi tempore. Tertio considero quod in tempore nulla est proportio, quia est commune, sicut aer et sol. Ex his sequitur quod praestatio vsurarum non habet causam, quia in solo tempore non potest fundari obligatio, ff. *de actio. et oblig.* l. *Obligationum fere* § *Placet*" [*Commentaria*, in C. 1.1.1, nn.30-31 (ed. cit. VI fol. 6va)]).

PART 1, QUESTION 8

480 **Vtrum ... permictatur**: "Whether usury is permitted in any case."

481-84 **Ad .viii.**[m] **... canonica**: The structure of this question follows Gottofredo in noting seven titles to payment beyond the principal. Ridolfi supplements this catalogue from the list in Hostiensis' *Summa*. For a discussion of these titles, see McLaughlin, "Teaching of the Canonists," 1: 125-44; and Noonan, *Scholastic Analysis of Usury*, 100-15.

485-89 **Primus ... secunda**: The rightful owner of a pledge may recover it from an unjust possessor by withholding the fruits. For X 5.19.1, see n. 145-64. X 5.19.8 confirms ecclesiastical exemption from the general rule that the fruits of pledges must be applied to the reduction of the principal but here applies it to monastic fiefs. Ridolfi notes in Part 2, question 49 that Hostiensis approves the title for laymen as well and in question 50 that the same holds for lease-holders (*emphyteuta*) and sometimes for those who hold the usufruct of a property.

490-94 **Secundus ... questione .47.**: A guarantor who has been forced to borrow in order to cover the bad debts of another can sue to recover any usury he paid. In X 3.22.3, Master S., who guaranteed debts contracted with Bolognese merchants by Peter of Blois, the chancellor of the Archbishop of Canterbury, complains that he is being harassed by the creditors for repayment of principal and usuries. Lucius III (1181-85) orders Peter to release his guarantor from his obligation and indemnify him for his losses.

The principle, however, was questioned on the grounds that a debtor should not be held liable for damages arising from an illicit contract, such as usury, which was entered into by his guarantor (see McLaughlin, "Teaching of the Canonists," 1: 131). In his *quaestio disputata* on the rule *Damnum*, Johannes Andreae surveys the opinions on whether this rule holds without exception. Ridolfi summarizes his conclusions in Part 2, question 47 as follows. (1) A guarantor may not demand from his debtor usury that he has paid to a third party nor any other thing that is not owed if the debtor is unaware of the guarantor's undertaking to the third party; (2) nor may he demand usury from a debtor who is aware of, but has not consented to, such an arrangement; nor (3) from a debtor who is aware and consents to, but has not mandated, the arrangement; nor (4) from a debtor who has mandated with regard only to the principal; nor (5) from a debtor who has given him a general mandate, since a general mandate cannot include something that is not owed (such as usury). (6) But a creditor may demand usury from a debtor who has mandated with respect to usury, albeit under another legitimate title, such as *mora* (7); likewise if the debtor has explicitly sworn an oath to pay any such usuries; or (8) if he has sworn to indemnify the guarantor for his damages; but not (9), even though the debtor mandated for usury, unless he swore an oath to pay usury or to indemnify the guarantor; nor (10) if usury was paid by the guarantor through some error. Fraud invalidates any case in which a guarantor could otherwise legitimately seek usury from his debtor (11). In any case in which a guarantor cannot recover usury from his creditor (12).

495-97 .3.us casus ... *legibus*: The title to "canonical usury" is based on Decretum Grat. C.12 q.2 c.10, a spurious addition to a letter of Pope Eusebius (d. 310) ordering those who steal ecclesiastical offerings to make a fourfold restitution.

498-504 .4.us ... *oblitus*: "'Usury' may be sought as interest (*interesse*), for example, in contracts of good faith, where it is not really usury but the difference [between what the creditor has lost and what he would have gained] had there been no delay in repayment." The *locus classicus* for the distinction between usury and interest as compensation for damages sustained by a party to a contract is Dig. 17.2.60: "According to Labeo, where a partner delays paying in profits made in the partnership business and spends the money on his own account, he obliged to pay interest as well; not technically as interest but as compensation for the interest not received through delay." Interest is sought in contracts of good faith, that is, in "real" contracts (*intra rem*) such as *commodatum*, the gratuitous loan of a nonfungible, deposit and pledge, which involve delivery of a thing, and in purely consensual contracts, such as purchase-sale, lease and partnership. Interest here does not represent profit but damages. Hence, in Dig. 19.1.21.3, a seller who is late delivering a good is not liable for the buyer's opportunity costs, but only for the value of the thing sold: "When the seller is responsible for nondelivery of an object, every benefit to the buyer is taken into account provided that it stands in close connection with this matter. If he could have completed a deal and made a profit from wine, this should not be reckoned in, no more than if he buys wheat and his household suffers from starvation because it was not delivered; he receives the price of the grain, not the price of slaves killed by starvation. An obligation does not increase because it is carried out slowly, although it would grow greater if wine were worth more today, and rightly so; for if the wine had been delivered, I as buyer would have it, and if not, that which should have been delivered previously is due now." However, "increments must be received with caution" lest they involve some form of dishonest gain, which is condemned at Decretum Grat. C.14 q.4 c.4, where clerics are forbidden to engage in lending or trade for profit.

504-19 **Ad predicta ... questione .119.**: C. 4.32.15 permits a creditor to impose a penalty of four times the principal of a loan, provided the value of the penalty does not exceed the legal rate of usury. In the gloss to this rescript, Accursius (d. 1263) rejects both the size of the penalty and the concept of legal usury on the grounds of fraud, while allowing genuine compensatory interest in delay: "condemnabo in tantam quantitatem nomine poenae, quanta est legitima usura, quod non placet; quia sic semper posset quis stipulari nomine poenae etiam vsuram ... dic ergo quantum interest" (gl. ord. ad C. 4.32.15, v. *Vltra* [ed. cit. col. 959]). Accursius' comments, however, raise a further problem: though a real contract, loan is not classed among contracts of good faith, but rather among contracts of strict law (*contractus stricti iuris*), in which a judge may consider only the terms of the contract and not issues of equity. In the case of loans, *interesse* is *extra rem*. Does the gloss then mean that interest may be sought in any contract whatsoever, whether of good faith or strict law? According to Bartolus and Baldus, interest in a money loan can be sought only if there is a formal agreement, for, as Bartolus notes, "in nummis non venit intrinsecum interesse, ideo venit extrinsecum" (*Commentaria*, in Dig. 45.1.68, n.2 [ed. cit. VI fol. 24rb]). Baldus writes: "I ask: to what extent may interest be sought? The gloss replies that it may be sought in any contract ... But against this oppose the fact that this interest is *extra rem*, which should not be considered ... for it is one thing in things, another in money, to which interest does not attach except *extra rem* and therefore it may be sought on the basis of an agreement" ("Sed quero an quatenus interesse possit peti. Respondit glosa quod sic in quocunque contractu ... Sed contra hoc oppone quia istud est interesse extra rem, quod non debet considerari ... aliud est in rebus, aliud in pecunia, in qua non cadit nisi interesse extra rem et ideo peti potest ex conuentione" [*Commentaria*, in C. 4.32.15, n.26 (ed. cit. VII fol. 90ra)]). This said, however, the conditions governing interest in contracts of good faith apply in contracts of strict law, that is, the interest must not be a form of profit, but a way to avoid damages arising from the debtor's failure to repay. Hence, at X 2.25.6, the gloss notes that "usury in delay does not enter into a contract of strict law unless it has been specifically promised" ("non veniunt vsurae ex mora in contractibus stricti iuris nisi specialiter sint promissae" [gl. ord. ad X 2.25.6, v. *Bona fidei* (ed. cit. col. 841)]). Or, as Baldus puts it in his comments on C. 4.32.19, we can say that conventional and legitimate interest enters every contract, if we assume an agreement to that effect; but if there is no agreement, then it can be sought only in contracts of good faith.

520-22 **Quintus ... tangetur**: In a contract of lease or hire, something may legitimately be received beyond the principal (because ownership and risk do not pass to the lessee).

523 **.vi.us ...** ***ciuitate***: In a credit sale, the vendor may charge more than a good is currently worth on the market if there is real uncertainty about the value of the good in the future, when payment will be made. On X 5.19.6, see n. 145-64.

524-32 **.vii.us ...** ***usuris***: X 5.19.16, a decretal of Innocent III (1198-1216), states that in the case of an unpaid dowry, a son-in-law is not bound to apply the fruits of land pledged by his father-in-law towards the reduction of the balance owing on the dowry. The reason is that the revenue of the dowry itself is often insufficient to sustain the burdens (*onera*) of matrimony. The opinions are reviewed in Part 2, questions 51-54.

Apart from the exceptions noted here and in n. 145-64, the fruits of pledges must be applied to the reduction of the principal. The gloss to X 5.19.1 defines fruits as what remains after the creditor has deducted reasonable expenses incurred in reaping them: "expensae istae non debent esse superfluae ... et illae tantum sunt deducendae quae in ipsam rem necessario factae sunt et pro fructibus colligendis" (gl. ord. ad X 5.19.1, v. *Deductis expensis* [ed. cit. col. 1733]). But it is conceivable that a creditor might manage the pledge in such a way that there are never any fruits surplus to his deductions. Should fruits then be calculated with respect to the amount the pledge would yield if honestly managed rather than with respect to the amounts actually received by the creditor? In his comments on X 5.19.1, Johannes Andreae notes the opinion of Hostiensis that the creditor is not held to potential fruits if he does not cultivate a pledge of land, unless he can be shown to be acting in bad faith. Fraud may be presumed and potential fruits calculated if he does not lease out the pledge, though he would normally do so, and likewise, even if he is accustomed to let his land to others, if there is a tenant prepared to lease the pledge.

533-38 Ostiensis uero ... i. questione: In his discussion of the "exceptions" to the usury prohibition in his *Summa*, Hostiensis notes that as a rule a lender may not exact anything in excess of the principal, but that this generalization does not hold in thirteen cases, twelve of which he summarizes in hexameters:

> Feuda, fideiussor, pro dote, stipendia cleri,
> Venditio fructus, cui uelle iure nocere,
> Vendens sub dubio, precium post tempora soluens,
> Poena nec in fraudem, lex commissoria, gratis
> dans, socii pompa: plus sorte modis datur istis.
> (*Summa*, X 5.19, *de usuris*, n.7 [ed. cit. col. 1623]).

The thirteenth case is that of labour expended by the lender in connection with the loan. Three of these Hostiensis does not regard as loans in the strict sense. In *socii pompa*, a fungible, usually coin, is leased for purposes of display (*ad pompam*). Since ownership does not pass to the lessee, this is a lease contract, not a loan. In the case of *venditio fructus*, the revenues of a portion of land are sold and although the purchaser might receive more in revenues than he paid, the element of uncertainty makes this a legitimate contract of sale. By the *lex commissaria*, a seller retains the right to regain possession by refunding the price within a certain period; meanwhile, the purchaser enjoys the revenues deriving from the thing sold. Provided the contract does not conceal a loan on security, it is legitimate. Of the remaining titles in Hostiensis' list, those not cited in the list of Gottofredo reproduced by Ridolfi are *cui uelle iure nocere, precium post tempora soluens* and *gratis dans*. The first derives from a passage of Ambrose included in the Decretum to the effect that usury may be required of anyone you are permitted to harm with arms: "ubi ius belli, ibi ius usurae" (C.14 q.4 c.12). Hostiensis nevertheless notes with approval the gloss to this canon that says that since you should not want to harm anybody, so you ought not to demand usury of anybody (gl. ord. ad Decretum Grat. C.14 q.4

c.12, v. *Cui* [ed. cit. col. 1099]; *Summa*, X 5.19 *de usuris*, n.8 [ed. cit. col. 1622]). The second case is that of a buyer who fails to make payment by the agreed date; the seller may then claim damages (*interesse*) incurred through the purchaser's breach of contract. *Gratis dans* refers to the principle whereby a debtor may freely offer a gift to his creditor. There must be no agreement to this effect and the gift must not constitute the creditor's primary motive for extending the loan in the first place (*Summa*, X 5.19 *de usuris*, n.7 [ed. cit. cols. 1620-21]). The glosses to Decretum Grat. dictum Grat. ante C.14 q.3 c.1 and to X 5.19.8 offer broadly the same categories as Hostiensis and Gottofredo do.

In addition to the cases noted by Hostiensis and Gottofredo, Baldus discusses the extrinsic titles *damnum emergens* and *lucrum cessans*. With respect to *damnum emergens*, loss sustained by the lender as a result of lending, he maintains that if the loss is real the creditor may claim damages, though he hesitates to permit provision for loss from the beginning of the contract: "Moreover, usury is sought for *damnum emergens* and may be so sought provided emergent damages can be proved; they may not be sought under this title, but under the title of interest ... For such interest will not be proved by means of an agreement, for example, if something was promised under the title of agreed interest if the principal was not paid. For future things could not be appraised from the beginning [of the contract] because they did not yet have a definite quantity or nature" ("Item petuntur vt damnum emergens, tunc possunt peti, dummodo probetur emergentia damni; nec petantur sub suo nomine, sed sub nomine interesse ... Non enim probabitur istud interesse per pactum, verbi gratia, si aliquid est promissum nomine interesse conuenti, si non soluatur sors. Futura enim non potuerunt a principio taxari, quia non habuerunt certam quantitatem vel naturam" [*Commentaria*, in C. 1.1.1, nn.31-32 (ed. cit. VI fol. 6va)]). He notes that *lucrum cessans*, potential profit foregone by the lender, is generally disapproved: "Sometimes usury is sought under the pretense of interest for profit foregone, though usually this is illicit, according to those who say that interest is not considered in profit" ("Interdum vsurae petuntur praetenso interesse lucri cessantis, tunc regulariter non possunt peti secundum illos, qui dicunt quod interesse non consideratur in lucro" [ibid. n.32]). See also Introduction, pp. 63-65.

538-46 Sed rectius ... uide: In article 4 of his *quaestio* on *Peccatum*, Johannes Andreae, following Gerard of Siena, replies to the argument that usury is permissible because both canon and civil law allow something to be received beyond the principal in certain cases, such as that of dotal pledges (see n. 524-32). Civil law, of course, allows usury in most cases, but in this respect it has been overridden by divine and canon law, which permit it in no case. The "exceptions" in canon law are only apparent (*prima facie*) and therefore it is accurate to say that usury is never permitted. The same observation is made by Hostiensis and Goffredo.

547-55 Et in articulo ... uide: In article 3 of his *quaestio* on *Peccatum*, Johannes Andreae discusses whether usury is permissible in terms of the end sought, namely, the attainment of some good or the avoidance of some evil. Permission can be conceded in three ways: (1) by simply setting aside the penalty for an illegal act; (2) by removing impediments to the performance of the act; or (3) by actively assisting in the performance of the act. An evil may be tolerated for the sake of a good that will result or in order to avoid a greater evil. In the latter case, a corporeal evil may be tolerated to avoid a spiritual (and by definition greater) evil, a lesser spiritual evil to avoid a greater spiritual one or a lesser corporeal evil to avoid a greater corporeal one. Considering the three types of law, natural, civil and canon, in the light of these categories, it is clear that natural law can never tolerate usury, because it is by nature vicious and therefore contrary to natural law (see nn. 420-38 to 461-66). Civil law can and does permit usury by imposing no penalties on usurers (the first mode of permission). Canon law, however, forbids usury absolutely and allows no extrinsic considerations to override this prohibition. Therefore, it is forbidden to engage in usury even to redeem captives from the Saracens (X 5.19.4; see n. 583-94). Indeed, it cannot be argued that a greater evil can be avoided through usury, for usury is, after a fashion, the greatest of evils, since it shows contempt for God, nature, scripture and law. He concludes: "for all these reasons I conclude that canon law can in no way concede or permit a usurious contract in order to avoid a greater evil, because, generally speaking, there does not appear to be a greater evil that could be avoided by usury" ("propter quae omnia concludo quod ius canonicum nullo modo debet concedere vel permittere contractum vsurarium propter maius malum vitandum, quia regulariter loquendo non apparet aliquod maius in ipso, quod per ipsum valeat euitari" [*Novella*, ad VI *de reg. iur.* 4, *Peccatum*, n.22 (ed. cit. fol. 64va)]).

556-61 Tractat ... preteribo: In article 5 of his *quaestio* on *Peccatum*, Johannes Andreae examines the apparent contradiction between civil and canon law on usury. He first draws a distinction between a prohibition in natural law and a prohibition in positive law. Natural law prohibits a vice simply by recognizing it as such, positive law by means of a threat to punish. Secondly, although the two kinds of positive law, canon and civil, are both founded on natural law and both exist to foster the common good, they do so in different ways. Civil law promotes the common good of civil society (*societas civiliter vivens*) through legal justice and civic harmony (*amicitia civilis*); canon law the common good of the community of the faithful (*societas regulariter secundum fidem in Deum tendens*) through heavenly friendship (*amicitia coelestis*). Something prohibited in natural law may be permitted in civil law because of the different modes of prohibition, the latter omitting to threaten a penalty. Something permitted in civil law may be forbidden in canon law because of the divergent objectives of the two systems. The good of civil society, for example, is better served by the promotion of civic harmony than by strict adherence to legal justice, which, in certain matters, civil law prefers to leave to divine judgement. Usury, though forbidden by natural law, is not an impediment to civil society and therefore civil law declines to threaten penalties. The object of canon law, on the other hand, is to guide people to God. This cannot be done without charity; mortal sin is a violation of charity and therefore forbidden. Usury is sinful in itself and therefore the canons condemn it as an impediment to the common good of the faithful. On the subject of usury, then, civil law is not opposed to canon law; it merely omits to prohibit something whose prohibition properly falls within the sphere of canon law. It would be otherwise if civil law flatly contradicted canon law by removing impediments to usury or promoting its exercise (the second and third modes of permission noted in article 3; see n. 547-55). In that case, the civil law would be void. But this does not appear to be the case, since Justinian, who compiled and promulgated the corpus of civil law, prescribed adherence to the first four general councils of the church (Nov. 131), including the council of Nicea, which forbade usury.

In his comments on the rubric to the title *de usuris* in the *Decretals*, Johannes Andreae cites Innocent IV's remarks more fully than Ridolfi does, particularly Innocent's suggestion that usury might be justifiable in terms of natural law: "Therefore usury, from which almost every evil arises, is generally prohibited. For even if a case could be found where, by natural law, which nature has implanted in men, usury was not a sin, nevertheless, on account of all the evils that flow from it, it is forbidden in every case, although some will deny this, saying, perhaps rightly, that a case cannot be found in which even by the instinct of nature it is not forbidden" ("Generaliter ergo prohibeatur, ex qua fere omnia mala prouenirent. Nam etsi inueniri posset casus quo iure naturali, quod natura homini indidit, usura non esset peccatum, tamen propter multorum malorum sequelam omni casu est prohibita, licet quidam id negent, et forte non male, secundum eum, dicentes non esse reperiri casum, quo et instinctu naturae non prohibeatur" [*Novella*, ad X 5.19 rubr., n.2 (ed. cit V fol. 72ra)]). He then refers the reader to his discussion of usury as naturally vicious in the *quaestio* on *Peccatum*. The comments of John of Legnano on X 5.19.19 derive from those of Johannes Andreae.

On the relationship between Innocent's social critique of usury and the natural law argument in the fourteenth century, see n. 377-96; on this passage in particular, see Spicciani, *Capitale e interesse*, 68.

PART 1, QUESTION 9

562 **Vtrum ... peccatum:** "Is it a sin to accept a loan at usury?" That is, does a borrower sin by implicating his creditor in the vice of receiving something beyond the principal?

563-74 **Ad nonum ... mortaliter:** Guido de Baysio treats this question in his comments on Decretum Grat. C.22 q.1 c.16, itself a passage from Augustine on the validity of oaths sworn by false gods, the principle being that you may legitimately benefit from the false belief of another and, by extension, from his sin, provided you are not the cause of either. Applying this principle to the case of usury, Guido, on the authority of Huguccio and Thomas Aquinas, concludes that it is not a sin to borrow at usury. Thomas' argument is found in *Summa theologiae*, secunda secundae, q. 78, art. 4: although no one is permitted to induce another to commit the sin of usury, you may borrow from one who is accustomed to lending at usury if some good is served, such as the relief of your own necessity or that of another. Likewise, one who falls among thieves does not sin if, under threat of death, he hands over his goods, though the thieves sin by taking them. The example from Jeremiah suggests that the need must be pressing and real: "[When they came into the city, Ishmael ... and the men with him slew them, and cast them into a cistern. But there were ten men among them who said to Ishmael,] 'Do not kill us, for we have stores of wheat, barley, oil and honey hidden in the fields'" (*Ier* 41.7-8).

575-82 **Sed Bernardus ... animo:** In his commentary on Decretum Grat. C.14

q.4 c.10, Guido cites the opinion of Bernardus Compostellanus Antiquus (fl. ca. 1210) that he who borrows at usury either causes the lender to sin or at least provides an occasion for him to sin. In the latter case–if, for example, the creditor already intends to lend at usury–the borrower is not guilty of sin, but if the borrower's request induces someone who would not otherwise lend at usury to do so, the borrower himself sins. Decretum Grat. C.22 q.1 c.16 (see n. 567-75), C.23 q.5 c.8 and c. 19 provide analogies. According to Augustine in the second canon, it is not a sin to kill in the course of your duty or by accident: "God forbid that something which we do or intend for good and licit reasons should be imputed to us as a fault if as a result of it some ill should befall someone against our will" ("Absit, ut ea, que propter bonum ac licitum facimus aut habemus, si quid per hec preter nostram uoluntatem cuiquam mali acciderit, nobis imputetur"). In Decretum Grat. C.23 q.5 c.19, Jerome argues that sometimes one who creates the conditions for a death is more culpable than he who actually kills, and so we must distinguish between murder, judicial execution and killing in self-defence: "When a man kills a man, it is very different whether the killing arises from a desire to harm or to steal something (such as an enemy or a thief does), or in the order of punishment or obedience (such as a judge or an executioner) or from the need to escape or give aid, as a traveler kills a highwayman or a soldier an enemy" ("Cum homo ab homine occiditur, multum distat, utrum fiat nocendi cupiditate uel iniuste aliquid auferendi [sicut fit ab inimico, sicut a latrone], an ulciscendi uel obediendi ordine [sicut a iudice, sicut a carnifice], uel euadendi uel subueniendi necessitate, sicut interimitur latro a viatore, hostis a milite").

583-631 Iohannes ... maius: This passage is closely modelled on Johannes Andreae's review of the opinions in his *Novella* on X 5.19.4.

583-94 Iohannes ... *Dilectus* .i.: X 5.19.4 is a decretal addressed to the Archbishop of Palermo by Alexander III forbidding anyone to borrow at usury in order to redeem captives from the Saracens: since scripture forbids Christians to lie on behalf of others, much more does it forbid them to be involved in the crime of usury ("quum scriptura sacra prohibeat pro alterius vita mentiri, multo magis prohibendus est quis, ne etiam pro redimenda vita captivi usurarum crimine involvatur"). In his comments, Johannes Andreae notes that on the basis of this text, particularly the expression *involvatur*, many regard borrowing at usury to be as sinful as lending, for if there were no borrowers, there would be no lenders, and he who gives occasion for injury would appear to have given the injury itself (X 5.36.9). He rejects this reading, however, in his comments on X 5.3.8 (see n. 310-17), as does Hostiensis in his remarks on X 5.19.4, as too rigid. Hostiensis adds that if it were correct, oaths would not be binding in usurious contracts, whereas they are according to X 2.24.1, which requires creditors to release debtors from their sworn obligations (the creditors' right to impose such oaths is not questioned), and according to X 2.24.6 (see n. 74-78).

In a *quaestio* on the title *de iureiurando*, Damasus (fl. 1217) concludes that it is not a sin to pay usury because the debtor is in the position of one who pays to be free of vexation: "Solution: say that it is not a sin to pay usury, although some say otherwise, for if you usurp my right and do not permit me to enjoy it unless I give you something, by giving I do not sin, but you sin by receiving, [as in] X 5.3.28"

("Solutio: dic quod non est peccatum soluere usuras, licet quidam aliter dixerunt, si enim inuadas ius meum et non aliter permittas me uti eo nisi dare tibi aliud, ego quidem dando non pecco, tu autem recipiendo peccas, extra *de symo. Dilecti* in .i[i]." [*Quaestiones, de iureiurando* (MS cit. fol. 30rb)]).

X 5.3.28 deals with the case of the prior of Pontefract who bribed the archdeacon of York to stop obstructing his right to fill certain benefices. Since the archdeacon continues as before, Celestine III (1191-98) orders that he repay the sum. The gloss notes that this decretal allows you to buy off ill-treatment ("Nota: per hanc decretalem quod licitum est alicui redimere vexationem suam" [gl. ord. ad X 5.3.28, casus (ed. cit. col. 1624)]) and adds later that "the same should be said of an unjustly interdicted benefice or office and an unjust excommunication, namely, that he who pays for the return of his office or benefice or for the lifting of the excommunication does not commit simony, though he who accepts the payment does. He who pays acquires no right, but pays simply to retain or redeem a right previously obtained, which is licit" ("Idem dicendum est de beneficio vel officio iniuste interdicto et excommunicatione iniusta: scilicet quod non committit simoniam qui dat pro sua restitutione officii vel beneficii, vel absolutione excommunicationis, vel interdicti; sed ille qui recipit simoniam committit. Qui dat nullum ius acquirit, sed dat vt ius acquisitum retineat vel redimat, quod licitum est" [ibid., v. *Restituere quod accepit* (ed. cit. col. 1624)]).

595-633 **Innocentius ... questione**: A paraphrase of Johannes Andreae's summary of Innocent IV's comments on X 5.19.4. The argument goes as follows: some say that you may borrow at usury to perform a good work but not for dissipation. Others maintain that the good that will follow from borrowing at usury must be weighed against the good that will follow from not borrowing. If a genuine good will follow, such as feeding the poor or building a church, and no good will come from denying the lender an occasion to sin–because he is prepared to lend and there are others prepared to borrow–then a greater good is accomplished by borrowing than by not borrowing. Indeed, in such circumstances, you may even solicit the loan because although a usurer always sins when he lends at usury, he sins less when he lends in a good cause. But if the usurer no longer wishes to lend or if he no longer has any customers, you should abstain, for in this case a greater good would follow from not borrowing than from borrowing. A third position is that if a usurer is prepared to lend and there are others who wish to borrow, you are free to borrow for any purpose except one that is itself sinful. Nevertheless, given a choice between two evils, you should choose the lesser. And so, in a time of dearth it is less sinful for a lender to charge for his money or goods than for him to hide them. John of Legnano rehearses Innocent's analysis in his comments on X 5.19.5.

Johannes Andreae also discusses whether usury is permissible because of the end sought in his *quaestio* on *Peccatum* (see n. 547-55).

PART 1, QUESTION 10

634-35 **Vtrum ... fenerari**: "Whether one can be dispensed from the sin of lending at usury."

636-38 **Ad decimum ...** ***Super eo***: The terms of X 5.19.4 seem to preclude the possibility of dispensing a usurer from sin: "super hoc dispensationem aliquam posse fieri non videmus."

638-40 **Iohannes ... questione .55.**: In his comments on X 5.19.4, Johannes Andreae notes that an exception to this principle is the case of usury exacted from an enemy, at least according to one interpretation of Decretum Grat. C.14 q.4 c.12 (see n. 533-38). Part 2, question 55 reviews the opinions on this question.

640-43 **Sed in ... meus**: X 5.19.7 lays down penalties for non-repentant usurers: suspension and deposition from office for clerics and excommunication for laymen until restitution has been made. The gloss adds that the bishop at his discretion may dispense from these penalties: "Can a bishop dispense from such penalties? I say that he can after satisfaction and penance, because this is not prohibited and is in fact proved by this decretal. In the past it was said that such cases should be sent to the pope; therefore conclude that bishops may deal mercifully with such people" ("Sed nunquid episcopus potest cum tali dispensare? Dico quod sic, post satisfactionem et poenitentiam, quia hoc non prohibetur, et hoc probatur per hanc decretalem. In antiqua dicebatur quod ad praesentiam papae tales mittantur; vnde collige quod episcopi cum talibus misericorditer agere possunt" [gl. ord. ad X 5.19.7, v. *Suspendas* (ed. cit. col. 1737)]). Gottofredo and John of Legnano make the same observation.

643-46 **Et uide ... questionis**: Decretum Grat. C.14 q.5. c.15, an extract from a letter of Augustine, states that he who violently extorts something from another must make restitution: "We are of the view that, following the example of Zacheus the publican, he who, contrary to the law of human society, takes something by theft, rapine, deceit, seizure or usurpation is obliged to restore it rather than confer it as a gift" ("Qui uero contra ius societatis humanae furtis, rapinis, calumpniis, obpressionibus, inuasionibus aliqua abstulerit, reddenda potius quam donanda censemus, Zachei publicani exemplo"). Commenting on this passage, Guido de Baysio notes that in matters that are mortally sinful according to divine law, such as theft and rapine, no bishop, not even the pope, can dispense from penance and restitution; in things that are mortally sinful by positive law no one inferior to the pope can dispense without his permission: "Note that Hostiensis said that in matters in which divine law says there is mortal sin, such as theft and rapine, ... a bishop, even the pope, cannot dispense from penance and restitution, as some say. But in matters in which positive law says there is mortal sin, dispensation is forbidden to bishops or inferiors of the pope: none can dispense [from restitution] or penance except the pope alone or one whom he has especially empowered" ("Et nota quod Hostiensis dicebat quod in his in quibus est mortale peccatum secundum legem diuinam, vt in furto et rapina ... dispensare non potest episcopus, nec etiam papa, vt aliqui dicunt, quominus penitentiam agat et restitutio fiat. ... In his vero in quibus mortale peccatum est secundum ius positiuum, et est episcopis siue inferioribus pape interdicta dispensatio nullus dispensare vel penitentiam prestare potest, nisi solus papa vel is cui papa specialiter commiserit" [*Rosarium*, ad Decretum Grat. C.14 q.5. c.15, n.4 (ed. cit. fol. 209va)]). For the comments of Johannes Andreae in article 3 of the *questio* on *Peccatum*, see n. 547-55.

PART 1, QUESTION 11

647 Quomodo ... detegatur: "How a usurer may be detected."

648-50 Ad undecimum ... remissionibus: Hostiensis says that a usurious contract may be detected in the external forum by means of witnesses and evidence. If, for example, it can be established before a judge by reliable testimony that a creditor, having refused a loan, preferred to buy property from his debtor with a provision that the latter might repurchase it at the end of a certain period, the creditor can be condemned as a usurer, since the transaction is a loan on security rather than a real sale, as in X 3.17.5 (see n. 650-52). Again, if the terms of the contract are weighted unfairly in favour of a creditor who is a notorious usurer, usury may be presumed, as in X 3.21.4 (see n. 770-76). Penalties can be proof of a usurious contract, particularly if the creditor is a notorious usurer: "You should know that a penalty pegged to a specific quantity creates a presumption of usury ... It is otherwise if it is attached to a specific thing or a deed, assuming, of course, that this is done by one who is not a usurer" ("Ut tamen scias, poenam in quantitate appositam praesumptionem vsurae inducere ... secus si speciei uel facto apponatur, subaudi ab illo qui non est usurarius" [*Summa*, X 5.19 *de usuris*, n.9 (ed. cit. col. 1628)]).

650-52 et per ea ... *diocesi*: X 3.17.5 describes a contract of sale in which the buyer agrees to resell to the seller in seven to nine years at barely half the original price; meanwhile the buyer enjoys the fruits. Innocent III declares the transaction a loan on security rather than a sale. The gloss notes that the smallness of the resale price creates a presumption of fraud. For X 3.21.4, see n. 770-76. The gloss remarks that "from the quality of the person a contract may be presumed in fraud of usury" or if the penalty exceeds the "normal rate of usury" as defined by Roman law: "ita ex qualitate personae praesumitur talis contractus in fraudem vsurarum factus. Idem potest dici in contractu vbi poena apponitur quae excedit legitimum modum vsurarum" (gl. ord. ad X 3.21.4, v. *Consueuerit* [ed. cit. col. 1144]). For X 2.24.32, see n. 994-97. The gloss observes that reputation alone is insufficient to prove fraud but is valid in combination with other proofs: "Et ita patet quod qualitercumque aliquid sit diuulgatum per famam, seu quasi notorium, non sufficit ad probationem ... sed cum aliis adminiculis sufficit" (gl. ord. ad X 2.24.32, v. *Ex fama* [ed. cit. col. 829]). X 5.19.15 suggests that a church court may prosecute manifest usurers even in the absence of formal accusations: "Since there are doubtless many usurers, indeed manifest usurers, in your diocese against whom no accuser has come forward ... we reply to your fraternity that, although no accuser has come forward, if it can be established by other proofs that they are manifest usurers, you may freely impose on them the punishment of usurers published in the Lateran Council" ("Quum in diocesi tua sint quam plurimi usurarii, de quibus minime dubitatur, quin sint usurarii manifesti, contra quos ... nullus accusator apparet ... Fraternitati tuae taliter respondemus, quod, licet contra eos non appareat accusator, si tamen aliis argumentis illos constiterit esse usurarios manifestos, in eos poenam in Lateranensi concilio contra usurarios editam libere poteris exercere"). The gloss notes that reputation alone is usually insufficient to prove usury: "If you understand 'manifest' as 'notorious,' there is no need for other evidence ... But if you mean manifest but not notorious, according to this decretal clear proof is needed for due process ... To this it could be said that 'notorious' does not possess the solidity of fact and so certain proofs are also necessary. Or say that established reputation shows that they are usurers and therefore through reputation and other proofs they are punished, because reputation alone is insufficient to convict" ("Si intelligas manifestos, id est, notorios, non est opus aliis argumentis.... Si autem loquitur de manifestis non notoriis, secundum hoc euidens probatio requiritur secundum iuris ordinem .... Ad hoc posset dici, quod illud notorium non habet facti perseuerantiam, vnde aliqua requiruntur argumenta. Vel dic quod solemnis fama docet ipsos esse vsurarios et ideo per famam et alia argumenta puniuntur, quia sola fama non sufficit ad condemnationem" [gl. ord. ad X 5.19.15, v. *Manifestos* (ed. cit. col. 1742)]).

652-54 **et per Baldum ... nigro**: In his commentary on C. 4.32.15, Baldus reviews Hostiensis and adds a number of illustrations, particularly of fraudulent penal clauses. He adds that to prove an agreement usurious "it is sufficient to show that it was thus previously agreed by the parties, even though the notary and legal witnesses of the act know nothing about it; if it can be proved by other witnesses [this is enough], as Innocent elegantly argues at X 3.16.1, which he understands to mean when it was previously agreed with a firm intention; it is otherwise if it was just considered, for many things are considered but not done" ("Scias etiam quod ad probandum contractum feneratitium sufficit probare quod ita erat preordinatum a partibus, licet tabellio et testes instrumentarii de hoc nihil sciant, si probatur per aliquos testes, ut eleganter ponit Innocentius in dicta c. *Gravis*, quod intelligit quando erat preordinatum sic firmando, secus si solummodo fit ratiocinando, quia multa dicuntur quae non fiunt" [*Commentaria*, in C. 4.32.15, n.12 (ed. cit. VI fol. 89va)]).

PART 1, QUESTION 12

655 **Que sit eorum pena**: "What penalties usurers are subject to."

On juristic opinion in general, see McLaughlin, "Teaching of the Canonists," 2: 1-22. On enforcement, see Helmholz, "Usury and the Medieval English Church Courts," 364-80.

656-59 **Ad duodecimum ...** ***pena***: Gottofredo and Hostiensis note that manifest usurers are subject to the triple penalty imposed by III Lateran of (1) exclusion from sacramental communion, (2) refusal of their pious offerings and (3) denial of burial: "usurarii manifesti nec ad communionem altaris admittuntur, nec Christianam, si in hoc peccato decesserint, accipiunt sepulturam, sed nec uiuorum oblationes recipi debent" (Hostiensis, *summa*, X 5.19 *de usuris*, n.10 [ed. cit. col. 1628]). Clerics who receive the offerings of usurers are suspended. The objective of these penalties is to compel the usurer to make restitution. Hostiensis adds that a usurer is "manifest" or "notorious" by the publicity of his activities: "he is a usurer who maintains a table ready for lending money at usury to all comers" ("qui usurarius mensam tenet paratam ad pecuniam mutuandam cuilibet sub usuris" [ibid.])–in which case he incurs the penalties automatically–or "by law" (*notorius iuris*), for example, through the publication of his name in church by the bishop or because he has confessed to or been convicted of usury through the testimony of witnesses. The church may denounce a usurer even when no accuser is prepared to come forward or sue for restitution.

Both jurists note that some penalties may be imposed only by a court. Hostiensis says that in the case of a cleric guilty of usury, he will first be suspended from his office and benefice and then, if he persists, degraded. A layman will be subjected to the penalties listed above and if he persists, subjected to full excommunication from the community.

Heirs of usurers are obligated to make restitution and if they fail to do so are subject to the same penalties as the testator. This rule applies to heirs unrelated to the deceased as well as to direct heirs, since, for purposes of restitution, the estate of a usurer is regarded as a single thing owed to his debtors.

660-64 **Additur ... occurret**: VI 5.5.2, a decree of II Lyons, renders void the testaments of manifest usurers who fail to make provision for full restitution and denies them burial: "Even though notorious usurers have made definite or general provision in their wills regarding restitution in the matter of illegally charged interest, church burial shall nevertheless be denied them till full satisfaction has been made to those to whom it is due, if they are available; in the case of absence, to those who are authorized to act for them. If these are also absent, it is to be made to the ordinary of the locality, or to his vicar, or to the testator's parish priest, in the presence of witnesses residing in that parish (in this case the ordinary, vicar and rector may by the authority of this constitution receive in their name and in the presence of witnesses a pledge on which legal action may be based), or at the request of the ordinary a pledge concerning the restitution to be made may be given to a competent notary. If the amount of usury received is known, this is always to be expressed in the aforesaid pledge, otherwise the amount is to be determined by him who receives the pledge. However, he may not knowingly fix this amount at a lower figure than what he believes to be the correct one, otherwise he shall be bound to make satisfaction for the remainder. All religious and others who dare in contravention of this constitution to admit notorious usurers to ecclesiastical burial, we decree that they incur the penalty prescribed by the Lateran Council against usurers. No one may witness the wills of notorious usurers, and no one may hear their confession or give them absolution, unless they make full restitution or give a satisfactory pledge to that effect, in so far as their resources permit. Wills of notorious usurers that do not follow this injunction are *ipso iure* invalid" (trans. Gilchrist, *Economic Activity*, 195-96, appendix). Clem. 3.7.1, a decree of the Council of Vienne, imposes automatic excommunication on clerics who bury public usurers: "Eos, qui ... usurarios manifestos scienter sepelire praesumunt, decernimus ipso facto excommunicationis sententiae subiacere." Another decree of II Lyons (=VI 5.5.1) is designed to make it impossible for usurers to do business: "Desiring to check the canker of usury which devours souls and exhausts resources, we command that the constitution of the Lateran Council against usurers be inviolably observed under threat of divine malediction. And since the fewer the opportunities given to usurers the more easily will the practice of usury be destroyed, we decree by this constitution that no community or association, nor any individual, whatever their office, rank or status, shall permit strangers and non-residents of their estates, who publicly practise or wish to practise usury, to rent offices for this purpose on their territory or to retain those that they already have, or permit them to dwell elsewhere, but they shall expel all known usurers from their territory within three months and shall not permit them to return in the future. No one shall lease or under any other title whatsoever let them have the use of their houses for the purpose of practising usury. Those who act otherwise, if they are churchmen, patriarchs, archbishops, or bishops incur suspension; individuals of lower rank incur excommunication, and communities and other associations are placed under interdict. If, through obstinacy, they despise these censures for more than a month, their territories shall be placed and remain under interdict so long as the usurers remain there. If, however, they are laymen, then, notwithstanding any privilege, let their ordinaries restrain them from such excesses by ecclesiastical censure" (trans. Gilchrist, *Economic Activity*, 194-95, appendix). A second decree of the Council of Vienne (=Clem. 5.5.1) excommunicates public officials who tolerate usury: "Reliable sources inform us that certain communities in violation of the law, both human and divine, approve the practice of usury. By their statutes confirmed by oath they not only permit the exaction and payment of usury, but deliberately compel debtors to pay it. They also try by heavy statutory penalties and various other means and threats to prevent recovery by individuals who demand repayment of excessive interest. For our part, we want to put an end to these abuses and so we decree, with the approval of the council, that all civil officials of these communities, that is, magistrates, rulers, consuls, judges, lawyers and other similar officials, who in future make, write or draw up statutes of this kind or knowingly decide that usury may be paid or in case of it having been paid may not be freely and fully restored when its return is demanded, incur the sentence of excommunication. They shall incur the same sentence if they do not within three months remove such statutes from the books of those communities (if they have the power to do so), or if they presume in any way to observe the said statutes or customs to the same effect" (trans. Gilchrist, *Economic Activity*, 206, appendix). Usurers and suspected usurers are compelled to produce their accounts: "Moreover, since money-lenders frequently conclude loan-contracts in an occult or fraudulent manner, which makes it difficult to convict them on a charge of usury, we decree that they should be forced by ecclesiastical censure to produce their books on such occasions" (trans. Gilchrist, ibid.). Finally, the council declares it equivalent to heresy to maintain that usury is not a sin: "Finally, if anyone falls into the error of believing and affirming that it is not a sin to practice usury, we decree that he is to be punished as a heretic, and we strictly command the ordinaries of the localities and the inquisitors to proceed against those suspected of such errors in the same way as they would proceed against those accused publicly or suspected of heresy" (trans. Gilchrist, ibid.).

665-67 **An autem ... dicam**: What of notaries who knowingly draft usurious instruments? Hostiensis says that "they are perjurers, because when they were made notaries they swore that they would not do this, therefore they may not thereafter witness or confect public instruments. For a perjurer cannot be a witness even when he has done penance ... and therefore [such notaries] are *infames* [persons condemned for crimes or private wrongs], to whom participation in legitimate transactions is prohibited" ("Quid de notariis, qui super vsuris scienter conficiunt instrumenta? Periuri sunt, quia quando creantur, iurant quod hoc non facient, ergo de cetero nec testificari poterunt nec publica conficere instrumenta. Periurus enim testificari non potest, quantumcumque poenitentiam egerit ... ex hoc etiam sunt infames, quibus sunt actus legitimi interdicti" [*Summa*, X 5.19 *de usuris*, n.8 (ed. cit. col. 1627)]).

What of a prelate who authenticates a usurious contract? Hostiensis remarks that "if the prelate is not aware of the contents ... and therefore does not understand [that the contract is usurious], his action is foolish, but he does not really consent.... But if he has read it and discovered the truth, he is complicit in usury, even if he does not benefit, for subscription ... induces consent and approval ... And since prelatial seals render documents authentic ... the laity, misled into thinking the church approves such contracts, sin with greater confidence" ("Etiam si praelatus non legit tenorem ... et ideo non intelligit, fatue agit, sed in veritate non consentit.... Si vero legit et veritatem inuenit particeps est usurarum, etsi non commodi, nam subscriptio ... consensum et approbationem inducit.... Et cum sigilla praelatorum reddant instrumenta authentica ... laici per hoc credentes contractus huiusmodi per ecclesiam approbari, securius peccant" [ibid.]).

Commentary: Part 2

Casus

673 ***Consuluit***: X 5.19.10 is a letter of Urban III ruling on three potentially usurious transactions. As the basis of Ridolfi's analysis, it is worth citing here in full:

"Your devotion has sought our opinion on (1) whether he who will not lend unless he is assured of receiving in return more than he lent–although there is no explicit agreement to this effect–should be treated in the internal forum as if he was a usurer, (2) whether he is guilty of the same offence [of quasi-usury] who–again without a formal agreement–refuses to postpone settlement of a debt unless he receives some profit and likewise (3) a merchant who sells goods on credit for a much higher price than he would receive if the price were paid immediately. The truth of the matter in all three cases is clear in the gospel of Luke [6.35] where it is said 'Lend, expecting nothing in return.' Since all usury and increase is forbidden in the law, such men should be considered evil-doers on account of their intention to profit and effectively compelled in the penitential forum to restore what they have received" ("Consuluit nos tua devotio, an ille in iudicio animarum quasi usurarius debeat iudicari, qui non alias mutuo traditurus, eo proposito mutuam pecuniam credit, ut, licet omni conventione cessante, plus tamen sorte recipiat; et utrum eodem reatu criminis involvatur, qui, ut vulgo dicitur, non aliter parabolam iuramenti concedit, donec, quamvis sine exactione, emolumentum aliquod inde percipiat; et an negotiator poena consimili debeat condemnari, qui merces suas longe maiori pretio distrahit, si ad solutionem faciendam prolixioris temporis dilatio prorogetur, quam si ei in continenti pretium persolvatur. Verum quia, quid in his casibus tenendum sit, ex evangelio Lucae manifeste cognoscitur, in quo dicitur: 'Date mutuum, nihil inde sperantes': huiusmodi homines pro intentione lucri, quam habent, quum omnis usura et superabundantia prohibeatur in lege, iudicandi sunt male agere, et ad ea, quae taliter sunt accepta, restituenda, in animarum iudicio efficaciter inducendi").

673-95 Casus ... dicam: Ridolfi derives the *casus* (summary) and illustrations from Johannes Andreae's *novella* and Hostiensis' comments on X 5.19.10.

673-76 Casus ... dicit: See n. 687.

680-81 Quasi ... proprie: X 5.19.10 considers usury by intention or tacit usury rather than usury proper or formal, which is expressed in a contract.

681-82 Inuoluatur ... fine: The word "involvatur" is also used in X 5.19.4 (see n. 583-94).

682 Parabolam ... Ostiensem: Hostiensis' cryptic annotation summarizes an older tradition of commentary. Gottofredo defined *parabola* as "a prolongation of the term within which the debtor was bound by oath to pay" ("idest termini pro-

rogationem in quo debitor per iuramentum soluere tenetur" [*Apparatus*, ad X 5.19.10 (MS cit. fol. 163r)]). According to Vincentius Hispanus (d. 1248), the term meant "to prolong. For he was in debt, having obliged himself by oath to pay it on the third day; and he kept me waiting, according to which the Lombards say 'la parola'" ("idest prolongare. Debebat enim sibi eam iuratus ad tertium diem dare, et ipse prolongauit michi, secundum quod Lombardi dicunt 'la parola'" [*Apparatus*, ad X 5.19.10 (MS cit. fol. 158r)]). Because of the prominence of north Italians in money-lending, "Lombard" was a common term for "usurer."

682-84 **aliter ... questione .vi.**: Johannes Andreae adds a further definition from Jerome: "a parable is a shadow or veil of the truth."

685-86 **In lege ... capitulo**: "Law" in the sense of the Pentateuchal law. The basic provision concerning usury is found at *Dt* 23.19-20: "You shall not lend upon interest to your brother, interest on money, interest on victuals, interest on anything that is lent for interest. To a foreigner you may lend upon interest, but to your brother you shall not lend upon interest," while *Ez* 18.8-17 affirms that "[if a man] does not lend at interest or take any increase, withholds his hand from iniquity, executes true justice between man and man, walks in my statutes, and is careful to observe my ordinances–he is righteous, he shall surely live, says the Lord God ... [He who] withholds his hand from iniquity, takes no interest or increase, observes my ordinances, and walks in my statutes; he shall not die for his father's iniquity." For a discussion of medieval interpretations of these passages, see Benjamin Nelson, *The Idea of Usury: From Tribal Brotherhood to Universal Otherhood*, 2nd ed. (Chicago and London: University of Chicago Press, 1969), 3-28.

686 **Taliter ... intentione**: Ridolfi, following Johannes Andreae, glosses the adverb *taliter* to mean "with such an intention," that is, with the intention to profit.

687-95 **Collige ... dicam**: A list of six *notabilia*, briefly noting legal principles arising from X 5.19.10.

687 **Collige ... summario**: The summary at lines 673-76 states that "(1) he who lends intending to receive more than the principal, (2) he who refuses to postpone repayment without receiving more and (3) he who sells for more on credit is bound in the penitential forum."

687-88 **.2.°, quod ... usurarius**: "A mental usurer is not properly speaking a usurer, but like a usurer" (see n. 680-81).

688-90 **.3.°, ex ... *Iudeos***: The pope's use of the word *vulgo* is authority for arguing from popular proverbs. In X 5.6.13 Innocent III forbids Jews to have Christian nurses and servants, invoking a popular proverb: "Jews ... should not be so ungrateful to us Christians that they repay our kindness with hatred and our familiarity with contempt; for when, in our kindness, we admit them to intimacy, they call down on us the same punishment that, according to the common saying, a mouse in a bag, a snake in the lap or a fire in the belly customarily draw down on their hosts" ("[Iudaei] ... ingrati tamen nobis esse non debent, ut reddant Christianis pro gratia contumelium et de familiaritate contemptum, qui, tanquam misericorditer in nostram familiaritatem admissi, nobis illam retributionem impendunt, quam, iuxta vulgare proverbium, mus in pera, serpens in gremio, et ignis in sinu suis consueverunt hospitibus exhibere").

690-93 **.4.°, nota ... *nostram***: This notation reflects Hostiensis' gloss on X

5.19.10 at *concedit*: "that is, he was accustomed to concede, for this is not expressed in an agreement according to what follows, but people with this intention were accustomed to offer freely, knowing that otherwise they laboured in vain; and so the custom of the family head must be considered" ("id est, concedere consueuit, non enim hoc in pactum deducitur, prout sequitur, sed homines hac intentione consueuerunt ei gratis offerre, scientes quod alias frustratorie laborarent, sic ergo spectatur consuetudo patris familias" [*Commentaria*, ad X 5.19.10 (ed. cit. V fol. 57va)]). That is, it is the habit and custom of the lender not to extend credit unless he has been offered a gift. To establish what is customary, one considers the practice of the head of the family. At Dig. 22.1.13, a debtor who promised six percent on a loan actually paid less and is sued by the creditor's heir. Scaevola holds that if the debtor paid the lesser rate for a long period of time he may successfully raise a defence on the grounds that the creditor consented to the lesser rate. The remaining citations provide analogous cases in which custom determines the legitimacy of an act. Dig. 13.7.12 notes that an administrator of one who is accustomed to borrow on pledges may bring an action for the return of a pledge. Decretum Grat. D.47 c.2, a canon of the council of Nicea, affirms the customary rule that clerics are forbidden to lend at usury. X 2.30.5 notes that a confirmation of temporal administration obtained by a regular cleric is void if it does not mention his status as a religious. If it does, it is a forgery, since the pope does not customarily grant such confirmations to the regular clergy.

693-94 **Item nota ... totum**: For Decretum Grat. C.14 q.3, see nn. 44-45 and 79-83.

694-95 **Vltimo ... dicam**: "There is a great difference between the judgement of a court (*iudicium fori*) and the judgement of heaven (*iudicium poli*)," that is, between judgement in the external forum (ecclesiastical court) and the internal forum (conscience, the sacrament of penance or confession). For the gloss to X 5.19.10, see Introduction, pp. 85-86.

696-1002 **.i. oppositio.... capitulo .xvi.°**: The eight *oppositiones* examine a series of apparent contradictions between the provisions of X 5.19.10 and other authorities.

PART 2, OPPOSITIO 1

696-97 **Vtrum ... peccatum**: "Whether a secondary hope of profit from a loan alone constitutes usury."

698-709 **Oppone ... *pio***: With respect to the first and second cases of X 5.19.10, the pope's reply seems "to press too hard" (for the tag, see n. 232-39) by denying creditors any hope of remuneration, even for necessities. But Alanus' gloss distinguishes between primary and secondary hope of profit, characterizing the latter as licit: "*Hoping*: add in the case of a loan in hope grounded primary on anticipation of profit; I do not, however, consider it wicked to hope secondarily for something or even to accept it on such grounds" ("*Sperantes*: supple 'causa mutui' in spe lucri principaliter posita; secundario tamen aliquid sperare non puto malum ... nec etiam recipere ex tali spe" [gl. ord. ad X 5.19.10, v. *Sperantes* (ed. cit. col.

1739)]). Decretum Grat. D.61 c.7 and D.59 c.2 condemn the "immoderate ambition" of those who without due preparation seek high ecclesiastical office, although the second canon allows that someone who has proceeded properly through the various orders to the priesthood may legitimately aspire to the episcopate. Decretum Grat. C.1 q.2 c.2 forbids a bishop to demand anything for consecrating a church, though he may accept a gift offered by the founder of his own free will.

709-14 **Imo naturaliter ... *Ordinationes***: The gloss adds that debtors are under a natural obligation to make a counter- or return-gift (*antidoron* Latin *antidotum*) to their benefactors: "immo naturaliter debitor est illi [creditori] obligatus ad *antidora* (gl. ord. ad X 5.19.10, v. *Sperantes* [ed. cit. col. 1739]). X 3.26.7 condemns clerics who bequeath to non-clerics goods acquired through the church on the principle that "in the offices of charity we are obligated first to those from whom we are conscious of having received a benefit" ("Quum in officiis caritatis primo loco illis teneamur obnoxii, a quibus beneficium nos cognoscimus recipisse ... "). Dig. 5.3.25.11 confirms the principle of return-gift in discussing the liability of wrongful possessors in good faith: "if they have made a gift, they will not be deemed to have become richer in spite of the fact that they have put someone under a moral obligation to make a return-gift."

Gottofredo notes that a judge who entertains a primary hope of remuneration appears to sell justice. He cites Decretum Grat. C.11 q.3 c.66, which forbids judges to receive gifts, and Decretum Grat. C.1 q.1 c.113, which declares simoniacal ordinations invalid.

PART 2, *OPPOSITIO* 2

715-16 **Vtrum ... mutui**: "Whether the natural obligation to make a return-gift can be expressed in a contract."

717-21 **Oppone ... Consuluit**: Two decretals describe situations in which the recipient of something is contractually obliged to do something in return. X 3.5.11 declares that a chapter can attach to a vacant prebend duties that a new incumbent is bound to fulfil. X 1.6.4 makes the delivery of the *pallium* to a newly elected archbishop conditional on his first swearing an oath of fidelity to the pope.

722-31 **Solutio ... lucri**: Hostiensis asks whether it is usurious for a lender to ask for a loan in return and notes that, according to the gloss on Decretum Grat. C.14 q.3 c.1, Gottofredo and Raymond, it is, for although the debtor is naturally bound to make a return-gift, to put such a natural obligation into the form of a civil contract or agreement savours of profit and therefore of usury. Hostiensis queries this conclusion on the grounds that nothing accedes to the principal in such a transaction, nor does there appear to be any increase. Moreover, in X 3.5.11 and 1.6.4 obligations are exacted that would otherwise be simoniacal. Secondly, even in things spritual, exchanges and compensation are permissible; and finally, a benefactor may licitly expect a reward. Nevertheless, he concludes, because of the uncertainty attaching to credit transactions, it is safer to adhere to the opinion of Gottofredo and Raymond. This is the *communis opinio* reflected in the *glossa ordinaria* to Clem. 5.5.1. I have been unable to consult a manuscript of Stephanus Hugonetti's *Apparatus in Clementinas*.

732-40 **Archydiaconus ... inerat:** Guido de Baysio provides a rationale for not allowing the natural obligation of a return-gift to be expressed formally in an agreement: a return-gift is not a debt as such, but in a formal agreement it becomes an obligation and thus an increase on the principal: "antidotum non est debitum simpliciter, et ideo dum deducitur in pactum est obligatio; et ita plus promittitur" (*Rosarium*, ad Decretum Grat. C.14 q.3 c.1, n.6 [ed. cit. fol. 207va]). In the case of X 3.5.11 and 1.6.4, the obligations arise from the very nature of the things in question and therefore to express them in an agreement is to do nothing more than declare what is already implicit.

740-42 **Et vide ... questione:** In Part 2, question 35, Ridolfi asks whether a creditor cannot at least contract some service or favour from the debtor. According to Johannes Calderinus, he cannot, since any increase on the principal, be it money, something measurable by money or, indeed, anything else, is usury.

PART 2, *OPPOSITIO* 3

743-45 **Vtrum ... tenebatur:** "Whether a creditor can make an agreement with a corporation (*uniuersitas*) by which he receives tax relief in lieu of interest."

746-50 **Oppone ... et cetera:** In his comments on the title *de usuris* in the *Speculum iuris*, William Durant (ca. 1236-1296) offers arguments for and against in the following case but fails to come to a conclusion. A city borrowed a sum of money from a citizen with an agreement that the citizen would be exempt from taxes (*collectae*) until the debt was repaid. At length, the city repaid the debt, but proceeded to demand payment of the unpaid taxes on the grounds that they were usury. On the one hand, it appears that the unpaid taxes were usury since the citizen profited by his exemption. Moreover, since all propertied citizens must pay taxes, the exempt citizen was guilty of theft from his co-citizens and his exemption a substitute for the direct payment of usury. On the other hand, it is not usurious to keep what is yours, and it is one thing to rob someone else and quite another to avoid losing what rightfully belongs to you. Likewise, one must consider the difference between profit and the costs incurred by the citizen-lender, and between avoiding damages and receiving profit.

751-58 **Solutio ... finem:** Johannes Andreae cites William's case in his *novella* on X 5.19.10, where he refers us to his own discussion of speculative commodity sales at X 5.19.19. Here the case is the reverse of that in X 5.19.6 (see n. 145-64): a buyer pays less than the current market value of a commodity for delivery at a future date. Gregory IX declares the transaction licit if there is uncertainty about the future value of the commodity. If, however, the buyer is certain that the future value will be greater than the amount paid, the transaction is usurious. Following Hostiensis, Johannes Andreae notes that although it is conceivable that the value will be less, such cases are rare. To avoid usury and the obligation to make restitution, the buyer should pay for delivery at the corresponding season; for example, he should pay in summer for delivery the following summer. By analogy, the citizen in William's case may accept the tax relief if no taxes have been already levied, so that there is genuine uncertainty about his profit. This opinion is reproduced by John of Legnano in his commentary on X 5.19.10 and by Johannes Calderinus in his *repetitio* on X 5.19.19.

PART 2, *OPPOSITIO* 4

759-61 **Vtrum ... mensura:** "Whether usury can be committed outside a *mutuum* contract and, if so, whether the norms of X 5.19.6 apply in things that do not consist in number, weight and measure." *Oppositiones* 5 to 7 address the same question.

762-70 **Oppone ... decretalis ista:** For X 5.19.6, see n. 145-64. There appears to be a contradiction between X 5.19.6, which allows credit sales at a higher price where there is uncertainty about the future value of the commodity, and X 5.19.10, which forbids credit sales completely. Ridolfi appeals to the gloss to X 5.19.10, which says that the cases are not opposed but different: X 5.19.6 pertains to the external forum and X 5.19.10 to the internal. Alternatively, the gloss adds, it might be said that X 5.19.6 deals with the formal and X 5.19.10 with the intentional aspects of a usurious transaction.

770-76 **Nec habet ... et .ii.:** For X 5.19.6 and the gloss, see n. 145-64. X 3.21.4 describes a contract of sale that incorporates provisions (1) that the original seller may repurchase the thing sold within a certain period of time, (2) that the fruits will be counted against the resale price, but (3) that the original seller will be charged a premium to redeem the property. It is noted that the original purchaser is accustomed to lend at usury. Is the transaction a genuine contract of sale or a usurious loan on security? Innocent III declares the transaction usurious because provisions (2) and (3) would be meaningless in a genuine contract of sale and because the original purchaser is a known usurer, whose status creates a presumption of fraud. He notes, however, that a clause permitting a sale to be broken does not in itself render a transaction fraudulent.

The maxim "quodcumque ei nomen imponas" etc. is from C.14 q.3 c.3 (see n. 44-45), although the gloss attributes it to Decretum Grat. C.14 q.3 c.1-2.

776-86 **Et, ut ... doctores:** Ridolfi cites three decretals in support of his contention that any contract can be questioned on the grounds of intention. X 2.24.7 holds debtors to their oaths not to seek repossession of pledges until the debt has been paid. Lenders are required to apply the fruits of such pledges to the reduction of the principal and if they fail to make restitution of any excess they can be excommunicated. In his gloss, Bernard of Parma notes that some regard the pope as having no authority in cases of possession except where they involve usury or perjury. Since there is an oath in the present case, the pope can require restitution on the grounds of sin. For X 3.17.5, see n. 650-52. The gloss observes that the underlying intention of the contract rather than the mere words should be considered: "emptione pignoris causa facta, non quod scriptum est sed quod suggestum est inspicitur" (gl. ord. ad X 3.17.5, v. *Emptionis* [ed. cit. col. 1126]). For X 3.21.4, see n. 770-76. The gloss notes: "non quod scriptum est, sed quod gestum est, inspicitur" (gl. ord. ad X 3.21.4, v. *Obligatis* [ed. cit. col. 1143]). X 3.21.6: if a creditor or his successor has received sufficient fruits from a pledge to extinguish the debt, the pledge should be restored to the debtor. In the case considered in the decretal, the creditor's heir had in turn pledged the original pledge to yet another creditor.

Tancred (1185-1236) notes that the first creditor could not commit the pledge to a second for more than the amount for which it had been committed to him. Since the debt has been extinguished, from a legal point of view the pledge had no value that he could dispose of.

787-96 **Ego non ... dixit**: So far as the transactions themselves are concerned, Ridolfi sees no contradiction between X 5.19.10 and X 5.19.6, since both deal with inflated credit sales. But because credit sales are not formally usurious, X 5.19.6 distinguishes between licit and illicit transactions: where there is uncertainty about the future value of the commodity, the transaction is licit; otherwise, it is not. In conclusion, the pope urges the faithful to refrain from such sales because their inner motivations cannot be hidden from God. However, as Ridolfi observes, X 5.19.10 assumes that the intentions of those who engage in such transactions are necessarily usurious. X 5.19.6, then, appears to allow greater moral latitude to buyers and sellers on credit and so to undermine the more stringent provisions of X 5.19.10. This is also the opinion expressed by Bernard of Pavia in a gloss to X 5.19.6, where he notes that X 5.19.10 puts the contrary argument. Ridolfi suggests that X 5.19.6 should be interpreted in terms of X 5.19.10 and both in terms of X 5.19.19, where Gregory IX adds a new criterion for judging the intentions of a seller on credit, namely, whether he is willing to sell now at a discount. If he is, then it may be assumed that he is acting usuriously. The gloss to X 5.19.19 applies this principle to X 5.19.6: "*He would not sell at the time*: otherwise he is not excused, because if he would sell at the time for less but in the certain knowledge that he would receive more at a later time, it is usury and so you should read X 5.19.6, as I have noted there" ("*Tempore non fuerat venditurus*: alias non excusatur, quia si tunc fuerat venditurus pro minori et ex certa scientia plus recipiat alio termino, vsura est, et sic intellige supra eodem *In ciuitate*, vt ibi etiam dixi" [gl. ord. ad X 5.19.19, v. *Tempore non fuerat venditurus* (ed. cit. col. 1745)]).

797-802 **Aliam ... Baldus**: Baldus says that X 5.19.6 censures credit sales only in cases where the thing sold is a fungible, for usury can be committed only in such things (see nn. 335-48 to 358-62). It is otherwise in the sale of a non-fungible, such as a house or a farm (see n. 420-88), where the purchaser enjoys the use of the thing, "for here it seems that there should be a consideration for time" ("In contrarium videtur quia consideratio temporis non debet esse sterilis" [*Commentaria*, in 4.32.rubr., nn.11-12 (ed. cit. VII fol. 88ra)]). Baldus cites C. 4.49.5, which states that if the purchaser of a farm pays part of the price and takes possession, he owes usury on the remainder of the price from the time he began to enjoy the fruits.

803-17 **Hoc dictum ... uide**: Ridolfi objects that number, weight and measure are formal characteristics of a usurious contract, but contracts in fraud of usury often do not embody the formal characteristics. For the opinion of Gottofredo, see n. 335-48. Baldus' observation, however, may proceed if we read "especially" (*presertim*) instead of "only" (*tantum*), for then it would agree with the gloss to X 5.19.8, where Laurentius Hispanus notes that usury may be sought in delay as quasi-*interesse*: "usury can also be sought according to the canons when, for example, I sell and convey to you an estate and you receive the fruits but do not pay me the price at term ... this sort of usury is sought not as quasi-usury but as quasi-interest" ("vsurae possunt peti etiam secundum canones, vt cum vendo tibi praedium et trado, et percipis fructus nec soluis mihi pretium ad terminum ... quia huiusmodi vsurae non quasi vsurae sed quasi interesse petuntur" [gl. ord. ad X 5.19.8, v. *de feudo* (ed. cit. col. 1737)]). Hostiensis also notes the title to quasi-interest for deferred payment in sales: "ex quasi autem mora veniunt vsurae; vt ecce emptor re sibi tradita non soluit precium" (*Summa*, ad X 5.19 *de usuris*, n.6 [ed. cit. col. 1617]).

817-22 **Quod etiam ... questionibus:** For C. 4.49.5, see n. 797-802. The gloss asserts without qualification that in this case delay gives title to usury: "Which is just, as when usury may be sought as quasi-interest; what it says here of usury also obtains in canon law, according to Azo" ("Quae adeo iusta est, vt cum quasi interesse petantur vsure: de vsuris etiam iure canonum obtineat quod hic dicit, secundum Azonem" [gl. ord. ad C. 4.49.5, v. *Ratio* (ed. cit. col. 1035)]). This is also the opinion of Bartolus at Dig. 19.1.13.26. The fragment reports the opinion of Papinian that "if the parties agree to the seller's being owed double if the price is not paid on time, this special clause is evidently an evasion of the imperial constitutions because it exceeds the statutory rate of interest." Accursius observes that "insofar as the clause does not exceed the statutory rate, it is valid ... just as in any monetary debt a penalty beyond the statutory rate is invalid.... Is what is said here true in every case? According to John [Bassian?] and Bulgarus (d. ca. 1158) it is not, unless the seller was accustomed to lend at usury.... Say instead, according to Azo, that fraud is always presumed to the extent that the charge exceeds the statutory rate. But according to us, who hold that usury may not be paid, ... shall we penalize the purchaser for the statutory rate? I reply that we shall, if he received the fruits so that he was liable for interest" ("et ita in eo quod non excedit, valet ... sicut in quolibet pecuniario debito poena vltra legitimum modum vsurarum promissa non valet ... Item an hoc est verum semper quod hic dicitur. Respondeo secundum Ioannem et Bulgarum non. Sed si erat solitus venditor foenerare ... dic aequis secundum Azonem quod semper presumitur fraus ex quantitate pecuniae quae excedit legitimum modum. Sed secundum nos qui dicimus vsuras non praestari ... nunquid condemnabimus emptorem hoc casu in legitimis vsuris? Respondeo sic, si ille fructus percepit vt sic loco interesse succedat" [gl. ord. ad Dig. 19.1.13.26, v. *Excedit* (ed. cit. I p. 966b)]).

Ridolfi takes the more cautious position that if the sum paid in delay is disproportionately high in relation to the fruits, fraud must be presumed. For Part 2, questions 15, 16 and 18, see nn. 2004-13 to 2165-82 and 1895-96 to 1970-86.

PART 2, *OPPOSITIO* 5

824-28 **Oppone ... suprafatam:** The third case of X 5.19.10 involves a contract of sale, but *Lc* 6.35 refers to a loan and is therefore irrelevant.

829-34 **Solutio ... antepenultima:** In his comments on X 5.19.6, Johannes Andreae follows Gottofredo in observing that in formal terms usury can be committed only in a loan, while X 5.19.6 deals with a contract of sale. In this decretal and in the third question of X 5.19.10, we have cases of mental usury because the buyer on credit is effectively granted a loan that is repayable with profit: "in contractu ergo uenditionis non committitur usura quoad formam, si ex mente scilicet, ut fingatur precium hoc casu ab emptore uenditori traditum et sibi postea mutuatum cum lucro" (*Novella*, ad X 5.19.6, n.6 [ed. cit. V fol. 74rb]).

PART 2, *OPPOSITIO* 6

836-40 **Oppone ... et cetera**: The credit sale described in X 5.19.10 is licit because buyers and sellers are permitted to deceive one another to the extent of half the just price.

Originally a remedy for sellers of land, the Roman law title of *laesio enormis* (C. 4.44.2) was extended by medieval civilians to buyers as well as sellers and made applicable to all sales transactions. The title permits a party to a sale to appeal a price that varies by more than half the current market or legally regulated price. In such cases, the sale may be rescinded and the original price refunded or the fair value paid. *Laesio enormis* was recognized as a canonical title by Alexander III (1159-81) in X 3.17.3. It was endorsed by Innocent III in X 3.17.6. On the development of *laesio enormis* doctrine, see Baldwin, *Medieval Theories*, 22-27, 42-46.

841-45 **Solutio ... finali**: The provisions of *laesio enormis* permit deception of up to half the just price, but according to Innocent IV, though such deception may pass in the external forum, it will be condemned in the internal forum if it is intentional, as Bernard of Parma notes in the gloss to X 5.19.10 (see n. 762-70).

846-61 **Sed dicit ...** ***ciuitate***: Johannes Calderinus asks whether, in view of its inspired character, canon law can be said to approve deception of any kind (Decretum Grat. D.50 c.29 ascribes the penalty for adulterous clerics to "the laws of the ancient fathers written at the prompting of the Holy Spirit" ["tituli antiquorum Patrum sancto Spiritu suggerente conscripti"]). The answer is that it cannot, if by deception you mean fraud rather than uncertainty about the value of the thing itself. But uncertainty does not enter into the present case because both parties are clear about the current price. The gloss to X 5.19.6 confirms this when it observes that in this case the buyers are not mistaken about the current or just price of the commodity; they knowingly pay more in order to defer payment. In other words, if it were a question of price deception, usury would not be an issue: "Non decepti in iusto pretio, sed scienter plus emerunt propter dilationem solutionis" (gl. ord. ad X 5.19.6, v. *Comparant* [ed. cit. col. 1736]).

Nor is it a sale, because the difference in price represents a charge for delaying payment, which makes the transaction a loan in all but name. For X 3.17.5, see n. 650-52. Laurentius Hispanus notes that the low resale price creates a presumption that it is a loan on security and not a genuine sale. If there were no fraud, the purchaser would licitly enjoy the fruits, though the sale could be rescinded by the seller and the land resold at its current price. And so, he concludes, the intention of the parties must be considered: "et ita potius considerandum est quod agitur inter contrahentes" (gl. ord. ad X 3.17.5, v. *Patet* [ed. cit. col. 1126]). In the gloss to X 5.19.6, Bernard of Parma observes that prices are not set by the desires of individuals but by common estimate. A credit sale at a higher price presupposes a knowledge of the current price, which is intentionally exceeded: "'pretia enim rerum non ex affectu singulorum sed communiter aestimantur' [Dig. 35.2.63.pr.] ... sed hic non fuit emptio facta aestimatione comuni" (gl. ord. ad X 5.19.6, v. *Non valent* [ed. cit. col. 1736]).

PART 2, *OPPOSITIO* 7

863-66 **Oppone ... fuerit**: "A thing is worth as much as it can be sold for." The maxim is from Bernard of Parma's gloss to X 5.19.6. Bernard, in turn, takes it from Accursius' gloss to Dig. 35.2.63.pr. This formulation of price doctrine was deduced by medieval civilians from suggestions in the Roman law texts cited by Bernard (Dig. 36.1.1.16, 35.2.82, 47.2.52.29). Medieval theorists understood it to mean that the value of a thing is its current market or lawfully regulated price (see Baldwin, *Medieval Theories*, 20-21; 28-29; 54), but Ridolfi cites it in its literal sense as an objection to X 5.19.10, implying that a higher price for delayed repayment is just because the buyer is willing to pay it.

867 **Solue ... secunda**: See n. 846-61.

PART 2, *OPPOSITIO* 8

868-70 **Vtrum ... et cetera**: "Whether it is a sin or usury to receive something beyond the principal from one who willingly offers it. If so, why? And what weight should be given to the dispositions of the creditor and the debtor in such cases?"

871-75 **Oppone ... et cetera**: In the first and third cases of X 5.19.10–that of the creditor who hopes for a profit on his loan and that of the credit sale–it appears that there is no sin or obligation to make restitution, for what one licitly accepts is not subject to restitution.

875-77 **Maior ... symilibus**: Not all levies are unjust. Decretum Grat. C.14 q.5 c.15 notes that physicians justly demand their fees and labourers their wages, even if their clients or employers pay unwillingly. X 3.39.6 is a decree of IV Lateran (1215) that regulates the size of prelates' retinues when conducting visitations and forbids bishops to impose undue taxes and exactions on their clergy, though it allows them to demand moderate aids for manifest and reasonable cause. In X 3.39.14, Innocent III declares that monasteries must contribute to the expenses of a provincial conducting a visitation of his province, and in X 3.39.23 he defines the procurations due to legates and nuncios of the apostolic see. X 5.39.54 allows needy preachers and confessors to accept alms from usurers. The gloss notes that X 5.19.3 forbids the reception of alms given by usurers. It adds later that there is no contradiction between the canons because the preachers are in fact working on behalf of those to whom the usurers' ill-gotten gains truly belong and from whom alms may licitly be accepted.

877-80 **Minor ... li. .vi.**: One may accept what is freely given. In Decretum Grat. D.18 c.8, Leo IV (847-55) declares that priests attending synods cannot be required to make offerings to the bishop, since such a requirement might discourage attendance or reception of the synod's decrees, but he rules that voluntary offerings need not be rejected. Decretum Grat C.1 q.2 c.1 forbids the imposition of a fee for the consecration of a church, but permits free-will offerings. For X 5.3.30, see n. 310-17. The gloss to VI *de reg. iur.* 4 notes that if a person from whom a thing has been taken freely forgives the debt, satisfaction is understood to have been made, whether or not there has been actual restitution: "*Restituatur*: quod dicit de restitutione, intelligas nisi is cui facienda est restitutio liberaliter remitteret; quia satisfactum intelligitur qualitercunque satisfaciat ... licet proprie verbis inhaerendo aliud sit restituere, aliud remittere" (gl. ord. ad VI *de reg. iur.* 4, *Peccatum*, v. *Restituatur* [ed. cit. col. 719]).

880-85 Sed in ... assummere: But since the debtor often presses interest on his creditor, he has no claim to restitution, for, according to Dig. 12.6.1, if someone pays what is not due and does so knowingly, the payment is not recoverable. Dig. 50.17.53 adds that "what can be reclaimed, if given in error, is a gift if given designedly." VI *de reg. iur.* 27 observes that no injury or fraud is committed against him who understands and consents to a transaction: "Scienti et consentienti non fit iniuria neque dolus." Quoting Cicero, Valerius Maximus observes, "how foolish it is to maintain that, when we have asked for them, we should not accept goods from those who offer them."

885-89 Et si ... symilibus: Nor can it be objected that no one should be enriched at the expense of another, since the debtor in these cases acts freely, and, as VI *de reg. iur.* 86 notes, "damages that you knowingly sustain through your own fault should be laid to your own account, not to that of others" ("Damnum, quod quis sua culpa sentit, sibi debet, non aliis, imputare"). Dig. 3.5.22 states that an administrator of another's goods who makes a payment that is not due is liable for the amount he mistakenly disbursed.

890-901 Solutio ... recipere: Ridolfi adopts the solution of Johannes Calderinus: the foregoing considerations hold true in transactions that are by nature licit, but they cannot in themselves render an illicit contract, such as usury, licit. Calderinus sees an analogy in X 2.2.12 and X 5.39.36. The first declares that a cleric cannot renounce his clerical immunity and submit to the judgement of a lay tribunal, even when he has sworn an oath to do so and his adversary is in agreement. The second forbids clerics to submit voluntarily to floggings, even if such punishments are customary in the region. Johannes Andreae, John of Legnano and Gregory of Rimini make similar observations.

902-14 Et si ... Quodsi: In the case of one who will not lend unless he is assured of receiving more in return, there is an implicit agreement, at least on the part of the lender, that amounts to usury, since intention alone constitutes usury. And even if the debtor acts willingly, it can be said in accordance with Decretum Grat. C.14 q.5 c.15 (see n. 875-77) that some things given willingly can be accepted only with sin, as in the case of a judge who accepts bribes in return for a favorable verdict. Decretum Grat. C.1 q.1 c.21 notes that simoniacs intentionally purchase the Holy Spirit and are therefore more culpable than blasphemers. VI 1.3.11 forbids someone to whom the pope delegates judicial authority to accept anything from the parties to a suit beyond freely offered and necessary expenses; any excess must be restored, regardless of the willingness of the donors. VI 3.20.2, a constitution of II Lyons, forbids archiepiscopal visitors and their households to exact procurations beyond their necessary expenses, even from those who are willing to pay. Clem. 5.3.2, a constitution of the council of Vienne, excommunicates inquisitors who use their office to engage in extortion or to justify the confiscation of church property. The sentence cannot be lifted until restitution has been made, notwithstanding the willingness of the donors.

914-15 **Hinc ... intendit**: "Usury is a lawful bandit who declares in advance what he intends to do." Johannes Andreae quotes the saying in his *quaestio* on the rule *Peccatum*. It derives from a letter on household management attributed to Bernard of Clairvaux and addressed to one Raymond, Lord of Castrum Ambruossi.

916-20 **Potest ... *symo***: But in neither the first nor the third case of X 5.19.10 can it be said that the debtor or purchaser is acting freely, since each is presumed to be constrained by his need for credit, and his will "disturbed and in a sense violated." Johannes Calderinus cites the analogous case of X 5.3.23, in which a candidate for ecclesiastical office has the support of a majority of the electors, while the votes of his opponents are bought by a friend with the knowledge and consent of the candidate: "amicus tuus de conscientia tua et voluntate, turbata ei, qui magister discordiae videbatur, certae quantitatis munus exsolvit, et sic, contradictio conquevit." The election is invalid by reason of simony.

921-28 **Sed oppone ... *iureiuran.***: It can be objected that this is true only if an explicit agreement intervenes. Ridolfi replies that the debtor is constrained by his fear that the creditor will recall in the loan on short notice. Dig. 12.6.26.3 states that one who pays usury under the mistaken impression that he owes a principal sum can recover what he has paid and will not be regarded as one who knowingly paid what he did not owe (see also n. 880-85). But Accursius notes that the opposite held in a case in which a debtor was threatened with recall of principal on which he had not promised to pay usury, but agreed to do so for the sake of an extension. He nevertheless had an action for recovery of what he paid, since he acted under duress: "contra videbatur: quia cum ad sortem soluendam vrgeretur debitor, quia vsurae non fuerant promissae et ideo non currebant, promisit usuras et soluit. Repetit quidem, licet sciens se non debere promisit; fecit enim respectu sortis etiam vt benigniorem haberet creditorem in dando dilatione sortis soluendae" (gl. ord. ad Dig. 12.6.26.2, v. *Indebitum* [ed. cit. I p. 701a]). For X 2.24.6, see n. 74-79. The gloss observes that even those who swear to pay usury may sue to recover what they have paid or for a release from their oath: "You should say that in canon law, usury is not owed and should never be paid ... and therefore usury paid can be sought as something that was not owed, notwithstanding the fact that something not owed but willingly paid cannot be recovered. But he pays from fear of his oath [to the creditor], though what he does from fear will not bind him. Alternatively, by one law he is bound to pay on account of his oath but by another law he recovers because something not owed has been paid; and thus the debtor has an action for recovery of what he paid, and thus he has an action against his creditor to r-elease him from his oath ... So when [the decretal] says 'they should be compelled,' read 'since they did not seek to be obsolved from their oath'" ("Ad hoc dicas quod vsurae indebitae sunt iure canonico et in nullo casu conceduntur ... et ideo solutae peti possunt tamquam indebitae, non obstat eo quod dicitur indebitum scienter solutum non repetitur; quia hoc fit metu iuramenti, vnde sibi non praeiudicat quod per metum facit. Vel sic, vno iure soluere tenetur propter iuramentum, sed alio iure repetit: quia indebitae solutae sunt, et sicut habet debitor actionem ad petendum solutum, ita habet actionem aduersus creditorem vt eum liberet a iuramento ... Et quod dicit 'cogendi sunt' intellige 'cum non petunt absolui a iuramento'" [gl. ord. ad X 2.24.6, v. *Cogendi sunt* (ed. cit. cols. 799-800)]).

928-36 **Vel si ... conclusione .vii.**[a]: Alternatively, the debtor may feel constrained to pay in order to guarantee future access to credit. Ridolfi refers to the argument of Decretum Grat. C.10 q.2 c.2, an imperial constitution outlining conditions under which ecclesiastical property may be sold or pledged in payment of debts. If the debts cannot be satisfied by pledging movables, the bishop and chapter may offer the creditor a field on the condition that the creditor can prove that the proceeds will be applied to the benefit of the church. The gloss asks what creditor would be prepared to contract with the church under such conditions, since few could be certain to what use this money might be put. Let it suffice that the church can be shown to have needed money, "lest we manage the affairs of the church so closely that we throw them into confusion" ("ne si nimia subtilitate circa res ecclesiarum laboremus, illa subtilitas eis in perniciem vertatur" [gl. ord. ad Decretum Grat. C.10 q.2 c.2, v. *Probat* (ed. cit. col. 929)]). In his *quaestio* on *Damnum* (see n. 885-89), Johannes Andreae asks whether a guarantor can recover usury that he has paid on behalf of a defaulting debtor who had promised usury for the sake of an extension of the term for repayment. In section four of the question, he notes that a guarantor has the same remedies as a debtor (see n. 921-28). For Part 2, question 47, see n. 490-94.

937-53 **Sed ratio ... questionem .ix.**: We might conclude from the foregoing that a creditor who receives anything in excess of the principal is always guilty of usury, but this is not so. Provided there is no agreement and the creditor does not primarily intend to profit, there is no sin. For this reason, according to Ridolfi, Johannes Calderinus cites the three cases of X 5.19.19, the first involving a sea-loan (see Introduction, p. 59, n. 26), the second the sale of a speculative commodity (see n. 751-58) and the third a credit sale (see n. 787-96). The pope approves the latter two if there is real uncertainty about the future value of the commodities, but presumably he could have condemned all three on the grounds of the borrower's need. If, however, we consider the psychology of the creditor rather than that of the debtor, it is clear that even if the debtor acted without constraint, a corrupt intention in the creditor renders the transaction usurious. For Part 2, question 3, see nn. 1021-22 to 1134-42; for questions 6 and 7, nn. 1210-18 to 1447-73; for question 9, nn. 1514-18 to 1592-1600.

954-67 **Item plus ... et cetera**: Nor should we jump to the conclusion that the debtor is necessarily constrained, since "through the employment of excessive subtlety many things are lost and brought to ruin." The maxim is derived from C. 6.49.7.pr., in which Justinian permits a guardian to receive restitution on behalf of a ward who is a fiduciary heir without the customary sureties, "lest by employing excessive subtlety with respect to the ward's property it be brought to ruin" ("ne, dum nimia subtilitate circa res utimur pupillares, ipsa subtilitas ad perniciem eorum revertatur"). In C. 6.38.4, Justinian directs that in testaments naming two guardians the words *et* and *aut* should have the same force, "lest, while the question of who should be tutor is in doubt, wards' property should perish" ("ne, dum dubitatur, apud quem debet esse tutela, in medio res pupillorum depereant"). The maxim is invoked in the gloss to Decretum Grat. C.10 q.2 c.2. For the opinion of Fredericus Petruccius, see Part 2, question 7, nn. 1260-62 to 1447-73.

968-94 **Preterea ... *Scribam*:** This is confirmed by Johannes Andreae, who writes in his *quaestio* on *Peccatum* that "a gift that is not preceded by a request or an agreement is presumed to be gratuitous and freely offered and consequently not subject to restitution." Ridolfi's own observation confirms that many debtors offer something beyond the principal in recognition of the profits they acquired by means of the capital the creditor made available. In adjudicating such a case, then, a judge must consider the character of the giver and whether he acts with discrimination (*discretio*), and therefore freely, or from real coercion. X 2.23.3 is *Prv* 20.11–"even a child makes himself known by his acts whether what he does is pure and right"–along with Jerome's commentary to the effect that you may assume that the inner disposition of one whom you observe to follow virtue and the commandments of God is pure. The gloss adds "that is, it is presumed and argued that from externalities you may make presumptions about internal states" ("id est, presumitur et est argutum per exteriora praesumi de interioribus" [gl. ord. ad X 2.23.3, v. *Intelligitur* (ed. cit. col. 786)]).

Other considerations will include the degree to which the debtor profited, whether the creditor was accustomed to recall loans on which he could expect no profit, the relationship between the parties and so on. The citations illustrate the observation that a man's future behaviour can be predicted from his past actions. Decretum Grat. C.23 q.5 c.24, from Jerome's commentary on the letter to Titus, states that those who are faithful in earthly things will be faithful in the things of God. X 2.23.6, an extract from Gregory the Great's letter appointing Maximus, bishop of Syracuse, papal vicar in Sicily, notes that the office is conferred in virtue of the bishop's character, that is, his inner qualities, not his status as occupant of an important see. X 2.23.9 is an excerpt from Jerome on *Os* 8.12 ("Were I to write for them my laws"), who observes "from those already given and ignored it seems that they will neglect these as well" ("Ex prius datis, et neglectis apparet, quod has negligent").

994-97 **Accedant ... questionibus:** X 2.24.32 declares that in cases of usury, judges may, when other proofs are wanting, exact from the litigants an oath to speak the truth. Commenting on this decretal, Johannes Andreae, following Hostiensis, lists circumstances that the judge should consider; Ridolfi's list at 979-90 largely corresponds to that of Johannes Andreae. X 3.17.5 (see n. 650-52) concerns presumptions. Johannes Andreae, again following Hostiensis, notes that if a lender prefers to purchase the goods of a borrower on the condition that the latter repurchase within a certain term over accepting them as security, usury should be presumed, especially if the price is low. When such agreements are employed by otherwise notorious usurers, fraud is automatically presumed: "a presumption against usurers is easily formed, because they are the worst class of men.... For they engage in all manner of barratries, now buying, now buying in part, now selling in part, which are truly barratries, which lead to hell" ("de facili contra usurarios praesumendum; quia pessimum genus hominum ... faciunt enim multas baratrias, nunc emendo, nunc partim emendo, nunc partim uendendo, quae uere sunt baratariae, scilicet ad Baratrum perducentes" [*Novella*, ad X 3.17.5, n.3 (ed. cit. V fol. 80vb)]). He reports his own observation that usurers have largely abandoned pure loan contracts in favour of conditional sales, such as the one X 3.17.5 describes, or variants designed to evade the canonical ban, such as two separate contracts, one a contract of sale, the second a promise to repurchase. Other usurers refuse an instrument of liberation to those who have paid principal and usury lest it be produced in an action against them for recovery. In other cases, debtors are required to pay third parties, who in turn pay the original creditor, and in this way the debtor is prevented from suing for restitution. Again, contracts can be drawn in different currencies, so that variations in the rate of exchange conceal a loan. In yet other cases, usury is committed by means of a fraudulent sale of non-existent or worthless merchandise. Other usurers attempt to evade the presumption of fraud by having their contracts drawn up in the names of others who are not related to them and whose transactions are not therefore automatically presumed to be fraudulent (ibid., n.4).

For Part 2, question 10, see nn. 1601 to 1645-51. Question 62 asks whether a debtor who has unwillingly forgiven his creditor any obligation to make restitution can nevertheless sue the estate if the creditor makes provision for restitution in his will. Ridolfi cites Johannes Andreae to the effect that he can if the creditor was accustomed to practice usury; otherwise not.

998-1002 **Sed quid ... capitulo .xvi.°**: Ridolfi concludes that if a creditor's intentions are just, he will not usually be guilty of usury if he accepts something beyond the principal, even if the debtor's motivations are mixed. The proposition is qualified in Part 2, question 9 (see nn. 1524-37 to 1592-1600).

In *City of God* 1.16, Augustine asks whether the victim of another's sin is nevertheless somehow complicit: "In the first place, then, let the principle be stated and affirmed that the virtue whereby a good life is lived controls the members of the body from its seat in the mind and that the body becomes holy through the exercise of a holy will, and while such a will remains unshaken and steadfast, no matter what anyone else does with the body or in the body that a person has no power to avoid without sin on his own part, no blame attaches to the one who suffers it" (trans. George E. McCracken, [Cambridge, MA: Harvard University Press, 1957-72], 1: 75).

Part 2, Question 1

1004-6 **Modo ... illa**: Precisely what transaction does the second question of X 5.19.10 describe, namely, is he who refuses to grant a *parabola iuramenti* without a gift, even in the absence of an agreement to this effect, to be considered a usurer in the internal forum?

1007-15 **Respondeo ... et cetera**: The term for the repayment of a loan approaches and the debtor requests a postponement to which the creditor accedes on the implicit understanding that the debtor will pay something beyond the principal. Sometimes there is an agreement restricting the movements of the debtor such that he cannot possibly repay the debt without buying the creditor's permission to go elsewhere on business or for work.

Part 2, Question 2

1017-18 **Secundo ... precepto**: Whether *Lc* 6.35, "Lend, expecting nothing in return," is a divine precept.

1019-20 Solutio ... *Dilectissimis*: On the authority of Gottofredo, Ridolfi replies that it is a precept in cases of necessity or times of dearth, when all things must be shared. The two citations from Gratian touch on the community of goods. Decretum Grat. D.47 c.8, an excerpt from a sermon of Ambrose on *Lc* 12.16 ("The land of a rich man brought forth plentifully"), condemns the rich who refuse to share with the poor: "But you into whose laps the gifts of God have fallen, do you think you do no evil when you hang on to what so many need for life? ... The bread that you hoard belongs to the hungry; the garments you flaunt are the garb of the naked; the money you conceal in the earth is the ransom and quittance of the wretched. You should know, then, that you usurp the goods of all those you could help if you wanted" ("Tu uero susceptis muneribus Dei, et in sinum tuum redactis, nichil te putas agere iniquum, si tam multorum uitae subsidia solus obtineas? ... Esurientium panis est, quem tu detines; nudorum indumentum est, quod tu recludis; miserorum redemptio est et absolutio pecunia, quam tu in terra defodis. Tantorum te ergo scias inuadere bona, quantis possis prestare quod uelis"). In Decretum Grat. C.12 q.1 c.2, Clement of Rome praises the example of the Apostles who held their property in common, "for the use of all things that are in the world should be common to all men. But through wickedness one said that this was his and another that that was his, and so was division among mortals created ... But [among the apostles] all who had houses or fields sold them and the money and other things they had they placed at the feet of the apostles ... and these they divided among them to each according to his need" ("Communis enim usus omnium, que sunt in hoc mundo, omnibus hominibus esse debuit. Sed per iniquitatem alius hoc dixit esse suum, et alius istud, et sic inter mortales facta diuisio ... Omnes uero, qui domos uel agros possidebant, uendebant eos, et precia eorum et reliquas res, quas habebant, offerebant, ponentes ante pedes apostolorum ... et diuidebant singulis, prout cuique opus erat").

PART 2, QUESTION 3

1021-22 **Vtrum ... sortem**: "Whether an intentional usurer is bound to make restitution of what he has received in excess of the principal."

1023-29 **.3.° quero ... *Consuluit***: For Alanus' gloss to X 5.19.10, see n. 698-709. For the opinions of Gottofredo and Hostiensis on secondary intention, see n. 112-20. In his comments on X 5.19.10, Johannes Andreae follows Gottofredo and Hostiensis. In his *quaestio* on *Peccatum*, Johannes Andreae observes that a primary intention to profit makes a usurer: "ubi sola intentio et sola spes lucri est principalis causa mutui, ibi ex sola intentione et spe lucri constituitur homo vsurarius" (*Novella* ad VI *de reg. iur.* 4, *Peccatum*, n. 8 [ed. cit. fol. 62vb]). But, as Ridolfi observes, X 5.19.10 deals with cases of primary rather than secondary intention to profit.

1030-43 **Sed quid ... mentalis**: If those who primarily intend to profit receive nothing, they should do penance. But are they bound to make restitution of anything they do receive? Some say that they are not unless they force the debtor to pay, say, by denying an extension for repayment, by receiving guarantees worth more than the sum lent or by refusing to release the debtor from a promise not to absent himself until the debt is paid. But X 5.19.10 does not explain what constitutes an exaction, as the canons do in other cases. For example, in X 2.20.47, Innocent III establishes rules for the admission of evidence in causes of consanguineous marriages: testimony concerning identity and relationship can be taken from those who affirm that they are not acting from personal motives and may refer to people by name, by adequate demonstration or circumlocution. X 4.14.7 says that witnesses must be able to distinguish degrees of relationship and to designate persons either by name or by some equivalent evidence ("nominibus propriis vel aequipollentibus indiciis"). Dig. 12.1.6 states that "there is a fixed claim when the identity or quantity of the subject matter of the obligation is indicated by a name or the quality and quantity are shown by a description which substitutes for a name.... it does not matter at all whether a thing is called by its name, pointed out with a finger, or described in words." Dig. 6.1.6 states that someone suing *in rem* must be specific about the thing he seeks, whether he claims the whole or a part, specifying the weight, if the thing is measured in that way, the number, if the goods are manufactured, and so on.

X 5.3.46 absolves from the penalties of simony abbots who obtained their spirituals and temporals not through an explicit simoniacal agreement but only in intention. Therefore, just as mental simony can be forgiven by penance without restitution, so should mental usury.

1044-52 **Alii ... columpna:** Ridolfi cites a succession of authorities to show that the safer opinion is that a usurer in intention who has received an increment on a loan is always obliged to make restitution, whether the debtor acted under implied duress or not: "qui principalem habet intentionem ad vsuram, licet vsurarius sit, non tenetur restituere ... nisi forte aliquid faceret quare debitor, etsi non voluntarie, tamen necessario ei daret ... Alii tamen dicunt quod semper tenetur restituere, et est tutius" (Innocentius IV, *Commentaria*, ad X 5.19.10 [ed. cit. fol. 517vb]). Johannes Andreae and John of Legnano emphasize that the usurer in intention is bound in the confessional, and this, Ridolfi suggests, is how the gloss to X 5.19.10 should be interpreted. For the text of the gloss, see Introduction, pp. 85-86.

1052-65 **licet ... disputans:** As reported in Johannes Andreae's *quaestio* on *Peccatum*, Gerard of Siena was of the view that a usurer in intention is bound to make restitution only when his intentions are externally expressed in such a way that the debtor is placed under an obligation, thus creating an implicit agreement that has the force of an explicit one. Gerard distinguishes between "mental usury," which is vicious but does not involve restitution, since there is no agreement, and "vocal usury," which is both vicious and subject to restitution, since it involves an explicit agreement or at least an implicit mutual understanding. Paulus de Liazariis is of the same opinion: "This is true, namely, that 'mental usury ought to be restored,' when the creditor's perverse intention somehow becomes known to the debtor, say because he was accustomed to lend at usury ... for then it is censured as usury by agreement, the agreement being silently understood. It is different when the creditor's intention is not known to the debtor: intention alone does not create an obligation to make restitution, since it takes the form of neither an implicit nor an explicit agreement or obligation, and so the debtor seems to give freely" ("Et hoc quod dico, 'vsura mentalis debet restitui' est verum quando praua creditoris intentio innotescit debitori quomodocumque, puta ex eo quod facere consueuit ... tunc enim usura censetur pactionalis, pacto tacite intellecto. Secus si debitori non innotescit intentio, tunc sola mens non obligat ad restitutionem cum non fit pactum uel exactio implicite uel explicite et sic dans gratis uidetur donare" [*Lectura*, in Clem. 5.5.1, v. *Solvantur usurae* (MS cit. fol. 240rb-va)]).

1066-88 **Et quia ... Hec ille**: Gerard offers three arguments in support of his position. (1) Since the formal element in usury is the exaction of something beyond the principal by an explicit agreement or something equivalent, where there is no such exaction, there is also no usury and therefore no need for restitution. He adds, however, that the lender's unexpressed intention to profit is vicious. (2) If you accept as a free gift something that you intended to steal, although you are a thief by intention, you are not in deed and therefore not bound to make restitution. Similarly, if your debtor offers you a gift, you are not bound to make restitution, even if you inwardly desired it, provided the debtor does not offer it under duress or as a result of an explicit agreement. (3) The rationale for the restitution of usury consists in the fact that it is not paid freely but is unjustly extorted from the debtor by the creditor through an agreement. But where the creditor's corrupt intention is unexpressed or unknown to the debtor, the latter's gift cannot be said to have been extorted and there is no obligation to make restitution.

1089-98 **Sed tu ... distinguendo**: Johannes Andreae, here paraphrased and expanded by Ridolfi, rejects Gerard's insistence on *pactum* as an index of usury, arguing that he weakens his case by suggesting in the third argument that the debtor's awareness of the creditor's intentions is sufficient to establish an obligation to make restitution, since in this case there is no agreement or exaction arising from an agreement. Johannes Andreae prefers the juristic distinction between the primary and secondary intentions of the lender, which "preserves the authority of the gospel 'lend, expecting nothing in return,' while tempering its rigour."

1099-1110 **Non uidetur ... responsione**: Ridolfi considers the response insufficient and suggests that the problem lies in the definition of usury as "profit owed or exacted in a loan." He prefers his own definition of usury as "profit from a loan primarily intended as such."

1111-18 **Ad secundum ... dilucidabo**: The cases of the would-be thief and the usurer are not really similar. The recipient in the first case does not receive the gift as the result of his corrupt intention. The usurer, by contrast, is led by a primary desire to profit, since he would not otherwise have lent, and therefore what he receives is tainted by a corrupt intention and should be restored to the debtor.

1119-31 **Sed uenio ... meo**: Following Johannes Andreae, Ridolfi denies that restitution is owed because usury has been extorted from the debtor; rather, the whole transaction is rendered vicious by the primary intention of the creditor, whether this is known to the debtor or not. The creditor's real offence is against charity, since he would not lend without the expectation of profit. For Gregory of Rimini's definition of usury, see nn. 51-54 to 63-71, 132-44 to 318-22, 2467-93 to 2623-29.

1132-33 **Quare autem ... *de sy.***: Commenting on Decretum Grat. C.14 q.3 c.1, Guido de Baysio asks why mental usurers must make restitution while mental simoniacs are not penalized. In reply, he notes the opinion of Hostiensis at X 5.3.46 that in simony both parties are guilty and therefore neither can be compensated by restitution, while in usurious transactions, the payee is guilty and the payer is not. Commenting on the same decretal, Johannes Andreae and John of Legnano maintain that it is a greater offence against charity to expect profit from a loan than to expect some return from a benefit that is in the gift of the benefactor, as is the case in simony. In both cases, ownership passes to the recipient, but a debtor is under a legal obligation to repay the sum lent, while no such obligation exists in a gift. Since the creditor therefore sustains less damage than the giver of a gift, it is fitting that his desire to profit be restrained.

1134-42 Sed ... questione: "But note that if he who paid something beyond the principal releases [the creditor from the obligation to make restitution], he will be free, just as he would be freed if there had been a release from usury paid as a result of an agreement. Indeed, even if [the debtor] did not release his creditor but made a gift to him whose hope and intention were corrupt, provided the debtor did not give with respect to the loan [the creditor would be under no obligation to make restitution], just as we say in the case of the [would-be] thief."

In support of this contention, Ridolfi cites Alexander III in X 3.28.4: if, as a result of an illness, someone offers himself and all his goods to a monastery, his parish church has a right to its portion; it is otherwise in the case of one who does so in good health, since he is free to dispose his goods as he pleases, conferring them on religious institutions or even on private persons. In X 3.26.15, Innocent III settles the respective rights of bishop and cathedral chapter over pious legacies. If something is left to a bishop in his personal capacity, for example, by a relative, the chapter has no rights. It is otherwise if the bishop and the church are named as legatees or the church alone. In such cases, the rules on canonical shares apply, since "the private disposition of a testator cannot override the general disposition of the canon" ("privata dispositio testatoris non potest generalem constitutionem canonis immutare"). Both decretals are concerned with the disposal of donations or gifts, and in both the disposition or condition of the donor determines the division and possession of the goods.

For the opinion of Gregory of Rimini and Ridolfi's critique, see nn. 2494-2531, 2694-2725 to 2726-44.

Part 2, Question 4

1145-46 Sed quere ... intentionem: "What if a creditor is sued for restitution in an ecclesiastical court and admits his corrupt intentions: is he then bound to make restitution?"

1147-52 Respondet ... meus: Hostiensis, followed by Johannes Andreae and John of Legnano, says that it depends on the nature of the suit. If the creditor is sued for restitution of usury proper instead of usury by intention, he must be absolved because the suit is improperly framed. He cites X 2.1.6, a decretal of Alexander III, which declares that the plaintiff must explain clearly what right he is seeking, and X 4.11.7, in which Innocent III requires those who are aware of an impediment of compaternity to a proposed marriage to declare it. Hostiensis nevertheless agrees that the present case might be considered unusual because of the spiritual dangers of usury. If the suit is in fact for restitution of intentional usury and the creditor admits to a corrupt intention, he is bound to make restitution.

1153-57 **Aduerte ... usura**: The gloss says that "intention plus effect make a man a usurer." Citing Tancred, Vincentius Hispanus adds that only that which is unequivocally usury is subject to restitution: "quod non esset si non esset usura" (*Apparatus*, ad X 5.19.10, v. *Inducendi* [MS cit. fol. 158v]).

1158-70 **Preterea ... publicationem**: Ridolfi cites four canons in support of the principle that what has been publicly confessed may be judged in the public forum. Decretum Grat. D.32 c.11 excludes from office those in major orders who openly live unchaste lives; those who sin secretly will be judged by God. Decretum Grat. C.2 q.1 c.6 observes that the church tolerates many occult sinners who will be condemned by divine judgement. Decretum Grat. C.2 q.5 c.20 forbids the application of torture to obtain confessions in ecclesiastical processes; a free and public confession may be the subject of trial, but secret sins are left to divine judgement. Decretum Grat. C.32 q.5 c.23 observes that although the Christian religion equally condemns adultery by either spouse, it is more difficult to prove adultery in the case of a male, whose sins are hidden. Nevertheless, in the absence of proof, there can be no punishment. X 1.31.2 declares that if a priest knows informally or through confession that one of his flock is guilty of a crime but unwilling to amend, he should not accuse him openly, but rather anonymously, as Christ did Judas when he said, "One of you will betray me" (*Mc* 14.8). Unless the priest can prove guilt judicially, he should not excommunicate the transgressor but confine himself to private admonitions.

The gloss to X 5.19.10 notes that mental usurers "on account of their intention are to be judged evil-doers in the internal forum and induced, though not compelled, to restore what they have received, nor are they to be punished as usurers though, in truth, in the sight of God, they are usurers, since they are bound to make restitution" ("Isti propter intentionem quam habuerunt, iudicandi sunt in iudicio animae male agere et inducendi sunt, sed non compellendi, vt si recepta restituant, nec tamquam vsurarii puniendi sunt, sed reuera quoad Deum vsurarii videntur, quia restituere tenentur sic accepta" [gl. ord. ad X 5.19.10, v. *Male agere* (ed. cit. col. 1739)]). If mental usurers are guilty before publication and obliged to make restitution, even more so are they after.

1171-77 **Preterea ... his**: Moreover, the church prefers simplicity to subtlety. X 1.38.9 declares that letters of appointment are to be interpreted in their obvious sense and in accordance with the intentions of the author. In this case, letters appointing episcopal vicars are to be understood to include full authority for them to act as the bishop's proctors. For X 2.1.6, see n. 1147-52; the relevant passage reads: "You shall take care lest, as is too often the case, your inquiry is too subtle: you should inquire simply into the facts themselves and the truth of the matter in accordance with the form of the canons" ("Provideatis attentius, ne ita subtiliter, sicut a multis fieri solet, cuiusmodi actio intentetur, inquiratis, sed simpliciter et pure factum ipsum, et rei veritatem secundum formam canonum ... investigare curetis"). X 5.40.6 is an extract from Hilary of Poitiers' treatise on the Trinity: "the meaning of what has been said is to be determined from the intention of the speaker, for things are not subordinate to words but words to things" ("Intelligentia dictorum ex causis est assumenda dicendi, quia non sermoni res, sed rei sermo subiectus").

1178-82 **Preterea ... symilibus**: In Roman law, possession is restricted to corporeal things; possession of incorporeal things, such as rights, obligations and so forth, is described as "like possession" (*quasi possessio*). Ridolfi's citations, however, show that incorporeal things are often discussed in the same terms as corporeal things. X 2.1.15, for example, notes that "you possessed the right of presentation to the said church" ("tu ius patronatus ipsius ecclesiae possidebas"). X 2.27.18, 3.36.6 and 3.38.19 refer in similar terms to rights of presentation. X 3.7.6 alludes to the possession of the right to institute incumbents and to oversee the administration of vacant benefices, and VI 2.5.2 to the legitimate possession of the right to receive benefices.

1182-93 **Bene facit ... Ostiensis**: In X 2.28.18, Innocent III on appeal overturns the presentation and induction of a priest on the grounds that he had not been presented by the patron of the living and finds in favour of a rival candidate who could demonstrate such presentation. Johannes Andreae, citing Innocent IV, notes that in using the word *adiudicantes* the pope also "intends to confirm and induct, since power does not consist in mere words," and that, as Hostiensis says, "the prince's sentence confers full rights, nor does it need additional qualifications" ("Papa adiudicat illi ecclesiam, per quod intendit illum confirmasse uel instituisse, cum non sit uis in uerbis.... Nam, ut dicit Hostiensis, sententia principis plenum ius conferat, nec aliis adminiculis eget" [*Novella*, ad X 2.27.18, n.13 (ed. cit. II fol. 238ra)]). X 2.28.34 says that an oppressed person who seeks the protection of a superior is considered an appellant, even though he may not describe his action as an appeal.

On X 2.27.18, Johannes Andreae follows Hostiensis in observing that the pope uses the term *irritandam* ("it should be void") rather than *irritam* ("it was void"), since, if the case had not been appealed, the earlier sentence upholding the original presentation and induction would have stood. In other cases, a sentence might be null from the outset because it contradicts the law or the common good. In yet others, such as matrimonial causes, a sentence might be null in truth but upheld in fact until proof is forthcoming and anyone wishing to overturn the sentence heard. Ridolfi considers the case of a publicly self-confessed mental usurer to fall into the latter class. He notes, however, that Paulus de Liazariis holds the opinion of Hostiensis outlined in n. 1147-52.

PART 2, QUESTION 5

1194-95 **Vtrum ... *usur.***: "Will an action by *condictio* lie against an intentional usurer on the basis of X 5.19.10?"

1199-1204 **Respondeo ... refert**: Innocent IV poses but does not answer the question in his commentary on X 5.19.10. Ridolfi follows Johannes Andreae who, in his comments on the gloss, deduces from the argument of Hostiensis outlined above in Part 2, question 4 (n. 1147-52) that such an action will indeed lie against a publicly self-confessed usurer, provided it is correctly framed.

PART 2, QUESTION 6

1210-18 **.vi.° quere ... obnoxius:** A creditor whose principal but unexpressed intention is profit lends without an explicit demand for usury. Repaying the principal, the debtor offers an additional ten percent, declaring that he does so in recognition of the service done him by the creditor, regardless of the latter's real intention. If the creditor accepts the interest on these terms, is he liable to restitution?

1219-25 **Videtur ... finem:** It would appear that he is, because it is not the debtor's but the creditor's primary intention that renders the transaction vicious. For the argument of Johannes Andreae cited here, see nn. 1111-18 and 1119-31.

1226-35 **In contrarium ... restitutionem:** It may be argued on the contrary that if the creditor understands the ten percent to be a freely-given gift and accepts it as such, he is, despite his corrupt intention, guilty only of sin, which may be absolved by contrition, and not bound to make restitution as well. Moreover, if a creditor is released by the debtor from the obligation to make restitution, his liability ceases. Since such a release is implicit in the free nature of the gift, the creditor is not obliged to make restitution (for the argument regarding release, see n. 1134-42).

1236-48 **Videtur ... similibus:** Ridolfi takes a middle position: if the creditor's primary intention persists, the gift is corrupted by association and must be restored, but if the creditor's original desire for profit has been replaced by charity, he is not obliged to make restitution, especially if his change of heart becomes known to the debtor before the offer. In support of his conclusion, Ridolfi cites Decretum Grat. D.50 c.18 and Johannes Andreae's *novella* on X 1.3.38. The first is from Gregory the Great's *Moralia*: "'Iron is taken out of the earth' [*Iob* 28.2] when a strong soldier of the church is separated from his former worldly activities. He should not therefore be despised for what he was, since he now begins to be what he was not" ("Ferrum de terra tollitur, cum fortis propugnator ecclesiae a terrena, quam prius tenuit, actione separatur. Non ergo in eo debet despici, quod fuit, quia iam incipit esse quod non fuit"). In X 1.3.38, Gregory IX lays down the procedure to be followed when the pope accidentally mandates the collation of two candidates to the same benefice. The second is to be refused, since it is not the intention of the pope to burden the church in question with two incumbents. However, Johannes Andreae, following Innocent IV, observes that the second is to be preferred if the first candidate renounces his letter of mandate, falls under an ecclesiastical ban, marries or otherwise renounces the clerical state. In such a case, the intention expressed in the second mandate is to be implemented. Likewise in our case: if the intention of the creditor changes from greed to charity, it is the second that should take precedence.

1248-59 **Et idem ... fieret:** The same holds true, Ridolfi argues, if the creditor intends to accept usury that he will restore to the debtor in the event that the latter does not absolve him from the obligation to do so. But if the debtor declines to accept restitution and insists on the donative character of the usury, it is as if restitution had been made and a gift then presented to the creditor, or as if the debtor had absolved his creditor from his obligation to make restitution. Ridolfi's authorities for this argument are Dino of Mugello (fl. 1279-ca. 1298), Johannes Andreae and Fredericus Petruccius, whose arguments are discussed in question 7.

PART 2, QUESTION 7

1260-62 **Vtrum ... restitutione**: "Whether the release of a usurer from the obligation to make restitution suffices to free him in the forum of conscience when no actual restitution takes place."

1266-67 **Vbi sciendum ... sic**: For the gloss, see n. 310-17.

1267-70 **Dynus ... *Proculo***: Dino of Mugello notes that some hold the opinion of the gloss, while others maintain that in cases of sin the letter of the law must be observed. Since "to restore" means to return a thing to its original state, the restitution must be real: "Alii dicunt quod non liberatur quis, quia verbis regulae inhaerendum est in dubio, cum de peccato agatur. Restituere autem est rem in primo statu reponere" (*Commentaria in regulas iuris*, in 4, *Peccatum*, nn.5-6 [ed. cit. p. 60]). He concedes, however, that if the creditor is released when he is on the point of returning the thing, it is as if restitution has been made: "Non absurdum tamen dici potest quod si res erat restitutioni parata, et tunc fiat remissio, quod habeatur perinde acsi res esset restituta et postea per eum cui restitutio facta fuit donata sit restituenti" (*ibid.* n.7). Dino's citations from the *Digest* refer to analogous cases: Dig. 24.1.3.12 asks whether the prohibition of gifts between spouses can be circumvented by requiring the husband's debtor to pay his wife. Paul replies that it cannot and that such money becomes the husband's property, for even if gifts between spouses were not void, the effect of the transaction would be to transfer the money from the debtor to the husband and then from the husband to the wife, "but because of the short time between the two actions, one is obsured." At Dig. 23.3.49, a husband lends part of his wife's dowry, but releases the debtor when he becomes insolvent. Is the husband liable? He is, "for the position is the same as where he had received the money and then donated it to the promisor." Similarly, Dig. 12.1.15 states that "if you owe me money under a mandate and we agree that you may keep it as a loan, the money is deemed to have passed to me and back to you again." Dig. 46.3.79 describes a valid discharge of a debt obligation: "Should I direct you to put money or anything else which you owe me where I can see it, the result is that you are released at once and that it becomes mine. For in such a case, no one else having physical control of the thing [or money], it is acquired by me, and in a sense, there is deemed to be a delivery by the long hand."

1270 ***Proculo***: The text of Dino of Mugello that I consulted has *Pecuniam*, which indeed makes more sense in the light of the title (*de solutionibus*) and the content of the *lex* itself.

1271-73 **Fuit ... restituta**: I have been unable to identify the theologians who maintain that mere readiness to make restitution is insufficient.

1273-75 **Iohannes ... secus**: Commenting on the gloss to *Peccatum*, Johannes Andreae accepts the opinion of Dino, but requires that the creditor offering restitution be rightly motivated. One who does not actually intend to make restitution is not free from sin: "multum puto in his animum ponderandum, nec tutum puto illum, qui gerit in mente non restituere, remissione non facta" (*Novella*, ad VI *de reg. iur.* 4, *Peccatum*, n.3 [ed. cit. fol. 62rb]).

1275-77 **Et uide ... adoptiuo**: In his *additiones* to the title *de usuris* of the *Speculum iuris*, Johannes Andreae asks whether a debtor can sue the heir of a repentant usurer for recovery of usury paid, despite having released the usurer from the obligation to make restitution. He can, provided the remission was granted involuntarily. But this can be determined only by inference (*coniectura*) from the material facts of the case. Was, for example, the rate of usury moderate (twelve percent a year or less), since such rates are routinely remitted by debtors? But in other circumstances, even a high rate might be voluntarily remitted if the debtor benefited greatly from the loan, for example, if he stood to forfeit a rich inheritance unless certain pious legacies were paid immediately or if he had succeeded in having a capital penalty converted to a fine payable within a specified period of time. In such cases, the usurer's heir should not be compelled to repay the remitted usury. Johannes Andreae maintains that his opinion is not at variance with that of Dino (see n. 1267-77), since, according to the gloss to Clem. 5.5.1 (v. *Non esse Peccatum* [ed. cit. col. 258]), without repentance even restitution will not release a usurer from the penalties of sin. But the usurer's inner stance can be inferred only from the circumstances and from his known behaviour, and therefore it must be asked whether the usury charged was excessive, whether the creditor habitually lent at usury and customarily sought releases from debtors and, above all, whether he was in a position to penalize debtors who refused to remit the obligation to make restitution, for example, by burdening them with taxes and public duties. In such cases, the presumption must be that the debtor acted under compulsion, "since no one is assumed willigly to throw away his money" ("non sponte praesumitur quis iactare pecunias suas" [*Additiones in Speculum iuris*, in 4.4 *de usuris*, v. *Libellus concipitur* (ed. cit. II pp. 501b-502a]).

1276-77 **cum suo consuluit adoptiuo**: This opinion was framed in cooperation with Johannes Calderinus, who was Johannes Andreae's son by adoption (Schulte, *Quellen und Literatur des Canonischen Rechts*, 2: 247).

1277-93 **Fredericus ... *Eos***: Two *quaestiones disputatae* of Fredericus Petruccius, numbered 18 and 22 in his *Consilia et questiones*, address the question in virtually identical terms. Ridolfi seems to be paraphrasing *quaestio* 18. Petruccius gives a qualified assent to the position of the gloss to *Peccatum*: if a debtor is not acting under duress or from fear, he may, even at the instance of an unrepentant usurer or out of consideration of the favours done him, remit the usurer's obligation to make restitution. This does not, however, absolve the usurer of sin, for just as the usurer offends both God and neighbour, he must also satisfy both. X 5.19.5, a decretal of Alexander III, requires that property acquired through usury be sold and the proceeds returned to those from whom it had been taken so that usurers might be freed not only from the penalty but from the sin of usury. In X 5.12.6, Alexander III directs that although those who seize the goods of a murdered man (the case is that of Thomas Becket) are not to be punished for homicide, they are nevertheless both bound to restore the goods to those to whom they rightfully belong and obliged to perform due penance.

1293-99 **Hanc opinionem ... titulo**: In discussing what constitutes satisfaction of the usurer's obligation to make restitution, both Hostiensis and Guido de Baysio cite Dig. 13.7.9.3, where satisfaction is defined as "anything that suits the lender in the absence of actual payment." Hostiensis rejects the theologians' position that satisfaction involves complete restitution: "But if a usurer pays and offers part of what he owes but then freely and without any formal agreement asks forgiveness of the rest, and his debtor freely remits this, the usurer is free, nor is he obliged to any additional restitution, just as he would be free if he had accepted a free offering" ("Sin autem vsurarius partem liberaliter et sine pacto soluat et offerat, et de alia parte misericordiam petat et debitor liberaliter remittat, liberatus est creditor, nec tenetur vlterius ad restitutionem, sicut nec teneretur si gratis recepisset gratis oblatum" [*Summa*, ad X 5.19 *de usuris*, n.12 (ed. cit. col. 1633)]). Care, however, must be taken to ascertain the debtor's liberty of action, for "if the debtor is poor or weak and the usurer rich and powerful, I do not presume that the debtor sincerely frees the usurer" ("si debitor est pauper et inops, et vsurarius diues et potens, non praesumo quod debitor ipsum usurarium ex corde liberet" [ibid.]). Hostiensis urges moderation in exacting restitution: "I do not write this in favour of usurers, for I owe them nothing. But neither do I want to be so unfair as to favour the theologians and drive people to desperation and lay snares for their souls ... Therefore it should be said and held that, provided there was no agreement, a usurer may ask or a court order that part of the amount owed in restitution be forgiven, and I say that a usurer so forgiven is thereby absolved" ("Non scribo hoc in fauorem vsurariorum, quia nec eis astrictus sum; sed nolo a rationabili recedere, vt theologis faueam et in desperantiam inducam homines, ac parem laqueum animarum ... Dicendum est igitur et tenendum quod precibus possit vel iussu iudicis sine pactione partium remissio fieri, et sic dicam talem vsurarium absolutum" [ibid. col. 1634]).

Lapo da Castiglionchio reports Petruccius' argument in his *repetitio* on X 5.19.6. On the composition of Lapo's *repetitio*, see Introduction, pp. 81-82, and n. 2186-94.

1300-1305 **Quid tenendum ... li. .vi.**: Great care must be exercised in pronouncing on questions that concern salvation. Decretum Grat. D.42 c.2, taken from John Chrysostom's commentary on Hebrews, urges the clergy to accept guests without discrimination since, like Abraham, they may entertain angels unawares. Our text echoes VI 1.6.3, which observes of the election of popes that "the greater the risk, the more carefully one must weigh the action" ("Ubi periculum maius intenditur, ibi procul dubio est plenius consulendum") and forbids cardinals to accept income from the papal camera for the duration of a conclave.

1305-10 **cautum ... quorundam**: The teaching of Johannes Andreae on this point is that remission of the obligation is inadequate unless the usurer has a real inner disposition to make restitution. The safer procedure, according to Dino, is to ensure that the usurer has the money at hand to return. According to the theologians, it must actually be offered. The safest opinion, according to "certain others," who are not identified, is that the money must first be restored and then replaced in the hands of the usurer by the person remitting the obligation.

1311-13 **Sed de ... ostendatur**: Ridolfi, however, considers Petruccius' opinion good in law and conscience. The remainder of the question analyzes Petruccius' argument.

1314-19 **Et quod ... minus**: If the owner of a thing that has been stolen wills that it remain in the possession of the thief, the latter is relieved of any obligation to make restitution. Dig. 41.3.32.pr. states that "if a thief should buy the stolen thing from its owner and hold it as having been delivered, he ceases to possess it as stolen and begins to possess it as his own." Dig. 43.26.6.3 says that "someone who has ejected someone else by force and has then asked him for the property by *precarium* ceases to possess it by force and takes possession of it by *precarium*, and does not think that he is relinquishing possession when he begins to be a possessor with the consent of the person he ejected; for if he had bought it from him, he would now begin to take ownership of it as buyer." A *precarium* is "what is conceded to one who asks for it for his use for as long as the person who has made the concession suffers it" (Dig. 43.26.1.pr.).

1319-25 **Quod autem ... *afferamus***: That theft (*furtum*) and rapine (theft with violence) are more serious than usury is clear from the penalties for these crimes. The citations, taken from Petruccius' *quaestio*, refer to titles in the *Digest* and *Code* rather than to specific *leges*, so a general synopsis will suffice. The penalties for theft and rapine were similar. A distinction was, however, made between manifest and non-manifest theft: the former was theft detected in the act (Inst. 4.1.3) and punishable by a fourfold penalty; the latter by a twofold penalty (Inst. 4.1.5; C. 6.2.11). As a species of aggravated manifest theft, rapine carried a penalty of four times the value of the thing stolen and, in the case of free persons, the disability of infamy, that is, loss of legal and political privileges (C. 9.12.8). Both theft and rapine were delicts (private injuries) and remedies were originally pursued through private actions. From the later Republic, however, public criminal prosecutions became more common (Dig. 47.2.93), and no action for delict lay against a thief prosecuted in this way (Dig. 47.2.57). Penalties in a successful public prosecution might involve simple restitution or restitution plus damages. *Vis armata* referred to the dispossession of someone of his property by use of weapons. A successful action for repossession would result in restitution plus damages (Dig. 43.16.1).

In Decretum Grat. C.24 q.1 c.21, Jerome notes that scripture inflicts various punishments on the wicked. He concludes: "who can doubt that the more wicked deed is more severely punished?" ("Quis iam dubitauerit, hoc esse sceleratius commissum, quod est grauius uindicatum?")

1325-29 **Secunda ... symilibus:** The citations illustrate the principle that even in serious crimes, worthy satisfaction and amendment liberate from sin. X 5.17.2 states that one who robs or otherwise violates a church shall be denied penance and burial unless he makes restitution or gives full security to make amends. X 5.19.18, a decree of IV Lateran, accuses Jews of charging Christian debtors such excessive usury that the church is becoming impoverished through unpaid tithes. Christians are therefore forbidden to associate or do business with Jews until the latter make adequate compensation. For VI 5.5.2, see n. 660-64. X 3.28.14 orders that one who has been excommunicated because of "manifest excesses" (murder, arson, violence to clerics, incest) but absolved on the point of death should be buried in the parish cemetery and his heirs compelled by ecclesiastical censure to make satisfaction. X 5.17.5 makes a similar provision with respect to arsonists.

1329-33 **Sed satisfactum ... intelligitur:** Satisfaction is understood to be whatever satisfies the creditor. Dig. 2.8.1 observes that "the giving of security means the same as the giving of satisfaction. For just as we are said to satisfy someone whose request we are fulfilling, so we are said to give security to our adversary when, on account of what he claims from us, such security is given that we make him safe on this head by the provision of guarantors." For Dig. 13.7.9.3, see n. 1293-99.

1334-39 **.3.ª ratio ... remictere:** He who can give can also remit and vice versa. For VI 1.3.11, see n. 902-14. X 2.20.10 concerns the case of a priest denied canonical induction because he had simoniacally promised to remit the parishioners the five barrels of wine that were customarily paid the pastor of the church. Dig. 3.6.2 states that "anyone who has been released from an obligation can be considered to have taken money, and it is the same if a loan has been made interest-free or a thing has been leased out or sold for too little. And it does not matter whether anyone has received money himself or ordered it to be given to someone else or ratified its receipt in his name."

1339-44 **.4.ª ratio ... li. vi.:** In some cases, an obligation to make restitution cannot be remitted, such as in that noted in VI 1.3.11 (see n. 902-14). VI 3.20.2 imposes a double penalty on episcopal visitors and their entourages who demand non-monetary gifts or provisions on the occasion of visitations, notwithstanding any remission of the obligation to make restitution. The existence of such rules implies that in other cases the norm concerning remission of the obligation to make restitution stands. VI 3.3.1, for example, forbids prebendaries and canons who fail to attend the offices to receive "manual" benefices, that is, daily allowances of money or food, and requires those who have done so to make restitution. Exceptions are made for the ill, those subject to "just and reasonable bodily necessity" ("iusta et rationabilis corporalis necessitas") and those occupied by necessary church business. The gloss, however, observes that this decretal contradicts VI 1.6.30, which explicitly denies clergy pursuing church business at the papal curia the right to receive such allowances. The gloss concludes that the chapter is not bound to grant manual benefices to curial clergy, but if it should, they are not obliged to make restitution. On the gloss to VI *de reg. iur.* 4, *Peccatum*, see n. 877-80.

1345-63 **Sed quia ... remissio:** Responses to the first three arguments.

1346-56 **A significatione ... eligenda:** Dig. 32.1.69 states the principle that "one ought only to depart from the sense of the words [of a testament] when it is clear that the testator meant something else." Likewise, X 5.40.8, taken from a letter of Gregory the Great, urges attention to the sense rather than the letter: "I ask that word not translate word but sense translate sense, because generally when you attend to verbal particulars you overlook their real sense" ("rogo, non verbum ex verbo, sed sensum ex sensu transferri, quia plerumque, dum proprietas verborum attenditur, sensus veritatis amittitur"). The three citations from the title of the *Digest* on the meaning of expressions define "restitution." Dig. 50.16.22 states that "more is conveyed by restitution than by presentation; for 'to present' is to provide the presence of something, 'to restore' is also to make someone the owner and hand over the produce." Dig. 50.16.81 says that "when the praetor says, *ut opus factum restituatur*, a plaintiff must recover any loss involved; for every benefit of a plaintiff is included in the word 'restitution.'" Dig. 50.16.75 states that "someone is regarded as 'restoring' who has restored the thing which he would have had as *actor* if a controversy had not arisen over it." Dig. 22.1.38.4 notes that "in the Fabian and Paulian actions in which alienations in fraud of creditors are revoked, fruits are included, since the praetor aims at fully undoing the alienation. This is not unfair, since 'restore,' which he uses here, has a wide meaning and covers fruits." Likewise, C. 2.47.1.pr. asserts that "he against whom lies a judgement for *restitutio in integrum* should no more withhold profit than damages, and therefore he should also restore anything he obtained through purchase-sale or any other contract" ("Qui restituitur in integrum, sicut in damno morari non debet, ita nec in lucro: et ideo quidquid ad eum pervenit vel ex emptione vel ex venditione vel ex alio contractu, hoc debet restituere"). In C. 9.51.1, the emperor Antoninus Pius restores Iulianus Licinianus to his province, "and that you may know what *in integrum* means: I restore you to your honours and your order and all other things" ("Restituo te in integrum provinciae tuae ... Ut autem scias, quid sit in integrum: honoribus et ordini tuo et omnibus ceteris").

1356-60 **Secunda ... remissionem:** Usury may be recovered despite an oath not to do so. In X 2.24.20, Innocent III requires the heirs of a repentant usurer to make full restitution even to debtors who had promised not to seek such restitution.

1360-63 **Tertia ... remissio:** Dig. 12.6.1 states that "if someone mistakenly pays what is not due he can recover it by this *condictio* [*indebiti*]. However, if he knows the money is not owed, the payment is not recoverable." Petruccius asks why usury that is payed knowingly may be recovered, since the payment is *ipso facto* invalid.

1363-89 **Sed dicit ... Fredericus:** Resolutions of the arguments *contra*.

1363-64 **Sed dicit ... uide:** To the third argument *contra*. For X 2.24.6, see n. 74-78, and for the gloss, see n. 921-28.

1364-65 **Ad secundum ... tangam:** See below, nn. 1443-47 and 1447-73.

1365-80 **Sed ad ... finali:** On X 5.40.8, see n. 1346-56. The gloss adds: "one should not always have recourse to the strict meaning of the words, but rather one should consider what the testator intended and what the custom of the region is ... nor should more attention be given to the words than to the will [of the testator]" ("Non enim semper ad proprietatem verborum incurrendum est sed videndum est quid testator senserit; in qua presumptione sunt qui morantur in eo loco ... nec plus verbum quam voluntas inspici debet" [gl. ord. ad X 5.40.8, v. *Proprietas* (ed. cit. col. 1934)]). Dig. 22.3.25.pr. states that when there is a dispute about money paid but not owed, the burden of proof is on the payer to show that he paid as the result of fraud or ignorance, for "no payer is ever so careless as to throw his money around and waste it on debts not owed, especially if the payer is a careful and diligent head of his household, who would not easily be credited with a mistake." In Decretum Grat. C.14 q.6 c.1, from which VI *de reg. iur.* 4, *Peccatum* is taken, Augustine remarks that "if a another's property taken sinfully could be restored but is not, there is no true penitence but merely a pretence" ("Si res aliena, propter quam peccatum est, reddi possit, et non redditur, penitencia non agitur, sed simulatur"). However, the term he uses is not the juridically precise *restituere*, but the looser *reddere*. Dig. 50.16.94 notes that "The word 'restore,' although it has the meaning of 'give back,' acquires also by itself the meaning of give." Decretum Grat. D.20 c.1 dictum Grat. ante c.1 suggests that the sayings of some popes are more authoritative than those of the church fathers: "Hence the sayings of certain popes seem to be preferable to the determinations of Augustine, Jerome and other treatises" ("Unde nonnullorum Pontificum constitutis Augustini, Ieronimi atque aliorum tractatorum dicta eis uidentur esse preferenda"). X 5.17.2 threatens manifest thieves and violators of churches with denial of absolution and burial unless they guarantee amendment or intention to amend. X 5.18.5 says that one who has robbed a church but has subsequently confessed and made satisfaction for his theft may be raised to orders, provided the crime was not a matter of public knowledge.

1380-89 **Preterea ... Fredericus**: Petruccius poses the hypothetical case of an injury (*damnum*) involving no seizure by or transfer of property to the agent of the injury. Properly speaking, "restitution" has no place here, but rather "satisfaction." Nevertheless, in a more general sense, satisfaction would involve assigning compensation equivalent to the injury–*restituere* in the juridical sense. In Petruccius' second case, a usurer owes his debtor a hundred by way of restitution but wants to delay repayment. In order to perform his Easter duty in good conscience, he proposes drawing up a contract of loan or deposit in the amount of the sum owed payable at a later date. The debtor is satisfied, and Petruccius concludes that the usurer's obligation to make restitution is fulfilled.

1390-97 **Sed cum ... obligationis**: Petruccius' central contention is that a usurer may be freed by the debtor from the obligation to make restitution. But in the last case, Ridolfi observes, the usurer clearly intends to make restitution, and the new contract offers the debtor both proof of his intentions and the means to recover usury already paid.

1398-1412 **Sed contra ... *indebito***: For Johannes Andreae's opinion, see n. 1111-18. In the case described by Johannes Andreae, both the motive of the usurer and the freedom of the debtor are unclear. In X 1.9.5, it is argued against a claimant to a benefice that he had freely renounced it and therefore cannot seek it again; what evidence should be admitted? Clement III replies that the judge must carefully consider the nature of the renunciation, "for it scarcely seems likely that anyone, without good reasons, would lightly resign a benefice that he had gone to great expense and effort to obtain and by which he ought to be supported, and therefore we believe ... that if the judge should find that the party acted as a result of force, fear, pressure, monetary considerations, extortion or, in particular, an oath, which it is scarcely believed he would offer freely and is almost always bad, he should not hesitate to admit the evidence, unless a canonical defence is advanced" ("respondemus, quod nulla ratio hoc verisimile reddit, ut quisquam beneficium multis forte expensis et laboribus acquisitum, quo sustenari debet, facile sine magna causa sua sponte resignet, ideoque supervacuum esse non credimus, causam resignationis diligenter inquiri, quam si forte probabililem, id est, non vi, nec metu, nec oppresione, nec interventu pecuniae, nec promissione extortam iudex invenerit, maxime si non intervenerit iuramentum, quod vix fieri de voluntate propria creditur, quod fere semper a malo est, nisi replicatio canonica fuerit opposita, admittere non postponat"). X 2.23.10 asserts that solid proofs are required of one who would prove something that is unlikely, and in such cases judges should beware of accepting proofs that are not borne out by common repute or that derive from witnesses who are likely to give false testimony. On Dig. 22.3.25.pr., see n. 1365-80.

1412-18 **Secus ... *usuca.***: The Authentic *Siue a me* notes a case in which consent is insufficient: unless certain conditions are met, a husband cannot alienate dotal property even with his wife's consent. But it is different in the present case. Dig. 6.1.77 states that the recipient of a gift of land has good title even though the gift was made by letter. The gloss observes that "if you acquire something, and afterwards you are found in possession of it, the presumption is that you hold possession by reason of purchase" ("Sed sumitur hic argumentum quod si tu emeris rem aliquam, et postea in eius possessionem reperiaris, presumitur te habere possessionem ex causa emptionis" [gl. ord. ad Dig. 6.1.77, v. *Sufficiebat* (ed. cit. I p. 440a)]). Bartolus asks whether one who has title and possession from different people may usucapt: "In cases where I have title from one and possession from another, sometimes possession precedes title, and here without doubt *usucapio* proceeds, or a true or putative title may intervene.... The reason is that I have changed the cause of possession and begin to possess in virtue of the title.... Note, however, that he from whom I have title knew that I was in possession, otherwise it is different" ("Secundo casu, quando habeo titulum ab vno, possessionem ab alio, et hoc constat: et quandoque possessio praecedit titulum, et tunc sine dubio usucapio procedit, siue superueniat titulus verus vel putatiuus ... Et est ratio quia muto causam possessionis et incipio ex titulo possidere ... Quod intellige, si ille a quo incepi habere titulum sciebat me possidere, alias secus" [*Commentaria*, ad Dig. 41.3.29, n.4 (ed. cit. V fol. 99va-b)]).

1419-30 **Immo plus ... furto**: If a mental usurer is under no obligation to return usury offered as a free gift, much less is the creditor in the present case.

1431-34 **Immo etiam ... recipere**: On X 5.19.7, see n. 640-43. The wording of the decretal is significant here: "You shall forbid your parishioners to *accept* usury" ("Praeterea parochianis tuis usuras recipere interdicas"). Johannes Andreae observes that according to this decretal it is forbidden not only to demand but to accept usury: "*Recipere*: ergo non solum exigere sed etiam recipere prohibentur" (*Novella*, ad X 5.19.7, n.1 [ed. cit. V fol. 74va]). He cites Decretum Grat. D.47 c.1: "a bishop, priest or deacon who demands usury from his debtors and does not desist shall be deposed" ("Episcopus aut presbiter aut diaconus usuras a debitoribus exigens, aut desinat, aut certe deponatur"). John of Legnano's interpretation follows Johannes Andreae. Ridolfi maintains that the argument is irrelevant to the present case because "what I receive from those who willingly pay usury I do not receive as usury."

1434-42 **Nec obstat ... remissionem**: For Johannes Andreae's comments on the gloss to X 5.3.27, see n. 240-57. Ridolfi claims that this passage has no bearing on the case at hand, since here only the debtor can testify as to the freedom of his action in remitting the creditor's obligation to repay usury.

1443-47 **Contra ... precedente**: See nn. 1398-1412 to 1419-30.

1447-73 **Sed obicies ... futurum**: Ridolfi poses and resolves the objection that although the usurer, whose intention has always been corrupt, has satisfied the debtor, he has not satisfied God. The usurer may be absolved of the obligation to make restitution, but he is still obliged to exhibit contrition, both for lending at usury and for persevering with a hardened (Pharaonic) heart in his determination not to make restitution. The saying of Gregory IX introducing X 1.4.11 (a definition of the relative authority of custom) reads: "The graver the sins, the longer they hold fast the unhappy soul [of the sinner]" ("[Quum] tanto sint graviora peccata, quanto diutius infelicem animam detinent alligatam ... ").

PART 2, QUESTION 8

1474-1513 **viii.[a] questio ... questione .lxxxi.**: Question 8 summarizes a *consultatio* of Fredericus Petruccius, numbered 184 in the Venice 1508 edition of his *Consilia et questiones*. It has two parts. The first (1478-96) asks why a debtor who has formally agreed not to seek restitution of usury may nevertheless do so, while one who has remitted may not; the second (1497-1513) whether an agreement made after usury has been paid (and the creditor is under a moral obligation to make restitution) has the same force as remission.

1478-80 **Sed quere ... liberatio** For X 2.24.20, see n. 1356-60.

1481-86 **Respondeo ...** ***Solutionis***: The two cases of *pactum*, one not to seek restitution and the other granting remission are distinct. He who remits something owed transfers it to the debtor and dissolves the obligation. This is the burden of Dig. 46.3.54, which states that "the term 'performance' pertains to any release, however effected, and relates to the substance of the obligation rather than to the payment of coins," and of Dig. 50.16.176: "In the designation 'settlement,' it has been decided that every kind of satisfaction must be included. We say that someone who has done what he promised to do 'settles.'"

1487-96 **At qui ...** ***solu.***: By contrast, he who agrees not to seek restitution does not dissolve the substance of the usurer's obligation, but merely agrees to refrain from enforcing his own claims. Such an agreement, however, constitutes a *nudum pactum*, a simple, formless agreement, which, in contrast to a contract or a *stipulatio*, "gives rise not to an obligation but to a defence" (Dig. 2.14.7.4). If the claimant is excluded from recovering usury paid by the defendent's invocation of the *exceptio*, he may oppose a *replicatio*, or rejoinder, to the effect that the agreement is one condemned by X 2.24.20. Such a course is not open to him who remits and so "remission seems to be stronger than agreement," although they appear to have similar effects in extinguishing a natural obligation, that is, an obligation, like the one under discussion, for which there was no formal action. Dig. 46.3.95.4 observes that "a natural obligation is automatically removed not only by payment of the money but also by a lawful pact or by an oath; the equitable bond which alone sustains it is dissolved by the equity of the pact."

1497-1502 **Tandem ... soluente**: The *replicatio* based on X 2.24.20 in essence asserts that an agreement to forego restitution concluded before restitution could be made is void. Dig. 2.14.27.4 states that "pacts founded on a shameful ground are not to be enforced. An example would be, if I make a pact that I will not bring the action for theft or insult if you commit either of these delicts. For it is generally beneficial that there be fear of the penalty for theft or insult. But after these delicts have been committed, we can make a pact [not to sue]." Dig. 23.3.41.3 provides an analogy to the present case: "Where a dowry is promised subject to a condition by a woman's debtor and afterward, before the husband can claim it, the debtor becomes insolvent, it is settled that the risk is the wife's; for the husband is not held to have accepted the claim at a time when he could not have collected it."

1499 l. *Cum unus*: The *incipit* of Dig. 2.14.27.4 is *Si unus*. The corruption probably derives from the textual tradition of Petruccius' *consilia* reflected in the edition I consulted, where the text at this point also reads *Cum unus*. A reader of F_1 supplied the correct *incipit* in the margin.

1502-13 **Immo ita ... questione .lxxxi.**: The case is otherwise when the pact to forego restitution is concluded after restitution could have been made, for then it has the same effect as a release or a gift. If the usurer is sued for restitution, he may successfully oppose the *exceptio*; if he makes restitution, an action for recovery of a payment made in error (*condictio indebiti*) is open to him. The rationale is that after the agreement the usury ceases to be the subject of a natural obligation and becomes that of a civil obligation. Petruccius cites Dig. 46.3.95.4 (see n. 1487-96) and Dig. 12.6.26.3: "We understand a payment not to have been due not only when it is altogether not owed but also when a claim to it is barred by a perpetual defense; for that too can be recovered, unless the payer knows the defense protects him." C. 1.18.10 states that a payment not due in law can be recovered by *condictio indebiti* only if paid as the result of an error of fact, but not if paid through ignorance of the law. The gloss argues, however, that if the thing is owed in law and not by a natural obligation, an error either of fact or of law is grounds for action: "Si debitum est iure ciuili, sed naturaliter indebitum, solutum per errorem iuris vel facti repetitur" (gl. ord. ad C. 1.18.10, v. *Cum quis* [ed. cit. col. 255]). Petruccius observes that the circumstances for recovery of usury in X 2.24.20 are quite different: there the usurer directs his heirs to restore usury to anyone who could show that he had paid it, not to anyone to whom he owed restitution, and so makes fact rather than law the determining condition for repayment. Otherwise the heirs would be obliged to repay nobody.

Ridolfi offers a critique of Petruccius' argument in Part 2, question 81.

PART 2, QUESTION 9

1514-18 **Vtrum ... restitutionem**: "Whether a creditor who has lent from charity but received something beyond the principal is bound to make restitution if the debtor was in a sense constrained, for example, by the consideration that if he failed to do so he would be unable to obtain credit in future or by some other similar consideration."

1524-37 **Hunc passum ... *Consuluit***: Although it is always safer to make restitution, provided the creditor acted from pure motives in accepting something beyond the pricipal and does not suffer from conscientious scruples, he is not bound to make restitution, even if he discovers after the fact that the debtor was not acting freely. For at the time of the transaction, the creditor was acting in good faith, notwithstanding the debtor's state of mind, about which he could know nothing. For the comments of Hostiensis, see n. 1577-86.

1538-59 **Ad predicta ... factas**: VI *de reg. iur.* 73 states that "something done legitimately should not be undone though some mishap occur as a result of which it would not have been begun" ("Factum legitime retractari non debet, licet casus postea eveniat, a quo non potuit inchoari"). The gloss gives the examples of a man who goes mad after marriage, who learns that his wife is related to him by affinity and so on. In none of these cases does the new factor invalidate an action originally undertaken in good faith. For the definitions of Hostiensis and Gottofredo, see nn. 44-45 to 47-51 and 79-83 to 132-44. On Gregory of Rimini's analysis, see nn. 164-231 and 2459-60 to 2611-22. These definitions pose no contradiction since the creditor's intentions were legitimate both at the time of the loan and at the moment of receiving the gift.

But Johannes Andreae's comments on X 1.3.43 seem to rule out this conclusion. The decretal punishes abuses of papal rescripts, among them the fraudulent use of a rescript by another person of the same name; offenders are liable for costs and damages. In his comments on this text, Johannes Andreae cites the opinion of Hostiensis that if the recipient of the rescript genuinely believed it had been granted to him, he is not liable; but if he used it after becoming aware that such use would be fraudulent, he is. But Ridolfi argues that the cases are not really analogous, for in Johannes Andreae's example, the recipient becomes aware of the fraud before completing the act for which he required the rescript, while in the present case the creditor learns of the debtor's true disposition only after the latter has paid.

1560-68 Pro et ... fides: This cluster of citations considers whether one who is unconsciously an unjust possessor may acquire ownership by means of long uncontested occupancy (*praescriptio longi temporis*), an institution virtually identical to *usucapio*. Canon and Roman law diverged on prescription, the former generally requiring good faith at all stages of the process. For a discussion and bibliography, see Kuehn, *Law, Family, and Women*, 108-111.

The gloss to Decretum Grat. C.14 q.6 c.1 (for this canon, see n. 1365-80) observes that the canon appears to invalidate the claims of the possessor, since duration does not diminish but rather increase the sin of one who occupies the property of another; moreover, good faith is required at every stage of prescription. But if the possessor remains unaware that the land belongs to another for the term of the prescription–that is, if he is acting subjectively in good faith–he legitimately prescribes, even if he should subsequently learn the true facts, though some maintain that prescribed property held for purposes of profit should be restored if the possessor is disturbed in conscience. Decretum Grat. C.34 q.2 c.5 asks whether a woman who marries a man whom she mistakenly believes to be free is an adulteress. The answer is that she is not so long as she remains ignorant of the truth. The canon perceives an analogy to the law of property: "just as in property law one is rightly called a possessor in good faith so long as he is unaware that he possesses the property of someone else. But when he becomes aware of the truth and fails to withdraw from the property, then he is considered to be in bad faith and will rightly be described as an unjust possessor" ("... sicut in iure praediorum tamdiu quisque bonae fidei possessor rectissime dicitur, quamdiu se possidere ignorat alienum. Cum uero scierit, nec ab aliena possessione recesserit, tunc malae fidei perhibetur, tunc iuste iniustus vocabitur"). The gloss observes, however, that "it does not say 'possessed' [but 'possesses']; for when prescription is complete, he does not know that he 'possesses' but that he 'possessed' somebody else's property; since at that point he has no awareness of possessing the property of another, he is not bound to make restitution" ("Non dicit 'possedisse,' nam post completam praescriptionem non scit se possidere alienum, sed possedisse; nec habet tunc conscientiam rei alienae, vnde non tenetur restituere" [gl. ord. ad Decretum Grat. C.34 q.2 c.5, v. *Possidere* (ed. cit. col. 1919)]). X 2.26.5 and 20 declare that a possessor in bad faith may not acquire ownership by prescription. The gloss to X 2.26.5 notes the above arguments and approves the opinion that the possessor in the situation discussed here need not make restitution: "Others say–and this appears to be the truer opinion–that he is not bound to return it, for it no longer belongs to someone else but in fact is his own and he possesses it justly" ("Alii dicunt, quod videtur verius, quod non tenetur eam amplius reddere, quia iam non esset aliena, immo sua et iuste eam possidet" [gl. ord. ad X 2.26.5, v. *Nouerit* (ed. cit. col. 856)]). X 2.26.20 contains a reference to time: "It is not fitting that one who prescribes at any moment in time be aware that the thing belongs to another" ("Oportet, ut qui praescribit in nulla temporis parte rei habeat conscientiam alienae"). The gloss interprets this as a reference to the period of time necessary to prescribe, not to time after prescription has been successfully completed: "*Nulla temporis*: scilicet ipsius praescriptionis. Si enim post completam praescriptionem sciat rem alienam, non dicitur ideo mala fide possidere" [ibid. ad X 2.26.20, v. *Nulla temporis* (ed. cit. col. 875)]). VI *de reg. iur.* 2 states that "a possessor in bad faith will not prescribe at any time" ("Possessor malae fidei ullo tempore non praescribit"). The gloss approves the above opinions, but adds that in some cases it may be necessary to prove title as well: "say in short that if the common law or presumption is not against the possessor, good faith is sufficient. Otherwise it is necessary to adduce and prove title, unless it is can be adduced that the prescription is from time immemorial" ("dic breviter quod si ius commune vel praesumptio non est contra possessorem, sufficit bona fides; alias necesse est allegari titulum et probari, nisi allegetur praescriptio tanti temporis cuius contrarii non sit memoria" [gl. ord. ad VI *de reg. iur.* 2, *Possessor* (ed. cit. col. 715)]).

Ridolfi prefers the doctrine of the glosses to Decretum Grat. C.14 q.6 c.1, X 2.26.5 and 20, which allow for a knowledge of unjust possession after the fact.

1568-77 Potest ... consilio .223.: This parenthetical passage illustrates the proposition that the law can make what is mine yours. Several of the texts cited here are analyzed in detail by Pennington, *Prince and the Law*, 8-164.

X 1.2.7 declares that lay statutes concerning church property are *ultra vires*. Innocent IV maintains that this is also true of laws affecting the property rights of laymen, with the exception of "just cause": "Nor may they legislate on the property rights of laymen, since such a statute would injure the rights of another, rights which pertain to someone or are acquired by natural law, such as ownership, obligations and so forth. Such rights are not conferred by civil law or by the emperor, like actions ... Hence a rescript or pragmatic sanction or annotation prejudicial to such rights is invalid ... for natural rights are perpetual ... I say, then, that a law or rescript prejudicial to natural law is void, unless there should be just cause, lest the two be brought into conflict" ("Super rebus etiam laicorum hoc statuere non possent, cum tale statutum esset in laesionem iuris alterius et eius iuris, quod ad aliquem spectat vel acquiritur de iure naturali, vt sunt dominia, obligationes et huiusmodi. Et non datur a iure ciuili, vel ab Imperatore vt actiones.... Vnde rescriptum vel pragmatica sanctio vel annotatio concessum in praeiudicium talis iuris non valet.... Nam et naturalia iura sunt perpetua ... Et dico non valere legem vel rescriptum in praeiudicium naturalis iuris, nisi iusta causa interueniat, ne sint contraria" [*Commentaria*, ad X 1.2.7, nn.2-3 (ed. cit. fol. 3va)]). X 5.36.8 declares that a communal statute by which citizens promise not to sue for damages arising from factional strife does not preclude claims for expenses. Citing X 1.2.7, Innocent observes that the commune may legislate to the prejudice of its own members: "Say that they could legislate to their disadvantage, for just as they obliged themselves to provide for damages by their own statute, they could overturn the obligation with a general statute made by those who rule the city" ("Vel dic quod potuerunt in eorum praeiudicium statuere, nam ... sicut statuto suo se obligauera[n]t ad damna refarcienda, ... ita statuto generaliter facto per illos tantum, per quos regitur ciuitas, potuerunt obligationem tollere" [ibid. ad X 5.36.8 (ed. cit. fol. 541rb)]). The gloss to X 2.26.5 notes that "the author of a canon or a *lex* can give me someone else's property, and I shall be secure" ("Conditor canonis vel legis potest mihi dare rem alienam, et tutus ero" [gl. ord. ad X 2.26.5, v. *Noverit* (ed. cit. col. 856)]).

The gloss to C. 7.37.3 reviews various interpretations of the phrase "all things belong to the prince" (*omnia principis*). Martinus (d. ca. 1158) held that all things belonged to the prince in the sense of ownership (*ad proprietatem*), while Bulgarus maintained that the phrase just referred to his protection of and jurisdiction over all things (*ad protectionem vel iurisdictionem*). The gloss prefers to read the text as "all things that pertain to the imperial fisc and patrimony belong to the prince; and so my book does not belong to the prince, and I have an action for recovery that he does not have" ("Vel verius omnia sunt sua, scilicet fiscalia et patrimonialia ... Vnde codex meus non est principis, sed mihi pro eo datur rei vindicatio directa, non principi" [gl. ord. ad C. 7.37.3, v. *Omnia principis* (ed. cit. col. 1867)]). This is the opinion approved by the gloss to the constitution *Omnem*, which introduces the *Digest*.

In his own comments on *Omnem*, Bartolus reviews the opinions and concludes: "Could the emperor, simply by making a law, take away my ownership without just cause? I say no ... But what about a city? I say that a city even less than the emperor can make a law that strips me of ownership without just cause" ("Numquid legem condendo possit [Imperator] simpliciter auferre dominium rei meae sine aliqua causa? Et dico quod non ... Item quero quid de ciuitate? Dico idem multo fortius quod etiam legem condendo dominium rei meae sine causa auferre non potest" [*Commentaria*, in Dig. Prooemium II, const. *Omnem*, nn.4-5 (ed. cit. I fol. 4rb)]). At Dig. 6.1.15 and 42.5.37, he gives two examples of just cause. Ulpian says at Dig. 6.1.15.2 that an unsuccessful defendant in an action for *vindicatio* of a parcel of land that has been expropriated for veterans must hand over even the token sum he had been paid. Bartolus deduces that the prince or a city may for just cause take away my right and give it to another: "Vltimo nota quod princeps ex causa potest auferre ius meum seu rem meam et dare alteri. Idem puto in Republica alicuius ciuitatis" (ibid., in 6.1.15, n.1 [ed. cit. I fol. 171ra]). Dig. 42.5.37 states that by its own statute the city of Coela Syria has priority over other creditors with claims to the property of a deceased debtor. The gloss suggests that this was a privilege granted by the emperor, though it concedes that a city could make such a law in its own right. Bartolus prefers the latter opinion: "I ask whether a city could pass a statute prejudicial to the rights of a private person ... Innocent ... says that it may not, but the truth is that it can by making a generally applicable law, as here ... But it cannot by passing a law applicable to a single person" ("Quaero vtrum ciuitas posset facere statutum per quod auferatur ius priuati ... Innocentius ... dicit quod non, sed veritas est quod potest facere faciendo legem vniuersalem, vt hic ... Sed faciendo legem priuatam contra vnum, hoc non potest" [ibid., in Dig. 42.5.37, n.1 (ed. cit. V fol. 128ra)]).

The gloss to Decretum Grat. C.9 q.3 c.21 remarks that just as the pope can call on the services of any cleric, the emperor may take away anyone's slave. And just as the latter can take away anyone's property, the pope may deprive a cleric of his benefice, abolish rights of presentation and depose a bishop; but he should not exercise these rights simultaneously because "he would throw the whole church into confusion" ("Sed numquid omnes simul? Non, quia sic vniuersalem ecclesiam turbaret, quod esse non debet" [gl. ord. ad Decretum Grat. C.9 q.3 c.21, v. *Ad nos* (ed. cit. col. 920)]). Commenting on the gloss, Guido de Baysio cites both Innocent's argument that the prince cannot take away my property and C. 7.37.3: "The prince can indeed take away a perpetual or temporal action, but if he wants to deprive me of my property by rescript he cannot, because ownership of things pertains to natural law ... and natural law is immutable." ("Princeps bene potest auferre actionem perpetuam et temporalem, sed si vult auferre rem meam ex rescripto non potest, quia dominia rerum sunt de iure nature ... et naturalia immutabilia sunt" [*Rosarium*, ad Decretum Grat. C.9 q.3 c.21, n.1 (ed. cit. fol. 170rb)]). The gloss to Gratian's *dictum* placed after Decretum Grat. C.23 q.8 c.22 notes that as Pharoah bought land during the famine in Egypt, likewise the emperor does not own all things; for a person does not buy what is already his own: "*Emeret*: et ita non sunt omnia Imperatoris, quia nemo potest rem suam emere" (gl. ord. ad Decretum Grat. C.23 q.8 c.22 dictum Grat. post c.22, v. *Emeret* [ed. cit. cols. 1436-37]). Commenting on the same passage, Guido de Baysio notes Hostiensis' doctrine that the prince's jurisdiction extends to *dominium maius* and *proprietas*, but prefers the opinion that all things belong to the prince in virtue of jurisdiction: "You should say therefore that all things belong to the emperor with respect to general jurisdiction ... And so, everyone in the kingdom of France is subject to the power and rule of the king of France, and over them he has the power of general jurisdiction and authority, for the word 'authority' may be understood in several ways" ("Dicas ergo quod omnia sunt imperatoris quoad iurisdictionem generalem ... vnde omnes homines qui sunt in regno Francie sunt sub potestate et principatu regis Francie et in eis habet imperium generalis iurisdictionis et potestatis, nam verbum potestatis pluribus modis accipitur" [*Rosarium* ad Decretum Grat. C.23 q.8 c.22 dictum Grat. post c.22, nn.5-6 (fol. 267ra)]).

Oldradus de Ponte's *consilium* 223 considers whether the king can set aside rights of primogeniture. His review of the opinions on the prince's authority over private property rights parallels that of the jurists cited above.

1577-86 **Quam ... contrarium:** In his *quaestio* on the rule *Possessor*, Johannes Andreae notes that the common opinion of the canonists is that a knowledge of unjust possession acquired after the period necessary for prescription has elapsed does not invalidate possession in good faith.

Hostiensis accepts the common opinion, observing that theologians hold the opposite: "But what if after prescription he becomes aware that he possesses the property of another, say he learned for certain that the coins he prescribed belonged to Martin: should he return them to Martin? The theologians say that he should ... while the masters of the canons commonly say the opposite, because according to both laws once prescription is complete he who prescribed is secure ... It seems to me that on this question the conscience of the theologians is too angelic ... Therefore, if somebody who has legitimately prescribed thinks that he sins mortally by retaining the thing prescribed, I do not consider him theological so much as fraudulent, for he fears what is unworthy of suspicion.... Nevertheless, if his conscience cannot be calmed, he should follow his conscience and return the thing, for otherwise he will not avoid danger" ("Sed quid si iam completa praescriptione conscientiam rei alienae incipiat habere, puta audiuit et pro certo quod haeres quas praescripsit erant Martini: numquid ipsas debet reddere Martino? Theologi dicunt quod sic ... Magistri canonum communiter contradicunt, quia completa praescriptione tutus est qui praescripsit secundum vtrumque ius ... Mihi videtur quod in hac quaestione conscientia theologorum est nimis angelica ... igitur si quis credit peccare mortaliter retinendo rem praescriptam legitime, ipsum non theologum iudico, sed fraudulosum, cum id timeat quod nulla suspicione est dignum.... Si tamen eius conscientia ratificari non potest, reddat rem et sequatur conscientiam, nam aliter ... periculum non euadet" [Summa, X 2.26 *de praescriptionibus*, rubricella *de praescriptione rerum immobilium*, n.3 (ed. cit col. 726)]). X 5.3.18 refers to "the over-scrupulousness that hesitates over things in which there is nothhing at all to fear" ("leges ... tenuem religionem [vocant] quae in talibus haesitat, ubi non est aliquatenus haesitandum").

At X 2.26.5, Johannes Andreae attributes to Huguccio the opinion that restitution is due whenever the possessor discovers himself to be or to have been in bad faith, but the gloss to Decretum Grat. C.34 q.2 c.5 makes clear that Huguccio shared the common opinion, with the exception that if the possessor's conscience was troubled, he should make restitution.

1586-91 **Or quia ... scripta:** In the sixth question of his *quaestio disputata* on *Possessor*, Johannes Andreae deals at length with the question of whether bad faith emerging after a completed prescription necessitates restitution. The *quaestio* is largely a critique of Gerard of Siena's rigorist (*pertinax*) opinion that subsequent bad faith invalidates prescription. In reply, Johannes Andreae adduces the common opinion of the jurists and Thomas Aquinas, concluding that the possessor is not obliged to make restitution unless, as Hostiensis and Raymund observe, he is troubled in conscience.

1592-1600 **Et que ... li. .vi.:** For *oppositio* 8, see nn. 937-53 to 998-1002. For the opinion of Gregory of Rimini, see nn. 2467-93 to 2494-2531. Ridolfi concludes that it is always safer to make restitution, but that there is a probable opinion in favour of the creditor.

X 2.26.17 says that one who possesses in the name of another will not prescribe; nor will he do so in his own name if there is a presumption against him, unless he has good faith and title. The gloss observes that both the canons and the laws require good faith in one who prescribes and that "good faith is always presumed unless it is proven to the contrary, since the law says that ignorance is presumed unless knowledge is proven" ("haec bona fides semper praesumitur, nisi probetur contrarium, cum lex dicat, praesumitur ignorantia nisi probetur scientia" [gl. ord. ad X 2.26.17, v. *Bona fides* (ed. cit. col. 869)]). Moreover, he who is in doubt is held to be acting in good faith: "Item, etsi habeat conscientiam dubiam, bona fide dicitur" (ibid.).

The gloss to VI 2.14.3 distinguishes between ownership (*dominium*) and quasi-ownership (*quasi dominium*), the latter representing the status, for example, of a purchaser in good faith who has property from one who is not in fact the owner. If the *quasi dominus* loses possession before completion of *usucapio*, he has an action for recovery called *actio Publiciana in rem*, for which he must prove title, delivery and good faith at the time of the transaction, "which is presumed unless the contrary be demonstrated" ("oportet eum probare ... bonam fidem tempore emptionis et traditionis, quod praesumitur, nisi contrarium probetur" [gl. ord. ad VI 2.14.3, v. *Dominii vel quasi* (ed. cit. col. 345)]).

PART 2, QUESTION 10

1601-3 **Vtrum ... recipere**: "Assuming there is no agreement, can it be presumed that a debtor who gives something in excess of the principal does so freely? Second, can it be presumed that the recipient receives such a gift in good conscience?"

1607-11 **Ad primum ...** ***uerisimile***: On *oppositio* 8, see nn. 937-53 to 998-1002. On Dig. 22.3.25.pr., see n. 1365-80. On X 1.9.5 and 2.23.10, see n. 1398-1412. X 2.13.2 states that the renunciation of one who has been forcibly removed from his benefice cannot be adduced to hinder his petition for reinstatement, "because it is unlikely that he who renounces his rights after despoliation did so freely" ("... quia non est verisimile, quod sponte iuri suo renunciaverit qui renunciat spoliatus").

1611-17 **In contrarium ... contingit**: For Gerard of Siena's position, see nn. 1052-65 and 1066-88; for Johannes Andreae's critique, see n. 1089-98.

For X 3.26.7 and Dig. 5.3.25.11, see n. 709-14. X 3.24.1, from the letters of Gregory the Great, characterizes the liberal man as one who considers himself to owe what he freely gives: "From a certain nobility he imposes on himself the rule that he regards what he gives freely as a debt and, lest it redound to his benefit, he views himself as having given nothing" ("Hanc sibi quodammodo nobilitas legem imponit, ut debere se quod sponte tribuit existimet, et, nisi in beneficiis suis creverit, nihil se praestitisse putet").

1618-27 **Solutio ...** ***Cum ita***: If the principal debt is extinct at the time of payment, the debtor can be presumed to be acting freely; otherwise not. For the gloss to Dig. 12.6.26.2 and X 2.24.6, see n. 921-28.

But on the basis of the considerations noted in *oppositio* 8 (see nn. 968-91 and 994-97), the presumption that the debtor is not acting freely might be overturned, "for," as Ridolfi observes, "a presumption can be overthrown by another presumption." In X 2.23.11, a free woman who has cohabited for more than ten years with a serf denies that he is her husband, despite his production of an instrument in which they describe one another as spouses. In such cases, local opinion of the union should be taken into account, and if the couple were reputed to have lived together as husband and wife, the union should be deemed a marriage. In X 2.23.14, the bishop of Auxerre has confessed to heresy but later retracts. Since either his confession was a lie or his retraction a perjury, there is a strong presumption against him. Innocent III, however, declines to condemn him on presumption alone, urging the bishop of Nevers to obtain sureties in addition to his oath to determine whether his retraction is sincere.

The principle holds true particularly in cases where the debtor acknowledges in writing that he acts freely, since there is then no room for conjecture. Dig. 45.1.137.2 states that if I agree to pay at Ephesus, a reasonable period of time is implicit in the agreement. Reasonable time is "the time which the conscientious head of a household would need to do what is promised." That is, I need not proceed by imperial post but neither must I dawdle; when such time has elapsed I am liable for payment. But if I should chance to arrive at Ephesus before the time, I must pay at once "since there is no room for conjecture when the actual time taken is established."

1627-39 Et ita ... questione .78.: The latter opinion is held "by many distinguished doctors," whom Ridolfi reviews in Part 2, question 78, but he excepts cases where fraud can be demonstrated, "for we know by experience that debtors are often in such need that they will do or write or admit whatever their creditors want in order to put off repayment." VI 1.7.2: I have a papal letter providing me to the next vacant prebend in a certain church. Although this promises to be a rich benefice, I am prevented from obtaining it by the resignation of one who holds a poor benefice. Boniface VIII rules that if the latter appears, on the basis of reasonable inference, to have acted fraudulently, I am not bound to accept the poor benefice but am entitled to the next vacancy comparable to the one in the expectation of which I obtained letters. If the prebend who resigned subsequently obtained the rich benefice and if fraud can be demonstrated, he is to be deprived. The gloss notes that fraud may be proven by "clear inferences": "*Coniecturas*: nota quod dolus probatur ex perspicuis coniecturis ... et qui eum allegat, probare illum debet" (gl. ord. ad VI 1.7.2, v. *Coniecturas* [ed. cit. col. 184]). For Johannes Andreae's comments on X 3.17.5, see n. 994-97.

Nevertheless, a written declaration will stand unless the contrary is proven. X 3.12.1: the office of chancellor to the archbishop of Milan having been vacant for a year, Innocent III nominated his own candidate in accordance with the provisions of IV Lateran. The archbishop replied that he was unable to implement the pope's directive because he had sequestrated the revenues in order to pay his debts. Subsequently, however, he asserted that he had secretly appointed a relative to the benefice ten months previously. Moreover, after receiving the pope's mandate, he invested his relative publicly with the episcopal seals, though he later denied doing so. Since the appointment was made secretly and was therefore suspect, and since the archbishop's testimony was contradictory, the presumption was against him. Clem. 2.7.1 states that apostolic letters in which the pope makes known his own action and intention are to be accepted as probative. The gloss notes that they are not equally probative if they describe the action of another although they create a presumption that stands unless the opposite can be proven: "Quid si talia narrata super quibus fundatur intentio papae non sunt de facto suo? Per hanc litteram videtur quod illa non probent ... Satis puto quod talia verba probant saltem praesumptiue, ex quo super illis fundatur intentio papae, ita quod praesumptioni stabitur nisi contrarium probetur" (gl. ord. ad Clem. 2.7.1, v. *Fecisse narramus* [ed. cit. col. 104]).

1640 **Ad secundum membrum:** The second part of the question is: "Can it be presumed that the recipient of something beyond the principal does so in good conscience?"

1640-44 **Ad secundum ... diceretur:** No one is presumed to be guilty in the absence of evidence. In X 1.12.1, Innocent III declares that candidates for episcopal consecration are presumed worthy unless something can be proved against them, just as in ordinations to the inferior orders, he whom the archdeacon does not know to be unworthy is presumed worthy. In Decretum Grat. C.1 q.7 c.26 (=C. 9.27.6) Theodosius and Valentinian express the principle that no one is presumed to act in a way prejudicial to his salvation: "And although we judge no one who despises the oath so unmindful of divine fear that he would place convenience before his own salvation, nevertheless in order to join the necessity of penalty to fear of salvation, if anyone dares disregard the proffered oath we concede everyone the power to accuse not only the recipients but the givers [of provincial honours] of, as it were, a public offence, with a fourfold penalty to be imposed on anyone who shall be convicted" ("Et licet neminem diuini timoris, contempnendo iureiurando, arbitremur inmemorem, ut saluti propriae ullum commodum anteponat, tamen ut ad salutis timorem ex necessitate periculi subiugetur, si quis ausus fuerit prebita sacramenta negligere, non modo aduersus accipientem, sed etiam aduersus dantem accusandi cunctis tamquam crimen publicum concedimus facultatem, quadrupli pena eo, qui conuictus fuerit, modis omnibus feriendo"). X 5.12.18 describes a case in which a priest attacked a thief who was robbing his church; the thief was then set upon by a mob and died of his wounds. Fearing for his salvation, the priest asks whether he is guilty of homicide. He is if it can be established that he struck the fatal blow, but he should be suspended if he intended to do murder, "since in this case it is safer to abstain from celebrating" ("... etsi forte non homicida non sit, a sacerdotali officio abstinere debet, quum in hoc casu cessare sit tutius quam temere celebrare"). Decretum Grat. D.6 de poen. c.3 forbids penitents to confess to a priest other than their own parish priest, unless the latter is incapable because of ignorance of administering the sacrament. The gloss notes that a confessor can accept the bare word of a penitent that his priest is incapable, since it is unlikely that anybody would lie in the context of the sacrament: "Sed numquid credet ille extraneus sacerdos simplici verbo eius poenitentis qui dicit suum sacerdotem imperitum? Sic, quia non est verisimile quod cum mendacio veniat ad poenitentiam" (gl. ord. ad Decretum Grat. D.6 de poen. c.3, v. *Pro ignorantia* [ed. cit. col. 1897]). Clem. 5.7.1 forbids religious, on pain of excommunication, to administer the sacraments to clerics or laymen without the permission of the parish priest. The gloss asks, "but is it so if the religious believes a parishioner who says he has such permission?" and replies in the negative, because "no one is presumed to be unmindful of his own salvation" ("sed nunquid credet religiosus parochiano dicenti se habere talem licentiam? Videtur quod sic ... quia non est praesumendus immemor suae salutis" [gl. ord. ad Clem. 5.7.1, v. *Non habita* (ed. cit. col. 263)]).

1645-51 **Accedat ... prontus:** For Johannes Andreae's comments, see n. 1275-77. For Part 2, question 62, see n. 1322-26.

PART 2, QUESTION 11

1652-53 **Vtrum ... emat:** "Whether it is licit to buy the revenues of an estate for the purchaser's lifetime or for some other designated period."

Questions 11 to 18 deal with *census* contracts (see Introduction, pp. 80-83, 98-99).

1657-79 **Respondeo ... Innocentium:** In his commentary on X 5.19.6 (for this decretal, see n. 145-64), Innocent IV discusses *census* contracts in the context of *venditio sub dubio*, noting three opinions, of which he approves the third. (1) The contract is licit if the return promised the investor does not exceed what he could by common estimate expect from land bought for the same amount. He alleges X 5.19.10 and refers presumably to the third case–that of a credit sale–though Ridolfi does not consider it pertinent. (2) If the purchase is perpetual, however great the return with respect to the price, the contract is licit because, according to Dig. 4.4.16.4, "contracting parties are in the course of nature allowed to overreach each other." (3) Innocent prefers to assimilate a series of concrete examples of *census* contracts based on existing property revenues or unfree labour to purchase-sale agreements (see Introduction, pp. 82-83). Since *census* was not a Roman law contract, Innocent's citations are rather tangential. In C. 1.2.10, Theodosius and Valentinian declare that ships of more than two thousand *modii* capacity may not be used by public or ecclesiastical dignitaries before public goods have been transhipped. The title *de hereditate vel actione vendita* (C. 4.39) deals generally with the sale of inheritances and actionable rights.

1680-87 **Ostiensis ...** ***fundum*:** In his *novella* on X 5.19.6, Johannes Andreae follows Hostiensis in observing that a perpetual or limited *census* contract is usually licit unless the creditor's profit exceeds the just price by more than half or unless it represents an attempt to circumvent the usury prohibition. The remainder of his comments reproduce the argument of Innocent IV on X 5.19.6. For X 3.17.5, see n. 650-52; for Dig. 19.1.13.26, see n. 817-22. In C. 4.32.26, Justinian sets rates of interest, limiting those on loans to six percent a year (half of one percent a month). X 5.19.13 states that despite a debtor's oath not to seek restitution a judge can compel a usurer to make restitution, "lest [usurers] be allowed to benefit by deceit and fraud" ("... ne dolo et fraude contingat eos commodum reportare").

In the remaining two citations, the canonists detect analogies to the redeemable character of many *census* agreements. C. 4.54.2 states that if an estate is sold on the condition that the seller or his heirs may redeem it by paying a specific price, the seller can compel performance by an *actio praescriptis verbis,* a general action adaptable to various situations, or by an *actio ex vendito,* a right of action against the buyer for payment, if the buyer or his heir refuses to restore the property on being offered the agreed price. In C. 4.54.6, an estate is delivered to a buyer for a low price in consideration of delivery of a specific thing (*certa res*) agreed between the parties; when the condition is not fulfilled, the estate should be returned to the seller.

1688-91 **Sed oppone ... pretium:** The licitness of *census* contracts may be questioned on the grounds that over a long period the returns to the buyer will exceed the price he paid; such a discrepancy might render a credit transaction usurious. For X 5.19.6, see n. 145-64; for X 5.19.19, n. 751-58; for the third response of X 5.19.10, see n. 673.

1692-1711 **Soluit ... *ciuitate*:** Innocent replies to this objection by asserting that *census* are contracts of sale and are therefore no more vitiated by profit than other sales. Moreover, in contrast to the cases cited in objection, here there is an element of uncertainty about the future value of the return that guarantees the licitness of the contract.

1712-31 **Est ergo ... emant:** Innocent's argument assumes that the buyer obtains rights to an existing income, but what if the *census* is created specifically for the purpose of the contract? Innocent reports the opinion of those who consider such contracts licit on the grounds that they involve no loan but rather a sale and because there remains an element of risk. Nevertheless, as Ridolfi observes, he counsels the faithful to abstain from such agreements. Despite this qualification, John of Legnano attributes approval of such contracts to Innocent. Others maintain that Johannes Andreae approves newly created *census* in his commentary on the rubric of the title *de usuris* of the *Speculum iuris*. There he describes the case of an investor who purchases for a thousand a *census* that by common estimate will yield a total of 1500 over ten years (a return of five percent a year). In support of the investor, Johannes Andreae points out that he risks his capital, which could be more profitably invested in land: "on behalf of the buyer it may be said that he submits his thousand to fortune, from which he endures various mishaps, for example, of war, sterility and so forth. Again, even assuming that sterility ceased for most of the ten years, he would still have only five hundred *lire* fruit or profit. And he could certainly have got a better return, that is, more than fifty a year, through a genuine purchase" ("pro emptore facit quod submittit etiam ille mille fortunae, ex quo nullos casus excipit, hostilitatis, sterilitatis, vel alios. Item dato quod cesset omnis sterilitas in capite decem annorum, non haberet nisi quingentas libras de fructu, vel lucro. Et certe plus habuisset communiter ex reditu vere emptionem faciendo de mille, scilicet vltra quinquaginta annuatim" [*Additiones in Speculum iuris*, in 4.4 *de usuris*, super rubr. (ed. cit. II p. 500b)]).

For the views of Lapo da Castiglionchio, see nn. 3668-71 to 3752-71.

1732-57 **Ego autem ... tempore:** In this passage, Ridolfi states his own position on newly created *census* and discusses two different readings of Johannes Andreae on the same topic (see also Noonan, *Scholastic Analysis of Usury*, 161, n. 35). (1) Ridolfi holds that such agreements will usually, though not necessarily, be presumed in fraud of usury. For this position he claims the authority of Innocent IV and Johannes Andreae; indeed, the latter's *novella* on X 5.19.6 simply reproduces Innocent's commentary and concluding reservations *verbatim*. (2) Moreover, Ridolfi contends, Johannes Andreae maintains this position in his commentary on the *Speculum iuris*. This is confirmed if, as some claim, Johannes Andreae's reservations about newly created *census* expressed in his *novella* on X 5.19.6 apply only in cases in which both the term and the return are guaranteed, for in the *Speculum iuris* commentary he suggests that such agreements approach usury, referring the reader to his earlier comments: "note that this doubt applies to misfortunes in the fruits, for if the fruits were certain, for example, rental returns not subject to chance, and if the term is set, the contract approximates usury, on which I write more in my comments on the gloss to X 5.19.6" ("adverte, quia hoc dubium facit infortunium in fructibus, quia si fructus essent certi, puta censuales reditus non submissi fortunae, et tempus certum, plus trahetur contractus ad vsuram, de quo latius scripsi eodem titulo *In ciuitate* in magna glosa" [*Additiones in Speculum iuris*, in 4.4 *de usuris*, super rubr. (ed. cit. II p. 500b)]). (3) Yet others maintain that Johannes Andreae intended to censure all *census* contracts that embodied such terms, including established *census*. Ridolfi notes, however, that the jurist defers to the position of Innocent and Hostiensis, who are quite explicit in their approval of established *census*, "provided there is no fraud or deception." (4) This last point lends support to the proposition that newly created *census* are illicit, but Ridolfi questions whether this is the only or necessarily the correct deduction from Innocent's argument.

For a summary of Part 2, question 60, see n. 1816-39.

1758-78 **Item ... memorata**: Ridolfi proposes that any *census*, including established *census*, in which the return and the term are guaranteed should be presumed fraudulent, particularly when the purchaser is accustomed to lend at usury. On X 3.21.4, see n. 770-76. Johannes Andreae's concluding comment on the rubric to the title *de usuris* in the *Speculum iuris* notes that "the foregoing apply especially when the buyer is not a usurer, for when he is, the contract must be presumed suspect" ("procedunt maxime praedicta vbi emens vsurarius non est; vbi enim talis esset, praesumeretur facile contra contractum" [*Additiones in Speculum iuris*, in 4.4 *de usuris*, super rubr. (ed. cit. II p. 501a)]). This conclusion is not at variance with the opinions of Innocent and Hostiensis, who restrict their approval to forms of *census* in which there is no fraud or deception.

1778-85 **Istud autem ... preterire**: All authorities agree in condemning as unlawful an agreement whereby the seller of the *census* obliges himself to more than the returns of the property.

PART 2, QUESTION 12

1786-89 **Constituit ... licitus**: "Someone creates a *census* of one florin on a house and sells it for ten with a provision that he may repurchase for the same amount. But if the *census* were sold for its true price, without the additional agreement, it would be worth twenty. Is this contract licit?"

This question reports John of Legnano's discussion of the case in his commentary on X 5.19.10.

1795-1801 **Arguit ... *Illo uos***: John of Legnano offers four arguments against the contract. (1) The contract is illicit because money, which cannot be the object of a sale, is here sold. Dig. 46.1.42 states that "money cannot be quantified in terms of merchandise in the way that merchandise, measured by quantity or number, may be assessed in money." Dig. 18.1.1 contains an account of the origin of money as a medium of exchange and measure of value: "But since it did not always and easily happen that when you had something which I wanted, I, for my part, had something that you were willing to accept, a material was selected which, being given a stable value by the state, avoided the problems of barter by providing a constant medium of exchange. That material, struck in due form by the mint demonstrates its utility and title not by its substance as such but by its quantity, so that no longer are the things exchanged both called wares but one of them is termed the price." (2) The contract also separates the use of a thing from the thing itself and (3) sells it for less than it is worth. (4) Finally, because there is a payment beyond the principal, the transaction approximates usury. For X 3.17.5, see n. 650-52; for X 3.21.4, see n. 770-76.

1802-7 **In contrarium ... *tabernas*:** There are four arguments in favour of the contract. (1) It is not a loan as defined by Decretum Grat. C.14 q.3 c.1: "If you lend, that is, if you make a loan of money to someone from whom you expect more than you gave, be it money or anything else, you are a usurer" ("si feneraueris hominem, id est si tu mutuum dederis pecuniam tuam, a quo plus quam dedisti expectes, non pecuniam solam, sed aliquid plus quam dedisti ... fenerator es"). (2) X 3.17.3 permits deception of up to half the just price (see n. 836-40). (3) Moreover, a purchase is not invalid if the buyer receives more than the price he paid. (4) The contract involves the sale of a right (*ius*) and rights are vendible. Dig. 18.4 deals with sales of inheritances and rights of action. Like any other thing, an inheritance can be sold, and since it represents "all the rights which the dead man possessed" (Dig. 50.16.24), the sale of an inheritance involves the sale of rights to actions (cf. Dig. 18.4.1.8, 20). Dig. 18.1.32 notes that when someone who conducts business on public land sells his premises, he does not sell the land but simply the right to trade there.

1808-16 **Soluit ... *causa*:** The solution distinguishes first between personal and real *census*. Personal *census* were based on the labour of the seller and were generally condemned (Noonan, *Scholastic Analysis of Usury*, 162). John of Legnano offers little by way of argument, except to suggest that in its *ad hoc* character this kind of *census* approximates a loan. On Decretum Grat. C.14 q.3 c.3, see n. 44-45. Decretum Grat. C.12 q.2 c.36 declares the sale of church property by parish priests void. By contrast, provided there is no fraud, a real *census* is a licit sale, for it involves a vendible right and a price. For Dig. 4.4.16.4, see n. 1657-79; for X 3.17.3, see n. 836-40. X 3.17.6 directs that a seller who has received less than half the just price has an action for recovery of the thing sold or for supplementary payment.

1816-39 **Sed aliquando ... partis:** In the case of newly created *census*, the same restrictions apply. However, real *census* that contain an agreement to repurchase for more or less than the sale price should be presumed to be in fraud of usury. For X 3.21.4, see n. 770-76; for X 3.17.5, see n. 650-52. Although John concedes the licitness of pacts to repurchase at the sale price, Ridolfi believes the same restrictions should apply (he makes the same observation in Part 2, question 60). For *dubium* 8 of the *Questio montis*, see Introduction, pp. 98-99, and n. 3705-24.

PART 2, QUESTION 13

1840-43 **Vtrum ... teneatur:** "I buy from someone who owns property a guaranteed *census* of ten baskets of grain for a sum with which I could purchase a field producing the same quantity of grain. Moreover, the *census* is not derived from a specific parcel of land but secured by the seller's property in general. Is the contract usurious?"

Ridolfi's principal authority for this question is John of Legnano's commentary on X 5.19.19.

1848-51 **Dubium ... reale:** The contract is questionable because it seems to give rise to a personal rather than a real *census*.

1852-59 **Soluit ... fine:** John of Legnano regards the contract as licit provided it is founded on and in proportion to the seller's *bona* that is, the totality of his real property and rights. Such *iura realia* are vendible according to Dig. 18.4 (see n. 1802-7). The jurist recognizes, however, that the contract leaves room for corrupt motives.

1858-59 **Cum tu:** F_1 reads *Cum tu* (X 5.19.5) and the citation is the same in the manuscript of John of Legnano that I consulted. The reference, however, is to the end of X 5.19.6: "the thoughts of men cannot be hid from almighty God" ("... quum cogitationes hominum omnipotenti Deo nequeant occultari"). The gloss observes: "God is witness to our secrets, from whom neither the character of the sin nor the disposition of the sinner is hid" ("secretorum Deus cognitor est ... quem non latet peccati qualitas neque peccantis affectus" [gl. ord. ad X 5.19.6, v. *Occultari* (ed. cit. col. 1737)]).

1860-78 **Non recte ... repetitione:** Ridolfi observes that the issue here is not the form in which the *census* is paid–since if the agreement were usurious, it would be so whether the medium was money or things (on Decretum Grat. C.14 q.3 c.3, see n. 44-45)–or the seller's right to create a *census* on his goods in general and to sell it, but whether he sells a right to the usufruct (*ius in re*) or a right giving rise to a personal action (*actio personalis*). The issue is discussed by Bartolus of Sassoferrato in his commentary on Dig. 31.1.88.15, where he describes the case of someone who creates a hundred-year *census* on the fruits of his property. If he creates a usufruct and sells it, he alienates it, a transaction implicit in C. 4.51.7, which forbids the alienation of the property of another. But if he does not establish a right of usufruct, then he simply sells a personal action and there is no alienation. In Dig. 18.1.81.1, Lucius Titius promises to provide annually a hundred bushels of grain from his estate to that of Gaius Seius. If he sells the estate, the purchaser is not obliged to Gaius Seius for the grain. In Dig. 33.1.21.pr., a legacy of a proportion of an estate's revenues continues to be owed even when the estate has been sold. Dig. 7.1.20 provides a criterion for distinguishing the intention in such a contract: "If a man frames a legacy in the following terms: 'I give and bequeath the annual fruits of the Cornelian estate to Gaius Maevius,' these words should be construed as amounting to a legacy of the usufruct of the estate."

I have been unable to consult a text of Johannes de Fantutiis' commentary on the Clementines or of Ridolfi's *repetitio* on Decretum Grat. C.12 q.2 c.52.

1874 **uel ne:** *Recte* an non.

PART 2, QUESTION 14

1879-82 **Habet ... usura:** "By statute or custom the rulers of a city sell to a buyer and his heirs five or ten florins annually from the city revenues (*pecunia*) in exchange for a hundred florins down, which is devoted to the benefit of the city. Is the agreement usurious?"

This question is from John of Legnano's commentary on X 5.19.19.

1887-94 **Solutio ... dubio:** Since money is a measure of value, it cannot be sold (for Dig. 46.1.42 and 18.1.1, see n. 1795-1801). But if the *census* is established on the goods of the city as a whole it is licit, as was concluded in the previous question. Ridolfi accepts this opinion, provided there are safeguards against fraud. The question is also dealt with in *dubium* 8 of the *Questio montis* (see Introduction, pp. 98-99, and nn. 3668-71 to 3752-71).

Part 2, question 15

1895-96 **Emit ... licitus:** "Titius buys from a church for a fixed sum of money certain properties to be held for life. Is such a contract licit?"

1900-1903 **Respondeo ... contrahitur:** Raymond of Penyafort asserts that such purchases are licit provided the age and health of the buyer are not such as to create a presumption of fraud. Gottofredo suggests that the contract might be permissible on the grounds of risk, but in the end judges it illicit: "But I am of the opposite opinion, since those engaging in such contracts hope to live a long time and expect that they will receive more from the fruits of these properties than they paid. And, as I said earlier, the vice of usury consists in hope alone" ("Sed puto contrarium, eo quod homines sperant viuere et sic taliter contrahentes credunt se amplius percepturos de possessionum prouentibus quam sit pecunia quam dederunt. Et sicut in principio dictum est sola spe contrahitur vitium vsurarum" [*Summa*, ad X 5.19 *de usuris*, n.12 (ed. cit. p. 444b)]).

1903-12 **Fatentur ... Huguccionem:** Gottofredo, however, approves the contract of *precaria*, in which a donor who wishes to retain the fruits of his donation for life is granted the usufruct of additional church land on the condition that both his donation and the *precaria* revert to the church's ownership after his death. Under this agreement, the authority for which is a canon of the council of Meaux (845) included in Gratian's *Decretum* (C.10 q.2 c.4), the donor may be granted the usufruct of property worth up to twice the value of his donation (three times if he transfers ownership and fruits immediately). Guido de Baysio says in his commentary: "At the first gloss where it says 'it is given to the church' add 'but this contract is no longer in use among us.' But it ought to be, as is clear from the text of that canon. Say someone wishes to give the ownership of his farm to the church so that he might receive the usufruct of another farm belonging to the church. If he wishes to retain the usufruct of the farm he gives to the church, let him receive double from the church's farms, so that if he receives fifty *sextarii* from his own land, he will get an additional hundred from the church's estates. But if he makes over ownership as well as usufruct, he should get triple: for example, if he has fifty *sextarii* from the farm he gave to the church, he will receive 150 from the church. And since this kind of *precaria* does not seem to benefit the church very much, it says that such a *precaria* cannot be transmitted to heirs and the church cannot be compelled to do so, according to Huguccio" ("In prima glosa ibi 'datur ecclesie,' adde sub: 'sed talis contractus nunc non est in vsu apud nos.' Sed sic debet fieri, vt ex litera istius c. colligitur. Ecce aliquis vult dare proprietatem predii sui ecclesie vt recipiat vsumfructum in predio ecclesie. Si vult retinere vsumfructum in predio quod dat ecclesie, accipiet de prediis ecclesie vsumfructum in duplum. Puta de proprio praedio colligit l. sextarios recipiet ergo de fundis ecclesie c. sextarios. Si vero statim vult tradere predium suum ecclesie et quoad vsumfructum et quoad proprietatem, tunc accipiet de prediis ecclesie triplum. Verbi gratia, accepit de predio quod dat ecclesie l. sextarios; accipiet de prediis ecclesie cl. sextarios. Et quia huiusmodi precaria non videtur multum expedire ecclesie dicit quod talis precaria non potest transmitti ad heredes et quod ecclesia non potest cogi ad eam faciendam, secundum Huguccionem" [*Rosarium*, ad Decretum Grat. C.10 q.2 c.4 (ed. cit. fol. 173va)]).

1912-26 **Sed Ostiensis ... titulo:** According to Hostiensis, Raymond and Gottofredo's criticisms of ecclesiastical *census* are equally applicable to *precariae*: "With all due respect, [my predecessors'] reasoning appears faulty, for if people can anticipate profit in *precaria*, they can in *census* too, and therefore it, too, is licit ... unless it is made in fraud of usury" ("Certe, salua pace ipsorum, minus bene videntur sensisse: nam ita homines possunt sperare lucrum in hoc ultimo contractu, sicut in primo, et adeo licitus est contractus primus ... nisi in fraudem fiat" [*Summa*, ad X 5.19 *de usuris*, n.8 (ed. cit. col. 1626)]). Johannes Andreae and Guido de Baysio cite Hostiensis' opinion with approval. Commenting on C. 3.28.12, Cino of Pistoia (ca. 1270-1336/37) and Baldus de Ubaldis note that one may lawfully purchase a life *census* provided the price is proportional to the length of time one is likely to live. Dig. 35.2.68 cites Ulpian's formula for the calculation of alimentary and usufructuary legacies: "From birth to the twenty-fifth year, the amount of thirty years' maintenance will be assessed and the Falcidian quota thereof be due; between twenty and twenty-five, the amount up to twenty-eight; between twenty-five and thirty, the amount of twenty-five; between thirty and thirty-five, the amount of twenty-two; between thirty-five and forty, the amount of twenty; between forty and fifty there will be a computation of as many years as are lacking to sixty, with one year's remission; between fifty and fifty-five, the amount of nine years; between fifty-five and sixty, the amount of seven years; for any age over sixty, the amount of five years. Ulpian says that we observe this rule also for the computation of a usufruct. Still, it has been the practice for the computation from birth to thirty to be of thirty but from thirty of as many years as are lacking to sixty. The computation never goes beyond thirty."

1927-37 **Sed ego ... ibi:** Ridolfi rejects the argument that the problem here is one of excessive profits: the question is whether there has been deception beyond half the just price. For Johannes Andreae on X 5.19.6, see n. 1680-87. In X 3.13.11, a monastery is compelled by financial necessity to enfeoff an estate to a layman, whose profit in the first year alone has exceeded his investment. Innocent III orders the fief revoked if it emerges that the monastery has suffered undue loss through the transaction.

1938-44 **Quid autem ... Ostiensem:** What of those who buy fruits for a specific price for life? At C. 4.32.14 Baldus discusses the factors that must be considered by an ecclesiastical judge: "Here the doctors consider a question that is often disputed by theologians and that is, is it licit to buy at a set price fruits for life? And it seems that it is, for the contract cannot be considered unjust in terms of the price, because it is unknown how long the buyer will live ... On the other hand, it appears that although we cannot be certain about how long the buyer will live, it is possible to make certain inferences ... Because the usufruct ends with the life, a specific price is arrived at and thus it is bought and sold ... And so, having considered the quality of the person and his age, an ecclesiastical judge will determine whether the contract is unjust, as in X 5.19.19, according to Peter and Cino" ("Vnde quaerunt hic doctores de vna questione de qua disputant fratres religiosi quotidie, videlicet, numquid sit licitum alicui emere certo pretio fructus ad vitam? Et videtur quod sic, nam iste contractus non potest videri iniustus in quantitate pretii, quia quantum viuet ignoratur ... In contrarium videtur quod licet non possumus habere aliquid certum de vita eius, tamen ad coniecturam eundum est ... Hinc est quod vsusfructus vita finitur, tamen certo pretio aestimatur, ideo emitur et venditur ... vnde inspecta qualitate personarum et aetate et in via fori ecclesiastici debet iudex arbitrari vtrum iste contractus censeatur iustus vel iniustus, vt *de vsur*. c. *Nauiganti*, secundum Petrum et Cynum" [*Commentaria*, in C.4.32.14, n.1 (ed. cit. VII fol. 89rb)]). Hostiensis includes the sale of fruits among the "exceptions" to the usury prohibition: "Twelfth exception: when I sell the fruits for a period of time. For although the buyer may receive more from the fruits [than he paid], nevertheless by reason of uncertainty, he is not bound to compensate me" ("Duodecimo, quando uendo fructus ad tempus; licet enim plus satis percipiat emptor de fructibus, non tamen tenetur mihi aliud sarcire ratione incertitudinis" [*Summa*, X 5.19 *de usuris*, n.8 (ed. cit. cols. 1622-23)]). This opinion is cited by Guido de Baysio in his comments on Decretum Grat. C.14 q.4 c.9. For Part 2, question 11, see nn. 1657-79 to 1712-31. For questions 17 and 18, see nn. 1987-89 to 2165-82.

PART 2, QUESTION 16

1945-46 **Que et ... precedente:** "What constitutes deception beyond half the just price in the purchase of a *census* from a church?"

1947-51 **Sed quia ... dimidiam:** The opinion of Hostiensis noted at the end of the last question is normally cited with the qualification that such sales are licit provided there is no deception beyond half the just price (see n. 836-40)

1952-69 **Vbi sciendum ... Lapus:** Lapo da Castiglionchio observes that the variety of *census* contracts makes generalization difficult, but that the canons indicate how they might be assessed by a judge. A constitution of the emperor Leo (457-74) included in the *Decretum* (C.10 q.2 c.2.11 et c.3) allows stewards of ecclesiastical property to sell the usufruct on the condition that the property revert to ecclesiastical ownership at the end of a specified term and that the purchaser concede an equivalent amount of his own property to the church. The gloss summarizes the constitution noting that "he who accepts an ecclesiastical property should agree that when the time has elapsed, he will restore to the church what he got plus an equal amount of his own property of the same quality along with what he got, including the same number of slaves and serfs, which will belong to the church in perpetuity" ("ille qui accipit rem ecclesiae debet facere pactum vt finito tempore restituat ecclesiae quod accepit ab ea et tantundem de suo eiusdem bonitatis et reditus cum eo quod accepit et cum totidem mancipiis et colonis, quod perpetuo penes ecclesiam remanebit"). But it also cites Huguccio's reading: "Huguccio briefly summarizes this case as follows: this law says that someone wants to receive the usufruct of a church estate for a certain period of time or until his death. He cannot do this unless he immediately confers on the church the ownership of an equivalent estate of his own and so for the agreed period he will enjoy the usufruct of both estates. Afterwards, full rights to both will pass to the church" ("Huguccio vero casum ponit breuiter sic: hic dicitur in hac lege, aliquis vult accipere praedium ecclesiae in vsumfructum vsque ad certum tempus vel vsque ad mortem suam. Non potest hoc facere nisi statim praedium suum aeque bonum per omnia conferat ecclesiae quoad proprietatem, et sic vsque ad statutum tempus retinebit vtrumque praedium quoad vsumfructum. Postea vtrumque perueniet ad ecclesiam pleno iure" [gl. ord. ad Decretum Grat. C.10 q.2 c.2.11, casus (ed. cit. cols. 931-32)]). For Decretum Grat. C.10 q.2 c.4, see n. 1903-12. The gloss notes an objection to C.10 q.2 c.2.11 and suggests that the triple *precaria* applies when the grantee is old or infirm and therefore unlikely to enjoy the fruits for very long: "*Double*: this seems to contradict *Si oeconomus*, where it is said that only so much will be given. Either the law is more generous on this point than the canon or the canon refers to the case in which an old or feeble man receives the usufruct" ("*Duplum*: videtur contradicere illi supra eadem ⟨causa⟩ *Si oeconomus* vbi dicitur quod tantundem dari debet: sed lex illa benignior est canone, vel canon loquitur in eo casu cum senex est vel debilis qui recipit rem ecclesiae" [gl. ord. ad C.10 q.2 c.4, v. *Duplum* (ed. cit. col. 933)]). Huguccio remarks that "such may not transmit the right to their sons or heirs, but possess it only during their lives; and this *capitulum* seems to contradict the earlier law, namely *Si oeconomus*" ("scilicet ita ut ad filios uel heredes tales ius non transmittant, sed tantum in diebus uite sue habeant, et uidetur hoc capitulum contradicere legi superiori, scilicet *Si yconomus*" [*Summa decretorum*, ad C.10 q.2 c.4, v. *Tantum in suo nomine* (MS cit. fol. 206r)]). Laurentius Hispanus says "so that such a right may not pass to inheriting sons, but that they might enjoy it only during their lives, *precariae* are here called usufructs" ("prima, scilicet, ut ad filios heredes tale ius non transeat, set tantum in diebus uite sue habeant; precarie hic dicuntur ususfructus" [*Apparatus in Decretum*, ad C.10 q.2 c.4, v. *Tantum in suo nomine* (MS cit. fol. 45r)]).

1970-86 **Quod clarius ... Cogita**: For Guido de Baysio and Gottofredo on Decretum Grat. C.10 q.2 c.4, see n. 1903-12. On the basis of these texts, Ridolfi offers the following rules: (1) if the *precaria* is worth more than twice that of a price to be paid after the purchaser's death, there is deception beyond half the just price. (2) If the purchaser pays at the time of the contract, then deception is present only if the *precaria* is more than three times the price. (3) In cases where the purchaser is unlikely to live very long, the church may sell a *precaria* worth more than twice or three times the price paid, since the church is likely to benefit. For Johannes Teutonicus' gloss to Decretum Grat. C.10 q.2 c.4, v. *Duplum*, see n. 1952-69. Ridolfi, however, is unwilling to assert (3) without qualification, since the canons speak of no more than a triple *precaria*. For the opinion of Cino of Pistoia, see n. 1912-26.

PART 2, QUESTION 17

1987-89 **Vendit ... contractus:** "What if someone sells the fruits of an estate for a period of ten years for a thousand, although the estate is by common estimate worth 150 a year. Is this contract lawful on the part of the buyer?"

The question and response are from Johannes Andreae's commentary on the rubric *de usuris* of the *Speculum iuris*.

1993-2000 **Refert ... licitum:** Johannes Andreae approves the contract provided the purchaser's return is not guaranteed against risk and he could earn a better return by buying land (see n. 1712-31).

PART 2, QUESTION 18

2004-12 **Sed quid ... contractus:** "Is the following contract, commonly called *ubbia*, licit? You give a hundred to a monastery on the condition that for the rest of your life and that of anyone else named by you the monastery will pay an annuity of sixteen percent. The monastery pledges its goods as security and retains the option to rescind the contract during your life by repaying the principal."

2014-29 **Videtur ... dicam:** The contract would appear to be licit because it has all the elements of a sale, namely a price (the principal) and a vendible thing (the annual return). For Part 2, question 11, see nn. 1657-79 to 1692-1711. Lapo da Castiglionchio analyzed a similar annuity based on the revenues of the commune of Florence; his opinions are discussed in *dubium* 8 of the *Questio montis* (see Introduction, pp. 98-99, and nn. 3668-71 to 3752-71.

2030-38 **Preterea ... consilium:** Moreover, the investor in the present case cannot recover his principal, which is not the case in a loan. Ridolfi cites *consilium* 207 of Oldradus de Ponte on a similar annuity. The monastery of St. Denis sold the Archbishop of Rheims a life annuity of four hundred *livres parisis* for 2400 *livres*. Of this sum, the monastery would pay the estate of the archbishop a thousand *livres* less funeral expenses and the portion of the second year's annuity already disbursed if he died within two years of the agreement. The archbishop, however, has survived for fifteen years and the monastery wants the contract declared usurious. Oldradus considers the contract licit on the grounds that it does not conform to the definition of usury as "profit owed or exacted in a loan contract." Here there is no loan, since there is no principal that must be repaid nor does a profit accrue to the principal sum. Instead, the principal is entirely consumed. What, then, should we call the contract? A purchase-sale in which the object of the sale is the right to a certain return. If the monastery objects that it was deceived in the price, since the archbishop lived longer than he was expected to, one can respond that in sales the parties may circumvent one another. Moreover, such an objection amounts to a denial of nature and no action can be allowed on such grounds. Again, the monastery's challenge should not be allowed since it would scarcely have entertained a counter-challenge of illicitness if the archbishop had died the day after solemnizing the agreement. Finally, Hostiensis and all the authorities who comment on X 5.19.6 hold that the risk implicit in such agreements removes any presumption of usury.

2039-51 **Credo ... moriantur:** Ridolfi, however, suggests that *ubbia* is illicit mainly because the returns are founded on the person of the seller rather than on property (see n. 1808-16). In such a case what is sold is not the right to a return but rather money itself, which is nonvendible (for Dig. 46.1.42, see n. 1795-1801). Secondly, the agreement is not a purchase-sale but the unnamed contract (*contractus innominatus*) described as *do ut facias*, "I give you something so that you will do something for me." But because it is likely that the purchaser will recover the principal within a relatively short time (principal and profit if the seller invokes his right to rescind the agreement), the contract is in fact a *mutuum* under another name.

2051-68 **Ad predicta ... decipient**: The comments of Innocent IV, Hostiensis and Johannes Andreae on X 5.19.6 address *census* founded on real property or persons other than the contracting parties, such as serfs. Those entering such agreements should ensure that the return is founded on real property.

2069-80 **Possent ... questionibus**: In his *novella* on X 5.19.6, Johannes Andreae cites Gottofredo's opinion that a contract may be *de facto* usurious but formally licit (see n. 829-34). Ridolfi notes, however, that because the terms of *ubbia* contracts vary greatly, care must be taken to consider variables such as the sums and property involved, the age of the purchaser and so on before pronouncing them in fraud of usury. For Johannes Andreae's comments on X 3.17.5, see n. 994-97; on William Durand's opinion in the *Speculum iuris*, see n. 1275-77.

2081-2159 **Post supra ... Pinu**: A *consilium* of John of Legnano and Laurentius de Pinu on the lawfulness of a contract similar to the *ubbia* contract. I have been unable to locate a manuscript of this *consilium*.

2084-95 **Abbas ... teneatur**: The subject of the *consilium* is the following contract: the monastery of St. Mary receives from the convent of St. G. an irrevocable gift of two hundred ducats on the condition that it pay the latter ten ducats (five percent) a year in perpetuity. The monastery of St. Mary, however, may rescind the agreement at any time by restoring the two-hundred-ducat principal to the convent of St. G.

2096-2100 **Concludunt ... *contra***: The jurists conclude that although the contract is not formally a loan, but rather a *donatio*, it can be construed to be in fraud of usury. The gloss to Decretum Grat. C.14 q.3 c.3 discusses fraud, citing Dig. 1.3.30, which declares that "fraud on the statute is practised when one does that which the statute does not wish anyone to do, yet which it has failed expressly to prohibit" or, in the words of the gloss itself, "he commits fraud on the law who observes the words of the law but evades its intention" ("Ille vero facit fraudem legi, qui obseruat verba legis, sed mentem eius circunuenit" [gl. ord. ad Decretum Grat. C.14 q.3 c.3, v. *Praecepta* (ed. cit. col. 1096)]). The gloss goes on to distinguish four species of fraud: (1) from thing to thing (*de re ad rem*), for example, when payment of interest on a money loan is made in some other medium to avoid the appearance of usury; (2) from person to person (*de persona ad personam*), for example, when someone exacts usury through the agency of someone else; (3) from contract to contract (*de vno contractu ad alium contractum*), for example, when a woman makes a gift to her husband but disguises it as a sale to evade the ban on gifts between spouses; and (4) in another form of fraud from contract to contract, when, for example, a woman constitutes herself principal debtor contrary to the *senatus consultum Velleianum*, which forbids women to undertake liability for others (citing Dig. 16.1.8.8: "If [a creditor] agrees with his debtor that he will provide someone to assume his debt and a formal release is granted to the debtor, then he provides a woman who was protected under the provisions of the *senatus consultum*, a *condictio* can be brought against him as if he had not provided [a substitute debtor]; for what is the difference between not providing one and providing one of such a kind?").

2100-2105 **Quod probat ... pro .c.**: The agreements additional to the *donatio* render the agreement the innominate contract *do ut facias*, which can be enforced by an *actio praescriptis verbis*. The gloss to the Code states that a *pactum* attached to a contract shapes the action arising from it: "Say that an agreement made on the spot so that something might be done for the stipulator is actionable on the basis of the stipulation and on the basis of the agreement by an *actio praescriptis verbis*" ("Tu dic ... pactum fieri incontinenti, vt aliquid fiat stipulatori, et agitur ex stipulatione informata et ex pacto praescriptis verbis" [gl. ord. ad C. 2.3.27, casus (ed. cit. col. 344-45)]). The contract in the present case, then, is to be understood as follows: "I give you two hundred so that you may pay me an annuity of five percent."

2105-24 **Aut ergo ... proposita**: What does the payment represent? Either the fruit of the principal or a charge for its use. But neither is licit, since money is naturally sterile and the use of money is its consumption. Dig. 12.1.19 refers to money used in repaying a loan or in paying a debt as "consumed." In Dig. 12.1.11, a fugitive slave makes you a loan with his master's money: does his master have an action (*condictio*) for recovery? Yes, since "the property in the coins will not pass to the recipient ... The coins can be vindicated if they still survive, or an action for production can be brought if they have ceased to exist through fraud; if without fraud you have used them up, I can bring a *condictio* against you." As it stands, Ridolfi's text suggests that the sterility and consumptibility arguments appear in the gloss to VI *de reg. iur.* 4, *Peccatum*: they do not, but Johannes Andreae cites the consumptibility argument in his *quaestio* on the same text (see n. 446-55). The analysis applies only to fungibles; the use of non-fungibles has a value distinct from the things themselves. C. 8.53.28 indicates that in certain things ownership can be separated from use. Decretum Grat. C.12 q.2 c.44 says that *precariae* and exchanges made during the vacancy of a see may be rescinded.

2125-35 **Demonstrat ... eos**: The additional agreement in this contract creates a presumption of usury, since it is contrary to the nature of a gift (*donatio*), which the contract claims to be. C. 8.54.4 states that conditions cannot be attached to a gift after the fact. Nor can gifts be revoked except under exceptional circumstances. X 3.24.10 allows a donor to revoke a gift to someone who does him violence or threatens him or his property with violence. For the gloss to X 3.21.4 and 3.17.5, see n. 776-86; to X 5.19.6, see n. 145-64; to X 5.19.10, see Introduction, pp. 85-86; to Decretum Grat. C.14 q.3 c.3, see n. 2096-2100.

2136-45 **Hic nulla ... q. .3.**: It may be objected that it is not inconsistent with the nature of a gift to give the donee the right to revoke; but the fact that the gift is not gratuitous renders the contract one of *do ut facias* rather than gift. The right to rescind the contract makes it in effect a loan and therefore in fraud of usury.

2146-59 **Et tandem ... Pinu**: The jurists conclude (1) that the contract is illicit, (2) that it is not binding, (3) that the monastery of St. Mary can seek release and

(4) that the annuity should be deducted from the principal.

2160-64 **Aduertatis ... questione .xviii.**: Ridolfi considers this case analogous to his own despite the absence of a provision whereby the seller of the annuity pledges his property as security.

2165-82 **Sed unum ... partis**: The content of the text and gloss at X 3.21.4, however, seems to contradict the conclusion of John of Legnano and Laurentius de Pinu that the agreement to rescind without deducting the annuity from the principal creates a presumption of usury. X 3.21.4 does not censure conditional sales nor do conditions in themselves create a presumption of fraud (see n. 770-76). The gloss adds: "when a contract is created with the condition that the buyer may rescind the sale if he is unsatisfied, the buyer has up to sixty days to do so and no more, unless the condition is that he may rescind whenever he wishes" ("cum contractus sub hac forma celebratur, vt liceat emptori a contractu discedere, si emptio displiceat sibi, tunc vsque ad sexaginta dies potest emptor a contractu discedere, non vltra, nisi hoc dictum sit, quod quandocunque velit, possit recedere a contractu" [gl. ord. ad X 3.21.4, v. *Proximos annos* (ed. cit. col. 1143)]). The contract considered in X 3.21.4, however, provides that fruits will be counted against the resale price and that a premium will be charged; and these provisions create a presumption of usury. The gloss asks why the premium is illicit: "But it seems that the buyer should not be impeded by the fact that he receives something additional, since he calculates the fruits in the money to be recovered and by receiving the fruits, he makes them his own" ("Sed videtur quod hoc non debeat obstare emptori, quod aliquid ultra recipiat, ex quo fructus perceptos computat in pecunia recipienda, nam percipiendo fructus suos facit" [gl. ord. ad X 3.21.4, v. *Praesumitur* (ed. cit. col. 1143)]). According to Dig. 18.2.2.1, when a thing is sold with an *in diem addictio* (an agreement that the sale will be annulled if the seller receives a better offer by a certain date), the buyer has a right "to usucapt his purchase and profit by its fruits and accessions to it." But according to Dig. 18.2.6, this holds only if no second purchaser appears, for then the buyer must restore interim fruits to the seller. In his *novella* on X 3.21.4, Johannes Andreae notes that although these conditions apply in cases of *ad diem addictio*, they do not if the contract specifies that the sale may be rescinded if it displeases the buyer, for then the interim fruits belong to the latter and he is not bound to make restitution: "It is otherwise if there was an agreement to rescind the sale if it was displeasing, because then the fruits are the buyer's and he is only obliged to restore what he received after the quantity on which they agreed has been produced, authenticated and deposited by the seller.... The reason may be that in the first case the main issue was the utility of the seller, in the second solely the pleasure of the buyer" ("Secus, si fuisset pactum de ea resoluenda si displiceret uenditio, quia tunc emptor omnino facit fructus suos, nec tenetur restituere nisi perceptos post oblatam consignatam et depositam a uenditore quantitatem, de qua conuenit ... Et potest esse ratio: quia primo casu principaliter agitur de utilitate uenditoris; secundo de solo ipsius placito" [*Novella*, ad X 3.21.4, n.6 (ed. cit. III fol. 90ra)]). If the same principle were applied in the present case, it could be argued that the buyer had an absolute right to retain the fruits. Indeed, concludes Ridolfi, if there were an agreement to apply the annuity to the reduction of the principal, this in itself might create a presumption of fraud, as in X 3.21.4. Nevertheless, he concludes, the analysis of John of Legnano and Laurentius de Pinu may be valid in cases concerning newly created *census*.

Commentary: Part 3

Question 5: *Questio montis*

Thema

2185-2264 **Vltimo ... uideamus:** The *Questio montis* is the fifth question of Part 3 and is subdivided into eight *dubia*. The *thema* serves as an introduction to the *questio* as a whole and summarizes the material facts that give rise to the legal problem.

2186-94 **Et pro ... recitabo:** On Gregory of Rimini's *quaestio* on the public debt of Venice, see Introduction, pp. 68-70, 79-80; on Francesco da Empoli's *Questio de monte*, pp. 72-75.

On Lapo da Castiglionchio, see Introduction, pp. 81-82. His *repetitio* on X 5.19.6 is divided into two questions: the first addresses the legitimacy of the public debt in general and the second asks whether the city can create new creditors by selling life annuities. (1) is subdivided into five questions: (1a) Do creditors of the *monte dell'uno tre* and *monte dell'uno due* licitly receive profit on their shares? (1b) Can they sell their rights in the two *monti*? (1c) Can others licitly purchase such rights? (1d) In virtue of the contract of sale, can the purchasers licitly receive the profit assigned to the original creditors? (1e) Assuming the original creditors illicitly received profit, can they, by virtue of the city's permission, sell a claim to the principal even though they have already received more in interest?

2191 **adversatur:** The manuscript reads *adversa*. I suggest the expansion *adversatur*: "and on many points Francesco da Empoli is opposed (to Gregory of Rimini)." Other possibilities are *adversarii* ⟨*sunt*⟩ and *adversantur*: "and on many points they are opposed."

2195-2244 **Facti prius ... et cetera:** A statement of the material "facts" (*factum*), the "things done." The passage echoes and paraphrases legislative provisions of the Florentine government.

2195-97 **Facti prius ... compellitur:** Although some funds, such as the *monte dell'uno tre* and *monte dell'uno due*, were designed to attract investments, *prestanze* were usually conceived of as involuntary or compulsory advances to the government in times of need–*onera* or obligations–rather than voluntary investments.

2197-99 **statuitque ... sortem:** On rates of interest, see Introduction, pp. 30-35, 46-47. Ridolfi's analysis focuses on the consolidation of 1381, which paid five percent.

2199-2200 **Et ita ... montis:** In popular discourse, owners of public debt credits were termed "creditors of the *monte*," a semantic point of significance in the controversy.

2200-2204 **Et contingit ... sortem:** Interest on *monte* credits was described as compensation "until the commune should repay the principal," but since no term for repayment was set and loans were effectively irredeemable, over time interest payments could equal or exceed the principal sum. Conversely, the unwillingness or inability of the government to assign tax revenues for the payment of interest could result in a loss to creditors.

2201 **ab eis iura habentibus:** On the legislation of 1344 that made *monte* credits transferable, see Introduction, p. 30. This and subsequent enactments refrained from explicitly authorizing the transfer of rights to interest, though participants in the credit market clearly understood themselves to be trading claims to both principal and interest (Kirshner, "Encumbering Private Claims," 22-23). On the market in credits, see Introduction, pp. 30-33, 40-41.

2205-21 **Et insuper ... retinere:** On the legislation of 1383 designed to avert the suggestion that the *monte* was usurious, see Introduction, p. 55.

2222-26 **Et quod ... condita:** The legislation of 1344 and subsequent reforms assured creditors of their interest *in perpetuum* (see Introduction, pp. 30-31).

2226-29 **Et sic ... memoratis:** The consolidations of 1345 and 1381 were retroactive insofar as they established a uniform rate of five percent for all outstanding loans, some of which, like those of the *monte dell'uno tre* and *monte dell'uno due*, had paid rates of ten to fifteen percent.

2230-31 **Et quod ... suis:** Usually only citizens of Florence and its territories could hold *monte* credits. However, non-resident foreign notables were sometimes granted citizenship privileges for this purpose; see Becker, *Florence in Transition*, 2: 178-79; Kirshner, "Papa Eugenio IV"; and idem, "Reading Bernardino's Sermon," 548, n. 2).

2232-35 **Et quod ... ut supra:** A reference to the government's right to accept credits ceded to it by testament and expressed in the provision of June 1383 (ed. and trans. Trexler in "Florence," 208, n. 287). In a survey of wills drawn up in Florence between 1350 and 1500 Kirshner finds no evidence of restitution of interest paid on *monte* credits ("From Usury to Public Finance," 240), while Trexler finds only one example in the public records ("Florence," 150, n. 118). There are, however, instances in the earliest *monte* registers of creditors ceding credits to the city *pro amore* (Kirshner, "Franco Sacchetti," 568, n. 44).

2236-42 **Sanciuit ... reuenditionis:** This passage is from Lapo's *repetitio* and refers to the *monte dell'uno tre* and *monte dell'uno due*. In the legislation of 1343-45 establishing the original consolidation, the government did not reserve the right to redeem credits as they came on the market, as was the practice in Venice and Genoa (Kirshner, "From Usury to Public Finance," 20). From the 1350s onward, temporary commissions for the liquidation of the debt were periodically created with authority to repurchase credits at market value (idem, "Franco Sacchetti," 579, n. 63), while the reform of 1381 undertook to retire the debt over a period of several years (see Introduction, p. 46). In 1389, the *Ufficiali alla diminuzione del monte* (Officials for the liquidation of the debt) were established as a permanent commission (Guidi, *Il governo*, 2: 268).

2243-44 **Et insuper ... et cetera:** On the *syndicus ad indulgendum*, see Introduction, p. 54.

2245-64 **Modo hinc ... uideamus:** Ridolfi calls the eight subsidiary questions of the *Questio montis dubia*, uncertain or contested propositions. In structure, the *dubia* are the same as scholastic *quaestiones*. On the *dubium* as a form of scholastic discourse, see M. Plezia, ed., *Lexicon mediae et infimae latinitatis Polonorum* (Wroclaw, 1972), s.v. *Dubius*. Ridolfi may also intend to suggest that these questions are *res dubiae*, doubtful cases arising from ambiguous formulations in legal acts or instruments (cf. Dig. 34.5 *passim*; Berger, *Encyclopedic Dictionary*, s.v. *Res dubiae*). According to Dig. 50.17.56, "in doubtful cases, the more generous view is always to be preferred," a procedure that might be said to characterize Ridolfi's overall approach to the *monte*.

QUESTIO MONTIS, DUBIUM 1

2265-67 Vtrum ... prelibati: "Whether *prestanze* may be imposed and the citizens compelled to pay them, and whether they may receive the allotted increment in good conscience." For a discussion, see Introduction, pp. 87-89.

2270-71 Primo ... *Placet*: Contributions may be exacted from citizens only with the permission of the prince. C. 10.19.1 is a constitution of Constantine (307-37) forbidding the imperial couriers and police to collect unpaid tribute without first obtaining certification of indebtedness from a municipal notary. In C. 10.48.8, Constantius (337-50) restricts the right of magistrates to impose tribute on provincials without imperial sanction.

2272-74 Secundo ... de hoc: By the institution of interest-bearing credits in the *monte*, the government has created an occasion of sin for the citizens, since if there were no borrowers there would be no lenders and therefore no usurers. For this reading of X 5.19.4, see n. 583-94.

2275-94 In contrarium ... et cetera: This passage is based on *consilium* 180 of Bartolus, who argues that "in circumstances of pressing necessity any city or corporation can impose a special levy" ("collectam specialem vnaqueque ciuitas uel vniuersitas pro necessitate sibi incumbenti imponere potest" [*Consilia, quaestiones et tractatus*, consilium 180, nn.1-2 (ed. cit. X fol. 43ra)]).

2275-80 In contrarium ... *uni. no.*: Although the imposition of universal levies is an imperial prerogative, necessity justifies cities and corporations in requiring extraordinary contributions (*collecta*) from their constituencies for the maintenance of "public utility" (*utilitas rei publicae*) (see Introduction, pp. 87-88).

In C. 8.11.12, Theodosius (379-95) advises provincial governors that the inhabitants of cities are responsible for the building and maintenance of walls and that to meet this necessity authorities shall impose mandatory levies on citizens in accordance with their means. He adds that every effort is to be made to ensure that the burden is equitably distributed. At Dig. 3.4.1.2, Gaius states that after due warning the praetor may seize and sell the property of a corporation (*universitas*) in settlement of its debts. Accursius asks in the gloss: "But what if they have no common property? What will the creditor do? I reply: they will be compelled to levy a contribution so that they do have something in common, for 'one who can bring it about that he satisfy a condition is regarded as already able to do so' [Dig. 50.17.174]" ("Sed quid si nihil habent commune; quid faciet creditor? Respondeo: compellentur facere collectam vt aliquid habeant commune, nam 'qui potest facere, vt possit [condicioni parere, iam posse videtur]'" [gl. ord. ad Dig. 3.4.1.2, v. *Pro-*

consul (ed. cit. I p. 193a)]).

2281-89 **Et ista ... *uerberato*:** A digression on how public necessity can justify the seizure and sale of citizens' goods. At Dig. 13.7.43.1, Scaevola holds that containers in the possession of a creditor as a pledge against a loan may be temporarily seized without compensation for damage by officials responsible for the grain supply for use at harvest time. Dig. 18.6.13 reports that the aedile ordered the destruction of couches that had been purchased but left standing in the street. If they had been delivered to the purchaser or if their non-delivery was his responsibility, he had no claim to compensation. At Dig. 7.1.27.3, Ulpian notes that "occupiers of land generally sell a fixed portion of the fruits of their land to the municipal authorities at a low price, and they often pay taxes due to the imperial treasury in the same way." At Dig. 8.4.13.1, Ulpian observes that "if it is established that there are stone quarries on your land, then, without your permission, no one who does not have a right to do so can quarry stone, either in a private capacity or in the name of the state, that is, unless a custom exists in respect of these quarries to the effect that if anyone wishes to quarry stone from them, he may do so, providing he first of all gives the owner the usual indemnification." For Dig. 6.1.15.2, see n. 1568-77.

2289-94 **Ad propositum ... et cetera:** Dig. 50.4.6.5 defines *munera patrimonii* as encumbrances on the property (*patrimonium*) of the citizens of a municipality: "But in fact the *munera*, which are imposed on *patrimonia*, are of two kinds; for some are imposed on owners of property, whether they are *municipes* or not, some only on *municipes* or *incolae*. Levies, which relate to land or buildings, are imposed on their owners; but *munera*, which are held to be patrimonial, are only imposed on *municipes* or *incolae*." Authentic 7.1 deals with the legitimation of natural offspring, which is effected by offering them to the *curia* of the city where they were born or, in the case of rural settlements, the city to which they are subject. In the gloss, Accursius remarks that villas and castles are subject to special levies (*collectae*) by the city: "Nota villas et castra sub ciuitate facere collectam" (gl. ord. ad Auth. 7.1, v. *Persoluat* [ed. cit. fols. 67vb-68ra]). In his comments on X 5.39.53, a decretal of Honorius III (1216-26) imposing excommunication on the officials of communes that have adopted statutes that infringe on ecclesiastical liberties, Innocent IV observes that although a corporation (*universitas*) as such cannot sin or commit a crime, it can be guilty of a civil offence and may be punished with pecuniary fines that will be executed against the common goods of the corporation or, if these are lacking, by way of compulsory pro-rated contributions from the members: "Item dicunt quidam, quod fiet collecta pro soluendis huiusmodi poenis per libram et solidum" (*Commentaria*, ad X 5.39.53, n.2 [ed. cit. fol. 559va]). Innocent's opinion is echoed by William Durant, who maintains that if a corporation is in the position of an insolvent debtor, members are obliged to contribute to a common fund: "What if a corporation is a debtor and the corporation has nothing that may be seized? Is everyone obliged to contribute? I reply, yes" ("Quid si vniuersitas est debitrix, nec est in vniuersitate quid possideatur, nunquid tenentur omnes ad contributionem? Respondeo: dic quod sic" [*Speculum iuris*, 2.3 *de executione sententiae*, n.5 (ed. cit. I p. 823b)]). Dig. 42.1.4.2 states that "the representative of the citizens of a municipality can refuse to accept the decision [against the municipality]; for the action to enforce the judgement will be given against the citizens as such [and not the representative]." In his commentary on this fragment, Bartolus follows William Durant in noting that if the citizens have no common fund, then a compulsory contribution must be imposed. But what form will the contribution take? Bartolus notes Innocent's opinion that *collectae* are pro-rated contributions, which Bartolus understands to be equivalent to *munera patrimonii*, and observes that this is the appropriate form when a judgement lies against the corporation because of "a contract of loan, purchase or such like" undertaken in fulfilment of the responsibilities of the corporation itself on the strength of anticipated revenues: "It seems to me that we must examine the reason for the judgement. Say the judgement was against the corporation because of a contract of loan, purchase or the like; if the loan was contracted for a reason which pertains to an obligation imposed on the corporation according to the value of the patrimony, then the levy should be pro-rated ... And I think the same holds if something was received by way of a loan or something bought for settling a patrimonial obligation or a mixed one" ("Mihi autem videtur quod debemus inspicere causam quare facta est condemnatio. Pone quod est condemnata vniuersitas ex contractu mutui, emptionis vel simili. Si enim mutuum fuit acceptum pro causa que respicit onus vniuersitatis pro viribus patrimonii ... tunc imponetur per solidum et libram.... Et idem intelligo si aliquid fuit acceptum mutuo vel aliquid est emptum pro expediendo aliquo munere patrimoniali vel mixto" [*Commentaria*, in Dig. 42.1.4.2, nn.1-2 (ed. cit. V fol. 106va)]). In the case of contracts undertaken on the strength or in the place of *munera personalia*–obligations fulfilled by personal work (such as serving in the militia)–*collectae* will take the form of *per capita* contributions: "But if [the contract was made] to meet some personal obligation, for example, a statutory obligation to serve in the army and so forth, and if an arrangement is subsequently made that they can pay something and not go, the levy should be imposed *per capita*. For just as, because of the money they paid, they enjoyed individual relief, so should they pay individually" ("Si vero pro expediendo aliquo munere personali, vt puta ex forma statuti quilibet debet ire ad exercitum vel ad quid aliud, tunc si deuentum est ad compositionem quod soluant aliquid et non vadant, tunc imponetur ista collecta per capita. Sicut enim pro ea pecunia quam soluerunt senserunt releuamentum per capita, ita per capita soluant" [ibid. n.3 (ed. cit. V fol. 106va)]). In doubtful cases, "levies should be imposed in accordance with the value of persons' patrimonies" ("In dubio vbi hoc non liqueret, collecta imponitur personis pro viribus patrimonii" [ibid. n.4 (ed. cit. V fol. 106va)]).

2295-99 Contra ... mutuantium: In reply to the second *ratio*, Ridolfi first denies that it is a sin to borrow at usury (see n. 583-94). Second, he anticipates the argument of the second *dubium* to the effect that the operation of the *monte* involves neither the government nor its creditors in usury.

2299-2305 Nec etiam ... capitale: Third, he maintains that the government has not created an occasion of sin for the creditors, since they could expect better returns from legitimate business or property investments, particularly given that the principal of a forced loan is in practice irredeemable and interest payments often irregular (see Introduction, pp. 32-33, 47).

2305-9 Sed cum ... fuerat: Ridolfi distinguishes between returns on the *monte comune* and on new funds such as the *monte dell'uno tre* and *monte dell'uno due*: "But since it is unlikely that interest and principal will be lost, even if this reasoning holds now and in the time of the *monte vecchio* when there [was and] is legislation disbursing five percent to lenders, nevertheless it does not with regard to former times when first fifteen percent and then ten percent were decreed."

2309-14 **Fuit enim ... tantum .v.**: On the various *monti* and the rates of interest paid on them, see Introduction, pp. 28-52, *passim*.

2314-18 **Cum enim ... dubitari**: The only justification for the higher rates paid on the *monte dell'uno tre* and *monte dell'uno due* would be an imminent threat to the commune's existence and the consequent risk to the investor of losing his investment. Under normal conditions such rates would be excessive and conducive to lending.

2318-21 **Sed ubi ... questione**: See nn. 562 to 595-633.

2322-24 **Sciendum tamen ... consultus**: For a discussion of Guido de Belloreguardo's *consilium* on the *monte*, see Introduction, pp. 67-68.

2324-37 **respondit ... recipientis**: Guido condemns a statute decreeing interest on the public debt as contrary to the public good (*bonum publicum*). He cites Gratian's account of the function of law as the prescription of good and the prohibition of evil: "The office of secular or ecclesiastical laws is to command what ought to be done, to prohibit what is wicked; or to permit the licit, such as seeking rewards, or the illicit, such as giving a *libellus* of repudiation, in order to avoid something worse" ("Officium vero secularium, siue ecclesiasticarum legum est, precipere quod necesse est fieri, prohibere quod malum est fieri; permittere uel licita, ut premium petere, uel quedam illicita, ut dare libellum repudii, ne fiant grauiora" [Decretum Grat. D.3 dictum Gr. post c.3]). He also cites Isidore of Seville's classification of law as permissive, preventive, punitive or preceptive: "All law either permits something, such as a man's seeking a reward; or prevents something, such as the marriage of nuns; or punishes something, such as the execution of murderers, for human life is regulated by rewards and punishments, or it enjoins something, such as 'Love the Lord your God'" ("Omnis autem lex aut permittit aliquid, ut: uir fortis petat premium; aut vetat, ut: sacrarum uirginum nuptias nulli petere liceat; aut punit, ut: qui cedem fecerit, capite plectatur; eius enim premio aut pena vita moderatur humana; aut precipit, ut: 'Dilige Dominum Deum tuum'" [Decretum Grat. D.3, c.4]). The legislation governing the operation of the *monte* fails to meet these criteria because: (1) it impoverishes the commune by refusing to apply interest payments to the liquidation of the principal; (2) it encourages greed; (3) it places private profit before the common good; and (4) it induces citizens to commit the sin of usury.

2338-48 **Et si ... propositum**: On Guido's rejection of the argument from necessity, see Introduction, pp. 67-68, 88-89.

2349-62 **Secundo ... Guido**: If the policy of paying five percent or more on *prestanze* is approved, it follows that usury is also approved, since the object of defending the common good would be served just as well by openly borrowing at similar rates.

2363-67 **Quid dicendum ... questione**: In response to the rigorist position of Guido, Ridolfi devotes the remainder of the *dubium* to elaborating the argument that necessity and the common good justify the institution of interest-bearing *prestanze*.

2368-76 **Ad responsiones ... concordantiis:** What is possible is not always desirable. Decretum Grat. C.2 q.1 c.7 is a letter of Gregory the Great instructing his legate in Spain to review the deposition of two bishops by a secular magnate. Gregory directs the legate to investigate the truth or falsehood of the charges and the procedures followed. The gloss asks, "why does he order an inquiry into whether due process was observed when they were deposed by someone other than his own delegate, for which reason they should be immediately reinstated? Say that it was to avoid disgracing the count" ("Sed quare iubet inquiri, scilicet an ordo iuris fuerit seruatus, cum ipsi depositi essent a non suo iudice, vnde statim deberent retitui? Dic quod hoc fuit propter scandalum comitioli" [gl. ord. ad Decretum Grat. C.2 q.1 c.7, v. *In primis* (ed. cit. col. 644)]). In X 4.1.17, Lucius III directs that a woman who has solemnly promised to contract a marriage may not be compelled to marry if she subsequently changes her mind, since "marriage ought to be free" and "compulsory unions often turn out badly" ("quum libera debeant esse matrimonia ... quum coactiones difficiles soleant exitus frequenter habere").

2376-88 Et melius ... ab alio: For Ridolfi's emphasis on the superiority of consent over force in meeting the government's fiscal requirements, see Introduction, pp. 88-89, 102. Ridolfi rejects as impractical Guido's suggestion that only citizens who can demonstrate loss be compensated. Moreover, "a law for the good of the republic ought to be the same for all, lest the scrupulous be distressed" (see n. 2745-56).

2389-97 Preterea ... fiorino: The government should seek the love of its citizens (see Introduction, p. 89). The sentiment was a commonplace in ancient and medieval political discourse. In his second *Philippic* against Mark Antony, Cicero asks: "Is it not better to die a thousand deaths than to be unable to live in your own city without an armed guard? Believe me, there is no protection in guards: you would be better protected by the love and good will of the people than by arms" ("Non igitur miliens perire est melius quam in sua civitate sine armatorum praesidio non posse vivere? Sed nullum est istuc, mihi crede, praesidium: caritate te et benevolentia civium saeptum oportet esse, non armis" [*Oratio Philippica* 2.44.112, ed. cit.]). Petrarch advises Francesco da Carrara, Lord of Padua: "... nothing is more foolish, nothing is more destructive to the stability of the state, than to wish to be dreaded by everyone. Many princes, both in antiquity and in modern times, have wanted nothing more than to be feared and have believed that nothing is more useful than fear and cruelty in maintaining their power. Concerning this belief we have an example in the case of the barbaric emperor named Maximinus. In fact, nothing is farther from the truth than these opinions; rather it is much more advantageous to be loved than to be feared, unless we are speaking of the way in which a devoted child fears a good father. Any other kind of fear is diametrically opposed to what a ruler should desire. Rulers in general want to reign for a long time and to lead their lives in security, but to be feared is opposed to both of these desires, and to be loved is consistent with both" ("How a Ruler Ought to Govern his State," trans. Benjamin G. Kohl in *The Earthly Republic*, 42).

I have been unable to find another example of the proverb "good the *soldo* that is better than the florin" ("buono è quel soldo che meglora il fiorino"), but its meaning is clear. It plays on the difference in value between the florin and the *soldo*. The latter, the *grosso da soldi*, was a silver coin worth 5s 6d (66d) in terms of the mainly copper *monete piccioli da denari*, the money used in daily transactions. The florin was a virtually pure gold coin worth 76s 6d (918d) in *monete piccioli* or 13.91 times the *grosso da soldi* (Mario Bernocchi, *Le monete della Repubblica fiorentina* [Florence: Leo S. Olschki, 1974], 3: 117). In strictly monetary terms, then, a *soldo* could never be "better than a florin." But a *soldo* paid willingly by a citizen is of greater value than a florin extorted from him by force.

2397-2400 **Dici profecto ... perdens:** On the commune's similarity to God himself, see Introduction, pp. 89, 104.

Stimulus amoris (Goad of Love) was the title of several medieval devotional manuals that circulated under the names of Bernard of Clairvaux, Bonaventure and the thirteenth-century Franciscan Giacomo da Milano (*Dictionnaire de Spiritualité*, s.v. "Jacques de Milan"). I have been unable to locate the quotation in any of Bernard's authentic tractates on the love of God (J. Leclercq and H. M. Rochais, ed. *Sancti Bernardi Opera*, vol. 3, *Tractatus et Opuscula* [Rome: Editiones Cistercienses, 1963]) or any of the various tracts attributed to him and published in *PL* 184. Nor have I been able to find it in either recension of Giacomo da Milano's *Stimulus amoris*: one attributed to Bonaventure (A.-C. Peltier, ed., *Opera omnia sancti Bonaventurae*, vol. 12 [Paris, 1868]) and the other edited by the Florentine Franciscans (*Stimulus amoris fr. Iacobi Mediolanensis* [Quaracchi-Florence: Typographia Collegii S. Bonaventurae, 1905]). The quotation, however, is a borrowing from Augustine, *Confessions* 1.4.

2400-11 **Pro hoc ... et cetera:** X 3.25.5, a canon of the Council of Toledo (525), permits a cleric to enjoy the fruits of improvements he has made in his glebe for the remainder of his life, even if he loses his benefice for some reason–indeed, according to Innocent, Hostiensis and Johannes Andreae, even if he is deprived of it for a crime. Ridolfi interprets this as a reward for improving church property and applies it by analogy to citizens who "improve" the commune by their contributions and are "rewarded" by interest payments. This idea is reinforced by reference to C. 3.28.35.1, where Justinian cites the opinion of Papinian that a son may challenge his father's will on the grounds of unjust disinheritance even if he promised not to do so, since filial obedience is better elicited by rewards than by binding obligations.

For Gregory of Rimini's argument from Aristotle, see below, n. 2467-93.

2412-15 **Quid ultra ... recurramus:** On Ridolfi's citation of Livy and Valerius Maximus in response to Guido de Belloreguardo, see Introduction, p. 104.

An example from Livy is the senate's institution of military pay in the late fifth century after a successful campaign against the Volsci, a measure that Livy saw as the beginning of a reconciliation of the social orders: "This [campaign] was followed by a boon which the senate, at the most opportune moment, conferred on the plebeians. Before the question was mooted either by the plebs or their tribunes, the senate decreed that the soldiery should receive pay from the public treasury. Previously, each man had served at his own expense. Nothing, it is recorded, was ever welcomed by the plebs with such delight; they crowded round the senate-house, grasped the hands of the senators as they came out, acknowledged that they were rightly called 'Fathers,' and declared that after what they had done no one would ever spare his person or his blood, as long as any strength remained, for so generous a country" (*Ab urbe condita* 4.59.11-60.1, trans. W. M. Roberts [London: J. M. Dent, 1912; rep. 1926], 1: 286-87).

Valerius says that Cnaeus Fulvius Flaccus refused a triumph awarded him by the senate "on account of his good deeds" (*ob res bene gestas* [*Factorum et dictorum memorabilium* 2.8.3 (ed. cit. p. 95)]). He writes of Valerius Poplicola, the consular colleague of Brutus, that he "afterwards filled the office of consul three times in a way highly satisfactory to the Roman people and he added to the glory of their ancestors by many great deeds. But when he died, his patrimony was insufficient to cover the cost of his funeral, so it was paid for out of public funds" ("... idemque [Valerius] postea tres consulatus acceptissimos populo Romano gessit et plurimorum ac maximorum operum praetexto titulum imaginum suarum amplificauit, cum interim ... patrimonio ne ad exequiarum quidem impensam sufficiente decessit, ideoque publica pecunia ductae sunt" [ibid. 4.4.1, (ed. cit. p. 188)]).

2416-33 **Ad secundam ... questione**: Ridolfi's refutation of Guido's conclusion at 2349-62 considers the moral options open to the government: even in the name of self-defence, extortion and robbery are not legitimate means to extract revenue. He makes a comparison to killing, which, in certain circumstances, can benefit the republic. To kill malefactors is a good because it punishes crime and serves as a deterrent, but to kill the innocent is more damaging than beneficial. By analogy, even if the city needs money it is not justified in seeking it either through charging or paying usury.

2434-49 **Et si ... rehabebo**: A reiteration of the argument that the statutory rate of five percent on *monte* credits is insufficient to attract lenders whose primary motivation is profit (see n. 2299-2305).

2440-41 **experientia media omnium magistra**: The tag is inspired by VI 1.6.6, which says "experience is the most effective teacher of affairs" ("magistra rerum efficax experientia").

2447 **uolam**: I.e. *velim* (see 2448).

2450-58 **Hec procedunt ... Clenkoh**: Guido's conclusion stands only if we make no distinction between the intentions of those lending to the government in the form of *prestanze* and the motivations of usurers who lend for profit. If no distinction is made, *prestanze* must be condemned, since even the common good cannot excuse sin. The notion that we must not consent to sin for the sake of a bodily good is from X 5.38.13: "Moreover, since the soul is much more valuable than the body, we forbid under threat of anathema any doctor to recommend to the sick for the sake of physical health anything that may endanger their souls" ("Ceterum, quum anima sit multo pretiosior corpore, sub interminatione anathematis prohibemus, ne quis medicorum pro corporali salute aliquid aegroto suadeat, quod in periculum animae convertatur").

QUESTIO MONTIS, DUBIUM 2

2459-60 **Vtrum ... incrementum**: "Whether those who pay *prestanze* may licitly accept an increment on them." On this *dubium*, see Introduction, pp. 89-93.

2461-66 **Videamus ... elucescat:** *Dubium* 2 is a response to Gregory of Rimini's critique of forced loans in his *quaestio disputata* on the public debt of Venice. On Gregory's theses, see Introduction, pp. 68-70.

Gregory sets out two questions in the *proemium* to his *quaestio*: (1) whether creditors of the public debt may licitly receive five percent interest and (2) whether others may purchase such credits and enjoy the same profits. Ridolfi addresses the second question in *dubia* 5 and 6. In support of an affirmative reply to the first question, Gregory adduces six reasons: (1) it is licit to accept a freely-given gift; (2) lenders should be indemnified for lost profits; (3) those who lend out of charity may accept a free gift from the borrower; (4) creditors should receive compensation for the risk to their capital; (5) in the case of *prestiti*, the end–the support of widows and orphans–justifies the means; and (6) what the pope has allowed cannot be called illicit. A negative determination is suggested by Decretum Grat. C.14 q.3 c.3: "anything added to the principal is usury" and "whatever name you give it, it is usury." Gregory's determination of the question is contained in article 3 of the *quaestio* and his detailed responses to these six justifications in article 4.

2467-2629 **Dicit ... potui:** A close, at points *verbatim*, summary of the argument of articles 3 and 4 of Gregory's *quaestio disputata*.

2467-93 **Dicit ... antepone:** Gregory begins by examining the intention of the creditors: do they lend with the intention of profiting? If so, they are guilty of usury and obliged to make restitution. The proof rests on the fact that there is no logical distinction between a government loan and a personal loan. If an intention to profit by a loan to an individual is usurious, so is a similar intention in a government creditor. Indeed, it might be said that the latter sins more since, according to Augustine, the common good should come before that of the individual. In the *Ethics*, after identifying the goal of politics as the *bonum humanum*, Aristotle observes that "if the end is the same for a single man and for a state, that of the state seems at all events something greater and more complete whether to attain or to preserve; though it is worthwhile to attain the end merely for one man, it is finer and more godlike to attain it for a nation or for city-states" (*Ethics* 1.2.1094b6-10, trans. W. D. Ross [ed. cit. p. 936]).

2494-2531 **Sed si ... mutuo:** What are the government's intentions? If creditors interpret interest payments as profit on a loan, they are guilty of usury and obliged to make restitution. Likewise if creditors neglect "clear evidence" of the government's real, as opposed to its expressed, intentions, since "feigned ignorance is no excuse." For example, if the government allots profits on the basis of the amount lent rather than in proportion to the loss incurred by individual creditors or if it rewards only those who lend it money and ignores other kinds of service, usury may be presumed. In summary, creditors may enjoy their profits in good conscience only if they have no intention of profiting by their loans and the government no intention of paying interest on a loan.

2532-50 **In secundo ... et cetera:** The profit is licit, however, if the creditors' motives are charitable and the government's intentions compensatory. In the latter case, creditors are in the position of guarantors (*fideiussores*) who, according to X 3.22.2, have the right to be indemnified for losses they incur through fulfilling their obligation to cover bad debts. Citing VI *de reg. iur.* 86, Gregory limits this title to those who lend under compulsion rather than by choice: "If anyone incurs a loss that is his own fault, the responsibility is his own, not others'" ("Damnum, quod quis sua culpa sentit, sibi debet, non aliis, imputare").

2551-72 **Et intelligit ... sapientis:** Gregory elaborates his conception of damage in article 4 in his reply to the second argument in favour of interest-bearing *prestiti*. *Damnum* can be understood either as (1) a simple loss or "diminution of property" or (2) the loss of anticipated profit from the sum lent. In both cases, creditors who have really suffered damages are entitled to indemnification in the form of *interesse*. Those who plead lost profits must, however, be engaged in a business or trade in which they would otherwise have invested the money lent to the government. Compensation should not be uniform, but adjusted annually to reflect profits that a lender might reasonably–that is, "according to the informed judgement of a prudent man"–expect from his trade in the period during which he has been deprived of his capital, "since it happens that profit is not always uniform, but sometimes less, sometimes more, and, from time to time, there is no profit at all, but a loss."

2573-84 **Sentit ... solutionem:** Ridolfi maintains that Gregory's endorsement of *damnum* takes no account of the peculiar position of citizens who can be forced, under circumstances of necessity, to lend to the government even without compensation. If these factors are considered, Gregory's analysis differs little from that of Guido de Belloreguardo, who maintains that creditors are entitled to nothing more than the restitution of their capital (see Introduction, pp. 68, 88). Ridolfi adds that a citizen in this position could licitly seek and accept indemnification, though the government is under no obligation to pay it.

2585-2610 **Sed quid ... tribuatur:** As qualified by Gregory, *damnum* and spontaneous gift cannot be invoked to justify the fiscal practices of Venice (or Florence). He concludes his analysis in article 3 by observing that profit paid on *prestiti* is paid in return for a loan. The proof of this is that all creditors are paid a uniform rate directly proportionate to the size of their loans. If payments were truly compensatory, they would reflect the damage sustained by individual lenders and this would vary in accordance with their resources and circumstances. In practice, however, the bigger the loan, the bigger the profit. Moreover, so long as the principal of the public debt remains unpaid, any profit offered to creditors must be considered payment for a loan and therefore usury.

2611-22 **Et subdit ... Deus:** Gregory concludes by noting that if the government is truly moved by benevolence, it does well to offer creditors rewards, for, as Aristotle observes, "without friends no one would choose to live, though he had all other goods; even rich men and those in possession of office and of dominating power are thought to need friends most of all; for what is the use of such prosperity without the opportunity of beneficence, which is exercised chiefly and in its most laudable form towards friends?" (*Ethics* 8.1.1155a5-10, trans. W. D.Ross [ed. cit. p. 1058]).

2623-29 **Ex quibus ... potui:** Gregory's conclusions are reported by Lapo da Castiglionchio, though he restricts their application to creditors of the *monte dell' uno tre* and *monte dell'uno due*: "for these [reasons], we may conclude that he considered the first creditors of the said *monte dell'uno tre* and *monte dell'uno due* to receive profit illicitly" ("ex quibus satis euidenter colligitur eum sensisse quod praedicti primi creditores dictorum montium de l'un tre et de l'un due minus licite percipiant lucrum praedictum" [*Allegationes*, allegatio 137, n.10 (ed. cit. fol. 163va)]).

2630-37 **Contrarium ... assero:** On Francesco da Empoli and Nicholas de Anglia, see Introduction, pp. 70-71.

2638-89 **Quid dicendum ... casu:** Ridolfi outlines his position on the moral status of creditors of the public debt and sketches a preliminary critique of Gregory's analysis.

2638-46 **Quid dicendum ... spetialius:** Other things being equal, all government creditors, willing and unwilling, may licitly hope for profit on their loans, provided this is not their primary intention. On Ridolfi's definition of usury as "profit from a loan principally intended as such," see Introduction, pp. 86-87, and Part 1, question 1, nn. 54-56, 232-39 to 290-301.

2647-74 **Tunc quis ... conscientie:** Creditors' primary motivation is not profit since they lend in obedience to the command of the government or from charity in order to help the city in its necessity, since, after God, they owe their first loyalty to the community. Nor would they otherwise be inclined to lend, since their capital could be more profitably invested in other, legitimate, ways. The transaction is usurious only if the government is an unwilling debtor and this is known to the creditors. But the city cannot be constrained by its own subjects and declares in its legislation that it offers profit to the creditors freely. If it pays unwillingly, citizens have no means of knowing this with certainty, since, to paraphrase Dig. 45.1.137.2, "there is room for conjecture in uncertain things, but not in certain" (see n. 1618-27). On scrupulous creditors, see nn. 1524-37 and 1577-86.

2675-89 **Superest ... casu:** According to the canonists, intentional profit from a loan is not always usury. One must distinguish between primary and secondary intention as Augustine, in Decretum Grat. C.1 q.1 c.47, distinguishes between the effects of heretical or simoniacal baptism, which remits sin but does not incorporate the recipient into the body of Christ unless he renounces his heresy or greed, and the effects of orthodox baptism. A secondary intention to profit is not usually usurious, unless the creditor knows or believes the debtor to be acting under compulsion, which is not the case here.

2690-2905 **Sed nunc ... foret:** A detailed examination of Gregory's critique of the motivations of *montisti*.

2694-2725 **Et primo ... symilibus:** Gregory's account of the government's motivations (see n. 2494-2531) discounts the creditors' charitable motives. Nor can it be said that the government cannot be constrained by citizens, since it may prefer to avoid unnecessary inconvenience and expense by offering creditors a return on their loans. So, for example, when the government urgently requires funds, it offers a higher rate of interest and rewards citizens who pay promptly with a bonus. Nor can citizens plead ignorance of the government's motives, since the legislators are themselves citizens. As X 1.3.41 states: "you cannot plead ignorance of your own action" ("de facto suo certus esse debet"); and VI *de reg. iur.* 31: "it is not necessary to further apprise him who is certain" ("Eum, qui certus est, certiorari ulterius non oportet"). Therefore, even if the citizens are moved by charity, their knowledge of the government's corrupt intention necessarily influences their motivation. For Decretum Grat. D.50 c.18, see n. 1236-48.

2726-44 **Hic attendendum ... questione:** In response, Ridolfi alleges that in practice citizens do not all act from the same motives. Some lend with a view to profit and these without doubt are usurers. Others, however, are moved by patriotism or forced to lend and these do not sin. Moreover, while he acknowledges that creditors' intentions are "governed by the intention of the commune," he denies that the government's intention is corrupt: payments are a free gift in recognition of creditors' service and compensation for the damages they sustain in lending. For X 3.24.1, see n. 1611-17; for X 3.26.7, see n. 709-14. For Part 1, question 1, see nn. 240-57 to 310-17. On whether a debtor may be presumed to give freely, see nn. 1601-1603 to 1645-51.

2745-56 **Et cum ... glosa:** For Ridolfi's response to Gregory's argument that interest payments should be adjusted on an individual basis (see n. 2585-2610), see Introduction, pp. 90-91.

The citations emphasize that strict justice must sometimes be tempered in the interests of the common good. The gloss to X 1.2.6 notes that "a statute or constitution should be just and moral and the same for all" ("Et statutum siue constitutio debet esse iusta et honesta et communis omnibus" [gl. ord. ad X 1.2.6, v. *Constitutum* (ed. cit. col. 18)]). Decretum Grat. D.50 c.25 is from a letter of Augustine on the rule that penitents should not be admitted or, in the case of clerics, readmitted, to the clerical order. He allows, however, that in cases where its application is likely to lead to disruptions, the rule should be relaxed. X 5.41.3 states that "it is better to allow a scandal than to renounce the truth" ("Utilius scandalum nasci permittitur, quam veritas relinquatur"). The gloss, citing D.50 c.25, notes that truth in the sense of justice or discipline (that is, law) is sometimes relaxed to avoid scandal ("in his duabus quandoque alique omittuntur propter scandalum"), though such departures should be seen as exceptional ("sed quando ius commune dispensabile est propter scandalum receditur a iure communi" [gl. ord. ad X 5.41.3, v. *Veritas* (ed. cit. col. 1963)]).

2756-62 **sicut in ... infinite:** Distinctions between members of corporate bodies are not necessarily based on merit. According to X 1.33.15, seniority of rank and emolument is a function of office: "We desire that he who is of the higher order, even if he was admitted later, should be preferred in the distribution of emoluments" ("Et qui maior est ordine, etiamsi postea sit receptus, in portione percipienda esse volumus potiorem"). X 1.33.1 adds that, other things being equal, he who was appointed first in time is to be considered senior to another in the same order: "Let this be the difference in honour, that he be considered foremost and senior who has first been appointed by the diliberation and joint action of the community" ("Sit honoris ista distinctio, ut ipse prior et maior habeatur, qui prius communitatis consilio et concordi fuerit actione ordinatus").

2763-76 **Preterea ... merentur:** Therefore, all creditors, whatever they deserve individually, are compensated at the modest rate of five percent, which corresponds to the return that might be expected on land (see n. 2299-2305). Since it is impossible in practice to calculate individual loss and gain, this policy has the advantage of not rewarding unworthy creditors more than they merit.

2777-90 **Nec insuper ... questione:** The allocation of compensation while the public debt remains unpaid and the termination of payments when it has been paid (see n. 2585-2610) do not create a presumption of usury. Payments cease because the loss to the creditors has been made good. Ridolfi draws an analogy to the case of one who, with no primary intention to profit, lends a merchant a thousand florins for ten years. The merchant earns a profit of twenty percent a year on this sum, out of which he pays his creditor eight percent a year in acknowledgement of his liberality. In the tenth year, the merchant repays the principal and ceases to pay the eight percent gift. Since the creditor in this transaction is not condemned as a usurer, neither should government creditors be condemned. The intentions of debtors and creditors are analyzed in Part 2, question 10 (see n. 1601-3 to 1645-51).

2791-2801 **Quot insuper ... concordantiis:** Real damages sustained by citizens are known only to God. In X 3.12.1, Innocent III remarks that although the pope occupies the place of God on earth, he cannot be expected to have knowledge of things done in secret ("etsi locum Dei teneamus in terris, non tamen de occultis potuimus divinare"). For the case, see n. 1627-39.

2802-4 **Nec insuper ... nostris:** The objection that the government neglects to reward other types of service (see n. 2494-2531) is rejected by Ridolfi on the grounds of experience: "in our day we see it done often, albeit without fanfare."

2805-9 **Preterea ... recurri:** See n. 2647-74.

2810-34 **Ad vltimum ... questione .56.:** For X 3.24.1, see n. 1611-17.

For Ridolfi's discussion of the objection that the legislators who decree compensation on the public debt are also the government's principal creditors (see n. 2694-2725), see Introduction, pp. 91-92. Four citations illustrate the proposition that a person may function in various capacities concurrently. X 3.8.15 speaks of circumstances in which a bishop has, in addition to his prelatial status, the standing and rights of a canon in his cathedral chapter for purposes of collation. At VI 2.15.11, the bishop, acting in his capacity as a prelate, cooperates with the chapter in making appointments and any appeal must be heard by the bishop's superior. This would not be the case if the bishop had canonical rights in the chapter, since he could hear any appeal in his episcopal role.

In X 1.6.18, Innocent III informs the chapter of Capua that it must obtain twofold permission to elect a bishop: "You should seek our assent in our royal capacity as well as the grace of apostolic confirmation" ("a nobis vice regia postuletis assensum, et apostolicae confirmationis gratiam requiratis"). The gloss notes that the pope's regal assent alone does not confer administrative authority: "But [the bishop] could not administer on the basis of [royal] assent alone, because the pope does not consent to his election as pope but as king ... and so a double consent is sought" ("Sed ex tali assensu administrare non posset, quia non consentit in eum tanquam papa, sed tanquam rex ... Et sic duplex consensus exigitur" [gl. ord. ad X 1.6.18, v. *Regia* (ed. Lyons 1496-1509, fol. 23rb)]). X 1.6.21 relates a case in which the archbishop of Milan, having been called upon to arbitrate a disputed episcopal election, appointed a bishop and confirmed his election. The gloss asks how one and the same person can both elect and confirm: "But does it not therefore appear that he who elected also confirmed? ... But it is not so, since he elected as arbitrator and confirmed as archbishop" ("Sed nonne eo ipso quod elegit, confirmasse videtur

... Sed non est verum quoniam tanquam arbiter elegit et tanquam archiepiscopus confirmauit" [gl. ord. ad X 1.6.21, v. *Confirmauit* (ed. Lyons 1584, col. 135)]).

Two further citations suggest the opposite conclusion. In X 5.33.16, Innocent III determines that the canons of the chapel of the duke of Burgundy enjoy exemption from episcopal jurisdiction when they function as canons but not when they hold cures as parish priests: "We command therefore that insofar as they are exempt with regard to the chapel you shall reverently defer to their apostolic privileges, but insofar as they are acknowledged to come within your jurisdiction with respect to parish churches and so forth, you may freely prosecute them for recovery of what is owed your office" ("Mandamus, quatenus, in quantum exempti sunt eiusdem ratione capellae, apostolicis privilegiis deferas reverenter; sed, in quantum ratione parochialium ecclesiarum vel alias iurisdictionem tuam respicere dignoscuntur, officii tui debitum in eosdem libere prosequaris"). Part 2, question 56 reviews opinions on whether "individuals are bound to make restitution of usury received by their city or college," and cites with approval the view of Hostiensis and John of Legnano that "governors and those having the power to prohibit" such contracts are so bound.

2835-52 Secundo ... incrementi: On *prestanzoni*, which paid rates of eight or ten percent, see Introduction, p. 92.

2853-2905 Ex quibus ... foret: A marginal note in Ridolfi's hand describes this passage as a "conclusion restricting the above" ("Conclusio limitans suprascriptam").

2853-60 Ex quibus ... habuerunt: On Ridolfi's position on the motivations of legislators, see Introduction, pp. 91-92.

2861-89 Quo autem ... blandiente: On the conditions under which Ridolfi considered rates exceeding five percent licit, see Introduction, p. 92.

2890-2905 Et si ... foret: When rates exceed five percent citizens cannot shield themselves by appealing to the decisions of others, because the more attractive terms are a temptation to profit absent from the standard rate. Such creditors are guilty of usury by intention but not necessarily bound to make restitution. In contrast, those who accept compensation at the traditional rate are explicitly exempted from restitution by the terms of the legislation. On the obligation to make restitution, see Part 2, questions 6 and 7 (nn. 1236-48 to 1248-59 and 1447-30). In all cases, those who are uneasy in conscience should make restitution, as should those who profit where the government's intention is not expressly stated in a clause like the one described in the *thema*.

2907-98 Sed incidit ... *Sacerdos*: A related *dubium*, which arises from the practice of offering a premium for early payment of *prestanze*.

2907-21 Sed incidit ... soluissent: For Ridolfi's examples, see Introduction, pp. 92-93.

2914 procurarunt: I.e. *procurauerunt*.

2921-31 Videtur ... subesse: It seems that in the cases given creditors are guilty of usury, since anyone who lends with a primary intention to profit is a usurer. X 1.2.3, from Augustine's commentary on Hebrews, was read by canonists as an injunction to judge similar cases similarly: "'For when there is a change in the priesthood, there is necessarily a change in the law as well' [*Hbr* 7.12]. Since both were given at once by the same God under the same covenant, what is said of the one must also be understood of the other" ("'Translato sacerdotio necesse est ut legis translatio fiat.' Quia enim simul et ab eodem, et sub eadem sponsione utraque data sunt, quod de uno dicitur necesse est ut de altero intelligatur"). The gloss adds that "where there is the same reason, there should also be the same law, and like cases should be judged similarly" ("Arguit quod vbi est eadem ratio, ibi debet esse idem ius, et quod de similibus idem iudicium est habendum" [gl. ord. ad X 1.2.3, v. *Quod de uno* (ed. cit. col. 16)]).

2932-38 **In contrarium ... conuerso:** On the other hand, it seems that a difference in the underlying rationale changes the nature of an agreement and therefore the disposition of the law. In Decretum Grat. C.1 q.1 c.26, Gregory the Great remarks that an unsound foundation vitiates the whole structure: "Paul says, 'No other foundation can any one lay than that which is laid, which is Jesus Christ [1 *Cor*. 3.11],' and therefore it is proved that where Christ is not the foundation, there is nothing good about the superstructure" ("Cum Paulus dicat: 'Fundamentum aliud nemo potest ponere, preter id, quod positum est, quod est Christus Iesus,' consequenter probatur, quia ubi Christus non est fundamentum, nullum boni operis est superedificium").

Moreover, if the principal issue fails, so does that which is accessory to it. VI *de reg. iur.* 42 states that "it is fitting that the nature of the accessory conform to that of the principal" ("Accessorium naturam sequi congruit principalis"). The maxim is cited in VI 1.14.9, where Boniface VIII declares that the death of the pope does not invalidate the mandate of a judge delegate: "we consider it fitting that just as a letter of grace–even if it has not yet been put into effect–is not rendered void by the death of the one who concedes it, so neither should a power conceded to judges delegate be voided, since it is fitting that, as subordinate to the said letter of grace, it conform to the nature of the principal" ("aequum esse censemus, ut, sicut ipsa gratia, licet nondum sit in eius exsecutione processum, morte non perimitur concedentis, sic nec etiam re integra perimatur exsecutoribus data potestas, quam, veluti gratiae predictae accessoriam, naturam sequi congruit principalis").

2938-44 **Item sepe ... corruptionem:** Often, however, things that are reproved principally are allowed in an accessory manner. In X 3.9.1, Innocent III forbids any change in the condition of a church when it is vacant. The gloss notes that "when a church is vacant, the clergy may not disperse its property ... nor may the bishop alienate the property of a vacant church which is subject to him ... But Huguccio said that if there is pressing need, the clergy may alienate something ... Again, in minor churches the bishop may, on the death of the priest, alienate something on the grounds of necessity" ("Vacante enim ecclesia clerici non possunt disponere aliquid de rebus ecclesiae ... Nec episcopus bona ecclesiae vacantis sibi subiectae alienare potest ... Huguccio tamen dicebat, quod si sit magna necessitas clerici possunt aliqua alienare ... Item in minoribus ecclesiis potest episcopus aliqua alienare propter necessitatem, mortuo sacerdote" [gl. ord. ad X 3.9.1, v. *Sede vacante* (ed. cit. col. 1089)]).

X 1.6.54 forbids clergy to hold multiple benefices involving the cure of souls. The gloss, however, notes five cases in which pluralism is permitted: when one church is dependent on another; when a second benefice is held *in commendam*;

when the benefices are poor; when the cleric is poor; and when the pope dispenses the pluralist. These cases are summed up in two verses:

Paupertas, pendens, defectus, gratia, seruans:
Ecclesias retinere duas dat quodlibet horum.
(gl. ord. ad X 1.6.54, v. *Intitulatum* [ed. cit. col. 202]).

VI 3.4.6 declares that a cleric who holds a benefice with a cure of souls may also accept a prebend to which a parish church is attached without violating the provisions of IV Lateran that forbid pluralism. VI 3.4.15: the pope provides a cleric to the next vacant prebend in a church; subsequently he provides another candidate to the next vacant dignity and prebend. A dignity with a prebend comes vacant: which candidate is to be provided? If the prebend is annexed to the dignity, the second, otherwise the first, though normally the latter would have priority at law. Clem. 3.2.2 declares that a letter providing a cleric to the next vacant benefice does not include hospitals or alms-houses unless these are specified. The gloss adds: "Note that if the hospital is the principal to which a church or chapel accedes, it is not encompassed by the letter, as here. But if this is reversed so that the church is the principal to which the hospital accedes, then I do not consider this decretal to apply, but rather that then an appointment will proceed by accessory right that would fail by the principal" ("Et aduerte, quia si hospitale sit principale cui accedit ecclesia uel capella, per literas non debetur, vt hic. Si vero conuertas quod ecclesia sit principale habens annexum hospitale, tunc non puto hoc locum habere, sed tunc iure accessorii veniet quid principaliter non veniret" [gl. ord. ad Clem. 3.2.2, v. *Ecclesias* (ed. cit. col. 150)]).

Dig. 8.3.18 deals with *servitutes* or easements, in this case a right of way that crosses several estates. If I make use of the servitude to cross only one estate do I lose my right to cross the others? Ulpian replies that "the whole servitude is lost or the whole retained. Thus, if I do not exercise my right over any of the estates, the whole servitude is lost; if I exercise it over one of the estates only, the whole servitude is still kept." But in Dig. 8.6.10, Paul observes that a right of way attached to an estate that I co-own with my ward cannot be lost through desuetude "on account of the interests of the *pupillus*."

Finally, a "quality," a secondary or accidental characteristic, may be corrupt without corrupting the "subject" or underlying reality.

2945-60 **Nunc ad ... usura**: In the present case, the loan that constitutes the underlying subject is not usurious: the lenders are not guided by a primary intention to profit but by patriotic motives, and in any event they would be compelled to lend even without profit. Nor is the government's intention corrupt. By extension it is wrong to suggest that the secondary quality–the desire to obtain a premium for lending–is corrupt or illicit.

2960-72 **Probatur ... alteratio**: For the parallel case cited by Ridolfi, see Introduction, pp. 92-93.

2973-85 **Et si ... corpus**: But something good in itself may be corrupted by a supervening quality, as the body is weakened by disease and the conscience debased by sin.

In a parenthesis (2974-85), Ridolfi gives a number of examples. It is good to give alms, but if you do so for reasons of display rather than charity, it would be better to abstain. Paul remarks at 1 *Cor* 13.2-3 that "if I have prophetic powers, and understand all mysteries and all knowledge, and if I have faith, so as to remove mountains, but have not love, I am nothing. If I give away all I have, and if I deliver my body to be burned, but have not love, I gain nothing." This text is cited by Gratian at Decretum Grat. D.3 de poen. c.49 and Augustine at Decretum Grat. D.4 de cons. c.31. Commenting on *Gal* 5.26 ("Let us have no self-conceit, no provoking of one another, no envy of one another"), Jerome remarks that "giving alms for the sake of praise is a 'self-conceit'; likewise long prayers and the pallor that comes from fasting ... and, though I hesitate to say so (but it must be said), martyrdom itself, if received for the sake of the brethren's admiration and praise is nothing but a vain shedding of blood, for the Apostle, the vessel of election, says, 'if I deliver my body to be burned, but have not love, I gain nothing'" ("Eleemosyna si ob laudem fiat, inanis est gloria: longa oratio, pallor ex ieiunio sequens ... et quod dudum timeo dicere sed dicendum est, martyrium ipsum, si ideo fiat ut admirationi et laudi habeamur a fratribus, frustra sanguis effusus est. Loquatur apostolus, loquatur electionis vas: 'Si tradideram corpus meum, ut glorier, charitatem autem non habeam nihil mihi prodest'").

In Decretum Grat. C.8 q.1 c.11, Augustine observes of 1 *Tim* 3.1 ("If any one aspires to the office of bishop, he desires a noble task"), that "a bishop who loves pre-eminence, not good works, should understand that he is no bishop" (*City of God* 19.19, trans. W. C. Greene [ed. cit. 6: 203]). According to Boniface VIII in VI 3.4.4, a papal grace provides the candidate to a benefice not a guaranteed income: "Although in the matter of benefices the fullest interpretationn should generally be adopted, nevertheless letters concerning future benefices should be interpreted narrowly because of the element of self-interest. Therefore, if we command that someone be provided up to a specific sum, our intention is not to provide him to a pension but only to ecclesiastical benefices" ("Quamvis plenissima sit alias in beneficiis interpretatio facienda: litterae tamen super obtinendis beneficiis impetratae debent, quum sint ambitiose, restringi. Et ideo, si alicui usque ad certam summam provideri mandamus, ei non in pensione, sed in beneficiis ecclesiasticis tantum volumus provideri"). Likewise, to lend freely to your neighbour is laudable, but wicked if the motive is avarice.

2986-96 respondeatur ... transformet: These examples have no parallel in the present case because the end sought–the gift or compensation for loss–is itself good. And "that of which the end is good, is itself good." I have been unable to locate this passage in the *Ethics*, but Ridolfi might be referring to the place where Aristotle discusses the good or end of human action: "What then is the good of each? Surely that for whose sake everything else is done. In medicine this is health, in strategy victory, in architecture a house, and in any other sphere something else, and in every action and pursuit the end; for it is for the sake of this that all men do whatever else they do. Therefore, if there is an end for all that we do, this will be the good achievable by action" (*Ethics* 1.7.1097a18-23, trans. Ross [ed. cit. p. 941]).

Ovid places the sentiment "the result proves all actions" in the mouth of the Thracians who condemn their queen Phyllis for threatening to kill herself after being abandoned by Demophoon. Phyllis replies by cursing those who maintain that the end justifies the means (*Heroides* 2.85-86).

On Part 2, question 7, see nn. 1260-62 to 1447-73.

2996-98 Facit ... *Sacerdos*: A parallel case of simony poses a possible objection to Ridolfi's conclusion. For VI 3.3.1, see n. 1339-44. The gloss poses the following problem: "An arrangement is made in a church whereby he who attends an office will have so much [in manual benefices]. A canon attends the office principally for the money. Does he commit simony? ... Solution: say, as Hostiensis does ... that such do not commit real simony, since no explicit agreement is involved. Nevertheless, they sin gravely and commit mental simony and must do adequate penance" ("Ordinatio est in ecclesia, qui vadit ad talem horam tantum habebit et cetera. Vadit canonicus ad horam principaliter pro denario: numquid simoniam committit? ... Solutio: dic secundum Hostiensem ... quod tales non committunt veram simoniam, cum nulla expressa pactio intercedat; peccant tamen grauiter et mentalem simoniam committunt, et per poenitentiam satis faciunt" [gl. ord. ad VI 3.3.1, v. *Receperit* (ed. cit. col. 385)]). The case and solution are cited by Guido de Baysio in his comments on Decretum Grat. C.1 q.2 c.9.

Questio montis, dubium 3

2999-3001 Posito ... peccato: "Are those who illicitly receive [increments on their *prestanze*] freed from sin and the the obligation to make restitution in virtue of the 'gift, forgiveness, and liberation' [referred to in the statute]?" See Introduction, pp. 54-55, 91-92.

3005-14 Hic passus ... *ciuitate*: The case is parallel to that of the creditor who has been released from the obligation to make restitution dealt with in Part 2, question 7 (see n. 1260-62 to 1447-73). Lapo da Castiglionchio's discussion of the problem in *allegatio* 137 also follows that of Fredericus Petruccius. The dictum of Augustine, "sin is not forgiven unless the thing stolen has been restored," occurs in slightly different forms at X 5.19.5 ("non remittatur peccatum, nisi restituatur ablatum") and VI *de reg. iur.* 4 ("Peccatum non dimittitur, nisi restituatur ablatum").

3015-29 Sed ego ... partis: Ridolfi excepts the case of the citizen whose consent to the statute is necessary and who acts from motives of self-interest. Such a lender must not only do penance but is also obliged to make complete restitution. For X 1.4.11, see n. 1447-73. For X 2.23.3, see n. 968-97.

Questio montis, dubium 4

3030-31 An dicti ... crediti: "May creditors licitly sell the claim (*ius*) they have over the *monte* in virtue of their credit?" See Introduction, p. 94.

3035-44 Ad quod ... predictus: In article 3 of his *quaestio disputata*, Gregory of Rimini maintains that a creditor may sell the right to any principal that remains after the deduction of interest payments he has received (see Introduction, p. 79). Lapo da Castiglionchio reports Gregory's opinion in *allegatio* 137.

3045-53 Et ego ... lucro: Ridolfi agrees that creditors may sell their claims to the *monte*, but considers their rights more extensive than Gregory or Lapo admit.

For Ridolfi's argument that interest payments are not a method of amortizing the loan, see nn. 2459-60 to 2890-2905.

QUESTIO MONTIS, DUBIUM 5

3054 **Vtrum ... emant**: "Whether others may licitly purchase claims in the public debt from creditors." On this *dubium*, see Introduction, pp. 94-96.

3055-67 **Ad quintum ... eum**: In article 3 of his *quaestio disputata*, Gregory of Rimini argues that purchasers of debt credits are usurers if their object is profit, for they either contract a loan or agree to postpone settlement of the debt in return for interest. In support, he alleges X 5.19.10, which condemns as usurers those who refuse to grant an extension of the term for repayment without an implicit agreement to pay more than the principal (see nn. 673 and 682).

3068-81 *Dictam ... Castiglonchio*: Lapo da Castiglionchio criticizes Gregory's conclusions in *allegatio* 137 on two grounds. First, the question is not whether buyers licitly purchase debt credits from the original creditors, but whether the creditors licitly sell them. If they ask for no more than the principal or for no more than they are legitimately entitled to, the sale is licit. Secondly, the transaction is not a loan but a contract of purchase-sale (*emptio venditio*), in which the purchaser may be motivated by a desire for profit. For X 3.17.3 and 6, see n. 836-40. The gloss to both canons notes that parties to a purchase-sale may circumvent one another without invalidating the contract: "But if I am deceived for less than half the just price, I have no action, for it is licit for contracting parties to deceive one another by up to half the just price" ("Si autem sum deceptus minus dimidia iusti pretii, non possum agere ad aliquid, quia licitum est contrahentibus sese inuicem decipere vsque ad dimidiam iusti pretii" [gl. ord. ad X 3.17.3, v. *Deceptione* (ed. cit. col. 1124)]). In other words, participants in the public debt market may legitimately expect to profit from their transactions.

3082-3107 **Iuri ... usurarii**: On Ridolfi's critique of Gregory and Lapo, see Introduction, pp. 94-95.

3091-98 **Quem quidem ... li. .vi.**: Ridolfi interprets X 2.1.6–which suggests that although a plaintiff must make clear what right he is seeking he need not name a specific action (see n. 1147-52)–as an injunction to consider the truth of the matter rather than the mere form.

VI *de reg. iur.* 46 expresses the principle that substitutes are to be judged by the norms that apply to those whom they replace: "He who succeeds to the legal position of another must accept his rights" ("Is, qui in ius succedit alterius, eo iure, quo ille, uti debebit"). The remaining citations provide additional illustrations. Decretum Grat. C.18 q.2 c.30 forbids a bishop to exact anything from a monastery beyond what was agreed at the time of foundation. X 2.1.11 states that the successor of one who has seized a benefice by force may be sued in virtue of a rescript authorizing action against his predecessor. In X 2.2.17, Gregory IX orders the bishop of Durham to satisfy the creditors of his predecessor. X 2.13.18, a decree of IV Lateran, renders anyone who knowingly accepts a benefice that has been illegally appropriated liable for restitution to the rightful incumbent, since "he, as it were, succeeds the spoliator in his wickedness so that, with regard to spiritual danger, there is scarcely any difference between them" ("quum spoliatori quasi succedat in vitium eo, quod non multum intersit, quoad periculum animae").

3108-18 **Preterea ... meum:** Moreover, in cases of fraud by means of a fictitious transaction ("from contract to contract"), the contract should be judged not by its form but by the truth of the matter. For X 3.17.5 and gloss, see nn. 650-52 and 776-86; for X 3.21.6, 2.24.7 and their respective glosses, see n. 776-86; for X 3.21.4 and gloss, see nn. 770-76 and 776-86; for 5.19.6 and gloss, see n. 145-64.

The rubric of C. 4.22 translates, "what is really being done is more valid than what is apparently being done," and the title as a whole is concerned with fictitious transactions in which the illicit intention of the parties is disguised under the form of a legal contract. It emphasizes the importance of "the truth of the matter" (*veritas rei*) rather than the formal characteristics of the contract. A contract made "in appearance" (*simulate*) was void because of the parties' defective intention, as was the illegal act they intended (Berger, *Encyclopedic Dictionary*, s.v. *Simulare*). Dig. 24.1.5.5 cites the jurist Julian's opinion "in connection with sales [between husband and wife], that where property is sold for less than its value, this will have no effect. But according to Neratius ... a sale between husband and wife for the purpose of making a gift will only have no effect if the husband did not intend to sell the property at all, but pretended to sell it so as to make a gift of it." For Dig. 16.1.8.8 and the gloss to Decretum Grat. C.14 q.3 c.3, see n. 2096-2100. Dig. 1.3.29 says that "it is a contravention of the law if someone does what the law forbids, but fraudulently, in that he sticks to the words of the law but evades its sense." The gloss notes that fraud against the law is sometimes committed "from one contract to another" citing as an example Dig. 24.1.5.5. For Part 2, question 18, see nn. 2081-2159 to 2165-82.

3119-41 **Sed huic ... usura:** The objection fails because the parties understand themselves to be participating in a purchase-sale agreement. See Introduction, pp. 94-95.

3142-56 **Sed si ... peccatum:** In *dubium* 5, the central issue is whether *monte* credits are licitly bought and sold; whether buyers licitly receive profit from credits is the subject of *dubium* 6. Ridolfi anticipates the objections of Gregory of Rimini concerning buyers' motivation (see nn. 3055-67). If we concede, with Ridolfi, that in most cases profit is licitly received and even desired by the original creditors, then the same should apply to buyers of credits.

3157-72 **Tolle ... sortem:** Ridolfi proposes two analogies. (1) The creditor of a loan for which the security is an estate is guilty of usury if he appropriates the revenues rather than applying them to the reduction of the principal, and likewise anyone who succeeds him as creditor. For X 3.17.5, see n. 650-52; for X 3.21.4, see n. 770-76; for X 5.19.1, see n. 145-64. But if the creditor should convert the loan into a purchase, he would licitly receive the income, and similarly anyone who in turn bought it from him, even if he paid less than the original principal. (2) A son-in-law who accepts a pledge from his father-in-law in lieu of an unpaid dowry is not required to apply the fruits to the reduction of the sum owed (see n. 524-32). If he were to sell his rights the buyer would enjoy the same privilege, despite the fact that if the latter had received the same property from the father-in-law as security against a loan he would be bound by the usual rules governing pledges. Francesco da Empoli comes to the opposite conclusion in his *Questio de monte* (ed. cit., pp. 39-41).

3172-76 **Nec obstat ... meum**: Commenting on the rubric *de usuris* in the Code, Baldus discusses a similar problem. A son-in-law raises a loan by pledging income he enjoys in lieu of dowry to his creditor: can the creditor licitly receive the income without applying it to the principal? Baldus says that he cannot, because the rationale for usury in this case is specific to the son-in-law and "whenever a person is the direct cause of a privilege, the privilege is altered when the person is altered" ("mutatione personae mutuatur priuilegium quoties persona est immediata causa priuilegii" [*Commentaria*, in C. 4.32.rubr., n.13 (ed. cit. VII fol. 88ra)]). In Part 2, question 54, Ridolfi notes Baldus' opinion along with that of his own master John of Legnano (who in turn cites the *Collectarius* [?Johannes Goffridi, fl. 1344-60]), who held that the transaction might be licit if the son-in-law pledges the income "along with every right [in the dotal pledge] that pertains to him" ("cum omni iure sibi competente" [F_1 fol. 37r; *TUI* 7, fol. 26rb-va]). This case cannot be cited in objection to the foregoing analogy because Baldus and John of Legnano were speaking of pledges rather than sales.

3177-87 **Et per ... inlicitum**: Purchasers of *monte* credits, then, cannot be accused of usury, even though they are motivated by a desire for profit, since (1) the profit on such shares is licit, and (2) in a purchase-sale contract, unlike a loan, a primary intention to profit is permissible, provided the profit itself is licit.

3188-3216 **Nec obstat ... *Sancimus***: On Ridolfi's view of the relationship between the buyer of a *monte* credit and the commune, see Introduction, p. 95. For Decretun Grat. C.1 q.7 c.26, see n. 1640-44.

3217-25 **Tolle ... principali**: Another analogy illustrating the principle that the same end may be sought through different contracts, one of which may be illicit. I may freely buy from you a farm worth a thousand for a thousand and enjoy the fruits; but if you want to pledge the farm to me this would not be allowed, though in both cases my object is the fruits. In the second transaction my desire for profit is rendered illicit by reason of your intention expressed in the proposed contract. The purchase of *monte* credits with a view to gain, like my purchase of the farm, is licit. But it would be otherwise if the buyer of *monte* credits were prepared to conclude the same transaction with the city directly, since he would then be as guilty as one who lends to the city with a primary intention to profit. Ridolfi adds, however, that buyers of credits should not be automatically presumed to have this intention (see nn. 3649-60 and 3661-67).

3226-31 **Sed inquies ... decretalis**: Does the purchase of *monte* credits not violate the usury prohibition in the way that the credit sale condemned in X 5.19.10 does? For the third case of X 5.19.10, see n. 673; for X 5.19.6, see n. 145-64; for X 5.19.19, see n. 751-58; and on the relationship of the three, see n. 787-96. For Johannes Andreae's comments on the gloss to X 5.19.6, see n. 829-34.

3232-56 **Respondeo ... Innocentium**: Ridolfi replies that the cases are not parallel and cites as authority Innocent IV's commentary on X 5.19.6, where he analyzes *census* contracts in terms of purchase-sale (see nn. 1657-79 and 1692-1711). Ridolfi observes that in the case censured by X 5.19.10, a merchant selling a thing on credit charges a premium of two percent of the market value and so "sells time." And in general, according to Innocent, a purchase-sale contract can be censured as usurious only if the price reflects a premium for delay in payment (X 5.19.6) or a discount for delayed delivery (X 5.19.19). *Monte* credits, however, are sold at their market price and there is no delay in payment or delivery.

3257-67 **Hoc ultimo ... uiuis**: Innocent adds that the sale of *census* rents is justifiable if the parties believe they may be worth less in the future than they are at present, or even if there is a measure of uncertainty about their future value. Ridolfi applies this observation to the traffic in *monte* credits: the uncertainty of ever recovering the principal of such loans is an encumbrance that reduces their value.

3268-80 **Sed inquiet ... commictitur**: But it might be objected that the present case does fall within the terms of X 5.19.6 and X 5.19.19, for the thing sold is the sum of money originally lent to the government: if this were taken into account, the price would far exceed the amount actually paid, which in practice is never more than half the face value of the credit. The difference, then, must represent the sale of the time during which the buyer postpones enjoyment of the principal.

3281-3318 **Sed tu ... aperiam**: Ridolfi replies that (1) the money originally lent to the government as money is nonvendible; (2) what is sold is a right or title to this money, which is vendible; (3) the principal sum in practice is non-recoverable (see n. 3257-67); but (4) even if it were recoverable, this would simply serve to enhance the value of the *ius*, since it is this, not the principal as such, that is the subject of the sale. A more accurate parallel to the present case is the sale of a property encumbered by a servitude: a house subject to a year's servitude will sell for more than one subject to a perpetual servitude. Likewise, a buyer will pay more to acquire the usufruct as well as the ownership of a farm than he would to acquire ownership alone, postponing the enjoyment of the usufruct until the death of the seller. As neither of these cases falls within the purview of X 5.19.6 or 5.19.19, neither does the present case. For Johannes Andreae and Gottofredo on credit sales, see n. 829-34. Though not cited by Ridolfi, Francesco da Empoli makes a similar argument in his *Questio de monte*.

QUESTIO MONTIS, DUBIUM 6

3319-20 **Posito ... uenditores**: "Granted that credits may licitly be bought and sold, do buyers of public debt credits licitly receive the profit that was enjoyed by the sellers?" On this *dubium*, see Introduction, p. 96.

3325-37 **In quo ... Gregorius**: A paraphrase of the conclusion to article 3 of Gregory of Rimini's *quaestio* (for an analysis of this passage, see also Kirshner, "From Usury to Public Finance," 189). Gregory argues that the moral restrictions that apply to government creditors also apply to buyers of credits. And just as the former sinned if they lent with the intention to profit, so do the latter; indeed more so, because they act voluntarily, whereas the former were, in a sense, compelled to lend. Nor, since they are motivated by greed rather than necessity, may buyers ascribe their losses to the actions of the government.

3338-56 **His addit ... dubito**: Lapo da Castiglionchio queries Gregory's rationale for applying a single standard to buyers and the original creditors, since the former cannot be held responsible for the intentions of either the government or the sellers. Indeed, even if the same standards are applied, the contention that buyers cannot purchase and enjoy any licit rights to profit enjoyed by the original creditors is not borne out by reason or Gregory's own arguments elsewhere. Lapo therefore concludes that Gregory did not intend a wholesale condemnation of the traffic in debt credits. Kirshner is of the view that "while Gregory established rigid, if not impossible, conditions under which the Venetian citizen could purchase stock, he hesitated to condemn speculation in itself" ("From Usury to Public Finance," 189).

3357-64 **Ego autem ... soluissent:** Ridolfi demurs, attributing a thoroughly rigorist position to Gregory (see Introduction, p. 96).

3365-74 **Sed aduertendum ... sentio:** On Francesco da Empoli's defence of the market in *monte* credits, see Introduction, pp. 73-75.

3375-81 **Conclusio ... uide:** A reiteration of the conclusion of *dubium* 5 that any rights the primary creditors receive from the government may be sold and enjoyed in good conscience by the purchasers.

3381-85 **Vt michi ... potui:** On Peter of Ancharano's *quaestio disputata* on the public debt, see Introduction, pp. 82-84.

3386-3400 **Et istud ... de usuris:** For Ridolfi's critique of the rigorist position for its effects on the psychology of participants in the market, see Introduction, p. 96. The citations emphasize the importance of moderation. *Medium tenuere* [i.e. *tenuerunt*] *beati* ("The blessed keep to the middle") is proverbial, but the sentiment is expressed in X 1.27.1, which admonishes sextons to see to the church lights "so that oil is not wasted by too much light, nor the church underlit by too little; but let all things be done with discretion" ("ne aut supra modum lucendo oleum depereat, aut minus lucendo obscurior sit ecclesia; sed omnia cum discretione agantur"). The gloss takes the opportunity to observe that "one should keep to the middle way" ("et sic via media tenenda est" [gl. ord. ad X 1.27.1, v. *Modum* (ed. Lyons 1496-1509, fol. 56ra)]).

The proverb "qui nimis emungit, sanguinem elicit" ("he who presses too hard draws blood") is cited in X 1.9.10 by Innocent III, who urges discretion in the exercise of episcopal discipline (for Guido de Baysio and Johannes Andreae on VI 5.5.2, see n. 232-39). The maxim "through the employment of excessive subtlety many things are lost and brought to ruin" is from C. 6.49.7 and C. 6.38.4 (see n. 954-67) and invoked in the gloss to Decretum Grat. C.10 q.2 c.2, X 1.6.44 and X 2.1.6.

3401-6 **Non dico ... *Dilecti*:** The law aims at equity rather than harshness. In VI 2.14.3 Innocent IV condemns those who, on the grounds of rigour, "wish to know more than is fitting," declaring that in suits for possession based on an alleged gift or sale, the judge must consider the circumstances, especially the time and place of the transaction described in the petition. But when simple ownership is claimed, "it is not necessary, opportune or even possible to investigate these attendant factors. And although it may appear otherwise to inquisitive persons who are accustomed to debate matters of little significance, in a case in which the claim is non-specific it nevertheless seems better that such matters should be determined with dispatch than dragged out through undue subtlety, especially since it is acknowledged that out of clemency equity permits some things in the common interest that run contrary to the severity of the law" ("Sed quum est in genere absque alicuius causae declaratione petitum, non sic oportet accepti iudicii tempus inspici, quia non requiruntur, nec sunt opportuna, nec attendi possunt huiusmodi comitantia in hoc casu. Et licet aliquibus curiosis, qui de iis, quae non multum expediunt, saepe disceptant, aliter forsan appareat, quando actum est causa aliqua non expressa: utilius tamen videtur negotia tali expediri compendio, quam per quandam exactam subtilitatem longo dispendio prorogari, praesertim quum nonnulla pro utilitate communi contra iuris asperitatem ex aequitatis mansuetudine tolerari noscantur"). X 2.1.6 urges judges to consider simply the facts and the truth of the matter; see n. 1171-77.

3406-8 **Quia tamen ... feci**: Ridolfi finally recommends a tutiorist position: "in doubt choose the safer way," that is, the position in favour of the moral principle. In the present case, this translates into abstention from the market in *monte* credits, which Ridolfi claims has always been his own practice. Contrast Peter of Ancharano, who argues that the principle of "in dubio via tutior est eligenda" has no application here (Kirshner, "From Usury to Public Finance," 200).

QUESTIO MONTIS, DUBIUM 7

3409-12 **Quid de ... describuntur**: "What of those who pay *prestanze* on behalf of others, from whom they sometimes receive a certain amount per florin, sometimes nothing, and are then described as creditors in their place?" This *dubium* is discussed in the Introduction, pp. 96-97 and brokerage practices at 43-44.

3416-33 **Reperio ... eos**: Ridolfi notes that previous analyses of this transaction, such as Guido de Belloregardo's *consilium* on the Florentine *monte*, focus on whether the broker ("Martin") is bound to make restitution of his fee to the citizen ("Peter"). On the one hand, it can be argued that he is not because by paying the fee Peter averts the damage and inconvenience he would incur by meeting his assessed loan. On the other hand, the transaction is analogous to a loan since Martin in effect "lends" Peter the amount of the assessment, which is "repaid" by transfer of title plus the fifty percent fee. To the first argument the critics reply that although Peter benefits from the transaction this does not justify Martin's charging for a loan.

3427-28 **si prestitisset ... isto**: Alhough "Martin" is the subject of *prestitisset*, *sibi* refers to "Peter"; the subject of *prouidisset* and *dedisset* is "Peter."

3431-32 **tamen ... prestat**: The grammatical subject is "Martin."

3434-37 **Examinemus ... qualis**: Ridolfi will first identify the nature of the contract in question and secondly determine whether the transaction is licit.

3438-51 **Et uidetur ... concordantiis**: The transaction seems to be a purchase-sale contract in which Peter is deemed to have paid his *prestanza* of ten and then sold his rights to this sum to Martin for five. According to the principle of logical economy, this case can be assimilated to the sale of a *monte* credit discussed in the preceding three *dubia*. Clem. 1.2.3 declares that a judge appointed by the pope to adjudicate a disputed benefice requires no further mandate to collate the successful litigant, and in this way "redundancy is avoided" (*ut evitetur circuitus*). The gloss adds that "it is vain to do with many what could be done as well with few" ("nam frustra fit per plura quod aeque commode possit fieri per pauciora" [gl. ord. ad Clem. 1.2.3, casus (ed. cit. col. 24)]).

3452-64 **Preterea ... nostro:** Alternatively, assuming that the five paid to the city by Martin was a loan to Peter, inasmuch as both parties agree that all rights and liabilities should pass to Martin, it is *as if* Peter had repaid the five to Martin and then received it back as the price of his rights in the public debt. The citations illustrate the principle that "whatever achieves the object serves the turn." For X 2.20.47 and Dig. 12.1.6, see n. 1030-43. The gloss adds that "it does not matter that any term of specification, like the 'blind' slave or the 'florid' one, is used" ("*An uocabulis*: vt seruum caecum vel rubeum. Sic nota: nil referre quid horum fiat" [gl. ord. ad Dig. 12.1.6, v. *An uocabulis* (ed. cit. I p. 648b)]). VI 1.3.2 explains the meaning of the phrase "certain others" when used in papal letters: "Since many articles of law criticize lack of precision, we are led to decree that by the general phrase 'certain others,' which we frequently insert into our letters, we mean no more than the three or four in judgement whose names the plaintiff included in his summons" ("Quum in multis iuris articulis infinitas reprobetur, provide duximus statuendum, ut per illum generalem clausulam 'quidam alii,' quae frequenter in literis nostris inseritur, ultra tres uel quatuor in iudicium non trahantur, quorum nomina in primo citatorio exprimat impetrator").

Nor is there any deception beyond the just price since Peter could not have received more than five for his credit on the open market.

3465-67 **In contrarium ... principio:** The contract seems to be a loan (*mutuum*) because Martin, not Peter, is described in the registers of the *monte* as the lender. Creditors of the public debt did not receive certificates: assignment, purchase and transfer of credits were book transactions.

3468-79 **Item ante ... centenario:** The contract is not a sale because Peter has no rights to sell until he has paid his *prestanza*. Instead, for the sake of the five he receives from Peter and anticipated profit from the government, Martin voluntarily makes himself a creditor at an effective rate of ten percent. The transaction, however, is disguised as a loan to Peter of five, which he repays, thus making it appear that Martin receives profit at the legal rate of five percent.

3480-3505 **Soluendo ... patet:** The transaction is the innominate contract *do ut facias*, which is enforceable by an *actio praescriptis verbis* (see Introduction, p. 97 and n. 2039-51). For C. 2.3.27, see n. 2100-2105.

3506-13 **Preterea ... cedo:** The parties to such contracts are commonly referred to as "buyers" and "sellers," though strictly speaking this is inaccurate. In X 3.5.16, Innocent III directs that clerics be ordained to a title or benefice, since the word "cleric" is derived from the Greek *kleros*, which means "portion" or "inheritance."

3514-71 **Nec obstat ... principio:** A discussion of the principle that an anticipated right grounded in the immediate circumstances can be alienated (see Introduction, p. 97).

3514-20 **Nec obstat ... *de dona.*:** Peter has an anticipated right grounded in the immediate circumstances, namely, the government's declared intention to pay compensatory interest. Such an expectation, moreover, is vendible. At C. 8.53.3, the emperor Decius (249-51) declares that "it is fitting that with the full agreement of the donor an anticipated right to sue may be transferred" ("Spem futurae actionis plena intercedente donatoris voluntate posse transferri non immerito placuit").

3520-32 **Vnde aduertendum ... l. .ii.**: The illustrations are from the sixth *quaestio* of Bartolus' commentary on Dig. 45.1.122.6. At Dig. 12.4.8, the jurist Neratius observes that a dowry given for a marriage between parties one of whom is below the lawful age (and therefore unable to consummate) is non-recoverable while the union lasts for "property given in this way before a marriage is entered is given, so to speak, as a potential dowry. So long as the potential remains, there is no recovery." According to Dig. 40.7.1, a *statuliber*, is "[a slave] who has freedom arranged [in his master's will] to take effect on completion of a period or fulfillment of a condition." Thus, although any slave may hope for his liberty, he is a *statuliber* only if his hope has a basis in his circumstances, specifically, according to Dig. 40.7.2, that "at least one of the heirs instituted has entered on the inheritance." Otherwise, "if he is alienated or usucapted or manumitted at an earlier stage, his hope of the freedom arranged lapses."

3533-44 **Similiter ... questione**: This example is a highly compressed version of the first *oppositio* of Bartolus' commentary on Dig. 45.1.122.6. The case described in the fragment is as follows: two brothers divide an inheritance and mutually stipulate that neither will challenge the division, each promising to pay a penalty if he does so. One brother dies and the survivor sues the heirs for the inheritance on the ground that it was a *fideicommissum* left him by their father. He loses his suit and must pay the penalty because such a claim was encompassed by the agreement between the brothers. Bartolus observes: "But if brother should succeed brother directly, perhaps by way of pupillary substitution, then it could be said that there was an expectation, as in Dig. 40.7.2" ("Sed si frater succederet fratri directo, forte ex vigore substitutionis pupillaris, tunc posset dici spem subesse, ut l. 2 supra *de statulib*. [Dig. 40.7.2; see n. 3520-32]" [*Commentaria*, in Dig. 45.1.122.6, n.4 (ed. cit. VI fol. 45ra)]). However, the case would be determined otherwise if one brother succeeded the other by way of intestacy. In this case, any prior agreement that involved cession of future rights would have had no basis in the circumstances at the time it was made, since the first brother might subsequently make a testament.

Dig. 34.3.6 illustrates the principle that someone cannot be said to have an interest simply because he might succeed another. In the testament of his emancipated son's creditor, a father is forgiven liabilities arising from the son's use of his *peculium*. *Peculium* was property granted to a son or slave under the authority of the father or master for his free use, though it remained the property of the father or master (Berger, *Encyclopedic Dictionary*, s.v. *Peculium*). Javolenus concludes that the "father will have an action insofar as he is due to pay anything on the *peculium* or from benefit taken. For [only] that in which he shall have an interest will belong to the father on the ground of the legacies." In virtue of this release can the father also sue to have the son forgiven any further obligation to the heir, since it is "an object of interest to the father to maintain the son's right intact"? The jurist concludes that he cannot: "nothing further is due to the father on the wording of that kind of will other than that he pay none of what he has been obliged to pay the heir." The gloss observes that the father's interest in the son's release consists in the fact that he might succeed to his obligations: "His right: namely, of the father, that is, in succeeding to the son, as a patron succeeds a freedman" ("*Ius eius*, scilicet patris, quod est in succedendo filio ut patronatus liberto" [gl. ord. ad Dig. 34.3.6, v. *Ius eius* (ed. cit. III p. 693b)]).

3545-53 Potest ... totum: A cleric cannot, strictly speaking, be said to have an expectation of a benefice unless he has some immediate ground for hope, such as a letter of expectancy granting him the next vacant benefice in a specific church. The citations illustrate at length the mechanism of expectancies. X 3.5.19, for example, declares that a cleric who has been provided to a canonry by a papal mandate shall enjoy a daily stipend until a prebend becomes available, while VI 3.4.13 quashes a collation made by a chapter in ignorance of the claim of a papal providee. X 1.3.7, 1.3.19 and 1.3.40 relate to procedural or circumstantial impediments to the execution of mandates, while others, such as X 1.29.12, 1.3.30, 1.3.38 and 39, VI 1.3.12-14 and 3.7.1, deal with disputes arising from multiple provisions to the same benefice.

3554-60 Potest ... *rescrip*.: Clem. 1.2.4 states that "You appear to renounce a grace that you be provided to a dignity or benefice if, before obtaining the benefice, you obtain another" ("Gratiae, ut de dignitate vel beneficio curato tibi provideatur, renunciare videris, si ante adeptionem eiusdem aliud beneficium pacifice assequaris"). Ridolfi draws the conclusion that you cannot properly be said to renounce an expectation for which you have no immediate grounds but only a generalized hope.

3561-71 Preterea ... principio: While on probation before taking his vows, a novice is not properly a religious, though he enjoys the immunity granted members of religious orders in virtue of his expectation of profession. VI 5.11.21 therefore declares that "Although one who enters religion may not be considered a religious in effect until he is privately or publicly professed, nevertheless anyone who assaults him shall not escape the bond of excommunication imposed by the canon" ("Quamvis autem is, qui religionem ingreditur, religiosus censeri cum effectu non possit, donec sit tacite vel expresse professus: si quis tamen violentas manus in eum iniiciat, excommunicationis latae a canone vinculum non evadit"). Johannes Andreae notes in his commentary that "since we consider a novice a religious, though not yet definitively a religious, he is tried in an ecclesiastical court" ("Cum igitur, vt dixi in textu, censeamus nouitium religiosum, licet commutabiliter, propter hoc conuenimus eum in foro ecclesiastico" [*Novella*, ad VI 5.11.21, n.2 (ed. cit. fol. 169vb)]). He makes the same observation in his commentary on VI 3.14.4, which directs that the benefice of a cleric who has entered religion shall not be conferred on another without his agreement before the completion of his novitiate, "unless he is resolved that he wishes to change his way of life entirely, or he makes his profession or knowingly takes the habit" ("Beneficium illius, qui religionem ingreditur, non est infra probationis annum alicui conferendum, nisi ad id ipsius accedat assensus, aut constet, quod vitam voluerit absolute mutare, vel professionem expressam fecerit, seu scienter habitum receperit professorum").

Ridolfi's allegation of Clem. 1.2.5 and gloss seems to apply to the argument of 3514-71 as a whole and suggests that an anticipated right must have a real, as opposed to an apparent, basis in the circumstances. The decretal states that "a letter granting you collation to the next vacant benefice does not extend to a benefice created after the date of the letter" ("Literas nostras, super conferendo tibi beneficio vacaturo directas, ad beneficium, post datam ipsarum creatum, statuimus non extendi"). The *casus* illustrates this with an example in which a cleric seeks and obtains in January a grace from the pope providing him to the next vacant benefice in his region. In November, a new chapel is endowed and duly licensed by the bishop. The cleric presents his grace, but is refused collation because his letter dated January refers only to foundations existing at that time. The bishop's action is upheld by the pope. The gloss notes that the measure is directed "against those who would enjoy the fruits of their graces too quickly" ("est inductum contra illos qui nimis cito volunt habere fructum de gratiis suis" [gl. ord. ad Clem. 1.2.5, casus (ed. cit. col. 26)]). It adds that the rule holds "even if [the benefice is created] shortly after ... therefore we must consider whether the benefice existed at the time the grace was given, just as we consider the age of the petitioner" ("etiam si paulo post ... inspicimus ergo an extaret beneficium tempore datae, sicut inspicimus aetatem impetrantis illo tempore" [ibid., ad v. *Post datam* (col. 27)]).

3572-79 **Ad aliud ... uerissimum**: In reply to the objection at 3465-67, Ridolfi argues that Martin should be described properly as neither a purchaser nor a lender, but as one who enters an innominate contract to absolve Peter from his obligation to the community and having done so, is rightly described as the government's creditor in his place.

3580-89 **Ex quo ... solutio**: The resolution of both questions posed at the beginning of the *dubium*–is Martin bound to restore five to Peter and is the transaction licit?–is clear from the foregoing argument: Martin is not bound to make restitution, while the transaction, as one that approximates purchase-sale, is licit (see n. 3119-41 and Introduction, p. 97).

3590-3617 **Sed quoad ... posita**: If the argument that Martin is bound to make restitution were carried to its logical conclusion, the purchaser in any sale of corporeal or incorporeal rights would be bound to compensate the seller for fluctuations in value. You, for example, buy a field at its market value of a hundred. In time it declines in value by half and you sell it to Martin for fifty. Martin is not obliged to make up your loss. Similarly, Peter sells a credit with a nominal value of ten for its market value of five, the difference being dictated by doubt about the government's ability to repay this sum.

In response to the objection that a change in market value involves the passage of time, Ridolfi modifies his example. I purchase for some reason or have credited to me by a defaulting debtor a right or title to a hundred and I immediately sell it to you for its market value of fifty: you are not thereby bound to make up the difference.

3618-25 **Sed contra ... principalis**: Ridolfi's conclusion that the transaction is licit may, however, be questioned with respect to the present hope or expectation of future profit that is sold. If hope of profit from a loan makes a usurer (X 5.19.10), then the seller of such a hope in the present case is a usurer and *a fortiori* the buyer.

3626-48 **Solue ... solutionem**: Ridoli replies by distinguishing between a primary and secondary intention to profit. At best, the desire for the five percent constitutes a secondary hope of profit, since lenders are coerced into lending. Nor can anyone object that this hope precedes or is concomitant with the lender's compliance with the government's decree, for, on the basis of experience, he knows that "compulsion and payment are certain." For X 2.23.6 and 9, see n. 968-94. This certainty constitutes an immediate cause such that it is as if he had paid, for hope must follow, not precede, payment. For VI 1.6.6, see n. 2440-41.

3649-60 **Sit ... *Nauiganti*:** The transaction is illicit if Martin's intention is fraudulent (see Introduction, p. 97). The citations illustrate the principle that intention is the criterion of licitness. For X 1.3.38, see n. 1236-48. At X 1.6.54, Gregory IX notes that a papal permission to hold multiple benefices obtained under false pretenses is void "since it was not our intention to dispense him from holding so many benefices, especially those with cure of souls, nor was it our intention to concede anything new, but that as an indulgence he might retain the benefices he already had" ("quum intentionis nostrae non fuerit, secum in tot beneficiis, praesertim habentibus curam animarum, dispensare, nec intentionis nostrae fuerit, aliquid de nouo concedere, sed ut per indulgentiam posset habita licite retinere"). For X 1.38.9, see n. 1171-77. X 2.24.16 states that one who has sworn to obey a command is not bound to obey if it is contrary to a prior oath; X 2.24.18 that one who knowingly swears to do something illicit is not bound by the oath, whereas if he does so in ignorance he should fulfil it; and X 2.24.25 that spouses may not separate, even if they have agreed to do so by a solemn oath, unless they intend to live continently. In X 3.5.36, Gregory IX forbids the division of a prebend for the sake of augmenting another since "it was not our intention that for the sake of renewing the said canon's prebend another prebend should be broken up" ("nostrae intentionis non exstitit, ut pro integratione praebendae supradicti canonici praebenda de novo aliqua scinderetur"). In X 3.5.38, he quashes a collation that exceeded the intention of the letter of provision: "Therefore, since the mandate does not extend to such offices and since it was not our intention to appoint the candidate to a rectorship or dignity–since the letter pertained only to a simple benefice–we declare the institution void" ("Quum igitur mandatum huiusmodi se ad talia non extendat, nec ad rectoriam vel dignitatem nostra feratur intentio, quum pro simplici beneficio iussio nostra manat: mandamus ... institutionem huiusmodi ... non tenere"). For X 3.17.5, see n. 650-52; for X 3.21.4, see n. 770-76. For X 5.19.19, see n. 751-58; for X 5.19.6, see n. 145-64.

3661-67 **Hoc autem ... uulgaria:** For Ridolfi's discussion of presumptions in Part 2, question 10, see nn. 1601-3 to 1645-51. These criteria can be applied in an earthly forum but the inner motivations of the purchasers of *monte* credits can finally be known and judged only in the divine tribunal.

QUESTIO MONTIS, DUBIUM 8

3668-71 **Quid si ... nominandi:** "What if the government creates new creditors by, for example, selling annuities for the life of the purchaser and one other named by him at a rate that corresponds to the rate paid creditors of the *monte* under the terms mentioned above in the *thema*?" See Introduction, pp. 98-99.

The question is treated by Lapo da Castiglionchio in *allegatio* 137 where he discusses annuities bearing interest rates that correspond to those of the *monte dell'uno tre* and *monte dell'uno due*, namely, fifteen and ten percent. The terms of this contract further specify that the government may redeem the credit at will for twenty-eight percent of the face value (see n. 2236-42) and that at the death of the buyer and his nominee the annuity will cease.

3677-87 **Et in ... questione**: For Lapo's opinion, see Introduction, p. 98. The opinions of Innocent and Hostiensis on *census* contracts are discussed in Part 2, question 11 (see nn. 1657-79 to 1778-85).

3688-3704 **Sed stat ... relinquitur**: For Ridolfi's discussion of deception beyond half the just price and the authorities cited here, see Part 2, question 16 (nn. 1945-46 to 1970-86).

3705-24 **Michi stat ... approbandum**: Ridolfi concludes that the contract is open to fraud except under certain conditions. He gives three reasons for hesitation. (1) Although it may be argued that because the annuity is based on the city's property (*bona*) it represents the sale of a real, as opposed to a personal, *census*, Ridolfi remains sceptical. He treats the question at length in Part 2, questions 13 and 14 (see nn. 1840-43 to 1887-94). (2) The contract is similar to the annuity condemned in Part 2, question 18 (see nn. 2004-13 to 2165-82), despite the fact that the contract there is described as a *donatio* and this as a sale. (3) The fact that the government retains the right to redeem the credit at will for less than the sale price creates a presumption of fraud (see Part 2, question 12; nn. 1786-89 to 1816-39).

3725-51 **Ad hoc ... notatis**: The following conditions must be met if the *census* is to be considered licit. (1) The return on the *census* must not be excessive but reasonable (*conueniens*). Ridolfi characterizes the rates on the *monte dell'uno tre* and *monte dell'uno due* as excessive in *dubium* 1 (see n. 2314-18). Given that these funds had been abolished in 1380, Ridolfi here seems to approve a rate corresponding to the current statutory return on *monte* shares of five percent. (2) It must be a real *census* based on the existing goods or real property of the commune and not a claim on the person of the commune (see nn. 1879-82 to 1887-94). (3) The agreement should not permit the termination of the contract on payment of more or less than the purchase price (see n. 1816-39). Ridolfi adds, however, that redemption at a discount is permissible if participation in the fund is open to all citizens without distinction; but if it figures in an agreement between the city and an individual it is presumed to be in fraud of usury. (4) The purchaser must not be someone who is accustomed to lend at usury.

3752-71 **Aduertendum ... uenditor**: The sale of annuities for life or some other indefinite period does not invalidate them but the contrary, for if both the term and the return were fixed, the contract would be presumed fraudulent. For Part 2, question 11, see nn. 1652-53 to 1778-85. But it might be objected that a life or perpetual term is, in a sense, fixed and guarantees a certain return; how, then, does it differ from, for example, a fifteen-year term with a guaranteed return of fifty percent? Ridolfi replies that in the latter case the fixed term implies a fictitious sale whereas the perpetual character of the former does not necessarily represent a guaranteed return–for example, in a life annuity, the purchaser might die immediately or before the accumulated profit exceeds the principal–but rather indicates a real sale in which the buyer possesses the thing bought in perpetuity and the seller the price.

3773-74 **die xiiii.ª ... m.°cccc.°iii.°**: Modern style, 14 February 1404.

3777-86 **Et si ... in nouella**: The apology for errors and prolixity is conventional. At X 3.12.1, Johannes Andreae observes on the authority of Hostiensis that "those who write much are excusable because although such detail is unnecessary for the learned, it is useful for beginners and for posterity.... It is better to weary the learned with references than to rob the young of what they ought to know.... In the prologue to his letters Cassiodorus says that it takes great skill to avoid what pleases the learned and, Hostiensis adds, to spare the unlearned complexities and subtleties, for both the gloss and the law should be common" ("Notat Hostiensis excusabiles multa scribentes, quae licet prouectis non sint necessaria, nouis et posteris possunt esse profutura ... melius est doctos onerare scitis quam iuuenes fraudare dicendis.... Cassiodorus in prologo epistolarum: Plerumque peritiae genus est uitare quod placeat doctis; subdebat Hostiensis: parcant et rudes quoad alta et subtilia, nam glosa sicut et lex debet esse communis" [*Novella*, ad X 3.12.1, n.4 (ed. cit. III fol. 68vb)]).

Glossary

The glossary includes legal and economic terms, examples of non-standard usage and words not easily recognized because of their spelling. Lemmas appear in the nominative of nouns and adjectives and the infinitive of verbs if these forms occur in the text. Otherwise words are given as they first appear, followed by the nominative or infinitive in brackets. Reference is to the number of the line in which the term makes its first or sole appearance in the text.

ACCAFFINITATES (*accaffinitas*) contract retaining mercenaries negotiated by an agent (*accaffinans*, *accaffoius*) who financed it by loans at interest (10).

ACCATTIS (*accattum*; It. *accatto*) short-term, compulsory but redeemable loan to the commune at rates of eight or ten percent a year (2838). Also the form ACCATTONIBUS (*accattone*; It. *accattone*) literally, a "big *accatto*" (2714). *See also* MONTE, PRESTANTIAS, PRESTANZONIBUS.

ACTIONEM (*actio*) right to sue in a trial (1332). ACTIO PRESCRIPTIS VERBIS an action to compel performance in a contract that did not conform to one of the standard types (2102-3). ACTIO PERSONALIS (CL *actio in personam*) required the defendant to give (*dare*), do (*facere*) or perform (*prestare*) something in fulfilment of a contractual obligation (1872). *See* CONTRACTUS.

ADDITIONE (*additio*) explanatory comment or gloss on a legal text (841-42).

ALIENATIO alienation, transfer of legal ownership (*dominium*) (1870). *See* DOMINI, DOMINIUM.

ALLEGAT (*allegare*) allege or adduce a legal authority (894).

ALLEGATIS (*allegatus*) adduced in a legal argument (344). *See* ALLEGAT.

ANTIDOTUM (=*antidonum*; Greek *antidoron*) counter- or return-gift acknowledging a favour (710).

APPARATU (*apparatus*) commentary, series of glosses on a legal text (23).

ARBITRIUM considered judgement of a jurist (*sapiens*) or an upright man (*vir bonus*) (978). *See* ARBITROR.

ARBITROR (*arbitrari*) judge on the basis of expertise or as an upright man (235).

BAROCCOLA (*baroccolum*; It. *baroccolo*) (10). *See* RETRANGULAS.

BENEFICIUM favour, service, benefit (292); an ecclesiastical office to which income was attached (485). *See also* GRATIAM, LITERIS.

BONA a person's property, including, in a legal sense, rights and debts (568).

BONA FIDES honesty, good faith of a legal agent in the fulfilment of an obligation or the exercise of a right, or the honest belief, even if mistaken, that he was not violating the right of another (499). *See also* CONTRACTUS, POSSESSOR MALE FIDEI.

CAMBIA (*cambium*; It. *cambio*) exchange of money from one currency to another that often concealed usury (9).

CANON church law, as opposed to a civil enactment (*lex*); in the text, a fragment of Gratian's *Decretum* (444); fixed annual payment of a rent (1676). *See also* DECRETALIS, LEX.

CANONICA canonical, pertaining to church law (484). *See* CANON.

CANONISTA canonist, church lawyer (1584). Syn. CANONUM DOCTOR. *See* CANON.

CANONUM DOCTORI (*canonum doctor*) doctor of the canons, canonist, church lawyer (2626). Syn. CANONISTA. *See* CANON.

CANTANTIA (*cantare*) expressing the meaning of a text (779).

CAPITALE principal of a loan (syn. *sors*) (925); nominal value of a *monte* credit (2198); purchase price of a *census* (2050); capital, money, credit or merchandise accumulated for business purposes (3164). *See also* CENSUS, MUTUUM, SORS.

CAPITULUM chapter or subdivision of a text (149); assembly of the clergy of a collegiate church or convent of religious (2084).

CARISTIA dearth (382).

CASUS case or instance (36); a summary of the material facts of a case or a summary of a text noting significant divisions and terms (673).

CAUTIONES (*cautio*) guaranty for performance of an obligation (1036).

CEDERE cede or transfer a right or an action to somebody else (3470).

CENSUALES (*censualis*) arising from a census (1744). *See* CENSUS.

CENSUS contract in which an annual return (*redditus*) from productive property was sold for a cash payment (*capitale*) (1682). CENSUS PERSONALIS a *census* based on the total goods (*bona*) of the seller (1833). CENSUS IN RE, CENSUS REALIS a *census* tied to a productive property (1813). *See also* BONA, CAPITALE, REDDITUS.

CIVILIS according to private law, as opposed to *criminalis*, a criminal matter; according to civil law, as opposed to *naturalis*, by nature or natural law (551). *See also* IUS, NATURALIS, OBLIGATIO.

CIVILITER by means of a private suit, as opposed to a criminal procedure (*criminaliter*); in accordance with civil law, as opposed to natural law (*naturaliter*) (1320). *See also* CRIMINALITER, IUS, NATURALITER.

CLEMENTINA (CONSTITUTIONE) (*clementina constitutio*) decree contained in the *Constitutiones Clementinae* of Clement V (1305-1314), promulgated in 1317 (397). *See also* CANON, DECRETALIS.

COLLA yoke, task (11).

COLLECTAS (collecta) compulsory contribution, levy, tax on members of a corporation (744).

COMITATINIS (*comitatinus;* It. *contadino*) inhabitant of the *contado* (*comitatus*) (2230). *See* COMITATU.

COMITATU (*comitatus*; It. *contado*) territory directly subject to Florence and liable to direct taxation, in contrast to *districtus* (districts), cities and territories of more recent acquisition, which retained their distinctive fiscal and administrative structures (2207). *See also* DISTRICTUALIBUS.

COMPETENS belonging, relevant or pertaining to a specific case or legal agent, as in the phrase *actio sibi competens* (1333). *See* COMPETIT.

COMPETIT (*competere*) belong, be relevant or pertinent to a specific case or actor, as in the phrase *ius competit Petro* (3287).

COMPRESTANS (*comprestare)* citizen making a compulsory loan to the commune (3426). *See also* PRESTANTIAS.

COMUNE in addition to its usual sense, a commune, a republican city-state (2020). Syn. COMUNITAS.

COMUNIONEM (*comunio*) sacrament of Holy Communion (1386).

COMUNIS OPINIO opinion expressing a broad consensus of jurists in virtue of which it possessed particular authority (139).

COMUNITAS commune, republican city-state (9). Syn. COMUNE.

CONCIVIUM (*concivis*) fellow-citizen (7).

CONCOMITANS accompanying, concomitant (192). *See* CONCOMITETUR.

CONCOMITANTER concomitantly (182). *See* CONCOMITETUR.

CONCOMITETUR (*concomitari*) accompany (204).

CONCOMUNICAT (*concomunicare*) impart, communicate (2698).

CONDITIO (CL *condictio*) action or remedy alleging unjust enrichment (1194-95). The *condictio* varied depending on the material facts of the suit. Those applicable to usury included: (a) *condictio indebiti*, a *condictio* for payment not due; (b) *condictio certi* for a specific thing; (c) *condictio incerti* for a non-specific thing; (d) *condictio ob iniustam causam* for the recovery of money paid as a result of an illegality, such as duress; and (e) *condictio triticaria* for the return of a quantity of a fungible, such as wheat or oil, delivered in a loan. Not to be confused with *conditio*, also used in the text in the usual sense of "condition." *See also* ACTIONEM.

CONDUCTIONIS (*conductio*). *See* LOCATIONIS ET CONDUCTIONIS.

CONSILIUM in addition to its usual sense of "opinion" or "judgement," the formal, written opinion of a jurist on a specific point of law usually in response to a request from a judge or a party to a suit; the written judgement of a theologian (966). *See* CONSULERE.

CONSULENTIS (*consulens*) expert who pronounced a legal or theological opinion (*consilium*) (1006). *See* CONSULERE.

CONSULERE pronounce a legal or theological opinion (*consilium*) (1276). CUM SIGILLO CONSULERE to deliver a legal opinion subscribed and sealed by the jurisconsult (2636-37). *See also* CONSILIUM.

CONTRACTUS contract, an agreement between two parties to create an actionable obligation (50). Contracts were categorized as: (a) consensual contracts such as *emptio venditio* (sale) and *locatio conductio* (rent); (b) "real" contracts, which involved delivery of a thing (*res*), such as *mutuum* (loan), *depositum* (deposit), *commodatum* (gratuitous loan of a non-fungible thing) and *pignus* (pledge); (c) contracts involving certain set forms of words, such as *stipulatio*; and (d) contracts creating a written obligation in the form of entries in an account book. CONTRACTUS BONE FIDEI, comprising most contracts in groups (a) and (b), required *bona fides* (good faith) in their performance, and suits arising from them were judged from the perspective of equity and honesty (499). CONTRACTUS STRICTI IURIS were enforced strictly with regard to the terms of the contract. In Roman law, loans of fungibles (*mutua*) fell within this category (512). CONTRACTUS INNOMINATUS was a bilateral contract lacking a specific name in which each party agreed to do or give something, such as "I give you something so that you may do something" (*do ut facias*) (2045). *See also* BONA FIDES, DEPOSITUM, EMPTIONIS ET VENDITIONIS, FRAUS, LOCATIONIS ET CONDUCTIONIS, MUTUUM, OBLIGATIO, PACTUM, PIGNUS.

CONTRAENDA i.e. *contrahenda* (*contrahere*) concluding a contract, contracting (1873). *See* CONTRACTUS.

CONVENIT (*convenire*) agree to a transaction or to settle a dispute (58).

CONVENTIO agreement between parties to a transaction or dispute (508). *See* CONVENIT.

CONVENTIONALI (*conventionalis*) based on an agreement (*conventio*) or contract between the parties in contrast to a requirement imposed by a judge (1431). *See* CONVENIT.

CONVENTUS convent, religious house; members of a convent viewed as a collective entity (2032-33).

CORBIUM (*corba*; CL *corbis*) a dry measure roughly equivalent to ten bushels (1841).

CREDITOR one to whom something was due at law, one who had an action to recover his due; the lender in a *mutuum* (188). *See also* CREDITUM, DEBITOR.

CREDITUM thing owed as a result of a legal transaction, principal of a loan (1483); a right to the principal of a compulsory government loan, which could be sold (2023-24). *See also* CREDITOR, DEBITOR.

CRIMINALITER by means of a criminal procedure as opposed to a civil suit (1320). *See also* CIVILITER.

DAMPNUM i.e. *damnum* damage or loss sustained by a creditor as a result of lending (501).

DARE in a legal sense, give something with the intention of making the recipient the owner (70). *See also* DOMINI, DOMINIUM, DONATARIUS, DONUM.

DEBITOR debtor, one who owed something as a result of a legal transaction; one from whom money could be exacted against his will; one who owed the principal of a loan (110). *See also* CREDITOR, CREDITUM, DEBITUM.

DEBITUM debt, thing owed to a creditor as a result of a legal transaction (75). *See also* CREDITOR, CREDITUM, DEBITOR.

DECRETALIS (LITTERA) decretal, a papal letter or rescript responding to a specific problem, ruling on a point of law or promulgating a conciliar canon and included in one of the systematic compilations of papal law, the *Liber extravagantium decretalium* of Gregory IX (1234) or the *Liber sextus decretalium* of Boniface VIII (1298) (20). *See also* CANON.

DE FACILI easily (820).

DEPOSITARIUS trustee, depositary (154). *See* DEPOSITUM.

DEPOSITUM deposit, a thing placed in trust. The trustee (*depositarius*) could not make use of it and was required to return it on demand with any proceeds or, in the case of delay, with interest (156).

DE PRESENTI at present, immediately (284).

DIMIDIAM (*dimidia*) IUSTI PRETII half of the just price, that is, of the market or legally regulated price of a thing. In canon law, sales that exceeded or fell short of the just price by half could be rescinded (838).

DISTRICTUALIBUS (*districtuales*; It. *distrettuali*) inhabitants of the "district" (*districtus*; It. *distretto*), that is, cities and territories more recently subject to Florence than the *contado* (*comitatus*) and retaining their traditional fiscal and administrative apparatus (2230-31). *See also* COMITATU.

DOLUS fraud, deceit used to defraud another (849).

DOMINI (*dominus*) in a legal sense, the owner, as opposed to the possessor or usufructuary of a thing (1317). Equivalent to It. *Messer*, a title accorded those, such as lawyers and church or public officials, who enjoyed the dignity of knighthood (247). Teacher (69). DOMINA woman of high social status (2006). *See also* DOMINIUM, USUSFRUCTUS.

DOMINIUM legal ownership of a thing, as opposed to mere possession (*possessio*) (472). Lordship, rule (2491-92). *See* DOMINI.

DONATARIUS donee (1112-13). *See* DARE, DONATIO, DONUM.

DONATIO gift, as opposed to the payment of a debt (969). Syn. DONUM. *See* DARE.

DONUM gift, as opposed to the payment of a debt (390). *See* DARE.

DUBIUM doubtful case, question (31). Syn. QUESTIO.

DUCATOS (*ducatus*) ducat, a Venetian gold coin comparable in value and fineness to the florin (2086). *See also* FLORENORUM.

EMPHYTEOSI (*emphyteosis*; CL *emphyteusis*) long-term, alienable lease that gave the leaseholder complete use of the thing leased and ownership of its fruits (488). *See also* FRUCTUS, USUSFRUCTUS.

EMPTIO (ET VENDITIO) contract of purchase and sale in which a thing (*merces*; CL *merx*) was exchanged for money (1720). CONTRACTUS EMPTITIUS ET VENDITITIUS a purchase-sale contract (3200). *See also* MERCES.

EST DARE "there is," "it is possible to give" or "to adduce" (160).

EXACTIO enforcement of an obligation to pay a debt (50). *See* EXIGERE.

EXCEPTIO defence that did not challenge the legality of the plaintiff's claim but alleged circumstances that invalidated it (76).

EXCIPIENDI (*excipere*) plead an *exceptio* (1503). *See* EXCEPTIO.

EXIGERE enforce payment of a debt (87). *See* EXACTIO.

EX QUO since (14).

EXTIMARI i.e. *estimari* estimate, assess, appraise (2609).

EXTIMATIO i.e. *estimatio* estimate, assessment, appraisal (434). See EXTIMARI.

EXTO i.e. *esto* (116).

FACERE in addition to its usual meanings, to support, help, or be of service, particularly with respect to authorities cited in an argument, as in the expressions *facit quod infra dixi, facit ad materiam quod dixit Johannes Andree, in contrarium videtur facere, contra rationes eius facere videtur glossa, bene facit in argumentum*, and so on (298).

FACTUM (*factum*) fact, thing done, in contrast to law (IUS); a matter of fact as opposed to a matter of law (1504).

FARAONICO (*faraonicus*) i.e., *pharaonico*, in the manner of Pharaoh, that is, with a hardened heart (*Ex* 4.21) (1469).

FENERARI lend at interest, to practise usury (from *fenus*, interest paid on a loan) (38).

FENERATOR usurer (1294-95). *See* FENERARI.

FENERATORIUS usurious (1811) *See* FENERARI.

FIDEICOMMISSI (*fideicommissum*) obligation to pay a sum or transfer property to a third party imposed on an heir by testament (3539).

FIDEIUSSOR guarantor of a debt (490). *See also* SATISDATIO.

FIORINO (It.) florin (2397). *See* FLORENORUM.

FLORENORUM (*florenus*; It. *fiorino*) florin, a virtually pure gold coin worth in 1404 s. 76 d. 6 in the *monete piccioli da denari*, the petty silver (but in fact largely copper) money used in daily transactions, or 13.91 times the silver *grosso da soldi* or *soldo*. The florin was used in trade and large transactions and was the basis of the Florentine money-of-account (1762). *See also* LIBRAS, SOLDO.

FORI (*forum*) court (694). IUDICIALE FORUM (847), FORUM CONTENTIOSUM (1143), FORUM ECCLESIASTICUM (3564) ecclesiastical court. FORUM CONSCIENTIE court of conscience, sacrament of penance (1260). *See also* IUDICIUM.

FRAUDATUR (*fraudare*) defraud (3667). *See* FRAUS.

FRAUDOLOSUM (*fraudolosus*) fraudulent (1820). *See* FRAUS.

FRAUDULENTAM (*fraudulentus*) fraudulent (821). *See* FRAUS.

FRAUS fraud, a transaction undertaken to deprive another of a legal advantage (95). A contract IN FRAUDEM USURARUM was a transaction that was not formally a loan but achieved the same end as a loan at usury (774). FRAUS DE CONTRACTU AD CONTRACTUM fraud from one contract to another in which a formally licit agreement concealed an illicit transaction (1833-34). *See also* CONTRACTUS, USURA.

FRUCTUS fruits, income from productive property (e.g. fields or mines) or legal transactions (e.g. rent from a lease), which normally belonged to the owner (87).

GENERALI STUDIO (*generale studium*) university (3773).

GLOSA (CL *glossa*) gloss, explanatory comment on a legal text; the standard apparatus of glosses (*glossa ordinaria*) on a text (139). GLOSA NOTABILIS gloss of particular significance (2279). *See also* NOTABILI.

GLOSATOR (CL *glossator*) author of one of the *glossae ordinariae* (504). *See* GLOSA.

GRATIAM (*gratia*) grace, a papal letter appointing a cleric to a benefice (3556). *See also* BENEFICIUM, LITERIS.

GROSSO MODO (It.) more generally (1383).

GUERRE (*guerra*; It. *guerra*) war (2311).

IMMOBILIA (CL *res immobiles*) immovables, land or buildings (2792). *See* MOBILIA, RES.

IMPRESTITIS (*imprestitum*; It. *imprestito*) compulsory loan to the commune of Venice analogous to the Florentine *prestanza* (3383).

IN CONTINENTI immediately (2101).

INDISTINCTE without distinction, without exception (136). *See* INDISTINCTUM.

INDISTINCTUM undifferentiated (1755-56).

INHIRI i.e. *iniri* (3574).

INSTRUMENTA (*instrumentum*) tool (384); document recording a legal transaction and having probative value when drawn up by a notary or other public official (665).

INTERESSE (CL *id quod interest*) compensation representing the difference between what a party to a contract had lost and what he would have gained if he had not entered into the transaction or if it had been fulfilled; legitimate compensation for damages sustained by a party to a loan as opposed to *usurae* (498). *See also* MUTUUM, USURA.

IUDICIUM judgement (115). IUDICIUM ECCLESIE proceedings or judgement of an ecclesiastical court (764). Syn. IUDICIUM MILITANS (114), IUDICIUM FORI (694), IUDICIUM CONTENTIOSUM (1145-46) proceedings or judgement of a terrestrial court. ANIMARUM IUDICIUM (184-85), IUDICIUM ANIME (765) judgement of conscience exercised in the sacrament of penance. Syn. IUDICIUM POLI (694-95), IUDICIUM TRIUMPHANS (114-15) judgement of heaven. IUDICIUM PRUDENTIS VIRI (2559) considered judgement of an upright man. *See also* FORI.

IURAMENTUM oath (77).

IURISTARUM (*iurista*) jurist, lawyer (408). *See* IUS.

IUS law in the broadest sense, equivalent to the German *Recht* (8). A specific legal provision (syn. LEX, CANON, DECRETALIS) (344). A right, the legal capacity of a person to do something, such as to acquire or dispose of a thing or to claim something from another (211). IUS REALE (CL *ius in re aliena*) a right over the property of another, such as servitude, pledge (*pignus*) or *emphyteusis*, which limited the owner's exercise of his ownership rights (1851). IUS NATURALE (550) natural law, natural right, law of nations, in contrast to IUS CIVILE (551) positive law, the sum of the rules and principles of Roman law and IUS CANONICUM (484) positive law of the church. UTRIUSQUE IURIS DOCTOR (3382) doctor of canon and civil law. *See also* CANON, DECRETALIS, LEX, NATURALIS, NATURALITER.

IUS INCORPORALE (CL *res incorporalis*) intangible thing, a right (3599). IUS CORPORALE (CL *res corporalis*) tangible thing (3599). *See* RES.

IUXTE i.e. *iuste* (2344).

LAUDA (*laudum*) protocol of a judicial decision; the judgement or finding itself (780).

LEGENS ORDINARIE university reader or lecturer on the mandatory ("ordinary") curricular texts (3773).

LEX law, a civil legislative enactment, as opposed to IUS, equivalent to the German *Gesetz* (2227); one of the constituent fragments of the *Institutiones*, *Digesta* or *Codex* (1354); divine law as expressed in the Pentateuch (685); law in the broad sense (syn. IUS) (91). LEX CANONIZATA imperial enactment included in a canonical collection (1957). *See also* CANON, IUS.

LIBELLI (*libellus*) petition of a plaintiff initiating a lawsuit (1646); a pamphlet (2398).

LIBRAS (*libra*; It. *lira*) money-of-account equivalent to 20 *solidi* or 240 *denarii* (1924). *See also* FLORENORUM and SOLDO.

LITERIS (*litere*; CL *litterae*) papal letter appointing a cleric to a benefice (1552). LITERE EXPECTATIVE papal letter appointing a cleric to the next vacant benefice in a church (3548-49). *See also* BENEFICIUM, GRATIAM.

LOCABILIBUS (*locabile*) rentable (450). *See* LOCATIONIS ET CONDUCTIONIS.

LOCATIONIS (*locatio*) ET CONDUCTIONIS (*conductio*) (CL *locatio conductio*) contract of lease and hire of property or services (160).

LUCRUM profit (41). LUCRUM CESSANS anticipated profit forgone as a consequence of lending (2768).

MAGISTRALIS pertaining to a magistrate or public office-holder (2826).

MALEGRATIBUS TUIS (*malegrates tuae*; It. *tuo malgrado*) against your will (1453). MALEGRATIBUS SUIS against his will (3637).

MERCANTIIS (*mercantia*; It. *mercanzia*) trade, business, commerce (2784). Syn. MERCIMONIA.

MERCES (=CL *merx*) thing sold in a contract of purchase-sale (866); fee, recompense (=CL *merces*) (2288). *See* EMPTIONIS ET VENDITIONIS.

MERCIMONIA (*mercimonium*) trade, commerce (985). Syn. *mercantia*. *See* MERCANTIIS.

MERCURIALI (QUESTIONE) (*mercurialis questio*) lit. "Wednesday question." The *quaestiones disputatae* on the title *de regulis iuris* of the *Liber sextus* by the Bolognese canonist Johannes Andreae, so called because they were disputed on Wednesdays (*dies Mercurii*; It. *mercoledi*) (271).

MERITO (*meritum*; It. *merito*) entitlement, compensatory *interesse* (2211). *See* INTERESSE.

MOBILIA (CL *res mobiles*) movables (2792). *See also* IMMOBILIA, RES.

MONS consolidated public debt of Florence, the *monte comune* (9). The MONS VETUS (2307) was the original consolidation of 1343-45. The text refers to the fifteen and ten percent funds established in the 1350s and 1360s (the *monte dell'uno tre* and *monte dell'uno due*) collectively as the MONS NOVUS (2313) and the new consolidation of 1381 at five percent as the MONS NOVISSIMUS (2314). The public debt of Venice was also called the MONS (53).

MORA (*mora*) default, delay in payment of a debt for which the debtor was liable to a penalty in the form of *interesse* (369). *See also* INTERESSE, PENA.

MUTUANS lender (113). *See* MUTUARE.

MUTUARE lend, contract a mutuum (49). *See* MUTUUM.

MUTUATIONEM (*mutuatio*) a lending, a loan, equivalent to MUTUUM (203).

MUTUUM loan of fungibles, including money, which the debtor was obliged to repay in the same quantity and quality. The principal sum was called *sors* or *capitale* (36). *Mutuum* was a gratuitous contract; in classical Roman law an agreement to pay interest (*usurae*) was embodied in a separate, unilateral contract called *stipulatio* or *pactum*. Medieval jurists called compensation for failure to meet the terms of the contract *interesse*. *See also* CAPITALE, INTERESSE, PACTUM, SORS, USURA.

NATURALIS natural, according to nature; often contrasted to *ciuilis*, according to law (427). *See also* CIVILIS, IUS, OBLIGATIO.

NATURALITER according to natural law, as opposed to *civiliter*, by law (35). *See also* CIVILITER, IUS.

NECESSITATA constrained (2863). *See* NECESSITATIS.

NECESSITATIS (*necessitas*) in law, exigency, need or compulsion to which an actor might be subject (567).

NOTABILI (*notabile*) noteworthy, of general significance (687).

NOTABILITER in a noteworthy or significant way (404).

NUMERATA counted out (524).

OBLIGATIO moral duty or a legal obligation to give, do or perform something arising from a contract or a wrongdoing (*delictum*) (61). CIVILIS OBLIGATIO was a legal obligation enforceable by an action (716) in contrast to a NATURALIS OBLIGATIO, which was not (715). OBLIGATIO PERSONALIS obligation enforceable against an individual (1821). *See also* ACTIONEM.

OPPOSITIO potential objection to the proposed interpretation of a text met by distinctions and additional authorities (27).

OR (It.) now, but (1586).

ORDINIS (*ordo*) HEREMITARUM order of the Hermits of St. Augustine, Augustinian friars (52). ORDO MINORUM order of Friars Minor, Franciscan friars (2191). ORDO PREDICATORUM order of Friars Preacher, Dominican friars (2636).

PACISCI conclude a *pactum* (41). *See* PACTUM.

PACTIO (49). *See* PACTUM.

PACTUM agreement that did not conform to any of the recognized categories of contract and was therefore unenforceable except as a defence (EXCEPTIO) or when appended to a contract in order to modify its terms (75). Syn. PACTIO. PACTUM NUDUM a simple, formless agreement in contrast to a contract (1489). *See also* CONTRACTUS, EXCEPTIO.

PARABOLAM (*parabola*) IURAMENTI postponement or extension of the term for payment of a debt (674).

PENA (CL *poena*) penalty, fine (39).

PER PRINCIPALIUS principally, above all (=*principaliter*) (1066).

PETERE sue, seek something by means of a legal process (35). *See also* ACTIONEM, PETITIONE.

PETITIONE (*petitio*) action for the recovery of a thing (1148). *See also* ACTIONEM.

PIGNORAVIT (*pignorare*; CL *pignerare*) give as a pledge (3174). *See* PIGNUS.

PIGNUS (*pignus*) pledge or security for a debt, as in the expression *in pignus recipere* ("to receive as a pledge"); the agreement under which security was pledged (486). Also CONTRACTUS PIGNORATITIUS contract of pledge (3162).

POSSESSOR MALE FIDEI one who possessed a thing in the knowledge that he was not the lawful owner, contrasted to a *possessor bonae fidei* (1565-66). *See also* BONA FIDES, DOMINI, DOMINIUM.

PRATICA (It.; ML *practica*) practice, custom (778).

PREBENDAM (*prebenda*) prebend, a stipend paid to a member of a collegiate church from endowments (3547).

PRECARIARUM (*precaria*) contract in which a donor gave property to the church in return for a life usufruct in the gift (1909). *See also* USUSFRUCTUS.

PRESCRIBIT (*prescribere*) to acquire possession by *praescriptio* (1566). *See* PRESCRIPTIONI.

PRESCRIPTIONI (*prescriptio*; CL *praescriptio longi temporis*) mode of acquiring ownership through possession for a period of ten years in the case of parties from the same region or twenty in the case of those from foreign cities. Canon law required good faith in prescription (1564). *See* BONA FIDES.

PRESTANTIAS (*prestantia*; It. *prestanza*) compulsory loan to the commune. The text restricts the term to loans at five percent a year (2196-97). *See also* ACCATTIS, PRESTANZONIBUS.

PRESTANTUR (*prestare*) offer, give, pay, perform (92); pay a *prestanza* (2345).

PRESTANZONIBUS (It. *prestanzone*) literally a "big *prestanza*" paying interest of eight or ten percent a year (2713-14). *See also* ACCATTIS, PRESTANTIAS.

PRESTATIO payment, performance (2106). *See* PRESTANTUR.

PROLISSUM i.e. *prolixum* (1700).

PRONTE i.e. *prompte* (2706).

PRONTUS i.e. *promptus* (1651).

PROVISIO (It. *provvisione*) commission or sum invested in a business venture, compensatory *interesse* (2211); in Florence, a legislative provision approved by the Council of the Popolo and the Council of the Commune (2222). *See* INTERESSE.

PULEDRIS (*puledrus*; It. *puledro*) foal (3405).

PUPILLOS (*pupillus*) person below the age of puberty, ward under the legal guardianship of a tutor (2797).

PUR (It. *pure*) still, however (1579).

QUESTIO (CL *quaestio*) problem cast in the form of a question on which pertinent authorities were brought to bear dialectically and the contradictions resolved (25).

QUICDQUAM i.e. *quicquam* or *quidquam* (1757).

REDDITUS (CL *reditus*) income, revenue, returns (1652). CENSUALES REDDITUS revenues from a *census* (1744). *See* CENSUS.

REFORMATIONE (*reformatio*; It. *riformagione*) legislative act of the commune of Florence (2234).

REMICTERE i.e. *remittere* release from an obligation, forgive a harm (640-41); refer to a passage in a legal authority (1581).

REMISSIO remission from an obligation (1135); reference to a legal authority (Syn. *allegatio*) (409). See ALLEGAT, REMICTERE.

REPETITIONEM (*repetitio*) detailed exegesis of a legal text involving the systematic treatment of a single topic (19).

REPLICABIT (*replicare*) advance a *replicatio* (1491). *See* REPLICATIONIS.

REPLICATIONIS (*replicatio*) *exceptio* advanced by the plaintiff in reply to an *exceptio* put forward by the defendant (1492). *See* EXCEPTIO.

RES thing that was the subject of a right (49). *Res* could be "corporeal" (physical objects, *mobilia* or *immobilia*) or "incorporeal" (*iura*, rights). RES NUMERABILES, PONDERABILES VEL MENSURABILES, RES QUE CONSISTUNT IN PONDERE, NUMERO VEL MENSURA things that could be counted, weighed or measured, i.e. fungibles, such as wine, grain, oil or specie (346-48). *See also* IMMOBILIA, IUS, MOBILIA, MUTUUM.

RESTITUERE restore a thing to its original legal condition so that the creditor had the use of it that he had before the debtor had damaged it (219-20).

RESTITUTIO restoration of a thing to its original legal condition (61). *See* RESTITUERE.

RETRANGULAS (*retrangula*; It. *ritràngola*) a usurious transaction in which A, a retrangulator (It. *ritagliatore*), bought goods on credit from B for a sum that was paid by A's debtor (C). The difference between the sum A lent to C and the amount C paid B represented A's profit (10). Syn. BAROCCOLA.

SACRE PAGINE (*sacra pagina*) sacred scripture, the Bible. SACRE PAGINE PROFESSOR, MAGISTER, DOCTOR a master or doctor of theology, theologian (2187-88).

SATISDATIO security given by the guarantor (*fideiussor*) of a debt (3266). *See* FIDEIUSSOR.

SATISFACTIO fulfilment of an obligation in a way other than that specified in the agreement (1326). *See* SOLUTIO.

SECURITATES (*securitas*) surety for a loan for which the guarantor charged a percentage; mercantile insurance (9-10).

SERVITIUM voluntary service, benefit (281).

SERVITUTEM (*servitus*) servitude, a right over the property of another, such as a right of way or the right to use a building or land of another (*servitus praediorum*). When the right, such as a usufruct, was attached to a specific person it was called a personal servitude (*servitus personarum*) (3264). *See also* USUSFRUCTUS.

SIGILLANTES (*sigillare*) affix a seal (*sigillum*) (666).

SINDICUM (*sindicus*) syndic, public official (2243).

SOLDO (It.; ML *solidus*) the *grosso da soldi*, a silver coin originally worth 12 *denari* but by 1402 valued at s. 5 d. 6 (d. 66) in terms of the mainly copper *monete piccioli da denari*, the money used in daily transactions (2397). *See also* FLORENORUM, LIBRAS.

SOLUTIO payment, fulfilment of a legal obligation (49).

SORS principal of a loan (11). Syn. CAPITALE. *See* MUTUUM

STATULIBER slave conditionally manumitted in his master's will (3525).

SUBSTITUTIONIS (*substitutio*) PUPILLARIS appointment of a substitute to an heir below the age of puberty as a precaution against the possibility that the principal heir might die before reaching the age at which he could legally make a will (3542).

SUMMA systematic compendium on a topic or series of topics (17); a compendium organized according to the titles of the *Liber extra* (48).

TAMTUM i.e *tantum* (2202).

TENORE (*tenor*) content, import of a legal act (2808).

THEMA theme, topic of analysis (2084).

THEOLOGORUM (*theologus*) theologian (408). Also TEOLOGUS (3092). SACRE THEOLOGIE MAGISTER master of sacred theology, theologian (52).

TITULO (*titulus*) title, subdivision of a legal compilation (48); title, cause of ownership (2086).

TRAFFICARE trade, traffic in goods (2301).

TRAFFICO (*trafficus*; It. *traffico*) trade, traffic in goods (2884).

TRANSACTIONIS (*transactio*) informal extrajudicial settlement between parties to a dispute (3535).

TRANSACTUM (*transigere*) conclude a *transactio* (3534). *See* TRANSACTIONIS.

UBBIE (*ubbia*; It. *ubbia*) life annuity (2001).

UNIVERSITAS corporation, association of individuals treated for legal purposes as a unit (744).

USURA usury, interest paid on a loan (*mutuum*), often in the plural (*usure*) (1). *See also* INTERESSE, MUTUUM.

USURARIUS usurer (38); usurious (194). *See* USURA.

USUSFRUCTUS usufruct, the right to use the property of another and to take the income from it without diminishing its capital value. Usufruct was a personal servitude (489). *See also* SERVITUTEM.

VALOR value (415).

VENDICARE (CL *vindicare*) claim a place, come into play, as in the phrase *vendicare sibi locum* (1962).

VIDERE when used as a substantive, view or opinion (972).

PRINCIPAL SOURCES

S. Battaglia and G. B. Squarotti, ed., *Grande dizionario della lingua italiana.*
A. Berger, *Encyclopedic Dictionary of Roman Law.*
M. Bernocchi, *Le monete della Repubblica fiorentina.*
E. Conti, *L'imposta diretta a Firenze nel Quattrocento* (1427-1494), 375-78, glossary.
E. Conti, ed., Matteo Palmieri, *Ricordi fiscali (1427-74)*, 281-332, glossary.
E. Conti et al., ed., *Le "Consulte" e "Pratiche" della Repubblica fiorentina nel Quattrocento*, Vol. 1: 1401, 333-43, glossary.
C. du Fresne du Cange, *Glossarium mediae et infimae latinitatis.*
F. Edler, *Glossary of Mediaeval Terms of Business: Italian Series, 1200-1600.*
R. Latham, ed., *Revised Medieval Latin Word-List from British and Irish Sources.*
R. Naz, ed., *Dictionnaire de droit canonique.*
J. F. Neiermeyer et al., *Mediae latinitatis lexicon minus.*
M. Plezia, ed., *Lexicon mediae et infimae latinitatis Polonorum.*
J. Pryor, *Business Contracts of Medieval Provence.*

Appendix
Notes on Ridolfi's Authorities

ALANUS ANGLICUS. *See* DECRETALES GREGORII IX.

AUTHENTICAE constitutions (*novellae*) issued by the emperor Justinian (527-65) after the publication of the CODEX in 534. 134 of these were collected in the sixth century under the title *Authenticum*. Medieval civilians grouped the 97 *authenticae* they considered relevant in their time into nine *collationes* and inserted individual *authenticae* into related titles of the CODEX. Several constitutions of the emperors Frederick I (1152-90) and Frederick II (1197-1250) were also interpolated into the CODEX as *authenticae*. The *glossa ordinaria* to the *Authenticum* was written by FRANCISCUS ACCURSIUS (*See* CODEX).

BALDUS DE UBALDIS (DE PERUSIO) ca. 1327-1400, the most influential civilian of the late fourteenth century. A native of Perugia, he studied canon law there under FREDERICUS PETRUCCIUS. After further studies in Pisa under the civilian BARTOLUS OF SASSOFERRATO, he was elected to a chair in civil law in Perugia in 1351. As a citizen, he was active in local politics and diplomacy. Although he spent most of his career in his native city (1351-57, 1365-76, 1379-90), he was much sought after as a lecturer and spent considerable periods at the universities of Pisa (1357-58), Florence (1359-64), Padua (1376-79) and Pavia (1390-1400), where he also taught canon law. Among his most famous pupils was the canonist PETER OF ANCHARANO. A prolific author, Baldus commented on the entire *Corpus iuris civilis* and produced over two thousand *consilia* on specific points of law. Though best known as a civilian, Baldus also commented extensively on the LIBER EXTRA, the LIBER SEXTUS and the CONSTITUTIONES CLEMENTINAE.

BARTHOLOMEW OF BRESCIA. *See* GRATIAN.

BARTOLUS OF SASSOFERRATO (BARTOLUS DE SAXOFERRATO) ca. 1313-57. The most influential civilian of the first half of the fourteenth century, he studied law under CINO OF PISTOIA at Perugia and later at Bologna, where he received his doctorate in 1334. He became a magistrate and professor of law at Pisa in 1339 and occupied a chair at Perugia from 1343 until his death. His most distinguished pupil was BALDUS DE UBALDIS. Bartolus wrote commentaries on all of the *Corpus iuris civilis*, several hundred *consilia* and a series of treatises on politics and government.

BERNARD OF PARMA. *See* DECRETALES GREGORII IX.

BERNARDUS COMPESTELLANUS ANTIQUUS. *See* DECRETALES GREGORII IX.

CINO OF PISTOIA (CINUS DE PISTORIO) ca. 1270-1336/37. He studied civil law at Bologna between 1292 and 1302 and then at Orleans under Petrus de Bellapertica and Jacobus de Ravannis, the first jurists to apply the techniques of Aristotelian dialectic developed in the Paris schools to the exegesis of civil law. Cino is generally credited with popularizing these techniques in Italy, thus marking a break from the earlier glossarial method of FRANCISCUS ACCURSIUS. A professor of civil law at Perugia, Cino counted BARTOLUS OF SASSORERRATO among his pupils. He was also an important vernacular poet and a friend of Dante; his death was commemorated by Petrarch. He wrote commentaries on the CODEX and the DIGESTUM VETUS.

CODEX the codification of imperial legislation commissioned by the emperor Justinian in 533 and published in the following year. It superseded all previous codifications, including an earlier collection of 529. The *Codex* was compiled by a committee of jurists who selected and edited imperial constitutions beginning with Hadrian (117-38). The resulting selection was divided into twelve books, each containing a number of titles within which individual constitutions were arranged chronologically. Medieval civilians treated the first nine books as a unit, while books 10-12 were known as the *tres libri*. The *glossa ordinaria* to the INSTITUTIONES, DIGESTA, *Codex* and *Novellae* of Justinian was written by the Bolognese civilian FRANCISCUS ACCURSIUS (fl. 1191-1263) who completed it around 1230. It incorporated earlier apparatuses on the *Codex* by Azo (fl. 1191-1220) and on the DIGESTA by Hugolinus (fl. 1197-1238).

CONSTITUTIONES CLEMENTINAE a collection of 106 decretals and conciliar canons commissioned by Clement V (1305-14) and promulgated with revisions in 1317 by John XXII (1316-34). It was significant as the last authoritative collection of medieval canon law and the first publication of the decrees of the Council of Vienne (1311-12). The *glossa ordinaria* on the *Clementinae* was written by JOHANNES ANDREAE.

DAMASUS a Hungarian, he first studied, then taught canon law at Bologna until 1217. He wrote commentaries on the first three *compilationes antiquae* (*see* DECRETALES GREGORII IX), the constitutions of IV Lateran, as well as *quaestiones* and two *summae* on papal decretals. He was notable for his extensive use of Roman law concepts in the explication of canon law.

DECRETALES GREGORII IX, *Liber extravagantium decretalium*, *Liber extra* or simply the *Extra*, an edition of decretals commissioned by Gregory IX (1227-41), who was himself a lawyer, and drawn from earlier collections of papal law known as the *quinque compilationes antiquae*. The arrangement and editing of this material was entrusted to a committee under the direction of RAYMOND OF PENYAFORT, who arranged the decretals in five books dealing broadly with the following topics inherited from earlier systematic collections: (1) ecclesiastical judges, (2) procedure, (3) clerics, (4) marriage and (5) crimes and penalties. The books were subdivided into titles on specific topics, which in turn contained individual decretals arranged chronologically. Promulgated in 1234, the *Liber extra* superseded previous collections as the "authentic" or authoritative statement of papal law. The *Liber extra* was itself modified by the subsequent inclusion of *novellae decretales* issued by Gregory's successor INNOCENT IV (1243-54). The *glossa ordinaria* on the *Extra* was written by BERNARD OF PARMA (BERNARDUS PARMENSIS DE BOTONE), a Bolognese canonist who composed successive versions of his apparatus of glosses between 1241 and his death in 1266. Bernard's gloss incorporated earlier glosses on the *compilationes antiquae* by TANCRED (1185-1236), the leading Bolognese canonist of the early thirteenth century, as well as material by ALANUS ANGLICUS (fl. 1190-1215), BERNARDUS COMPESTELLANUS ANTIQUUS (fl. ca. 1210), LAURENTIUS HISPANUS (d. 1248) and VINCENTIUS HISPANUS (d. 1248).

DECRETUM GRATIANI. *See* GRATIAN.

DIGESTA or *Pandectae* the compilation of classical Roman jurisprudence commissioned by the emperor Justinian in 530 and published in 533. Under the chairmanship of the jurist Tribonian, the compilers excerpted and edited passages from some nine thousand texts, which they then distributed among fifty books subdivided into titles. The resulting *catena* of excerpts superseded all existing books of Roman jurisprudence. Medieval civilians divided the *Digesta* into three parts reflecting the stages in which the text was recovered: the *Digestum vetus* (Dig. 1.1-24.2), the *Infortiatum* (Dig. 24.3-38.17) and the *Digestum novum* (Dig. 39.1-50.17). The *glossa ordinaria* to the *Digesta* was written by FRANCISCUS ACCURSIUS (*see* CODEX).

DIGESTUM VETUS, DIGESTUM NOVUM. *See* DIGESTA.

DINO (ROSONI) OF MUGELLO (DINUS DE MUGELLO) fl. 1279-ca. 1298. A Florentine, he obtained a doctorate in civil law in 1279 and a chair at Pistoia, which he occupied until 1284. He taught in Bologna from 1285 to 1296, when he accepted an appointment to the papal *studium* in Rome. He died there soon after 1298. He wrote commentaries on the DIGESTUM NOVUM and INFORTIATUM, a collection of contradictory glosses on the *Corpus iuris civilis* and an influential commentary on the title *de regulis iuris* of the LIBER SEXTUS.

FRANCESCO DA EMPOLI (FRANCISCUS DE EMPOLI) d. 1370. Little is known about his early life, but he lectured on theology at Oxford in the mid-1340s as a member of the Franciscan order. He was vicar of the convent of Santa Croce in Florence in 1347, reader in theology at the University of Florence in 1359 and provincial minister of the Franciscans of Tuscany from 1360 to 1367. He is known for his *Questio de monte* of 1353-54 in defence of the *monte comune.*

FRANCISCUS ACCURSIUS. *See* CODEX.

FREDERICUS PETRUCCIUS (DE SENIS) fl. 1322-1343. Little is known about his life or career beyond the fact that he taught canon law at Siena between 1322 and 1326 and at Perugia between 1333 and 1343, where BALDUS DE UBALDIS was one of his pupils. His *Consilia et quaestiones* were much cited. A rigorist tract attacking the public debt of Florence was attributed to him in the fifteenth century, although it was in fact written by the Florentine Dominican Domenico Pantaleoni.

GERARD OF SIENA (GHERARDUS DE SENIS) d. 1336. A native of Siena, Augustinian friar and theologian. After studies in Italy, possibly at Bologna, he went to Paris, where he became a master of the Sentences in 1329. In addition to part of a commentary on the *Sentences* of Peter Lombard, his extant works include two treatises *de usuris* and *de praescriptionibus*. The former, an important formulation of the natural law argument against usury, was reported and analyzed by JOHANNES ANDREAE in his *quaestio* on the rule *Peccatum* in the LIBER SEXTUS.

GOTTOFREDO DA TRANI (GOFFREDUS TRANENSIS) d. 1245. A native of Apulia, he studied in Bologna, where he was a pupil of the civilian Azo and a contemporary of Sinibaldus Fliscus, later Innocent IV. He taught civil law at Naples and Bologna. In 1240 he became a judge of the Roman Rota, the papal court of appeal, and was made a cardinal in 1244. He wrote an apparatus of glosses on the LIBER EXTRA and a *summa* on the titles of the DECRETALES GREGORII IX, which influenced BERNARD OF PARMA in his composition of the *glossa ordinaria.*

GRATIAN (GRATIANUS) little is known with certainty about this canonist who was active in Bologna between 1135 and 1145. His systematic compilation of canonical material drawn from the church fathers, the canons of the church councils and papal sources, the *Concordia discordantium canonum*, commonly known as the DECRETUM, was completed around 1140. A version of the DECRETUM that included extensive additions and interpolations was received as the standard textbook of canon law in the schools. The gloss written by JOHANNES TEUTONICUS (fl. 1210-1245) and completed soon after 1215 became the *glossa ordinaria* to the DECRETUM. Johannes' gloss was revised in the light of the LIBER EXTRA and augmented by the Bolognese canonist BARTHOLOMEW OF BRESCIA (BARTHOLOMEUS BRIXIENSIS) (fl. 1234-1258). It was this composite text that was cited as the ordinary gloss by subsequent canonists.

GREGORY OF RIMINI (GREGORIUS DE ARIMINO) d. 1358. An Augustinian friar and theologian, he studied in Paris between 1323 and 1329 and later taught theology at Padua, Bologna and Perugia. From 1341, he lectured on the Sentences of Peter Lombard at Paris, becoming a doctor in 1345. He was elected Prior-General of his order in 1357. His extant works include a commentary on the Sentences in the nominalist tradition of Duns Scotus and a *tractatus* or *quaestio disputata* on the public debt of Venice written in the last year of his life.

GUIDO DE BAYSIO ("ARCHYDIACONUS") b. ca. 1246-1256. He was a native of Baiso, near Modena. After taking a doctorate in canon law at Reggio, he went to Bologna in 1286, where he set up as a private teacher of law. Among his pupils was JOHANNES ANDREAE. His nickname ("the Archdeacon") derives from his appointment to the archdeaconry of Bologna in 1296. He finally obtained a chair in canon law in 1301, but four years later joined the papal court in Avignon as a judge of the *Audientia litterarum contradictarum*. He died in 1313. His reputation among late medieval canonists rested on his commentary on the DECRETUM, entitled *Rosarium*. Completed in 1300, the *Rosarium* preserved glosses by the early thirteenth-century decretists HUGUCCIO, LAURENTIUS HISPANUS and VINCENTIUS HISPANUS that had been omitted from the ordinary gloss. He also wrote an influential commentary on the LIBER SEXTUS.

GUIDO DE BELLOREGUARDO d. 1377. Prior-General of the Augustinians from 1371 to 1377, he wrote a condemnation of the *monte comune* known through Ridolfi's report of it in the *Tractatus de usuris*.

GUILLELMUS DE MONTE LAUDUNO d. 1343. A native of the county of Quercy in France, he was a Cluniac monk and doctor of canon law of Paris. He taught at the University of Toulouse until 1314 and a few years later was appointed Abbot of Saint-Jean de Montierneuf in Poitiers. His works include commentaries on the LIBER SEXTUS, the CONSTITUTIONES CLEMENTINAE and an apparatus of glosses on the *Extravagantes* of John XXII.

GUILLELMUS REDONENSIS fl. 1240-1245. Nothing is known about him except that he was a Dominican and wrote the standard commentary on RAYMOND OF PENYAFORT's *Summa de poenitentia*. Guillelmus' gloss was often incorrectly attributed to John of Friburg.

HOSTIENSIS (HENRICUS DE SUGUSIO) b. ca. 1200. The most influential canonist of the thirteenth century, he studied canon law at Bologna in the

1220s and lectured on the LIBER EXTRA in Paris in 1239. Appointed to a succession of sees by his contemporary at Bologna INNOCENT IV, he was made cardinal bishop of Ostia (hence his nickname) by Urban IV in 1262. His most influential work was his *summa* on the decretals, completed around 1253. When he died in 1271 he had just finished a *lectura* (commentary) on the decretals.

HUGUCCIO fl. 1180-1210. A Bolognese canonist and one of the most influential commentators on the DECRETUM, Huguccio left his *summa* on Gratian unfinished on his appointment to the see of Ferrara in 1190. His glosses were known to late medieval canonists through the *glossa ordinaria* of JOHANNES TEUTONICUS and the works of GUIDO DE BAYSIO and JOHANNES ANDREAE.

INFORTIATUM. *See* DIGESTA.

INNOCENT IV (SINIBALDUS FLISCUS) ca. 1200-1254. A native of Genoa, he taught canon law at Bologna until he joined the papal curia as a consultor in 1226. He was made a cardinal in 1227 and elected pope in 1243. His pontificate was dominated by his conflict with Frederick II, whom he deposed at the first council of Lyons in 1245. Innocent's own legislative activity was embodied in three *collectiones novellarum* later inserted into the LIBER EXTRA. In his capacity as a private doctor, he was in the unique position of being able to comment (sometimes disparagingly) on his own decretals in his influential apparatus of glosses on the LIBER EXTRA.

INSTITUTIONES an introductory handbook of Roman law published by Justinian along with the DIGESTA. It was based on an earlier text of the same title by the jurist Gaius (fl. 161). The *glossa ordinaria* on the *Institutiones* was written by FRANCISCUS ACCURSIUS.

JESSELINUS DE CASSANIS (GENZELLINUS, ZENZELINUS) d. 1334/35. Probably a native of southern France, he is referred to in a document of 1317 as a professor of canon law at Montpellier. By the early 1320s, he was in Avignon in the service of Cardinal Arnaldus de Via. In 1326 he was appointed auditor of the Rota. His works include commentaries on the LIBER SEXTUS, the CONSTITUTIONES CLEMENTINAE and the *Extravagantes* of John XXII.

JOHANNES ANDREAE b. ca. 1270. A native of Rifredo, near Florence, he studied canon law at Bologna under GUIDO DE BAYSIO. A professor of canon law at Bologna from 1301 until his death in the first visitation of the plague in 1348, he was the most celebrated canonist of his day and was described by BALDUS as the "*iuris canonici fons et tuba*" (fount and trumpet of canon law). Among his pupils were JOHANNES CALDERINUS, whom he adopted as his heir, and PAULUS DE LIAZARIIS. A layman, he was active in civic affairs, serving the city as a diplomat and the university as a legislator. Revealed in his writings as a man of wide curiosity and humane culture, he was a friend of the humanist Petrarch and the lawyer-poet CINO OF PISTOIA. As a canonist, he was consulted by Clement V and his opinions were cited by John XXII. During his career, he wrote apparatuses of glosses on all the collections of decretal law, of which two, on the LIBER SEXTUS (1301) and the CONSTITUTIONES CLEMENTINAE (1322), became the *glossae ordinariae*. He produced apparatuses supplementary to the ordinary glosses on the LIBER EXTRA and LIBER SEXTUS called *Novella compilatio glossarum* or *Novella commentaria*, as well as a series of influential *additiones* (glosses) to the *Speculum iudiciale* of WILLIAM DURANT. He also wrote a multitude of treatises on various aspects of the law, a biography of Jerome and a number of *quaestiones disputatae*, some of which, based on the maxims of the title *de regulis iuris* of the LIBER SEXTUS, he published under the title *Quaestiones mercuriales* (Wednesday Questions), because they were debated on Wednesdays during the academic term.

JOHANNES CALDERINUS d. 1365. He obtained a doctorate in Bologna in 1326, where he taught until his death in the plague of 1365. Adoptive son of JOHANNES ANDREAE and father of Gaspar Calderinus, who was also a distinguished canonist, he was active in the politics and diplomacy of Bologna. Many treatises and *additiones* are attributed to him, but his most influential work was a collection of *distinctiones et repetitiones* on the LIBER EXTRA.

JOHANNES DE FANTUTIIS d. 1391. Little is known about him beyond the fact that he received a doctorate in 1370 and engaged in private tuition in Bologna from 1377. His most distinguished pupil was Lorenzo Ridolfi. He wrote *consilia* in collaboration with JOHANNES CALDERINUS and BALDUS DE UBALDIS among others, as well as commentaries on the DECRETUM and CONSTITUTIONES CLEMENTINAE.

JOHANNES FAVENTINUS d. ca. 1187. He taught the DECRETUM at Bologna and published an influential apparatus of glosses in 1171.

JOHANNES TEUTONICUS. *See* GRATIAN.

JOHN KLENKOCK (JOHANNES CLENKOH, KLENKLOK) fl. 1374. A German Augustinian friar and theologian, he wrote a critique of the *monte comune* that is preserved in the appendix to *Questio montis* of Ridolfi's *Tractatus de usuris*.

JOHN OF LEGNANO (JOHANNES DE LIGNANO) b. ca. 1320. Born into a noble Milanese family, he studied under PAULUS DE LIAZARIIS at Bologna, receiving doctorates in canon law in 1351 and civil law in 1352. He lectured on the LIBER EXTRA from 1381 until his death in 1383. He was a teacher of Lorenzo Ridolfi, who refers to him as *dominus meus* in his writings. Active in diplomacy and public affairs, he also wrote influential commentaries on the LIBER EXTRA and the CONSTITUTIONES CLEMENTINAE, *consilia* and treatises on topics in both laws, most notably on the law of war.

LAPO DA CASTIGLIONCHIO (LAPUS DE CASTIGLONCHIO) d. 1381. A Florentine statesman, he studied at Bologna under JOHN OF LEGNANO and JOHANNES CALDERINUS, taking his doctorate in 1353. He lectured on canon law at the University of Florence in 1357-58 and again from 1362 to 1369. A leading proponent of "narrow" oligarchic government, he ran afoul of the Ciompi regime and was exiled in 1378. He taught canon law for a year in Padua in 1379 and died in Rome in 1381. Among his extant works are collections of *allegationes*, *repetitiones* on the LIBER EXTRA and assorted tractates.

LAURENTIUS DE PINU d. ca. 1398. A Bolognese, he lectured at Bologna on the LIBER EXTRA from 1365 until his death. Lorenzo Ridolfi was among his pupils. He wrote a *lectura* on the DECRETUM, *consilia* and a *Tractatus de iuribus incorporalibus*.

LAURENTIUS HISPANUS. *See* DECRETALES GREGORII IX.

LIBER EXTRA. *See* DECRETALES GREGORII IX.

LIBER SEXTUS DECRETALIUM a compilation of decretals and conciliar canons issued subsequent to the promulgation of the DECRETALES GREGORII IX. Commissioned by Boniface VIII (1294-1303) as a supplement to the five books of the LIBER EXTRA–hence its name ("Sixth Book of Decretals"), although it retains the fivefold internal organization of the earlier collection –the *Liber sextus* was promulgated in 1298. It is particularly noteworthy for the inclusion of the decrees of I Lyons (1245) and II Lyons (1274) and for the title *de regulis iuris* at the end of the fifth book, which contains forty-eight rules or maxims of law. The *glossa ordinaria* to the *Liber sextus* was written by JOHANNES ANDREAE.

NICHOLAS DE ANGLIA probably to be identified with a Nicholas de Anglia who taught in the Dominican *studium* at Padua in 1402, he wrote a *quaestio disputata* on the public debt of Venice sometime in the last quarter of the fourteenth century. Ridolfi cites him as "a certain English Dominican master."

OLDRADUS DE PONTE (LAUDENSIS) d. after 1337. From Lodi, he studied civil law at Bologna under DINO OF MUGELLO and taught at Padua from 1307 to 1311. In 1311 he entered the service of cardinal Peter Colonna and went to Avignon where he functioned as an advocate and probably an assessor in the court of the Rota until his death. Although he wrote commentaries on the civil law (now lost), he is best known for the more than three hundred *consilia* he wrote and collected.

PAULUS DE LIAZARIIS d. 1356. A pupil of JOHANNES ANDREAE, he taught canon law in Bologna from 1321 and in Perugia from 1325 to 1333, after which he returned to Bologna. His most distinguished pupil was JOHN OF LEGNANO. His extant writings include a *lectura* and *apostillae* on the CONSTITUTIONES CLEMENTINAE, *repetitiones* on the titles of the LIBER EXTRA, *quaestiones*, *consilia* and a treatise on possession and ownership.

PETER OF ANCHARANO (PETRUS DE ANCHARANO) b. ca. 1333, he studied civil law under BALDUS DE UBALDIS at Perugia and canon law at Bologna under Bartholomeus de Saliceto. From 1384 until his death in Bologna in 1416, he was employed as a legal consultant and law professor in various cities including Venice (1384-87, 1390-92), Siena (1387-90), Ferrara (1402-05) and Bologna (1395-1402, 1405-16). His *Quaestio disputata de monte Venetorum uel Florentinorum* was delivered at Bologna in 1398. Other extant works include commentaries on the LIBER EXTRA, *lecturae* on the LIBER SEXTUS and the CONSTITUTIONES CLEMENTINAE, *repetitiones* on the LIBER EXTRA and a collection of *consilia*.

RAYMOND OF PENYAFORT (RAYMUNDUS DE PENNAFORTE) ca. 1180-1275. A Catalan, he studied canon law at Bologna from 1210 to 1221 and lectured during the last three years on the DECRETUM and the fourth *compilatio antiqua*. In 1222, he entered the Dominican order in Barcelona and served as Master-General of the order from 1238 to 1240. In 1230, he was appointed by Gregory IX to supervise the compilation of the LIBER EXTRA. A prolific writer, Raymond wrote an important *Summa de poenitentia* (ca. 1222-34) and *Summa de matrimonio* (ca. 1235).

STEPHANUS (HUGONETTI) PROVINCIALIS b. ca. 1280. A native of Narbonne, he was an auditor of the Rota by 1319. Papal governor of Lombardy from 1320 to 1330, he was made bishop of Bologna in 1330, dying there two years later. He was author of an apparatus of glosses on the CONSTITUTIONES CLEMENTINAE.

TANCRED. *See* DECRETALES GREGORII IX.

THOMAS AQUINAS ca. 1225-74. He was educated at Monte Cassino and the university of Naples between 1231 and 1244. In the latter year he joined the Dominican order and went to Paris where he studied theology from 1245 to 1248. Admitted master of theology of Paris in 1256, he taught there until 1259, after which he taught in Italy. He returned to Paris in

1269. A prolific author, he was best known for his *Summa theologiae*, a synthesis of dogmatic and moral theology, and for his commentaries on the works of Aristotle.

VINCENTIUS HISPANUS. *See* DECRETALES GREGORII IX.

WILLIAM DURANT (GUILLELMUS DURANTIS, "SPECULATOR") b. ca. 1236 at Beziers in Provence, he was a pupil of BERNARD OF PARMA and a protegé of HOSTIENSIS. He lectured at Modena, but spent most of his career in papal administration. He was appointed Auditor-General of the Roman Rota in 1267 and bishop of Mende in Provence in 1286. A papal governor in Italy and France between 1278 and 1282, he died governor of the Romagna in 1296. His most influential work was the *Speculum iudiciale* (hence his nickname "Speculator"), a treatise on judicial procedure that drew on his experience in the Rota. It was first published in 1276 and revised between 1287 and 1291.

ZENZELINUS. *See* JESSELINUS DE CASSANIS.

PRINCIPAL SOURCES

A. Berger, *Encyclopedic Dictionary of Roman Law.*

James A. Brundage, *Medieval Canon Law.*

J. A. Clarence Smith, *Medieval Law Teachers and Writers, Civilian and Canonist.*

F. L. Cross, ed., *The Oxford Dictionary of the Christian Church.* 2nd ed.

J. Kirshner, "Francesco da Empoli." In *Dizionario biografico degli Italiani,* 49.

——, "The Moral Theology of Public Finance."

——, "Reading Bernardino's Sermon."

O. Langholm, *Economics in the Medieval Schools.*

L. Martines, *Lawyers and Statecraft in Renaissance Florence.*

J. P. McCall, "The Writings of John of Legnano with a List of Manuscripts," *Traditio* 23 (1967): 415-37.

W. P. Müller, "The Recovery of Justinian's Digest."

R. Naz, ed. *Dictionnaire de droit canonique.*

K. Park, "Readers at the Florentine Studio."

K. Pennington, Bio-bibliography of Medieval Canonists (unpublished).

——, "Henricus de Segusio (Hostiensis)" in *Popes, Canonists and Texts, 1150-1550.*

J. F. von Schulte, *Die Geschichte der Quellen und Literatur des Canonischen Rechts.*

Bibliography

A. Manuscripts Cited

Augsburg, Staats- und Stadtbibliothek, 2° Cod. Aug. 388, fols. 6r-87r (Lorenzo Ridolfi, *Tractatus de usuris*)

Florence, Archivio di Stato, Arte dei giudici e notai o proconsolo 670
—, Carte Strozziane, Terza serie, 41/1-20
—, Catasto 66
—, Catasto 395
—, Catasto 437
—, Catasto 438
—, Catasto 489
—, Mercanzia 19
—, Monte comune o delle Graticole 3137
—, Notarile antecosimiano 9040
—, Notarile antecosimiano 9042
—, Provvisioni, Registri 103

Florence, Biblioteca Nazionale Centrale, Conventi soppressi 1721, fols. 1ra-102vb (Lorenzo Ridolfi, *Tractatus de usuris*)
—, Fondo principale II, III, 366 [formerly Magliabechiano xxix, 184] (Lorenzo Ridolfi, *Tractatus de usuris*)
—, Fondo principale II, III, 370 [formerly Magliabechiano xxix, 185] (Lorenzo Ridolfi, *Tertius liber consiliorum*)
—, Magliabechiano vi, 134 (*Orationes*)
—, Magliabechiano xxix, 171 (Lorenzo Ridolfi, *Repertorium iuris*)
—, Magliabechiano xxix, 172 (*Consilia, legalia*)
—, Magliabechiano xxix, 179, fols. 278v-288r (Peter of Ancharano, *Quaestio disputata de Monte Venetorum vel Florentinorum*)
—, Panciatichi 147 (Lorenzo Ridolfi, *Zibaldone*)

Florence, Biblioteca Medicea-Laurenziana, Conventi Soppressi 264, fols. 56r-118v (Lorenzo Ridolfi, *Tractatus de usuris*)
—, Edili 54 (John of Legnano, *Commentaria in librum IV et V Decretalium*)

Florence, Biblioteca Riccardiana, 1667 (*Vita, miracoli e transito di S. Girolamo*)

Klosterneuburg, Stiftsbibliothek, 655 (Johannes Faventinus, *Summa decretorum*)

Lons-le-Saunier, Archives départementales du Jura, 16, fols. 2ra-313ra, 325rb-483vb (Huguccio, *Summa decretorum*)
Lucca, Biblioteca Capitolare Feliniana, 311, fols. 193ra-249vb (Lorenzo Ridolfi, *Tractatus de usuris*)

Messina, Università di Messina, Biblioteca della facoltà di giurisprudenza, A.1 (Lorenzo Ridolfi, *Consilia, 1388-98*)
Munich, Bayerische Staatsbibliothek, Clm 7580, fols. 216r-293r (Lorenzo Ridolfi, *Tractatus de usuris*)
—, Clm 8786 (John of Legnano, *Commentaria in libros I-II Decretalium*)
—, Clm 8787 (John of Legnano, *Commentaria in libros III-V Decretalium*)
—, Clm 26669, fols. 1r-84v (Lorenzo Ridolfi, *Tractatus de usuris*)

Paris, Bibliothèque nationale, lat. 3968, fols. 9v-33v (Vincentius Hispanus, *Apparatus glossarum ad Decretales Gregorii IX*)
—, lat. 15402 (Gottofredo da Trani, *Apparatus glossarum in Decretales Gregorii IX*)
—, nouv. acq. lat. 1802, fols. 1ra-88rb (Lorenzo Ridolfi, *Tractatus de usuris*)

Rome, Biblioteca Angelica, 625, fols. 209r-225r (Gerard of Siena, *Tractatus de usuris et de prescriptionibus*)

Vatican City, Biblioteca Apostolica Vaticana, Borghese 261, fols. 19r-44v (Damasus, *Quaestiones*)
—, Ottob. lat. 3335, fols. i-iv, 1r-120v (Lorenzo Ridolfi, *Tractatus de usuris*)
—, Pal. lat. 658 (Laurentius Hispanus, *Apparatus in Decretum*)
—, Pal. lat. 788, fols. 61r-115r (Lorenzo Ridolfi, *Tractatus de usuris*)
—, Ross. 685, fols. 272r-315v. s. xv (Lorenzo Ridolfi, *Tractatus de usuris*)
—, Ross. 1038, fols. 308r-368r. s. xv (Lorenzo Ridolfi, *Tractatus de usuris*)
—, Vat. lat. 1452, fols. 163ra-247vb (Paulus de Liazariis, *Lectura in Constitutiones Clementinas*)
—, Vat. lat. 2652 (Johannes Calderinus et Gaspar Calderinus, *Repetitiones et distinctiones in Decretales*)
Vienna, Österreichische Nationalbibliothek, 4139, fols. 71r-172r (Lorenzo Ridolfi, *Tractatus de usuris*)

B. Printed Primary Sources

Alexander Lombard. *Tractatus de usuris*. Edited by A.-M. Hamelin in *Un traité de morale économique au XIVe siècle: le 'Tractatus de usuris' de maître Alexandre d'Alexandrie*. Analecta mediaevalia Namurcensia, no. 14. Louvain, Montreal and Lille: Nauwelaerts, Librairie Franciscaine and Librairie Giard, 1962.

Ambrose. *De Tobia*. Edited by Carolus Schenkl. Corpus Scriptorum Ecclesiasticorum Latinorum, vol. 32. Vienna, Prague and Leipzig: F. Tempsky and G. Freytag, 1887.

Aristotle. *The Basic Works of Aristotle*. Edited by Richard McKeon. New York: Random House, 1941.

—. *Ethica Nicomachea*. Translatio Roberti Grosseteste, recensio recognita. Edited by Renatus Antonius Gauthier. *Aristoteles Latinus*, vol. XXVI.1-3, fasc. 4. Leiden and Brussels: E. J. Brill and Desclée de Brouwer, 1973.

Augustine. *De ciuitate Dei*. Edited by Bernardus Dombart. 4th ed. rev. Alphonsus Kalb. 2 vols. Leipzig: Teubner, 1928-29. Reprint Corpus Christianorum, Series Latina, nos. 47-48. Turnhout: Brepols, 1955.

—. *The City of God Against the Pagans*. Translated by George E. McCracken, William M. Green, D. Wiesen, Philip Levine, E. M. Sanford and William C. Greene. 7 vols. Loeb Classical Library. Cambridge, MA: Harvard University Press, 1957-72.

—. *Confessions*. Translated by William Watts. 2 vols. Loeb Classical Library. Cambridge, MA: Harvard University Press, 1977.

—. *Confessionum libri XIII*. Edited by Martinus Skutella. Rev. Lucas Verheijen. Corpus Christianorum, Series Latina, no. 27. Turnhout: Brepols, 1981.

—. *Epistulae*. Edited by Albertus Goldbacher. Corpus Scriptorum Ecclesiasticorum Latinorum, vol. 57. Vienna and Leipzig: F. Tempsky and G. Freytag, 1911.

Bartolus of Sassoferrato. *Bartoli a Saxoferrato ... omnia quae extant opera*. 11 vols. Venice: Iuntae, 1602-1603.

Bernard of Clairvaux. *Sancti Bernardi Opera*. Edited by J. Leclercq, H. M. Rochais et al. 8 vols. Rome: Editiones Cistercienses, 1957-77.

—. *Sancti Bernardi ... Opera Omnia*. Edited by Jean Mabillon and J.-P. Migne. Patrologiae Cursus, Series Latina, vols. 182-85. Paris: J.-P. Migne, 1854-55.

Bernardino of Siena. *Opera Omnia*. Vol. 4, *Quadragesimale de evangelio aeterno, sermones XXVII-LIII*. Quaracchi-Florence: Typographia Collegii S. Bonaventurae, 1956.

Bible. *Biblia sacra iuxta vulgatam versionem*. Edited by Roger Gryson et al. 4th rev. ed. Stuttgart: Deutsche Bibelgesellschaft, 1994.

—. *The Holy Bible*. Revised Standard Version. London: Oxford University Press, 1962.

Bonaventure. *Opera omnia*. Edited by A.-C. Peltier. 15 vols. Paris: Ludovicus Vives, 1864-71.

Boniface VIII. *Sextus Decretalium liber ... Ioannis Andreae ... aliorumque ... virorum commentariis explicatior redditus*. Lyons: Hugo à Porta, 1559.

Boyer, John W. and Julius Kirshner, ed. *University of Chicago Readings in Western Civilization*. Vol. 4, *Medieval Europe*, edited and translated by Julius Kirshner and Karl F. Morrison. Chicago and London: University of Chicago Press, 1986.

Brucker, Gene A., ed. *Firenze nel Rinascimento*. Florence: La Nuova Italia, 1969.

—, ed. and trans. *The Society of Renaissance Florence: A Documentary Study*. New York: Harper and Row, 1971.

Cicero, Marcus Tullius. *De natura deorum*. Edited by Arthur Stanley Pease. 2 vols. Cambridge, MA: Harvard University Press, 1955-58.

—. *Orationes. Pro Milone, Pro Marcello, Pro Ligario, Pro Rege Deiotaro, Philippicae XIV*. Edited by Albert Curtis Clark. 2nd ed. Oxford: Clarendon Press, 1918.

Cino of Pistoia. *In Codicem et aliquot titulos ... Digesti ueteris commentaria*. 2 vols. Frankfurt: Sigismundus Feyerabendt, 1578. Reprint Turin: Bottega d'Erasmo, 1964.

Clement V. *Clementis Quinti Constitutiones ... glossis ... Ioannis Imolae ... aliorumque doctorum commentariis elucidiores redditae*. Lyons: Hugo à Porta, 1559.

Conti, Elio, Maria Cristina Frassineti, Daniela de Rosa, Magda Cavaciocchi and Renzo Ninci, ed. *Le "Consulte" e "Pratiche" della Repubblica fiorentina nel Quattrocento*. Vol. 1, *1401: Cancellierato di Coluccio Salutati*. Università degli studi di Firenze, Fonti di storia medievale e umanistica. Florence: Università di Firenze, 1981.

Corpus iuris canonici. Edited by Aemilius Friedberg. 2 vols. Leipzig: B. Tauchnitz, 1879. Reprint Graz: Akademische Druck- u. Verlagsanstalt, 1959.

De Angelis, Laura, Renzo Ninci and Paolo Pirillo, ed. *Le Consulte e Pratiche della Repubblica fiorentina (1405-1406)*. Istituto storico italiano per il Medio Evo, Fonti per la storia dell'Italia Medievale, Antiquitates, no. 5. Rome: Istituto storico italiano per il Medio Evo, 1996.

Dino of Mugello. *Commentaria in regulas iuris*. Venice: [n.p.] 1570.

Diplovatatius, Thomas. *Liber de claris iuris consultis, pars posterior*. Edited by Fritz Schultz, Hermann Kantorowicz and Giuseppe Rabotti. *Studia Gratiana* 10 (1968).

Durant, Willam. *Speculum iuris ... cum Johannis Andreae, Baldi de Ubaldis ... theorematibus*. 2 vols. Venice: [n.p.] 1576.

Gherardi, Alessandro, ed. *Statuti della Università e Studio fiorentino dell'anno MCCCLXXXVII seguiti da un'appendice di documenti dal MCCCXX al*

MCCCCLXXII. Documenti di storia italiana pubblicati a cura delle R. Deputazioni sugli studi di storia patria di Toscana, dell'Umbria e delle Marche, vol. 7. Florence: M. Cellini, 1881. Reprint Bologna: Forni, 1973.

Giacomo da Milano. *Stimulus amoris fr. Iacobi Mediolanensis*. Quaracchi-Florence: Typographia Collegii S. Bonaventurae, 1905.

Gottofredo da Trani. *Summa super titulis Decretalium*. Lyons, 1519. Reprint Darmstadt: Scientia Verlag Aalen, 1968.

Gratian. *Decretum Gratiani [cum glossis]*. Paris: Gulielmus Merlin, Gulielmus Desboys and Sebastianus Niuellius, 1561.

Gregory IX. *Decretales Domini Gregorii Papae IX ... una cum glossis*. Lyons: [n.p.] 1584.

—. [*Decretalium libri V cum glossis*.] Lyons: Johann Siber, 1496-1509.

Gregory of Rimini. *Tractatus de imprestantiis Venetorum et de usura*. Reggio Emilia: Ludovicus de Mazalis, 1508.

Guido de Baysio. *Lectura ... super Decreto, quam ipse Rosarium appellauit*. Lyons: Johannes de Jonuelle, 1516.

—. *In sextum Decretalium commentaria*. Venice: Iuntae, 1606.

Hostiensis (Henricus de Segusio). *In Decretalium libros commentaria*. 5 vols. Venice: Iuntae, 1581. Reprint 2 vols., Turin: Bottega d'Erasmo, 1965.

—. *Summa Aurea*. Venice: Iacobus Vitalis, 1574. Reprint Turin: Bottega d'Erasmo, 1963.

Innocent IV (Sinibaldus Fliscus). *Commentaria ... super libros quinque Decretalium*. Frankfurt: Hieronymus Feyerabendt, 1570. Reprint Frankfurt: Minerva, 1968.

Jerome. *Commentarius in epistolam ad Galathos*. Patrologiae Cursus, Series Latina, vol. 26. Paris: J.-P. Migne, 1884.

—. *Epistolae*. Patrologiae Cursus, Series Latina, vol. 22. Paris: J.-P. Migne, 1854.

Johannes Andreae. *In quinque Decretalium libros novella commentaria*. 6 vols. Venice: Franciscus Franciscius, 1581. Reprint 4 vols., Turin: Bottega d'Erasmo, 1963.

—. *In sextum Decretalium commentaria et in titulum de regulis iuris novella commentaria*. 2 vols. Venice: Franciscus Franciscius, 1581. Reprint 1 vol., Turin: Bottega d'Erasmo, 1963.

Justinian. *Codicis Sacratissimi Imperatoris Iustiniani Perpetui Augusti libri duodecim Accursii commentariis*. Geneva: Theodorus de Iuges, 1625.

—. *Corpus iuris civilis*. Edited by Theodor Mommsen, Paul Krueger, Rudolf Schoell and Wilhelm Kroll. 3 vols. Berlin: Weidmann, 1892-95. Reprint 1954.

—. *The Digest of Justinian*. Edited and translated by Alan Watson et al. 4 vols. Philadelphia: University of Pennsylvania Press, 1985.

—. [*Digesta I*] *Digestum vetus D. Iustiniani sacratissimi principis [cum glossis]*. Lyons: Hugo à Porta, 1549.
—. [*Digesta II*] *Infortiatum: pandectarum iuris civilis tomus secundus [cum glossis]*. Lyons: Hugo à Porta, 1550.
—. [*Digesta III*] *Digestum novum: pandectarum iuris civilis tomus tertius [cum glossis]*. Lyons: Hugo à Porta, 1550.
—. *Imperatoris Iustiniani Institutionum libri quattuor*. Edited with commentary by J. B. Moyle. 5th ed. Oxford: Clarendon Press, 1912.
—. *Volumen de Tortis. [Novellae, Codex X-XII, Glossa Accursii]*. Venice: Battista Torti, 1492.

Kirshner, Julius, ed. "A Document of the Meeting of the Chapter General in Florence (1365)." *Archivum Franciscanum Historicum* 62 (1969): 392-99.
Kohl, Benjamin G. and Ronald G. Witt, ed. and trans. *The Earthly Republic: Italian Humanists on Government and Society*. Philadelphia: University of Pennsylvania Press, 1978.

Lapo da Castiglionchio. *Allegationes*. Venice: Johannes Variscus, 1571.
Livy. *Ab Vrbe Condita*. Edited by C. F. Walters, R. S. Conway, S. K. Johnson and A. H. McDonald. 5 vols. Oxford: Clarendon Press, 1914-65.
—. *History of Rome*. Translated by W. M. Roberts. 4 vols. London: J. M. Dent and Sons, 1912.
Lopez, Robert S. and Irving W. Raymond, ed. and trans. *Medieval Trade in the Mediterranean World*. New York and London: Columbia University Press, 1955.

Ninci, Renzo, ed. *Le Consulte e Pratiche della Repubblica fiorentina (1404)*. Istituto storico italiano per il Medio Evo, Fonti per la storia d'Italia, no. 115. Rome: Istituto storico italiano per il Medio Evo, 1991.

Oldradus de Ponte. *Consilia seu responsa*. Frankfurt: Sigismundus Feyerabent, 1576.
—. [*Consilia et quaestiones*.] Rome: Adam Rot, 1472.
Olivi, Peter John. *Tractatus de emptionibus et venditionibus, de usuris, de restitutionibus*. Edited by Giacomo Todeschini in *Un trattato di economia politica francescana: il "De emptionibus et venditionibus, de usuris, de restitutionibus" di Pietro di Giovanni Olivi*. Istituto storico italiano per il Medio Evo, Studi storici, fasc. 125-26, pp. 51-108. Rome: Istituto storico italiano per il Medio Evo, 1980.
Ovid. *Heroides*. Edited by Henricus Dörrie. Berlin: 1971.

Palmieri, Matteo. *Ricordi fiscali (1427-74)*. Edited by Elio Conti. Istituto storico italiano per il Medio Evo, Studi storici, fasc. 132-35. Rome: Istituto storico italiano per il Medio Evo, 1983.

Petrarch, Francesco. *Rerum Senilium liber XIIII. Ad magnificum Franciscum de Carraria Padue dominum. Epistola I. Qualis esse debeat qui rem publicam regit*. Edited by Vincenzo Ussani. Padua: Collegium Typographorum Patavinum, 1922.

Petruccius, Fredericus. *Consilia et Questiones*. Venice: Paganinus de Paganinis, 1508.

Pryor, John, ed. *Business Contracts of Medieval Provence: Selected "Notulae" from the Cartulary of Giraud Amalric of Marseilles, 1248*. Studies and Texts 54. Toronto: Pontifical Institute of Mediaeval Studies, 1981.

Raymond of Penyafort. *Summa Sancti Raymundi de Peniafort ... de Poenitentia et Matrimonio cum glossis Ioannis de Friburgo*. Rome: Ioannes Tallinus, 1603. Reprint Farnborough, 1967.

Ridolfi, Lorenzo. *Tractatus de usuris*. In *Tractatus universi iuris, duce et auspice Gregorio XIII ... in unum congesti*, vol. 7, fols. 15ra-50rb. Venice: [Franciscus Zilettus], 1584.

Spagnesi, Enrico. *Utiliter edoceri: Atti inediti degli Ufficiali dello Studio fiorentino (1391-96)*. Università di Firenze, Pubblicazioni della facoltà di giurisprudenza, no. 34. Milan: Giuffrè, 1979.

Stefani, Marchionne di Coppo. *Cronica fiorentina*. Edited by Niccolò Rodolico. Rerum italicarum scriptores, vol. 30, part 1. Città di Castello: Lapi, 1903-13.

Tartagnis, Alexander de. *Consilia*. 4 vols. Venice: Bernardinus de Benalis, 1499.

Thomas Aquinas. *Opera omnia*. Vol. 9: *Secunda secundae Summae Theologiae*. Rome: S. C. Propaganda Fide, 1897.

Ubaldis, Baldus de. *Baldi Ubaldi Perusini ... in [Corpus iuris civilis] commentaria*. 10 vols. Venice: Haeredes Georgii Varisci, 1615-16.

Valerius Maximus. *Factorum et dictorum memorabilium libri novem*. Edited by Carolus Kempf. Stuttgart: B. G. Teubner, 1966.

Vespasiano da Bisticci. *Le vite*. Edited by Aulo Greco. 2 vols. Florence: Istituto Nazionale di Studi sul Rinascimento, 1970-76.

—. *Renaissance Princes, Popes, and Prelates: The Vespasiano Memoirs: Lives of Illustrious Men of the XVth Century*. Translated by William George and Emily Waters. New York: Harper and Row, 1900.

Villani, Giovanni. *Nuova Cronica*. Edited by Giuseppe Porta. 3 vols. Parma: Ugo Guanda, 1990.

Villani, Matteo and Filippo Villani. *Cronica*. Edited by Ignazio Moutier. 6 vols. Florence: Magheri, 1825-26.

Vincke, Johannes. *Beiträge zur Kirchen- und Rechtsgeschichte*. Vol. 3,

Schriftstücke zum Pisaner Konzil: Ein Kampf um die öffentliche Meinung. Bonn: Peter Hanstein, 1942.

C. Secondary Sources

Abbondanza, Roberto. "Gli atti degli Ufficiali dello Studio fiorentino dal maggio al settembre 1388." *Archivio storico italiano* 117 (1959): 80-110.

Antonelli, Giovanni. "La magistratura degli Otto di Guardia a Firenze." *Archivio storico italiano* 92 (1954): 3-39.

Armstrong, Lawrin. "The Politics of Usury in *Trecento* Florence: The *Questio de monte* of Francesco da Empoli." *Mediaeval Studies* 61 (1999): 1-44.

—. "The *Tractatus de materia montis* of Lorenzo Ridolfi." In *Proceedings of the Twelfth International Economic History Congress, Madrid, 1998, Session D: Recent Doctoral Research in Economic History*, ed. Clara-Eugenia Núñez, 15-23. Madrid: Universidad Nacional de Educación a Distancia and Fundación Fomento de la Historia Económica, 1998.

—. "The *Tractatus de materia montis* of Lorenzo Ridolfi: Edited from Florence, Biblioteca Nazionale Centrale, Fondo Principale II, III, 366." PhD thesis, University of Toronto, 1996.

Ascheri, Mario. "Analecta manoscritta consiliare (1285-1354)." *Bulletin of Medieval Canon Law* 15 (1985): 61-94.

—. "*Consilium sapientis*, perizia medica e *res iudicata*: Diritto dei 'dottori' e istituzioni communali." In *Proceedings of the Fifth International Congress of Medieval Canon Law, Salamanca, 21-25 September 1976*, Monumenta iuris canonici, series C: Subsidia, vol. 6, ed. Stephan Kuttner and Kenneth Pennington, 533-79. Vatican City: Biblioteca Apostolica Vaticana, 1980.

—. "Rechtsprechungs-Konsiliensammlungen-Italien." In *Handbuch der Quellen und Literatur der neueren europäischen Privatrechtsgeschichte*, vol. 2, *Neuere Zeit (1500-1800): Das Zeitalter des gemeinen Rechts*, part 2, *Gesetzgebung und Rechtssprechung*, ed. Helmut Coing, 1113-1222. Munich: C. H. Beck'sche, 1976.

Astorri, Antonella. *La Mercanzia a Firenze nella prima metà del Trecento: Il potere dei grandi mercanti*. Biblioteca storica toscana, no. 34. Florence: Leo S. Olschki, 1998.

Baldwin, John W. "The Medieval Merchant before the Bar of Canon Law." *Papers of the Michigan Academy of Science, Arts and Letters* 44 (1959): 287-99.

—. *The Medieval Theories of the Just Price: Romanists, Canonists, and Theologians in the Twelfth and Thirteenth Centuries*. Transactions of the American Philosophical Society, n.s. 49, part 4. Philadelphia: American Philosophical Society, 1959.

Barbadoro, Bernardino. *Le finanze della Repubblica fiorentina: Imposta diretta e debito pubblico fino all'istituzione del Monte*. Biblioteca storica toscana, no. 5. Florence: Leo S. Olschki, 1929.

Barducci, Roberto. "... *Cum parva difficultate civium predictorum* ...: Spunti introduttivi per un regesto della legislazione finanziaria fiorentina del Trecento." In *Renaissance Studies in Honor of Craig Hugh Smyth*, ed. Andrew Morrogh, Fiorella Superbi Gioffredi, Piero Morselli and Eve Borsook. 2 vols., 1: 3-15. Florence: Giunta Barbèra, 1985.

—. "Politica e speculazione finanziaria a Firenze dopo la crisi del primo Trecento (1343-1358)." *Archivio storico italiano* 137 (1979): 177-219.

—. "Le riforme finanziarie nel Tumulto dei Ciompi." In *Il Tumulto dei Ciompi: Un momento di storia fiorentina ed europea*, 95-102. Florence: Leo S. Olschki, 1981.

Baron, Hans. *The Crisis of the Early Italian Renaissance: Civic Humanism and Republican Liberty in an Age of Classicism and Tyranny*. 2 vols. Princeton: Princeton University Press, 1955. Rev. ed. in 1 vol. Princeton: Princeton University Press, 1966.

—. *From Petrarch to Leonardo Bruni: Studies in Humanistic and Political Literature*. Chicago and London: University of Chicago Press, 1968.

—. *Humanistic and Political Literature in Florence and Venice at the Beginning of the the Quattrocento: Studies in Criticism and Chronology*. Cambridge, MA: Harvard University Press, 1955.

—. *In Search of Florentine Civic Humanism: Essays on the Transition from Medieval to Modern Thought*. 2 vols. Princeton: Princeton University Press, 1988.

—. "Leonardo Bruni: 'Professional Rhetorician' or 'Civic Humanist'?" *Past and Present* 36 (1967): 21-37.

Baumgärtner, Ingrid, ed. *Consilia im späten Mittelalter: Zum historischen Aussagewert einer Quellengattung*. Sigmaringen: Jan Thorbecke, 1995.

—. "Stadtgeschichte und Consilia im italienischen Spätmittelalter: eine Quellengattung und ihre Möglichkeiten." *Zeitschrift für historische Forschung* 17 (1990): 129-54.

Bayley, Charles Calvert. *War and Society in Renaissance Florence: The 'De militia' of Leonardo Bruni*. Toronto: University of Toronto Press, 1961.

Becker, Marvin B. "Church and State in Florence on the Eve of the Renaissance (1343-1382)." *Speculum* 37 (1962): 509-27.

—. "Economic Change and the Emerging Florentine Territorial State." *Studies in the Renaissance* 13 (1966): 7-39.

—. "An Essay on the *Novi Cives* and Florentine Politics, 1343-1382." *Mediaeval Studies* 24 (1962): 35-82.

—. *Florence in Transition*. 2 vols. Baltimore: Johns Hopkins Press, 1967-68.

—. "The Florentine Territorial State and Civic Humanism in the Early Renaissance." In *Florentine Studies: Politics and Society in Renaissance Florence*, ed. Nicolai Rubinstein, 109-39. London: Faber and Faber, 1968.

—. "Some Economic Implications of the Conflict Between Church and State in Trecento Florence." *Mediaeval Studies* 21 (1959): 1-16.

—. "A Study in Political Failure: The Florentine Magnates, 1280-1343." *Mediaeval Studies* 27 (1965): 246-308.

—. "Three Cases Concerning the Restitution of Usury in Mediaeval Florence." *Journal of Economic History* 17 (1957): 445-50.

— and Gene A. Brucker. "The *Arti Minori* in Florentine Politics, 1342-1378." *Mediaeval Studies* 18 (1956): 93-104.

Bellomo, Manlio. *The Common Legal Past of Europe, 1000-1800*. Translated by Lydia G. Cochrane. Studies in Medieval and Early Modern Canon Law, no. 4. Washington, DC: Catholic University of America, 1995.

Berger, Adolf. *Encyclopedic Dictionary of Roman Law*. Transactions of the American Philosophical Society, n.s., no. 43, part 2. Philadelphia: American Philosophical Society, 1953.

Bernocchi, Mario. *Le monete della Repubblica fiorentina*. 5 vols. Florence: Leo S. Olschki, 1974-85.

Black, Antony. "The Individual and Society." In The *Cambridge History of Medieval Political Thought, c. 350-c. 1450*, ed. James H. Burns, 588-606. Cambridge: Cambridge University Press, 1988.

Blomeyer, Arwed. "Aus der Consilienpraxis zum kanonischen Zinsverbot." *Zeitschrift der Savigny-Stiftung für Rechtsgeschichte, kanonistische Abteilung* 66 (1980): 317-35.

Bocock, Robert. *Hegemony*. London and New York: Tavistock Publications, 1986.

Brown, Alison. "De-masking Renaissance republicanism." In *Renaissance Civic Humanism: Reappraisals and Reflections*, ed. James Hankins, 179-99. Cambridge: Cambridge University Press, 2000.

—. "Florence, Renaissance and Early Modern State: Reappraisals." *Journal of Modern History* 56 (1984): 285-300. Repr. in idem, *The Medici in Florence*, 307-26.

—. "The Guelf Party in 15th Century Florence: The Transition from Communal to Medicean State." *Rinascimento* 20 (1980): 41-86. Repr. in idem, *The Medici in Florence*, 103-50.

—. *The Medici in Florence: The exercise and language of power*. Italian Medieval and Renaissance Studies, University of Western Australia, no. 3. Florence and Perth, Australia: Leo S. Olschki and University of Western Australia Press, 1992.

Brucker, Gene A. "The Ciompi Revolution." In *Florentine Studies: Politics and Society in Renaissance Florence*, ed. Nicolai Rubinstein, 314-56. London: Faber and Faber, 1968. Repr. in idem, *Renaissance Florence: Society, Culture, and Religion*, 37-79.

—. *The Civic World of Early Renaissance Florence*. Princeton: Princeton University Press, 1977.

—. "Un documento fiorentino sulla guerra, sulla finanza e sulla amministrazione pubblica (1375)." *Archivio storico italiano* 115 (1957): 165-76.

—. "Florence and its University, 1348-1434." In *Action and Conviction in Early Modern Europe: Essays in Memory of E. H. Harbison*, ed. Theodore K. Rabb and Jerrold E. Seigel, 220-36. Princeton: Princeton University Press, 1969. Repr. in idem, *Renaissance Florence: Society, Culture, and Religion*, 109-205.

—. *Florentine Politics and Society, 1343-1378*. Princeton: Princeton University Press, 1962.

—. "The Florentine *Popolo minuto* and its Political Role, 1340-1450." In *Violence and Civil Disorder in Italian Cities, 1200-1500*. UCLA Centre for Medieval and Renaissance Studies Contributions, no. 5, ed. Lauro Martines, 155-83. Berkeley, Los Angeles and London: University of California Press, 1972. Repr. in idem, *Renaissance Florence: Society, Culture, and Religion*, 81-109.

—. "The Ghibelline Trial of Matteo Villani (1362)." *Medievalia et Humanistica* 13 (1960): 48-55. Repr. in idem, *Renaissance Florence: Society, Culture, and Religion*, 29-36.

—. "Humanism, Politics and the Social Order in Early Renaissance Florence." In *Florence and Venice: Comparisons and Relations*, vol. 1, *Quattrocento*, ed. Christine Smith and Salvatore Camporeale, 3-11. Florence: La Nuova Italia, 1979. Repr. in idem, *Renaissance Florence: Society, Culture, and Religion*, 237-45.

—. "The Medici in the Fourteenth Century." *Speculum* 32 (1957): 1-26. Repr. in idem, *Renaissance Florence: Society, Culture, and Religion*, 3-28.

—. *Renaissance Florence*. Berkeley, Los Angeles and London: University of California Press, 1969.

—. *Renaissance Florence: Society, Culture, and Religion*. Goldbach: Keip, 1994.

Brundage, James A. *Medieval Canon Law*. London and New York: Longman, 1995.

Buckland, W. W. *A Text-Book of Roman Law from Augustus to Justinian*. 3rd ed. Revised by Peter Stein. Cambridge: Cambridge University Press, 1963.

Caferro, William. *Mercenary Companies and the Decline of Siena*. Baltimore and London: Johns Hopkins University Press, 1998.

Carocci, Guido. *La Famiglia dei Ridolfi di Piazza: Notizie storiche e genealogiche*. Florence: Giuseppe Civelli, 1889.

Le carte Strozziane del r. Archivio di Stato in Firenze, Inventario. 3 vols. Florence: Ministero dell'Interno, 1884-91.

Cavallar, Osvaldo. *Francesco Guicciardini giurista: I ricordi degli onorari*. Università di Firenze, Centro di studi per la storia del pensiero giuridico moderno, Biblioteca per la storia del pensiero giuridico moderno, no. 36. Milan: Giuffrè, 1991.

Cipolla, Carlo M. *The Monetary Policy of Fourteenth-Century Florence*. Berkeley, Los Angeles and London: University of California Press, 1982.

Clavero, Bartolomé. *Antidora: Antropología católica de la economía moderna*. Università di Firenze, Centro di studi per la storia del pensiero giuridico moderno, Biblioteca per la storia del pensiero giuridico moderno, no. 39. Milan: Giuffrè, 1991.

Cohn, Samuel Kline, Jr. *Creating the Florentine State: Peasants and Rebellion, 1348-1434*. Cambridge: Cambridge University Press, 1999.

—. *The Laboring Classes in Renaissance Florence*. New York, London and Toronto: Academic Press, 1980.

Coing, Helmut. "Die juristische Facultät und ihr Lehrprogramm." In *Handbuch der Quellen und Literatur der neueren europäischen Privatrechtsgeschichte*, vol. 1, *Mittelalter (1100-1500): Die gelehrten Rechte und die Gesetzgebung*, ed. Helmut Coing, 39-128. Munich: C. H. Beck'sche, 1973.

Colli, Vincenzo. "I *libri consiliorum*: Note sulla formazione e diffusione delle raccolte di consilia dei giuristi dei secoli XIV-XV." In *Consilia im späten Mittelalter: Zum historischen Aussagewert einer Quellengattung*, ed. Ingrid Baumgärtner, 225-35. Sigmaringen: Jan Thorbecke, 1995.

Collins, Hugh. *Marxism and Law*. Oxford and New York: Oxford University Press, 1982.

Conti, Elio. *L'imposta diretta a Firenze nel Quattrocento (1427-1494)*. Istituto storico italiano per il Medio Evo, Studi storici, fasc. 136-39. Rome: Istituto storico italiano per il Medio Evo, 1984.

Curtius, Ernst Robert. *European Literature and the Latin Middle Ages*. Translated by Willard R. Trask. Bollingen Series, no. 36. Princeton: Princeton University Press, 1953.

D'Amico, Franca Sinatti and Hugo Nicolini. *Indices corporis iuris civilis iuxta vetustiores editiones cum criticis collatas*. Ius Romanorum Medii Aevi, subsidia, no. 1. 3 vols. in 5. Milan: Giuffrè, 1964.

Davies, Jonathan. *Florence and its University During the Early Renaissance*. Education and Society in the Middle Ages and Renaissance, no. 8. Leiden, Boston and Cologne: E. J. Brill, 1998.

De La Roncière, Charles-M. "Indirect Taxes or 'Gabelles' at Florence in the Fourteenth Century: The Evolution of Tariffs and Problems of Collection." Translated by Janet Sondheimer. In *Florentine Studies: Politics and Society in Renaissance Florence*, ed. Nicolai Rubinstein, 140-92. London: Faber and Faber, 1968.

—. *Prix et Salaires à Florence au XIVe Siècle (1280-1380)*. Collection de l'École française de Rome, no. 59. Rome: L'École française de Rome, 1982.

De Roover, Raymond. *Business, Banking, and Economic Thought in Late Medieval and Early Modern Europe: Selected Studies of Raymond de Roover*. Edited by Julius Kirshner. Chicago and London: University of Chicago Press, 1974.

—. *Money, Banking and Credit in Mediaeval Bruges: Italian Merchant-Bankers, Lombards and Money-Changers, A Study in the Origins of Banking*. Cambridge, MA: Mediaeval Academy of America, 1948.

—. "The Organization of Trade." In *Cambridge Economic History of Europe*, vol. 3, *Economic Organization and Policies in the Middle Ages*, ed. M. M. Postan and E. E. Rich, 42-118. Cambridge: Cambridge University Press, 1963.

—. *La pensée économique des scolastiques: doctrine et méthodes*. Montreal and Paris: Institut d'études médiévales and J. Vrin, 1971.

—. *The Rise and Decline of the Medici Bank, 1397-1494*. Cambridge, MA: Harvard University Press, 1963.

—. "Il trattato di fra Santi Rucellai sul cambio, il monte comune e il monte delle doti." *Archivio storico italiano* 111 (1953): 3-41.

Doren, Alfred. *Le arti fiorentine*. Translated by Giovanni Battista Klein. 2 vols. Florence: Felice Le Monnier, 1940-48.

Eagleton, Terry. *Ideology: An Introduction*. London and New York: Verso, 1991.

Eckstein, Nicholas A. *The District of the Green Dragon: Neighbourhood Life and Social Change in Renaissance Florence*. Istituto Nazionale di Studi sul Rinascimento, Quaderni di Rinascimento, no. 22. Florence: Leo S. Olschki, 1995.

Edler, Florence. *Glossary of Mediaeval Terms of Business: Italian Series, 1200-1600*. Cambridge, MA: Mediaeval Academy of America, 1934.

—. "Restitution in Renaissance Florence." In *Studi in onore di Armando Sapori*, 773-80. 2 vols. Milan: Istituto Editoriale Cisalpino, 1957.

Epstein, Stephan R. "Cities, Regions and the Late Medieval Crisis: Sicily and Tuscany Compared." *Past and Present* 130 (1991): 3-50.

Fubini, Riccardo. "From Social to Political Representation in Renaissance Florence." In *City States in Classical Antiquity and Medieval Italy: Athens and Rome, Florence and Venice*, ed. Anthony Molho, Kurt Raaflaub and Julia Emlen, 223-39. Stuttgart: Franz Steiner, 1991.

—. "Renaissance Historian: the Career of Hans Baron." *Journal of Modern History* 64 (1992): 541-74.

Fumagalli, Edoardo. "I trattati di fra Santi Rucellai." *Aevum* 51 (1977): 289-332.

Galassi, Francesco. "Buying a Passport to Heaven: Usury, Restitution, and the Merchants of Medieval Genoa." *Religion* 22 (1992): 313-26.

Gilchrist, John. *The Church and Economic Activity in the Middle Ages*. London, Melbourne and Toronto: Macmillan, 1969.

Ginatempo, Maria. *Prima del debito: Finanziamento della spesa pubblica e gestione del deficit nelle grandi città toscane (1200-1350 ca.)*. Biblioteca storica toscana, no. 38. Florence: Leo S. Olschki, 2000.

Ginori-Lisci, Leonardo. *I Palazzi di Firenze nella storia e nell'arte*. 2 vols. Florence: Cassa di Risparmio di Firenze, 1972.

Goldthwaite, Richard A. *The Building of Renaissance Florence: An Economic and Social History*. Baltimore and London: Johns Hopkins Press, 1980.

Gramsci, Antonio. *Quaderni del Carcere*. Edited by Valentino Gerratana. 4 vols. Turin: Einaudi, 1977.

Green, Louis. *Chronicle into History: An Essay on the Interpretation of History in Florentine Fourteenth-Century Chronicles*. Cambridge: Cambridge University Press, 1972.

Guida generale degli Archivi di Stato italiani. Vol. 2. Rome: Ministero per i Beni Culturali e Ambientali, Ufficio Centrale per i Beni Archivistici, 1983.

Guidi, Guidubaldo. *Il Governo della città-repubblica di Firenze del primo Quattrocento*. 3 vols. Biblioteca storica toscana, no. 20. Florence: Leo S. Olschki, 1981.

Halm, Carolus, Georgius Thomas and Gulielmus Meyer. *Catalogus Codicum Latinorum Bibliothecae Regiae Monacensis*. Vol. 3, part 3. Munich: Bibliotheca Regia, 1873.

Halm, Carolus and Gulielmus Meyer. *Catalogus Codicum Latinorum Bibliothecae Regiae Monacensis*. Vol. 4, part 4. Munich: Bibliotheca Regia, 1881. Reprint Wiesbaden: Otto Harrassowitz, 1969.

Hankins, James. "The Baron Thesis after Forty Years and Some Recent Studies of Leonardo Bruni." *Journal of the History of Ideas* 56 (1995): 309-38.

—, ed. *Renaissance Civic Humanism: Reappraisals and Reflections*. Cambridge: Cambridge University Press, 2000.

—. "Rhetoric, history, and ideology: the civic panegyrics of Leonardo Bruni." In *Renaissance Civic Humanism: Reappraisals and Reflections*, ed. James Hankins, 143-78. Cambridge: Cambridge University Press, 2000.

Hay, Douglas, "Property, Authority and the Criminal Law." In *Albion's Fatal Tree: Crime and Society in Eighteenth-Century England*, ed. Douglas Hay, Peter Linebaugh, John G. Rule, Edward P. Thompson and Cal Winslow, 17-63. Harmondsworth: Penguin, 1977.

Helmholz, R. H. "Usury and the Medieval English Church Courts." *Speculum* 61 (1986): 364-80.

Henderson, John. *Piety and Charity in Late Medieval Florence*. Chicago and London: University of Chicago Press, 1997.

Herde, Peter. "Politik und Rhetorik in Florenz am Vorabend der Renaissance: Die ideologische Rechtfertigung der Florentiner Aussenpolitik durch Coluccio Salutati." *Archiv für Kulturgeschichte* 47 (1965): 141-220.

—. "Politische Verhaltensweisen der Florentiner Oligarchie 1382-1402." In *Geschichte und Verfassungsgefüge: Frankfurter Festgabe für Walter Schlesinger*, 156-249. Wiesbaden: Steiner, 1973.

Herlihy, David. "Family and Property in Renaissance Florence." In *The Medieval City*, ed. Harry A. Miskimin, David Herlihy and Abraham L. Udovitch, 3-24. New Haven and London: Yale University Press, 1977.

—. "The Rulers of Florence, 1282-1530." In *City States in Classical Antiquity and Medieval Italy: Athens and Rome, Florence and Venice*, ed. Anthony Molho, Kurt Raaflaub and Julia Emlen, 197-221. Stuttgart: Franz Steiner, 1991. Repr. in idem, *Women, Family and Society*, 353-80.

—. *Women, Family and Society in Medieval Europe: Historical Essays*, 1978-91. Edited by Anthony Molho. Providence and Oxford: Berghahn, 1995.

— and Christiane Klapisch-Zuber. *Tuscans and Their Families: A Study of the Florentine Catasto of 1427*. New Haven and London: Yale University Press, 1985.

Hörnqvist, Mikael. "The two myths of civic humanism." In *Renaissance Civic Humanism: Reappraisals and Reflections*, ed. James Hankins, 105-42. Cambridge: Cambridge University Press, 2000.

Hoshino, Hidetoshi. *L'arte della Lana in Firenze nel basso medioevo: Il commercio della Lana e il mercato dei panni fiorentini nei secoli XIII-XV*. Biblioteca storica toscana, no. 31. Florence: Leo S. Olschki, 1980.

Hunecke, Volker. "The Conference on the Tumulto dei Ciompi held in Florence 16-19 September 1979." *Journal of Italian History* 2 (1979): 280-92.

—. "Il Tumulto dei Ciompi--600 Jahre danach: Bemerkungen zum Forschungsstand." *Quellen und Forschungen aus italienischen Archiven und Bibliotheken* 58 (1978): 360-410.

Hunt, Alan. *Explorations in Law and Society: Toward a Constitutive Theory of Law*. New York and London: Routledge, 1993.

Hunt, Edwin S. *The medieval super-companies: A study of the Peruzzi Company of Florence*. Cambridge and New York: Cambridge University Press, 1994.

Hyde, John Kenneth. "Contemporary Views on Faction and Civil Strife in Thirteenth- and Fourteenth-Century Italy." In *Violence and Civil Disorder in Italian Cities, 1200-1500*. UCLA Centre for Medieval and Renaissance Studies Contributions, no. 5, ed. Lauro Martines, 273-307. Berkeley, Los Angeles and London: University of California Press, 1972.

—. *Society and Politics in Medieval Italy: The Evolution of the Civil Life, 1000-1350*. London and Basingstoke: Macmillan, 1973.

Indici e Cataloghi, VII: I Codici Panciatichiani della r. Biblioteca Nazionale Centrale di Firenze. Vol. 1, fasc. 3. Rome: Ministero della Pubblica Istruzione, 1891.

Jones, Philip. "Communes and Despots: The City State in Late Medieval Italy." *Transactions of the Royal Historical Society*, 5th series, 15 (1965): 71-96.

—. "Florentine Families and Florentine Diaries in the Fourteenth Century." *Papers of the British School at Rome* n.s. 11 (1956): 183-205.

—. *The Italian City-State: From Commune to Signoria*. Oxford: Clarendon Press, 1997.

Jurdjevic, Mark. "Civic Humanism and the Rise of the Medici." *Renaissance Quarterly* 52 (1999): 994-1020.

Kantorowicz, Hermann. "Citations in the Later Middle Ages (1935)." Translated by W. H. Bryson. In W. H. Bryson, *Dictionary of Sigla and Abbreviations to and in Law Books Before 1607*, 3-16. Charlottesville: University Press of Virginia, 1975.

Kaye, Harvey J. *The Education of Desire: Marxists and the Writing of History*. New York and London: Routledge, 1992.

Kent, Dale. "The Florentine *Reggimento* in the Fifteenth Century." *Renaissance Quarterly* 28 (1975): 575-638.

—. *The Rise of the Medici: Faction in Florence, 1426-1434*. Oxford: Oxford University Press, 1978.

— and Francis W. Kent. *Neighbours and Neighbourhood in Renaissance Florence: The District of the Red Lion in the Fifteenth Century*. Harvard Center for Italian Renaissance Studies, no. 6. Locust Valley, NY: J. J. Augustin, 1982.

Kent, Francis W. *Household and Lineage in Renaissance Florence: The Family Life of the Capponi, Ginori, and Rucellai*. Princeton: Princeton University Press, 1977.

Kirshner, Julius. "*Ars imitatur naturam*: A *Consilium* of Baldus on Naturalization in Florence." *Viator* 5 (1974): 289-331.

—. "Baldus de Ubaldis on Disinheritance: Contexts, Controversies, Consilia." *Ius Commune: Zeitschrift für Europäische Rechtsgeschichte* 27 (2000): 186-87.

—. "Citizen Cain of Florence." In *La Toscane et les Toscans autour de la Renaissance: Cadres de vie, société, croyances: Mélanges offerts à Charles-M. de La Roncière*, 175-89. Aix-en-Provence: L'Université de Provence, 1999.

—. "*Civitas sibi faciat civem*: Bartolus of Sassoferrato's Doctrine on the Making of a Citizen." *Speculum* 48 (1973): 694-713.

—. "Conscience and Public Finance: A *Questio disputata* of John of Legnano on the Public Debt of Genoa." In *Philosophy and Humanism: Renaissance Essays in Honor of Paul Oskar Kristeller*, ed. Edward P. Mahoney, 434-53. Leiden: E. J. Brill, 1976.

—. "*Consilia* as Authority in Late Medieval Italy: The Case of Florence." In *Legal Consulting in the Civil Law Tradition*, ed. Mario Ascheri, Ingrid Baumgärtner and Julius Kirshner, 107-40. Berkeley: The Robbins Collection, 1999.

—. "Encumbering Private Claims to Public Debt in Renaissance Florence." In *The Growth of the Bank as Institution and the Development of Money-Business Law*, ed. Vito Piergiovanni, 19-75. Berlin: Duncker and Humblot, 1993.

—. "Francesco da Empoli." In *Dizionario biografico degli Italiani*, vol. 49. Rome: Istituto della Enciclopedia italiana, 1997.

—. "From Usury to Public Finance: The Ecclesiastical Controversy over the Public Debts of Florence, Genoa and Venice (1300-1500)." PhD thesis, Columbia University, 1970.

—. "The Moral Theology of Public Finance: A Study and Edition of Nicholas de Anglia's *Quaestio disputata* on the Public Debt of Venice." *Archivum Fratrum Praedicatorum* 40 (1970): 47-72.

—. "A Note on the Authorship of Domenico Pantaleoni's Tract on the *Monte Comune* of Florence." *Archivum Fratrum Praedicatorum* 43 (1973): 73-81.

—. "Paolo di Castro on *Cives ex privilegio*: A Controversy over the Legal Qualifications for Public Office in Early Fifteenth-Century Florence." In *Renaissance Studies in Honor of Hans Baron*, ed. Anthony Molho and John A. Tedeschi, 227-64. Dekalb: Northern Illinois University Press, 1971.

—. "Papa Eugenio IV e il monte comune: documenti su investimento e speculazione nel debito pubblico di Firenze." *Archivio storico italiano* 127 (1969): 339-82.

—. *Pursuing Honor While Avoiding Sin: The 'Monte delle doti' of Florence.*

Quaderni di Studi senesi, no. 41. Milan: Giuffrè, 1978.

—. "A *Quaestio de usuris* Falsely Attributed to Bartolus of Sassoferrato." *Renaissance Quarterly* 22 (1969): 256-61.

—. "Raymond de Roover on Scholastic Economic Thought." In *Business, Banking and Economic Thought in Late Medieval and Early Modern Europe: Selected Studies of Raymond de Roover*, ed. Julius Kirshner, 15-36. Chicago and London: University of Chicago Press, 1974.

—. "Reading Bernardino's Sermon on the Public Debt." In *Atti del simposio internazionale cateriniano-bernardiniano: Siena, 17-20 aprile 1980*, ed. Domenico Maffei and Paolo Nardi, 547-622. Siena: Accademia senese degli Intronati, 1982.

—. "Some Problems in the Interpretation of Legal Texts re. the Italian City-States." *Archiv für Begriffsgeschichte* 19 (1975): 16-27.

—. "Storm over the *Monte Comune*: Genesis of the Moral Controversy over the Public Debt of Florence." *Archivum Fratrum Praedicatorum* 53 (1983): 219-76.

—. "'*Ubi est ille*?': Franco Sacchetti on the *monte comune* of Florence." *Speculum* 59 (1984): 556-84.

— and Kimberly Lo Prete. "Peter John Olivi's Treatises on Contracts of Sale, Usury and Restitution: Minorite Economics or Minor Works?" *Quaderni fiorentini per la storia del pensiero giuridico moderno* 13 (1984): 233-86.

— and Anthony Molho. "The Dowry Fund and the Marriage Market in Early Quattrocento Florence." *Journal of Modern History* 50 (1978): 403-38.

Klapisch-Zuber, Christiane. "'Kin, Friends, and Neighbors': The Urban Territory of Merchant Family in 1400." In *Women, Family, and Ritual in Renaissance Italy*, translated by Lydia Cochrane, 68-93. Chicago and London: University of Chicago Press, 1985.

—. "Ruptures de parenté et changements d'identité chez les magnats florentins du XIVe siècle." *Annales: Economies, Sociétés, Civilisations* 43 (1988): 1205-40.

Kristeller, Paul Oskar. *Iter Italicum: A Finding List of Uncatalogued or Incompletely Catalogued Humanistic Manuscripts of the Renaissance in Italian and Other Libraries*. 7 vols. London and Leiden: E. J. Brill, 1963-1997.

Kuehn, Thomas. *Law, Family, and Women: Toward a Legal Anthropology of Renaissance Italy*. Chicago and London: University of Chicago Press, 1991.

Kuttner, Stephan, ed. *A Catalogue of Canon and Roman Law Manuscripts in the Vatican Library*. Vol. 1, *Codices Vaticani latini 541-2299*. Studi e testi, no. 322. Vatican City: Biblioteca Apostolica Vaticana, 1986.

—. *A Catalogue of Canon and Roman Law Manuscripts in the Vatican Library*. Vol. 2, *Codices Vaticani latini 2300-2746*. Studi e testi, no. 328. Vatican City: Biblioteca Apostolica Vaticana, 1987.

—. Introduction to Johannes Andreae, *In quinque Decretalium libros novella commentaria*. 6 vols. Venice: Franciscus Franciscius, 1581. Reprint 4 vols., Turin: Bottega d'Erasmo, 1963. Vol. 1, i-xiv.

—. "Notes on the Presentation of Text and Apparatus in Editing Works of the Decretists and Decretalists." *Traditio* 15 (1959): 452-64.

Langholm, Odd. *The Aristotelian Analysis of Usury*. Bergen, Oslo, Stavanger and Tromsø: Universitetsforlaget, 1984.

—. *Economics in the Medieval Schools: Wealth, Exchange, Value, Money and Usury According to the Paris Theological Tradition, 1200-1350*. Studien und Texte zur Geistesgeschichte des Mittelalters, no. 29. Leiden, New York and Cologne: E. J. Brill, 1992.

—. "The Medieval Schoolmen (1200-1400)." In *Ancient and Medieval Ideas and Concepts of Social Justice*, ed. S. Todd Lowry and Barry Gordon, 439-501. Leiden, New York and Cologne, 1998.

—. *Price and Value in the Aristotelian Tradition: A study in scholastic economic sources*. Bergen, Oslo and Tromsø: Universitetsforlaget, 1979.

Lansing, Carol. *The Florentine Magnates: Lineage and Faction in a Medieval Commune*. Princeton: Princeton University Press, 1991.

Lears, T. J. Jackson. "The Concept of Cultural Hegemony: Problems and Possibilities." *American Historical Review* 90 (1985): 567-93.

Le Goff, Jacques. "The Usurer and Purgatory." In *The Dawn of Modern Banking*, 25-52. New Haven and London: Yale University Press, 1979.

—. *Your Money or Your Life: Economy and Religion in the Middle Ages*. Translated by Patricia Ranum. New York: Zone Books, 1988.

Lesnick, Daniel R. *Preaching in Medieval Florence: The Social World of Franciscan and Dominican Preaching*. Athens, GA, and London: University of Georgia Press, 1989.

Lopez, Roberto S. *Intervista sulla città medievale*. Edited by Marino Berengo. Rome: Laterza, 1984.

Marks, L. F. "The Financial Oligarchy in Florence under Lorenzo." In *Italian Renaissance Studies: A Tribute to Cecilia M. Ady*, ed. E. F. Jacob, 123-47. London: Faber and Faber, 1960.

Martines, Lauro. "Forced Loans: Political and Social Strain in *Quattrocento* Florence." *Journal of Modern History* 60 (1988): 300-11.

—. *Lawyers and Statecraft in Renaissance Florence*. Princeton: Princeton University Press, 1968.

—. "Political Conflict in the Italian City States." *Government and Opposition* 3 (1968): 69-91.

—. *Power and Imagination: City-States in Renaissance Italy*. Baltimore: Johns Hopkins University Press, 1979.

—. *The Social World of the Florentine Humanists, 1390-1460*. London:

Routledge and Kegan Paul, 1963.
Martino, Federico. "Un consilium inedito in materia di usura di Lorenzo Ridolfi." *Il diritto ecclesiastico* 80 (1969): 335-52.
—. "Umanisti, giuristi, uomini di stato a Firenze fra Trecento e Quattrocento: Lorenzo d'Antonio Ridolfi." In *Studi in memoria di Mario Condorelli*, 3 vols., 3: 179-200. Milan: Giuffrè, 1988.
Mazzatinti, Giuseppe. *Inventari dei manoscritti delle biblioteche d'Italia*. Vol. 10. Forli: Luigi Bordandini, 1900. Reprint Florence: Leo S. Olschki, 1955.
McCall, John P. "The Writings of John of Legnano with a List of Manuscripts." *Traditio* 23 (1967): 415-37.
McLaughlin, Terence P. "The Teaching of the Canonists on Usury (XII, XIII and XIV Centuries)." *Mediaeval Studies* 1 (1939): 81-147; 2 (1940): 1-22.
Meek, Christine. "Il debito pubblico nella storia finanziaria di Lucca nel XIV secolo." *Actum Luce* 3 (1974): 7-46.
Milner, Stephen J. "Citing the *Ringhiera*: The Politics of Place and Public Address in Trecento Florence." *Italian Studies* 55 (2000): 53-82.
Molho, Anthony. "The Brancacci Chapel: Studies in its Iconography and History." *Journal of the Warburg and Courtauld Institutes* 40 (1977): 50-98.
—. "Cosimo de' Medici: *Pater patriae* or *Padrino*?" *Stanford Italian Review* 1 (1979): 5-33.
—. "Créanciers de Florence en 1347: Un aperçu statistique du quartier de Santo Spirito." In *La Toscane et les Toscans autour de la Renaissance: Cadres de vie, société, croyances: Mélanges offerts à Charles-M. de La Roncière*, 77-93. Aix-en-Provence: L'Université de Provence, 1999.
—. "The Florentine Oligarchy and the *Balie* of the Late Trecento." *Speculum* 43 (1968): 23-51.
—. *Florentine Public Finances in the Early Renaissance, 1400-1433*. Cambridge, MA: Harvard University Press, 1971.
—. *Marriage Alliance in Late Medieval Florence*. Cambridge, MA, and London: Harvard University Press, 1994.
—. "Politics and the Ruling Class in Early Renaissance Florence." *Nuova rivista storica* 52 (1968): 401-20.
—. "The State and Public Finance: A Hypothesis Based on the History of Late Medieval Florence." In *The Origins of the State in Italy, 1300-1600*, ed. Julius Kirshner, 97-135. Chicago: University of Chicago Press, 1995.
—. "Tre Città-stato e i loro debiti pubblici: Quesiti e ipotesi sulla storia di Firenze, Genova e Venezia." In *Italia 1350-1450: Tra crisi, trasformazione, sviluppo: tredicesimo convegno di studi, Pistoia, 10-13 maggio 1991*, 185-215. Pistoia: Centro italiano di studi di storia e d'arte, 1993.

Mollat, Michel. *The Poor in the Middle Ages: An Essay in Social History.* Translated by Arthur Goldhammer. New Haven and London: Yale University Press, 1986.

Moulakis, Athanasios. "Civic humanism, realist constitutionalism, and Francesco Guicciardini's *Discorso di Logrogno.*" In *Renaissance Civic Humanism: Reappraisals and Reflections*, ed. James Hankins, 200-222. Cambridge: Cambridge University Press, 2000.

Müller, Wolfgang P. "The Recovery of Justinian's Digest in the Middle Ages," *Bulletin of Medieval Canon Law*, n.s. 19 (1989): 1-29.

Munro, John H. "The International Law Merchant and the Evolution of Negotiable Credit in Late-Medieval England and the Low Countries." In *Banchi pubblici, banchi privati e monti di pietà nell'Europa preindustriale: Amministrazione, techniche operative e ruoli economici*, Atti della società ligure di storia patria, n.s. 31, fasc. 1, 49-80. Genoa: Società ligure di storia patria, 1991. Repr. in idem, *Textiles, Towns and Trade*, X.

—. "The 'New Institutional Economics' and the Changing Fortunes of Fairs in Medieval and Early Modern Europe: The Textile Trades, Warfare, and Transaction Costs." *Vierteljahrschrift für Sozial- und Wirtschaftsgeschichte* 88 (2001): 1-47.

—. Review of *A Financial Revolution in the Hapsburg Netherlands: Renten and Renteniers in the County of Holland, 1515-1565*, by James D. Tracey. *American Historical Review* 92 (1987): 434-35

—. "Textile Technology" and "Textile Workers." In *The Dictionary of the Middle Ages*, ed. Joseph Strayer et al., vol. 11, 693-715. New York: Charles Scribner's Sons, 1988. Repr. in idem, *Textiles, Towns and Trade*, 1-35.

—. *Textiles, Towns and Trade: Essays in the history of late-medieval England and the Low Countries*. Aldershot: Variorum, 1994.

Najemy, John M. "*Audiant Omnes Artes*: Corporate Origins of the Ciompi Revolution." In *Il Tumulto dei Ciompi: Un momento di storia fiorentina ed europea*, 59-93. Florence: Leo S. Olschki, 1981.

—. "Civic humanism and Florentine politics." In *Renaissance Civic Humanism: Reappraisals and Reflections*, ed. James Hankins, 75-104. Cambridge: Cambridge University Press, 2000.

—. *Corporatism and Consensus in Florentine Electoral Politics, 1280-1400.* Chapel Hill: University of North Carolina Press, 1982.

—. "The Dialogue of Power in Florentine Politics." In *City States in Classical Antiquity and Medieval Italy: Athens and Rome, Florence and Venice*, ed. Anthony Molho, Kurt Raaflaub and Julia Emlen, 269-88. Stuttgart: Franz Steiner, 1991.

—. "Guild Republicanism in Trecento Florence: The Successes and Ultimate

Failure of Corporate Politics." *American Historical Review* 84 (1979): 53-71.
—. Review of *In Search of Florentine Civic Humanism* by Hans Baron. *Renaissance Quarterly* 45 (1992): 340-50.
Narducci, Henricus. *Catalogus codicum manuscriptorum praeter Graecos et orientales in Biblioteca Angelica.* Vol. 1. Rome: Ludovicus Cecchini, 1893.
Naz, Raoul, ed. *Dictionnaire de droit canonique.* 7 vols. Paris: Letouzey et Ané, 1935-65.
Nelson, Benjamin. *The Idea of Usury: From Tribal Brotherhood to Universal Otherhood.* 2nd ed. Chicago and London: University of Chicago Press, 1969.
—. "The Usurer and the Merchant Prince: Italian Businessmen and the Ecclesiastical Law of Restitution, 1100-1550." *Journal of Economic History*, supplement 7 (1947): 104-22.
Ninci, Renzo. "Lo 'Squittino del Mangione': il consolidamento legale di un regime (1404)." *Bulletino dell'Istituto storico italiano per il Medio Evo e Archivio muratoriano* 94 (1988): 155-250.
Noonan, John T. *The Scholastic Analysis of Usury.* Cambridge, MA: Harvard University Press, 1957.

Origo, Iris. *The Merchant of Prato: Francesco di Marco Datini.* London: The Reprint Society, 1957.
Ottokar, Nicola. *Il comune di Firenze alla fine del Dugento.* Florence: Vallecchi, 1926. 2nd ed. Turin: Einaudi, 1962.

Park, Katharine. "The Readers at the Florentine Studio according to Communal Fiscal Records (1357-1380, 1413-1446)." *Rinascimento*, n.s. 20 (1980): 249-310.
Pastoureau, Michel. "Stratégies héraldiques et changements d'armoires chez les magnats florentins du XIVe siècle." *Annales: Economies, Sociétés, Civilisations* 43 (1988): 1241-54
Pazzaglini, Peter R. and Catherine A. Hawks. *Consilia: A Bibliography of Holdings in the Library of Congress and Certain Other Collections in the United States.* Washington, DC: Library of Congress, 1990.
Pennington, Kenneth. "Bio-bibliography of Medieval Canonists" (unpublished).
—. "Henricus de Segusio (Hostiensis)." In *Popes, Canonists and Texts, 1150-1550.* Aldershot, Hampshire and Brookfield, VT: Variorum, 1993.
—. *The Prince and the Law, 1200-1600: Sovereignty and Rights in the Western Legal Tradition.* Berkeley, Los Angeles and London: University of California Press, 1993.
Pirillo, Paolo. *Costruzione di un contado: I fiorentini e il loro territorio nel*

basso Medioevo. Florence: Le Lettere, 2001.

Plezia, Marian, ed. *Lexicon mediae et infimae latinitatis Polonorum*. 7 vols. Wroclaw, Warsaw, Kracow and Gdansk, 1953.

Post, Gaines. *Studies in Medieval Legal Thought: Public Law and the State, 1100-1322*. Princeton: Princeton University Press, 1964.

Rashdall, Hastings. *The Universities of Europe in the Middle Ages*. 2nd ed. Edited by F. M. Powicke. 3 vols. Oxford: Clarendon Press, 1936.

Raveggi, Sergio, Massimo Tarassi, Daniela Medici and Patrizia Parenti. *Ghibellini, guelfi e popolo grasso: I detentori del potere politico a Firenze nella seconda metà del Dugento*. Florence: La Nuova Italia, 1978.

Riesenberg, Peter. "The Consilia Literature: A Prospectus." *Manuscripta* 6 (1962): 3-22.

Rigg, A. George. "Morphology and Syntax." In *Medieval Latin: An Introduction and Bibliographical Guide*, ed. Frank A. C. Mantello and A. George Rigg, 83-92. Washington, DC: Catholic University of America Press, 1996.

Rocke, Michael. *Forbidden Friendships: Homosexuality and Male Culture in Renaissance Florence*. New York and Oxford: Oxford University Press, 1996.

Rodolico, Niccolò. *I Ciompi: Una pagina di storia del proletariato operaio*. 3rd ed. Florence: Sansoni, 1980.

—. *La democrazia fiorentina nel suo tramonto (1378-1382)*. Bologna: Nicola Zanichelli, 1905.

—. *Il popolo minuto: Note di storia fiorentina (1343-1378)*. Florence: Leo S. Olschki, 1968.

Roettgen, Steffi. *Wandmalerei der Frührenaissance in Italien*. Vol. 1, *Anfänge und Entfaltung 1400-1470*. Munich: Hirmer, 1996.

Rossi, Guido. *Consilium sapientis iudiciale: Studi e ricerche per la storia del processo romano-canonico*. Vol. 1: *Secoli XII-XIII*. Seminario giuridico della Università di Bologna, no. 18. Milan: Giuffrè, 1958.

Rubinstein, Nicolai. *The Government of Florence Under the Medici (1434 to 1494)*. 2nd ed. Oxford: Clarendon Press, 1997.

—. *The Palazzo Vecchio, 1298-1532: Government, Architecture, and Imagery in the Civic Palace of the Florentine Republic*. Oxford: Clarendon Press, 1995.

Rutenburg, Victor. *Popolo e movimenti popolari nell'Italia del '300 e '400*. Translated by Gianpiero Borghini. Bologna: Mulino, 1971.

Salvemini, Gaetano. *Magnati e popolani in Firenze dal 1280 al 1295*. Florence: G. Carnesecchi, 1899. Reprint Turin: Einaudi, 1960.

Santarelli, Umberto. "'Maxima fuit Florentiae altercatio': l'usura e i montes." In *Banchi pubblici, banchi privati e monti di pietà nell'Europa preindustriale: Amministrazione, techniche operative e ruoli economici*, Atti della società ligure di storia patria, n.s. 31, fasc. 1, 81-94. Genoa: Società ligure di storia patria, 1991.

Sapori, Armando. "L'interesse del denaro a Firenze nel Trecento." In *Studi di storia economica (secoli XIII, XIV, XV)*. 3rd ed., 3 vols., 1: 223-43. Florence: Sansoni, 1955-1967.

Schnapper, Bernard. "La répression de l'usure et l'évolution économique (XIIIe-XVIe siècles)." *Tijdschrift voor rechtsgeschiedenis* 37 (1969): 47-75.

Schulte, Johann Friedrich von. *Die Geschichte der Quellen und Literatur des canonischen Rechts*. 3 vols. Stuttgart: F. Enke, 1875-80; reprint Graz: Akademische Druck- u. Verlagsanstalt, 1956.

Seigel, Jerrold E. "Civic Humanism or Ciceronian Rhetoric?" *Past and Present* 34 (1966): 3-48.

Shatzmiller, Joseph. *Shylock Reconsidered: Jews, Moneylending, and Medieval Society*. Berkeley, Los Angeles and London: University of California Press, 1990.

Smith, John Ashton Clarence. *Medieval Law Teachers and Writers, Civilian and Canonist*. Ottawa: University of Ottawa Press, 1975.

Spicciani, Amleto. *Capitale e interesse tra mercatura e povertà nei teologi e canonisti dei secoli XIII-XV*. Rome: Jouvence, 1990.

Stella, Alessandro. *La révolte des Ciompi: les hommes, les lieux, le travail*. Paris: L'École des hautes études en sciences sociales, 1993.

Stevenson, Henry and Giovanni Battista de Rossi. *Codices Palatini latini Bibliothecae Vaticanae*. Vol. 1. Vatican City: Typographeum Vaticanum, 1886.

Swanson, Robert N. *Universities, Academics and the Great Schism*. Cambridge: Cambridge University Press, 1979.

Tabacco, Giovanni. *Egemonie sociali e strutture del potere nel medioevo italiano*. Turin: Einaudi, 1974.

Tabulae codicum manu scriptorum praeter graecos et orientales in Bibliotheca palatina Vindobonensi asservatorum. Vol. 3. Vienna: Caroli Geroldi Filius, 1869. Reprint Graz: Akademische Druck- u. Verlagsanstalt, 1965.

Trachtenberg, Marvin. *Dominion of the Eye: Urbanism, Art, and Power in Early Modern Florence*. Cambridge: Cambridge University Press, 1997.

Tracy, James D. *A Financial Revolution in the Hapsburg Netherlands: Renten and Renteniers in the County of Holland, 1515-1565*. Berkeley and London: University of California Press, 1985.

Trexler, Richard C. "Charity and the Defense of Urban Elites in the Italian Communes." In *The Rich, the Well Born, and the Powerful: Elites and Upper Classes in History*, ed. Frederic Cople Jaher, 64-109. Urbana, Chicago and London: University of Illinois Press, 1973.

—. "Florence, by the grace of the Lord Pope ...." *Studies in Medieval and Renaissance History* 9 (1972): 117-215.

—. "Follow the flag: the Ciompi revolt seen from the streets." *Bibliothèque d'Humanisme et Renaissance* 46 (1984): 357-92. Repr. in idem, *Power and Dependence in Renaissance Florence* 3: 30-60.

—. "Herald of the Ciompi: The Authorship of an Anonymous Florentine Chronicle." *Quellen und Forschungen aus italienischen Archiven und Bibliotheken* 65 (1985): 159-91. Repr. in idem, *Power and Dependence in Renaissance Florence* 3: 6-29.

—. "Neighbours and Comrades: The Revolutionaries of Florence, 1378." *Social Analysis* 14 (December 1983): 53-106. Repr. in idem, *Power and Dependence in Renaissance Florence* 3: 61-126.

—. *Power and Dependence in Renaissance Florence*. Vol. 3, *The Workers of Renaissance Florence*. Binghamton, NY: Center for Medieval and Early Renaissance Studies, 1993.

—. *Public Life in Renaissance Florence*. Ithaca, NY: Cornell University Press, 1980.

Tunberg, Terence O. "Prose Styles and Cursus." In *Medieval Latin: An Introduction and Bibliographical Guide*, ed. Frank A. C. Mantello and A. George Rigg, 111-21. Washington, DC: Catholic University of America Press, 1996.

Van der Wee, Herman. "Monetary, Credit, and Banking Systems." In *Cambridge Economic History of Europe*, vol. 5, *The Economic Organization of Early Modern Europe*, ed. E. E. Rich and Charles Wilson, 310-35. Cambridge: Cambridge University Press, 1977.

Viller, M., F. Cavallera, J. de Guibert, A. Rayez, A. Derville and A. Solignac, ed. *Dictionnaire de spiritualité*. Paris: Beauchesne, 1937-.

Waley, Daniel. "The Army of the Florentine Republic from the Twelfth to the Fourteenth Century." In *Florentine Studies: Politics and Society in Renaissance Florence*, ed. Nicolai Rubinstein, 70-108. London: Faber and Faber, 1968.

—. *The Italian City-Republics*. 3rd ed. London and New York: Longman, 1988.

Walter, Hans, ed. *Proverbia sententiaeque latinitatis Medii Aevi: Lateinische Sprichwörter und Sentenzen des Mittelalters in alphabetischer Anordnung*. 9 vols. Göttingen: Vandenhoeck and Ruprecht, 1963-86.

West, Martin L. *Textual Criticism and Editorial Technique*. Stuttgart: E. B. Teubner, 1973.

Witt, Ronald G. "The Crisis after Forty Years." *American Historical Review* 101 (1996): 110-18

—. "Florentine politics and the ruling class, 1382-1407." *Journal of Medi-*

eval and Renaissance Studies 5 (1975): 243-67.

—. *Hercules at the Crossroads: The Life, Works, and Thought of Coluccio Salutati.* Duke Monographs in Medieval and Renaissance Studies, no. 6. Durham, NC: Duke University Press, 1983.

Zorzi, Andrea. *L'amministrazione della giustizia penale nella Repubblica fiorentina: Aspetti e problemi.* Biblioteca storica toscana, no. 23. Florence: Leo S. Olschki, 1988.

—. "I fiorentini e gli uffici pubblici nel primo Quattrocento: Concorrenza, abusi, illegalità." *Quaderni storici* 66 (1987): 725-51.

Index of Citations

A. Corpus iuris canonici

Decretum Gratiani
- D.1 dictum Grat. ante c.1: 277
- D.3 dictum Grat. post c.3: 214, 354
- D.3 c.4: 214, 354
- D.4 c.6: 267
- D.18 c.8: 163, 304
- D.20 dictum Grat. ante c.1: 181, 322-23
- D.32 c.11: 173, 314
- D.35 c.4: 209
- D.42 c.2: 178, 319
- D.46 c.10: 271
- D.47 c.1: 183, 324
- D.47 c.2: 155, 297
- D.47 c.3: 144, 273
- D.47 c.8: 144, 146, 168, 273, 276, 310
- D.50 c.18: 176, 227, 316, 361
- D.50 c.25: 228, 361
- D.50 c.29: 162, 303
- D.59 c.2: 156, 298
- D.61 c.7: 156, 298
- D.88 c.11: 277
- C.1 q.1 c.21: 164, 305
- C.1 q.1 c.26: 233, 364
- C.1 q.1 c.47: 225, 360
- C.1 q.1 c.113: 156, 298
- C.1 q.2 c.1: 163, 304
- C.1 q.2 c.2: 156, 298
- C.1 q.2 c.4: 135, 265
- C.1 q.7 c.26 (=C.9.27.6): 95, 191, 243, 334, 370
- C.2 q.1 c.6: 173, 314
- C.2 q.1 c.7: 355
- C.2 q.5 c.20: 173, 314
- C.8 q.1 c.11: 235, 366
- C.10 q.2 c.2: 307
- C.10 q.2 c.2.11 (=C. 1.2.14.5): 202, 258, 342, 379
- C.10 q.2 c.3 (=C. 1.2.14.5): 202, 258, 342, 379
- C.10 q.2 c.4: 202, 258, 340, 343, 379
- C.11 q.3 c.66: 156, 298
- C.12 q.1 c.2: 168, 310
- C.12 q.2 c.10: 148, 281
- C.12 q.2 c.11: 134, 264
- C.12 q.2 c.36: 197, 338
- C.12 q.2 c.44: 207, 346
- C.14 q.3: 155, 268, 297
- C.14 q.3 c.1: 196, 338
- C.14 q.3 c.2: 138, 139, 266-67, 267
- C.14 q.3 c.3: 132, 134, 142, 159, 197, 198, 218, 262, 263, 270, 300, 338, 339, 358, 369
- C.14 q.3 c.4: 133, 134, 142, 263, 270
- C.14 q.3 dictum Grat. post c.4: 58n, 133, 263
- C.14 q.4 c.4: 148, 281-82
- C.14 q.4 c.9: 58n
- C.14 q.4 c.12: 153, 283, 289
- C.14 q.5 c.15: 162, 164, 289, 304, 305

C.14 q.6 c.1: 180, 181, 322
C.18 q.2 c.30: 238, 368
C.22 q.1 c.16: 151, 286, 287
C.22 q.2 c.4: 146, 276
C.23 q.5 c.8: 151, 287
C.23 q.5 c.19: 151, 287
C.23 q.5 c.24: 167, 308
C.24 q.1 c.21: 179, 320
C.32 q.5 c.23: 173, 314
C.34 q.2 c.5: 187, 327
D.3 de poen. c.49: 234, 366
D.6 de poen. c.3: 334
D.4 de cons. c.31: 234, 366

Glossa ordinaria to the *Decretum Gratiani*
ad C.2 q.1 c.7, v. *In primis*: 215, 355
ad C.9 q.3 c.21, v. *Ad nos*: 188, 330
ad C.10 q.2 c.2, v. *Probat*: 165, 166, 248-49, 307, 372
ad C.10 q.2 c.2.11, casus: 342-43
ad C.10 q.2 c.4, v. *Duplum*: 202, 203, 343
ad C.14 q.3 dictum Grat. ante c.1, v. *Quod autem*: 149, 284
ad C.14 q.3 c.1, v. *Plus quam*: 146-47, 157, 278, 298
ad C.14 q.3 c.1, v. *Expectes*: 157, 298
ad C.14 q.3 c.3, v. *Praecepta*: 207, 208, 239, 256, 345-46, 369
ad C.14 q.4 c.12, v. *Cui*: 283-84
ad C.14 q.6 c.1, v. *Nisi restituatur*: 187, 327, 328
ad C.23 q.8 dictum grat. post c. 22, v. *Emeret*: 188, 330
ad C.34 q.2 c.5, v. *Possidere*: 187, 189, 327-28, 331
ad D.6 de poen. c.3, v. *Pro ignorantia*: 191, 334

Liber extra
1.2.3, 233: 363-64
1.2.6: 227-28
1.2.7: 328
1.3.7: 253, 376
1.3.19: 253, 376
1.3.30: 253, 376
1.3.38: 253, 256, 316, 376, 378
1.3.39: 253, 376
1.3.40: 253, 376
1.3.41: 226, 360
1.3.43: 327
1.4.11: 184, 236, 324-25, 367
1.6.4: 157, 298, 299
1.6.18: 362
1.6.21: 230, 362
1.6.54: 233, 256, 364, 378
1.9.5: 182, 190, 323, 332
1.9.10: 156, 248, 297, 372
1.12.1: 191, 334
1.27.1: 248, 372
1.29.12: 253, 376
1.31.2: 173, 314
1.33.1: 228, 361
1.33.15: 228, 361
1.38.9: 174, 256, 314, 378
1.43.4: 134, 264
2.1.6: 173, 174, 238, 249, 313, 314, 368, 373
2.1.11: 238, 368
2.1.15: 174, 315
2.2.12: 163, 305
2.2.17: 238, 368
2.13.2: 190, 332
2.13.18: 238-39, 368-69
2.20.10: 180, 321
2.20.47: 169, 250, 311, 374
2.23.3: 167, 236, 308, 367
2.23.6: 167, 256, 308, 378
2.23.9: 167, 256, 308, 378
2.23.10: 182, 190, 323, 332
2.23.11: 190, 332-33

2.23.14: 190, 333
2.24.1: 151, 287
2.24.6: 133, 151, 263, 287, 306, 322
2.24.7: 133, 159, 239, 263, 300, 369
2.24.16: 256, 378
2.24.18: 256, 378
2.24.20: 180, 184, 185, 322, 325, 326
2.24.25: 256, 378
2.24.32: 154, 308
2.26.5: 187, 328
2.26.17: 331
2.26.20: 187, 328
2.27.18: 174, 315
2.28.34: 174, 315
2.30.5: 155, 297
3.5.11: 157, 298, 299
3.5.16: 252, 374
3.5.19: 253, 376
3.5.36: 256, 378
3.5.38: 256, 378
3.7.6: 174, 315
3.8.15: 230, 362
3.9.1: 233, 364
3.12.1: 191, 229, 333, 362
3.13.11: 201, 341
3.17.3: 161, 196, 197, 202, 238, 303, 338, 368
3.17.5: 59n, 154, 159, 193, 196, 197, 239, 241, 256, 290, 300, 303, 308, 335, 338, 369, 378
3.17.6: 161, 197, 238, 303, 338, 368
3.17.7: 202
3.21.4: 154, 159, 195, 196, 197, 209, 239, 241, 256, 290, 300, 337, 338, 347, 369, 378
3.21.6: 159, 239, 300-301, 369
3.22.2: 221, 358-59
3.22.3: 147, 280
3.24.1: 190, 227, 229, 332, 361, 362
3.24.10: 208, 346
3.25.5: 216, 356
3.26.7: 156, 190, 227, 298, 332, 361
3.26.15: 172, 313
3.28.4: 172, 313
3.28.14: 179, 320
3.36.3: 146, 276
3.36.6: 174, 315
3.38.19: 174, 315
3.39.6: 163, 304
3.39.14: 163, 304
3.39.23: 163, 304
4.1.17: 215, 355
4.11.7: 173, 313
4.14.7: 169, 311
5.3.1: 269
5.3.8: 269
5.3.9: 269
5.3.10: 269
5.3.18: 188, 331
5.3.21: 269
5.3.23: 165, 306
5.3.28: 152, 287, 288
5.3.30: 163, 269, 304
5.3.34: 140, 268
5.3.42: 269
5.3.46: 169, 311
5.6.13: 155, 296
5.12.6: 178, 318
5.12.18: 191, 334
5.17.2: 179, 181, 320, 323
5.17.5: 179, 320
5.18.5: 181, 323
5.19.1: 136, 147, 237, 241, 265, 280, 369
5.19.3: 59n, 304
5.19.4: 59n, 153, 155, 212, 285, 287, 288, 295, 351
5.19.5: 59n, 178, 198, 236, 318, 367
5.19.6: 59n, 81, 95, 149, 158,

198, 239, 243, 244, 256, 266, 282, 299, 300, 301, 335, 336, 339, 369, 370, 371, 378
5.19.7: 289, 324
5.19.8: 147, 280
5.19.10: 56, 76n, 80, 85, 95, 131, 133, 134, 136, 155, 158, 161, 168, 169, 175, 186, 192, 193, 237, 243, 244, 255, 256, 262, 263, 264, 266, 268, 295, 297, 300, 301, 302, 303, 304, 306, 309, 310, 315, 335, 336, 368, 370, 370-71, 377
5.19.13: 193, 335
5.19.15: 154, 290
5.19.16: 149, 241, 282-83
5.19.18: 179, 320
5.19.19: 59n, 95, 193, 201, 243, 244, 256, 301, 307, 336, 342, 370, 371, 378
5.33.16: 230, 363
5.36.8: 329
5.36.9: 151, 287
5.37.7: 134, 264
5.38.13: 218, 357
5.39.36: 163, 305
5.39.54: 163, 304
5.40.6: 174, 314-15
5.40.8: 180, 181, 321, 322
5.41.3: 361
5.41.4: 71

Glossa ordinaria to the *Liber extra*
ad 1.2.3, v. *Quod de uno*: 233, 363-64
ad 1.2.6, v. *Constitutum*: 227-28, 361
ad 1.6.18, v. *Regia*: 230, 362
ad 1.6.21, v. *Confirmauit*: 230, 362-63
ad 1.6.44, v. *Administrent*: 249, 372
ad 1.6.54, v. *Intitulatum*: 233, 365
ad 1.27.1, v. *Modum*: 248, 372
ad 2.1.6, v. *Subtiliter*: 249, 372
ad 2.23.3, v. *Intelligitur*: 167, 308
ad 2.24.6, v. *Cogendi sunt*: 165, 181, 190, 306-7, 322, 332
ad 2.24.7, v. *Ad restituendum*: 159, 239, 300, 369
ad 2.24.32, v. *Ex fama*: 154, 290
ad 2.25.6, v. *Bona fidei*: 148, 282
ad 2.26.5, v. *Nouerit*: 187, 328, 329
ad 2.26.17, v. *Bona fides*: 189, 331-32
ad 2.26.20, v. *Nulla temporis*:, 187, 328
ad 3.9.1, v. *Sede vacante*: 233, 364
ad 3.17.3, v. *Deceptione*: 238, 368
ad 3.17.5, v. *Emptionis*: 159, 208, 239, 300, 346, 369
ad 3.17.5, v. *Patet*: 162, 303
ad 3.17.5, v. *Dimidiam*: 154, 290
ad 3.17.6, v. *Dimidiam*: 238, 368
ad 3.21.4, v. *Obligatis*: 159, 208, 239, 300, 346, 369
ad 3.21.4, v. *Proximos annos*: 209, 347
ad 3.21.4, v. *Praesumitur*: 209, 347
ad 3.21.4, v. *Consueuerit*: 154, 290
ad 3.21.6, v. *Extenuassent*: 159, 239, 301, 369
ad 5.3.10, v. *Procurationem*: 141, 269
ad 5.3.27, v. *Interueniente*: 140, 183, 268, 324
ad 5.3.28, casus: 288

ad 5.3.28, v. *Restituere quod accepit*: 288
ad 5.19.1, v. *Deductis expensis*: 283
ad 5.19.1, v. *Beneficium*: 136, 265-66
ad 5.19.6, v. *Comparant*: 162, 303
ad 5.19.6, v. *Non valent*: 162, 240, 303-4, 304
ad 5.19.6, v. *Ex tali forma*: 136, 159, 208, 239, 266, 300, 346, 369
ad 5.19.6, v. *Vsurarum*: 159, 266, 301
ad 5.19.6, v. *Venditores*: 159
ad 5.19.6, v. *Occultari*: 198, 339
ad 5.19.7, v. *Suspendas*: 153, 289
ad 5.19.8, v. *De feudo*: 149, 160, 284, 301-2
ad 5.19.10, casus: 85-86, 155-56, 169, 208, 297, 311, 346
ad 5.19.10, v. *Sperantes*: 156, 168, 297-98, 298, 310
ad 5.19.10, v. *Male agere*: 158, 161, 173, 300, 303, 314
ad 5.19.13, casus: 193
ad 5.19.15, v. *Manifestos*: 154, 290-91
ad 5.19.19, v. *Tempore non fuerat venditurus*: 159, 301
ad 5.39.54, v. *Vel alio* et v. *Quasi gerunt causam eorum*: 163, 304
ad 5.40.8, v. *Proprietas*: 181, 322
ad 5.41.3, v. *Veritas*: 228, 361

Liber Sextus
1.3.2: 250, 374
1.3.11: 164, 179, 180, 305, 321
1.3.12: 253, 376
1.3.13: 253, 376
1.3.14: 253, 376
1.6.3: 178, 319
1.6.6: 218, 256, 357, 378
1.6.30: 321
1.7.2: 191, 333
1.14.9: 233, 364
2.5.2: 174, 315
2.14.3: 249, 372-73
2.15.11: 230, 362
3.3.1: 321, 367
3.4.1-41: 253, 376
3.4.4: 235, 366
3.4.6: 233, 365
3.4.13: 253, 376
3.4.15: 233, 365
3.7.1-8: 253, 376
3.14.4: 254, 376
3.20.2: 164, 180, 305, 321
5.5.1: 154, 292-93
5.5.2: 154, 179, 292, 320
5.11.21: 254, 376
de reg. iur. 2: 187, 328
de reg. iur. 4: 180, 236, 322, 367
de reg. iur. 27: 163, 305
de reg. iur. 31: 226, 360
de reg. iur. 42: 233, 364
de reg. iur. 46: 239, 368
de reg. iur. 73: 186, 326
de reg. iur. 86: 163, 221, 305, 359

Glossa ordinaria to the *Liber Sextus*
ad 1.7.2, v. *Coniecturas*: 191, 333
ad 2.14.3, v. *Dominii vel quasi*: 189, 332
ad 3.3.1, v. *Receperit*: 235, 367
ad 3.3.1, v. *Vtilitas*: 180, 321
ad *de reg. iur.* 2, *Possessor*, v. *Possessor*: 187, 328
ad *de reg. iur.* 4, *Peccatum*, v. *Restituatur*: 163, 177, 180, 304-5, 317, 318, 321
ad *de reg. iur.* 46, *Is, qui in ius*,

casus: 239
ad *de reg. iur.* 73, *Factum legitime*, v. *Factum legitime*: 186, 326-27

Constitutiones Clementinae
1.2.3: 250, 373
1.2.4: 253, 376
1.2.5: 376-77
2.7.1: 333
3.2.2: 233, 365
3.7.1: 154, 292
3.11.2: 146, 276
5.3.2: 164, 305-6
5.5.1: 60n, 154, 293
5.7.1: 334

Glossa ordinaria to the *Constitutiones Clementinae*
ad 1.2.3, casus: 250, 373-74
ad 1.2.5, casus et v. *Post datam*: 254, 377
ad 2.7.1, v. *Fecisse narramus*: 191, 333-34
ad 3.2.2, v. *Ecclesias*: 233, 365
ad 5.5.1, v. *Proximi*: 144, 274
ad 5.5.1, v. *Onera*: 157, 298
ad 5.5.1, v. *Non esse peccatum*: 318
ad 5.7.1, v. *Non habita*: 191, 334-35

Extravagantes Communes
3.5.1: 99n
3.5.2: 99n

B. Canonists

Damasus
Quaestiones, *de iureiurando*: 151, 213, 287-88, 353

Dino of Mugello
Commentaria in *de reg. iur.* 4, *Peccatum*: 177, 316, 317, 318, 319

Fredericus Petruccius
Consilia, quaestio 18: 166, 177, 307, 316, 318, 319, 367
—, quaestio 22: 177, 307, 316, 318, 319, 367
—, consilium 184: 184, 325

Gottofredo da Trani
Apparatus ad X 5.19.6, v. *Alias merces*: 243, 246, 371
— ad X 5.19.6, v. *Forma*: 206, 345
— ad X 5.19.6, v. *Nisi dubium sit*: 160, 161, 301, 302-3
— ad X 5.19.7, v. *Excommunicationis*: 153
— ad X 5.19.8, v. *Clericorum*: 149-50
— ad X 5.19.10, v. *Date mutuum*: 168, 310
— ad X 5.19.10, v. *Sperantes*: 156, 157, 168, 295-96, 298, 310
— ad X 5.19.10, v. *Intentione*: 156, 298
Summa, X 2.26 *de prescriptionibus*: 188
—, X 5.19 *de usuris*: 132, 133, 134, 141, 142, 143, 147, 153, 154, 186, 200, 203, 262, 263-64, 264-65, 270, 271, 272, 280, 281-83, 289, 291, 298, 327, 340, 341, 343

Guido de Baysio
Rosarium ad Decretum Grat. C.1 q.2 c.9: 235, 367
— C.9 q.3 c.21: 188, 330
— C.10 q.2 c.4: 200, 203, 340-41, 343
— C.14 q.3 c.1: 157, 169, 172, 299, 312-13
— C.14 q.4 c.9: 200, 201, 341, 342
— C.14 q.4 c.10: 151, 286-87
— C.14 q.5 c.15: 153, 289
— C.22 q.1 c.16: 150, 286
— C.23 q.8 dictum Grat. post c.22: 188, 330
Commentaria ad VI 5.5.2: 138, 178, 249, 267, 318, 372
— ad VI 5.11.21: 254

Guillelmus Redonensis
Apparatus in Summam Raymundi 2.7 *de usuris*: 138, 266, 267

Hostiensis (Henricus de Segusio)
Commentaria ad X 1.3.43: 187, 327
— ad X 2.24.32: 167, 308
— ad X 2.27.18: 174, 315
— ad X 2.28.18: 174, 315
— ad X 3.12.1: 260, 380
— ad X 3.17.5: 167, 308-9
— ad X 3.25.5: 216, 356
— ad X 5.3.1: 141, 269
— ad X 5.3.46: 312-13
— ad X 5.19.2: 143-44, 273
— ad X 5.19.4: 151, 287
— ad X 5.19.6: 192, 201, 204, 205, 257, 335, 337, 341, 344, 345, 379
— ad X 5.19.10: 155, 169, 172, 295, 296-97, 313-14
— ad X 5.19.16: 63-64
Summa, X 2.26 *de praescriptionibus*, rubricella *de praescriptione rerum immobilium*: 186, 188, 188-89, 326-27, 331
— X 3.21 *de pignoribus*: 149, 283
— X 5.19 *de usuris*: 86n, 132, 133-134, 134-135, 141, 142, 143, 149, 153-154, 154, 157, 160, 168, 178, 186, 200, 201, 262, 263, 264-65, 270-73, 280, 283-84, 290-91, 293-94, 294, 298, 302, 310, 318-19, 327, 341, 342

Huguccio
Summa ad Decretum Grat. C.10 q.2 c.4, v. *Tantum in suo nomine*: 202, 343

Innocent IV (Sinibaldus Fliscus)
Commentaria ad X 1.2.7: 187-88, 328-29
— ad X 1.3.38: 176, 316
— ad X 2.26.20: 188
— ad X 2.27.18: 174, 315
— ad X 3.25.5: 216, 356
— ad X 5.3.1: 141, 269
— ad X 5.19 rubr.: 143, 273, 286
— ad X 5.19.1: 132, 133, 262, 263
— ad X 5.19.4: 152, 288
— ad X 5.19.6: 161, 192, 193, 194, 201, 204, 205, 244, 257, 303, 335, 336, 337, 341, 345, 370, 379
— ad X 5.19.10: 169, 175, 310-11, 311, 315
— ad X 5.36.8: 188, 329
— ad X 5.39.53: 213, 352

Jesselinus de Cassanis and Guillelmus de Monte Lauduno
Commentaria ad Clem. 5.5.1: 144, 274

Johannes Andreae
Novella ad X 1.3.38,: 176, 316
— ad X 1.3.43: 187, 327
— ad X 2.24.32: 167, 308
— ad X 2.26.5: 189, 331
— ad X 2.27.18: 174, 174-75, 315
— ad X 2.28.18: 174, 315
— ad X 3.12.1: 260, 380
— ad X 3.17.5: 167, 191, 206, 308-9, 333, 345
— ad X 3.21.4: 209, 347
— ad X 3.25.5: 216, 356
— ad X 5.3.1: 141, 269
— ad X 5.3.8: 141, 151, 269, 287
— ad X 5.3.9: 141, 269
— ad X 5.3.21: 141, 269
— ad X 5.3.27: 139, 140, 183, 267, 268, 324
— ad X 5.3.30: 141, 269
— ad X 5.3.42: 141, 269-70
— ad X 5.3.46: 172, 313
— ad X 5.19 rubr.: 143, 150, 273, 286
— ad X 5.19.1: 132, 133, 149, 262, 283
— ad X 5.19.4: 151, 152, 153, 287, 288, 289
— ad X 5.19.6: 161, 192, 195, 201, 204, 205, 206, 243, 246, 257, 302-03, 335, 336, 341, 344, 345, 370, 371, 379
— ad X 5.19.7: 183, 324
— ad X 5.19.10: 155, 158, 168, 169, 173, 175, 295, 296, 299, 310, 311, 313-14, 315
— ad X 5.19.19: 65, 158, 299
— ad VI 3.14.4: 254, 376
— ad VI 5.5.2: 138, 249, 267, 372
— ad VI 5.11.21: 254, 376
— ad VI *de reg. iur.* 2, *Possessor*: 188, 189, 330, 331
— ad VI *de reg. iur.* 4, *Peccatum*: 60n, 132, 139, 141, 143, 144, 145, 146, 147, 150, 153, 164, 166, 168-69, 170, 176, 177, 182, 190, 207, 262, 267-68, 270, 270-71, 274-76, 278, 279, 284-85, 286, 288, 289, 305, 306, 310, 311, 312, 316, 317, 323, 346
— ad VI *de reg. iur.* 86, *Damnum*: 147, 165, 280-81, 307
Additiones in Speculum iuris, in 4.4 *de usuris*, super rubr.: 194, 195, 200, 203, 336, 337, 341, 344
— in 4.4 *de usuris*, v. *Libellus concipitur*: 177, 191, 206, 319, 335, 345

Johannes Calderinus
Repetitio in X 5.19.19: 144-45, 146, 157, 158, 161, 163, 164, 164-65, 165, 274, 276, 276-277, 299, 299-300, 303, 305, 306, 307

Johannes de Fantutiis
Commentaria ad Clem. 3.4.1: 199, 339

Johannes Faventinus
Summa ad C.10 q.2 c.4: 203

John of Legnano
Commentaria ad X 2.26.20: 189
— ad X 3.21.4: 209
— ad X 5.3.46: 169-70, 172, 311, 313
— ad X 5.19.1: 133, 150
— ad X 5.19.5: 153, 288
— ad X 5.19.7: 183, 289, 324
— ad X 5.19.10: 158, 169, 173, 194, 196, 299, 311, 313-14, 336, 337
— ad X 5.19.19: 133, 142, 146,

147, 150, 161, 164, 169, 182, 198, 199, 263, 270, 277, 279, 286, 305, 311
Consilium: 206, 345

Lapo da Castiglionchio
Allegationes, allegatio 137: 81-82, 98, 178, 194, 202, 204, 210, 223, 236, 237, 238, 241, 247, 257, 259, 319, 336, 342, 344, 349, 350, 359-60, 367, 368, 371-72, 379

Laurentius de Pinu
Consilium: 206, 345

Laurentius Hispanus
Apparatus ad Decretum Grat. C.10 q.2 c.4, v. *Tantum in suo nomine*: 202, 343

Lorenzo Ridolfi
Repetitio in Decretum Grat. C.12 q.2 c.52: 199, 339

Repetitio in X 1.3.6: 15
Consilium de usuris: 37n

Oldradus de Ponte
Consilia seu responsa, consilium 207: 204, 344
Consilia et quaestiones, consilium 223: 188, 330

Paulus de Liazariis
Lectura in Clem. 5.5.1, v. *Solvantur usurae*: 170, 175, 311-12, 315

Peter of Ancharano
Quaestio disputata de imprestitis Venetiarum: 71, 82-84, 248, 372

Raymond of Penyafort
Summa de poenitentia, 2.7 *de usuris*: 134, 142, 157, 169, 200, 262, 270, 298, 340, 341

Stephanus Hugonetti
Commentaria ad Clem. 5.5.1: 157, 298

Vincentius Hispanus
Apparatus ad X 2.26.5, v. *Postquam*: 188
— ad X 5.19.10: 296
— ad X 5.19.10, v. *Inducendi*: 173, 314

William Durant
Speculum iuris, 2.3 *de executione sententiae*: 213, 352
—, 4.4 *de usuris*: 158, 299

C. *Corpus iuris civilis*

Institutiones
3.14.pr.: 57, 57n, 142, 147, 270, 278
3.14.2: 57n
3.24: 57n
4.1.3: 320
4.1.5: 320

Digest
1.3.29: 369
1.3.30: 207, 345
2.8.1: 179, 320-21
2.14.7.4: 185, 325
2.14.27.4: 185, 325
3.4.1.2: 351

3.5.22: 163, 305
3.6.2: 180, 321
4.4.16.4: 192, 197, 335, 338
5.3.20.11: 272
5.3.25.11: 156, 190, 298, 332
5.3.51.1: 264
6.1.6: 169, 311
6.1.15.2: 213, 329, 352
6.1.15.3: 272
6.1.77: 182, 324
7.1.20: 199, 339
7.1.27.3: 212-13, 352
8.3.18: 233, 365
8.4.13.1: 213, 352
8.6.10: 233, 365
12.1.2.2: 147, 278
12.1.5: 272
12.1.6: 169, 250, 311, 374
12.1.11: 207, 346
12.1.15: 177, 317
12.1.19: 207, 346
12.4.8: 252, 375
12.6.1: 163, 180-81, 305, 322
12.6.26.3: 185, 306, 326
13.6.5.3-5,8,9: 57n
13.7.6: 272
13.7.7: 272
13.7.9.3: 178, 179, 318, 321
13.7.12: 155, 297
13.7.43.1: 212, 352
16.1.8.8: 239, 346, 369
16.3.7.2: 134, 264
17.1.10.3: 272
17.2.60: 62n, 148, 272, 281
18.1.1: 196, 199, 337-38, 340
18.1.32: 196, 338
18.1.81.1: 199, 339
18.2.6: 347
18.4: 196, 198, 240, 338, 339
18.4.1.8: 338
18.4.1.20: 338
18.6.13: 212, 352
19.1.13.26: 193, 302, 335
19.1.21.3: 148, 281
22.1.2: 272
22.1.3.4: 264
22.1.6: 272
22.1.13: 155, 297
22.1.17.8: 264
22.1.21: 272
22.1.32.2: 272
22.1.38.4: 180, 321-22
22.1.38.7: 272
22.1.38.8: 272
22.1.38.10: 272
22.2.5: 271-72
22.3.25.pr.: 181, 182, 190, 322, 323, 332
23.3.41: 185, 325
23.3.49: 177, 317
24.1.3.12: 177, 317
24.1.5.5: 239, 369
30.47.6: 272
31.84: 272
32.1.69: 180, 321
33.1.21.pr.: 199, 339
34.3.6: 253, 375-76
35.2.63.pr.: 303
35.2.68: 201, 341
35.2.82: 162, 304
36.1.1.16: 162, 304
40.7.1: 252, 375
40.7.2: 252, 253, 375
41.3.32.pr.: 179, 319-20
42.1.4.2: 352-53
42.5.37: 329
43.16.1: 179, 320
43.26.1.pr.: 320
43.26.6.3: 179, 320
44.7.44.1: 280
45.1.114: 272
45.1.137.2: 190, 225, 229, 333, 360, 362
46.1.42: 196, 199, 205, 337, 340, 345
46.3.54: 185, 325

46.3.72.1: 272
46.3.79: 177, 317
46.3.85: 272
46.3.95.4: 185, 325, 326
47.2: 179, 320
47.2.52.29: 162, 304
47.2.57: 320
47.2.93: 320
50.4.6.5: 213, 352
50.16.22: 180, 321
50.16.24: 94-95n, 338
50.16.75: 180, 321
50.16.81: 180, 321
50.16.94: 181, 322
50.16.176: 185, 325
50.17.53: 163, 305
50.17.56: 351
50.17.174: 351

Glossa ordinaria to the *Digest*
ad Prooem. II, const. *Omnem*, v. *Sanctionem*: 188, 329
ad 1.3.29, v. *Prohibet*: 239, 369
ad 3.4.1.2, v. *Proconsul*: 212, 351-52
ad 6.1.77, v. *Sufficiebat*: 182, 324
ad 7.1.20, v. *Legatus esset*: 199
ad 12.1.6, v. *An uocabulis*: 250, 374
ad 12.6.26.2, v. *Indebitum*: 165, 190, 306, 332
ad 19.1.13.26, v. *Excedit*: 160, 302
ad 34.3.6, v. *Ius eius*: 253, 376
ad 35.2.63.pr., v. *Funguntur*: 304
ad 42.5.37, v. *Sua*: 188, 329

Code
1.2.10: 192, 335
1.18.10: 326
2.3.27: 251, 374
2.47.1.pr.: 180, 322
3.28.35.1: 217, 356
4.22: 239, 369
4.32.15: 282
4.32.26: 193, 335
4.32.26.2: 273
4.39: 192, 335
4.44.2: 161, 303
4.44.18: 161
4.49.5: 160, 272, 301, 302
4.51.7: 198-99, 339
4.54.2: 193, 335
4.54.6: 193, 335
6.2: 179, 320
6.2.11: 320
6.38.4: 166, 307, 372
6.38.4.1: 248
6.49.7.pr.: 166, 307
6.49.7: 248, 372
7.37.3: 330
8.11.12: 212, 351
8.33.2: 134, 264
8.37.1: 272
8.53.3: 252, 374-75
8.53.28: 207, 346
8.54.4: 208, 346
9.12: 179, 320
9.12.8: 320
9.51.1: 180, 322
10.19.1: 212, 351
10.48.8: 212, 351
Excerptum Nov. 6.1=Auth. 1.6: 273
Excerptum Nov. 61.1 = Auth. 62 coll. 5.14 post C. 4.29.21: 182, 323-24
Excerptum Nov. 34.1 = Auth. 36 coll. 4.5 post C. 4.32.16: 134, 264
Excerptum Nov. 7.pr. = Auth. 7 coll. 2.1 post C. 4.35.23: 192
Excerptum Nov. 83.1 = Auth. 6.11: 273
Excerptum Nov. 89.2 = Auth. 7.1 coll. 2.1: 213, 352

Glossa ordinaria to the *Code*
ad 1.18.10, v. *Cum quis*: 185, 326
ad 2.3.27, casus: 207, 346
ad 4.32.15, v. *Vltra*: 148, 282
ad 4.49.5, v. *Ratio*: 160, 302
ad 7.37.3, v. *Omnia principis*: 188, 329
ad excerptum Nov. 89.2=Auth. 7.1 coll. 2.1, v. *Persoluat*: 213, 352

Novellae Iustiniani
131: 286

D. Civilians

Baldus de Ubaldis
Commentaria in C. 1.1.1: 146, 147, 149, 278, 279-80, 284
— in C. 3.28.12: 201, 341-42
— in C. 4.32.rubr.: 159-60, 241, 301, 370
— in C. 4.32.14: 201, 342
— in C. 4.32.15: 148, 148-49, 154, 282, 291
— in C. 4.32.19: 148, 282
— in Dig. 6.1.15: 188, 329
— in Dig. 19.1.13.26: 160, 302
— in Dig. 31.1.88.15: 198, 339
— in Dig. 41.3.29: 182, 324
— in Dig. 42.1.4.2: 213, 353
— in Dig. 42.5.37: 188, 329-30
— in Dig. 45.1.68: 148, 282
— in Dig. 45.1.122.6: 253, 375-76
Consilia, quaestiones et tractatus, consilium 180: 213, 351

Bartolus of Sassoferrato
Commentaria in Dig. Prooem. II, const. *Omnem*: 188, 329

Cino of Pistoia
Commentaria in C. 3.28.12: 200, 341, 342, 343

E. Bible

Dt 23.19-20: 155, 296
Iob 28.2: 316
Ps 43.22: 232
Prv 20.11: 308
Prv 30.33: 138, 156, 267, 297
Ier 41.7-8: 151, 286
Ez 18.8-17: 155, 296
Os 8.12: 308
Mt 17.23-26: 103
Mt 22.21: 103n
Mc 1.7: 228
Mc 14.8: 314
Lc 6.35: 56, 76, 85, 155, 158, 161, 168, 268, 269, 295, 302, 309, 312
Lc 12.16: 273, 310
Io 1.27: 228
Io 11.50: 217
Io 18.14: 217
Rm 2.16: 173
1 Cor 3.11: 233, 364
1 Cor 5.6: 176
1 Cor 5.6-8: 176
1 Cor 11.14: 139

1 Cor 13.2-3: 234, 366
1 Cor 14.25: 232
Gal 5.26: 366
Gal 6.7: 70, 223
1 Tim 3.1: 235, 366
Hbr 7.12: 363

F. Classical Authors

Aristotle
Ethica Nicomachea 1.2.1094b6-10: 68n, 219, 358
— 1.7.1097a18-23: 235, 366
— 4.1.1121b,: 278
— 5.4.1132b10-15: 136, 265, 278
— 8.1.1155a5-10: 223, 359
Politica 1.9.1257a-b: 276, 278

Cicero
De natura deorum 3.84: 163, 305
Oratio Philippica 2.44.112: 216, 355

Livy
Ab urbe condita 4.59.11-60.2: 217, 356-57

Ovid
Heroides 2.85: 235, 366-67

Valerius Maximus
Factorum et dictorum memorabilium 1.1, ext. 3: 163, 305
— 2.8.3, 4.4.1: 217, 357

G. Medieval Authors

Alexander Lombard
Tractatus de usuris: 65

Ambrose
De Tobia 3.9: 224

Augustine
Confessiones 1.4: 216, 356
De ciuitate Dei 1.16: 167, 309
— 19.19: 366
Epistula 211.12: 68n, 103, 219, 358

Pseudo-Bernard of Clairvaux
Epistola ad Raymundum dominum Castri Ambruosii: 164, 306

Domenico Pantaleoni
Tractatus de monte communi: 71, 78-79

Francesco da Empoli
Questio de monte: 70, 73-75, 210, 223, 242, 244, 245, 247, 349, 360, 369-70, 371

Gerard of Siena
Tractatus de usuris et de prescriptionibus, q.1, art.2: 144, 270, 274, 275, 276, 278, 279, 311-12, 331

Gregory of Rimini
Tractatus de imprestantiis Venetorum et de usura: 68, 210, 349
Tractatus, proemium: 218, 358

—, art. 1: 86, 132, 135, 172, 186-87, 220, 263, 265-66, 267, 312, 327
—, art. 2: 146, 220, 277-78
—, art. 3: 68-70, 79-80, 140, 172, 217, 218, 219, 220, 222, 237, 246, 268, 313, 331, 358-60, 367, 368, 369, 371
—, art. 4: 69, 140, 164, 221, 268, 305, 358-59

Guido de Belloreguardo
Consilium de monte: 67, 79, 214, 249, 354, 373

Jerome
Epistola 121.6: 155, 296
Commentarius in epistolam ad Galatas 3, in *Gal* 5.14, 5.26: 234-35, 366

John Klenkock
Consilium de monte: 67, 79, 218

Nicholas de Anglia
Questio disputata de imprestitis Venetorum: 71, 80-81, 224, 360

Peter John Olivi
Tractatus de emptionibus et venditionibus, de usuris, de restitutionibus: 64
Quodlibet 1, qq. 16-17: 64n

Petrarch
Rerum Senilium liber XIII.I: 216, 355

Piero degli Strozzi
Tractatus super casu de monte communi: 70-71, 75-78

Thomas Aquinas
Summa theologiae, II-II, q.78, art. 1: 60, 276, 278-79
—, II-II, q.78, art. 2: 65
—, II-II, q.78, art. 4: 150, 286

General Index

accaffinitas, contract, 126, 131
accattum (compulsory loan), 92, 226, 230-32. *See also prestanza; prestanziati; prestanzone*
Alberti bank, 46
Albizzi: family, 51; Maso degli, politician, 49, 50n105
Alexander V, pope, 26
Alexander Lombard, theologian: on *lucrum cessans*, 65
Ambrosius de Vignate, theologian, 111
Ammirato, Scipione, 23
annuity (*census, redditus, rente, ubbia*), contract, 82-83, 192-209, 335-48; approved by popes, 99; criteria of licitness, 82, 192-96, 335-37; government, 98-99, 199, 257-60, 339-40, 378-80; public debt credits as, 80-84; as purchase-sale contract, 80-81, 82-83, 192-93, 197, 204, 334-36, 338, 344; redemption provision in, 99, 196-97, 204-6, 209, 258-59, 337-38, 344-45, 347-48, 379. *See also precaria*
antidotum. See donum
Antonino (Antonio di ser Niccolò Pierozzi), archbishop of Florence and theologian, 27, 111
Antonius de Butrio, canonist, 65, 103n10; on compulsory loans, 88n14
Aristotle: on common good, 68n59, 103, 219, 358; on commutative justice, 74n83, 278; on exchange, 3-4n7, 136, 265, 276, 278; on the good, 235, 366; on liberality, 223, 278, 359
Astesanus, theologian: on compulsory loans, 73n80
Augustine, 167, 216, 309, 356; on common good, 103, 219, 358
Azo, civilian: coins substantive *interesse*, 62

Baldus de Ubaldis. *See* Ubaldis, Baldus de
Barbadoro, Bernardino, 29n2
Bardi: bank, 29; Nanna di Niccolò de', wife of Lorenzo Ridolfi, 19n45; Tommaso di Piero di messer Rodolfo de', merchant, 41
Barducci, Roberto, 29n2, 44n75
baroccolum, contract, 125, 131
Baron, Hans, 3, 104-6
Baroni, Piero di Vannozzo, 40
Bartolomeo da San Concordio, theologian, 73n80
Bartolus of Sassoferrato, civilian, 71-72n71, 252-53, 375-76; on *collecta*, 87, 212-13, 351-53; on delay, 160, 302; on private property, 87-88, 188, 329-30
Barucci, Caterina di Angelo, wife of Lorenzo Ridolfi, 19n45
Becker, Marvin B., 8n3, 26n80, 31n18
Bellomo, Manlio, 17n39
Bernard of Clairvaux, 89, 104, 164, 216, 306, 356
Bernardino of Siena, theologian, 66n51; dependence on Ridolfi, 3n5, 111; on incredibility thesis, 84n123; on patriotism, 103n10; on public debt market, 80n80
Bernardus Compestellanus Antiquus,

canonist: on borrowing at usury, 151, 287
bill of exchange. *See cambium*
Black, Antony, 102-3n9
Boccaccio, Giovanni, humanist, 107
Bonaventure, theologian, 356
Boniface IX, pope, 25
bonum commune. *See* common good
bonum publicum. *See* common good
bonum rei publicae. *See* common good
brokers. *See* public debt brokers
Brown, Alison, 9-10n6, 107n26
Brucker, Gene A., 9-10n6, 10n7, 11n9, 12n12, 22, 22-23n59, 26n80, 31n18, 40, 41n66, 45n81, 50n105, 108
Bruni, Leonardo, humanist, 104-5, 122n27

Caesar, Julius, 104
Caferro, William, 56n11
Calderinus, Gasparus, canonist, 14; Johannes, canonist: on *collecta*, 158, 299-300; on gift, 157, 299; on intention, 163-66, 305-7; on just price, 161-62, 303-4; on *lucrum cessans*, 65; on speculative credit sales, 158, 299-300; on usury prohibition, 144-45, 146, 274, 276-77
Callistus III, pope: approves annuity, 99
cambium (exchange), contract, 59, 61n31, 125, 131, 309
canonical usury, interest title, 148, 281
capitale: investment capital, 64, 241, 308, 336, 358, 359, 360, 369; principal of a loan, 165, 166, 205, 210, 213, 224, 230
Castiglionchio: family, 51; Lapo da, canonist, 14, 68n58; on annuity, 98, 202, 257, 342-43, 379; on *monte dell'uno due* and *monte dell'uno tre*, 81-82, 223, 349, 359-60; on public debt market, 81-82, 94, 236-41, 367-69; on restitution, 178, 232, 319, 367; Ridolfi's dependence on, 87, 93, 210, 349
catasto (fiscal census) of 1427, 12-13n14, 41-42n67, 45n78, 100, 103n12. *See also estimo*; *prestanza*; *prestanziati*
Cavallar, Osvaldo, 16n30, 17-18n39
census. *See* annuity
Centueri, Guglielmo, theologian, 66; on compulsory loans, 70n67; on incredibility thesis, 84n123; on public debt market, 80
charity, 101. *See also* poverty
Charles IV, emperor, 34
Cicero, 89n16, 216n30, 355
Cino of Pistoia, civilian: on annuity, 200-201, 341
Ciompi (textile workers), 12, 13, 34n32; burden of *prestanze* on, 42-45, 51-52; elite fear of, 50-51; fiscal programme of, 45-46, 68; guild of, 10n8; revolt in 1378, 11-12. *See also* poverty; *sottoposti*; wages
civic humanism, 3, 104-5; as elite ideology, 107-10
collecta (corporate levy), 87, 158, 212-13, 299-300, 351-53
Colli, Vincenzo, 116
comitatus. *See contado*
commodatum (loan for use), contract, 57, 279
common good (*bonum commune*, *bonum publicum*, *bonum rei publicae*), 67, 89, 102-4, 214, 215, 231, 354-55
commune, council of, legislative assembly, 11, 46; opposes war *prestanze*, 47, 49
communis opinio (consensus opinion), 19, 86, 98, 138, 146, 189, 267, 278, 298, 330, 331
community of goods, 168, 310
compulsory loan. *See accattum*, *monte comune*, *prestanza*, *prestanziati*, *prestanzone*

condictio, action, 175, 315
condottieri (mercenaries), 29, 31n15, 126
Conservatori delle leggi (Defenders of the Laws), magistracy, 25
consilium: legal genre, 18-19, 37n45, 184, 188, 204, 206, 213, 325, 344, 345, 351; theological genre, 67, 126, 214, 249n33, 354, 373
Consolidated Stock of the Nation (British public debt), 99n47
Constitutiones Clementinae, canonical collection, 14, 15, 60
consulta (advisory council), 22-23, 24, 26, 47, 68, 106, 108. *See also* leadership elite; new men; patriciate; regime; *Signoria*
contado (county), 41-42, 210, 350
Conti, Elio, 23, 24n66, 106
Corbinelli: family, 13; Angelo, merchant, 38-39
Corsini: family, 13; Filippo, civilian, 19n43
credits (*credita*) in *monte comune*, 36, 44, 56, 66, 67, 87, 89, 212, 351, 357, 358, 379; alienability of, 30, 210-11, 236-57, 350, 367-78; derivative uses of, 38-39; description of interest on, 54-55, 65, 210-11, 349-50; immunity of owners from prosecution, 54-55, 210-11, 350; interest rates on, 30-35, 38n49, 46, 55, 70, 91, 92, 93, 210, 213-14, 231, 349-50, 353-54, 363; market value of, 32-34, 74-75, 76-77; ownership of, 37-38, 40-41, 51-52, 77-78, 91, 100, 110, 210-11, 229-30, 349-50, 362; redemption of, 30, 33-34, 46, 211, 350; speculation in, 32-33, 37, 40-41, 51, 72-84, 93-97, 236-57, 367-78; suspension of interest payments on, 33, 47, 68; in testament, 37, 38-39, 211, 350. *See also accattum*; *monte comune*; *monte dei cinque per cento interi*; *monte dell'uno due*; *monte dell'uno tre*; *monte libero dell' uno due*; *prestanza*; *prestanziati*; *prestanzone*
credit sale. *See* sale

damages. *See damnum*
Damasus, canonist: on borrowing at usury, 151, 213, 287-88
damnum (damages), interest title, 62, 81, 148; public debt interest as, 54-55, 65, 70, 210-11, 216, 221-23, 230-32, 355, 358-59, 361, 362
damnum emergens (damages incurred), interest title, 63, 65, 284
Datini, Francesco, merchant, 48, 49, 92n21
Davies, Jonathan, 15n28
Debt Officials. *See Ufficiali del monte*
Decretals of Gregory IX, canonical collection, 14, 58, 59
Decretum, canonical collection, 14, 15, 16, 58
Defenders of the Laws. *See Conservatori delle leggi*
de la Roncière, Charles-M., 32n19
delay. *See mora*
del Bene, Francesco di Jacopo, wool merchant, 40; Ricciardo di Francesco, civilian, 16, 20
della Scala, Mastino, lord of Verona, 33
de Roover, Raymond, 61nn31
Dieci di Balìa (Ten of War), magistracy, 24
Dietsalvi family, 51
Dino of Mugello, canonist: on restitution, 177-78, 317, 319
Diplovatatius, Thomas, 14, 17
distretto (district), 41-42, 210, 211, 350
Dominicans, Florentine, 78n95
donum (gift), 170-71, 207-8, 312, 345-46; interest title, 62, 87, 135-41,

265-70, 284; public debt interest as, 54, 55, 71, 75, 76, 79, 90, 91, 210-11, 216, 227-28, 234, 235-36, 361-62, 367; return-gift (*antidotum*), 87, 156-57, 175-77, 190, 298-99, 316
dotal pledge, interest title, 62, 149, 241, 282-83, 284, 370
do ut facias (I give that you may do), innominate contract, 97, 205, 207, 251, 254, 345, 346, 374, 377
dubium, scholastic genre, 211, 349, 350-51
Duns Scotus, John, theologian: on *damnum emergens*, 63n41
Duodici Buonuomini (Twelve Good Men), magistracy, 11, 23
Durant, William, canonist: on *collecta*, 213, 352-53; on government loans, 158, 299

Edward III, king of England, 29
Eight of Police. *See Otto di Guardia*
Eighty-One. *See Ottantuno*
electoral procedures, 20-22, 104-7. *See also* guilds; leadership elite; new men; officeholders; patriciate; regime; *Signoria*
emptio et venditio. *See* sale
Enemy, interest title, 283-84
estimo (fiscal census), 29; basis of taxes on the *contado*, 41-42n67; basis of urban tax and *prestanza* assessments, 41, 42-43n71; reintroduction proposed, 46, 68. *See also catasto*; *monte comune*; *prestanza*; *prestanziati*; property tax
Eugenius IV, pope, 83-84n122
exchange. *See cambium*

Fantutiis, Johannes de, canonist, 14
fenus (usury), 57, 271; *fenus nauticum* (sea loan), 59, 271-72, 307. *See also mutuum*; usurer; usury
fideiussor (guarantor), interest title, 147-48, 221, 280-81, 307, 358-59
Florence: population in 1427, 21n51; university of, 15-17
Francesco da Empoli, theologian, 72, 78, 110, 126; on compulsory loans, 70, 223, 360; on maritime insurance, 75; on public debt market, 73-75, 79n101, 94, 95, 95n30, 96n34, 244, 247-48, 371, 372; Ridolfi's dependence on, 87, 93, 210, 349
Franciscans, Florentine, 78n95
fraus (fraud): *de contractu ad contractum* (from contract to contract), 94, 197, 205, 207, 239-40, 256, 258, 345, 369; presumed, 98, 160, 190-91, 193-95, 197, 199, 206, 207-8, 209, 256-57, 258-60, 302, 309, 333-35, 335-37, 338, 339, 345, 346, 347-48, 378, 379-80; types of, 345-46. *See also mutuum*; sale; usury
fungibles: defined, 57; subject of loans, 142-43, 144-46, 270-71, 274-79. *See also mutuum*; usury
furtum. *See* theft

gabelles (consumption taxes), 32, 41, 46, 50; fund public debt, 30, 31, 34; social effects of, 44-45, 77-78, 100
Galassi, Francesco, 61n31
Genoa, 49, 108, 350; public debt controversy, 66n52, 73n80
gente nuova. *See* new men
Gerard of Siena, theologian: on intention, 170-71, 190, 311-12, 332; on prescription, 331; on usury and natural law, 60, 144-47, 274-79
Giacomo da Milano, theologian, 356
Giani, Gherardino di Niccolò Gherardini, 41
gift. *See donum*
Giugni, Domenico, 48
Gonfaloniere della Giustizia (Standard-Bearer of Justice), magistracy, 11, 12n13, 24. *See also* electoral pro-

cedures; officeholders; regime; *Signoria*
Gonzaga, Francesco, lord of Mantua, 23
Gottofredo da Trani, canonist: defines usury, 132, 133, 143, 262, 263-64, 271; on etymology of usury, 141, 270; on gift, 157, 298; on intention, 86, 135, 156, 265, 298; on interest titles, 143, 147-49, 272, 280-83; on loan as locus of usury, 134, 142, 160, 161, 264, 270, 301, 302-3; on *Lc* 6.35 as divine precept, 168, 310; on *parabola*, 295-96; on penalties of usurers, 153, 154, 289, 291-92; on *precaria*, 200, 340-41; on prescription, 188; usury permitted by no law, 149-50, 284
Gramsci, Antonio, 5, 106-7, 109
grandi. *See* patricians
Gratian, canonist, 95; defines usury, 58, 59, 132, 133, 262, 263
Great Schism, 23, 26
Gregory XI, pope: Florentine war with, 35, 43
Gregory XII, pope, 26, 49
Gregory of Rimini, theologian: on compulsory loans, 68-70; defines usury, 132, 133, 135-41, 172, 263, 265-68, 312; on intention, 68, 86, 89-90, 103n10, 135-41, 164, 218-23, 265-68, 305, 358-59; on intention of legislators, 68-69, 90-91, 219-23, 358-59; on *lucrum cessans*, 65; on public debt market, 79, 94, 96, 237-40, 246-47, 367-79, 371-72; Ridolfi's dependence on, 68, 87, 210, 349; on usury prohibition, 146, 277-78
guarantor. *See fideiussor*
Guelf Society, 9, 13, 41n66. *See also* magnate; patriciate
Guicciardini, Caterina di Luigi, wife of Lorenzo Ridolfi, 19n45; Francesco, civilian, 16n30, 17-18n39
Guidi, Guidubaldo, 11n9
Guido de Baysio, canonist: on borrowing at usury, 150-51, 286-87; on gift, 157, 299; on intention, 172, 312-13; on penalties of usurers, 138, 153, 267, 289; on *precaria*, 200-201, 340-42; on private property, 188, 330; on restitution, 172, 178, 188, 312-13, 318, 330
Guido de Belloreguardo, theologian, 126; on compulsory loans, 67-68, 88, 104, 214-15, 354; on public debt market, 79, 249, 373; Ridolfi's dependence on, 87
guild of judges and notaries. *See* lawyers.
guilds, 10-11. Major guilds, 29-30; composition of 9; dominance of 11, 21; in regime of 1378-82, 12. Minor guilds: oppose war *prestanze*, 47, 49-52, 102; in regime of 1343-48, 31-32; in regime of 1378-1382, 12; in regime of 1382-1434, 21-22. Textile workers' guilds: created 1378, 12; suppressed 1382, 21. *See also* Ciompi; new men; patriciate; *popolo*; *sottoposti*
Guillelmus Redonensis, canonist: on gift, 138, 266-67

Hankins, James, 3n6
Hay, Douglas, 109n39, 110
hegemony: defined, 106-7; and law 109-10
Helmholz, R. H., 61n30
Henderson, John, 101n4
Herlihy, David, 20n47, 21n51, 42-43n71
Hostiensis (Henricus de Segusio), canonist: on annuity, 82, 98, 192-93, 204, 335-36, 344; on borrowing at usury, 151, 287; on credit sales, 299; defines usury, 132, 133-35, 143, 263, 264-65, 271; on delay,

160, 302; on detection of usurers, 153-54, 167, 290-91, 308-9; on etymology of usury, 141, 270; on gift, 157, 298; on intention, 86, 135, 155-56, 168, 172-73, 265, 295-97, 310, 312-14; on interest titles, 61-62, 143, 149-50, 271-73, 283-84; on loan as locus of usury, 134, 264; on *lucrum cessans*, 63-64; on *parabola*, 155, 295-96; on penalties of usurers, 154, 291-92, 293-94; on *precaria*, 200-201, 341-42; on prescription, 186, 188, 331; on restitution, 172-73, 178, 312-14, 318-19; usury permitted by no law, 143, 149-50, 273, 284
Huguccio, canonist: on borrowing at usury, 150-51, 286; on *precaria*, 202, 343; on prescription, 331
Hunt, Alan, 109n37
Hunt, Edwin S., 29n5

imprestitum (Venetian compulsory loan), 84, 248
incredibility thesis, 83-84
Innocent IV (Sinibaldus Fliscus), pope and canonist: on annuity, 82, 98, 192-94, 201, 204, 244, 335-36, 341, 344, 370-71; on borrowing at usury, 152-53, 288; on *collecta*, 213, 352; defines usury, 132, 133, 262, 263; on gift, 133, 141, 263, 269; on intention, 169, 310-11; on just price, 161, 303; on *lucrum cessans*, 64; on prescription, 188, 330; on private property, 187-88, 328-29; on restitution, 169, 310-11; on sale of time, 95n32; on social effects of usury, 58, 143-44, 273-74
insurance, mercantile, 75, 76, 125-26
intention. *See* usury
interesse (compensation), interest title, 62-63, 64, 148-49, 222, 272, 281-82, 284, 301-2; public debt interest as, 54, 55, 56, 65, 70, 71, 73, 75, 77, 81, 89, 91, 92, 93, 94, 96, 100, 110, 228, 231, 234, 253, 210-11, 223, 349, 359, 374. *See also* credits; *monte comune*; usury

Johannes Andreae, canonist, 14; on annuity, 82, 98, 192-96, 203, 204, 335-37, 344; on borrowing at usury, 151-53, 287-88; on *collecta*, 158, 299; defines usury, 132, 133, 262, 263; on detection of usurers, 166-67, 308-9, 317-18; on gift, 133, 139, 140, 141, 263, 267-68, 269-70; on intention, 155-56, 163-64, 168-72, 173-75, 175, 175-77, 190-91, 295-97, 305, 310-13, 313-15, 315, 316, 317, 319, 332, 333, 335; on interest titles, 147-48, 149, 165, 280-81, 283, 307; on loan as locus of usury, 143, 270-71; on *lucrum cessans*, 65; on *parabola*, 155, 296; on penalties of usurers, 153, 289; on *precaria*, 200, 341; on prescription, 188, 330, 331; reports Gerard of Siena, 60n28, 144-47, 170-72, 189-90, 274-79, 311-12, 331, 332; on restitution, 138, 168-72, 173-75, 175, 175-77, 177, 182-83, 267, 310-13, 313-15, 315, 316, 317-18, 319, 323-24; on social effects of usury, 143-44, 273; on speculative credit sales, 158, 161, 299, 302-3; on usury and civil law, 150, 285-86; on usury and natural law, 144-47, 150, 274-79, 285-86; usury permitted by no law, 150, 284-85
Johannes Calderinus. *See* Calderinus, Johannes
Johannes Faventinus, canonist: on *precaria*, 203
John of Legnano, canonist, 14; on annuity, 194, 196-99, 206-9, 336, 337-40, 345-48; on *collecta*, 158, 299-

300; on gift, 133, 263; on intention, 163-64, 169-70, 172, 173, 305, 311, 313, 313-14; on just price, 161; on loan as locus of usury, 142-43, 270; on penalties of usurers, 153, 289; on prescription, 189; on speculative credit sales, 158, 299; on usury and natural law, 146, 277
Jones, Philip, 37
just price, 74-75, 95-96, 161-62, 202-3, 257-58, 303-4, 342-43, 368, 379

Kent, Dale, 41n65, 89n17, 111n47
Kent, Francis W., 41n65
Kirshner, Julius, 3-4n7, 29n2, 45-46n81, 53n1, 66-67n52, 68n58, 71n68, 71-72n71, 77, 77n92, 78n95, 83-84n122, 84n123, 88n14, 93, 109n36, 115n17, 126, 216n30, 372
Klapisch-Zuber, Christiane, 12-13n14, 20n47, 41-42n16,
Klenkock, John, theologian, 126; on compulsory loans, 67, 218; on public debt market, 79
Kuehn, Thomas, 3-4n7

Ladislaus, king of Naples, 24, 25
laesio enormis. *See* just price
Langholm, Odd, 3-4n7, 56n13, 274, 275
Lateran Council, Third: anti-usury measures, 57n20, 60, 291-93
Laurentius de Pinu, canonist, 14, 15; on annuity, 206-9, 345-47
Laurentius Hispanus, canonist: adopts substantive *interesse*, 62; on *precaria*, 202, 343
law: civil, 150, 285-86; common (*ius commune*), 17n39, 87, 328; history of, 3-4, 109; ideological function of, 109-10; natural, 60, 144-47, 150, 274-80, 284-86; pentateuchal, 296; relative autonomy of, 109
lawyers: class origins of, 13-14, 19-20; on compulsory loans, 71, 71-72n71; as diplomats, 25; education, 14-15; guild of judges and notaries, 10n8, 17, 18, 261; ideological function, 110; incomes, 19-20; professional activities, 17-19; prominence in regime of 1382-1434, 7; on public debt market, 81
leadership elite: coopt new men, 20-22, 22n57, 107, 110; hegemony threatened, 1-2, 47, 50-51; social composition of, 21-23, 105-6. *See also consulta*; electoral procedures; new men; patriciate; *pratica*; regime
Lears, T. J. Jackson, 106-7
lease and hire. *See locatio et conductio*
Le Goff, Jacques, 4
Lesnick, Daniel R., 78n95
lex commissaria, interest title, 283
Liber sextus, canonical collection, 14, 15, 60
Livy, 104, 217, 356-57
loan. *See mutuum*
locatio et conductio (lease and hire), contract, 57, 136, 149, 266, 279, 282
Lombard. *See* moneylender
Lopez, Roberto S., 8n3
Lucca, 33: Florentine treaty with, 49
lucrum cessans (profit forgone), interest title, 63-65, 66, 69, 90, 91, 228, 284
Lyons, Second Council of: anti-usury measures, 60, 292-93

magnates, social group, 8-9, 13, 29
Malatesta, Carlo, governor of Romagna, 25
Marks, L. F., 37n46
Martin V, pope: approves annuity, 99
Martines, Lauro, 3-4n7, 5n9, 8n3, 13, 19-20n46, 23n65, 25, 107n28
Martino, Federico, 19n43, 37n45,

115n17, 199n32
Massaccio, painter, 103
McLaughlin, T. P., 56n13
Medici: bank, 46; Cosimo de', 24, 25
Mercanzia (merchant tribunal), 9; *Offitiales super illicitis contractibus* (commission on illicit contracts), 125n41
mercenaries. *See condottieri*
merchants: and usury prohibition, 60-61, 63-64, 69, 77, 101n5, 123, 125-26, 228, 264, 273, 295, 368, 370-71
Milan, 23, 41; Florentine wars with, 1390-1404, 1-2, 23, 24, 25, 46-50, 88, 104-5; 1423-26, 24, 38n49; 1436-40, 24
miserabili (destitute), 42, 101. *See also* poverty
Misericordia, charitable fraternity, 36
Molho, Anthony, 5n9, 11n9, 21n51, 103n12, 111n47
moneylender, 86, 155, 296; penalties for, 60-61, 124-25. *See also* usurer; usury
mons novissimus. See monte comune
mons novus. See monte dell'uno due and *monte dell'uno tre*
mons vetus. See monte comune
monte comune (public debt), 15n27, 40, 37, 38n49, 39n55, 40, 42, 44, 55, 86, 90, 96, 97, 100, 109, 111, 210, 211, 212, 236, 237, 246, 251, 257, 259, 350, 351, 353, 367, 373, 374, 378; controversies over, 1-2, 4-5, 41-42, 45-46, 47-52, 53, 65-84, 87, 88-89, 93-95, 98, 102-3, 110, 123, 131, 210-60, 262, 349-80; corruption in administration of, 35-36; establishment of in 1343-45, 28-33, 213, 250; non-citizens invest in, 83-84n122, 350; novelty of, 31; pope guarantor of, 32; reformed in 1381, 46, 82, 213-14, 349, 354; size in 1343, 29, in 1350-58, 34n29, in 1381, 46, in 1407 and 1425, 50n107; voluntary loans to, 33-34, 46, 67, 95, 242, 370. *See also* credits
monte dei cinque per cento interi, 38n49, 92n23
monte dei prestanzoni, 38n49
monte delle doti (Dowry Fund), 39
monte dell'uno due (two-for-one *monte*), 35, 46, 213-14, 349-50, 353-54, 379
monte dell'uno tre (three-for-one *monte*), 34-35, 40, 46, 53, 213-14, 349-50, 353-54, 379
monte di Pisa, 38n49
monte libero dell'uno due, 35n38
monte vecchio. See monte comune
mora (delay), interest title, 62-63, 148, 160, 281, 301-2
Morelli, Giovanni, chronicler, 49
Moulakis, Athanasios, 27
Munro, John H., 36n40, 99n47
mutuum (loan): defined, 57; locus of usury, 2, 56-58, 59, 61, 65-66, 86, 109, 134, 142-43, 264, 270-71. *See also* fungibles; usury

Najemy, John M., 5n9, 8n3, 12n13, 22n57, 31-32n18, 107
Naples, 24, 25, 29
new men, social group, 10, 13, 21, 50; coopted by leadership elite, 20-22, 105-7, 110; create *monte comune*, 31-32; and Franciscans, 78n95; as *monte* speculators 36, 51, 77, 78; oppose war *prestanze*, 1-2, 47, 49-52, 102; political privileges restricted, 10n7, 51n111. *See also* electoral procedures; guilds; leadership elite; officeholders; patriciate; *popolo*; regime
Nicea, First Council of: anti-usury measures, 57n20, 286, 297
Nicholas V, pope: approves annuity, 99
Nicholas de Anglia, theologian: on

compulsory loans, 71, 88n14, 223-24, 360; on patriotism, 103n10; on public debt credits as *redditus*, 81; on public debt market, 80-81
Noonan, John T., 2-3, 56n13, 93, 95n32, 274, 275

officeholders, 1382-1434, 20-22, 21n51, 50-51, 105-6. *See also* electoral procedures; leadership elite; new men; patriciate; *Signoria*
Officers of Decency. *See Ufficiali dell' Onestà*
Officials for the liquidation of the debt. *See Ufficiali alla diminuzione del monte*
Officials of the University. *See Ufficiali dello Studio*
Offitiales super illicitis contractibus. *See Mercanzia*
Oldradus de Ponte, canonist: on annuity, 83n120, 204-5, 344; on private property, 188, 330
oligarchs. *See* leadership elite, patriciate
Olivi, Peter John, theologian: on *damnum emergens*, 63n41; on *lucrum cessans*, 64
Ordinances of Justice, constitutional statute, 10
Orsanmichele, charitable fraternity, 36, 38, 101
Ottantuno (Eighty-One), magistracy, 47, 48, 49, 50n109
Otto di Guardia (Eight of Police), magistracy, 25, 50
Ottokar, Nicola, 8-9n4

paghe sostenute (withheld interest), 38n49
Palmieri, Matteo, humanist, 37n47
Pantaleoni: family, 78n95; Domenico, theologian: attribution of *Tractatus de monte comuni*, 71n68; on compulsory loans, 70-71; on public debt market, 78-79
Paolo di Castro, canonist, 19n43
parabola (extension of debt term), 155, 168, 237, 295-96, 309, 310, 368
Parte Guelfa. *See* Guelf Society
partnership (*societas*), contract, 59, 148, 281
patriciate, social group, 8-10; and crisis of 1343, 29, 31-32; displaced by *popolo*, 11-12; and Dominicans, 78n95; hegemony of, 11, 20-23, 24, 46, 47, 50-51, 102, 105-7, 110; hostility to *monte comune*, 78; opposition to taxation, 41; and public debt market, 51. *See also consulta*; electoral procedures; guilds; *monte comune*; officeholders; popolo; property taxes; regime; *Signoria*
Paulus de Liazariis, canonist, 170, 175, 311-12, 315
pawnbrokers. *See* moneylenders
penalty. *See poena*
penance, sacrament, 61, 85, 153, 155-56, 159, 161, 169, 179, 236, 289, 295, 296, 297, 300, 303, 310, 311, 320, 367
Pennington, Kenneth, 102
Peruzzi: bank, 29; Ranieri de', 36
Peter of Ancharano, canonist, 19n43; on annuity, 82-83, 99; attribution of *Quaestio disputata de monte Venetorum vel Florentinorum*, 71-72n71; on compulsory loans, 71, 88n14; incredibility thesis, 83-84; on *lucrum cessans*, 65; on patriotism, 103n10; on public debt market, 82-83, 248, 372, 373
Peter the Chanter, theologian: on sale of time, 95n32
Petrarch, Francesco, humanist, 89n16, 107, 216n30, 355
Petruccius, Fredericus, canonist, 71n68;

on restitution, 177-78, 178-81, 184-85, 318-19, 319-23, 325-26
Piero di Ser Grifo, notary, 34
Pietro di Gentile da Castelfiorentino, Ser, notary, 36
Pisa, 23, 26, 41-42n67; Council of, 26; Florentine conquest of, 24, 38n49; Florentine wars with, 29, 35, 40, 213
Pitti family, 12
pledge, interest title, 136, 147, 149, 159, 265-66, 280, 283, 300-301. *See also* dotal pledge
poena (penalty), interest title, 62-63, 134, 148-49, 160, 264, 282, 284, 290, 302
popolo (people): as anti-oligarchic coalition, 10, 13, 49; as enfranchised citizen body, 8, 8n3, 10-11, 24, 102, 108, 110; *popolo minuto* (little people), 42-43n71. *See also* Ciompi; guilds; magnates; new men; patriciate; *sottoposti*
popolo, council of, legislative assembly, 11, 46; opposes war *prestanze*, 47, 49
poverty: defined, 101; and public debt, 41-45, 51-52, 77-78, 100; and usury, 57-58, 143-44, 273-74
praescriptio. *See* prescription
pratica (select committee), 22-23, 24n70, 49n103. *See also consulta*; leadership elite; regime; *Signoria*
precaria (canonical annuity), contract, 200-3, 340-44. *See also* annuity
prescription (*praescriptio*), mode of acquisition, 187-89, 327-32
prestanza (compulsory loan), 1, 2, 12-13n14, 29, 31, 33, 34, 35, 38n49, 39n4, 49, 55, 65, 86, 97, 102, 103, 104, 108; assessment of, 41, 42-45, 46, 47, 50; citizenship privileges linked to, 50-51; communal legislation on, 88, 210-11, 349-50; demands for abolition of, 45-46, 50; licitness of, 67-71, 87-93, 212-36, 351-67; paid by brokers, 43-44, 96-97, 100, 249-57, 373-78; paid *ad perdendum* (to be lost), 44, 47-48, 100; and poverty, 42-45, 47, 77-78, 100; premiums for payment of, 92-93, 332-35, 365-67; uncompensated loans proposed, 67-68, 214-15, 354
prestanziati (compulsory lenders), 41, 44, 47, 70, 71-72n71, 72, 75, 78, 79, 80, 87, 89, 94, 103
prestanzone (compulsory loan), 38n49, 92, 226, 230-32, 363
Priors of the guilds. *See Signoria*
private property, 102, 187-88, 215, 328-30
property taxes, 102, 215; abolished, 41; Ciompi demand reinstatement of, 45; reinstated, 29, 41. *See also estimo*; gabelles
public debt. *See monte comune, monte dei cinque per cento interi, monte dei prestanzoni, monte delle doti, monte dell'uno due, monte dell'uno tre, monte di Pisa, monte libero dell'uno due*
public debt brokers, 43-44, 96-97, 249-57, 373-78
public debt market, 30, 32-34, 40-41, 51-52, 72-84, 93-97, 100, 110, 236-57, 367-78. *See also* credits; *monte comune*; public debt brokers
purchase-sale. *See* sale

rapina. *See* theft
Raymond of Penyafort, canonist: on gift, 157, 298; on loan as locus of usury, 134, 142, 264, 270; on *precaria*, 200, 340-41
redditus. *See* annuity
regime: of 1343-1348, 11, 21n51, 30-32; of 1378-1382, 11-12, 21n51; of 1382-1434, 20-23, 46-52, 102, 105-7, 111n47; of 1434-1494, 37

Remigio of Florence, theologian: on common good, 102-3n9; on *lucrum cessans*, 65
rental contract. *See locatio et conductio*
rente. *See* annuity
repetitio (exposition), legal genre, 15, 81, 85, 131, 262
restitution. *See* usury
retrangula, contract, 125, 131
Ridolfi: family, 12-13, 24; Antonio, merchant, 13; Bernardo di Lorenzo, 117n21; Maddalena (Bartolomea) di Lorenzo, nun, 39
Ridolfi, Lorenzo di Antonio, canonist: born, 13; *Casa della Sapienza*, on board of, 16-17; *catasto* declarations, 12-13n14, 20n47, 37-38, 92n22, 117n21; college of doctors of law, member of, 17; *Conservatori delle leggi*, member of, 25; *consulte* and *pratiche*, participant in, 23-24, 26, 49n103, 108; devotion to Jerome, 19n45, 117n21, 261; *Dieci di Balìa*, member of, 24; diplomatic mission to Carlo Malatesta (1393), 25, to Filippo Mario Visconti (1420), 25, to Alexander V (1409), 26, to Boniface IX (1399), 25, (1392) 108, to Venice (1425), 25-26; education, 13-15; *Gonfaloniere della Giustizia*, 24; governor of Vico Pisano (1406), 24; on Great Schism, 26; humanist associations, 107-8; law practice, 17-20; magnate status, 13, 24; marriages, 19, 117n21; *Otto di Guardia*, member of, 25; political views, 2, 13, 26, 49, 89n17, 108; prior (1394), 24; property, 12-13n14, 20n47; public status, 2, 7-8, 19-20, 23-24, 26-27; readmitted to political privileges, 24; record in public office, 7, 24; *Ufficiali dell'Onestà*, member of, 25; *Ufficiali dello Studio*, member of, 16; university lecturer, 15-16; writes on prosody and rhetoric, 107-8
— Works: *Consilia*, 17-18n39, 113, 115, 116-17, 120n25; *Repertorium iuris*, 113, 115, 117; *Zibaldone*, 19n45, 107n29, 113, 117
—, —: *Tractatus de usuris*: classical precedents in, 104, 217, 356-57; composition of, 1-2, 85-86, 131-32, 261-62; *cursus* in, 261; *exordium topoi* in, 262; ideological function of, 2, 100-102, 109, 110; manuscripts of, 112-21; organization of, 112-13, 123, 131-32, 262; proverbs cited, 89, 96, 216, 248; as *repetitio*, 85, 131; sources of, 87, 93, 94, 123, 210, 349
—, —: *Tractatus de usuris*, topics: *accaffinitas*, 126; annuity, 82-83, 192-209, 335-48; anticipated rights, 252-54, 374-77; borrowing at usury, 150-52, 286-88; *cambium*, 125; common good, 89, 102-4, 214, 215, 231, 354-55; commune likened to God, 89, 90, 104, 216, 356; compulsory loans, 87-93, 210-11, 212-18, 349-51, 351-57; credit sales, 155, 158-62, 164-65, 165-66, 295, 296, 300-304, 306, 307; definition of usury, 86, 132-35, 143, 262-65, 271; detection of usury, 153-54, 166-67, 290-91, 308-9; discounting public debt credits, 95-96, 240-46, 369-71; etymology of usury, 141, 270; gift, 86-87, 135-41, 156-57, 175-77, 190, 265-70, 284, 298-99, 316; government annuity, 98-99, 199, 257-60, 339-40, 378-80; intention of creditors, 86-87, 89-90, 135-41, 155-57, 159, 161, 162, 162-67, 168-72, 172-75, 175-77, 185-89, 189-91, 218-35, 265-70, 295-99, 301, 302, 303, 304-9, 310-13, 313-15, 316, 326-32, 332-35, 357-59; intention of public debt legislators,

90-91, 219-23, 226-27, 229-31, 358-59, 360-61, 362-63; intention of public debt speculators, 95, 97, 237-57, 368-78; interest titles, 143, 147-49, 272-73, 280-84; loan locus of usury, 134, 142-43, 158-62, 264, 270-71, 300-304; *Lc* 6.35, 168, 309; *parabola*, 167-68, 309; payment of compulsory loans likened to charity, 103, 216, 355-56; penalties of usurers, 124-25, 153, 154, 288-89, 291-94; premiums for payment of compulsory loans, 92-93, 332-35, 365-67; prescription, 187-89, 327-32; *prestanzoni* and *accattoni*, 92, 230-32, 363; private property, 187-88, 328-30; public debt brokers, 96-97, 249-57, 273-78; public debt market, 93-97, 236-57, 367-78; public necessity, 87-88, 102, 110, 212-13; public utility, 87, 88, 216-18, 351-52, 355; restitution of public debt profits, 235-36, 367; restitution of usury, 124, 155, 162, 168-72, 172-75, 175, 175-77, 177-84, 184-85, 185-89, 295, 304, 309, 310-13, 313-15, 315, 316, 317-25, 325-26, 326-32; *retrangula* and *baroccolum*, 125; sales disguising usury, 159, 162, 167, 300, 303, 308-9; *securitas*, 125-26; social effects of compulsory loans, 89, 100, 143-44, 273-74; speculative commodity sales, 158, 159, 165-66, 299-300, 301, 307; spiritual and corporeal usury, 143, 271; uncompensated compulsory loans, 88-89, 102; uniform rates of public debt interest, 90-91, 222-23, 227-28, 361; usurious contracts, 123-24; usury and civil law, 150, 285-86; usury and natural law, 144-47, 150, 274-80, 284-86; usury permitted by no law, 149-50, 273, 284-86

Rinuccini: bank, 46; family, 51
Rocke, Michael, 26n80
Roettgen, Steffi, 103n12
Rubinstein, Nicolai, 35-36n39

Sacchetti: family, 51; Franco, 40n57; Giannozzo, 56
sale (*emptio et venditio*), contract: credit sale, 59, 155, 158-62, 164-65, 165-66, 295, 296, 300-304, 306, 307; disguising usury, 59, 159, 162, 167, 300, 303, 308-9; of public debt, 94-96, 97, 238-46, 248, 250-55, 368-71, 372, 373-77; of rights, 94-97, 196, 240, 252, 338, 374; speculative commodity sale, 158, 159, 165-66, 299-300, 301, 307
Salutati, Coluccio, humanist, 104, 105, 107-8, 122n27
Salvemini, Gaetano, 8-9n4
San Giovanni, urban quarter, 43nn72-73, 47
San Miniato, Florentine war with, 35, 41-42n67, 68
Santa Croce, Franciscan convent, 38, 72
Santa Maria Novella: Dominican convent, 36, 72; urban quarter, 44
Santo Spirito, urban quarter, 12-13
scrutiny. *See* electoral procedures
sea loan. *See fenus*
securitas, contract, 125, 131
Sedici Gonfalonieri (Sixteen Ward Standard-Bearers), magistracy, 11, 23
Siena, Florentine treaty with, 49
Signoria, chief magistracy, 11, 45: advised by *consulte* and *pratiche*, 22-23; appeals for ruling on public debt, 66; social composition of, 1378-82, 12, 12n13, 1382-1434, 21-22. *See also* electoral procedures; guilds; leadership elite; new men; officeholders; patriciate
Sixteen Ward Standard-Bearers. *See*

Sedici Gonfalonieri
societas. See partnership
socii pompa, interest title, 283
sottoposti (textile workers), 12-13; assessed loans, 42-43. *See also* Ciompi; poverty; wages
Spicciani, Amleto, 56n13, 63n39, 274
Standard-Bearer of Justice. *See Gonfaloniere della Giustizia*
Stefani, Marchionne di Coppo, chronicler, 40
Stella, Alessandro, 12n12, 43n72
Stimulus amoris, devotional tract, 89, 104, 216, 356
stipulatio, contract, 57
Strozzi: family, 51, 78n95; Antonio di Vanni, civilian, 115; Carlo di Tommaso, 115; Palla, 37; Piero, theologian, 72, 110, 126; attribution of *Tractatus super casu de monte communi*, 71n68; on compulsory loans, 70-71; on public debt market, 75-78; on scrupulous creditors, 56; Ridolfi's dependence on, 87
summa, legal genre, 131, 262
syndicus ad indulgendum (Syndic for Immunity), 54, 211, 350

Tartagnis, Alexander de, civilian, 111
tassa di lancie (military tax), 41-42n67, 50
tax revolts, 42
taxes. *See estimo*, gabelles, property taxes, *tassa di lancie*
Ten of War. *See Dieci di Balìa*
textile workers. *See* Ciompi, *sottoposti*
theft (*furtum, rapina*), 59, 164, 170, 171, 179, 182-84, 289, 299, 306, 312, 319-20
Thomas Aquinas, theologian, 79; on borrowing at usury, 150-51, 286; on common good, 102-3n9; on *damnum emergens*, 63; on *lucrum cessans*, 65; on usury and natural law, 60
time, sale of, 95, 245-46, 255, 280, 371, 377
tractatus, legal genre, 131, 262
Trexler, Richard C., 12n12, 32n21, 55
Tudeschis, Nicholas de, canonist, 102-3n9
turpe lucrum (dishonest profit), 58, 109, 281-82

Ubaldis, Angelo de, civilian, 19n. Baldus de, civilian, 116n20; on annuity, 201, 341-42; on compulsory loans, 71-72n71; on credit sales, 159-60, 301-2; on detection of usurers, 154, 291; on interest titles, 148-49, 149, 282, 284; on usury prohibition, 146, 147, 278, 279-80
ubbia. See annuity
Ufficiali alla diminuzione del monte (Officials for the liquidation of the debt), magistracy, 350
Ufficiali del monte (Debt Officials), magistracy, 33n25, 36-37, 46, 56
Ufficiali dell'Onestà (Officers of Decency), magistracy, 25
Ufficiali dello Studio (Officials of the University), magistracy, 16
university. *See* Florence
Urban III, pope: on usury, 56, 85, 295
usurer: *monte* credits forfeit, 37; testament of, 106, 154, 292, 309. *See also* moneylender; usury
usury, 56, 109, 132-35, 143, 262-65, 271; borrowing at, 150-53, 286-88, 213, 353; and civil law, 150, 285-86; and compulsory loans, 2-3, 53-56, 65-71, 212-236, 351-67; as crime, 59; detection of, 153-54, 166-67, 177, 258-60, 290-91, 308-9, 317-18, 379-80; etymology of, 141, 270; and exchange, 125; government victim of, 54, 55; and intention, 85-87, 89-90, 135-41, 155-57, 159, 161, 162,

162-67, 168-78, 186-91, 265-70, 295-99, 301, 302, 303, 304-9, 310–19, 326-35; interest titles, 61-65, 143, 147-49, 159-60, 272-73, 280-84, 301-2; legitimation of quasi-heretical, 60, 154, 293; loan locus of, 57-59, 134, 142-43, 264, 270-71; manifest (notorious), 60-61, 86, 99, 308-9; and natural law, 60, 144-47, 150, 274-80, 284-86; occult, 60-61, 85-86, 155-57, 159, 161, 162, 162-67, 265-70, 295-99, 301, 302, 303, 304-9; penalties for, 61, 124-25, 153, 154, 288-89, 291-94; permitted by no law, 149-50, 273, 278, 284-86; permitted in Byzantium, 57n20; prohibition extended to laity, 57; prohibition reinforces precommercial economic relations, 4, 57-58, 61n31, 109; public debt interest as, 54; and public debt market, 66, 72-84, 93-97, 109-10, 236-57, 367-78; restitution of, 59, 61, 124, 155, 162, 168-89, 295, 304, 309, 310-32; in sales, 59, 155, 158-62, 164-65, 165-67, 295, 296, 299-304, 306, 307, 308-9; social effects of, 58, 143-44, 273-74. *See also fenus*; moneylender; *monte comune*; usurer

utilitas rei publicae (public utility), 87, 88, 216-18, 351-52, 355

Uzzano, Niccolò da, politician, 17, 47n90

Valerius Maximus, 104, 217, 357

venditio fructus, interest title, 201, 283, 342

venditio sub dubio, interest title, 335

Venice: public debt controversy, 66-67n52, 70, 80, 132; Florentine alliance with, 25-26

Verona, Florentine war with, 29

Vespasiano da Bisticci, memorialist, 7, 17, 20n47, 26n78, 27, 111, 261, 262

Vienne, Council of: anti-usury measures, 60, 292-93

Villani, Giovanni, chronicler, 31n18, 32n19, 33-34; Matteo, chronicler, 33, 53, 72-73

Vincentius Hispanus, canonist: on *parabola*, 296; on prescription, 188; on restitution, 314

Vincke, Johannes, 26n82

Visconti, Filippo Maria, duke of Milan, 25, 33n24; Giangaleazzo, duke of Milan, 2n3, 25, 48, 104

wages, 14n23, 16n31. *See also* Ciompi; poverty; *sottoposti*

Walter of Brienne, duke of Athens, 29-30, 31

William Durant. *See* Durant, William

Witt, Ronald G., 21n53, 34n32

Zabarellis, Franciscus de, canonist, 16n31